T0185363

Communications in Computer and Information Science   1005

Commenced Publication in 2007
Founding and Former Series Editors:
Phoebe Chen, Alfredo Cuzzocrea, Xiaoyong Du, Orhun Kara, Ting Liu,
Krishna M. Sivalingam, Dominik Ślęzak, Takashi Washio, and Xiaokang Yang

More information about this series at http://www.springer.com/series/7899

Fuchun Sun · Huaping Liu ·
Dewen Hu (Eds.)

Cognitive Systems
and Signal Processing

4th International Conference, ICCSIP 2018
Beijing, China, November 29 – December 1, 2018
Revised Selected Papers, Part I

Editors
Fuchun Sun
Department of Computer Science
and Technology
Tsinghua University
Beijing, China

Huaping Liu ⓘ
Department of Computer Science
and Technology
Tsinghua University
Beijing, China

Dewen Hu
College of Mechatronics and Automation
National University of Defense Technology
Changsha, China

ISSN 1865-0929   ISSN 1865-0937 (electronic)
Communications in Computer and Information Science
ISBN 978-981-13-7982-6   ISBN 978-981-13-7983-3 (eBook)
https://doi.org/10.1007/978-981-13-7983-3

This Springer imprint is published by the registered company Springer Nature Singapore Pte Ltd.
The registered company address is: 152 Beach Road, #21-01/04 Gateway East, Singapore 189721, Singapore

Preface

Welcome to the proceedings of the International Conference on Cognitive Systems and Information Processing (ICCSIP 2018), which was held in Beijing, the capital of China, from November 29 to December 1, 2018. ICCSIP is the prestigious biennial conference on cognitive systems and information processing with past events held in Beijing (2012, 2014, 2016). Over the past few years, ICCSIP has matured into a well-established series of international conferences on cognitive information processing and related fields over the world. Similar to the previous event, ICCSIP 2018 provided an academic forum for the participants to share their new research findings and discuss emerging areas of research. It also established a stimulating environment for the participants to exchange ideas on future trends and opportunities of cognitive information processing research.

Currently, cognitive systems and information processing are applied in an increasing number of research domains such as cognitive sciences and technology, visual cognition and computation, big data and intelligent information processing, bioinformatics and applications. We believe that cognitive systems and information processing will certainly exhibit greater-than-ever advances in the near future. With the aim of promoting the research and technical innovation in relevant fields domestically and internationally, the fundamental objective of ICCSIP is defined as providing a premier forum for researchers and practitioners from academia, industry, and government to share their ideas, research results, and experiences.

This year, ICCSIP received 169 submissions, all of which are written in English. After a thorough reviewing process, 96 papers were selected for presentation as full papers, resulting in an approximate acceptance rate of 56%. The accepted papers not only address challenging issues in various aspects of cognitive systems and information processing but also showcase contributions from related disciplines that illuminate the state of the art. In addition to the contributed papers, the ICCSIP 2018 technical program included three plenary speeches by Prof. Qionghai Dai, Prof. Feiyue Wang, and Prof. Jianwei Zhang. We would also like to thank the members of the Advisory Committee for their guidance, the members of the international Program Committee and additional reviewers for reviewing the papers, and the members of the Publications Committee for checking the accepted papers in a short period of time. Last but not the least, we would like to thank all the speakers and authors as well as the participants for their great contributions that made ICCSIP2018 successful and all the hard work worthwhile.

December 2018

Fuchun Sun
Huaping Liu
Dewen Hu

Organization

ICCSIP 2018 was organized by the Cognitive Systems and Information Processing Society of Chinese Association for Artificial Intelligence, Cognitive Computing and Systems Society of Chinese Association of Automation, Tsinghua University, Science in China Press, Institute of Software Chinese Academy of Sciences.

Organization

Honorary Chairs

Bo Zhang	Tsinghua University, China
Deyi Li	Chinese Academy of Engineering, China

Advisory Committee Chairs

Nanning Zheng	Xi'an Jiaotong University, China
Wei Li	Beihang University, China
Lin Chen	Chinese Academy of Sciences, China
Ning Xi	Michigan State University, USA
Fuji Ren	Tokushima University, Japan
Donald C. Wunsch	Missouri University of Science and Technology, USA
Cesare Alippi	Politecnico di Milano, Italy
Yinxu Wang	University of Calgary, Canada
Philip Chen	University of Macau, SAR China

General Chairs

Fuchun Sun	Tsinghua University, China
Jennie Si	Arizona State University, USA
Jianwei Zhang	Universität Hamburg, Germany

Program Committee Chairs

Dewen Hu	National University of Defense Technology, China
Angelo Cangelosi	University of Manchester, UK
Michael Y. Wang	Hong Kong University of Science and Technology, SAR China
Chenglin Wen	Hangzhou Dianzi University, China
Changwen Zheng	Institute of Software, Chinese Academy of Sciences, China

Organizing Committee Chairs

Huaping Liu	Tsinghua University, China
Hong Cheng	University of Electronic Science and Technology, China
Guangbin Huang	Nanyang Technological University, Singapore

Plenary Sessions Chairs

Zengguang Hou	Institute of Automation, Chinese Academy of Sciences, China
Chenglin Wen	Hangzhou Dianzi University, China

Special Sessions Chairs

Fei Song	Science China Press, China
Yixu Song	Tsinghua University, China

Publications Chairs

Wei Li	California State University, USA
Quanbo Ge	Hangzhou Dianzi University, China

Publicity Chairs

Jianmin Li	Tsinghua University, China
Bin Fang	Tsinghua University, China

Finance Chair

Chunfang Liu	Tsinghua University, China

Registration Chair

Jianqin Yin	Beijing University of Posts and Telecommunications, China

Local Arrangements Chair

Zhongyi Chu	Beihang University, China

Electronic Review Chair

Xiaolin Hu	Tsinghua University, China

Program Committee

Fuchun Sun	Tsinghua University, China
Dewen Hu	National University of Defense Technology, China
Guojun Dai	Hangzhou Dianzi University, China
Zhiguang Qin	University of Electronic Science and Technology, China
Jingmin Xin	Xi'an Jiaotong University, China
Huaping Liu	Tsinghua University, China
Wanzeng Kong	Hangzhou Dianzi University, China
Yuanlong Yu	Fuzhou University, China
Chenglin Wen	Hangzhou Dianzi University, China
Zhiquan Feng	University of Jinan, China
Yi Ning	Henan University of Technology, China
Rui Nian	Ocean University of China, China
Fang Liu	Shenyang Ligong University, China
Meiqin Liu	Zhejiang University, China
Bin Xu	Northwestern Polytechnical University, China
Weihua Su	Academy of Military Medical Sciences, China
Yujian Li	Beijing University of Technology, China Science China Press, China
Ke Li	Beihang University, China
Yongming Li	Shaanxi Normal University, China
Shunli Li	Harbin Institute of Technology, China
Hongbo Li	Tsinghua University, China
Li Li	Tianjin Normal University, China
Tieshan Li	Dalian Maritime University, China
Zhijun Li	South China University of Technology, China
Xia Li	Shenzhen University, China
Dongfang Yang	Rocket Force University of Engineering, China
Ming Yang	Shanghai Jiao Tong University, China
Jian Yang	Nanjing University of Science and Technology, China
Fengge Wu	Chinese Academy of Sciences, China
Licheng Wu	Minzu University of China, China
Jian He	Beijing University of Technology, China
Haibo Min	Rocket Force University of Engineering, China
Hongqiao Wang	Rocket Force University of Engineering, China
Liejun Wang	Xinjiang University, China
Hui Shen	National University of Defense Technology, China
Pengfei Zhang	China North Vehicle Research Institute, China
Jianhai Zhang	Hangzhou Dianzi University, China
Chun Zhang	Tsinghua University, China
Jinxiang Chen	China Iron and Steel Research Institute Group, China
Liang Chen	Shenzhen University, China
Minnan Luo	Xi'an Jiaotong University, China
Xiong Luo	University of Science and Technology Beijing, China

Fan Zhou	Shenyang Ligong University, China
Erqiang Zhou	University of Electronic Science and Technology, China
Yucai Zhou	Changsha University of Science and Technology, China
Dongbin Zhao	Chinese Academy of Sciences, China
Yuntao Zhao	Shenyang Ligong University, China
Qingjie Zhao	Beijing Institute of Technology, China
Huijing Zhao	Peking University, China
Shiqiang Hu	Shanghai Jiao Tong University, China
Laihong Hu	Rocket Force University of Engineering, China
Ying Hu	Chinese Academy of Sciences, China
Zhansheng Duan	Xi'an Jiaotong University, China
Peijiang Yuan	Beihang University, China
Chen Guo	Dalian Maritime University, China
Deshuang Huang	Tongji University, China
Panfeng Huang	Northwestern Polytechnical University, China
Yongzhi Cao	Peking University, China
Rongxin Cui	Northwestern Polytechnical University, China
Quanbo Ge	Hangzhou Dianzi University, China
Hong Cheng	University of Electronic Science and Technology, China

Organizers

Cognitive Systems and Information Processing Society of Chinese Association for Artificial Intelligence
Cognitive Computing and Systems Society of Chinese Association of Automation
Tsinghua University
Science in China Press
Institute of Software Chinese Academy of Sciences

Technical Co-sponsors

IEEE Computational Intelligence Society
Science in China Series F: Information Sciences
National Natural Science Foundation Committee of China

Co-organizer

Beijing University of Posts and Telecommunications

Contents – Part I

Algorithms

Robotics

Contents – Part II

Deep Learning

Vision and Image

Automatic Analog Pointer Instruments Reading Using Panel Detection and Landmark Localization Networks

Keshan Yang, Zhansheng Duan[✉], and Kai Fang

Center for Information Engineering Science Research, Xi'an Jiaotong University,
Xi'an 710049, Shanxi, China
{yangkeshan,fangkai}@stu.xjtu.edu.cn,zsduan@mail.xjtu.edu.cn

Abstract. Analog pointer instruments are widely used in industrial automation. However, reading their values by human is time and labour consuming. Most current pointer reading algorithms lack universality and can not handle complex and varying application scenarios. Therefore, this paper proposes a general pointer instrument reading scheme based on CNN. Our main contributions are two folds. First, we combine two sub-networks into one backbone, which has shortened the inference time. Second, we propose a light-weighted sampling decoder, which makes our scheme achieve a higher accuracy. Comparing to other algorithms, our scheme can deal with the case in which the instrument is too difficult to read, e.g., there is more than one similar pointer in one panel. Also, our scheme only needs less than 100 ms on a typical laptop for a 512×512 image. It is fast enough and can satisfy most requirements in industrial automation.

Keywords: Pointer instrument reading · Panel detection · Landmark localization

1 Introduction

Due to historic reasons, analog pointer instruments such as piezometer and thermometer are still widely used in industrial automation. These instruments are usually read by human, which is time and labor consuming. Per the requirements of automation, it is necessary to develop such a scheme in which the computers can recognize (read) the instrument value online.

There are quite a few methods to read the value of pointer instrument, in which the methods based on computer vision are the easiest and non-invasive way. Lots of methods have been proposed in recent years on reading the pointer instruments based on computer vision [1–3]. These methods mainly consist of

Research supported in part by National Natural Science Foundation of China through grants 61673317 and 61673313, and the Fundamental Research Funds for the Central Universities of China.

© Springer Nature Singapore Pte Ltd. 2019
F. Sun et al. (Eds.): ICCSIP 2018, CCIS 1005, pp. 3–14, 2019.
https://doi.org/10.1007/978-981-13-7983-3_1

two steps: (a) image registration. (b) pointer localization. However, these methods have several problems. First, they can not handle the case when the panel is obscured. Second, pointer detection methods based on Hoff line transformation can not work when shapes of pointers are irregular. Finally, both image registration based on local binary descriptors like ORB [4] and pointer detection based on Hoff line transformation are time consuming.

In this paper, we present a novel CNN-based pointer instrument reading scheme to handle the above problems. More specifically, we combine the panel detection step and the pointer localization step into one step. By designing a network which has two sub-networks. One is the detection sub-network for detection task, and the other is the landmark localization sub-network used to find landmarks in the panel. Once landmarks in the panel are localized, we can easily figure out the reading by combining with some prior information. We have conducted some experiments on several types of pointer instruments. The results suggest that our scheme is not only cost-efficient, but also flexible and robust for practical consideration.

The rest of this paper is organized as follows. Section 2 is a more detailed description about the analog pointer instrument reading problem. The CNN network architecture and the training details are described in Sect. 3. The experiments are exhibited in Sect. 4. We conclude the paper in Sect. 5.

2   Pointer Instrument Reading Problem

There are many types of pointer instruments in industrial automation. To make the description in this section more representative, we take water meter as an example. Figure 1(a) shows an image of a water meter captured by a camera, which has 4 pointers and 4 panels. Our goal is to read the value of this instrument, which is $0.8976 \, \mathrm{m}^3$ in this water meter example.

In order to read the value of this water meter, two sub-problems for each image need to be solved. The first problem is whether all panels exist in the picture. The second problem is to find positions of different scale values, including zero scale value and full scale value, and positions of all pointers. This problem can be abstracted as a landmark localization problem, which are the 46 blue points and 4 red points showed in Fig. 1(b). The first problem can be treated as a classification problem or a detection problem. In this paper we treat it as a detection problem and design a light weighted sub-network to solve it. The second problem can be treated as a binary classification problem which is similar to human key points detection in [5]. We design a fast and accurate enough landmark localization sub-network to solve the second problem. Next we will describe the network design in more details.

3   Network Architecture

3.1   Panel Detection

In the practical situation, cameras are deployed at a fixed location, but the instruments may move or even rotate by themselves. Even if both the cameras

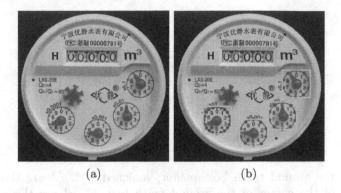

(a)   (b)

Fig. 1. A pointer instrument example. Our goal is to detect the four green bounding boxes and 46 blue points and 4 red points in (b). (Color figure online)

and the pointer instruments are fixed, the variation of the distance and viewing angle between them can also cause the zoom and tilt of panel images. It is impossible to assign different parameters, e.g., color and length of the pointer, for each pointer instrument or each camera. With a panel detector, we can narrow the hunting zone of landmarks to improve the accuracy and speed.

Inspired by recent CNN-based object detection work like SSD in [6], considering the speed and accuracy requirements of panel detection, we design a light-weighted network as our detector. Figure 2 shows its architecture. We first use a modified dilated-Resnet50 [7], in which the number of filters has been changed to one sixteenth of the original, as the backbone feature extractor to keep the whole model light weighted. After the backbone multiple convolutions with stride 2 are applied to generate multiple features of different resolutions. On each feature a convolution is applied as an anchor generator to provide multiple anchors, while each anchor represents a bounding box over the input image. At each training step, each ground truth box is assigned to at least one anchor. An anchor will be assigned to a ground truth box when its Intersection over Union (IoU) is greater than 0.7, and an anchor will be negative if its IoU between all ground truth boxes is less than 0.3.

Similar to Faster R-CNN [8], we use two types of losses to optimize the detection sub-network, i.e., the classification Cross-Entropy loss L_{cls} and smooth-L1 loss L_{loc}:

$$L_{cls} = -\frac{1}{N} \sum_{i \in Pos} \log(p_i^{cls}) \tag{1}$$

$$L_{loc} = \frac{1}{N} \sum_{i \in Pos} \sum_{j=0}^{3} \text{smooth}_{L1}(w_j p_{i,j}^{loc} - w_j l_i^{loc}) \tag{2}$$

$$l_i^{loc} = (l_i^{loc_{dx}}, l_i^{loc_{dy}}, l_i^{loc_{dw}}, l_i^{loc_{dh}}) \tag{3}$$

$$l_i^{loc_{dx}} = g_i^{cx} - anchor_i^{cx} \qquad (4)$$

$$l_i^{loc_{dy}} = g_i^{cy} - anchor_i^{cy} \qquad (5)$$

$$l_i^{loc_{dw}} = \log(\frac{g_i^w}{anchor_i^w}) \qquad (6)$$

$$l_i^{loc_{dh}} = \log(\frac{g_i^h}{anchor_i^h}) \qquad (7)$$

where g_i is the ground truth box $anchor_i$ assigned, g_i^{cx}, g_i^{cy} are the x and y coordinates of the center of the ground truth box, g_i^w, g_i^h are the width and height of the features. w is the weight of L_{loc} to decrease the gaps between the gradients of $g_i^{cx}, g_i^{cy}, g_i^w, g_i^h$.

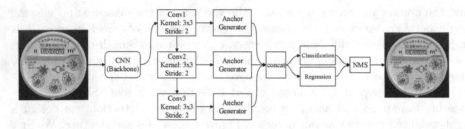

Fig. 2. Detection sub-network architecture. After the classification and location regression steps, the Non-Maximum Suppression (NMS) step is applied on all anchors. The outputs of this detection sub-network are the four green bounding boxes. (Color figure online)

3.2 Landmark Localization

The landmark localization sub-task is to find some points which are important, like zero scale point, full scale point, center of the panel, the pinpoint of the pointer, etc. Apparently, the accuracy of this sub-network decides the accuracy of the whole scheme.

Sub-network Architecture. Figure 3 shows the architecture of the landmark localization sub-network. Treating the task as a binary classification problem, it can be seen that the resolution of the output can not be too small. Therefore, we up-sample the output feature by a well designed decoder. After each bi-linear sampling step, a filtering module is applied to reduce the aliasing effect. On the other hand, the decoding speed may be very slow as the feature resolution increases. To keep the decoder light-weighted, we set the number of filters in all filtering modules equal to the number of landmarks, which can also ease over-fitting when the landmark training set is small.

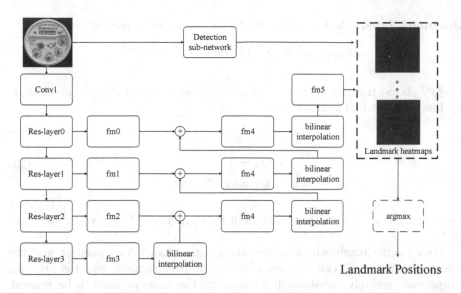

Fig. 3. Landmark localization sub-network of architecture.

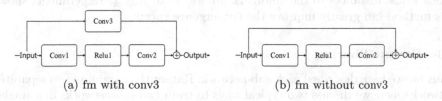

(a) fm with conv3   (b) fm without conv3

Fig. 4. Filtering module of the landmark localization sub-network. To reduce computational cost, conv3 is added when and only when the number of channels between the input and the output is different, and the number of filters in all filtering modules equals the number of landmarks.

Training Objective. We generate the landmark sub-network training objective using Gaussian distribution. More specifically, let $l^i, 1 \leq i \leq N_l$ stands for the i-th landmark, where N_l is the number of landmarks. l_x^i, l_y^i are the x and y coordinates of l^i. The training objective of l^i, denoted as T_i, is a gray picture with height and width equal the input image. $T_i(m, n)$ is calculated using Eq. (8), where σ is a hyper-parameter which is set to 7 and the strides are set to 1 because the width and height of the model outputs equal the width and height of the input image.

$$T_i(m, n) = \exp \left[-\frac{(x_0 - l_x^i)^2 + (y_0 - l_y^i)^2}{2\sigma^2} \right]$$

$$x_0 = stride * n + \frac{stride}{2} - 0.5 \qquad\qquad (8)$$

$$y_0 = stride * m + \frac{stride}{2} - 0.5$$

Landmark Loss. The loss of the landmark sub-network can be written as:

$$L_{landmark} = \sum_{i,m,n} (T_i(m,n) - P_i(m,n))^2 \qquad (9)$$

where T_i is the training objective of the i-th landmark and P_i is its prediction. The estimation of l_x^i and l_y^i are:

$$\hat{l}_x^i = p_i \% w$$
$$\hat{l}_y^i = (p_i - \hat{l}_x^i)/w \qquad (10)$$
$$p_i = \arg\max_k \ P_{f,i}(k)$$

where w and h are the width and height of P_i, $P_{f,i}(k) \in \mathrm{R}^{w*h}$ is a vector flattened by P_i.

Treating the pixels whose values are greater than 0.5 as positive and the others as negative, it can be seen that the positive samples and the negative samples are severely unbalanced. This makes the network hard to be trained. To solve this problem, in the first several epochs, we only evaluate the loss of pixels whose distances to the landmark are less than R_{mask}. Experiments show this method can greatly improve the convergence speed.

3.3   Feature Sharing

Thus far we have described each sub-network. Rather than training two separate networks, here we discuss two typical ways to train two sub-networks in a single network through feature sharing.

Alternating Training. In this way, we let $L_{keypoints}$ be zero, and the detection sub-network is first trained on Pascal VOC data set [9]. As the number of classes is different, parameters of some convolutions need to be reinitialized. Next we first train the detection sub-network using on-site panel detection data set, and then we train the landmark localization sub-network using on-site landmark data set. This process is iterated. We use the way of training in this paper.

Joint Training. It is also possible to treat two sub-networks as one network when training. More specifically, let $L = L_{detection} + L_{landmark}$, and back-propagation takes place as usual. It can be seen that each image needs both bounding box annotation and landmark annotation in this way, which is a strict constraint as the detection sub-network only needs about one hundred images but the landmark sub-network needs more.

3.4   Landmark Registration

In a few cases, the image may be wrapped as a result of the non-vertical perspective. Therefore, after finding the landmarks, it is necessary to compute an optimal affine transformation between the points of the input image and the template image to further improve the accuracy. In this paper, we find the optimal 2×2 matrix A and 2×1 vector b through the following linear least squares estimation:

$$\left[\hat{A}|\hat{b}\right] = \arg\min_{[A|b]} \sum_i \left\| d[i] - As[i]^T - b \right\|^2. \tag{11}$$

where s[i] and d[i] are the i-th landmarks from the input image and the template image, respectively. And $[A|b]$ has a form of

$$\begin{bmatrix} a_{11} & a_{12} & b_1 \\ a_{21} & a_{22} & b_2 \end{bmatrix} \tag{12}$$

4 Experimental Results

4.1 Experiments on VOC2007

Metrics. Same as VOC2007 detection task in [9], the standard metric we use to measure performance for detection task is the Mean Average Precision (mAP) at certain IoU (Intersection-over-Union). Given a bounding box predicted by the detection sub-network and a ground truth box, the IoU between them is defined as the ratio of the intersection area to the union area. Once the IoU threshold is given, the True Positive (TP), the True Negative (TN), the False Positive (FP), and the False Negative (FN) can be calculated. The Precision is defined as:

$$\text{Precision} = \frac{\text{TP}}{(\text{TP} + \text{FP})} \tag{13}$$

And the Recall is defined as:

$$\text{Recall} = \frac{\text{TP}}{(\text{TP} + \text{FN})} \tag{14}$$

As each bounding box predicted by the detection sub-network owns a score, a Precision-Recall curve, denoted as $P(r)$, as in Fig. 5 for each class can be built. The AP for each class and each image is the average of 11 Precisions at the points where Recall $= 0, 0.1, 0.2, 0.3, 0.4, 0.5, 0.6, 0.7, 0.8, 0.9, 1$. That is,

$$\text{AP} = \frac{1}{11} \sum_{r \in \{0, 0.1, \ldots, 1\}} P(r) \tag{15}$$

And the mean Average Precision (mAP) is calculated as:

$$\text{mAP} = \frac{1}{N_c} \frac{1}{N_{image}} \sum_{i=1}^{N_c} \sum_{j=1}^{N_{image}} \text{AP}_{i,j} \tag{16}$$

where N_c is the number of classes and N_{image} is the number of images. As is the standard for detection tasks, we use mAP with a 50% IoU threshold (mAP@0.5) as the evaluation metric for quality of the panel detection sub-network. Higher mAP for the detection sub-network is desirable.

Experimental Results. We first train the detection sub-network on VOC2007 training and validation set and test it on VOC2007 test set [9] as the on-site training set lacks diversity. It can be seen that the detection mAP is a little lower than the state-of-the-art detection model, but it is two times faster than SSD300 [6], which makes it possible to apply our scheme on low-performance computational platform. This is because we just use it as our pre-training step and we only optimize the network for our panel detection task but not for VOC detection challenge. In fact, in our experiments, our scheme works pretty well even though the on-site training set is small (Table 1).

Table 1. Experimental results on VOC2007 test data set

Model	mAP	FPS on P40	FPS on 1050ti	FPS on CPU
R-FCN [10]	82.3%	8	-	-
SSD300 [6]	74.3%	46	-	-
Ours (With landmark)	65.1%	50	14	2
Ours (No landmark)	65.1%	81	-	3.1

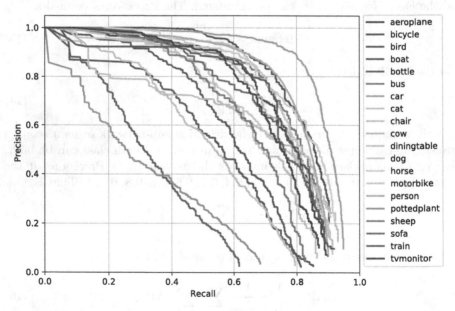

Fig. 5. Precision-Recall Curves on VOC 2007 test data set. The two classes with the lowest mAP are potted plants and bottles, which are mainly small targets and not so important for panel detection.

4.2   Experiments on Piezometer

Training Data Set Description. We collect about one hundred images for detection task and about three hundred images for the landmark localization task. To simulate the affine transformation caused by non vertical perspective view, we print several images on papers and then capture them by a camera. The detection data set contains 241 images and the landmark localization data set contains 826 images. Figure 6 shows an example of images in the training set. The instrument we want to read is one type of pressure indicator, whose full scale is 40 and scale division is 1, and it has one pointer. For each image, we annotate 7 positions as our landmarks: scale values of 0, 10, 20, 30, 40, head and tail of the pointer.

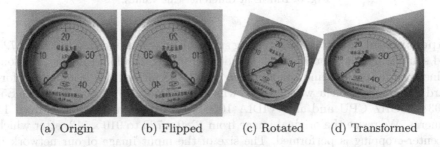

(a) Origin   (b) Flipped   (c) Rotated   (d) Transformed

Fig. 6. An example of images in our training data set. For each image, we perform random flipping, random rotating, random affine transformation to reduce overfitting.

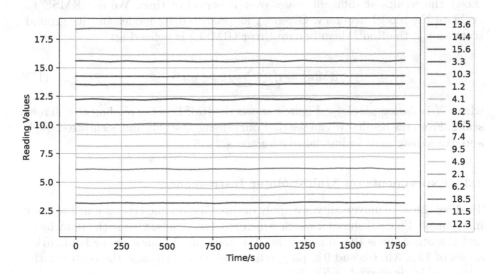

Fig. 7. Reading results on on-site data set when the true value is 1.2, 2.1, 3.3, 4.1, 4.9, 6.2, 7.4, 8.2, 9.5, 10.3, 11.5, 12.3, 13.6, 14.4, 15.6, 16.5, 18.5, 20.6 respectively.

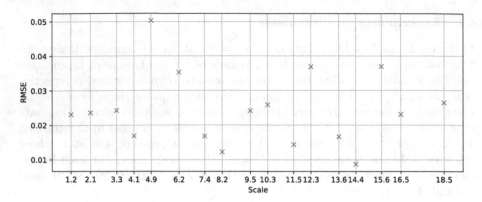

Fig. 8. RMSE at different scale values.

Experimental Setup. In the training stage, all images are resized to 1280×720 and some image augmentation like random cropping, random rotating, random affine transformation, and random resizing are performed. We conduct all forward experiments on a workstation, which is a Dell T7810 with an Intel E5-2603@1.6GHZ CPU and an NVIDIA 1050Ti GPU, to handle images from 14 cameras. We resize the original image from 1280×720 to 910×512, after which a center-cropping is performed. The size of the input image of our network is 512×512.

Experimental Results. We validate our model on on-site data set. Figure 7 shows the results at different scales over a period of time. We use RMSE to evaluate the model accuracy. Given y_p as predicted by model and its ground truth as y_{gt}, the Root Mean Square Error (RMSE) is defined as:

$$\text{RMSE} = \sqrt{\frac{1}{N} \sum (y_p - y_{gt})^2} \tag{17}$$

where N is the length of y_{gt}. Figure 8 shows the RMSE of the reading at different scales. From the results we can see that our scheme is stable and accurate enough and can satisfy most industrial requirements.

4.3 Experiments on Multi-pointer Instrument

To show the wide universality, we apply our method on one type of multi-pointer instrument. Figure 9 shows a watch which has two hands. One is the hour hand and the other one is the minute hand. We annotate 7 points as our landmarks: scales of 12 h, 3 h, 6 h and 9 h, pinpoints of the two hands and the center of the watch, which is showed in Fig. 9 (a).

The readings of the watch can be got by the following steps: (a) Get the landmark positions of the four fixed points (scales of 12 h, 3 h, 6 h and 9 h). (b)

Align the image by landmark registration with the four fixed points. (c) Get the landmark positions of the other three landmarks by letting the aligned image as the input. The reading of the minute hand is got by its included angle with vertical line, and the reading of the hour hand is got according to its nearest hour scale when the minute is less than 15′, and the previous nearest hour when the minute is greater than 15′. According to the experiments, the max error of the reading results can be controlled to less than 2′ with the above steps.

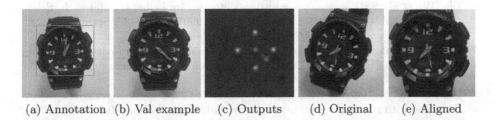

(a) Annotation   (b) Val example   (c) Outputs   (d) Original   (e) Aligned

Fig. 9. A multi-pointer watch. The watch has two hands, and we annotate 7 points as our landmarks, which are showed as the blue points in (a). (b) is an example image in the validation set. The landmark predictions are showed as blue points. (c) is the landmark localization sub-network outputs of (b). (e) is the image aligned by (d) according to the landmarks predicted by the landmark sub-network. (Color figure online)

5 Conclusion

This paper presents a novel CNN-based analog pointer instrument reading scheme. It adopts panel detection and landmark localization technology, and can handle the case in which the pointer instrument is difficult to read using traditional methods while weakening the camera setup requirements. The whole scheme has low complexity, good real-time, high recognition accuracy and no human intervention is required after being deployed. Next we will further improve the accuracy and have the scheme run on embedded devices to reduce deployment costs.

References

1. Han, J., Li, E., Tao, B., Lv, M.: Reading recognition method of analog measuring instruments based on improved hough transform. In: 2011 the 10th International Conference on Electronic Measurement and Instruments, vol. 3, pp. 337–340. IEEE (2011)
2. Yue, X., Min, Z., Zhou, X., Wang, P.: The research on auto-recognition method for analogy measuring instruments. In: 2010 International Conference on Computer, Mechatronics, Control and Electronic Engineering, vol. 2, pp. 207–210. IEEE (2010)

3. Yang, Z., Niu, W., Peng, X., Gao, Y., Qiao, Y., Dai, Y.: An image-based intelligent system for pointer instrument reading. In: 2014 the 4th IEEE International Conference on Information Science and Technology, pp. 780–783. IEEE (2014)
4. Rublee, E., Rabaud, V., Konolige, K., Bradski, G.: ORB: an efficient alternative to SIFT or SURF. In: 2011 IEEE International Conference on Computer Vision, pp. 2564–2571. IEEE (2011)
5. Wei, S., Ramakrishna, V., Kanade, T., Sheikh, Y.: Convolutional pose machines. In: IEEE Conference on Computer Vision and Pattern Recognition, pp. 4724–4732 (2016)
6. Liu, W., et al.: SSD: single shot multibox detector. In: Leibe, B., Matas, J., Sebe, N., Welling, M. (eds.) ECCV 2016. LNCS, vol. 9905, pp. 21–37. Springer, Cham (2016). https://doi.org/10.1007/978-3-319-46448-0_2
7. He, K.M., Zhang, X., Ren, S., Sun, J.: Deep residual learning for image recognition. In: 2016 IEEE Conference on Computer Vision and Pattern Recognition, pp. 770–778 (2016)
8. Ren, S., He, K., Girshick, R., Sun, J.: Faster R-CNN: towards real-time object detection with region proposal networks. In: Advances in Neural Information Processing Systems, pp. 91–99 (2015)
9. Everingham, M., Eslami, S.A., Van Gool, L., Williams, C.K., Winn, J., Zisserman, A.: The pascal visual object classes challenge: a retrospective. Int. J. Comput. Vis. 111(1), 98–136 (2015)
10. Dai, J., Li, Y., He, K., Sun, J.: R-FCN: object detection via region-based fully convolutional networks. In: Advances in Neural Information Processing Systems, pp. 379–387 (2016)

A Novel Remote Sensing Image Classification Method Based on Semi-supervised Fuzzy C-Means

Guozheng Feng, Jindong Xu[✉], Baode Fan, Tianyu Zhao, Xiao Sun, and Meng Zhu

School of Computer and Control Engineering, Yantai University, Yantai, China
xujindong1980@163.com

Abstract. Because of the uncertainty of remote sensing image and ill-posedness for model, the traditional unsupervised classification algorithm is difficult to model accurately in the classification process. The pattern recognition methods based on fuzzy set theory can manage the fuzziness of data effectively, such as fuzzy c-means clustering algorithm. Among them, the type-2 fuzzy c-means algorithm has better ability to control uncertainty. However, the semi-supervised method can use prior knowledge to deal with ill-posedness of algorithms more suitable. This paper proposes the method based on the semi-supervised adaptive interval type-2 fuzzy c-means (SS-AIT2FCM). In the interval type-2 fuzzy algorithm, soft constraint supervision is performed by a small number of labeled samples, which optimizes the iterative process of the algorithm and mines the optimal expression of the data, and reduces the ill-posedness of the algorithm itself. Experimental results indicate that SS-AIT2FCM can get more accurate clusters and more clear boundaries in the remote sensing image of serious mixed pixels, have an effective results to suppress the phenomenon of "isomorphic spectrum".

Keywords: Semi-supervised · Type-2 fuzzy set · Fuzzy c-means algorithm · Remote sensing image classification

1 Introduction

Remote sensing image classification is the basis and key of analysis and application in the field of remote sensing [1]. The ultimate goal of remote sensing image classification is to give a unique class label to each pixel in remote sensing image data. The inherent uncertainty of remote sensing image data and its ubiquitous phenomenon of "same object with different spectral" [2–4] often leads to the ill-posedness of the algorithm data, which has a certain degree of influence on the accuracy of the classification results and restricts the development and application of remote sensing technology. Traditional single remote sensing image classification techniques often cannot adapt to the processing needs of various remote sensing data [5, 6]. Therefore, it is urgent to study new classification algorithms that are more universal and adaptable to the current problems.

Semi-supervised classification of remote sensing image is based on prior knowledge, and then it introduces the classification training process for labeled class [1].

© Springer Nature Singapore Pte Ltd. 2019
F. Sun et al. (Eds.): ICCSIP 2018, CCIS 1005, pp. 15–25, 2019.
https://doi.org/10.1007/978-981-13-7983-3_2

Because of the ill-posedness of remote sensing image, statistical pattern cannot completely express the data distribution of remote sensing image, and classification results of pattern cannot be estimated or estimated inaccurately [7]. Introducing the method of semi-supervised can effectively solve this ill-posedness problem [8].

Fuzzy set mathematical theory is an effective mathematical method to express fuzziness and uncertainty [9]. Among them, type-1 fuzzy c-means algorithm (T1FCM) has been widely studied in the field of remote sensing image classification because it can solve the uncertainty of remote sensing data to some extent [10–12], but it is not ideal for the classification of remote sensing image data with density difference and large uncertainty [13]. Compared with type-1 fuzzy set, the type-2 fuzzy sets describe the uncertainty of data by constructing uncertain membership function [14]. Thus type-2 fuzzy set has better ability of describing multiple fuzzy uncertain information and is more suitable to deal with the multiple uncertainties in remote sensing image classification, such as remote sensing data and the uncertainty of its category [15]. But it is hard to be used in the classification of remote sensing image for its high computing complexity. The method of interval type-2 fuzzy classification technology can maintain good higher-order uncertainty description ability and can effectively reduce the computational complexity of the ordinary type-2 fuzzy set [16, 17].

At present, there are many algorithms based on interval type-2 fuzzy set. In 2014, Yu [16] applied the interval type-2 fuzzy c-means algorithm to solve the problem of remote sensing image classification, which based on using the distance of two different method to make membership interval, and obtained the accurate classification results. In 2015, Assas [18] compared the various hard structure modes of membership function interval and applied it to the remote sensing data experiment, and the experiment result proved that the interval type-2 fuzzy modeling has more accuracy and robustness than type-1 fuzzy modeling in remote sensing image classification. In 2016, He [19] proposed adaptive interval type-2 fuzzy c-means algorithm (AIT2FCM), which be modeled dynamically for membership interval by structuring adaptive factor of class the deviation. However, the research based on type-2 fuzzy set of clustering method in remote sensing image is still in the initial stage. Long [20] first proposed a semi-supervised type-2 fuzzy c-means clustering algorithm based on semi-supervised thought and two different fuzzy exponential models for interval type-2 fuzzy c-means, and it is used for classification and change detection of remote sensing images. However, its two different index modeling methods are prone to the problem of large categories of "swallowing" small categories.

Therefore, from the point of the well-posedness and complexity of the classification algorithm and the semi-supervised learning thought, this paper proposes a remote sensing image classification method based on semi-supervised adaptive interval type-2 fuzzy C-means, which will greatly improve the classification effect of remote sensing images.

2 Semi-supervised Adaptive Interval Type-2 Fuzzy C-Means

2.1 Objective Function

The key idea of the semi-supervised thinking in this paper is to conduct soft constraint supervision through a small number of labeled samples, to achieve optimization guidance for the algorithm iterative process, to mine the optimal expression of data, and to reduce the ill-posedness of the algorithm itself. Remote sensing image data is $X = \{x_1, x_2, \ldots, x_n\} (x_i = \{x_{i1}, x_{i2}, \ldots, x_{ip}\})$, $1 \leq i \leq n$. Combined with semi-supervised thinking, the objective function of SS-AIT2FCM algorithm is designed as follows:

$$J_t = (1 - \lambda) \sum_{j=1}^{c} \sum_{p=1}^{\|X^U\|} \left(u_{pj}^u\right)^m \left(d_{pj}\right)^2 + \lambda \sum_{j=1}^{c} \sum_{i=1}^{\|X^L\|} \left(u_{ij}^u\right)^m \left(d_{ij}\right)^2 \tag{1}$$

Where λ is the ratio of labeled sample points in data sample; X^U is the unlabeled sample set, X^L is the labeled sample set, $\|X^U\|$ and $\|X^L\|$ respectively are the number of samples in these sets; u_{ij}^u represents the membership degree of data point x_i^u belonging to the jth cluster; d_{ij} represents the distance between the data point x_i and the cluster centroid v_p, c is the number of clusters, and m is the fuzzy weight index.

2.2 Center Update

In order to improve classification accuracy and reduce unnecessary algorithm time, algorithm introduced the thought of semi-supervised learning, and designed from two aspects of the initial V^0 and centroid calculation formula. It can reduce the number of iterations of the algorithm and make up for the increase of algorithm time complexity caused by increasing the clustering accuracy.

Type-2 FCM algorithm is similar to type-1 FCM algorithm, if the center is initialized randomly, which means if we randomly initialize membership degree matrix, will not only increased the unnecessary iterative number of algorithm, but also caused unstable clustering results. Based on the semi-supervised thought, this paper proposes to initialize the center V^0 according to the expert knowledge (labeled sample set X^L), and then realize the initialization of membership degree. The initial center formula is as follows:

$$V^0 = \frac{\sum_{i=1}^{\|X^L\|} u_i^l x_i^l}{\sum_{i=1}^{\|X^L\|} u_i^l} \tag{2}$$

Where x_i^l is the ith point in labeled sample set X^L; u_i^l is the membership matrix of the label sample point x_i^l. If x_i^l belongs to the jth cluster, $u_{ij}^l = 1$, else $u_{ij}^l = 0$.

In order to give full play to the guiding role of labeled sample points in the algorithm, accelerate the stability speed of the center, and increase the accuracy of clustering results, the calculation formula of the center v_j is designed as follows:

$$v_j = \frac{\sum_{p=1}^{\|x^U\|} u_{pj}^u x_p^u}{\sum_{p=1}^{\|x^U\|} u_{pj}^u} + \lambda \left(\frac{\sum_{i=1}^{\|x^L\|} u_{ij}^l x_p^l}{\sum_{i=1}^{\|x^L\|} u_{ij}^l} - \frac{\sum_{p=1}^{\|x^U\|} u_{pj}^u x_p^u}{\sum_{p=1}^{\|x^U\|} u_{pj}^u} \right)$$

$$= (1 - \lambda) \frac{\sum_{p=1}^{\|x^U\|} u_{pj}^u x_p^u}{\sum_{p=1}^{\|x^U\|} u_{pj}^u} + \lambda \frac{\sum_{i=1}^{\|x^L\|} u_{ij}^l x_p^l}{\sum_{i=1}^{\|x^L\|} u_{ij}^l} \tag{3}$$

If $\lambda = 1$, that all samples are labeled sample, algorithm does not need iteration, if $\lambda = 0$, will be degraded for unsupervised clustering algorithm. The ratio λ is defined as follows:

$$\lambda = \frac{\|X^L\|}{\|X\|} = \frac{\|X^L\|}{\|X^L\| + \|X^U\|} \tag{4}$$

Where X is the datasets, and $\|X\|$ is the total number of datasets.

2.3 Fuzzy Construction and Defuzzification

The structure of the type-2 FCM membership interval thought a measure of maximum difference, to improve uncertainty expression ability. The membership interval of unlabeled sample is defined as follows:

$$\overline{U}^U = \left[\bar{u}_{ij}^u \right], \quad \bar{u}_{ij}^u = \left[\sum_{k=1}^{c} (L_{ij}/L_{ik})^{2/m-1} \right]^{-1} \tag{5}$$

$$\underline{U}^U = \left[\underline{u}_{ij}^u \right], \quad \underline{u}_{ij}^u = \left[\sum_{k=1}^{c} (S_{ij}/S_{ik})^{2/m-1} \right]^{-1} \tag{6}$$

Where $\bar{u}_{ij}^u$ and $\underline{u}_{ij}^u$ are upper and lower bounds of membership u_{ij}^u, $L_{ij} = mean\left(d_{ij}^x \right)$ is the average values between dimensions, $S_{ij} = max\left(d_{ij}^x \right)$ is the maximum values between dimensions, d_{ij}^x is the dimensional distance between unlabeled sample x_i^u and cluster center v_j.

The interval type-2 FCM algorithm needs to normalize the membership degree of the interval. In this paper, the adaptive factor γ [21] is introduced to dynamically adjust the membership width. The adaptive factor γ is as follows:

$$U^U = \overline{U}^U - \gamma(\overline{U}^U - \underline{U}^U) \tag{7}$$

Where $\gamma = \{\gamma_1, \gamma_2, \cdots \gamma_c\}$ is for each cluster. The meaning of the formula is that when data are divided into difference clusters, the adaptive factor γ will become larger in $[0, 1]$ if the mean-square error of the cluster becomes larger. And the membership descending value is extended immediately. As the number of iterations increases, γ tends to be a stable value. Positive correlation curve of adaptive factor γ calculation is defined as follows:

$$\gamma = 1 - 0.97exp(-5e^2) \tag{8}$$

Where $e = \{e_1, e_2, \cdots, e_j, \cdots, e_c\}$ is the mean-square error of the cluster, and defined as follows:

$$e_j = \frac{\sum_{i \in C_j} \left(u_{ij}^u\right)^m \delta\left(x_i^u, v_j\right)}{\|C_j\|}, \quad j = 1, 2, \cdots, c \tag{9}$$

Where $\delta\left(x_i^u, v_j\right)$ represents the deviation between the unlabeled sample points x_i^u and the center v_j in current cluster C_j. $\|C_j\|$ is the number of sample points in cluster C_j. The SS-AIT2FCM algorithm steps are as follows:

Step1: Firstly, certain expert knowledge of each classes is obtained in datasets X, and the sample labels is marked. Confirming labeled sample set X^L and unlabeled sample set X^U, determining clustering number c, iteration termination number T and threshold ε, initializing the number of iterations $t = 1$, the fuzzy weight index m, the membership matrix U^U of unlabeled sample points and objective function $J_0 = 0$.
Step2: According to Eq. (4), initialize the ratio λ of labeled sample. According to the method in Eq. (2), initialize the center V^0.
Step3: According to Eqs. (5) and (6), calculate membership degree interval $\left[\overline{U}^U, \underline{U}^U\right]$.
Step4: According to membership matrix U^U, obtain the mean-square-error of each cluster in method of Eq. (9), update the adaptive factor γ in method of Eq. (8), and update the descending membership matrix U^U in method of Eq. (7).
Step5: According to Eq. (3), update the center V.
Step6: According to Eq. (1), update the objective function J_t.
Step7: If $\|J_t - J_{t-1}\| \leq \varepsilon$ or $t \geq T$, stop; else $t = t + 1$, turn to **Step3**.

3   Experiment and Discussion

3.1   Experimental Data

To test the validity and adaptability of the algorithm, we select one multi-spectral data of SPOT5 satellite sensor (10 m spatial resolution) and one multi-spectral data of TM satellite sensor (30 m spatial resolution) as the experimental data, which are located in

Summer Palace, Beijing City, China, and Hengqin Island, Guangdong Province, China, respectively. They have a wide coverage and its features are rich in content, and there are obvious uncertainty, ambiguities and interferences.

The size of Summer Palace SPOT5 image data (east to Century City, west to Beijing Botanical Garden, south to Xingshikou Road, north to the Summer Palace) is 591 * 736 pixels. As shown in Table 1 below, the land is covered by the water, bare land, grassland, construction site, and woodland. This experimental data has obvious features, such as large coverage area, many shadows, and strong fuzziness. These features can exactly be used to prove the accuracy and adaptability of the algorithm in complex remote sensing image classification problem.

Table 1. Composition of the categories in Summer Palace SPOT5 image data.

Experimental data	Land cover	Describe
Summer Palace SPOT5	Water	River, Kunming reservoir
	Bare land	Main trunk road, residential district
	Grass	Grassland, greenbelt
	Construction site	Large buildings, airports
	Woodland	Mountain forest, landscape forest

The size of Hengqin Island TM image data (covers the entire big Hengqin Island and small Hengqin Island and its surrounding waters) is 452 * 795 pixels. As shown in Table 2 below, the land is covered by vegetation, farms, building land, clear water, turbid water, and wetland. This experimental data have fuzzy characteristics as the same pixel represents many kinds of ground objects and serious spectral overlaps. And it can effectively verify the feasibility and correctness of the semi-supervised fuzzy classification method.

Table 2. Composition of the categories in Hengqin Island TM image data.

Experimental data	Land cover	Describe
Hengqin Island TM	Vegetation	Grassland, forest land
	Farms	Raise oysters, water flooded rice fields
	Building land	Housing, roads, airport
	Clear water	Clear water
	Turbid water	Turbid water
	Wetland	Wetland

These experiments aims to verify the correctness and applicability of proposed algorithm for classification problem of more complex remote sensing image data. The algorithms used for comparison are FCM, KM-IT2FCM [16] and AIT2FCM [19]. There is no filtering, post-processing or other operations in the process of experiment. Moreover, in order to ensure the comparability of the final experimental results, the parameters (iteration termination number $T = 300$, threshold $\varepsilon = 10^{-5}$ and the fuzzy weight index $m = 2$) in the experiment were uniform. The classification effect of the algorithm is compared from visual interpretation and objective indicators.

3.2   Experimental Results Analysis

Figure 1(a) is RGB image of source image data combined by 1, 2, and 3 bands. The following three regional images are selected for the obvious classification of the differences in Fig. 1(a)–(e), namely Area. 1, Area. 2 and Area. 3. As shown in Fig. 1, the shadow of the mountain forest in the Area. 1 is severe, which increases the interference of the classification. The dark pixels of the forest wetland in the Area. 2 are serious, and the road and the central house are covered by the shadow of the trees, which increases the ambiguity of the classification. In the Area. 3, the waterways, roads, and grasses surrounding the roads are staggered.

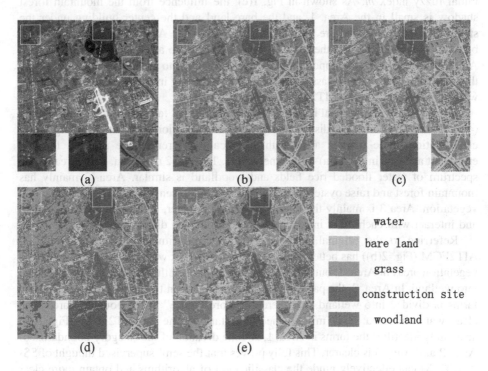

water
bare land
grass
construction site
woodland

Fig. 1. Experiment result of Summer Palace SPOT5 data based on different methods.

Referring to the experimental original image data, as shown in Fig. 1, type-1 FCM (Fig. 1(b)) based on single membership function has insufficient fuzzy expression ability for heterogeneous regions of remote sensing images with serious spectral aliasing, large coverage area and abundant features: In Fig. 1(b), the road and waterway are blurred, the waters and woodland categories are seriously misclassified, and grassland and woodland cannot be correctly distinguished. Because the shaded areas are similar to the waters, the shadow areas are misclassified into waters. As in Area. 1, the mountain shadow spectrum is similar to that of water, so the mountain shadow is misclassified into water. The KM-IT2FCM (Fig. 1(c)) based on the two fuzzy indices to construct the membership interval depends on the selection of the fuzzy index m, which is prone to the classification result of the large category "phagocytic" small category phenomenon: As shown in Fig. 1(c), the road and the waterway are misclassified, and the shadow of the mountain is divided into waters. The AIT2FCM (Fig. 1(d)) for constructing the membership interval based on the fuzzy distance metric has a degree of ill-posedness problems on the data and dependence on the selection of the fuzzy index m: In Fig. 1(d), the phenomenon of misclassification between categories is serious, and the boundary is not obvious. Referring to the experimental results of literature [19], the dependence of the algorithm on the selection of the fuzzy index m is shown to some extent. Only SS-AIT2FCM (Fig. 1(e)) obtained the classification results with high degree of aggregation and more obvious boundaries under the same initial fuzzy index m: As shown in Fig. 1(e), the influence from the mountain forest shadow is small in the Area. 1, and the bare land and the center building under the shadow of the forest land are accurately identified in the Area. 2, the clear boundary between the waterway and the road is obvious, and there are fewer "noise points" in Area 3. This indicates the importance of prior knowledge to the classification results of the algorithm in the rough classification of remote sensing images, and the validity and well-posedness of the SS-AIT2FCM algorithm.

Figure 2(a) is the original image of TM images based false color composite image (4, 3, 2 bands). In order to discuss the guiding role of prior information on algorithm classification, three marked areas with significant differences are selected for discriminant analysis in Fig. 2(a)–(d), namely Area. 1, Area. 2 and Area. 3. In Area. 1, the spectrum of water flooded rice fields and woodland is similar. Area. 2 mainly has mountain forest and raise oysters, which is susceptible to sensitive changes of mountain vegetation. Area 3 is mainly the farms and the clear water, and the two are connected and interact with each other in reality, so it is difficult to distinguish.

Referring to the original image data of the experiment, as shown in Fig. 2, AIT2FCM (Fig. 2(b)) has better completed the division of water flooded rice fields and vegetation areas in Area. 1, but the boundary area between the two categories is divided into wetland. In Area. 2, the partial boundary area between the mountain forest and the farms is divided into wetland, and there are more "noise" in the boundary area. The clear water in Area. 3 is misclassified into farms; The SS-AIT2FCM (Fig. 2(c)) accurately identifies the farms in Area. 1, and the division of the category boundaries of Area. 2 and Area. 3 is clearer. This fully proves that the semi-supervised thought of SS-AIT2FCM can effectively guide the classification of algorithms and obtain more clear and accurate category results.

Comparing experimental results of these algorithms for three groups of multi-spectral data, we measured a set of sample points (80) of complex and object spectrum aliasing area, and combined with the land use map and the historical data of previous years, respectively. As shown in Table 3, we can see the overall classification accuracy and KAPPA coefficient of SS-AIT2FCM is the highest in all algorithms, classification results consistent with the results of visual interpretation, and the algorithm execution time (CPU time) is the lowest, which proved that the addition of semi-supervised method can reduce

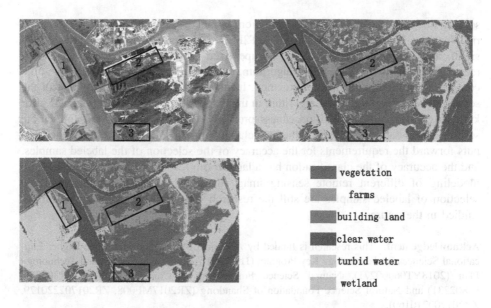

Fig. 2. Experiment result of Hengqin Island TM data based on different methods. (Color figure online)

the algorithm time while meeting the requirements of sophisticated category. For remote sensing images with serious spectral aliasing, large coverage and abundant features, SS-AIT2FCM has higher classification accuracy and better adaptability.

Table 3. Objective indicators comparison results of the classification algorithm

Experimental data	Classification algorithm	Overall accuracy	Kappa coefficient	CPU-time (s)
Summer Palace SPOT5	FCM	60%	0.552	116.548
	KM-IT2FCM ($m_1 = 1.5$, $m_2 = 4.5$)	80%	0.712	281.098
	AIT2FCM	64%	0.601	206.530
	SS-AIT2FCM ($\lambda = 0.01$)	89%	0.876	108.384
Hengqin Island TM	AIT2FCM	72%	0.640	319.378
	SS-AIT2FCM ($\lambda = 0.05$)	81%	0.745	144.746

4 Conclusion

This paper proposes a semi-supervised adaptive interval type-2 fuzzy c-means algorithm (SS-AIT2FCM). The SS-AIT2FCM apply the priori information to the initialization centroid and centroid calculation process, and fully exerts the guiding role of the labeled sample on the algorithm. The experimental results show that the interval type-2 fuzzy algorithm performs better than the type-1 fuzzy algorithm in remote sensing image data with low spatial resolution, large coverage area of mixed pixels and rich features. The accuracy of the SS-AIT2FCM algorithm with prior knowledge is significantly higher than that of the unsupervised algorithm, and it can effectively reduce the computation time of the algorithm, and make up for the increase of the time complexity of the type-2 fuzzy set method. It further validates the effectiveness of the semi-supervised method in the algorithm in this paper. The introduction of expert prior knowledge also solved the ill-posedness problem of the algorithm itself for remote sensing image data, and improved the final classification result. However, the algorithm puts forward the requirements for the accuracy of the selection of the labeled samples, and the accuracy of the classification has a large room for improvement. The matching modeling of different remote sensing image data and fuzzy algorithms, and the selection of labeled samples are still the research directions that need to be further studied in the future.

Acknowledgement. This research is funded by A Project of Shandong Province Higher Educational Science and Technology Key Program (J18KZ016), the Yantai Science and Technology Plan (2018YT06000271), Natural Science Foundation of China (61801414, 61802330, 61802331) and Natural Science Foundation of Shandong (ZR2017MF008, ZR201702220179, ZR201709210160).

References

1. Du, P.J., Xia, J.S., Xue, Z.H., et al.: Review of hyperspectral remote sensing image classification. J. Remote Sens. **20**(2), 236–256 (2016)
2. Xu, J.D., Yu, X.C., Pei, W.J., et al.: A remote sensing image fusion method based on feedback sparse component analysis. Comput. Geosci. **85**(PB), 115–123 (2015)
3. He, H., Liang, T.H., Hu, D., et al.: Remote sensing clustering analysis based on object-based interval modeling. Comput. Geosci. **94**, 131–139 (2016)
4. He, H., Yu, X.C., Hu, D.: Analysis and Application of Fuzzy Uncertainty Modeling. Science Press, Beijing (2016)
5. Xu, J.D., Ni, M.Y., Zhang, Y.J., et al.: Remote sensing image fusion method based on multiscale morphological component analysis. J. Appl. Remote Sens. **10**(2), 025018 (2016)
6. Gong, J.Y., Zhong, Y.F.: Survey of intelligent optical remote sensing image processing. J. Remote Sens. **20**(5), 733–747 (2016)
7. Persello, C., Bruzzone, L.: Active and semisupervised learning for the classification of remote sensing image. IEEE Trans. Geosci. Remote Sens. **52**(11), 6937–6956 (2014)
8. Crawford, M.M., Tuia, D., Yang, H.L.: Active learning: any value for classification of remotely sensed data? Proc. IEEE **101**(3), 593–608 (2013)
9. Zadeh, L.A.: Fuzzy set. Inf. Control **8**, 338–353 (1965)
10. Yu, X.C., He, H., Hu, D., et al.: Land cover classification of remote sensing imagery based on interval-valued data fuzzy c-means algorithm. Sci. China: Earth Sci. **57**(06), 1306–1313 (2014)
11. Liu, L.: A new fuzzy clustering method with neighborhood distance constraint for volcanic ash cloud. IEEE J. Mag. **4**(99), 7005–7013 (2016)
12. Choubin, B., Solaimani, K., Habibnejad, R M , et al · Watershed classification by remote sensing indices: a fuzzy c-means clustering approach. J. Mt. Sci. **14**(10), 2053–2063 (2017)

13. Hwang, C., Rhee, C.H.: Uncertain fuzzy clustering: interval type-2 fuzzy approach to c-means. IEEE Trans. Fuzzy Syst. **15**(1), 107–120 (2007)
14. Memon, K.H.: A histogram approach for determining fuzzy values of interval type-2 fuzzy c-means. Expert Syst. Appl. **91**, 27–35 (2018)
15. Huo, H.Y., Guo, J.F., Li, Z.L., et al.: Remote sensing of spatiotemporal changes in wetland geomorphology based on type 2 fuzzy sets: a case study of Beidahuang wetland from 1975 to 2015. Remote Sens. **9**(7), 683 (2017)
16. Yu, X.C., Zhou, W., He, H.: A method of remote sensing image auto classification based on interval type-2 fuzzy c-means. In: IEEE Proceedings of the International Conference on Fuzzy Systems, pp. 223–228 (2014)
17. Guo, J.F., Huo, H.Y.: An enhanced IT2FCM* algorithm integrating spectral indices and spatial information for multi-spectral remote sensing image clustering. Remote Sens. **9**(9), 960 (2017)
18. Assas, O.: Images segmentation based on interval type-2 Fuzzy C-Means. In: IEEE Proceedings of SAI Intelligent Systems Conference, pp. 773–781 (2015)
19. He, H., He, D., Yu, X.C.: Land cover classification based on adaptive interval type-2 fuzzy clustering. Chin. J. Geophys. **59**(6), 1983–1993 (2016)
20. Long, N., Mai, D.S., Pedrycz, W.: Semi-supervising Interval Type-2 Fuzzy C-Means clustering with spatial information for multi-spectral satellite image classification and change detection. Comput. Geosci. **83**, 1–16 (2015)
21. Li, H.X.: Variable domain adaptive fuzzy controller. Sci. China: Tech. Sci. (01), 32–42 (1999)

Vision-Based Joint Attention Detection for Autism Spectrum Disorders

Wanqi Zhang, Zhiyong Wang, and Honghai Liu[✉][iD]

State Key Laboratory of Mechanical System and Vibration,
Shanghai Jiao Tong University, Shanghai, China
{sissi_sjtu,yzwang_sjtu,honghai.liu}@sjtu.edu.cn

Abstract. Autism Spectrum Disorder (ASD) is one of the most common neurodevelopmental disorders in childhood. Its clinical symptoms mainly include narrow interests, stereotyped behavior and social communication disorders. There is still no cure for ASD. Only early detection and intervention can help to alleviate the symptoms and effects of ASD, so that ASD patients can adapt to the society and live a relatively normal life. Joint Attention is one of the core features of ASD and one of the key diagnostic indicators. In this paper, a detection test for Joint Attention is carried out among 8 non-ASD adults through a visual system which contains of one RGB camera and one Kinect. The result shows that the system can effectively detect the Joint Attention and has good accuracy.

Keywords: Autism Spectrum Disorder · Joint Attention · Visual system

1 Introduction

Autism Spectrum Disorder (ASD) is one of the most common neurodevelopmental disorders in childhood. Its clinical symptoms mainly include narrow interests, stereotyped behavior and social communication disorders. The first source of ASD's harmfulness is that ASD is global and extensive [1–3]. At the same time, the incidence of autism is still growing rapidly year by year [4]. The second source of harmfulness of ASD is that there is still no cure for it. Only early detection and intervention can help to alleviate the symptoms and effects of ASD, so that ASD patients can adapt to the society and live a relatively normal life. In addition, another harmful source of ASD is the shortage of corresponding medical resources. At present, the diagnosis and intervention of ASD are mostly done by professional rehabilitation doctors. However the number of such professionals is seriously imbalanced with the number of ASD patients, which causes most ASD patients to miss the best screening and intervention opportunities.

Supported by the National Natural Science Foundation of China (No. 61733011, 51575338).

ⓒ Springer Nature Singapore Pte Ltd. 2019
F. Sun et al. (Eds.): ICCSIP 2018, CCIS 1005, pp. 26–36, 2019.
https://doi.org/10.1007/978-981-13-7983-3_3

With the development of science and technology, human-computer interaction technology has gradually developed, broadening the communication methods between humans and computers. In the field of human-computer interaction, eye center positioning technology, face recognition technology, skeleton motion recognition technology, and hand gesture recognition technology have become more mature. Therefore, in recent years, combining these technologies with the diagnostic paradigm to assist in the diagnosis and treatment of ASD has become a hot trend. Whether in the process of manual diagnosis and treatment or in the process of computer-assisting diagnosis and treatment, behavior analysis is a common method. In this process, "Joint Attention (Hereinafter referred to as JA)" is an important paradigm. During the diagnosis, the children's response about this paradigm can be used to measure whether the subject has autism or not. Training about this paradigm can help improve children's social skills during the intervention. In this paper we use a machine vision detection system includes an RGB camera and Kinect, combined with multi-sensor data fusion technology and the above-mentioned technologies, to achieve the detection process of Joint Attention in ASD and estimation the detection accuracy of the system.

2   Related Works

This section reviews some of the previous work of others. Previously, the detection and intervention of JA was mainly done manually. Professional physicians interact with children. Through behavioral analysis, they manually judge whether children's JA development is defective, or train and correct behavior of JA of ASD children during the interaction process. In recent years, the development of artificial intelligence assisted systems has provided a new and useful tool for JA detection. Han et al. [5] used a wearable eye tracker during interacting with children, estimated the child's facial direction through the video which is recorded by the camera mounted on the eye tracker, and further analyzed gaze patterns to determine JA. The work in [6] compares the development differences of JA between typical developing children and children with ASD by Kinect sensors to capture social behavioral cues.

In the intervention of ASD, the use of human-machine interface for assistance has also become a development trend. Mei et al. proposed a new JA training method that uses customizable virtual tasks (CVH) and virtual reality (VR) games to assist with JA training. They developed a CVH with customizable [7]. Zheng et al. developed a new autonomous robotic system for JA training for ASD children and conducted four sessions of one-target interventions for six ASD children. It automatically tracks the behavior of the participants during the intervention and adaptively adjusts the interaction patterns based on the participants' performance. The results show that the autonomous robotic system can improve one-target joint attention performance in young children with ASD in an 8-month intervention. The result also suggested that it might cause good interactions in a more difficult task [8].

3   Paradigm and Detection Scene

JA refers to the process in which one person establishes eye contact with others, pays attention to the same object or event, and shares the attention between two people. JA develops from an early childhood and is an important part of the development of language, psychology and social cognition [9]. Psychologists have shown that the issue of JA is one of the core features of ASD and one of the key diagnostic indicators [10]. Therefore, whether in the process of artificial diagnosis and treatment of ASD or robot-assisted diagnosis and treatment of ASD, it is a common method to analyze whether a subject has JA problem or to train for JA.

The scene for detection is shown in Figs. 1 and 2. Figure 1 is a three-dimensional view of the scene, and Fig. 2 is a top view of the detected scene. The venue is 4 m * 2.5 m in size with a table and two chairs. The chairs are placed face to face on both sides of the table. During the test, the child is seated, the adult is sitting opposite, and the toys are placed on the table.

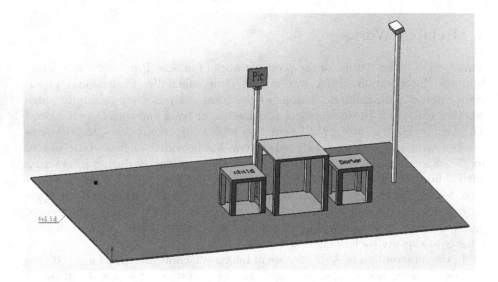

Fig. 1. A three-dimensional view of the detection scene for Joint Attention.

In this article, the testing process is as follows: Adult first gets the child's attention, if can't, then directly end this round of the test. If the adult gets childs attention successfully, give an instruction such as "Baby, look!", point at the picture on the left-front side of the child, and show it with gaze at the same time. If the child responds, the entire test ends. If the child does not respond, let the child play toys for 3 min before conducting the second round of testing. The second round of testing is the same as the first round. Each round is tested once, and there should be at least 3 min between two rounds. Among them, the

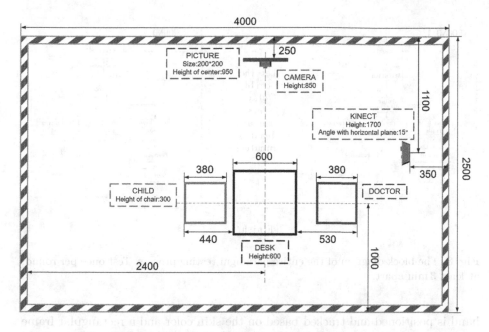

Fig. 2. A top view of the detection scene for Joint Attention.

"response" represents that the child turns head and looks at the picture that the adult points to within 10 s. There are three kinds of "no response" performances. (1) After 10 s from the finger pointing of the adult, the child turns to look at the picture, (2) the child turns head without looking at the picture, (3) the child looked at the adult, but did not turn his head to look at the picture. The testing process of JA is shown in the Fig. 3.

4   Method

4.1   Evaluation Indicator

In test of JA, the effective detection process begins with pointing behavior by adult, and the pointing represents the beginning of a round of testing. During the test, the system judges whether the adult has finger pointing behavior through gesture recognition. The next 10 s start from the time when the pointing behavior of adult occurs is key detection time range of the system. During this period of time, the system detects whether the child looks at the picture after the adult's pointing behavior by detecting and tracking the child's gaze, and further determines whether JA problem exists.

Adult pointing behavior is mainly reflected in the finger pointing gesture during the test, and the corresponding detecting technology is hand gesture recognition technology. Hand gesture recognition technology is based on deep learning. First of all, the video frame is converted to the YCbCr space. Then the

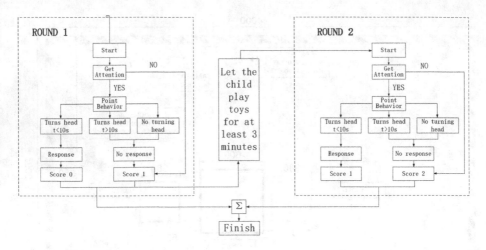

Fig. 3. The block diagram of the entire paradigm testing process. Test once per round, at least 3 min apart.

hand is positioned and tracked based on the skin color and a rectangular frame containing the hand is obtained. The hand gestures are then identified using a pre-trained model through a convolutional neural network.

For the JA test, the most important assessment point is a triangle which contains of the eye contact between child and adult, adults gaze or finger guiding child to look at the picture, and the childs gaze on the picture pointed by the adult, which is shown in Fig. 4. Therefore, in the evaluation of JA paradigm, children's gaze is the main concern. The premise of tracking gaze is to detect the face. In existing scenarios and systems, two sensors capture data in parallel. The confidence score of the acquired face is obtained with a predefined facial front as a standard, and the sensor with the highest facial confidence score at a certain moment is defined as the best sensor for this moment. After detecting the face, an improved support vector regression (SVR) method is used to locate the center of the eye based on facial feature localization. The method uses the original pixel values and the gradient intensity values calculated by convolution with the Sobel operator to train the model. In the positioning phase, the facial key points are first obtained, and the inner parts of the 12 points around the eyes (6 points are for one eye) are selected as the areas of interest, then the trained model is used for central location for the extracted regions of interest. After obtaining the position of the center of the eye, a two-eye model based method is used to estimate the gaze direction of the ASD child [11].

4.2 Algorithm Logic

Mapping the JA test process to the system algorithm is the prerequisite for accurate detection. The judgment for JA is mainly determined by the total score for all key points in the detection process. Recognition algorithm logic of

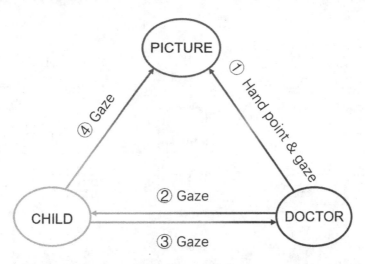

Fig. 4. For the JA test, the most important assessment point is a triangle which contains of the eye contact between child and adult, adults gaze or finger guiding child to look at the picture, and the childs gaze on the picture pointed by the adult.

JA is shown in Fig. 5. First, start the first round of testing, if the adult can not get the child's attention, then make a palm gesture, when the system detects this gesture, the first round will be ended and scored 1. If the adult successfully obtains the child's attention, then points to the picture on the left front of the child. The gesture of the index finger indicates the starting of timing and data detection. If the child looks at the picture in the first round of tests, then there is a response. At this time, the JA test is skipped and a total score of 0 is obtained. If the child does not look at the picture, there is no response. Score 1 and start the next round of test. Similarly, if the system detects an adult five-finger gesture in the second round of test, it means that the child's attention cannot be obtained, and the second round of the test will be ended and scored 2. If a pointing gesture is detected, the system starts timing and records the data. If the child in the second round of test responds, score 1; if there is no response, score 2. After the two rounds of testing, the total score of the two rounds is calculated, which is the total score for the JA test.

4.3 Data Collection and Analysis

The data acquisition system used in this paper is included in the 4×2.5 scene, which mainly includes a camera, a Kinect and their fixed bracket. The distribution, height and angle of the two vision sensors are given in Figs. 1 and 2, too. The system mainly collects gaze information of children in the range of 10 s after the pointing behavior of adults. It is worth noting that before using the system to collect data, two vision sensors should be calibrated to unify their coordinate system and world coordinate system to obtain accurate data.

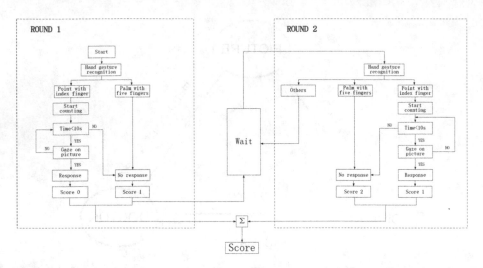

Fig. 5. Mapping the JA detection process to the system algorithm is the prerequisite for accurate JA detection. The judgment for JA is mainly determined by the total score for all key points in the detection process. Figure shows recognition algorithm logic of JA.

In the detection process of the paradigm JA, whether the child looks at the picture pointed by the adult is the most critical evaluation index, that is, by analyzing the child's gaze information to determine whether the child's sight-line is on the picture. During the analysis, this problem can be transformed into a geometric problem in three-dimensional space. That is, whether the gaze vector intersects with the picture pointed by the adult is calculated by the starting point and direction of the childs gaze. Considering the characteristics of people looking at objects, we first get the plane where the picture is located, and further define "gaze intersects with the picture" as the gaze vector intersects with the circle on the plane centered on the center of the picture with R as the radius (R is determined by the actual size of the image). Figure 6 shows a schematic diagram of the spatial model of this problem.

Assume that the coordinates of the starting point of the child's gaze is (x_C, y_C, z_C), direction of gaze vector is described as (V_x, V_y, V_z). Then determine the child's gaze vector in the form of parametric equations:

$$\begin{cases} x = x_C + V_x \cdot t \\ y = y_C + V_y \cdot t \\ z = z_C + V_z \cdot t \end{cases} \tag{1}$$

Assuming that the plane of the picture is $Ax + By + Cz + D = 0$, then the normal vector of this plane is (A, B, C) and obviously point $P = \left(-\frac{D}{3A}, -\frac{D}{3B}, -\frac{D}{3C}\right)$ is on this plane. Describe this plane with point P and the normal vectors:

$$A\left(x + \frac{D}{3A}\right) + B\left(y + \frac{D}{3B}\right) + C\left(z + \frac{D}{3D}\right) = 0 \tag{2}$$

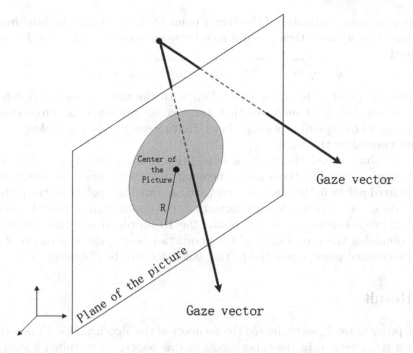

Fig. 6. During the analysis, the problem that whether the child looks at the picture pointed by the adult can be transformed into a geometric problem in three-dimensional space. That is, whether the gaze vector intersects with the picture pointed by the adult is calculated by the starting point and direction of the childs gaze.

Combine Eqs. (1) and (2) to obtain the expression of t:

$$t = \frac{A\left(-\frac{D}{3A} - x_C\right) + B\left(-\frac{D}{3B} - y_C\right) + C\left(-\frac{D}{3C} - z_C\right)}{A \cdot V_x + B \cdot V_y + C \cdot V_z} \tag{3}$$

In the expression of t in Eq. (3), if the denominator $A \cdot V_x + B \cdot V_y + C \cdot V_z$ equals to zero, it means that the gaze vector is parallel to the plane of the picture, and there is no intersection. This means that the child does not look at the picture pointed by the adult. If the denominator $A \cdot V_x + B \cdot V_y + C \cdot V_z$ is not equal to zero, substitute Eq. (3) into Eq. (1) to obtain intersection of the gaze vector and the plane of the picture. For convenience, write $A\left(-\frac{D}{3A} - x_C\right) + B\left(-\frac{D}{3B} - y_C\right) + C\left(-\frac{D}{3C} - z_C\right)$ as M, and its coordinates are

$$\begin{cases} x_I = x_C + V_x \cdot \dfrac{M}{A \cdot V_x + B \cdot V_y + C \cdot V_z} \\[2ex] y_I = y_C + V_y \cdot \dfrac{M}{A \cdot V_x + B \cdot V_y + C \cdot V_z} \\[2ex] z_I = z_C + V_z \cdot \dfrac{M}{A \cdot V_x + B \cdot V_y + C \cdot V_z} \end{cases} \tag{4}$$

Suppose the coordinates of the center point O of the picture pointed by the adult are (x_O, y_O, z_O), then the distance between point O and point I can be obtained

$$d = \sqrt{(x_C - x_O)^2 + (y_C - y_O)^2 + (z_C - z_O)^2} \tag{5}$$

Since the point O is in the same plane with the circle of radius R defined above, when $d < R$, it indicates that gaze vector intersects the projection of the picture in the two-dimensional plane. That means the child is looking at the picture pointed by the adult.

In the above calculation process, in addition to obtaining data such as gaze and gesture captured by the sensor, a necessary step is to obtain the positions of several fixed points in the medical scene, such as three key points on the picture. Since Kinect can capture depth information, the depth map of Kinect and the 2D RGB image can be matched to obtain the 3D coordinates of the fixed point. After obtaining the coordinates of the above two points, the expression of the two-dimensional plane where the picture is located can be obtained.

5   Result

In the previous work, we evaluated the accuracy of the algorithm for JA detection and got good results. In the experiments in this paper, we recruited 8 subjects (including 3 women and 5 men whose mean age is 25 years, no ASD patients), using the system and algorithm of this paper to get the score in JA test. In the process of being detected by the system, manual testing is also performed by professionals at the same time. The accuracy of the system score is evaluated by the score of manual testing as ground truth. In the experiment, the picture that the adult and the child shared attention was a picture, and the radius R of the circular range was set to 200 mm according to the size. Figure 7 shows the picture taken by the test system during the experiment.

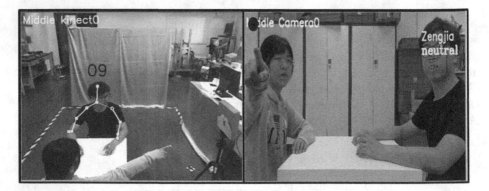

Fig. 7. The pictures taken by the test system during the experiment. The left shows the view of Kinect and the right shows the view of RGB camera.

The system scores of the 8 subjects during the test are given in the Table 1. All 8 subjects are healthy adults. There is no ASD patients and no defects in JA. The results of manual testing by professionals are all 0 points. However, in result of the system detection, subject 3 scored 3, which was inconsistent with the manual score.

Table 1. The scores given by detection system of the 8 subjects during the Joint Attention test.

Subject	Score		Total score
	Round 1	Round 2	
Subject 1	0	-	0
Subject 2	0	-	0
Subject 3	1	2	3
Subject 4	0	-	0
Subject 5	0	-	0
Subject 6	0	-	0
Subject 7	0	-	0
Subject 8	0	-	0

The experimental data of the subject was extracted and analyzed in a step-by-step manner, and the reason for the error was obtained. For subject 3, the gaze data detected by the system was confusing and the accuracy was poor. The reason may be that the subject's face is small and the system cannot accurately detect facial feature points. As mentioned above, one of the prerequisites for gaze detection is the central positioning of the eye, and an important step in the process of center positioning of the eye is to obtain facial feature points. Therefore, the subject's small face becomes the main cause of detection failure. This is also an aspect of the system and algorithm that needs to be improved in the future.

6   Conclusion

In this paper, a detection test for Joint Attention is carried out in 8 non-ASD adults through a computer vision system which contains of one RGB camera and one Kinect. The result shows that the system can effectively detect the JA and has good accuracy.

References

1. The National Autistic Society: What is Autism? (2014). www.autism.org.uk/about-autism
2. Zablotsky, B., Black, L.I., Maenner, M.J., et al.: Estimated prevalence of autism and other developmental disabilities following questionnaire changes in the 2014 National Health Interview Survey. Natl. Health Stat. Rep. **2015**(87), 1–20 (2015)
3. Cubells, J.: Prevalence of autism spectrum disorders in China. Shanghai Arch. Psychiatry **25**(3), 176–177 (2013)
4. Christensen, D.L., Baio, J., Braun, K.V., et al.: Prevalence and characteristics of autism spectrum disorder among children aged 8 years - autism and developmental disabilities monitoring network, 11 sites, United States, 2012. MMWR Surveill. Summ. **65**(3), 1C23 (2016)
5. Han, Y., Fathi, A., Abowd, G.D., et al.: Automated detection of mutual eye contact and joint attention using a single wearable camera system. In: International Meeting for Autism Research (2012)
6. Anzalone, S.M., Tilmont, E., Boucenna, S., et al.: How children with autism spectrum disorder behave and explore the 4-dimensional (spatial 3D+time) environment during a joint attention induction task with a robot. Res. Autism Spectr. Disord. **8**(7), 814–826 (2014)
7. Mei, C., Zahed, B.T., Mason, L., Ouarles, J.: Towards joint attention training for children with ASD - a VR game approach and eye gaze exploration. In: 2018 IEEE Conference on Virtual Reality and 3D User Interfaces, VR, Tuebingen/Reutlingen, Germany, pp. 289–296 (2018)
8. Zheng, Z., Nie, G., Swanson, A., Weitlauf, A., Warren, Z., Sarkar, N.: Longitudinal impact of autonomous robot-mediated joint attention intervention for young children with ASD. In: Agah, A., Cabibihan, J.-J., Howard, A.M., Salichs, M.A., He, H. (eds.) ICSR 2016. LNCS, vol. 9979, pp. 581–590. Springer, Cham (2016). https://doi.org/10.1007/978-3-319-47437-3_57
9. Mundy, P., Newell, L.: Attention, joint attention, and social cognition. Curr. Dir. Psychol. Sci. **16**(5), 269 (2007)
10. Osterling, J., Dawson, G.: Early recognition of children with autism: a study of first birthday home videotapes. J. Autism Dev. Disord. **24**(3), 247–257 (1994)
11. Esteban, P.G., Baxter, P., Belpaeme, T., et al.: How to build a supervised autonomous system for robot-enhanced therapy for children with autism spectrum disorder. Paladyn J. Behav. Robot. **8**(1), 18–38 (2017)

Multi-scale Local Receptive Field Based Online Sequential Extreme Learning Machine for Material Classification

Xinying Xu[1(✉)], Jing Fang[1], Qi Li[2], Gang Xie[1,3], Jun Xie[2], and Mifeng Ren[1]

[1] College of Electrical and Power Engineering,
Taiyuan University of Technology, Taiyuan, China
xuxinying@tyut.edu.cn
[2] College of Information and Computer Science,
Taiyuan University of Technology, Jinzhong, China
[3] School of Electronic and Information Engineering,
Taiyuan University of Science and Technology, Taiyuan, China

Abstract. Surface material classification has attracted a lot of attention from the academic and industrial communities. The surface material classification methods are for static object material data. However, in real industrial production, data cannot be generated overnight. It is generated continuously. In this work, we propose an algorithm named Multi-Scale Local Receptive Field Based Online Sequential Extreme Learning Machine (MSLRF-OSELM) for material classification, which not only can make dynamic training of networks by using data that are generated online of material images, but also can extract highly representative features from complex texture by multi-scale local receptive field. We conduct experiments on the public texture ALOT dataset and MNIST dataset. Experimental results verify the effectiveness of our algorithm and has good generalization performance.

Keywords: Dynamic · Multi-scale · Local receptive field · Surface material recognition

1 Introduction

Recently, surface material classification has attracted a lot of attention from the academic and industrial communities. Traditional scholars use static data for the classification of surface material. [1–3] selected different feature extraction methods for different data features. For material image, [1] proposed Average Gray Level (AGL) to represent image coarseness, edginess feature (IE) to represent image edginess, image glossiness (IG) [4], gray-level co-occurrence matrix (GLCM) to represent image line-likeness and roughness [4,5], image color distance feature (ICD) [6].

The surface material classification methods described above are for static object material data. However, in real industrial production, data cannot be

© Springer Nature Singapore Pte Ltd. 2019
F. Sun et al. (Eds.): ICCSIP 2018, CCIS 1005, pp. 37–53, 2019.
https://doi.org/10.1007/978-981-13-7983-3_4

generated overnight. It is generated continuously. Contemporary online learning develops technology from the industrial revolution to replace cheap labor and reduce the workload of workers. In the course of industrial production, massive amounts of data will be generated one after another. [7] proposed a family of cost-sensitive online classification algorithms with adaptive regularization. [8] proposed a novel online universal classifier capable of performing all the three types of classification. How to extract useful information from these online data is a major problem.

In this work, we propose an algorithm named Multi-Scale Local Receptive Field Based Online Sequential Extreme Learning Machine (MSLRF-OSELM) for material classification, which not only can make dynamic training of networks by using data that are generated online of material images, but also can extract highly representative features from complex texture by multi-scale local receptive field. The specific process of our structure is shown in Fig. 1. The architecture is consists of $p + 1$ MSLRF-NET. The BLOCK dataset generated online are successively entered into the corresponding network to updated the output weight β. We conduct experiments on the public texture ALOT dataset, which includes 250 material texture. Additionally, in order to verify that our method has strong generalization performance, we also conduct experiments on the MNIST dataset.

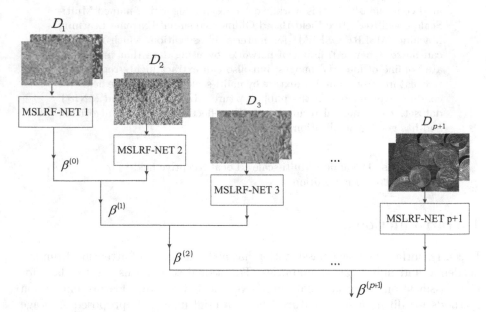

Fig. 1. The architecture of MSLRF-OSELM. The architecture is consists of $p + 1$ MSLRF-NET. The BLOCK dataset generated online are successively entered into the corresponding network.

The main contributions are summarized as follows:

1. We establish a novel online framework for surface material recognition task.
2. We develop an algorithm in which the scales of local receptive fields are diverse.
3. We conduct experiments on the public texture ALOT dataset and handwritten MNIST dataset. The obtained results show that the proposed method provides high efficiency and has strong generalization performance.

The rest of this paper are organized as follows. Section 2 briefly reviews the classic approaches of the Online Sequential Extreme Learning Machine (OSELM) and the Local Receptive Fields based Extreme Learning Machine (LRF-ELM). Section 3 describes the proposed framework. Section 4 shows the results of the experiments and compares the results with other methods. Conclusion and further works are presented in Sect. 5.

2   Relate Works

2.1   Online Sequential Extreme Learning Machine

In 2015, Huang et al. proposed the Local Receptive Fields based Extreme Learning Machine (LRF-ELM) and the extreme learning machine for regression and multiclass classification [9,10]. Although ELM algorithm has the advantages of fast speed and good generalization performance, when the training data is large, there are two problems that are the memory capacity is too large and the training time is too long. In response to the above problems, the Online Sequential Extreme Learning Machine (OSELM) algorithm is given in [11], the steps of OSELM mainly include two parts: the initial learning phase and the online learning phase.

(1) The initial learning phase.

The initial output weight $\beta^{(0)}$ of network is calculated by the initial dataset D_0, where $\{(\mathbf{x}_j, \mathbf{t}_j) | j \in [1, 2, \cdots, N_0]\}$. We suppose that D_0 has N_0 initial training samples, where $\mathbf{x}_j = [\mathbf{x}_{j1}, \mathbf{x}_{j2}, \cdots, \mathbf{x}_{jn}]$ is the j-th training sample, $\mathbf{Y}_j = [\mathbf{Y}_{j1}, \mathbf{Y}_{j2}, \cdots, \mathbf{Y}_{jm}]$ and $\mathbf{t}_j = [t_{j1}, t_{j2}, \cdots, t_{jm}]$ are the predict label and target label of the j-th training sample, respectively. There are n input neurons, L hidden neurons and m output neurons. The activation function of network is $G(\mathbf{x})$. Randomly generate input weights ω_i and bias b_i, where $i \in [1, 2, \cdots, L]$.

The initial output weight of network can be calculated by Eq. (1) as follows [12]:

$$\mathbf{H}_0 = \begin{pmatrix} G(\omega_1 \cdot \mathbf{x}_1 + b_1) & \cdots & G(\omega_L \cdot \mathbf{x}_1 + b_L) \\ \vdots & \cdots & \vdots \\ G(\omega_1 \cdot \mathbf{x}_{N_0} + b_1) & \cdots & G(\omega_L \cdot \mathbf{x}_{N_0} + b_L) \end{pmatrix}_{N_0 \times L} \tag{1}$$

Correspondingly, the initial output weight $\beta^{(0)}$ is calculated by Eq. (2) [13]:

$$\beta^{(0)} = \mathbf{P}_0^{-1} \mathbf{H}_0^T \mathbf{T}_0 \tag{2}$$

where $\mathbf{P}_0 = \mathbf{H}_0^T \mathbf{H}_0$, $\mathbf{T}_0 = [t_1, t_2, \cdots, t_N]^T$. Then, we set $k = 0$.

(2) The online learning phase.

The second phase is the online learning phase, in which the output weight β of network is updated sequentially by block dataset D_{k+1}, where $\{(\mathbf{x}_j, \mathbf{t}_j) | j \in [1, 2, \cdots, N_{k+1}]\}$.

If the block dataset is consisted with several training samples, the output weight $\beta^{(k+1)}$ is calculated by Eq. (3):

$$\begin{cases} \mathbf{P}_{k+1} = \mathbf{P}_k - \mathbf{P}_k \mathbf{H}_{k+1}^T \left(\mathbf{I} + \mathbf{H}_{k+1} \mathbf{P}_k \mathbf{H}_{k+1}^T \right)^{-1} \mathbf{H}_{k+1} \mathbf{P}_k \\ \beta^{(k+1)} = \beta^{(k)} + \mathbf{P}_{k+1} \mathbf{H}_{k+1}^T \left(\mathbf{T}_{k+1} - \mathbf{H}_{k+1} \beta^{(k)} \right) \end{cases} \tag{3}$$

If the block dataset is consisted with only one training sample, the output weight $\beta^{(k+1)}$ is calculated by Eq. (4):

$$\begin{cases} \mathbf{P}_{k+1} = \mathbf{P}_k - \dfrac{\mathbf{P}_k \mathbf{h}_{k+1} \mathbf{h}_{k+1}^T \mathbf{P}_k}{1 + \mathbf{h}_{k+1}^T \mathbf{P}_k \mathbf{h}_{k+1}} \\ \beta^{(k+1)} = \beta^{(k)} + \mathbf{P}_{k+1} \mathbf{h}_{k+1} \left(\mathbf{t}_{k+1}^T - \mathbf{h}_{k+1}^T \beta^{(k)} \right) \end{cases} \tag{4}$$

2.2 Local Receptive Fields Based Extreme Learning Machine

The Local Receptive Fields based Extreme Learning Machine (LRF-ELM) was proposed by Huang et al. [9], which is a generic architecture of ELM and can directly deal with images [10]. Figure 2 describes the detailed process of LRF-ELM. The links between input and hidden layer nodes are sparse and bounded by corresponding Local Receptive Fields. The local receptive field were sampled from any continuous probability distribution. In particular, the scale of local receptive field is only one scale. LRF-ELM can extract features by itself and classify the category of the image [14,15].

In general, the training phase of LRF-ELM consists of three basic operations:

(1) Feature mapping.

Randomly generate the initial weight matrix $\hat{\mathbf{A}}^{init}$ of the LRF-ELM by Eq. (5) [16,17]. It is noted that the size of the input image is $d \times d$, the size of local receptive field of the input layer is $r \times r$, where the size of r is fixed, so the size of the feature map should be $(d - r + 1) \times (d - r + 1)$, and we have

$$\begin{aligned} &\hat{\mathbf{A}}^{init} \in \mathbf{R}^{r^2 \times K} \\ &\hat{\mathbf{a}}_k \in \mathbf{R}^{r^2}, k = 1, 2, \ldots, K \end{aligned} \tag{5}$$

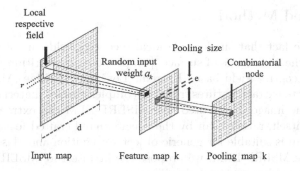

Local
respective
field

Pooling size

Random input
weight a_k

Combinatorial
node

r

e

d

Input map

Feature map k

Pooling map k

Fig. 2. The architecture of LRF-ELM.

Then, orthogonalize the $\hat{\mathbf{A}}^{init}$ by singular value decomposition (SVD) method. The input weight of the k-th feature map is $\mathbf{a}_k \in \mathbf{R}^{r \times r}$, which corresponds to $\hat{\mathbf{a}}_k \in \mathbf{R}^{r^2}$ column-wisely. The convolutional node (i, j) in the k-th feature map is calculated as Eq. (6):

$$\mathbf{C}_{i,j,k}(\mathbf{x}) = \sum_{m=1}^{r} \sum_{n=1}^{r} \mathbf{x}_{i+m-1,j+n-1} \cdot \mathbf{a}_{m,n,k}$$
$$i, j = 1, 2, \ldots, (d - r + 1)$$
(6)

(2) Square-root pooling and formulate the combinatorial node.

As shown in Fig. 2, the pooling size e denotes the distance between the center and the edge of the pooling area. And the pooling map is the same size as the feature map. $\mathbf{h}_{p,q,k}$ denotes the combinatorial node (p, q) in the k-th pooling map [18,19] that can be calculated as Eq. (7):

$$\mathbf{h}_{p,q,k} = \sqrt{\sum_{i=p-e}^{p+e} \sum_{j=q-e}^{q+e} \mathbf{C}^2_{i,j,k}}$$
$$p, q = 1, 2, \ldots, (d - r + 1)$$
$$if (i, j) \ is \ out \ of \ bound : \mathbf{C}_{i,j,k} = 0$$
(7)

In short, the values of all the combined nodes are concatenated into row vectors for each input sample. N samples forms N row vectors, that is the output matrix $\mathbf{H}$. $\mathbf{H} \in \mathbf{R}^{N \times K \cdot (d-r+1)^2}$.

(3) Calculate the β using the output matrix $\mathbf{H}$.

The training sample has its own target label $\mathbf{t}_j$, where $j = 1, 2, \cdots, N$. The output weights β can be calculated by the following Eq. (8) [20]:

$$\beta = \begin{cases} \mathbf{H}^T(\frac{\mathbf{I}}{C} + \mathbf{H}\mathbf{H}^T)^{-1}\mathbf{T} & N \le K \cdot (d - r + 1)^2 \\ (\frac{\mathbf{I}}{C} + \mathbf{H}^T\mathbf{H})^{-1}\mathbf{H}^T\mathbf{T} & N > K \cdot (d - r + 1)^2 \end{cases}$$
(8)

where C is the value of the regularization parameter, $\mathbf{H}^T$ is the transpose matrix of the output matrix $\mathbf{H}$ [21].

3   Proposed Method

Inspired by the fact that single scale local receptive field cannot extract more features from the wide range of surface, [15] propose an algorithm named Multi-Scale Local Receptive Field based Extreme Learning Machine (MSLRF-ELM), which is better to extract features from the complex surface material and classify the types of the image. It is noted that MSLRF-ELM can extract features by the algorithm itself, rather than by the specific hand-crafted feature extractor, so the algorithm is suitable for generic object recognition and classification. On the basis of the MSLRF-ELM, we propose the architecture MSLRF-OSELM to deal with online object material classification problems.

The MSLRF-OSELM contains the following steps:

(1) Initial learning phase based on multi-scale local receptive field.
(1.1) Color three-channel separation.

The downsampled image is separated by RGB three-channel color,and R,G,B single-channel image vectors are obtained respectively [22,23].
(1.2) Randomly generate and orthogonalize the initial weight for S scale channels.

The initial output weight $\beta^{(0)}$ of network is calculated by the initial dataset D_0, where $\{(\mathbf{x}_j,\mathbf{t}_j)|\ j \in [1,2,\cdots,N_0]\}$. We suppose that D_0 has N_0 initial

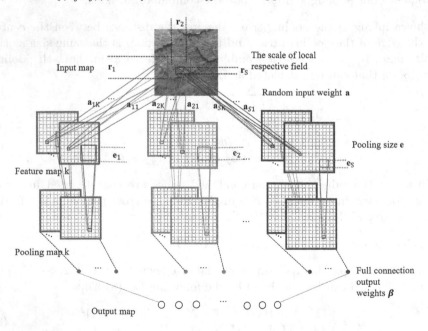

Fig. 3. The processing of MSLRF-ELM. The input image is the MeshFloorCloth, which is subsampled into $32 \times 32 \times 3$. In contrast to LRF-ELM, the MSLRF-ELM has S scale channels and the scale is $r_1, r_2, \cdots, r_S$, respectively. Each scale channel contains K feature maps. So the network can randomly generate $3 \times S \times K$ feature maps.

training samples, where $\mathbf{x}_j = [\mathbf{x}_{j1}, \mathbf{x}_{j2}, \cdots, \mathbf{x}_{jn}]$ is the j-th training sample, $\mathbf{Y}_j = [\mathbf{Y}_{j1}, \mathbf{Y}_{j2}, \cdots, \mathbf{Y}_{jm}]$ and $\mathbf{t}_j = [t_{j1}, t_{j2}, \cdots, t_{jm}]$ are the predict label and target label of the j-th training sample, respectively. There are n input neurons, L hidden neurons and m output neurons. The activation function of network is G(x).

As illustrated in Fig. 3, we suppose MSLRF-ELM has S-scale channels, and the scale is r_s, where $s = 1, 2, \ldots, S$. In order to obtain the thorough representation of the input image, each scale channel randomly generate K different input weights to obtain K different feature maps, so each color channel can randomly generate $S \times K$ feature maps. Please note that when the S scales of local receptive field are equal, MSLRF-ELM is equal to the traditional LRF-ELM [24].

According to Eq. (9), the network randomly generates initial weight matrix $\hat{\mathbf{A}}_c^{init(s)}$ of the s-th scale channel. We assume the input size is $d \times d$, therefore the size of s-th scale of Local Receptive Field is $(d - r_s + 1) \times (d - r_s + 1)$.

$$
\begin{aligned}
&\hat{\mathbf{A}}_c^{init(s)} \in \mathbf{R}^{r_s^2 \times k} \\
&\hat{\mathbf{A}}_c^{init(s)} = [\hat{\mathbf{a}}_{c1}^{init(s)}, \hat{\mathbf{a}}_{c2}^{init(s)}, \cdots, \hat{\mathbf{a}}_{cK}^{init(s)}] \\
&\hat{\mathbf{a}}_{ck}^{(s)} \in \mathbf{R}^{r_s^2} \\
&c \in \{R, G, B\} \\
&s = 1, 2, \ldots, S \\
&k = 1, 2, \ldots, K
\end{aligned}
\tag{9}
$$

(1.3) Then, orthogonalize the initial weight matrix $\hat{\mathbf{A}}_c^{init(s)}$ to obtain the orthogonal matrix $\hat{\mathbf{A}}_c^{(s)}$.

The SVD method is used to orthogonalize the initial weight matrix $\hat{\mathbf{A}}_c^{init(s)}$ to obtain the orthogonal matrix $\hat{\mathbf{A}}_c^{(s)}$. Each column of $\hat{\mathbf{A}}_c^{(s)}$ is an orthogonal basis. The input weight of the k-th feature map is $\mathbf{a}_{ck}^{(s)} \in \mathbf{R}^{r_s^2}$, which corresponds to $\hat{\mathbf{a}}_{ck}^{(s)}$ column-wisely.

(1.4) Multi-scale feature mapping.

The tradition method extracts the underlying features of the image through shallow learning, while the features extracted by convolution can eliminate the semantic gap between images. The $\mathbf{C}_{i,j,c,k}^{(s)}$ denotes convolutional node (i, j) of the k-th feature map in s-th scale channel of c color channel that is calculated as Eq. (10):

$$
\begin{aligned}
&\mathbf{C}_{i,j,c,k}^{(s)}(\mathbf{x}) = \sum_{m=1}^{r} \sum_{n=1}^{r} \mathbf{x}_{i+m-1,j+n-1}^c \cdot \mathbf{a}_{m,n,c,k}^{(s)} \\
&c \in \{R, G, B\}, \\
&s = 1, 2, \ldots, S \\
&k = 1, 2, \ldots, K \\
&i, j = 1, 2, \ldots, (d - r_s + 1)
\end{aligned}
\tag{10}
$$

(1.5) Multi-scale pooling.

The size of pooling is e_s, where $s = 1, 2, \ldots, S$. The symbol e_s denotes the distance between the center and the edge of the pooling area, which is shown in Fig. 3. The size of pooling map is the same as the feature map $(d - r_s + 1) \times (d - r_s + 1)$. $\mathbf{h}^{(s)}_{p,q,c,k}$ denotes the combinatorial node (p, q) of the k-th feature map in s-th scale channel of c color channel, which can be calculated by Eq. (11):

$$\mathbf{h}^{(s)}_{p,q,c,k} = \sqrt{\sum_{i=p-e}^{p+e} \sum_{j=q-e}^{q+e} \mathbf{C}^{2(s)}_{i,j,c,k}}$$
$$p, q = 1, 2, \ldots, (d - r_s + 1)$$
$$if (i, j) \ is \ out \ of \ bound : \mathbf{C}^{(s)}_{i,j,c,k} = 0 \tag{11}$$
$$c \in \{R, G, B\},$$
$$s = 1, 2, \ldots, S$$
$$k = 1, 2, \ldots, K$$

(1.6) Full connection.

Simply, in order to obtain the combinatorial layer matrix $\mathbf{H}_0 \in \mathbf{R}^{N_0} \times K \cdot \sum_{s=1}^{S} (d - r_s + 1)^2$, we concatenate the value of all combinatorial nodes into a row vector and put the rows of N_0 input samples together.

(1.7) Calculate the initial output weight $\boldsymbol{\beta}^{(0)}$.

Correspondingly, the initial output weight $\boldsymbol{\beta}^{(0)}$ is calculated by Eq. (12):

$$\boldsymbol{\beta}^{(0)} = \mathbf{P}_0^{-1} \mathbf{H}_0^T \mathbf{T}_0 \tag{12}$$

where $\mathbf{P}_0 = \mathbf{H}_0^T \mathbf{H}_0$, $\mathbf{T}_0 = [t_1, t_2, \cdots, t_{N_0}]^T$.

(1.8) Set $p = 0$.
  (2) The online learning phase based on multi-scale local receptive fields.
(2.1) Online multi-scale feature mapping for D_{p+1} dataset based on local receptive fields.

We assume that the online dataset D_{p+1} is $\{(\mathbf{x}_j, \mathbf{t}_j) | \ j \in [1, 2, \cdots, N_{p+1}]\}$. We put D_{p+1} into the multi-scale local receptive field were sampled from any continuous probability distribution. In particular, the scale of local receptive fields is only one scale network, according to the Eq. (13), we conduct multi-scale feature mapping operation to obtain $\mathbf{C}^{(s)(p+1)}_{i,j,c,k}(\mathbf{x}_{p+1})$. It is noted that the specific operation steps are the same as in step (1.4), in which S-scale channels, the initial weights and biases of each scale channel are equivalent to the settings in step (1.4).

$$\mathbf{C}^{(s)(p+1)}_{i,j,c,k}(\mathbf{x}_{p+1}) = \sum_{m=1}^{r} \sum_{n=1}^{r} \mathbf{x}^{c(p+1)}_{i+m-1,j+n-1} \cdot \mathbf{a}^{(s)}_{m,n,c,k}$$
$$c \in \{R, G, B\},$$
$$s = 1, 2, \ldots, S \tag{13}$$
$$k = 1, 2, \ldots, K^*$$
$$i, j = 1, 2, \ldots, (d - r_s + 1)$$

(2.2) Online multi-scale pooling for D_{p+1} dataset.

Following step (2.1), we perform a multi-scale pooling operation on the dataset D_{p+1}. The operation process is similar to step (1.5). The size of the multi-scale pooling is equivalent to the setting of the parameter in step (1.5). Multi-scale pooling values $\mathbf{h}_{u,v,c,k}^{(s)(p+1)}$ denotes the combinatorial node (u, v) of the k-th feature map in s-th scale channel, which can be calculated by Eq. (14):

$$
\mathbf{h}_{u,v,c,k}^{(s)(p+1)} = \sqrt{\sum_{i=u-e}^{u+e} \sum_{j=v-e}^{v+e} \mathbf{C}_{i,j,c,k}^{2(s)(p+1)}}
$$

$$
\begin{aligned}
&u, v = 1, 2, \ldots, (d - r_s + 1) \\
&if\,(i, j)\ is\ out\ of\ bound : \mathbf{C}_{i,j,c,k}^{(s)(p+1)} = 0 \\
&c \in \{R, G, B\}, \\
&s = 1, 2, \ldots, S \\
&k = 1, 2, \ldots, K
\end{aligned} \tag{14}
$$

(2.3) Full connection for D_{p+1} dataset.

Simply, in order to obtain the combinatorial layer matrix $\mathbf{H}_{p+1} \in \mathbf{R}^{N_{p+1}} \times K \cdot \sum_{s=1}^{S} (d - r_s + 1)^2$, we concatenate the value of all combinatorial nodes into a row vector and put the rows of N_{p+1} input samples together.

(2.4) Calculate the output weight $\beta^{(p+1)}$ for D_{p+1} dataset.

By observing, we have summarized the recursion formula (15):

$$
\begin{cases}
\mathbf{P}_{p+1} = \mathbf{P}_p + \mathbf{H}_{p+1}^T \mathbf{H}_{p+1} \\
\beta^{(p+1)} = \beta^{(p)} + \mathbf{P}_{p+1}^{-1} \mathbf{H}_{p+1}^T \left(\mathbf{T}_{p+1} - \mathbf{H}_{p+1}\beta^{(p)}\right)
\end{cases} \tag{15}
$$

According to Woodbury's theorem, $\mathbf{P}_{p+1}^{-1}$ can be derived from the following Eq. (16):

$$
\begin{aligned}
\mathbf{P}_{p+1}^{-1} &= \left(\mathbf{P}_p + \mathbf{H}_{p+1}^T \mathbf{H}_{p+1}\right)^{-1} = \mathbf{P}_p^{-1} \\
&-\mathbf{P}_p^{-1}\mathbf{H}_{p+1}^T \left(\mathbf{I} + \mathbf{H}_{p+1}\mathbf{P}_p^{-1}\mathbf{H}_{p+1}^T\right)^{-1} \times \mathbf{H}_{p+1}\mathbf{P}_p^{-1}
\end{aligned} \tag{16}
$$

Make $\mathbf{Q}_{p+1} = \mathbf{P}_{p+1}^{-1}$, if the block dataset is consisted with several training samples, the Eq. (15) can be updated as Eq. (17):

$$
\begin{cases}
\mathbf{Q}_{p+1} = \mathbf{Q}_p - \mathbf{Q}_p\mathbf{H}_{p+1}^T \left(\mathbf{I} + \mathbf{H}_{p+1}\mathbf{Q}_p\mathbf{H}_{p+1}^T\right)^{-1}\mathbf{H}_{p+1}\mathbf{Q}_p \\
\beta^{(p+1)} = \beta^{(p)} + \mathbf{Q}_{p+1}\mathbf{H}_{p+1}^T \left(\mathbf{T}_{p+1} - \mathbf{H}_{p+1}\beta^{(p)}\right)
\end{cases} \tag{17}
$$

If the block dataset is consisted with only one training sample, the output weight of the Eq. (15) can be updated as Eq. (18):

$$
\begin{cases}
\mathbf{Q}_{p+1} = \mathbf{Q}_p - \dfrac{\mathbf{Q}_p\mathbf{h}_{p+1}\mathbf{h}_{p+1}^T\mathbf{Q}_p}{1+\mathbf{h}_{p+1}^T\mathbf{Q}_p\mathbf{h}_{p+1}} \\
\beta^{(p+1)} = \beta^{(p)} + \mathbf{Q}_{p+1}\mathbf{h}_{p+1} \left(\mathbf{t}_{p+1}^T - \mathbf{h}_{p+1}^T\beta^{(p)}\right)
\end{cases} \tag{18}
$$

(2.5) Set $p = p + 1$, determine whether the D_{p+1} dataset is the last online dataset, and if so, we stop the online learning. Otherwise,repeat the steps (2.1)–(2.4) until the dataset is the last block dataset of the online training datasets.

(2.6) Calculate the output weight β by following Eq. (19):

$$\beta = \beta^{(p+1)} \tag{19}$$

4 Experiment Results

4.1 The ALOT Dataset

The ALOT (Amsterdam Library of Textures) dataset was established by a scholar in the field of computer vision, which contains 250 natural materials, such as wood fibers, white rice, sugar, onions, and wool blankets, etc. [25]. Figure 4 shows the part samples of ALOT dataset. The dataset is a collection of texture images under different lighting and viewing directions. Each type of texture is collected in six different lighting conditions, four different rotation angles that acquire image by four different rotation angle including 0, 60, 120 and 180°. In addition, each camera also collects a red spectral texture image. Therefore, the total number of each category is 100, the entire ALOT dataset consists of 25,000 images. The dataset consists of two parts: the color image and the grayscale image. The size of each image is 384 × 256.

Fig. 4. The part samples of ALOT dataset that consists of 250 categories. The dataset is available at http://aloi.science.uva.nl/public_alot/

4.2   Experiment Settings

In order to verify the effectiveness of MSLRF-OSELM, we use the ALOT dataset to conduct our online experiments. Firstly, we randomly generate 20 samples for each category as test samples and others as training samples. In our experiment, taking into account the computer memory and running speed, we downsample the ALOT dataset samples as 32×32. In view of the fact that the dataset images are derived from different conditions, we use a Zero Component Analysis (ZCA) [26] whitening transformation on all samples to reduce the interference information of the image. We turn static training samples into dynamic incremental training samples to train the online network.

In addition, in order to confirm that MSLRF-OSELM has good generalization performance, we use MNIST dataset to conduct another experiment. We select 10000 samples as testing samples and others as training samples. The process of online training network is similar to the processing of ALOT training dataset.

For ALOT dataset, we set 4 different scale of local receptive field of MSLRF-OSLRF that are 2 scales, 4 different scales 4(d), 4 same scales 4(s) and 8 scales. For MNIST dataset, we set 4 different scale of local receptive field of MSLRF-OSLRF that are 2 scales, 4 scales, 8 different scales 8(d) and 8 same scales 8(s). The specific settings are shown in Table 1.

To verify the effect of the size of BLOCK D_{p+1} dataset on the experimental results, we set different BLOCK sizes for the two datasets. For the ALOT dataset, we set the size of BLOCK as $\{10, 20, 40\}$. For MNIST, we set the size of BLOCK as $\{500, 1000, 2000\}$. In regard to MSLRF-OSELM, the most important parameter is the number of each scale channel. And taking the computational complexity and computer memory into account, we set the number of feature maps and pooling maps for each scale channel of ALOT and is $\{5, 10, 15, 20, 25\}$. We set the number of feature maps and pooling maps for each scale channel of MNIST is $\{2, 3, 4, 5, 6\}$.

Table 1. The parameters of MSLRF-OSELM network of different datasets on experiments.

The dataset	r_s								e_s								The scales
	r_1	r_2	r_3	r_4	r_5	r_6	r_7	r_8	e_1	e_2	e_3	e_4	e_5	e_6	e_7	e_8	
ALOT	4	6							3	5							2
	3	4	5	6					2	3	4	5					4(d)
	5	5	5	5					4	4	4	4					4(s)
	3	4	5	6	7	8	9	10	2	3	4	5	6	7	8	9	8
MNIST	3	5							2	4							2
	3	5	7	9					2	4	6	8					4
	3	5	7	9	11	13	15	17	2	4	6	8	10	12	14	16	8(d)
	10	10	10	10	10	10	10	10	9	9	9	9	9	9	9	9	8(s)

4.3   Overall Classification Accuracy Rate

In order to verify the effectiveness of our proposed online architecture for complex surface material, we conduct four different experiments on ALOT dataset of local receptive field with the multi-scale condition, in which local receptive field with 2 scales, 4(d) scales (the size of the 4 scales is different), and 4 scales(s) (the size of the 4 scales is same), 8 scales. The 10-fold cross-validation average accuracy rate of the combined effects of the three important parameters that includes the scale of local receptive field, the number of feature maps and the number of BLOCK dataset are shown in Table 2.

Table 2. The average testing accuracy of ALOT dataset (%).

Feature maps	2 scales			4(d) scales			4(s) scales			8 scales		
	10	20	40	10	20	40	10	20	40	10	20	40
5	93.32	93.84	94.42	95.24	95.6	96.42	94.53	94.82	95.27	93.73	94.22	94.63
10	93.62	93.95	94.12	95.76	96.14	96.92	94.97	95.43	95.89	94.35	94.81	95.23
15	95.65	96.72	97.38	96.23	96.52	97.39	95.24	95.77	96.36	95.52	95.93	96.95
20	95.82	95.9	96.17	96.8	97.07	97.83	95.85	95.54	96.51	95.15	95.74	96.58
25	95.31	96.01	96.08	96.03	96.45	97.2	95.78	95.43	96.58	95.41	95.2	95.63

From Table 2, we can observe when the number of feature maps of each scale channel is 20, the number of BLOCK dataset is 40, the classification of 2 scales, 4(d) scales, 4(s) scales and 8 scales of local receptive field are 96.17%, 97.83%, 96.51% and 96.58%, separately. From the results, we can know the classification of our proposed method with 4 different scales of local receptive field is performs better than the traditional LRF-ELM with 4 same scales of local receptive field. Therefore, we can observe the influence of scale of local receptive field on the accuracy of online network classification: the classification of our MSLRF-OSELM with 4 different scales of local receptive field outperforms better than the classification performance of 2 scales and 8 scales of local receptive field, the online network of multi-scale of local receptive field can extract highly representative rich features that benefits to the classification of object materials. Additionally, from Table 2, we also observe that when the number of BLOCK dataset is 40, sufficient samples can make the network have more discriminative features and help to classify the samples correctly.

In order to verify that our method has good generalization performance, we performed four different experiments in the same manner using the published MNIST dataset. The 10-fold cross-validation average accuracy rate of the combined effects of the three important parameters are shown in Table 3. From the Table 3, we can observe that when the number of feature maps of each scale channel is 5, the number of BLOCK dataset is 2000, the classification of 2 scales, 4 scales, 8(d) scales and 8(s) scales of local receptive field are 96.7%, 97.2%, 98.39% and 96.8%, separately. Our method with 8 different scales of local receptive field can achieve the best classification.

Table 3. The average testing accuracy of MNIST dataset (%).

Feature maps	2 scales			4 scales			8(d) scales			8(s) scales		
	500	1000	2000	500	1000	2000	500	1000	2000	500	1000	2000
2	94.06	95.35	95.99	95.63	95.83	95.57	96.56	96.83	97.32	94.73	94.5	95.6
3	94.4	95.5	96.1	96.29	96.01	96.2	97.23	97.38	97.6	95.92	96.2	96.13
4	96.4	96.17	96.62	96.41	96.59	96.34	97.25	97.56	97.73	96.54	96.85	96.36
5	95.89	96.2	96.7	96.44	96.81	97.2	97.92	97.92	98.39	96.53	96.51	96.8
6	96.58	96.48	96.65	96.17	96.8	96.62	97.38	97.66	97.85	96.85	96.65	96.78

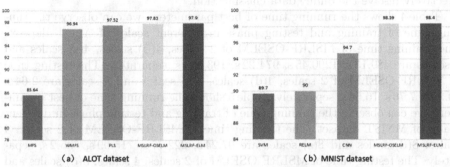

(a) ALOT dataset   (b) MNIST dataset

Fig. 5. The comparison of testing accuracy of different methods for ALOT and MNIST dataset (%).

To further illustrate the effectiveness of the our method (MSLRF-OSELM), we compare the experimental results of this methods with Multi-Fractal Spectrum (MFS) [27], Wavelet based Multi Fractal Spectrum (WMFS) [28], Partial Least Squares (PLS) [29,30], MSLRF-OSELM and MSLRF-ELM, as shown in Fig. 5(a). From Fig. 5(a), we can observe that the classification accuracy of MFS, WMFS, PLS, MSLRF-OSELM and MSLRF-ELM are 85.64%, 96.94%, 97.52%, 97.83% and 97.9%, separately. We also compare the experimental results of this methods on MNIST dataset with Support Vector Machine (SVM) [31], Regularized Extreme Learning Machine (RELM) [32], Convolutional Neural Network (CNN) [33], MSLRF-OSELM and MSLRF-ELM, as shown in Fig. 5(b). From Fig. 5(b), we can observe that the classification accuracy of SVM, RELM, CNN, MSLRF-OSELM and MSLRF-ELM are 89.7%, 90%, 94.7%, 98.39% and 98.4%, separately. It is noted that the MSLRF-ELM deals with static data, while our method MSLRF-OSELM deals with online data. The classification performance of MSLRF-OSELM is superior to other methods and can achieve the classification of MSLRF-ELM that effect of static data, therefore, the results demonstrate the effectiveness of our MSLRF-OSELM method.

In summary, we can conduct the following conclusions: multi-scale of local receptive field can extract highly representative rich features that benefits to the classification of object materials. We should select suitable scale of local receptive field and the number of BLOCK according to dataset. Sufficient samples can make the network have more discriminative features and help to classify the samples correctly.

4.4 Time Profiling

ELM and LRF-ELM with fast learning speed that require few computations. Although the MSLRF-OSELM network needs to train the network in batches during the online training of the network, it is worthwhile to inherit the advantages of the OSELM and LRF-ELM methods at the same time, and it can effectively resolve the online data classification.

Table 4 shows the running time of best parameters, we can observe the running time of training and testing phase in different scales of ALOT dataset. The training time of MSLRF-OSELM of 2 scales, 4(d) scales, 4(s) scales and 8 scales are 489.13 s, 1290.45 s, 974.22 s, 1933.24 s, separately. The testing time of MSLRF-OSELM of 2 scales, 4(d) scales, 4(s) scales and 8 scales are 2.64 s, 10.36 s, 7.76 s, 16.54 s, separately. Table 5 shows the running time of best parameters, we can observe the running time of training and testing phase in different scales of MNIST dataset. The training time of MSLRF-OSELM of 2 scales, 4 scales, 8(d) scales and 8(s) scales are 97.24 s, 222.77 s, 715.99 s, 685.2 s, separately. The testing time of MSLRF-OSELM of 2 scales, 4 scales, 8(d) scales and 8(s) scales are 8.25 s, 12.72 s, 19.25 s, 17.35 s, separately. From Tables 4 and 5, we can observe that as the network scale increases, the training network time is also increasing. Therefore, we should select appropriate scales of local receptive field according to the characteristics of the data itself.

Table 4. The running time of training and testing phase in different scales of ALOT dataset (s).

Phase	2 scales	4(d) scales	4(s) scales	8 scales
Training	489.13	1290.45	974.22	1933.24
Testing	2.64	10.36	7.76	16.54

Table 5. The running time of training and testing phase in different scales of MNIST dataset (s).

Phase	2 scales	4 scales	8 scales(d)	8 scales(s)
Training	97.24	222.77	715.99	685.2
Testing	8.25	12.72	19.25	17.35

In order to make our method more convincing, we compared the training and testing time profiling of our method with other methods. Table 6 shows the running time of ALOT dataset. The training time of MFS, WMFS, PLS, MSLRF-OSELM and MSLRF-ELM are 720.32 s, 738.05 s, 822.19 s, 1290.45 s,

238.09 s, separately. The testing time of MFS, WMFS, PLS, MSLRF-OSELM and MSLRF-ELM are 0.94 s, 1.15 s, 1.57 s, 10.36 s, 0.65 s, separately. Table 7 shows the running time of MNIST dataset. The training time of SVM, RELM, HOG+ELM, MSLRF-OSELM and MSLRF-ELM are 11.34 s, 3.23 s, 69.82 s, 715.99 s, 90.92 s, separately. The testing time of SVM, RELM, HOG+ELM, MSLRF-OSELM and MSLRF-ELM are 5.62 s, 0.94 s, 0.93 s, 19.25 s, 1.34 s, separately. From Tables 6 and 7, we can observe that the training and testing time cost of our method are the largest, but the classification results of our method can approach or exceed the classification performance of the above method to deal with the online data.

Table 6. The running time of different methods of ALOT dataset (s).

Methods	MFS	WMFS	PLS	MSLRF-OSELM	MSLRF-ELM
Training	720.32	738.05	822.19	1290.45	238.09
Testing	0.94	1.15	1.57	10.36	0.65

Table 7. The running time of different methods of MNIST dataset (s).

Methods	SVM	RELM	HOG+ELM	MSLRF-OSELM	MSLRF-ELM
Training	11.34	3.23	69.82	715.99	90.92
Testing	5.62	0.94	0.93	19.25	1.34

5 Conclusion

In this work, we establish an online classification architecture for surface material classification. The results demonstrate that the more scales of local receptive field are, the more high-level representative features can be extracted from the surface material. Additionally, our MSLRF-OSELM is an effective method for processing online object material classification and has strong generalization performance.

In our future work, we are planning to propose multi-modal fusion that combine acceleration and sound modality information to processing online object material classification tasks.

Acknowledgements. This work was supported in part by the National Natural Science Foundation of China under Grant 61503271 and Grant 201606159, in part by the Research Project Supported by Shanxi Scholarship Council of China under Grant 2016-044, Grant 2015-045.

References

1. Ojala, T., Pietikainen, M., Maenpaa, T.: Multiresolution gray-scale and rotation invariant texture classification with local binary patterns. IEEE Trans. Pattern Anal. Mach. Intell. **24**(7), 971–987 (2002)
2. Kuchenbecker, K.J., Fiene, J., Niemeyer, G.: Improving contact realism through event-based haptic feedback. IEEE Trans. Vis. Comput. Graph. **12**(2), 219–230 (2006)
3. Jones, L.A.: Kinesthetic sensing. In: Human and Machine Haptics. Citeseer (2000)
4. Tamura, H., Mori, S., Yamawaki, T.: Textural features corresponding to visual perception. IEEE Trans. Syst. Man Cybern. **8**(6), 460–473 (1978)
5. Motoyoshi, I., Nishida, S., Sharan, L., Adelson, E.H.: Image statistics and the perception of surface qualities. Nature **447**(7141), 206–209 (2007)
6. Sharma, G., Wu, W., Dalal, E.N.: The CIEDE2000 color-difference formula: implementation notes, supplementary test data, and mathematical observations. Color Res. Appl. **30**(1), 21–30 (2005)
7. Zhao, P., Zhang, Y., Wu, M., et al.: Adaptive cost-sensitive online classification. IEEE Trans. Knowl. Data Eng. **PP**(99), 1 (2018)
8. Meng, J.E., Venkatesan, R., Ning, W.: An online universal classifier for binary, multi-class and multi-label classification. In: IEEE International Conference on Systems, Man, and Cybernetics, pp. 003701–003706. IEEE (2017)
9. Huang, G.B., Bai, Z., Kasun, L.L.C., et al.: Local receptive fields based extreme learning machine. IEEE Comput. Intell. Mag. **10**(2), 18–29 (2015)
10. Huang, G.B., Zhou, H., Ding, X., Zhang, R.: Extreme learning machine for regression and multiclass classification. IEEE Trans. Syst. Man Cybern. Part B: Cybern. **42**(2), 513–529 (2012)
11. Lan, Y., Soh, Y.C., Huang, G.B.: Ensemble of online sequential extreme learning machine. Neurocomputing **72**(13), 3391–3395 (2009)
12. Lim, J., Pang, H.S., et al.: Low complexity adaptive forgetting factor for online sequential extreme; learning machine (OS-ELM) for application to nonstationary system; estimations. Neural Comput. Appl. **22**(3–4), 569–576 (2013)
13. Yan, W., Zhen, W., Huang, M., et al.: Ultra-short-term wind power prediction based on OS-ELM and bootstrap method. Autom. Electr. Power Syst. **38**(6), 14–19+122 (2014)
14. Lv, Q., Niu, X., Dou, Y., et al.: Classification of hyperspectral remote sensing image using hierarchical local-receptive-field-based extreme learning machine. IEEE Geosci. Remote Sens. Lett. **13**(3), 434–438 (2016)
15. Li, F., Liu, H., Xu, X.: Multi-modal local receptive field extreme learning machine for object recognition. In: 2016 International Joint Conference on Neural Networks, IJCNN, pp. 1696–1701. IEEE (2016)
16. Xie, S.J., Yoon, S., Yang, J., et al.: Feature component-based extreme learning machines for finger vein recognition. Cogn. Comput. **6**(3), 446–461 (2014)
17. Chacko, B.P., Krishnan, V.R.V., Raju, G., et al.: Handwritten character recognition using wavelet energy and extreme learning machine. Int. J. Mach. Learn. Cybern. **3**(2), 149–161 (2012)
18. Fu, A., Dong, C., Wang, L.: An experimental study on stability and generalization of extreme learning machines. Int. J. Mach. Learn. Cybern. **6**(1), 129–135 (2015)
19. Balasundaram, S., Gupta, D.: On optimization based extreme learning machine in primal for regression and classification by functional iterative method. Int. J. Mach. Learn. Cybern. **7**(5), 707–728 (2016)

20. Sachnev, V., Ramasamy, S., Sundaram, S., et al.: A cognitive ensemble of extreme learning machines for steganalysis based on risk-sensitive hinge loss function. Cogn. Comput. **7**(1), 103–110 (2015)

21. Yang, Y., Wu, Q.M.J.: Multilayer extreme learning machine with subnetwork nodes for representation learning. IEEE Trans. Cybern. **46**(11), 2570–2583 (2016)

22. Swain, G., Lenka, S.K.: A better RGB channel based image steganography technique. In: Krishna, P.V., Babu, M.R., Ariwa, E. (eds.) ObCom 2011. CCIS, vol. 270, pp. 470–478. Springer, Heidelberg (2012). https://doi.org/10.1007/978-3-642-29216-3_51

23. Tiwari, N., Shandilya, M.: Secure RGB image steganography from pixel indicator to triple algorithm-an incremental growth. Int. J. Secur. Appl. **4**(4), 53–62 (2010)

24. Fang, J., Xu, X., Liu, H., et al.: Local receptive field based extreme learning machine with three channels for histopathological image classification. Int. J. Mach. Learn. Cybern. 1–11 (2018)

25. Burghouts, G.J., Geusebroek, J.M.: Material-specific adaptation of color invariant features. Pattern Recogn. Lett. **30**(3), 306–313 (2009)

26. Krizhevsky, A., Hinton, G.: Learning multiple layers of features from tiny images. Master's thesis, Department of Computer Science, University of Toronto (2009)

27. Xu, Y., Ji, H., Fermüller, C.: Viewpoint invariant texture description using fractal analysis. Int. J. Comput. Vis. **83**(1), 85–100 (2009)

28. Zhang, L., Zhang, D.: Domain adaptation extreme learning machines for drift compensation in e-nose systems. IEEE Instrum. Meas. **64**(7), 1790–1801 (2015)

29. Zhou, X., Xie, L., Zhang, P., Zhang, Y.: Online object tracking based on CNN with metropolis-hasting re-sampling. In: ACM Multimedia, pp. 1163–1166. ACM (2015)

30. Quan, Y., Xu, Y., Sun, Y., Luo, Y.: Lacunarity analysis on image patterns for texture classification. In: CVPR, pp. 160–167. IEEE (2014)

31. Peng, P., Ma, Q.L., Hong, L.M.: The research of the parallel SMO algorithm for solving SVM. In: International Conference on Machine Learning and Cybernetics, pp. 1271–1274. IEEE (2009)

32. Gómez-Villafuertes, R., Rodríguez-Jiménez, F.J., Alastrue-Agudo, A., et al.: Purinergic receptors in spinal cord-derived ependymal stem/progenitor cells and their potential role in cell-based therapy for spinal cord injury. Cell Transpl. **24**(8), 1493 (2015)

33. Agarap, A.F.: An architecture combining convolutional neural network (CNN) and support vector machine (SVM) for image classification (2017)

Effect of Short-Term Micro-expression Training on the Micro-expression Recognition Performance of Preschool Children

Fangbing Qu, Supei Yan, Jiuqing Liang, and Jianping Wang[✉]

College of Preschool Education, Capital Normal University,
Beijing 100048, China
{qufangbing, liangjiuqing}@cnu.edu.cn,
sophie_pei0921@126.com, wjp_bjys@163.com

Abstract. Micro-expressions are facial expressions that are characterized by short durations, involuntary generation and low intensity, and they are regarded as unique cues revealing one's hidden emotions. Numerous researchers have studied the recognition of micro-expression, mainly focused on the recognition ability of college students or adults. However, researches from the perspective of child development are almost scanty considering the great significance of the development of expression recognition ability. To further facilitate development in this field, the present paper firstly aim to study the preschoolers' micro-expression recognition ability. Besides, the authors are also interested in the effect of micro-expression recognition training, whether micro-expression training can improve children's ability to recognize different emotion types of micro-expression. Results suggest that 5-years-old children's recognition accuracy was relatively low as 0.38. However, after a short term training through micro-expression training tool, the micro-expression recognition accuracy in post-test increased to 0.54, which was significantly higher than pre-test. No gender difference on micro-expression recognition was found. These findings extend our understandings of human's micro-expression recognition from the perspective of child development.

Keywords: Pre-school children · Micro-expression ·
Micro-expression training tool (METT) · Micro-expression recognition

1 Introduction

Researches on judgements of emotions of facial expressions has a long history in psychology, and has contributed greatly to the literature of emotion science and other fields. The ability involved in the recognition and comprehension of emotional facial expression, usually referred to as Emotion Recognition Ability, are essential to the development of healthy social behaviors. These skills are related to important developmental outcomes such as school readiness, enhanced language, literacy and mathematics skills in preschool [1–4]. Emotion recognition begins to develop in the preschool years and tends to predict social behavior and adjustment among preschool-aged children.

© Springer Nature Singapore Pte Ltd. 2019
F. Sun et al. (Eds.): ICCSIP 2018, CCIS 1005, pp. 54–62, 2019.
https://doi.org/10.1007/978-981-13-7983-3_5

Numerous researchers have studied the development patterns of children's emotion recognition [5, 6]. Researchers have evidenced that individual first exhibits the ability of facial expression recognition shortly after birth. For instance, Haviland and Lelwica [13] discovered that ten-week old babies can recognize emotions such as happiness, anger, and sadness [7]. Kalman and Andrews have also argued that such recognition only occurs between babies and their carers' faces, which implies that facial familiarity also has impact one's facial expression identification [7]. Children as young as two demonstrate the ability to accurately identify facial expressions of various emotions including happy, sad, angry and scared [9, 10]. Children ages four to five to be proved that they can accurately and reliably identify facial expressions of the six basic emotions of happy, sad, anger, fear, surprise and disgust [11, 12].

Children ages four to six constitute a special and rapid development period in one's physical, psychological, and social abilities, with the age of 5 being a particular milestone for children in developing the capability to recognize expressions [13]. Subsequent studies have suggested that children can successfully label facial expressions with accurate emotion labels. Izard additionally suggested that the age of six is a turning point in children's capability to recognize expressions [14]. This has been supported by other studies which have suggested that children are able to recognize happy facial expressions at subtle intensities at approximately 5 years old, although, they suggest that sensitivity to other types of expressions continues to develop until 10 years, and beyond [15, 16].

Among the past literatures investigating children's comprehension of emotions and their ability to recognize emotions, different kinds of stimuli has been employed, such as static facial expression images, cartoon expressions, facial expressions from different cultures, and simple expressions on stick figures [17]. Besides, several facial expression databases have also been developed to support the study on emotion recognition ability, such as the Japanese Female Facial Expression Database (JAFFE) [18]; the CMU Pose, Illumination and Expression (PIE) [19] and its new version, the Multi-PID database [20]; and the Genki-4 K database [21, 35]. However, the above databases mainly contains still and posed facial expression images, which is quite different with naturally expressed or spontaneous facial expressions [22]. Therefore, new facial expression databases with spontaneous facial expressions were developed, such as the Extended Cohn-Kanade Dataset (CK+) [23]; the Denver Intensity of Spontaneous Facial Action (DISFA) [24] and the Affectiva-MIT Facial Expression Dataset (AM-FED) [25]. All these improvement of facial expression stimuli have greatly improved the development of research on children's emotion recognition ability.

However, previous researches mainly focused on children's recognition of general facial expressions, usually called macro-expressions, which typically last for more than 1/2 of a second, up to 4 s [22]. Recently, another type of facial expression, micro-expression (ME), which is characterized by its involuntary occurrence, short duration and typically low intensity, has drawn the attention of affective computing researchers and psychologists [26]. Micro-expression is a special case of basic emotional expression, which was first discovered by Haggard and Issacs in 1966 when investigating clinical cases [27]. Later, Ekman and his colleges further studied the nature of micro-expression [28, 29]. After carefully study the recording of psychiatric interviews frame by frame, they found that the micro-expressions were emotional expressions that leaked out when individuals tried to inhibit or manage their facial expression, which may further indicate clues of concealment or deception. Therefore, the recognition of micro-expressions may serve great value in our daily communications and other significant fields such as homeland security, business, and other high-stakes situations [28, 30].

Considering the significant value of micro-expression in our daily life and other fields, it has been largely overlooked in research concerning children's facial expression recognition ability. Few studies have investigated children's performance on micro-expression recognition, which leaves great research spaces on this topic. Besides, the ability of micro-expression identification in young children may greatly help them in understanding the adult communication and better adapt to new challenges and environments. Therefore, the present study attempt to investigate to what extent can 5-years-old Chinese children recognize micro-expression?

In the literatures concerning micro-expression recognition, several paradigms and databases have been developed. The Japanese and Caucasian Brief Affect Recognition Test (JACBART) was first published to test one's performance on micro-expression recognition [31]. The JACBART created the appearance of more dynamic expressions, which include three emotional expression faces with two neutral face imposed before and after the emotional face, reducing the after effects of the stimuli. Then Ekman and Friesen developed a more usable and self-instructional training tool, the Micro Expression Training Tool (METT) [32]. The METT is presented as a stand-alone training tool, including a pre-test, a training section, practicing examples with feedback, a review section and a post-test. Facial stimuli in this training tool are elicited in special psychological experiments with necessary consistency and reliability of expression, poser, intensity and angle. Previous studies have applied the METT to different kinds of individuals aiming to improve their micro-expression recognition ability. For example, a METT training not only significantly improved Korean department store employees' ability to identify MEs (N = 81, 18% increase), but also led to higher social and communication skills scores [33]. Endres et al. applied the METT on medical students. After training, students showed a significant improvements in the recognition of micro-expression [34]. Researchers also have trained individuals with Schizophrenia to read facial expressions using METT. Results suggested a significant improvement in micro-expression recognition at post-test, illustrating the tool's effectiveness to different populations [33, 34]. Another study also suggested that the METT may improve one's ability in detecting deception [37].

Previous studies have mainly test the robustness of METT training on adult participants. However, few studies have focused on whether the METT training will be effective on children as young as 3–6 years old. Therefore, the second aim of present study is to test the effect of short-term METT training on preschool children.

Therefore, the present study aims to investigate the following two questions.

1. To what extent can preschoolers aged 5 recognize micro-expression?
2. Whether a short-term training of Micro-Expression Training Tool will improve the recognition performance of pre-school children?

Based on existing (albeit limited) findings, we expected preschooler's performance on micro-expression to differ between different emotions. Besides, as the special rapid developing stage of preschooler's emotion recognition and understanding ability, we hypothesized that there would be no gender difference between boy and girls. Regarding the effect of short-term METT training, we expected that a short-term training would improve preschooler's performance on micro-expression recognition.

2 Methodology

2.1 Participants

Forty 5-years old children were collected from a local kindergarten (21 females, 5 years old). All participants' parents signed an informed consent form and were told they have the right to terminate the experimental procedure if they found their children were uncomfortable. The institutional review board (IRB) of the College of Preschool Education, Capital Normal University approved the study protocol.

2.2 Materials and Procedure

Micro-Expression Training Tool was used (www.paulekman.com) [32]. 7 different emotional types of micro-expression were shown in a dynamic changing sequence (sad, angry, surprise, fear, disgust, contempt and happy) other than still emotional picture. Therefore, in total 14 micro-expressions of emotions (2 each of happy, angry, sad, disgust, surprise and contempt) were presented in the pre-test assessment. The micro-expressions were only presented with 15 ms, beginning and ending with neutral still facial images. Children were asked to label the micro-expressions with one of the seven emotion labels. The accuracy results were computed by score out the percentage of accurate times out of presented images.

- Pre-test: Children were presented with different micro-expressions shown with METT software. When the first micro-expression was shown in the monitor, they were asked to judge its emotion type. 14 micro-expressions were shown with 7 emotion types: sad, angry, surprise, fear, disgust, contempt and happy. Accuracy results were recorded during the pre-test.
- Training phase: Participants took part in a 15-mins training section and were presented with different emotional types of dynamic micro-expression, which were different with pre-test and post-test section. They were first asked to judge the emotional type of each micro-expression. When their response was wrong, the experimenter would present with the right answer and explain the difference between them. Results suggest that the participants usually confound the difference between angry and sad, surprise and fear, contempt and disgust. The participants were allowed to replay the dynamic micro-expression during the 15-mins training section.
- Post-test phase: After the 15-mins training section, participants took part in the post-test section and were present with dynamic micro-expression which were different from the pre-test and training phase. 14 dynamic MEs with 7 emotional types were presented and participants were asked to judge its emotional type. Accuracy results were recorded.

3 Results

3.1 Pre-test Results: Children's Micro-expression Recognition Ability

Descriptive statistic suggests that 5-year old children's recognition ability of micro-expression is higher for happy ME than other ME (happy > anger, $t = 6.2$, $p < 0.01$; happy > sad, $t = 7.5$, $p < 0.01$; happy > fear, $t = 8.2$, $p < 0.01$; happy > surprise, $t = 5.9$, $p < 0.01$; happy > disgust, $t = 8.4$, $p < 0.01$; happy > contempt, $t = 10.1$, $p < 0.01$). Recognition of anger ME was significantly better than sad and fear ME (all ps < 0.01).

3.2 Gender Difference of Children's Micro-expression Recognition Ability

Independent sample T test shows that there was no significant gender difference in the pre-test ($t = -0.13$, $p > 0.05$) (see Fig. 1), which suggest that participants as young as 5 years old may not show their difference in micro-expression ability between boy and girls. Same analysis was conducted on the post-test results, while no significant difference was found on ME recognition ability between male and female ($t = 0.629$, $p > 0.05$) (see Fig. 1).

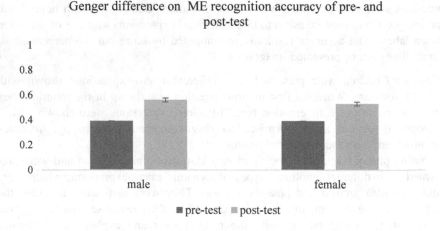

Fig. 1. Independent sample t test results of gender difference on ME recognition accuracy be in pre-test and post-test.

3.3 Training Effect: Comparison Between Pre- and Post-training

Paired T test analysis suggests a significant difference between children's pre- and post-test. After the 15-mins training, 5 years old children showed a significant increase in their ability in the ME recognition task ($t = -7.068$, $p < 0.001$) (see Fig. 2).

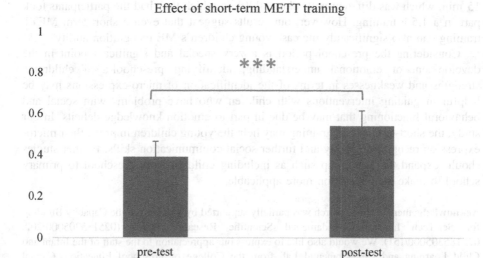

Fig. 2. Comparison of ME recognition accuracy before and after METT training.

4 Conclusion

In this paper, we tapped on the topic of children's ability of micro-expression recognition with the help of METT training. Among the age group of 5-year-old children, they showed a different recognition pattern depending the emotion type of micro-expression. They showed a higher recognition ability for happy micro-expression than the other emotion types. Besides, recognition accuracy was higher for anger than sad and fearful ME. No gender difference was found before and after the METT training.

A significant increase in ME recognition accuracy was found after the METT training.

Even 5 years old children show a comparative ability in micro-expression recognition task. While their performance show a different pattern for different emotional types. Recognition ability was better for happy ME than the other ME, which might attribute to the quite frequent occurrence of happy facial expressions in daily life, which can also explain the difference between anger ME and sad/fear. Angry facial expression has quite adaptive function in the evolution of human, which helps one to flight from a dangerous situation and keep alive.

No gender difference was found between boys and girls in their recognition accuracy of micro-expression both in pre- and post-test. This result suggests even after training, boys and girls didn't show difference in ME recognition. This result was in accord with Frank et al. [34]. In their study, the gender difference of ME recognition was also not found between male and female participants.

After a 15 min METT training, 5 year old children showed a significant increase in the accuracy of ME recognition, which suggest the effectiveness of short-term METT training on the development of children's ME recognition ability. Due to the limitation of preschool children's attention character, we have to limit the training time as short as

15 min, which was different with Ekman [30], in which they had the participants took part in a 1.5 h training. However, our results suggest that even a short term METT training can also significantly increase young children's ME recognition ability.

Considering the preschool period is a very special and significant point in the development of emotional understanding, identifying preschool-aged children's strengths and weaknesses in terms of the identification of micro-expressions may be helpful in guiding interventions with children who have problems with social and behavioral functioning that may be due in part to emotion knowledge deficits. In our study, the short-term METT training may help the young children improve their micro-expression recognition ability and further social communication skills. Further studies should expand the age group such as including children from preschool to primary school to make the conclusion more applicable.

Acknowledgement. This research was partially supported by grants from the Capacity Building for Sci-Tech Innovation-Fundamental Scientific Research Funds (025185305000/202, 025185305000/151). We would also like to express our appreciation to the staff of the Infant and Child Learning and Developmental Lab from the College of Preschool Education, Capital Normal University.

References

1. Campbell, S.B.: Behavior Problems in Preschool Children. Clinical and Developmental Issues, 2nd edn. Guilford Press, New York (2002)
2. Denham, S.A.: Social-emotional competence as a support for school readiness: what is it and how do we assess it? Early Edu. Dev. **17**, 57 (2006)
3. Raver, C.C.: Emotions matter: making the case for the role of children's emotional adjustment for their early school readiness. Soc. Policy Rep. **16**, 3–24 (2002)
4. Raver, C.C., Garner, P.W., Smith-Donald, R.: The roles of emotion regulation and emotion knowledge for children's academic readiness. In: Pianta, R.C., Cox, M.J., Snow, K.L. (eds.) School Readiness and the Transition to Kindergarten in the Era of Accountability, pp. 121–147. Paul H Brookes Publishing, Baltimore (2006)
5. Parker, A., Mathis, E., Kupersmidt, J.: How is this child feeling? Preschool-aged children's ability to recognize emotion in faces and body poses. Early Edu. Dev. **24**(2), 188–211 (2013)
6. Dalrymple, K.A., di Oleggio Castello, M.V., Elison, J.T., Gobbini, M.I.: Concurrent development of facial identity and expression discrimination. PLoS ONE **12**(6), 1–16 (2017)
7. Kahana-Kalman, R., Walker-Andrews, A.S.: The role of person familiarity in young infants' perception of emotional expressions. Child Dev. **72**(2), 352–369 (2001)
8. Gao, X., Maurer, D.: Influence of intensity on children's sensitivity to happy, sad, and fearful facial expressions. J. Exp. Child Psychol. **102**(4), 503–521 (2009)
9. Denham, S.A.: Social cognition, social behavior, and emotion in preschoolers: contextual validation. Child Dev. **57**, 194–201 (1986)
10. Wellman, H., Harris, P.L., Banerjee, M., Sinclair, A.: Early understanding of emotion: evidence from natural language. Cogn. Emot. **9**, 117–149 (1995)
11. Russell, J., Widen, S.: A label superiority effect in children's categorization of facial expressions. Soc. Dev. **11**(1), 30–52 (2002)
12. Widen, S., Russell, J.: Children acquire emotion categories gradually. Cogn. Dev. **23**(2), 291–312 (2008)

13. Haviland, J., Lelwica, M., Parke, R.D.: The induced affect response: 10-week-old infants' responses to three emotion expressions. Dev. Psychol. **23**(1), 97–104 (1987)
14. Grinspan, D., Hemphill, A., Nowicki, S.: Improving the ability of elementary school-age children to identify emotion in facial expression. J. Genet. Psychol. **164**(1), 88–100 (2003)
15. Gao, X., Maurer, D.: A happy story: developmental changes in children's sensitivity to facial expressions of varying intensities. J. Exp. Child Psychol. **107**(2), 67–86 (2010)
16. Ekman, P.: Telling lies: Clues to deceit in the marketplace, politics, and marriage. WW Norton & Company, New York (2009). (Revised edition)
17. Lyons, M., Akamatsu, S., Kamachi, M., Gyoba, J.: Coding facial expressions with gabor wavelets. In: Proceedings of 3rd IEEE International Conference on Automatic Face Gesture Recognition, pp. 200–205 (1998)
18. Sim, T., Baker, S., Bsat, M.: The CMU pose, illumination, and expression database. IEEE Trans. Pattern Anal. Mach. Intell. **25**(12), 1615–1618 (2003)
19. Gross, R., Matthews, I., Cohn, J., Kanade, T., Baker, S.: Multi-pie. Image Vis. Comput. **28** (5), 807–813 (2010)
20. Whitehill, J., Littlewort, G., Fasel, I., Bartlett, M., Movellan, J.: Toward practical smile detection. IEEE Trans. Pattern Anal. Mach. Intell. **31**(11), 2106–2111 (2009)
21. Qu, F., Wang, S.-J., Yan, W.-J., Fu, X.: CAS(ME)^2: a database of spontaneous macro-expressions and micro-expressions. In: Kurosu, M. (ed.) HCI 2016. LNCS, vol. 9733, pp. 48–59. Springer, Cham (2016). https://doi.org/10.1007/978-3-319-39513-5_5
22. Lucey, P., Cohn, J.F., Kanade, T., Saragih, J., Ambadar, Z., Matthews, I.: The extended Cohn-Kanade dataset (ck+): a complete dataset for action unit and emotion-specified expression. In: Proceedings of IEEE Computer Societ Conference on Computer Vision and Pattern Recognition Workshops, pp. 94–101 (2010)
23. Mavadati, S.M., Mahoor, M.H., Bartlett, K., Trinh, P., Cohn, J.F.: DISFA: a spontaneous facial action intensity database. IEEE Trans. Affect. Comput. **4**(2), 151–160 (2013)
24. McDuff, D., El Kaliouby, R., Senechal, T., Amr, M., Cohn, J.F., Picard, R.: Affectiva-mit facial expression dataset (am-fed): naturalistic and spontaneous facial expressions collected in-the-wild. In: Proceedings of IEEE Conference on Computer Vision Pattern Recognition Workshops, pp. 881–888 (2013)
25. Haggard, E.A., Isaacs, K.S.: Micromomentary facial expressions as indicators of ego mechanisms in psychotherapy. In: Gottschalk, L.A., Auerbach, A.H. (eds.) Methods of Research in Psychotherapy, pp. 154–165. Appleton Century Crofts, New York (1966)
26. Ekman, P., Friesen, W.V.: Nonverbal leakage and cues to deception. Psychiatry **32**, 88–106 (1969)
27. Ekman, P., Friesen, W.V.: Detecting deception from the body or the face. J. Pers. Soc. Psychol. **29**, 124–129 (1974)
28. Matsumoto, D., LeRoux, J., Wilson-Cohn, C., Raroque, J., Kooken, K., Ekman, P., et al.: A new test to measure emotion recognition ability: Matsumoto and Ekman's Japanese and caucasian brief affect recognition test (JACBART). J. Nonverbal Behav. **24**, 179–209 (2000)
29. Matsumoto, D., Hwang, H.S.: Evidence for training the ability to read microexpressions of emotion. Motiv. Emot. **35**(2), 181–191 (2011)
30. Ekman, P.: MicroExpression Training Tool (METT). University of California, San Francisco (2002)
31. Marsh, P.J., Green, M.J., Russell, T.A., McGuire, J., Harris, A., Coltheart, M.: Remediation of facial emotion recognition in schizophrenia: functional predictors, generalizability, and durability. Am. J. Psychiatr. Rehabil. **13**, 143–170 (2010)
32. Endres, J., Laidlaw, A.: Micro-expression recognition training in medical students: a pilot study. BMC Med. Educ. **9**(1), 47 (2009)

33. Russell, T.A., Green, M.J., Simpson, I., Coltheart, M.: Remediation of facial emotion perception in schizophrenia: concomitant changes in visual attention. Schizophr. Res. **103**, 248–256 (2008)
34. Frank, M.G., Herbasz, M., Sinuk, K.: I see how you feel: Training Laypeople and professionals' to recognize fleeting emotions. In: Proceedings of the Annual Meeting of the International Communication Association. Sheraton New York, pp. 88–95 (2009)
35. Qu, F., Wang, S.J., Yan, W.J., Li, H., Wu, S., Fu, X.: CAS(ME)^2: a database for spontaneous macro-expression and micro-expression spotting and recognition. IEEE Trans. Affect. Comput. **9**(4), 424–436 (2018)

Video-Based Person Re-identification
by Region Quality Estimation
and Attributes

Simin Xu[✉] and Shiqiang Hu

School of Aeronautics and Astronautics,
Shanghai Jiao Tong University,
Room A407 Aerospace Building, 800 Dongchuan Road,
Shanghai 200240, People's Republic of China
siminxu0613@sjtu.edu.cn

Abstract. Person re-identification (re-ID) has become a significant area
in automated video surveillance. The main challenge of this task lies
in changes of pedestrians' appearance across different cameras due to
occlusions and illumination variations. Video-based person re-ID provides more information about pedestrians, but how to aggregate useful
information of all frames is still an open issue. Although using region
quality estimation network (RQEN) can achieve relative good performance on standard datasets, it is limited by the alignment of all bounding boxes. If the position of person varies in bounding boxes, it will
influence the region generating unit, which thus decreases the accuracy
of re-ID. To solve this limitation, this paper proposes a network combining the quality estimation and attribute classification. While convolution
neural network can effectively learn global features, attribute recognition focus more on details. Therefore, our method achieves comparable
results on iLIDS-VID and PRID 2011 datasets with the help of attribute
classification.

Keywords: Person re-identification · Video-based ·
Attributes recognition

1 Introduction

Person re-identification aims to identify a given pedestrian in different cameras.
Given an image or video of a specific person, the process of person re-ID is
to determine whether this person has been observed by another camera [1].
Nowadays researchers attach great importance to relevant issues due to its broad
application and significant research sense.

A large amount of work has focused on two aspects: one is to obtain a robust
descriptor to extract reliable features of pedestrians [2–6]; another is to learn a
good distance metric [7–11]. In feature extraction, previous work can be divided
into hand-crafted features extraction and deep-learned features extraction. Since

© Springer Nature Singapore Pte Ltd. 2019
F. Sun et al. (Eds.): ICCSIP 2018, CCIS 1005, pp. 63–75, 2019.
https://doi.org/10.1007/978-981-13-7983-3_6

more large-scale datasets have been introduced, CNN-based deep learning models become increasingly popular and achieve good performance in person re-ID. In existing literature, person re-ID with single image has been explored extensively. Instead of limited information in one single image, researchers fix their eyes on video-based re-ID which provides richer temporal information of pedestrians. When building appearance models of pedestrians, a typical issue in video-based re-ID is how to aggregate information from a sequence of images. Karanam et al. [12] simply take the average of all the images, but this method produces undesired noise due to recognition failure caused by partial occlusions. To handle this challenge, Liu et al. [13] has proposed a quality aware network which aggregates all the images according to their quality. However, this network predicts the quality scores of all samples from the integral view and ignores which part causes noise. Song et al. [14] has improved the quality predictor by dividing all the frames into three regions and predicts the quality score of each part respectively. Through extracting the complementary region-based information between different frames, this region-based quality estimation network can obtain better results. Yet the performance of this network is limited by the quality of pedestrian alignment since all the frames are divided through the same standard. In this paper, we randomly select a certain number of pedestrians and then crop a small lower part of images of these people. The result turns out to be 22.4% and 6.2% lower than that in [14] on iLIDS-VID and PRID 2011 dataset respectively.

To address the situation above, we propose to use attribute labels as complementary cues to improve re-ID performance when images of pedestrians are misaligned. Attributes recognition e.g. age, gender and dressing, has significant applications in video surveillance and has been developed recently. Although person re-ID based on deep learned network can learn comparable robust features automatically, they rely more on global descriptors and ignore similar details between different identities. If two pedestrians are very similar in appearance, a CNN model fails to tell subtle differences while adding attributes recognition helps predict identities more precisely by local structures. Even when images are not complete such as the situation where lower parts are missing, the prominent attribute features won't be influenced. Therefore, this paper designs a multi-task model combining the aggregation method through region-based quality prediction and attributes recognition, which can reduce the impact caused by occlusion and misalignment. To evaluate the performance of our method, we conduct experiments on iLIDS-VID and PRID 2011 dataset for video-based person re-identification.

To sum up, main contributions of this paper are summarized as follows.

(1) In order to obtain misaligned datasets, we preprocess the images of video-based datasets iLIDS-VID and PRID 2011. First, we randomly select 50 pedestrians for iLIDS-VID and 30 for PRID 2011, then subtract the bottom part of all the images of these pedestrians and finally resize these images to make all the images the same size
(2) We have manually labeled a set of pedestrian attributes for the two datasets. Combining the attribute classification loss, identity prediction loss and

triplet loss, the method we proposed can achieve better performance on the processed datasets.

2 Related Work

Since CNN-based deep learning models became popular in 2014 [15], a large body of research focus on designing an effective net structure to obtain competitive accuracy. One major drawback of deep learning in re-ID is that training a model needs large-scale data volume. With the appearance of video-based re-ID, there is plenty of space for improvement since the scale of video-based datasets is typically larger than image-based datasets. Current video-based re-ID methods typically apply a max/average pooling layer to aggregate frame-level features into a global vector [16,17]. Inspired by the field of action recognition, some researchers propose using spatial-temporal features to re-identify pedestrians since each pedestrian has a sequence of images. Fernando et al. [18] design a descriptor that captures the video-wide temporal dynamics by learning to rank the frame-level features of a video. After that, more attention is paid to capturing temporal information between consecutive video frames. For example, McLaughlin et al. [17] extract features of frames through a CNN model, and then obtain the information flow between time-steps through feeding all these features into a recurrent final layer. However, all these works mentioned above utilize global features of video frames and ignore the complementary information in multiple sub-regions. Therefore, our work borrows the idea from [14] to take advantage of efficient sub-regions of different video frames.

As an auxiliary information of pedestrian features, we introduce attributes labels to help re-identify person of interest. In older works, attributes prediction has been investigated a lot in face recognition. Due to its comparable results, researchers start to employ this thought in person re-ID. Layne et al. [19] use SVM to train attribute detectors which predict 15 attribute features, e.g. hair color and bag type, to describe pedestrians. Li et al. [20] propose a deep learning framework which recognizes multiple attributes jointly. In addition to these works, several attribute datasets such as PETA and RAP are also released. The main idea of this paper is based on the net structure in [21], in which the CNN learns ID classification loss and attribute classification loss simultaneously and back-propagates the weighted sum of them.

The datasets we use are preprocessed, so parts of images may not contain whole body of pedestrians, which also causes misalignment between different pedestrians. Nevertheless, attribute predictions such as age or gender do not need entire features of identities. Combine attributes recognition and region-based quality estimation network, our proposed model obtains better results in flexible situations (Fig. 1).

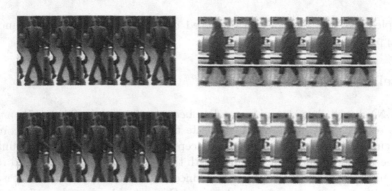

Fig. 1. Examples of images before and after being preprocessed. The first row shows the complete images of pedestrian and the second row shows the images which are subtracted the bottom part.

3 Proposed Method

3.1 Architecture Preview

Figure 2 illustrates an overview of our network, which consists CNN feature aggregation part and attribute prediction part. In order to fully employ inter-class differences and intra-class differences, we train frame-level and video-level features by introducing triplet loss. The triplet loss which usually consists three components, the anchor, the positive, and the negative, aims to reduce the distance between the anchor and the same, and push the different from the anchor. The inputs of our network should be images of one pedestrian under one of the two cameras and another pedestrian under both two cameras. Through the quality estimation unit, we can generate the video-level feature representations F_u, F_m, F_l which will be used for identity and attribute prediction. During training stage, our network predicts ID label and multiple attribute labels and back propagate the weighted sum of individual losses. During testing stage, we extract the Pool5 descriptors for retrieval. To predict ID label and attribute labels simultaneously, we introduce $M + 1$ fully connected layers, where M is the number of attributes. The total loss of our network consists ID classification loss, attribute classification loss and triplet loss. Suppose we have K identities and each identity has M attributes and an image set of n images. Let x_i denotes the i-th image, d_i and l_i^j denote the identity label and attribute label of image x_i respectively, where $j \in 1, 2, ..., M$ is the index of attribute classes. Given a training example x, let y be the ground-truth ID label and k be the predicted label, $p(k)$ denotes the predicted probability of each ID label $k \in 1, 2, ..., K$. Then the loss of ID classification can be computed as below:

$$L_{ID} = - \sum_{k=1}^{K} \log(p(k))q(k) \tag{1}$$

where $q(y) = 1$ and $q(k) = 0$ for all $k \neq q$.

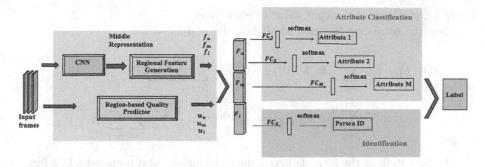

Fig. 2. An overview of the proposed method.

As for attribute prediction, we use the similar computation method to formulate M softmax losses. Let y_m be the ground-truth attribute label and j be the predicted attribute label, $p(j)$ denotes the predicted probability of each attribute label. The loss of attribute classification can be formulated by:

$$L_{att} = -\sum_{j=1}^{m} \log(p(j))q(j) \tag{2}$$

where m is the number of classes for a certain attribute and $q(y_m) = 1$ and $q(j) = 0$ for all $j \neq y_m$.

As a result, the overall loss of our network can be defined by following formulation:

$$L = L_{softmax} + L_t \tag{3}$$

$$L_{softmax} = \lambda L_{ID} + \frac{1}{M}\sum_{i=1}^{M} L_{att} \tag{4}$$

where L_t denotes the triplet loss, L_{ID} and L_{att} denote the cross entropy loss of identity classification and attribute classification. λ is a parameter that balances the two losses. The determination of λ will be discussed in Sect. 4.2.

3.2 Backpropagation Algorithm

One important process in convolutional neural network is to update parameters by backpropagation algorithm (BP algorithm), which makes the classification more accurate. This section gives a brief statement of the fine-tuning process of BP parameters under the multilayer neural network.

Given a set of data samples $((x^{(1)}, y^{(2)}), ..., (x^{(m)}, y^{(m)}))$, we use batch gradient descent (BGD) algorithm to update parameters of neural network. In person re-ID task, $x^{(i)}$ denote features of pedestrians and $y^{(i)}$ denote the ground truth labels of pedestrians. For a single sample $(x^{(i)}, y^{(i)})$, the cost function can be computed as follow:

$$J(W, b; x^{(i)}, y^{(i)}) = \frac{1}{2} \parallel h_{W,b}(x^{(i)}) - y^{(i)} \parallel^2 \tag{5}$$

where $h_{W,b}(x^{(i)})$ is the output value of each layer.

Then the total cost function of all samples is defined as:

$$J(W,b) = [\frac{1}{m} \sum_{i=1}^{m} J(W,b;x^{(i)},y^{(i)})] + \frac{\lambda}{2} \sum_{l=1}^{n_l-1} \sum_{i=1}^{s_l} \sum_{j=1}^{s_l} (W_{ij}^{(l)})^2$$

$$= [\frac{1}{m} \sum_{i=1}^{m} \frac{1}{2} \parallel h_{W,b}(x^{(i)}) - y^{(i)} \parallel^2] + \frac{\lambda}{2} \sum_{l=1}^{n_l-1} \sum_{i=1}^{s_l} \sum_{j=1}^{s_l} (W_{ij}^{(l)})^2 \qquad (6)$$

The first item in the formula is standard deviation (also represents loss function) and the second one is the regularization term, where λ is the regularization parameter, n_l is the number of deep neural network layers and s_l is the number of neurons of the lth layer.

Through minimizing the objective function $J(W,b)$ to solve the value of W,b, it is necessary to initialize each parameter W,b to a very small, near-zero random value, such as a normal distribution. Then the gradient descent algorithm updates parameters $W_{ij}^{(l)}$ and $b_i^{(l)}$ according to the following rules:

$$W_{ij}^{(l)} = W_{ij}^{(l)} - a\frac{\partial J(W,b)}{\partial W_{ij}} \qquad (7)$$

$$b_i^{(l)} = b_i - a\frac{\partial J(W,b)}{\partial b_i} \qquad (8)$$

where a denotes the learning rate. During the process of updating parameter, the solution of $\frac{\partial J(W,b)}{\partial W_{ij}}$ and $\frac{\partial J(W,b)}{\partial b_i}$ can be achieved by BP algorithm. The process of deriving from backward to forward step by step through chain rules is the key part of BP algorithm in deep convolutional neural network. We use pseudo code to implement one iteration of batch gradient descent algorithm as follows.

3.3   Quality Estimation Unit

In this paper, we use the same strategy in [14] to estimate the quality of frames. According to the landmarks of images, we divide images into three-part-division by location ratio 3:2:2 in height direction. The input images are sent into two different parts, one is for generating the middle representations through fully convolutional network and another is for predicting the quality scores of input images. Both the middle representation and the quality scores are sliced by the location ratio to represent the upper part, middle part and the lower part of images. Let $S = I_1, I_2, ..., I_n$ denote an image set of given pedestrian, $f_u(I_i)$, $f_m(I_i)$, $f_l(I_i)$ denote feature vectors of each part respectively and $\mu_u(I_i)$, $\mu_m(I_i)$, $\mu_l(I_i)$ denote the corresponding quality scores after being scaled to $[0,1]$. Then the final representation of given pedestrian can be computed by

$$F_{part}(S) = \sum_{i=1}^{n} \mu_{part}(I_i)f_{part}(I_i) \qquad (9)$$

where $F_{part}(S)$ denotes different region's feature representation of an image sequence, n is the number of images. Notice that $\sum_{i=1}^{n} \mu_{part}(I_i) = 1$ (Fig. 3).

Algorithm 1. Batch Gradient Descent Algorithm

---

1. For each layer in deep convolutional neural network.
   (a) Let $\Delta W^{(l)} := 0$, $\Delta b^{(l)} := 0$, where $\Delta W^{(l)}$ has the same dimension as $W^{(l)}$ and $\Delta b^{(l)}$ has the same dimension as $b^{(l)}$.
2. For $i = 1, 2, ..., m$
   (a) Compute $\nabla_{W^{(l)}} J(W, b; x, y)$ and $\nabla_{b^{(l)}} J(W, b; x, y)$ by BP algorithm.
   (b) Compute $\Delta W^{(l)}$ and $\Delta b^{(l)}$:

$$\Delta W^{(l)} := \Delta W^{(l)} + \nabla_{W^{(l)}} J(W, b; x, y)$$

$$\Delta b^{(l)} := \Delta b^{(l)} + \nabla_{b^{(l)}} J(W, b; x, y)$$

3. Update weight parameters by following formulas to minimize $J(W, b)$ until the network converges.

$$W^{(l)} = W^{(l)} - a\left[\frac{1}{m}\Delta W^{(l)} + \lambda W^{(l)}\right]$$

$$b^{(l)} = b^{(l)} - a\left[\frac{1}{m}\Delta b^{(l)}\right]$$

3.4 Attribute Annotation

In order to make a contrast with the results in [14], we use iLIDS-VID and PRID 2011 datasets for experiments and manually annotate the two datasets with attribute labels. With reference to previous works, the attributes we annotate in this paper are all ID-level rather than instance-level, which means these attributes are related to identities themselves instead of appearing for a short time. To some extent, if two images contain the same identity, their ID-level attributes should be matched.

For iLIDS-VID, we have labeled 26 attributes: gender (male, female), hair length (long, short), sleeve length (long, short), length of lower-body clothing (long, short), type of lower-body clothing (pants, dress), wearing hat (yes, no), carrying bag (yes, no), carrying backpack (yes, no), 8 colors of upper-body clothing (black, white, red, yellow, gray, blue, green, brown), 9 colors of lower-body clothing (black, white, purple, yellow, gray, blue, green, brown, red) and age (child, teenager, adult, old).

For PRID 2011, we similarly have labeled 31 attributes: age, gender, hair length, sleeve length, length of lower-body clothing, type of lower-body clothing, wearing hat, carrying bag, carrying backpack, carrying handbag (yes, no), hair color (light, dark), carrying clothes (yes, no), wearing sunglasses (yes, no), 11 colors of upper-body clothing (white, black, blue, brown, green, red, gray, pink,

Fig. 3. Samples of images divided by location ratio 3:2:2 in height.

green, orange, purple), 8 colors of lower-body clothing (black, blue, brown, gray, white, red, yellow, orange) (Fig. 4).

4   Experiments

4.1   Datasets and Evaluation Metric

PRID 2011. [22] dataset contains 200 pedestrians and each has 2 image sequences under two different cameras, in which the length of each image sequence varies from 5 to 675 frames. In our experiments, only sequences with more than 27 frames will be used. The images of this dataset are captured in an open area, so the background is rather clean and has little occlusion.

iLIDS-VID. [23] is a multi-shot dataset consisting of 600 image sequences of 300 identities. Each image sequence has a length of 23 to 192 frames. This dataset is created using videos from two non-overlapping cameras in an airport terminal. Due to its extremely heavy occlusion, this dataset is more challenging.

Evaluation metric. In our experiments, we use the same setting as [14] for comparison. For data splitting, we use half identities for training and another half for testing on both two datasets. Considering the relative small size of these two datasets, we repeat the experiments ten times and report the average results. For re-identification task, we use the Cumulative Matching Characteristic (CMC) curve, which implies the precision of retrieval.

4.2   Parameter Validation and Attribute Analysis

Parameter Validation. As mentioned in Sect. 3, λ is an important parameter which balances the ID classification loss and attribute classification loss. Since we repeat the experiments ten times, we can randomly choose one time for parameter validation. Obviously when λ is smaller, the contribution of person identity classification becomes less influential. We evaluate the re-ID performance from $\lambda = 3$ to $\lambda = 15$ and find that the result is better when $\lambda = 10$. Results with various value of λ is presented in Fig. 5.

Attribute Analysis. Before training, we first analyze the discriminative potential of how the attributes we have labeled can help person re-ID performance.

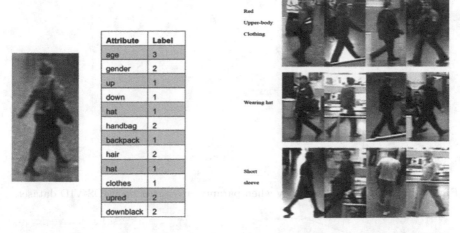

Attribute	Label
age	3
gender	2
up	1
down	1
hat	1
handbag	2
backpack	1
hair	2
hat	1
clothes	1
upred	2
downblack	2

Fig. 4. Attribute labels of a given pedestrian in iLIDS-VID dataset. For example, we use 1 to represent children, 2 for teenager, 3 for adult and 4 for old. The right part shows some representative attributes.

We assume perfect attribute detection and only use attribute features to obtain CMC curves in Fig. 6. Also we show the results with the random 10 attributes and 20 attributes. This figure shows that: (i) with more attributes being used, the re-ID performance can be better; and (ii) the re-ID accuracy (rank-1 accuracy) on the two datasets can reach 65.33% and 81% with all the attributes we have labeled, illustrating that attribute features are reliable to discriminate different people.

4.3 Comparison with Related Methods

The method we propose aims to improve the performance of re-ID on the datasets after preprocessing. In order to validate the effectiveness of our network, we construct two baselines for contrast. For baseline 1, we choose the GoogLeNet with batch normalization initialized with the ImageNet model [24]. Based on the pre-trained model, we set the number of neurons in the last FC layer to the number of training identities. During testing, we extract a 1024-dim feature vector from the pool5 layer for each query and gallery image. Then we calculate the Euclidean distance between the gallery and query features. For baseline 2, we adopt the method in [3] which achieves comparable results when the two datasets are not preprocessed.

The results of evaluation are presented in Tables 1 and 2. Since images of datasets are cropped, the accuracy of three methods all decrease. However, our method can achieve better performance because the cropped part doesn't influence the attribute recognition. On iLIDS-VID dataset, B1 only obtains a rank-1 accuracy of 50.7% and B2 increases the result by 4%. With the help of attribute classification, our model can achieve the accuracy of 63.3%, the improvement

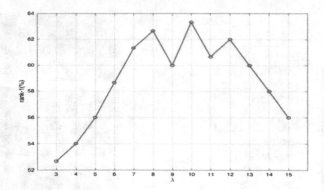

Fig. 5. The re-ID rank-1 accuracy when parameter λ varies on iLIDS-VID dataset.

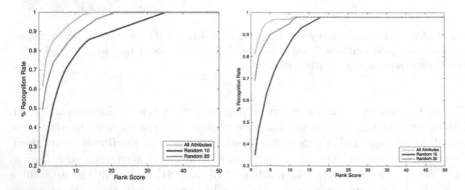

Fig. 6. Best case re-identification using attributes. Left figure shows the results on iLIDS-VID and the right one shows the results on PRID 2011.

over B1 and B2 is 12.6% and 8.6%. Also on PRID 2011 dataset, the comparison demonstrates that the method we proposed increases the accuracy by 10.0% and 4.4% compared to B1 and B2.

Tables 3 and 4 compare the result of our method with other state-of-the-art methods [16,17,25–27] which evaluated the performance of person re-ID on standard datasets. Although we cut off part of the images of datasets in our experiments, the method this paper proposes increases rank-1 accuracy by 5.3% on iLIDS-VID dataset and 9.6% on PRID 2011 dataset. The results show that our network combining with attributes classification does achieve effective and stable performance.

Table 1. Comparison with related method on iLIDS-VID

Matching rate(%)	iLIDS-VID			
Rank	1	5	10	20
Baseline 1	50.7	74.7	85.3	91.3
Baseline 2 (RQEN)	54.7	80.0	91.3	97.3
Ours	63.3	90.0	94.0	99.3

Table 2. Comparison with related method on PRID 2011

Matching rate(%)	PRID 2011			
Rank	1	5	10	20
Baseline 1	80.0	97.8	100.0	100.0
Baseline 2 (RQEN)	85.6	100.0	100.0	100.0
Ours	90.0	100.0	100.0	100.0

Table 3. Comparison with related method on iLIDS-VID

Matching rate(%)	iLIDS-VID			
Rank	1	5	10	20
CNN+SRM+TAM	55.2	86.5	-	97.0
CNN+XQDA	53.0	81.4	-	95.1
CNN+RNN	58	84	91	96
STA	44.3	71.7	83.7	91.7
TDL	56.3	87.6	95.6	98.3
Ours	63.3	90.0	94.0	99.3

Table 4. Comparison with related method on PRID 2011

Matching rate(%)	PRID 2011			
Rank	1	5	10	20
CNN+SRM+TAM	79.4	94.4	-	99.3
CNN+XQDA	77.3	93.5	-	99.3
CNN+RNN	70	90	95	97
STA	64.1	87.3	89.9	92.0
TDL	56.7	80.0	87.6	93.6
Ours	90.0	100.0	100.0	100.0

5   Conclusions

In this paper, we propose a network which combines the region-based quality estimation and attribute recognition for video-based person re-identification. First we preprocess the datasets and present the limitation of the method that relies on the quality prediction of upper, middle and lower part of images. To test the effectiveness of our method, we have annotated attribute labels of two video-based datasets. The experiment results show attributes can provide complementary information with CNN features, thus the combined network improves the performance of re-ID.

References

1. Bedagkar-Gala, A., Shah, S.K.: A survey of approaches and trends in person re-identification. Image Vis. Comput. **32**(4), 270–286 (2014)
2. Gray, D., Tao, H.: Viewpoint invariant pedestrian recognition with an ensemble of localized features. In: Forsyth, D., Torr, P., Zisserman, A. (eds.) ECCV 2008. LNCS, vol. 5302, pp. 262–275. Springer, Heidelberg (2008). https://doi.org/10.1007/978-3-540-88682-2_21
3. Zheng, W.S., Li, X., Xiang, T., et al.: Partial person re-identification. In: IEEE International Conference on Computer Vision, pp. 4678–4686. IEEE (2016)
4. Zhao, R., Ouyang, W., Wang, X.: Unsupervised salience learning for person re-identification. In: Computer Vision and Pattern Recognition, pp. 3586–3593. IEEE (2013)
5. Zhang, L., Xiang, T., Gong, S.: Learning a discriminative null space for person re-identification. In: Computer Vision and Pattern Recognition, pp. 1239–1248. IEEE (2016)
6. Weijer, J.V.D., Schmid, C., Verbeek, J., et al.: Learning color names for real-world applications. IEEE Trans. Image Process. **18**(7), 1512–1523 (2009)
7. Liu, Y.: Distance Metric Learning: A Comprehensive Survey. Michigan State Universiy, East Lansing (2006)
8. Hirzer, M.: Large scale metric learning from equivalence constraints. In: IEEE Conference on Computer Vision and Pattern Recognition, pp. 2288–2295. IEEE Computer Society (2012)
9. Davis, J.V., Kulis, B., Jain, P., et al.: Information-theoretic metric learning. In: Proceedings of the International Conference on Machine Learning, ICML 07, pp. 209–216 (2007)
10. Hirzer, M., Roth, P.M., Köstinger, M., Bischof, H.: Relaxed pairwise learned metric for person re-identification. In: Fitzgibbon, A., Lazebnik, S., Perona, P., Sato, Y., Schmid, C. (eds.) ECCV 2012. LNCS, vol. 7577, pp. 780–793. Springer, Heidelberg (2012). https://doi.org/10.1007/978-3-642-33783-3_56
11. Chen, D., Yuan, Z., Hua, G., et al.: Similarity learning on an explicit polynomial kernel feature map for person re-identification. In: Proceedings of Conference on Computer Vision and Pattern Recognition, pp. 1565–1573 (2015)
12. Karanam, S., Li, Y., Radke, R.J.: Sparse Re-id: block sparsity for person re-identification. In: IEEE Conference on Computer Vision and Pattern Recognition Workshops, pp. 33–40 IEEE (2015)
13. Liu, Y., Yan, J., Ouyang, W.: Quality aware network for set to set recognition, pp. 4694–4703 (2017)

14. Song, G., Leng, B., Liu, Y., et al.: Region-based quality estimation network for large-scale person re-identification (2017)
15. Yi, D., Lei, Z., Liao, S., et al.: Deep metric learning for person re-identification. In: International Conference on Pattern Recognition, pp. 34–39. IEEE (2014)
16. Zheng, L., et al.: MARS: a video benchmark for large-scale person re-identification. In: Leibe, B., Matas, J., Sebe, N., Welling, M. (eds.) ECCV 2016. LNCS, vol. 9910, pp. 868–884. Springer, Cham (2016). https://doi.org/10.1007/978-3-319-46466-4_52
17. Mclaughlin, N., Rincon, J.M.D., Miller, P.: Recurrent convolutional network for video-based person re-identification. In: Computer Vision and Pattern Recognition, pp. 1325–1334. IEEE (2016)
18. Fernando, B., Gavves, E., José, O.M., et al.: Rank pooling for action recognition. IEEE Trans. Pattern Anal. Mach. Intell. **39**(4), 773–787 (2017)
19. Layne, R., Hospedales, T.M., Gong, S.: Person Re-identification by attributes. In: BMVC (2012)
20. Li, D., Zhang, Z., Chen, X., et al.: A richly annotated dataset for pedestrian attribute recognition (2016)
21. Lin, Y., Zheng, L., Zheng, Z., et al.: Improving person re-identification by attribute and identity learning (2017)
22. Hirzer, M., Beleznai, C., Roth, P.M., Bischof, H.: Person re-identification by descriptive and discriminative classification. In: Heyden, A., Kahl, F. (eds.) SCIA 2011. LNCS, vol. 6688, pp. 91–102. Springer, Heidelberg (2011). https://doi.org/10.1007/978-3-642-21227-7_9
23. Wang, T., Gong, S., Zhu, X., et al.: Person re-identification by discriminative selection in video ranking. IEEE Trans. Pattern Anal. Mach. Intell. **38**(12), 2501–2514 (2016)
24. Ioffe, S., Szegedy, C.: Batch normalization: accelerating deep network training by reducing internal covariate shift, pp. 448–456 (2015)
25. Liu, K., Ma, B., Zhang, W., et al.: A spatio-temporal appearance representation for video-based pedestrian re-identification. In: IEEE International Conference on Computer Vision, pp. 3810–3818. IEEE (2015)
26. Zhou, Z., Huang, Y., Wang, W., et al.: See the forest for the trees: joint spatial and temporal recurrent neural networks for video-based person re-identification. In: IEEE Conference on Computer Vision and Pattern Recognition, pp. 6776–6785. IEEE (2017)
27. You, J., Wu, A., Li, X., et al.: Top-push video-based person re-identification. In: Computer Vision and Pattern Recognition, pp. 1345–1353. IEEE (2016)

A Preliminary Visual System
for Assistant Diagnosis of ASD:
Response to Name

Zhiyong Wang$^{(\boxtimes)}$, Jingjing Liu$^{(\boxtimes)}$, and Honghai Liu$^{(\boxtimes)}$![ORCID]

State Key Laboratory of Mechanical System and Vibration,
Shanghai Jiao Tong University, Shanghai, China
{yzwang_sjtu,lily121,honghai.liu}@sjtu.edu.cn

Abstract. Autism spectrum disorder (ASD) is a kind of developmental disorder which attracted a lot of attention for its urgency and pervasiveness. The rapid development of machine vision technologies have brought new ideas to the auxiliary diagnosis of ASD, such as face detection, gaze estimation, action recognition, etc. The paper proposed a preliminary visual system for assistant diagnosis of ASD in a core clinical testing scenario-Response to Name (NTR). The eye center localization and gaze estimation were applied to measure the responses of the subjects. The main contribution of the article is that an experimental paradigm was established from a visual engineering perspective. The results showed that this system could analyze the response of the child for NTR accurately.

Keywords: ASD · Response to Name · Gaze estimation

1 Introduction

Autism spectrum disorder (ASD) is a kind of pervasive developmental disorder involving various anomalies in social relations, behavior, etc [1]. In the recent decades, the prevalence of ASD has been increasing dramatically [2]. The prevalence rate of ASD is 1/5000 in 1975, but 1/59 in 2018 [3,4] in America. It is approximates to 1/100 in China, and the number is about 10 million in total with a huge number of them are children from 0 to 14. It is known that ASD is mainly manifested in three core symptoms: social impairments, communication difficulties, narrow interest and stereotypical and repetitive behaviors. Social impairments mean children have a qualitative defect in social communication. In infancy, children avoid eye contact, lack of interest in and reaction to human voices, do not expect to be held or the body is stiff and unwilling to be close to people when held. In early childhood, children with ASD still avoid eye contact, and often do not respond to their names. Although the exact cause of autism is

Supported by the National Natural Science Foundation of China (No. 61733011, 51575338).

F. Sun et al. (Eds.): ICCSIP 2018, CCIS 1005, pp. 76–86, 2019.
https://doi.org/10.1007/978-981-13-7983-3_7

unknown and there is no way to completely cure, research indicates that appropriate and scientific treatment can improve the condition. Especially in the early childhood, early diagnosis and intervention of autism will have a good effect on the improvement of their symptoms [5].

The diagnosis of autism ultimately boils down to the definition of symptoms. In the clinical diagnosis, the physicians observe the children's performance and determine if the children are lack of social interaction, joint attention, communication, and mental or behavioral flexibility by using some assessment scales and criteria [6]. Two common diagnostic classification systems are DSM-IV-TR (Diagnostic and statistical manual of mental disorders) and ICD-10 (International classification of Diseases). ADI-R (autism diagnostic interview-revised) and ADOS (Autism Diagnostic Observation Schedule) are considered to be the most standard tool in autism diagnosis. Compared with other assessment scales, they set a wider range of ages, expose more psychometric data, and better meet DSM and ICD standards. No matter in which scales and the clinical diagnosis, the RTN is a fundamental and essential process to test the basic cognitive function [7]. However, the drawbacks of this diagnostic mode based on assessment scales and the observation are evident. The main problems are as follows:

- **comprehensive observation is difficult.**
- **diagnosis consistency is poor.**
- **professional ability to diagnose is demanding.**

In order to solve or alleviate this problem, a number of studies have been pay attention to new techniques in auxiliary diagnosis and interventions for ASD. It is true that the children with ASD are always accompanied by abnormal symptoms in neurological activations, speech, face, body gestures or physiological response. Because ASD is a brain disorder, plenty of researchers focus on EEG (electroencephalo-graph) and sMRI (structural magnetic resonance imaging) to find some potential features. Whitford et al. [8] recorded the EEG and sMRI of the same subjects at the same time. The result shows that the curve of slow wave brain electrical power and cortical gray matter density decrease is approximately parallel as the age grows. Some of the studies pay attention to the physiological signals like, ECG (Electrocardiograph) and GSR (galvanic skin response), when the mood of children with ASD changes [9]. Accelerometers embedded in wristband could detect the users repetitive arm movements [10]. The facial features, especially the direction of eye gaze, are considered as important evaluation points since the autistic people have social deficits. The eye tracking and gaze estimation are regarded as a significant clue to assess ASD [11,12]. Besides, the head tracking was also applied to detect the response of the child [13]. Children with ASD use simple and single linguistic rules more often in speech production [14].

Although the above methods could provide some new evidence to ASD, they are still not applied to clinical diagnosis due to the cost, complexity, pertinence, etc. In this paper we proposed a novel noninvasive visual system to capture the symptoms and manifestations of the children during one core assessment scenario: Response to Name. The system is just a preliminary platform and the main contribution of the article is that a detailed experimental paradigm was established from a visual engineering perspective.

2   Method

2.1   Experimental Site

In the RTN test scene, there are three people involved in this experimental site including the child, one of his parents and one implementer who will call the child's name. Generally the implementer is the physician or another parent of the child, which depends on the child's reaction. The experimental site is fixed in a place of which the width is 2.5 m and length is 4 m. The positions of desk, chairs and sensors are also confirmed based on the size parameters of the children ranging from 2–6 years old and the sensors' range. The specific distribution parameters are showed in Fig. 1. The parent and the child sit face to face and the implementer stands about 45° behind the child in the left or right. There are some toys on the desk for the child to play.

2.2   Sensing System Framework

In order to gather the information of the child's RTN, we designed a visual system which contained a camera and a depth sensor. The camera can capture the face of the child with ASD, so the gaze and expression information can be analyzed. The camera we used is the Logitech BRIO with a highest resolution of 4K and three kinds of view: 65°, 78° and 90°. Besides, it can focus automatically and there are no physical knobs, which we will not worry about the accidentally touches from the child. As for the depth sensor, the Kinect 1.0 of Microsoft was chosen to record the voice detect the skeleton points information which can display the movements of the child. The specific location parameters of these sensors are also shown in Fig. 1.

2.3   Experimental Procedure

First, the descriptions of the positive and negative response for calling name were given by the experts. The details are as follows:

Positive response: The child turns his head to the implementer and makes eye contact to the implementer; Or the child turns his head to the implementer but makes no eye contact to the implementer.

Negative response: The child pauses for a moment without turning his head towards the implementer; Or the child answered "Yes" without turning his head to the implementer.

Second, the child and his parent would be invited to sit face to face. The child was provided two toys to play. If the child did not play the toys, the

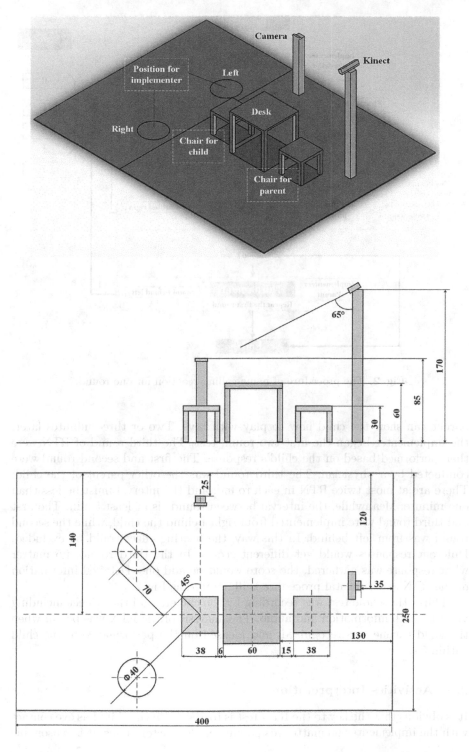

Fig. 1. The specific distribution parameters of the experimental site (cm).

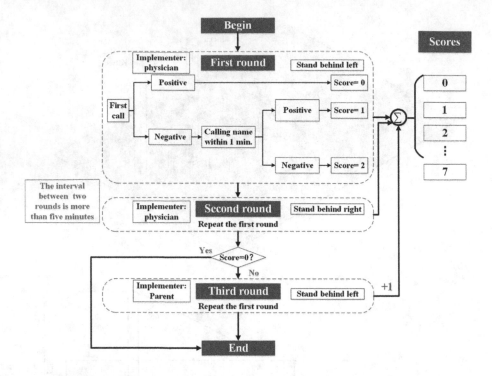

Fig. 2. The procedure of name-calling reaction for one round.

parent can show the child how to play with toys. Two or three minutes later, the implementer began the first two round test. The third round of RTN were then performed based on the child's response. The first and second round were conducted by a physician. The third round was the other parent of the child; There are at most twice RTN in each round, and the interval must be less than one minute. Meanwhile, the interval between rounds is at least 5 min. The first and third round were implemented from right behind the child, while the second round was from left behind. In this way, the hearing effect could be excluded. Different responses would get different scores. In the third round, no matter what response was gathered, the score would be add one. Detailed information of the RTN experimental procedure is illustrated as Fig. 2.

Third, the whole test was recording by the camera and the Kinect including videos, depth information and audio. The analysis of the RTN was begun when the child's name was recognized, and focused on the performance of the child within 5 s.

2.4   Activities Interpretation

It is obvious that the key to the RTN test is to observe if the child has eye contact with the implementer no matter his parents or the doctor. Thus, it is reasonable to use the gaze of child as a clue to evaluate the performance of the child. When the gaze is not available, the direction of face and head is employed to show the child's response. The key step to accurately estimate gaze is localization of the child's eye pupil center. Cai et al. [15] proposed an improved integrodifferential approach to represent gaze via efficiently and accurately localizing the eye center in lower resolution image. This proposed method takes advantage of the drastic intensity changes between the iris and the sclera and the grayscale of the eye center as well. The ratio derivative is formulated as follows:

$$
\begin{cases}
I_r = K_r * I \\
I'_{r+1} = K'_{r+1} * I \\
D_r = \frac{I'_{r+1}}{I_r} \\
\arg\max_{(r,x,y)}(D_r) \\
r \in [r_{\min}, r_{\max}]
\end{cases}
\tag{1}
$$

where K_r is the mask with a center weight and r stands for the radius of the circle inside the kernel. The mask without a center weight is represented as K'_{r+1}, whose radius is $r+1$. I_r and I'_{r+1} are the results of the convolution of the different masks with eye image I. D_r. stands for the ratio derivative calculated by the division of the convolution result image. r_{min} and r_{max} are set according to the size of the eye image representing the minimum and maximum of the radius r. The weights of the points around the circular arcs are of equal value and normalized to 1, and the weight of the center point is settled to a valid value. In order to locate the eye center and radius, the proposed method searches the maximum of different radii of D_r.

This method was applied to detect the eye pupil center for the base of the gaze estimation. In our experiment, we never fixed the head of the child with ASD, which brought a problem in the gaze estimation. In our system, the method provided in [16] was used to track the gaze of the child. They built a rotation invariant gaze estimation model based on the located facial features, eye center, head pose and the depth data gathered from Kinect. The principle of the gaze estimation is illustrated as shown in Fig. 3. The ellipse and circle in the image represent the eye and the iris, respectively. The center of two eye corners is assumed to be the eye center (x_c, y_c). Because of the low resolution in the eye area, the iris center is assumed to be the pupil center (x_p, y_p).

The gaze direction in the head coordinate system can be estimated by the following equations.

$$
\begin{cases}
\vartheta = \tan^{-1}(a_0 * (D_{CP} * \frac{\cos\alpha}{L} - a_1)) \\
\delta = \tan^{-1}(b_0 * (D_{CP} * \frac{\sin\alpha}{L} - b_1)) \\
D_{CP} = \sqrt{(x_p - x_c)^2 + (y_p - y_c)^2}
\end{cases}
\tag{2}
$$

where ϑ; δ stands for horizontal and vertical axial components of the gaze direction respectively. L is the Euclidean distance of the two eye corners. D_{cp} is the Euclidean distance of the eye center and pupil center. α is the intersection angle of the eye-pupil line and corner-corner line. a_0; a_1; b_0; b_1 are parameters that can be determined in the calibration stage.

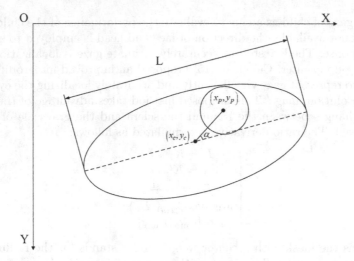

Fig. 3. The principle of gaze estimation.

Based on above gaze estimation method, the eye contact between the child and the implementer can be captured and recorded. The mutual gaze between the child and implementer was simplified by supposing the implementer was in a fixed posture and position. Thus, when the child looked at the implementer, we just measured the direction of child's gaze and calculated the intersection of the gaze and the bounded plane. This area was set to be circular with the center around the center between implementer's. Though implementer moved slightly certainly, the offset makes less influence to the result to judge the mutual gaze. The principle to judge eye contact is shown as Fig. 4.

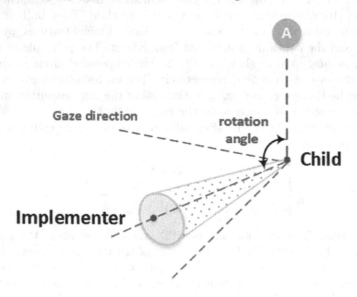

Fig. 4. The method to judge the eye contact.

3   Experiment Result

In our experiment, we invited ten normal adults to be the subjects of which average age is 24 years old. And there are nine male subjects and a female subject. They didn't know the experimental procedure beforehand. And we used a tennis ball and a cashmere doll as the toys. Some test scenes are shown in Fig. 5.

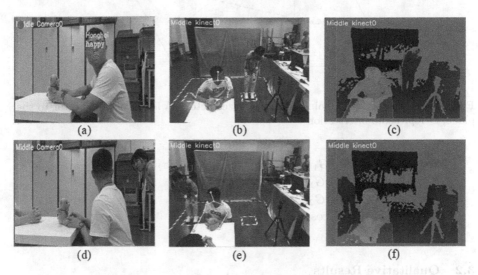

Fig. 5. (a) and (b) shown the status before and after calling name; (d) and (e) shown the views from different cameras at the same time; (c) and (f) shown the views from Kinect sensor.

3.1   Evaluation Method

There are two parameters to calculate: the intersection of the gaze and the fixed plane with a bound and the angle of the view. Meanwhile, the duration of eye contact is also considered. For the intersection, we used the method for calculating the intersection of a spatial line and a plane. H is the gaze start point which is decided by the facial feature point between the brows. And the plane now is fixed in the camera's vertical plane. The equation is shown below (Fig. 6).

$$\begin{cases} x = h_1 + g_1 * t \\ y = h_2 + g_2 * t \\ z = h_3 + g_3 * t \\ p_1 * (x - n_1) + p_2 * (y - n_2) + p_3 * (z - n_3) = 0 \end{cases} \tag{3}$$

For calculating the angle of the view, the method of calculating the angle between space vectors was used just as the followings. $G_1(x_1,y_1,z_1)$ and $G_2(x_2,y_2,z_2)$ are the gaze vectors.

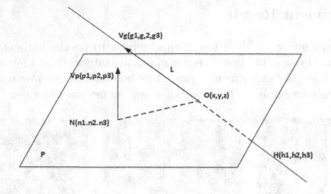

Fig. 6. H is the gaze start point; V_g is the gaze vector; V_p is the normal vector to the plane; O represents intersection

$$\begin{cases} G_1 * G_2 = x_1 x_2 + y_1 y_2 + z_1 z_2 \\ |G_1| = \sqrt{x_1{}^2 + y_1{}^2 + z_1{}^2} \\ |G_2| = \sqrt{x_2{}^2 + y_2{}^2 + z_2{}^2} \\ \cos\theta = \frac{G_1 * G_2}{|G_1||G_2|} \end{cases} \tag{4}$$

3.2 Qualitative Results

Because the subjects are normal adults, we only did two rounds of RTN testing. Totally, we got twenty responses to the test. The results of mutual gaze were detected as showed in Table 1. It is evident that our method can detect the eye contact accurately. If the intersections were in the circle, we considered the

Table 1. The results of mutual gaze detected

Subject	First round		Second round	
	True score	Calculated score	True score	Calculated score
1	0	0	0	0
2	0	0	0	0
3	0	1	0	0
4	0	0	0	1
5	0	0	0	0
6	0	0	0	0
7	0	0	0	0
8	0	0	0	0
9	0	0	0	1
10	0	0	0	0

mutual gaze were detected correctly. On the contrary, if the intersections are out of the circle, it is regarded as the miss detection of the eye contact. The accuracy of this method based on the distribution of the intersections is achieved 85%. It is acceptable for the using in name-calling reaction.

4 Conclusion

The paper proposed a preliminary visual system for assistant diagnosis of ASD in a core clinical testing scenario-Response to Name. Through advanced gaze estimation method, the gaze of the subjects were detected accurately. The intersection of the gaze and the fixed plane with a bound were mainly analyzed in this paper to judge the eye contact between the subject and implementer. The result shows that our system could be applied to the RTN test basically. Because the true children with ASD are complicated and changeable, the system and algorithm will be optimized and threshold of marking will be adjust in the future work. Meanwhile, more core clinical testing scenarios will be integrated for the early screening and diagnosis for ASD.

Combining the angle of the views, a more comprehensive system and evaluation indicator will be further studied.

References

1. Rogers, S.J., Pennington, B.F.: A theoretical approach to the deficits in infantile autism. Dev. Psychopathol. **3**(2), 137–162 (1991)
2. Xu, G., Strathearn, L., Liu, B., et al.: Prevalence of autism spectrum disorder among US children and adolescents, 2014–2016. JAMA **319**(1), 81–82 (2018)
3. Defilippis, E.M., Jaigirdar, T., Gaglani, S.M., Sakumoto, M., Punwani, V., Desai, R., et al.: Open osmosis: library of open educational resources (OER) for medical education (2015)
4. Baio, J., Wiggins, L., Christensen, D.L., et al.: Prevalence of autism spectrum disorder among children aged 8 years autism and developmental disabilities monitoring network, 11 sites, United States, 2014. MMWR Surveill. Summ. **67**(SS–6), 1–23 (2018). https://doi.org/10.15585/mmwr.ss6706a1
5. Liu, X., Wu, Q., Zhao, W., et al.: Technology-facilitated diagnosis and treatment of individuals with autism spectrum disorder: an engineering perspective. Appl. Sci. **7**(10), 1051 (2017)
6. Charman, T.: Why is joint attention a pivotal skill in autism? Philos. Trans. R. Soc. Lond. **358**(1430), 315–324 (2003)
7. Nadig, A.S., Ozonoff, S., Young, G.S., et al.: A prospective study of response to name in infants at risk for autism. Arch. Pediatr. Adolesc. Med. **161**(4), 378 (2007)
8. Whitford, T.J., Rennie, C.J., Grieve, S.M., et al.: Brain maturation in adolescence: concurrent changes in neuroanatomy and neurophysiology. Hum. Brain Mapp. **28**(3), 228–237 (2010)
9. Krupa, N., Anantharam, K., Sanker, M., et al.: Recognition of emotions in autistic children using physiological signals. Health Technol. **6**(2), 137–147 (2016)
10. Goodwin, M.S., Intille, S.S., Velicer, W.F., et al.: Sensor-enabled detection of stereotypical motor movements in persons with autism spectrum disorder. In: International Conference on Interaction Design and Children, pp. 109–112. ACM (2008)

11. Han, J., Kang, J., Ouyang, G., et al.: A study of EEG and eye tracking in children with autism. Chin. Sci. Bull. **63**, 1464–1473 (2018)
12. Guillon, Q., Hadjikhani, N., Baduel, S., et al.: Visual social attention in autism spectrum disorder: insights from eye tracking studies. Neurosci. Biobehav. Rev. **42**(5), 279–297 (2014)
13. Bidwell, J., Essa, I.A., Rozga, A., et al.: Measuring child visual attention using markerless head tracking from color and depth sensing cameras. In: ACM International Conference on Multimodal Interaction, pp. 447–454. ACM (2014)
14. Chin, I., Rubin, D., Tovar, A., et al.: Dense recordings of naturalistic interactions reveal both typical and atypical speech in one child with ASD. In: International Meeting for Autism Research (2012)
15. Cai, H., Liu, B., Zhang, J., et al.: Visual focus of attention estimation using eye center localization. IEEE Syst. J. **PP**(99), 1–6 (2017)
16. Cai, H., Zhou, X., Yu, H., et al.: Gaze estimation driven solution for interacting children with ASD. In: International Symposium on Micro-NanoMechatronics and Human Science, pp. 1–6. IEEE (2016)

Dynamic Detection and Tracking Based on Human Body Component Modeling

Jian He$^{(\boxtimes)}$ and Zihao Wang

Faculty of Information, Beijing University of Technology,
Beijing 100124, China
Jianhee@bjut.edu.cn

Abstract. Focus on the problem of dynamic human detection and tracking in complex scenes, a physical structure based Convolutional Nerual Network is proposed. Firstly, aiming at the modeling and analysis of the human body and its components, the human body detection algorithm adapted to complex scenes is proposed, and the convolutional neural network is designed to realize the model. Secondly, the human body tracking model based on convolutional neural network and off-line training is designed, and the human body tracking algorithm is optimized to realize fast and accurate tracking of human body. Using IOU, Euclidean distance and other algorithms, the relationship between the targets detected by the detection algorithms in two adjacent frames is established. Multi-modal fusion of multiple models using a state machine or the like, so that multiple models can work effectively at the same time. This experiment carried out simulation experiments on the bus video dataset. The experimental results show that the algorithm can effectively track the passengers who are obscured by each other on the bus, and the accuracy exceeds the current best algorithms, which proves the effectiveness of the algorithm.

Keywords: Target detection · Target tracking · Neural network

1 Introduction

In recent years, with the in-depth study of convolutional neural networks, the accuracy of target detection algorithms based on convolutional neural networks has been greatly improved compared with the algorithms of traditional artificial design feature extractors. Target detection algorithms based on convolutional neural networks are mainly divided into two categories: (1) two-step detection algorithms based on regional recommendations, such as: RCNN [1], Fast-RCNN [2], Faster-RCNN [3], FPN [4], etc.; (2) end-to-end one-step detection algorithms, such as: YOLOv3 [5], DSSD [6] and so on. Both types of algorithms have their own advantages and disadvantages: the two-step detection algorithm is better than the end-to-end detection algorithm in accuracy, and the end-to-end detection algorithm is faster than the two-step detection algorithm, which can basically achieve real-time. These algorithms have achieved good results in COCO [7], VOC [8] and other test data sets.

Although the above algorithm has a very high accuracy in most public data sets, the effect of the algorithm is not good in practical applications. The reason can be attributed to: the current public data set is too single in the sample size, scene, time period, illumination and other dimensions; and the different data collection standards are different, it is difficult to achieve cross-data set research and application. As shown in Fig. 1, YOLOv3 is very accurate in detecting humans on the COCO dataset. In the bus scene, human body detection cannot be performed accurately. In this regard, this paper can accurately detect the human body in the scene of severe occlusion and poor light.

Video-based target tracking methods can be divided into two categories: generating model methods and discriminating model methods. The method of generating the model: model the target area in the current frame, and find the area most similar to the background area is a negative sample to train the machine learning based classifier, and the next frame uses the trained classifier to find the optimal area. Such as: Struck [9], KCF [10], MIL [11]. With the success of CNN in the field of image recognition, researchers have used convolutional neural networks to extract feature maps and correlate them with target filtering, such as MDNet [12], TCNN [13], ECO [14]. Analysis of VOT 2017 results shows that most. discriminant model methods are on-line training methods, resulting in very slow target tracking speed, most of the algorithm speed is about 1 fps. In practical applications, multiple targets are simultaneously tracked, and the existing algorithms are difficult to meet the real-time processing requirements. In this paper, we optimize the existing target detection algorithm, analyze and refine the dependencies and attributes among the various parts of the human body through modeling. Then the human body is detected at the same time, and the human body component is detected. The human body detection algorithm is assisted by the human body component, so that it can work well in the actual environment with serious occlusion. In the aspect of tracking, this paper adopts the tracking model of off-line training, carries out pre-training on the open data set, as long as one forward propagation.

The target can be tracked, so as to improve the speed of the algorithm and detect multiple targets in real time. Finally, Kalman filter is used to predict the target trajectory in time series, and a multi-modal fusion decision-making method is proposed to make the two algorithms work together and improve the accuracy of human tracking and detection.

(1) COCO   (2) YOLOv3   (3) Our model   (4) Our model

Fig. 1. Effect of human body detection framework in this paper

2 Dynamic Human Body Detection and Tracking Method

2.1 Detection Model

When some features of the human body are occluded, the existing detection algorithm cannot accurately detect modeling and analysis of the human body, the calculation method of the credibility of the candidate frame is designed, which can improve the recall rate of the human detection frame.

Figure 1-2 shows the detection effect of YOLOv3. Most of the passengers on board are not detected, and the detection effect is not good. Figure 1-3 shows the detection of human body components by the model in this paper. Figure 1-4 shows the final output of the model. The candidate frame is filtered by the credibility analysis algorithm to accurately detect all passengers. The detection problem of the occluded human body is well solved.

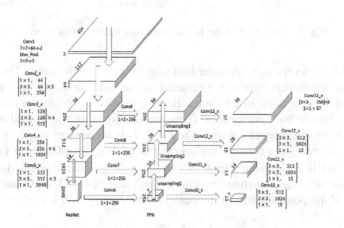

Fig. 2. Network structure

Network structure. As shown in Fig. 2, the network in this paper is a full convolutional neural network. The prediction of the detection frame refers to YOLOv3, and the picture is divided into n × n cells, and each cell predicts Network structure. As shown in Fig. 2, the network in this paper is a full convolutional neural network. The prediction of the detection frame refers to YOLOv3, and the picture is divided into n × n cells, and each cell predicts the detection frame. The prediction of the human body component is based on OpenPose [20], which outputs a heat map for each component. The main structure of the network is the first 49-layer network of ResNet51 [23]. On this basis, the feature pyramid structure is combined, so that the feature map contains different receptive semantic information, and the feature maps of multiple scales are output. Prediction of human body components. As shown in Fig. 1-3, the algorithm can detect the components of the human body and establish dependencies between the components. As shown in Fig. 2, the output of the network model conv13_x is a heat map of the pre-human body component, and its dimension is

$56 \times 56 \times 57$. The first two dimensions are the size of the feature map, and the last dimension is the pixel channel. The network predicts 19 human body components, each of which is represented by a pixel channel. On this basis, the network predicts 19 dependencies for each of the 19 components, each of which is represented by 2 pixel channels.

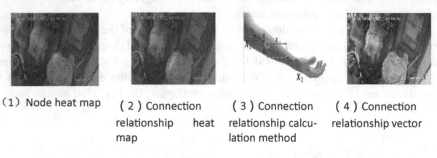

（1）Node heat map   （2）Connection relationship heat map   （3）Connection relationship calculation method   （4）Connection relationship vector

Fig. 3. The effect of the human detection frame in this paper

Figure 3-1 shows the right shoulder heat map of the network output. The heat map is a Gaussian distribution with $\sigma = 3$ centered on the right shoulder coordinate point. The heat map is then calculated by the following method to obtain the precise coordinates of the human body component: Gaussian filtering is first performed on the heat map outputted by the network, as shown in Eq. 1. I_σ is a Gaussian filtered picture, I is the original picture, * is a convolution operation, and $G_{(x,y)}$ is a Gaussian kernel. The Gaussian kernel is a Gaussian kernel of two-dimensional Gaussian filtering, and its calculation method is as shown in Formula 2. The value of σ is 3, and x and y are the coordinates of the point relative to the center of the convolution kernel.

$$I_\sigma = I * G_{(x,y)} \tag{1}$$

$$G_{(x,y)} = \frac{1}{2\pi\sigma^2} e^{-\frac{(x^2+y^2)}{2\sigma^2}} \tag{2}$$

Then, the filtered result is binarized according to formula 3:

$$I_{(x,y)} = \begin{cases} 1 \ if \ I_{(x,y)} > I_{(x\pm1,y\pm1)} \\ 0 \quad others \end{cases} \tag{3}$$

A point with a value of 1 is the exact coordinates of the body component.

Figure 3-4 shows the vector of the dependency. The pixel value in the figure is defined as follows: Fig. 3 is the dependence between the elbow x_1 and the hand x_2, where x is any point from x_1 to x_2, and the value is pointed by x_1. A unit vector of x_2, which is decomposed into a horizontal component $x_\rightarrow$ and a vertical component $x_\uparrow$ corresponds to the two pixel channels mentioned above. From Eq. 3, calculate the coordinate x_i of the elbow and the y_j of all the hands in the figure. Calculate the distance $L_{(i,j)}$ between any x_i and y_j by Eq. 4, Calculate the distance $L_{(i,j)}$ between any x_i and y_j, where v is the average of the aspect ratio of the human arm in the COCO data set. By v and $L_{(i,j)}$, we can estimate the arm The range of pixels. The range is divided into ten regions equally, and one point is randomly selected from each region, and the values predicted by the network of the ten points are multiplied by $x_{\rightarrow}$ and $x_{\uparrow}$ corresponding to the modified points, and then averaged in the modulo, get the credibility C, as shown in Eq. 5.

$$.L_{(i,j)} = |x_i - y_j| \quad W_{(i,j)} = v|x_i - y_j| \tag{4}$$

and v is the length of the human arm in the COCO data set. The average of the width ratio, through v and $L_{(i,j)}$, we can estimate the range of pixels contained in the arm. The range is divided into ten regions equally, and one point is randomly selected from each region, and the values predicted by the network of the ten points are multiplied by $x_{\rightarrow}$ and $x_{\uparrow}$ corresponding to the modified points, and then averaged in the modulo, get the credibility C, as shown in Eq. 5

$$C_{(ij)} = \sum_{k=1}^{10} \left| \left(x^k_{\rightarrow}, x^k_{\uparrow}\right) \cdot \left(x_{\rightarrow}, x_{\uparrow}\right) \right| \tag{5}$$

After obtaining $C_{(ij)}$, find the best two-dimensional matching according to the Hungarian algorithm.

This match relationship is the correct dependency. Think of the collection of dependencies as a forest, each person corresponds to a tree, we start from the head node, perform a breadth-first search, find out which nodes belong to the same person and finally get the results of Fig. 1-3. The sizes of the output feature maps of the detection frames, conv10_x, and conv12_x are 7×7, 14×14, and 28×28, respectively. Each pixel of the figure corresponds to a cell of the receptive field size in the original image. The cell is responsible for predicting the body information within its scope. We use the clustering method of mean drift to cluster the human body's callout boxes on COCO datasets, and analyze three different proportions of rectangular frames as the a priori frames for detection. Credibility. The reliability of the traditional method is the IOU of the detection frame and the label box. When the reliability is less than 0.5, the detection frame is considered to be an erroneous result. However, due to occlusion, low definition of the input picture, etc., the reliability is reduced, and the correct detection result is considered to be wrong. This paper proposes a method of joint detection to assist human detection. Calculate the minimum circumscribed rectangle of the network predicting each person's joint point, and find the detection result and the IOU of these circumscribed rectangles. If the IOU is greater than 0.7 and the credibility is lower than 0.5, the credibility of the test result is increased to 0.5. Then we perform a non-maximum suppression of the detection frame with a reliability greater than or equal to 0.5 to obtain the final detection result.

2.2   Single Target Tracking Model

Traditional single-target tracking algorithms are trained online, making the single-target tracking algorithm slow. The tracking algorithm in this paper aims to make the model learn certain human characteristics by offline training on the open human dataset, and has certain generalization ability. Online training is no longer performed at runtime, which greatly increases the speed of the algorithm. This paper optimizes the GOTURN [21] target detection algorithm and achieves excellent results in human tracking.

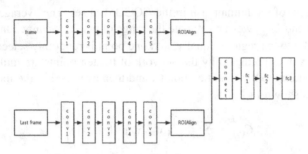

Fig. 4. Single target tracking network structure

Network structure. This paper improves the network structure of GOTURN, and adds the ROIAlign layer, so that the input can be any size image, while retaining the information of the picture scale. The network structure is shown in Fig. 4.

The network input is the image in the frame for the previous frame detection. And the image in the current frame that doubles the size of the previous frame detection frame. The feature is extracted by the convolutional network, and is pooled into the same size by the ROIAlign layer, input into the fully connected layer, and the current frame tracks the position of the target.

2.3   Target Tracking Process

In this paper, the state machine is used to analyze the target state, and the policy tree is used to judge whether the current target is the tracking target. As shown in Eq. 6, the equation has a state set S, a behavior set A, and a frame number T in which the state stays.

$$S(s_1, s_2, s_3, s_4)$$
$$T(t_1, t_2, t_3, t_4) \qquad (6)$$
$$A(a_1, a_2, a_3)$$

s_1 in S indicates that the target is detected; s_2 indicates that the target is detected and tracked; s_3 indicates that the target is not detected, but is still tracking; s_4 indicates that the target is not detected for a long time, and the target is not tracked. In the behavior set A, a_1 is the predicted target position of the next frame; a_2 is the IOU between the two frames before and after the calculation, and the best two-dimensional matching is calculated by the Hungarian algorithm; a_3 is the position of updating the current tracking target, when the target. When the state is currently s_2 or the previous state is s_1, the updated coordinates are the coordinates of the detected network output. When the target current state is s_3 and the previous state is s_2 or s_3, the updated coordinates are the coordinates of the target tracking model output. The decision process of this algorithm is shown as follow.

First, a_1 operation is performed on the target of the previous frame state s_2, s_3, and the coordinate set $s_{2/3}$ is generated, and the current frame image is input to the target detection network, and the detection result is obtained, and the state is s_1. The detection result and the coordinate set $s_{2/3}$ perform the a_2 operation. For the target with successful matching, the state is set to s_2, and the target setting state that is not matched to the target and the states are s_2 and s_1 is s_3, and the pair is not The target to the target and whose state is s_3, when its state dwell time t_3 is less than 3, the set state is s_3, and when it is equal to 3, the set state is s_4. For the target whose previous frame state is s_3, the target of the states s_2 and s_3 is subjected to the a_3 operation, and the result is input to the next frame.

3 PS-CNN Network Training

3.1 Training of Target Detection Model

Detect the loss function of the box. The loss function consists of the loss function of the detection frame and the loss function of the attitude detection. The detection part network outputs three different scale feature maps, and each cell outputs three different scale detection frames, and each detection frame corresponds to one credibility. We define the output of the detection frame of any (c_x, c_y) unit output as p_x, p_y, p_w, p_h, p_c corresponding to the length and width of the a priori frame a_w, a_h, the original size of the picture is (W, H), According to Eq. 7, the coordinates and length and width of the upper left corner of the detection frame of the output are calculated as b_x, b_y, b_w, b_h, and the reliability is c.

$$b_x = \sigma(p_x) + c_x$$
$$b_y = \sigma(p_y) + c_y$$
$$b_w = a_w e^{p_w} \tag{7}$$
$$b_h = a_h e^{p_h}$$
$$c = \sigma(p_c)$$

The coordinates and length and width of the upper left corner of the label of the detection target in the figure are x, y, w, h and the IOU of the prediction rectangle is c, which is output by any unit of a certain size s_k characteristic map calculated by Eq. 7.

$$loss = \sum_{k=1}^{3}\sum_{j=0}^{s_k^2}\sum_{i=0}^{3j} \lambda_{target}\left[(x_i - x)^2 + (y_i - y)^2 + (w_i - w)^2 + (h_i - h)^2\right]$$

$$+ \sum_{k=1}^{3}\sum_{j=0}^{s_k^2}\sum_{i=0}^{3j} \lambda_{obj}\left[(c_i - c)^2\right] \tag{8}$$

The coordinates and length and width of the upper left corner of a detection frame are x_i, y_i, w_i, h_i, and the reliability is c_i, and the loss function is shown in Eq. 8. When the target falls on the detecting unit, $\lambda\_target = 1$, $\lambda\_obj = 1$, and in other cases $\lambda\_target = 0$, $\lambda\_obj = 0.5$.

The loss function of attitude detection. The loss function of the attitude detection network is L1 loss as shown in Eq. 9. Where x is the heat map of the network output and $\hat{x}$ is the heat map we generated based on the label.

$$loss = sigma\, x - x \tag{9}$$

Our main job is to generate heat maps for training based on the annotation of the data. The COCO dataset provides annotations for the important nodes of 19 individuals. For each joint point, we generate a heat map. The generation method is as shown in Eq. 10, assuming that the joint points of the n categories in the figure, (x_i, y_i) are the coordinates of the joint points marked, and the value of any point (x, y) in the figure is $P_{(x,y)}$ As shown in the formula, the value of λ is 1.

$$P_{(x,y)} = \sum_{i=1}^{n} \lambda \frac{1}{2\pi\sigma^2} e^{-\frac{\left((x-x_i)^2 + (y-y_i)^2\right)}{2\sigma^2}} \tag{10}$$

There are 19 kinds of connection relationships among 19 individual body joint points. For a certain connection relationship, a unit vector is generated for points within the range of formula 4 according to the method of Fig. 4-6, and the point value outside the range is 0. Since one unit vector is composed of the values of the two components of vertical and horizontal, a total of 38 heat maps are generated. These heat maps are normalized to the size of the network output, then spelled into a three-bit matrix, and the output of the network is calculated for loss. Training steps. In this paper, the ResNet-51 part is pre-trained 200 times on ImageNet [24]. The number of training sessions per iteration is 20000, and the number of batches is 12. The first 49 layers of the pre-trained ResNet-51 are used for the model of the algorithm, and the algorithm model is trained on the COCO data set. During training, we adjusted the number of batches to 8 and the number of trainings to 10,000. First use $[10]^{\wedge}(-2)$.The learning rate is iterated 100 times, then iterated 50 times with the learning rate of $[10]^{\wedge}(-3)$, and finally iterated 50 times with the learning rate of $[10]^{\wedge}(-4)$ to obtain the final model parameters.

3.2   Training of Single Target Tracking Model

The loss function of the single target tracking model is L1 loss, and the loss between the predicted rectangular frame and the labeled rectangular frame is calculated, as shown in Eq. 9. The model was trained on the Caltech Pedestrian Dateset [25] dataset. The data set is a video data set, and each frame is marked with a detection frame of the human body. Using Sect. 2.2 we can see that the network is input in the forward propagation. The position information of the two frames before and after the input is relatively similar, so the generalization ability of the model is reduced during training. In the training, the content of the information in the current frame label is cyclically shifted to prevent the network from over-fitting.

4 Experimental Analysis

4.1 The Detection Result

The algorithm in this paper has achieved excellent results in real-world scenarios, surpassing some of the existing top-level algorithms. As shown in the results in Table 1, under the bus data set, the existing algorithm has greatly improved the recall rate relative to other algorithms, reaching a maximum of 74.2%, but the accuracy has not decreased much, being 47.3%. Finally achieved the highest F_1 Value, and can achieve a speed of 10 frames per second. And on the coco data set, the algorithm has also achieved high accuracy as shown on Table 2, which shows that the algorithm in this paper has strong generalization ability while making optimization for specific problems.

Table 1. Result on our bus dataset

Method	Backbone	AP_{75}	AP_{50}	AR_1	AR_{10}	F_1	Time
RCNN	VGG-16	20.5	43.6	89.7	19.4	26.9	24000
Fast-RCNN	VGG-16	23.9	46.5	90.6	37.6	41.6	1000
Faster-RCNN	ResNet-101+PN	34.0	54.1	93.1	56.2	55.1	172
Faster-RCNN	Inception-ResNetV2	32.7	51.5	92.8	54.7	53.1	90
TOLOv3 608	Darknet-53	28.7	52.9	91.5	46.8	50.0	51
DSSD513	ResNet-101	26.7	49.5	91.8	48.7	49.1	156
RetinaNet	ResNet-101+FPN	38.4	56.9	94.6	57.9	57.3	198
PS-CNN	ResNet-51+FPN	27.8	47.3	98.6	74.2	57.7	97

Table 2. Result on coco dataset

Method	Backbone	AP_{75}	AP_{50}	AR_1	AR_{10}	F_1	Time
RCNN	VGG-16	18.4	37.4	93.6	50.4	42.9	24000
Fast-RCNN	VGG-16	19.1	41.2	94.7	73.3	52.7	1000
Faster-RCNN	ResNet-101+FPN	39.0	59.1	97.1	78.9	67.5	172
Faster-RCNN	Inception-ResNetV2	36.7	55.5	96.3	76.4	64.2	90
TOLOv3 608	Darknet-53	23.2	48.0	95.7	70.5	52.6	51
DSSD513	ResNet-101	35.2	53.3	96.1	74.2	62.0	156
RetinaNet	ResNet-101+FPN	42.3	59.1	98.4	80.1	68.0	198
PS-CNN	ResNet-51+FPN	36.7	54.9	99.1	82.4	65.9	97

The results of this paper can be seen as a two-class problem of the human body and the background. For the two-category problem, the commonly used evaluation criteria are accuracy and recall rate. The formula for calculating the accuracy is:

$$AP = \frac{1}{n} \sum_{i=1}^{n} \frac{TP}{TP+FP} \tag{11}$$

The calculation formula for the recall rate is:

$$AR = \frac{1}{n} \sum_{i=1}^{n} \frac{TP}{TP+FN} \tag{12}$$

The mean of the correct rate and recall rate F_1:

$$\frac{2}{F_1} = \frac{1}{AP} + \frac{1}{AR}$$

$$F_1 = \frac{1}{n} \sum_{i=1}^{n} \frac{2TP}{2TP+FP+FN} \tag{13}$$

In the environment of severe occlusion, the algorithm ensures that the human target can still be accurately detected without being lost. The speed of the right.

4.2 Result of the Target Tracking Algorithm

The target tracking algorithm in this paper is based on the GoTurn network structure and is optimized for human body training. Therefore, in the tracking of the human body, the level of the top algorithms in the industry can be achieved, as show on Table 3 and the speed can reach about 100 fps, and real-time tracking of multiple targets can be performed in real time in a real scene. The algorithm realizes real-time tracking of each passenger on the bus dataset, and can be extended to count the number of people getting on and off, and track some practical applications such as specific passengers.

Table 3. Human tracking result

Method	Accuracy	Overlap
MDNet	67.48	37.82
KCF	51.47	29.64
Struck	48.77	28.94
MIL	56.75	33.89
TCNN	70.41	39.81
ECO	73.56	42.37
Ours	69.54	37.21

(a) result on our bus dataset

Method	Accuracy	Overlap	Speed(fps)
MDNet	67.48	37.82	1
KCF	51.47	29.64	178
Struck	48.77	28.94	20
MIL	56.75	33.89	38
TCNN	70.41	39.81	1.5
ECO	73.56	42.37	60
Ours	69.54	37.21	108

(b) result on VOT2015

5 Conclusion

This paper designs and implements a human body detection algorithm. By analyzing and modeling the human body structure, a credibility calculation method is established, and the output of the network model is further optimized, so that the detection algorithm can be in a complex scene. It still has a high precision. And improved GoTurn algorithm to optimize its tracking effect on the human body. Finally, a set of decision-making methods is established, which makes the algorithm of this paper have higher robustness. On the bus with serious occlusion, it can still accurately detect and track people. The algorithm in this paper is only highly robust to human detection. For other types of objects, the detection in complex scenes is still not effective. And the model does not compress, trim, etc., and does not optimize the acceleration of specific equipment, so it is not very efficient in efficiency. In the future, we will improve the robustness of the algorithm to other objects, and pruning the model to reduce its computational complexity, so that it can be embedded into embedded devices to enhance its practical application value.

References

1. Girshick, R., Donahue, J., Darrell, T., et al.: Rich feature hierarchies for accurate object detection and semantic segmentation. In: Proceedings of the IEEE Conference on Computer Vision and Pattern Recognition, pp. 580–587 (2014)
2. Girshick, R.: Fast R-CNN. In: Proceedings of the IEEE International Conference on Computer Vision, pp. 1440–1448 (2015)
3. Ren, S., He, K., Girshick, R., et al.: Faster R-CNN: towards real-time object detection with region proposal networks. In: Advances in Neural Information Processing Systems, pp. 91–99 (2015)
4. Lin, T.Y., Dollár, P., Girshick, R.B., et al.: Feature pyramid networks for object detection. CVPR 1(2), 4 (2017)
5. Redmon, J., Farhadi, A.: YOLOV3: an incremental improvement. arXiv preprint arXiv: 1804.02767 (2018)
6. Fu, C.Y., Liu, W., Ranga, A., et al.: DSSD: deconvolutional single shot detector. arXiv preprint arXiv:1701.06659 (2017)
7. Lin, T.Y., et al.: Microsoft COCO: common objects in context. In: Fleet, D., Pajdla, T., Schiele, B., Tuytelaars, T. (eds.) ECCV 2014. LNCS, vol. 8693, pp. 740–755. Springer, Cham (2014). https://doi.org/10.1007/978-3-319-10602-1_48
8. Everingham, M., Van Gool, L., Williams, C.K.I., et al.: The pascal visual object classes (VOC) challenge. Int. J. Comput. Vis. 88(2), 303–338 (2010)
9. Hare, S., Golodetz, S., Saffari, A., et al.: Struck: structured output tracking with kernels. IEEE Trans. Pattern Anal. Mach. Intell. 38(10), 2096–2109 (2016)
10. Henriques, J.F., Caseiro, R., Martins, P., et al.: High-speed tracking with kernelized correlation filters. IEEE Trans. Pattern Anal. Mach. Intell. 37(3), 583–596 (2015)
11. Babenko, B., Yang, M.H., Belongie, S.: Visual tracking with online multiple instance learning. In: IEEE Conference on Computer Vision and Pattern Recognition 2009, CVPR 2009, pp. 983–990. IEEE (2009)

12. Nam, H., Han, B.: Learning multi-domain convolutional neural networks for visual tracking. In: Proceedings of the IEEE Conference on Computer Vision and Pattern Recognition, pp. 4293–4302 (2016)
13. Nam, H., Baek, M., Han, B.: Modeling and propagating CNNs in a tree structure for visual tracking. arXiv preprint arXiv:1608.07242 (2016)
14. Danelljan, M., Bhat, G., Khan, F.S., et al.: ECO: efficient convolution operators for tracking. CVPR **1**(2), 3 (2017)
15. Dalal, N., Triggs, B.: Histograms of oriented gradients for human detection. In: IEEE Computer Society Conference on Computer Vision and Pattern Recognition 2005, CVPR 2005, vol. 1, pp. 886–893. IEEE (2005)
16. Platt, J.: Sequential minimal optimization: a fast algorithm for training support vector machines (1998)
17. Zitnick, C.L., Dollár, P.: Edge boxes: locating object proposals from edges. In: Fleet, D., Pajdla, T., Schiele, B., Tuytelaars, T. (eds.) ECCV 2014. LNCS, vol. 8693, pp. 391–405. Springer, Cham (2014). https://doi.org/10.1007/978-3-319-10602-1_26
18. Vojir, T., Noskova, J., Matas, J.: Robust scale-adaptive mean-shift for tracking. Pattern Recogn. Lett. **49**, 250–258 (2014)
19. He, K., Gkioxari, G., Dollár, P., et al.: Mask R-CNN. In: 2017 IEEE International Conference on Computer Vision (ICCV), pp. 2980–2988. IEEE (2017)
20. Cao, Z., Simon, T., Wei, S.E., et al.: Realtime multi-person 2D pose estimation using part affinity fields. arXiv preprint arXiv:1611.08050 (2016)
21. Held, D., Thrun, S., Savarese, S.: Learning to track at 100 FPS with deep regression networks. In: Leibe, B., Matas, J., Sebe, N., Welling, M. (eds.) ECCV 2016. LNCS, vol. 9905, pp. 749–765. Springer, Cham (2016). https://doi.org/10.1007/978-3-319-46448-0_45
22. Redmon, J., Divvala, S., Girshick, R., et al.: You only look once: unified, real-time object detection. In: Proceedings of the IEEE Conference on Computer Vision and Pattern Recognition, pp. 779–788 (2016)
23. He, K., Zhang, X., Ren, S., et al.: Deep residual learning for image recognition. In: Proceedings of the IEEE Conference on Computer Vision and Pattern Recognition, pp. 770–778 (2016)
24. Russakovsky, O., Deng, J., Su, H., et al.: Imagenet large scale visual recognition challenge. Int. J. Comput. Vis. **115**(3), 211–252 (2015)
25. Dollár, P., Wojek, C., Schiele, B., et al.: Pedestrian detection: a benchmark. In: IEEE Conference on Computer Vision and Pattern Recognition 2009, CVPR 2009, pp. 304–311. IEEE (2009)

A Real-Time Method for Marking the Extent of a Lipid Plaque Based on IV-OCT Imaging

Cheng Zhang[1], Jian He[1($\boxtimes$)], Weidong Wang[1], Shengqi Yang[1],
and Yuqing Zhang[2]

[1] Beijing University of Technology, Beijing 100124, China
Jianhee@bjut.edu.cn
[2] National Center for Cardiovascular Diseases, Beijing 100037, China

Abstract. Atherosclerotic plaques, the leading cause of heart attack, can be characterized from intravascular optical coherence tomography (IV-OCT) images by doctors. Since lipid accumulation is an important indication of atherosclerotic plaque, we introduced a new convolutional neural network, called Single Shot Plaque Marking Network (SSPM), to develop an automated method that highlights the extent of lipid plaques from IV-OCT images at real-time, which then would help doctors easily find the vulnerable plaque. Compared with previous available methods, our method is capable of marking the suspicious lipid plaque areas in real-time with better time-efficiency and competitive accuracy during the diagnosis. SSPM is tested on IV-OCT human coronary artery imaging dataset, and the result shows that our method is able to mark suspicious lipid-plaque areas at 91 fps on GPU, or 16 fps on CPU, with an accuracy of 87%.

Keywords: Detection algorithms · Artificial neural networks · Computational efficiency · Health and safety · Biology

1 Introduction

According to the disease statistics, cardio-vascular disease is the main cause of mortality and morbidity all over the world. Meanwhile, researches show that atherosclerosis is the key factor leading to cardio vascular disease. Atherosclerosis is a status when artery walls thicken because of the cholesterol accumulation within the walls of arteries [1]. Atherosclerotic plaques have a wide range of morphological and anatomical features along with different stages. For instance, in a stable plaque, the accumulation of collagen forming a fibrous plaque can bring about progressive stenosis. While in a vulnerable plaque, the set-up of lipids and necrotic core can cause unexpected thrombosis and heart attack [2]. Autopsy researches have revealed several histological features of the vulnerable plaques, such as a large lipid pool, a thin fibrous cap (<65 µm), and activated macrophages near the fibrous cap [3]. Since the vulnerable plaque has high risk of leading to heart attack and stroke, it is very important to identify and treat the plaque as early as possible [4].

Optical coherence tomography (OCT) is an intravascular imaging modality, which has the capability of providing cross-sectional images of tissue with a resolution of

© Springer Nature Singapore Pte Ltd. 2019
F. Sun et al. (Eds.): ICCSIP 2018, CCIS 1005, pp. 99–111, 2019.
https://doi.org/10.1007/978-981-13-7983-3_9

10 μm. OCT can be combined with any spectral technology, and its high resolution can make up for the defect of other imaging techniques, which could not identify extremely thin fiber caps [5]. According to the available research results, OCT is a promising imaging technique for the measurement of vulnerable plaques.

Though OCT has lots of advantages, it is hard for an untrained person to distinguish the differences between vulnerable plaque and non-plaque area. In particular, OCT has a rapid image acquisition speed which is more than 100 frame/s [6], a pullback can generate large amount of images. It requires lots of time to manually interpret such amount of images. Research shows that lipid accumulation is an important indication of atherosclerotic plaque [7], therefore, we introduced a new convolutional neural network to develop a real-time method for marking the extent of lipid plaque, which is fully automated with the potential for high throughput atherosclerotic plaque assessment. After marking the extent of lipid plaques, doctors can find the vulnerable plaque easily.

The remainder of this paper is organized as follows. Section 2 introduces the related works on plaque detection, their advantages and disadvantages are analyzed. Section 3 analyzes the reason why simultaneously processing multiple frames is unsuitable for marking the extent of a plaque at real time. Section 4 introduces our method in detail, including the model of the convolutional neural network, a unique loss function, and the way of training the network. Section 4 presents the implementation our method, and the experimental results based on an IV-OCT dataset is discussed. Accuracy and speed are compared between our method and previously proposed methods. Section 5 presents the conclusion, and the suggestion for future works.

2 Related Works

Researchers have tried their best to develop different technology to help doctor find vulnerable plaque. Since lipid accumulation is an important indication of atherosclerotic plaque [7], some automatic methods are developed to distinguish a lipid-rich plaque area (namely vulnerable plaque) from a non-plaque area. Prakash et al. [6] segmented the vulnerable plaque and the non-plaque areas by analyzing IV-OCT images and extracting their texture features [8]. Nam et al. [9] proposed a novel automatic plaque classification algorithm based on OCT imaging to characterize the lipid-rich plaques. This method has a remarkable prediction speed in finding lipids by using Gaussian center of mass (GCOM) as a metric algorithm [10]. Fleming et al. [11] introduced a model to detect lipids from OFDI (Optical frequency domain imaging or frequency domain OCT) data by developing a novel method called quadratic discriminant analysis. This method predicted the position of lipids and detected atherosclerotic plaques by attenuation analysis and backscattering analysis in a short execution time.

Some methods are presented to identify the types of the plaques. Rico-Jimenez et al. [12] presented an automatic plaque classification method to identify four kinds of plaques, including Intimal Thickening, Fibrotic-Lipid, Fibrotic and Superficial-Lipid. By enabling parallel computation, this method can allow high throughput in dealing with the recorded data.

A pixel-wise tissue classification method [13] was proposed to identify three types of plaques: fibrous, calcified and lipid-rich plaques. The textural features and optical attenuation coefficient values were used as classification criterion. Compared to other methods, feature extraction in above method required more computational resources. Intensity and texture based features were used to classify four plaque types in [14] from IV-OCT images. This method also adopted a random forest classifier to handle the features, and achieved a high accuracy. Gargesha et al. [15] estimated 3 types of atherosclerotic plaques by a SVM based classifier with 3-D data. It required a large amount of computational resource to extract features, including intensity, texture features, border sharpness, optical properties and 3-D shape characteristics.

Recently, convolutional neural network (CNN) has shown its advantages on the object detection field. By training on large data sets and designing complex networks and cost function, CNN can achieve both high accuracy and speed on detection tasks. The general object detection methods detect customized objects and can run at real-time. For instance, SSD [16] and Faster R-CNN [17], are typical millstones of the CNN detection approaches. However, these methods cannot be directly used on plaque detection. The reason is that the networks are huge and complex. They need a great number of samples to feed the training process. Especially in the condition of a very limited number of IV-OCT images, the network has to be specifically designed to fit for plaque detection.

There is a promising method using CNN to detect plaques [18] from Carotid Ultrasound images, which can achieve a relatively fast speed of 52 ms per frame (19 fps) on a professional GPU environment. Being different from the above methods, our research focuses on detecting plaques from IV-OCT images.

3 Method

The main idea of our method to divide each frame of the IV-OTC imaging into multiple regions, and predict each region according to the contextual features simultaneously. Our method included 4 steps, namely preprocessing, network design, loss design, and training label creation.

3.1 Convolutional Neural Network Design

A new convolutional neural network for our method is carefully designed, so as to process full image by single shot and predict all region simultaneously. It shortens both execution time and latency. The input of the network is polar-transformed intravascular image and the output is the predicted extent of the plaque. The network includes convolutional, max pooling and fully connected layers. Convolutional and pooling layers extract features from the whole image, fully connected layers output the prediction of regions. The architecture of the network is shown in Fig. 1, with 2 convolutional layers followed by 2 fully connected layers. The final layer does not use any activation function, meanwhile other layers use the leaky rectified linear activation function shown in Eq. (1).

$$\phi(x) = \begin{cases} x, & if\ x > 0 \\ 0.1x, & if\ x \leq 0 \end{cases} \tag{1}$$

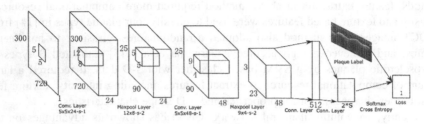

Fig. 1. Network architecture.

The last layer of the network has $2 * S$ outputs which describe the extent of the plaques. Number 2 represents 2 kinds of class for marking the extent of each plaque, namely plaque extents and non-plaque extents. Number S represents the horizontal position of polar-transformed IV-OCT image. The output layer is sliced into S pieces, and each piece has 2 scores which represent the evidence of plaque area and non-plaque area in the corresponding image area respectively.

Since a prediction is made by a single neural network, each neuron inside a layer can be individually computed. At the last layer, the score for each piece is computed simultaneously. As a result, our network maximizes the use of RAM, and minimizes the execution time of a single frame. It gives our method a higher time efficiency.

Preserving contextual information is essential for OCT plaque marking task [19]. However, traditional sliding window and region proposal-based techniques generally slice the input image into small pieces (shown in Fig. 2(a)) as the input, and then make predictions according to the evidence of each piece gradually. The sliced pieces will lose some contextual information about the image; it can't see the larger context, so it decreases the accuracy of extent marking. On the contrary, our method (shown in Fig. 2(b)) uses the whole image as the input for the network during training and test time. It implicitly encodes contextual information about plaques as well as their appearance. Hence, our method preserves the contextual information of the entire image. The last layer of network can predict each output region using different features extracted from the whole image, and mark the border of each output region as well.

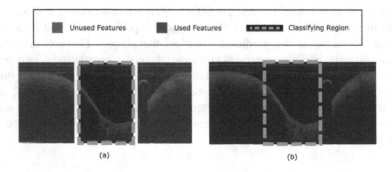

Fig. 2. (a) Image is sliced into pieces. (b) Features of the whole image is used

3.2 Loss Function Design

The loss function designed for gradient decent is shown in Eq. (2).

$$f = \frac{\lambda_{plaque} \sum_{i=0}^{S} I_i^{plague} \left(H_{y_i'}(y_i) \right)}{S} + \frac{\lambda_{normal} \sum_{i=0}^{S} I_i^{normal} \left(H_{y_i'}(y_i) \right)}{S} \tag{2}$$

In this loss function, S represents the horizontal position of transformed image. y_i is the predicted probability distribution of classes inside each region, y_i' is correct probability distribution of classes inside each region, which always has 1 class with 100% probability and others with 0% probabilities. Function $H_{y_i'}(y_i)$ represents the cross-entropy, which measuring the distance between two distributions. The output of this function indicates how inefficient the predictions are for describing the truth. Parameter I_i^{plague} represents if the correct label of region i is plaque area, and I_i^{normal} represents if the correct label of region i is non-plaque area. The design of this loss is inspired by YOLO, a state-of-the-art, real-time object detection system.

To adjust the sensitivity of model to plaque area, two parameters λ_{normal} and λ_{plaque} are added to the loss. In the training set, half of the training samples contain plaque areas. Since the samples are being sliced to regions, every region inside a non-plaque image is a non-plaque region, but only approximately 30%–50% of regions inside a plaque image are actually plaque regions. The network uses regions as training set to optimize its parameters, therefore the actual training set for the network is unbalanced. Without remedy, the score of non-plaque regions can overpower the score of plaque regions and diverge the training. Parameters λ_{normal} and λ_{plaque} are used to increase the loss for plaque regions, and decrease the loss for normal regions respectively.

The definition of $H_{y_i'}(y_i)$ is shown in (3). Parameter c is the number of types of regions. Although in this paper we only test our model on 2 types of regions, non-plaque region and plaque region, the model can actually handle more generalized situations, for example, the classification of four types of plaques by modifying parameter c.

$$H_{y'}(y) = -\sum_i^c y_i' \log(y_i) \tag{3}$$

As mentioned before, the output of our network are scores. Those scores represent evidence of a region being in certain classes. There are totally $(c * S)$ scores being generated. To convert those scores to S probability distributions over c classes, softmax regression is being adopted. This activation function shown in (4) produces positive numbers that add up to one. Parameter x represents c scores generated by the prediction of a region.

$$y_i = normalize(\exp(x)) = \frac{\exp(x_i)}{\sum_j \exp(x_j)} \tag{4}$$

The fully expanded loss function is shown in (5). The inputs of the function are the prediction value of the network x, correct label y', the number of class c, the number of region S, weight parameters λ_{normal} and λ_{plaque}. The output is the weighed mean of cross-entropy.

$$loss\left(x, y', c, S, \lambda_{normal}, \lambda_{plaque}\right)$$

$$= \lambda_{plaque} \frac{\sum_{i=0}^{S} I_i^{plague}\left(-\sum_i^c y_i' \log\left(\frac{e^{x_i}}{\sum_j e^{x_c}}\right)\right)}{S}$$

$$+ \lambda_{normal} \frac{\sum_{i=0}^{S} I_i^{normal}\left(-\sum_i^c y_i' \log\left(\frac{e^{x_i}}{\sum_j e^{x_c}}\right)\right)}{S} \quad (5)$$

To avoid over fitting, random dropout is adopted after the first connected layer of the network and the second connected layer of the alternative version of network.

3.3 Training

According to the loss function of the network, training samples must have same number of pieces as the last layer of the network. An operation called label segmentation is applied to acquire training labels from original labels, as shown in Fig. 3. Generally, it divides original labels into S regions with equal length and gives proper classes to each region.

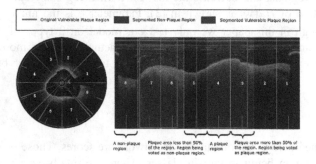

Fig. 3. An example of training labels

Non-plaque areas and vulnerable plaque areas are treated as two different classes. Each region only has one class label. When multiple types of areas appear inside a region, the biggest area is used as the class of the region, while other areas inside this region are deprecated. Note that, if there is only one type of area inside the region, its class is used as the class of the region.

4 Implementation and Experimental Analyzation

There are totally 2000 IV-OCT images provided by People's Liberation Army General Hospital. Among them, there are 1800 for the training set and 200 for test set respectively.

4.1 Implementation

During the creation of training labels, original plaque and non-plaque areas are sliced into S pieces. Apparently, changing the position of original plaque areas causes localization errors. Specifically, the increase of region number S will cause the decrease of localization error rate, if S is equal to width of whole image, then no localization error will be caused. However, the larger the S is, the more parameters are involved in the network. It means that more training samples are needed to produce satisfied results. Therefore, the number of S should be carefully chosen.

Figure 4 illustrates the relationship between S and localization error rate. The error rate decreases sharply at first and eventually becomes stable when there are more than 20 regions segmented.

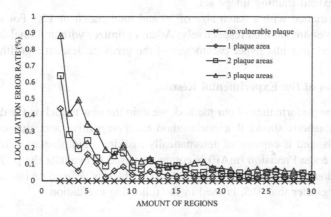

Fig. 4. Relationship between the amount of regions and the localization error rate which the segmentation process brings.

In our model, S is set to 23 which is considered sufficient to keep a low localization error. A visualized projection of segmented labels on image when S equals to 23 is shown in Fig. 5.

To increase the model sensitivity for plaques, Parameter λ_{normal} is set to .7, and λ_{plaque} is set to 1.0. Dropping rate for the dropout layer is set to .5 at training, and 1.0 at evaluation.

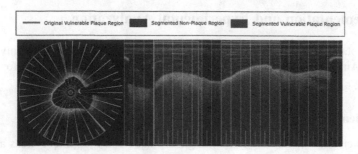

| Original Vulnerable Plaque Region | Segmented Non-Plaque Region | Segmented Vulnerable Plaque Region |

Fig. 5. Projection of segmented labels on image when S equals to 23

To make the training process more stable, the value of each pixel is normalized between 0 and 1. Initial weights are randomized using truncated normal distribution for symmetry breaking. Parameters for normal distribution (namely μ, and σ) are set to 0, and 0.1 respectively in our method.

For data augmentation, we randomly rotate the original OCT image by 0°–360°. Unlike unified object detection model, according to the imaging principle of IV-OCT, any degree of rotation can form a new valid sample. Also, samples are randomly mirrored to extend training image set.

Model is trained with a batch size of 50 and total epoch of 120. For each epoch, training samples are shuffled respectively. Adam optimizer with an initial learning rate of 10^{-4} is used to adjust hyper parameters of the gradient descent algorithm.

4.2   Analysis of the Experimental Results

To validate the performance of our method, we train the new model on the data set. The result of evaluations shows that our method has competitive accuracy compared to other methods, and is capable of automatically marking lipid plaques at real-time.

Mean Average Precision (mAP) is commonly used to evaluate the performance of object detection. The standard overlap criterion, which is defined as intersection over union (IOU) greater than 0.5, is used in the following evaluation.

Table 1. Evaluation result of lipid plaque marking

Correct prediction (TP)	IOU < 0.5 or duplicated prediction (FP)	No prediction made (FN)	Average precision	Recall
46	7	4	0.8679	0.9200

Evaluation result is shown in Table 1. In this evaluation, there are only two classes (non-plaque and lipid plaque), therefore, the mAP is equal to average precision, which is approximately 0.87. A high recall of 0.92 means most of the plaques are marked.

Considering plaque-area and non-plaque area as two different classes, classification tests are performed to evaluate the accuracy of the method. The result of the pixel-wise evaluation, as shown in Table 2, is the standard parameter used to compare our method to others. In this evaluation, predicted labels are compared with original labels marked by experts. According to the classification test, the overall accuracy of our method is 87%. This result is promising, but not the best considering we are only marking the extent of plaque and non-plaque area, without further classification of plaque types.

Additionally, a region-wise evaluation is performed. The purpose of this evaluation is to exclude the localization errors brought by training label segmentation. In this evaluation, predicted labels are compared with segmented labels.

Finally, we compute the accuracy loss caused by label segmentation, which cannot be remedied by adding more samples to the training set. The result shows in "Difference" line indicates that less than 1% of accuracy loss and precision loss is caused by label segmentation, which is acceptable.

Table 2. Pixel-wise classification results

	Accuracy	Sensitivity	Specificity	Precision
Pixel-wise	0.8683	0.7816	0.9383	0.9110
Regional	0.8713	0.7821	0.9434	0.9178
Difference	−0.003	−0.0005	−0.0051	−0.0068

Additionally, *fps* is introduced to evaluate the time-efficiency of our method, and the difference on the processing speed is compared between our method and others. The experimental result proves that our method has higher processing speed and capable of marking plaque extents in real-time. Since *fps* higher than 5 is considered as motion on human visual system [20], *fps* being 6 should be the base line for a method to be considered "running in real-time".

We evaluate the *fps* of our method under 3 different environments, and experimental results are shown in Fig. 6. The first one is double Nvidia Tesla M40 GPU, an expensive hardware made for machine learning, representing the professional GPU environment. The second one is GTX980M, a laptop hardware for daily using, representing the personal GPU environment. The third one is Intel i7 CPU only, representing the CPU environment. The OCT acquisition speed is presented as an upper limit of any OCT based algorithm's *fps*.

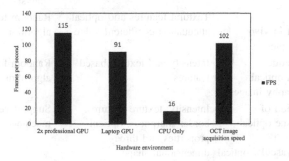

Fig. 6. Processing speed evaluation

On professional GPU, the algorithm runs at 115 *fps*, exceeding the OCT acquisition speed. This means each acquired image by OCT could be processed immediately. Laptop GPU executes the algorithm at 91 *fps*. This speed is sufficient for real-time analyzing. Without expensive graphical hardware, algorithm runs at 16 *fps* under CPU environment. Since the human processes this frame rate as motion, it is still proper to be considered a real-time application.

Benefited from the special designing of the network, our method runs 5.7 times faster with the support of GPU. By segmenting the training labels and designing the optimized loss function, the model gained the ability of predicting each region simultaneously. Prediction of each region is computed concurrently, and gathered after the work of all regions is done. In this way, our method can fulfill the bandwidth of CPU or GPU to execute the task for single image handling, thus acquiring high performance on processing speed.

Table 3 shows a general comparison of our method with other automatic plaque detection methods. The accuracy and average precision parameters are not listed, because the samples used for validation are various.

Table 3. Feature extractors, classifier and speed for each methods.

Method	Features used	Classifier	*fps* (CPU)
Ours	Convoluted pixel feature	Dense neural network	16.39
Texture based segmentation method	Spatial gray level dependence matrices	K-means clustering algorithm	Not provided
Characterization of lipid-rich plaques using spectroscopic optical coherence tomography	Gaussian center of mass	Lipid distribution function	0.19
Depth resolved detection of lipid using spectroscopic optical coherence tomography	Quadratic discriminant analysis	Discriminant functions	Not provided
Automatic classification of atherosclerotic plaques imaged with intravascular OCT	Morphological features	Threshold and linear discriminant analysis	0.66
Automated tissue characterization of in vivo atherosclerotic plaques	Textural features and optical attenuation coefficient value	Random forest algorithm	0.03
Atherosclerotic plaque characterization in optical coherence tomography images	Intensity and texture based features	Random forest algorithm	Not provided
Parameter estimation of atherosclerotic tissue optical properties from three-dimensional intravascular optical coherence tomography	Intensity, texture features, border sharpness, optical properties and three-dimensional shape characteristics	Support vector machine	Not provided

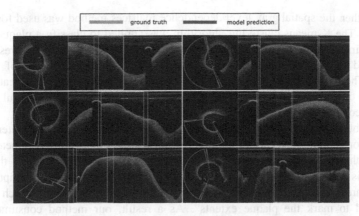

Fig. 7. Prediction of lipid plaque extents

The comparison on *fps* shows that our method outperforms other methods on execution speed, and fulfills the goal of marking the extents of lipid plaque in real-time. The supporting of GPU is optional, while a GPU environment can effectively accelerate the computation.

Figure 7 shows some typical results predicted by our method. In the image, Red box is the plaque position validated by human experts. Green box is the prediction result provided by our model. Two boxes are overlapping closely, indicates the model is capable of localizing lipid-rich vulnerable plaques.

In related work section, we issued an unconnected label problem to the automated tissue characterization paper. In our model, the label segmentation training acts like a mean filter to the class probability in the neutral area, thus reducing the probability of triggering this issue to 2%.

4.3 Discussion

Since our method only includes one network evaluation for marking the extent of a plaque, it makes our method handle IV-OCT image at real-time without any cost of other processing. However, it can be seen from Table 3 that our model uses the convoluted pixel feature for the classification, and the feature should be trained and extracted by convolutional layers. It makes our model larger which requires more training data so as to achieve the same accuracy with higher marking speed compared with other methods. Take the automated tissue characterization of in vivo atherosclerotic plaques by IV-OCT image as example [13], after a first preprocessing step including automatic guide-wire and lumen segmentation, the local attenuation coefficient was estimated and local gray scale features and geometrical features are computed. Finally the random forest algorithm was applied to classify based on these locally extracted values. Its *fps* is about 0.03. The texture based segmentation method [6] normalized each image file to achieve a uniform distribution of intensities, and used a threshold to perform automatic image segmentation to improve the image quality at first. And then the spatial gray level dependence matrices method was used for feature extraction. The K-means clustering algorithm was applied to classify a plaque at last.

Those image processing methods mentioned above extract general features such as texture and brightness, but the plaque classification only needs a part of them to proceed. Therefore, computational power used on the extraction of extra features are wasted. In our method, images are directly fed into the network, only useful features are being computed.

When building the convolutional neural network, the number of parameters inside the extractor is predefined. In our method, we randomly initialize the parameter of the extractor, then adjust them by training according to the loss function. In this way, extractor is being tuned to respond the plaque features exactly. Computational resources are effectively used. Samples are consumed to tell the model "which features are needed to mark the plaque extents". As a result, our method consumes more samples than other methods in training, and runs faster.

5   Conclusion

We introduce a real-time lipid plaque extent marking model for automatic plaque extent marking on OCT data. Our model achieves significantly faster speed and promising accuracy. Since IV-OCT samples are rare and normally not affordable, the model and training method is specially designed to avoid using large amount of samples. Relying on its fast prediction speed, this method can convey real-time plaque position information to the doctors during the operation, and help them find the vulnerable plaques immediately.

References

1. Allender, S., et al.: European cardiovascular disease statistics. Eur. Heart Netw. **3**, 11–35 (2008)
2. Davies, M.J.: Anatomic features in victims of sudden coronary death. Coronary artery pathology. Circulation **85**(1 Suppl.), I19–I24 (1992)
3. Lee, R.T., Libby, P.: The unstable atheroma. Arterioscler. Thromb. Vasc. Biol. **17**(10), 1859–1867 (1997)
4. Virmani, R., Kolodgie, F.D., Burke, A.P., Farb, A., Schwartz, S.M.: Lessons from sudden coronary death. Arterioscler. Thromb. Vasc. Biol. **20**(5), 1262–1275 (2000)
5. Drexler, W., Liu, M., Kumar, A., Kamali, T., Unterhuber, A., Leitgeb, R.A.: Optical coherence tomography today: speed, contrast, and multimodality. J. Biomed. Opt. **19**(7), 071412 (2014)
6. Prakash, A., Hewko, M., Sowa, M., Sherif, S.: Texture based segmentation method to detect atherosclerotic plaque from optical tomography images. In: European Conference on Biomedical Optics, p. 88020S (2013)
7. Hansson, G.K.: Inflammation, atherosclerosis, and coronary artery disease. N. Engl. J. Med. **352**(16), 1685–1695 (2005)
8. Haralick, R.M., Shanmugam, K., et al.: Textural features for image classification. IEEE Trans. Syst. Man Cybern. **SMC-3**(6), 610–621 (1973)

9. Nam, H.S., et al.: Characterization of lipid-rich plaques using spectroscopic optical coherence tomography. J. Biomed. Opt. **21**(7), 075004 (2016)
10. Jaedicke, V., et al.: Comparison of different metrics for analysis and visualization in spectroscopic optical coherence tomography. Biomed. Opt. Express **4**(12), 2945–2961 (2013)
11. Fleming, C.P., Eckert, J., Halpern, E.F., Gardecki, J.A., Tearney, G.J.: Depth resolved detection of lipid using spectroscopic optical coherence tomography. Biomed. Opt. Express **4**(8), 1269–1284 (2013)
12. Rico-Jimenez, J.J., Campos-Delgado, D.U., Villiger, M., Otsuka, K., Bouma, B.E., Jo, J.A.: Automatic classification of atherosclerotic plaques imaged with intravascular OCT. Biomed. Opt. Express **7**(10), 4069–4085 (2016)
13. Ughi, G.J., Adriaenssens, T., Sinnaeve, P., Desmet, W., D'hooge, J.: Automated tissue characterization of in vivo atherosclerotic plaques by intravascular optical coherence tomography images. Biomed. Opt. Express **4**(7), 1014–1030 (2013)
14. Athanasiou, L.S., Exarchos, T.P., Naka, K.K., Michalis, L.K., Prati, F., Fotiadis, D.I.: Atherosclerotic plaque characterization in optical coherence tomography images. In: Annual International Conference of the IEEE Engineering in Medicine and Biology Society, EMBC 2011, pp. 4485–4488 (2011)
15. Gargesha, M., et al.: Parameter estimation of atherosclerotic tissue optical properties from three-dimensional intravascular optical coherence tomography. J. Med. Imaging **2**(1), 016001 (2015)
16. Liu, W., et al.: SSD: single shot MultiBox detector. In: Leibe, B., Matas, J., Sebe, N., Welling, M. (eds.) ECCV 2016. LNCS, vol. 9905, pp. 21–37. Springer, Cham (2016). https://doi.org/10.1007/978-3-319-46448-0_2
17. Ren, S., He, K., Girshick, R., Sun, J.: Faster R-CNN: towards real-time object detection with region proposal networks. In: Advances in Neural Information Processing Systems, pp. 91–99 (2015)
18. Lekadir, K., et al.: A convolutional neural network for automatic characterization of plaque composition in carotid ultrasound. IEEE J. Biomed. Health Inform. **21**(1), 48–55 (2017)
19. Tearney, G.J., et al.: Consensus standards for acquisition, measurement, and reporting of intravascular optical coherence tomography studies. J. Am. Coll. Cardiol. **59**(12), 1058–1072 (2012)
20. Read, P., Meyer, M.-P.: Restoration of Motion Picture Film. Butterworth-Heinemann, Oxford (2000)

An Image Segmentation Model Based on Cascaded Multilevel Features

Xiao-Juan Zhang[1] and Xi-Li Wang[1,2(✉)]

[1] Shaanxi Normal University, No. 620 West Chang'an Street, Chang'an District,
Xi'an 710119, Shaanxi, China
wangxili@snnu.edu.cn
[2] Key Laboratory of Modern Teaching Technology, Ministry of Education,
Shaanxi Normal University, Xi'an 710119, China

Abstract. In deep convolutional networks for segmentation, resolution is significantly reduced by multiple pooling and convolution operations, which makes the prediction accuracy of pixel class reduced. Based on the deep convolutional coding-decoding network, an end-to-end image segmentation model by cascading multi-level features in encoder and decoder is proposed in this paper. Firstly, the last layer convolution feature of the first two convolution stages and all convolution layer features of the last three convolution stages in the encoder are selected, and the features of the latter three stages are added pixel by pixel through skip connection. Secondly, all the convolution layer features of the last three convolution stages in the decoder are selected to fuse pixel by pixel. Finally, the above multi-level features are cascaded in the way of channel splicing, and then sent to the new convolution layer to learn and make category prediction. In this paper, the experiments are carried out on the CUB_200_2011 and ISPRS Vaihingen datasets, and compared with the research results in the literature. The results show that the proposed model does better than the comparative methods, and has achieved good segmentation effect on common images and remote sensing images.

Keywords: Image segmentation · Convolutional coding-decoding network ·
Cascaded multi-level features

1 Introduction

Image segmentation refers to the process of dividing a set of pixels with similar features into several sub-regions of the image. It can also be regarded as assigning a unique label (or category) to each pixel in the image, so that pixels with the same label have some common visual characteristics, which makes the image easier to understand and analyze. At present, deep learning methods, especially Convolutional Neural Network (CNN), such as VGG [11], GoogleNet [12], ResNet [9], etc. have achieved remarkable results in the field of image processing. The advantage of CNN is that its multi-layer

Supported by The National Natural Science Foundation of China (No. 41471280, 61401265, 61701290, 61701289).

F. Sun et al. (Eds.): ICCSIP 2018, CCIS 1005, pp. 112–123, 2019.
https://doi.org/10.1007/978-981-13-7983-3_10

structure can automatically learn multi-level features from a large number of labeled samples. Zeiler [1] used deconvolution operation to visualize the features of multi-layer convolution neural networks in 2013. It was found that the shallower convolution layer (conv1, conv2) had smaller receptive field, and the learned features were basically local features such as color and edge. With the deepening of the network level, the receptive field of the deeper layer (conv3, conv4 and conv5) becomes larger, and the features learned were more distinctively global features. In 2014, Long et al. [2] proposed fully convolution network (FCN), which pioneered the use of convolution neural networks for semantic segmentation of images. The FCN converts the fully connected layer in the traditional CNN model into a convolution layer, which reduces the feature map size and enables feature extraction. In order to obtain the prediction category of each pixel, the smaller feature map is up-sampled to the same size of the original image by a deconvolution operation at the end of the network. Finally, pixel-by-pixel classification is performed on the prediction map to achieve segmentation of the input image. However, repeated pooling and convolution operations in FCN will reduce the resolution of the feature map and make the original image information lost seriously. Although the reduced feature map can be restored to the original size by deconvolution or bilinear interpolation, the lost information can not be completely restored, which leads to blurred target edges and incomplete details. In order to obtain accurate segmentation results, Long et al. proposed a hopping structure, in which the intermediate layer feature map and the deeper feature map were added and fused pixel by pixel. Among such methods FCN8s [2] structure had better performance. In 2015, Kendall et al. [3] proposed an encoding-decoding SegNet network that stores the max-pooling indices during the encoding stage and applies this indices in the up-sampling process of the decoding stage to produce a sparse feature maps. These feature maps are then convolved with a trainable decoder filter bank to produce dense feature maps. In 2015, Ronneberger et al. [19] proposed a U-Net model for medical image segmentation. It consists of a contraction path to extract context information and an expansion path to locate accurately. It copies and splices all the feature maps of the contraction path layers into the corresponding layers of the expansion path to improve the performance of the model. In the same year, Yu et al. [4] proposed the concept of dilated convolutions by sparsifying the interior of the convolution kernel and filling the sparse position by 0. The use of hole convolution, on the one hand, makes the receptive field larger, then can capture more context information. On the other hand, after the convolution, the resolution of the feature map is unchanged, so that the original image information can be retained more and the convolution calculation amount is not change. In 2016, Chen et al. [5] proposed an atrous spatial pyramid pooling (ASPP) structure to extract multi-scale feature maps by paralleling atrous convolution kernel with different ratios and finally perform multi-scale feature fusion to achieve accurate segmentation. Although convolution with different scales can effectively capture multi-scale information, the larger the atrous ratio is, the smaller the proportion of the effective feature weights in the atrous convolution kernel is, thus making the model unable to capture smaller targets in the image and insensitive to the details (such as edges) of the target, and resulting in grid phenomenon. Therefore, Chen et al. [7] proposed an improved atrous pyramid pooling structure in 2017 to improve this phenomenon and obtain finer segmentation results by integrating global information into the ASPP structure. Wang et al. [6] modified the dilated convolution and proposed the hybrid dilated convolution (HDC) framework. By designing the dilated ratio of all convolution kernels in the model to be zigzag, the network can meet the requirements of the segmentation of small objects and large objects at the same time. In addition, Lin et al. [18] proposed a general multi-path optimization network (RefineNet). The design of the model structure uses a jump structure. The coding part is based on RESNET. The decoded part of the RefineNet module used identity mapping to connect all feature graphs in the coding process to form a short-distance residual connection. The long-distance residual connection between the RefineNet module and the RESNET module allow gradients to propagate directly to any convolution layer in ResNet, thus achieving end-to-end network training. Zhao et al. [17] also proposed a PSPNet structure that integrates contexts of different regions to obtain global information. Its backbone network is Resnet 101 network with hole convolution. In the final pooling stage, an asynchronous pyramid pooling module is added to obtain multi-scale feature maps. In addition, the model uses one in training. An auxiliary loss is used to deal with the gradient vanishing problem in deep networks.

The above researches have explored the application of deep learning in image segmentation, but there are still some shortcomings. For deep convolution neural networks, repetitive pooling and convolution operations tend to reduce the resolution of feature maps and cause serious loss of detailed information. This drawback makes the segmentation accuracy difficult to improve effectively, whether by deepening the decoding process of the model or using the atrous convolution without losing the resolution of feature maps. We consider that features at all levels are helpful to semantic segmentation. High-level features are helpful for category recognition, and low-level features are helpful to enhance the details of segmentation results. Therefore, based on the convolutional coding-decoding network, we propose an image segmentation model with cascaded multi-level features. There are two main contributions in this paper: (1) The convolution features of the corresponding stages in the encoder and the decoder are cascaded by channel splicing, and then sent to a new convolution layer to further learn and implement the final category prediction. The idea of cascading multi-level features allows the model to make full use of the features learn at each stage of the encoding-decoding network and to obtain improved segmentation results. (2) Before cascading the convolution features of the last three stages in the encoder and decoder, this paper adds and fuses them pixel by pixel by jump connection. On the one hand, it can reduce the complexity of the model after cascading the multi-level features, and simplify the training of the model. On the other hand, this can involve the hierarchical dependence of the features extracted by the deeper convolutional layer, retain the local consistency of the features and improve segmentation performance.

2   Proposed Method

2.1   Image Segmentation Model Based on Cascaded Multilevel Features (CMLFDNN)

The SegNet [3] model is used as the segmentation backbone network, which consists of two components: encoder and decoder. Encoder contains 13 convolutional layers and 5 pooling layers. Decoder is fully mirrored with 13 convolutional layers and 5 unpooling layers. Pooling in the encoder uses the maximum pooling and saves the largest pooled index location. In the decoder, the decoding layer enlarges the smaller feature map by using the maximum pooling index to obtain the sparse feature map. The expanded position is filled with 0. The convolution operation is performed on the sparse feature map, so that the previously filled value (0) changes, thus the sparse feature map goes dense. The unpooling operation in the decoder of SegNet utilizes the maximum pooled index value to provide the location related to the features for densifying the sparse feature map, and enables the decoder to obtain the features containing abundant location information and more distinguishing features. Therefore more accurate segmentation results can be obtained. But it also has two drawbacks: Firstly, in decoding stage only the feature of the last pool layer of the coding stage is used, and the resolution of the feature map is too small. The decoding process established on this has great limitations to enhance segmentation performance. Secondly, the deep network lose much information due to multiple pooling and convolution operations. SegNet model only uses the feature of the last convolution layer in the decoding stage when making pixel prediction, and discards the features of other layers, so that the model can not get more precise segmentation results.

In the learning process of deep convolution neural network, different levels of convolution layer learn different levels of features. The shallow convolution layer learns local features. As the depth of the convolution layer deepens, the receptive field becomes larger, features learned by the deeper convolution layer contains more global features. Local features help to improve the detail of the segmentation results, and global features contribute to the identification of target categories. Based on the above analysis, a cascaded multi-level feature convolution neural network model (CMLFDNN) is proposed, whose structure is shown in Fig. 1.

The proposed CMLFDNN model adopts the features of all convolution stages in the encoder and the features of the last three convolution stages in the decoder. Specifically, first, in the encoder: select the convolution feature of the last layer of conv1 and conv2, and all the convolutional layer features of conv3, conv4 and conv5. In particular, the feature maps of conv3, conv4 and conv5 stages are expanded by layer-by-layer bilinear interpolation and fused pixel by pixel. Secondly, in the decoder, all the features of the last three stages (conv3_D, conv2_D, conv1_D) are selected and also fused layer by layer. Finally, all the above feature maps are cascaded by channel splicing, and then sent to the new convolutional layer and softmax layer for learning and the final segmentation result is obtained. The number of convolutional feature maps at each stage is indicated at the top of Fig. 1.

There are two differences between CMLFDNN model and SegNet model. First is in feature fusion: Before cascading the features of encoder and decoder, CMLFDNN

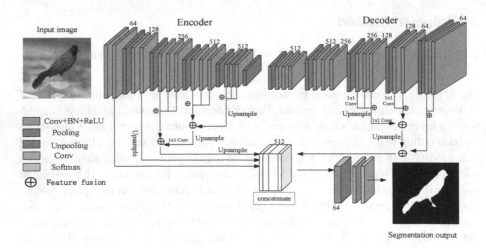

Fig. 1. The structure of CMLFDNN model.

model enlarges the features of the last three stages of encoder and decoder layer by layer, then adds and fuses them pixel by pixel. This not only considers the hierarchical dependence of the features extracted in different convolution stages, but also retains the local consistency of the features. Furthermore, this feature fusion does not introduce too many parameters for cascade operation, which simplifies the network training process. Comparatively, SegNet model does not fuse features. Second is in the features used in pixel category prediction: CMLFDNN model cascades all the convolution features of the encoder and the features of the last three convolution stages of the decoder in a channel splicing manner, which is equivalent to constructing a feature pool containing rich local and global features, and then feeding the features into a new convolution layer for dimensionality reduction and learning. The result is sent to the softmax layer for category prediction. While SegNet model only uses the feature of the last convolutional layer in the decoding stage for pixel class prediction. Compared to the SegNet model, CMLFDNN uses more information for category prediction.

2.2   Model Training and Parameters Setting

The experiments are implemented in a workstation equipped with a 64-bit 4Ubuntu system. The hardware configuration is an Intel(R) Xeon(R) CPU E5-2690 v3 2.6 GHz processor, 256 GB memory, and 4 TB hard disk. The entire model is trained using the Caffe deep learning platform. An NVIDIA Tesla K 40c 12 GB memory GPU is used to accelerate the training process. The network parameters are initialized using the VGG16 model pre-trained on the ImageNet data set, and the remaining layer parameters are initialized by the MSRA [8] initialization method. When only the number of inputs n is considered, weights obey the Gaussian distribution of mean value of 0 and variance of 2/n. In the training process, random gradient descent is used. The fixed learning rate is 0.0001, batch_size is 5, gamma is 1, weight decay is 0.0002, momentum is 0.99, and the maximum number of iterations is 100 000.

In the phase of network back propagation, cross entropy loss function is used to update the weights of the network.

$$Loss(l, p, \theta) = \frac{1}{N} \sum_{i=1}^{N} \sum_{k=1}^{K} -\sigma(l_i = k) \log p_{k,i} \tag{1}$$

Where l_i is the ground truth label of pixel i. $p_{k,i}$ represents the probability that i belongs to k-th class. K is the number of classes. N represents the total number of pixels in the batch. $\sigma(\bullet)$ is an indicator function, whose value takes 1 when $l_i = k$ and 0 otherwise. θ is the parameter set of the model.

3 Dataset Description and Evaluation Indexes

3.1 Dataset Description and Data Augmentation

3.1.1 ISPRS Vaihingen Dataset

It is 2D semantic label challenge subset in Vaihingen dataset [9]. It consists of 3-band IRRG (near infrared, infrared, green) image data, and the corresponding digital surface model (DSM) and normalized digital surface model (NDSM) data. The data set contains 33 images of different sizes. The ground sampling distance is 9 cm. Among them, there are 16 labeled images, each of which is tagged into six categories: impervious surfaces, buildings, low vegetation, trees, cars, and clutters/background. Twelve training sets, two validation sets and two test sets were randomly selected from 16 tagged images.

This dataset is relatively small for training deep networks. In our experiment, 256×256 image patches are used to train the network. For training and validation sets, a two-stage approach is used to augment the data. In the first stage, for a given image, due to the unequal size, the IRRG images and the corresponding ground truth image are cropped by a sliding window with a size of 256×256 and a step size of 128, and then three image patches whose positions are fixed (i.e. upper right corner, lower left corner and lower right corner) are extracted. In the second stage, all the patches are rotated at 90, 180 and 270° respectively, and then all the image blocks obtained by rotation are flipped horizontally and vertically. Finally, 15000 training samples and 2045 validation samples are obtained respectively.

3.1.2 Caltech-UCSD Birds200 Dataset

Caltech-UCSD Birds 200 [10] database contains 200 different species of birds, a total of 11,788 RGB images of different sizes. Some of the images have ground truth images. The birds in the dataset have different sizes, different postures, and complex in spectral and background. We randomly select 2000 images from tagged images as training set and 500 as validation set.

The number of training samples is far from adequate for network training effectively. Therefore we first normalizes the training set and the verification set to the size of 256×256. Secondly, all the images are rotated at 90, 180 and 270° respectively, and then all the image blocks obtained by rotation are flipped horizontally and vertically. Finally, 24000 training samples and 6000 validation samples are obtained respectively.

3.2 Evaluation Indexes

In this paper, we use the following indexes to evaluate the performance of the model on the above two datasets, namely F1 value, overall accuracy (OA), average precision (AP), and intersection over union (IOU). F1 value is the harmonic mean of precision (P) and recall (R). It is a comprehensive evaluation metric. Average precision (AP) is the average pixel classification accuracy of target and background. Their definitions are as follows:

$$F1 = \frac{2 * P * R}{P + R} \tag{2}$$

$$OA = \frac{TP + TN}{TP + FN + FP + TN} \tag{3}$$

$$AP = \int_0^1 P(R) dr \tag{4}$$

$$IOU(P_m, P_{gt}) = \frac{|P_m \cap P_{gt}|}{|P_m \cup P_{gt}|} \tag{5}$$

Where, $P = \frac{TP}{TP + FP}$, $R = \frac{TP}{TP + FN}$, P_{gt} is the set of pixels of the truth label map. P_m is the set of pixels of the predicted map. "$\cap$" and "$\cup$" represent intersection and union operations respectively. $|\bullet|$ represents the number of pixels in the group. TP: a prediction is positive and the actual value is also positive; FP: a prediction is positive but the actual value is negative; FN: a prediction is negative but the actual value is positive; TN: a prediction is negative and the actual value is also negative.

4   Experimental Results

4.1   ISPRS Vaihingen Dataset

4.1.1   Experimental Results

On ISPRS Vaihingen testset, the segmentation results of the proposed method and SegNet model are shown in Fig. 2. The input image sizes of all models are 256×256, and all of them are IRRG three-channel color images. The size of the predictive output is same as the input image. From top to bottom in Fig. 2 there are: input image, Ground truth map, SegNet segmentation result, and CMLFDNN segmentation result.

The objects in each map are of different sizes and shapes. There are complex situations such as shadow and occlusion in the scene. For example, the distribution of low vegetation and trees in the second, third and fifth images is concentrated. Due to the influence of the height of trees and buildings, there is a large area of shadow in the original image, and some shadows block the car and the road surface. Compared with

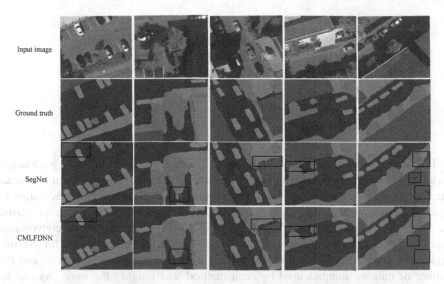

Fig. 2. Segmentation results by SegNet and CMLFDNN model on ISPRS Vaihingen testset, impervious surfaces: ■ buildings: ■ low vegetation: ■ trees: ■ cars: ■

SegNet, the segmentation results with significant differences are marked with black rectangles in Fig. 2. It can be seen that the segmentation result of the SegNet model have a lot misclassified pixels, targets are discontinuous and the target contours are not smooth. The segmentation result of CMLFDNN model is much close to the ground truth, and the targets are more complete and the details are clearer.

Table 1 shows the quantization results of each image in Fig. 2 and the whole testset. From Table 1, we can see that the proposed method can achieve the highest value in each index. The average F1 value and average IOU over the entire testset were 2.48% and 2.05% higher than those of SegNet model respectively. From the qualitative and quantitative results, the proposed method gets much better performance in urban remote sensing image segmentation.

Table 1. Segmentation results of deep models for five images and the entire testset.

Metric (%)	Image1		Image2		Image3		Image4		Image5		Testset avg.	
	F1	IOU	F1	IOU	F1	IOU	F1	IOU	F1	IOU	F1	IOU
SegNet	88.43	80.38	90.44	78.64	89.96	83.67	93.88	90.38	87.65	77.29	89.07	81.07
CMLF-DNN	90.23	82.32	92.79	80.02	92.17	84.97	96.25	92.01	91.31	81.28	91.55	83.12

4.1.2   Comparison with Existing Research Results

We also compare the proposed method with some existing methods with better segmentation performance in the literatures. The results are shown in Table 2. To consist with the comparative literatures, Table 2 lists F1 values for each category and overall accuracy (OA) of each method in the ISPRS Vaihingen dataset.

Table 2. Comparison with existing research results

Method	Imp surf	Building	Tree	Low veg	Car	OA
CNN+RF [11]	88.58	94.23	86.29	76.58	67.28	86.52
Dilation [12]	90.19	94.49	87.24	77.69	76.77	87.80
MLP [13]	91.69	95.24	88.12	79.44	78.42	88.92
SegNet	91.57	94.37	89.21	82.57	86.63	89.21
CMLFDNN	**93.24**	**95.89**	**90.24**	**85.46**	**87.74**	**90.97**

In the comparative methods, literature [11] proposes a CNN+RF segmentation model which combines CNN with random forest (RF). CNN is mainly used to extract features and RF is used for classification. The literature [12] uses atrous convolution to segment the remote sensing image, and uses CRF to smooth the segmentation result. The literature [13] concatenates the last convolution feature map of all convolution stages in a fully convolution network and sends them to another network for classification. The above experimental results are taken from the original literatures, and the number of training samples used by each method was roughly the same. As can be seen, the results of the proposed method is better than those of the comparative methods on F1 value in each category and the overall accuracy (OA) is the best. The overall accuracy is about 1.76% higher than that of the best results in the literature.

4.2 Caltech-UCSD Birds200 Dataset

4.2.1 Experimental Results

The segmentation results on Caltech-UCSD Birds200 are shown in Fig. 3. The input image of the network is 256 × 256 RGB image. The output of the network is prediction result of the same size as the input image. In Fig. 3, black represents the background and white represents the target (bird). From top to bottom in Fig. 3, there shows RGB image, ground truth map, SegNet segmentation result, and CMLFDNN segmentation result.

Fig. 3. Segmentation results of depth models on Caltech-UCSD Birds200 testset

In Fig. 3, the bird's species, shapes, spectral, and postures are various. The backgrounds are cluttered and the some of its spectral are similar to the targets. Extracting the target from the background is extremely challenging. As can be seen, deep models can deal with such challenges better. Compared with SegNet model, the segmentation results of the proposed method are closer to the ground truth. The segmented targets and details are more complete, misclassification and incorrect segmentation are greatly improved.

Table 3. Segmentation results of deep models for five images and the whole testset.

Metric (%)	Image1		Image2		Image3		Image4		Image5		Testset avg.	
	F1	IOU	F1	IOU	F1	IOU	F1	IOU	F1	IOU	F1	IOU
SegNet	90.91	83.34	85.40	74.52	93.91	88.51	92.78	86.53	79.46	65.93	86.89	77.86
CMLFDNN	93.20	87.27	89.05	80.27	94.81	90.14	94.97	90.42	89.47	80.95	91.69	83.87

Table 3 shows the quantitative results of the five images in Fig. 3 and the whole testset. As can be seen, the proposed method achieves the highest level on each index for the five images. The average F1 value and the average IOU value over the entire testset were 4.8% and 6.01% higher than those of the SegNet model respectively. Our method gets better results in this dataset.

4.2.2 Comparison with Existing Research Results

In this section, we compare our method with the methods in the literature with better segmentation performance. The results are shown in Table 4. To consist with the comparative literatures, Table 4 lists average precision (AP) and IOU values of the methods of the Caltech-UCSD Birds 200 dataset.

Table 4. Comparison with existing research results of the Caltech-UCSD Birds 200 dataset

Method	Bird-AP	Bird-IOU
MMBM1 [14]	90.42	75.92
Shape prior [15]	88.27	76.30
High-prior [16]	92.37	81.24
SegNet	85.29	77.39
CMLFDNN	**95.28**	**83.87**

In Table 4, a Boltzmann machine (MMBM) with maximized edges is proposed in literature [14], which simulates the joint distribution of hidden variables and output labels according to input observations. An iterative conditional pattern algorithm is derived to calculate the posterior probability of the target's distribution from the connection between image to label and image to hidden layer. Literature [15] uses the convolution layer of traditional CNN to extract global shape and local edge information, then uses fully connected parts to represent the shape specific to a given object class, and further refines segmentation results by matching segmentation mask patches with local features. Literature [16] proposes a conditional variational automatic encoder, which mainly consists of an image encoder for extracting high-level priors from images, a segmentation encoder for extracting high-level priors from segmentation, and a hybrid decoder for exporting segmentation results from high-level priors and input images. Then semantic segmentation is implemented via optimization problem that are parameterized by these components. The above experimental results are taken from the original literatures, and the number of training samples used are approximately the same. To our knowledge, literature [16] obtains the best segmentation result for this dataset so far. As can be seen from Table 4, the values of AP and IOU of our method are the highest, and are 2.91% and 2.63% higher than those of the best results in the literatures respectively. This demonstrates the good segmentation performance of the proposed method on this challenging birds dataset.

5   Conclusion

Multiple pooling and convolution operations in CNN reduce the resolution of the feature map and lost the image details, and make it difficult to improve segmentation accuracy effectively. Based on the convolutional coding-decoding network, this paper proposes an image segmentation model with cascaded multi-level features. The proposed model can make full use of the features extracted from the deep network to improve pixel class prediction. The proposed method is evaluated through experiments on the CUB_200_2011 and ISPRS Vaihingen datasets and is compared with existing research results. The experiment results show that the proposed method gets better results than current good image semantic segmentation methods. The targets segmented by our method are more complete, continuous and smooth.

References

1. Zeiler, M.D., Fergus, R.: Visualizing and understanding convolutional networks. In: Fleet, D., Pajdla, T., Schiele, B., Tuytelaars, T. (eds.) ECCV 2014. LNCS, vol. 8689, pp. 818–833. Springer, Cham (2014). https://doi.org/10.1007/978-3-319-10590-1_53
2. Long, J., Shelhamer, E., Darrell, T.: Fully convolutional networks for semantic segmentation. In: Proceedings of the IEEE Conference on Computer Vision and Pattern Recognition, pp. 3431–3440 (2015)
3. Badrinarayanan, V., Kendall, A., Cipolla, R.: SegNet: a deep convolutional encoder-decoder architecture for image segmentation. IEEE Trans. Pattern Anal. Mach. Intell. 39(12), 2481–2495 (2017)
4. Yu, F., Koltun, V.: Multi-scale context aggregation by dilated convolutions. In: ICLR 2015 (2015)
5. Chen, L.C., Papandreou, G., Kokkinos, I.: DeepLab: semantic image segmentation with deep convolutional nets, atrous convolution, and fully connected CRFs. IEEE Trans. Pattern Anal. Mach. Intell. 40(4), 834–848 (2018)

6. Wang, P., Chen, P., Yuan, Y.: Understanding convolution for semantic segmentation. In: IEEE Winter Conference on Applications of Computer Vision, pp. 1451–1460 (2018)
7. Chen, L.C., Papandreou, G., Schroff, F.: Rethinking atrous convolution for semantic image segmentation. arXiv preprint arXiv:1706.05587 (2017)
8. He, K., Zhang, X., Ren, S.: Delving deep into rectifiers: surpassing human-level performance on ImageNet classification. In: Proceedings of the IEEE International Conference on Computer Vision, pp. 1026–1034 (2015)
9. ISPRS Homepage. http://www2.isprs.org/commissions/comm2/wg4/vaihingen-2d-semantic-labeling-contest.html. Accessed 21 Dec 2017
10. Wah, C., Branson, S., Welinder, P., Perona, P., Belongie, S.: The Caltech-UCSD Birds-200-2011 dataset. Computation & Neural Systems Technical report, CNS-TR-2011-001 (2011)
11. Paisitkriangkrai, S., Sherrah, J., Janney, P., et al.: Effective semantic pixel labelling with convolutional networks and conditional random fields. In: Proceedings of the IEEE Conference on Computer Vision and Pattern Recognition Workshops, pp. 36–43 (2015)
12. Volpi, M., Tuia, D.: Dense semantic labeling of subdecimeter resolution images with convolutional neural networks. IEEE Trans. Geosci. Remote Sens. **55**(2), 881–893 (2017)
13. Maggiori, E., Tarabalka, Y., Charpiat, G.: High-resolution semantic labeling with convolutional neural networks. arXiv preprint arXiv:1611.01962 (2016)
14. Yang, J., Safar, S., Yang, M.H.: Max-margin boltzmann machines for object segmentation. In: Proceedings of the IEEE Conference on Computer Vision and Pattern Recognition, pp. 320–327 (2017)
15. Safar, S., Yang, M.H.: Learning shape priors for object segmentation via neural networks. In: 2015 IEEE International Conference on Image Processing, ICIP, pp. 1835–1839 (2015)
16. Zheng, H., Liu, Y., Ji, M., Wu, F., Fang, L.: Learning high-level prior with convolutional neural networks for semantic segmentation. Comput. Sci. (2015)
17. Zhao, H., Shi, J., Qi, X., Wang, X., Jia, J.: Pyramid scene parsing network. In: IEEE Conference on Computer Vision and Pattern Recognition, CVPR, pp. 2881–2890 (2017)
18. Lin, G., Milan, A., Shen, C., Reid, I.D.: RefineNet: multi-path refinement networks for high-resolution semantic segmentation. In: CVPR, vol. 1, no. 2, p. 5 (2017)
19. Ronneberger, O., Fischer, P., Brox, T.: U-Net: convolutional networks for biomedical image segmentation. In: Navab, N., Hornegger, J., Wells, W.M., Frangi, A.F. (eds.) MICCAI 2015. LNCS, vol. 9351, pp. 234–241. Springer, Cham (2015). https://doi.org/10.1007/978-3-319-24574-4_28

How to Understand the Basic Graphic Analysis Method

Zhenlin Xu[1], Fangqu Xu[1], Wen Xu[1], and Xiaohui Zou[2(✉)] (iD)

[1] Shanghai Shenyue Software Technology Co., Ltd., Room B10, North D., Bld. 8, No. 619 Longchang Road, Shanghai 200090, China
hyperien@qq.com, {xufangqu,cindyxu}@geomking.com
[2] SINO-US Searle Research Center (Beijing-Berkeley), Beijing, China
949309225@qq.com

Abstract. This paper aims to apply the understanding model to understand the Basic Graphic Analysis Method. The method steps are as follows: 1. Apply model A to understand its old terms, such as: Graphic, Natural and Symbolic Language; 2. Apply model B, to understand new terms, such as: the Basic Graphic Analysis Method and the Elementary Periodic Table as the set of basic graphics; 3. Apply model C, to understand the combination or expressions through following steps: step 1, decompose the graphic, natural and symbolic language contained in the geometric language in response to the actual problems on different cognitive levels of geometric language; step 2, analyze the visibility of graphic objects; step 3, deductive construct of graphic features. The result is to understand the Basic Graphic Analysis Method based on the recognition, analysis and application of basic graphs. The significance lies in the usage of the Elementary Periodic Table in the field as the set of basic graphics, to deconstruct any geometry problem and simplify the process, so that the geometry problem understanding could be more standardized, concise and traceable. Both human's cognitive structure and machine's information processing levels by the geometry problem could be therefore improved.

Keywords: Understanding Model Application · Geometric language · Natural language · Symbolic language · Basic Graphic Analysis Method

1 Introduction

This paper aims to apply the understanding model to understand the Basic Graphic Analysis Method. Among them, it involves a new concept the Elementary Periodic Table as the set of basic graphics. It is to transfer the concept and principle of the periodic table of elements in chemistry to the basic graphic collection in geometry. If this assumption is acceptable, then the computer-aided teaching software we designed can be further developed into artificial intelligence-assisted teaching software.

This is useful for both cognitive structure and information processing. To this end, we consider a series of bilingual cognitive features involved in geometry and its teaching software. Graphical, natural, and symbolic languages actually involve generalized translation. This goes far beyond the scope of geometry teaching and

F. Sun et al. (Eds.): ICCSIP 2018, CCIS 1005, pp. 124–131, 2019.
https://doi.org/10.1007/978-981-13-7983-3_11

computer-assisted instruction, and begins with the traditional artificial intelligence and a new generation of artificial intelligence. Thinking from this perspective, the meaning of our topic is different.

2 Geometric Language Used to Describe Any Plane Geometry Problem

Graphic, is the research object of geometry, plane graphic, is the research object of plane geometry. Any plane geometry problem, whether it's a proof, calculation or construction problem, will use a plane graphic and its various properties as the research object, assisted with natural and symbol language as its description part. Thus, the usage of three elements: graphic language, natural language and symbolic language could give the full description of any problem in geometry the combination of these three elements builds therefore the "geometric language" which could be used to describe any plane geometry problem [1].

Plane geometry is one of the most basic and important subjects in developing junior high school students' thinking ability (including intuitive thinking, logical thinking and innovation). In the specific age of junior middle school students' growth, no other subject could replace it inland and abroad [2].

However, plane geometry is precisely a subject that is difficult for teachers to teach and students to learn for a long time. The reason is that the geometric language, which is used to describe the plane geometry problem, covers graphic language, natural language and symbolic language. It transfers a lot of information from each dimension to the readers. The students, including some teachers, who have been trained by traditional plane geometry education methods, don't own the enough cognitive knowledge level of geometric language to deconstruct the important parts from three elements of geometric language, which could help them to understand and solve the plane geometry problem. It brings the result that the regularity of plane geometry problem analysis method couldn't be mastered by them [3].

Therefore, in order to explore the regularity of plane geometry problem analysis methods, help students and teachers to improve their cognitive knowledge of geometric language, Professor Fangqu Xu, one of Shanghai Shenyue Software Technology's founders, initiated and proposed a new analysis method – Basic Graphic Analysis Method. Basic Graphic Analysis Method helps students and teachers to deconstruct the most important element of geometric language – graphic language, so that the "elementary periodic table" in the plane geometry area – basic graphics set could be obtained (Fig. 1).

In order to provide an intuitive understanding of geometric language and Basic Graphic Analysis Method, let's make an example: [2]

Known: In $\triangle ABC$, $AB = AC$, $AD \perp BC$ the foot is D,

BE is the angle bisector of $\angle ABC$, over E draw $EF \perp BE$ intersect BC at point F,

$EG \perp BC$ the foot is G,

Proof: $DG = \frac{1}{4}$

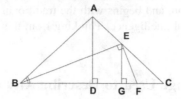

Fig. 1. Example graph

From this example it can be seen that the description of a plane geometry problem consists of following three parts:

(1) Graphic language
(2) Natural language
       Known: In △ABC, AB = AC, AD⊥BC the foot is D,
       BE is the angle bisector of ∠ABC, over E draw EF⊥BE intersect BC at point F,
       EG⊥BC the foot is G,
       Proof: DG = $\frac{1}{4}$BF
(3) Symbolic language
       △, =, ∠, ⊥

In these three parts, the plane graphic, which constitutes the graphic language and is treated as the research object of this problem, is the most important element deconstructed from the geometric language which describes the problem [5]. All other elements of geometric language – natural language and symbolic language, are combined with graphic language into a whole to describe the plane graphic and its properties. Therefore, the cognitive knowledge of geometric language could be converted to the cognitive knowledge of level of graphic language, actually plane graphics largely.

3   Visibility Analysis and Deductive Construction of Plane Graphics

If we do the further analysis of the plane graphics of above mentioned example, we can get:

In the conditions, BE is the angular bisection line of ∠ABC and the EF⊥BE, EF is therefore the perpendicular line of the angular bisection line BE. The angular bisection line and the perpendicular line of the angular bisector line appears, so that we can apply the proof using basic graphic – the important line in the isosceles triangle. This isosceles triangle is obtained by intersecting both sides of the perpendicular line of the angular bisector line and sides of the angle. The perpendicular line EF of the angular bisection line BE is now intersected with the side BC of the corner and not intersected with the other side BA, so they should be extended to the intersection, that is, extend line FE to intersect with BA's extension line at H, so that we can get △BEH ≅ △BEF, BH = BF, EH = EF. Here the important line in the isosceles triangle is the first basic graphic in this example (Fig. 2).

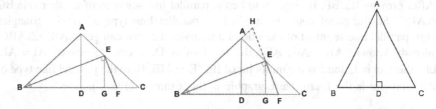

Fig. 2. First basic graphic

After proving BH = BF, to be proved result DG = $\frac{1}{4}$BF could be transformed into DG = $\frac{1}{2}$BH, this is the multiple relationship between two line segments. Because ∠BEH = 90°, so the multiple line segment BH becomes the hypotenuse of right △BEH, so that we can apply the proof using basic graphic – midline on the hypotenuse of a right triangle. Currently in the graphic, there is right triangle, but no midline on the hypotenuse, we should add it through taking the midpoint I of BH, connecting EI to intersect AD at point J, so that we get EI = $\frac{1}{2}$BH. The problem is now converted to prove DG = $\frac{1}{2}$EI. Here the midline on the hypotenuse of a right triangle is the second basic graphic in this example (Fig. 3).

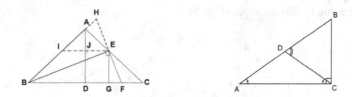

Fig. 3. Second basic graphic

After taking the midpoint I of BH, because point E is proved to be midpoint of FH, there exist two midpoints, which builds multiple midpoint problem, so that we can apply the proof using basic graphic – median of a triangle, and get IE//BF. Here the median of a triangle is the third basic graphic in this example (Fig. 4).

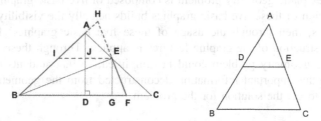

Fig. 4. Third basic graphic

After proving IE//BF, IE appears to be the parallel line segment of another side BC of △ABC. So the proof could be applied by parallel line type of similar triangles through parallel line segment of the side of a triangle, then we can get △AIE∽△ABC. As already known, AB = AC, AD⊥BC the foot is D, it can be proven AI = AE, AJ⊥IE the foot is J, and J is the midpoint of IE, JE = $\frac{1}{2}$IE. Here the parallel line type of similar triangles is the fourth basic graphic in this example (Fig. 5).

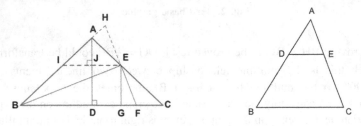

Fig. 5. Fourth basic graphic

Now the problem is converted into proving DG = JE. In known conditions EG⊥BC, the foot is G, so we can get EG//JD. Because EJ//GD, we can prove DG = JE in usage of parallel line properties, the analysis could then go to end. The usage parallel line is the fifth basic graphic in this example (Fig. 6).

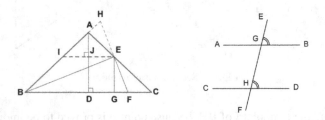

Fig. 6. Fifth basic graphic

Through the analysis of this example, it could be found that the plane graphic in such a complex plane geometry problem is composed of five basic graphics. Analysis and identification of these five basic graphics builds actually the visibility analysis of graphic objects; then through the usage of these five basic graphics' features, the deduction construction of the graphic features is applied. Through these two steps, a complex plane geometry problem could be simplified, so that students and teachers could capture the important information deconstructed from the geometric language and use them to get the solution for the problem.

4 Basic Graphics Set and Basic Graphic Analysis Method

The result is to understand that the Basic Graphic Analysis Method based on the recognition, analysis and application of basic graphs. Extensively, using the method described above to analyse thousands of plane geometry graphics, we could come to the conclusion that the number of basic graphics in plane geometry subject is 32. These 32 basic graphics constitute the basic elements of plane geometry, and their infinite combination will deduce an infinitely changed plane geometry. The 32 basic graphics are divided into 7 types (Fig. 7):

1. parallel line
2. isosceles triangle
3. angle related to circle
4. congruent triangles
5. similar triangles
6. triangle with special angle
7. triangle related to area method [4].

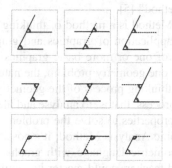

Fig. 7. Basic graphics in parallel line as example

For every single basic graphic in it there exists a complete system consisting of standardized description, property, position property, application condition and application method. For example, for midline on the hypotenuse of a right triangle mentioned above as second basic graphic, it has the following characters (Fig. 8) (Table 1):

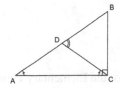

Fig. 8. Basic graphic "midline on the hypotenuse of a right triangle"

Table 1. Properties of *Basic graphic "midline on the hypotenuse of a right triangle"*

Item	Description
Graphic description	Midline on the hypotenuse of a right triangle
Property	$\triangle ABC, \angle ACB = 90°$ $AD = BD \Leftrightarrow CD = AD = \frac{1}{2}AB$ $AD = BD \Leftrightarrow \angle DAC = \angle DCA, \angle BDC = 2\angle DAC$
Position property	Midline on the hypotenuse of a right triangle
Application condition	It exists midline on the hypotenuse of a right triangle
Application method	If it exists midline on the hypotenuse of a right triangle, could use properties of the basic graphic "midline on the hypotenuse of a right triangle" to do the calculation or proof

In plane geometry subject, according to the conditions and conclusions of the problem, the analysis method to analyse and identify one or more basic graphics, apply the properties of these basic graphics and then solve the plane geometry problem is the "Basic Graphic Analysis Method" [5].

Basic Graphic Analysis Method is a method of thinking and analysis based on the identification, analysis and application of graphics and graphic properties. Any geometric graphic is composed of one or more basic graphics. When a number of basic graphics are combined to be one geometry problem, the nature of the basic graphics is hidden. So the analysis and thinking process of the geometry problem is essentially to reverse this comprehensive process, that is, to analyse and identify these basic graphics, the use the basic graphics' properties to solve the problem.

By using the Basic Graphic Analysis Method, it's possible to deconstruct of plane graphics and so on, the geometric language with graphic language as its essential element, so that students and teachers could master its regularity. Any plane geometry problem could be simplified, become more standardized, concise and traceable, so that the cognitive knowledge of geometric language by students and teachers could be improved and the plane geometry problem becomes easier to understand and solve [6].

Additionally, per Basic Graphic Analysis Method, the human content information processing by geometric language could be standardised and formulated, and it builds a possible method for the machine formal information processing of geometric language based on the basic graphics reality in every single plane geometry graphic, so that the understanding of geometric language both by human and machine and their combined translation becomes possible.

5 Conclusions

The significance lies in the usage of the Elementary Periodic Table in the field as the set of basic graphics, to deconstruct any geometry problem and simplify the process, so that the problem understanding could be more standardized, concise and traceable. It builds a solid base of bilingual cognitive features by geometry that not only the human' cognitive structure by geometry problem could be standardized and improved, but also information processing by computer for geometry problem could be established.

Since the publication, after years of development, the Basic Graphic Analysis Method has been widely applied and achieved good results. In future, besides the more standardized and accurate description per Basic Graphic Analysis Method, the research direction will focus on the combination of Basic Graphic Analysis Method and modern Information Technology, including programming language, interface language, audio/video form, etc., in the area of human content information processing and machine formal information processing, so that Basic Graphic Analysis Method could be spread and mastered by human in a more simple and easier way and help both human and machine to better conduct and understand geometric language. In this paper, as the Understanding Model Application (UMA) 18: How to Understand the Basic Graphic Analysis Method, the emphasis is mainly on reading and learning from the standpoint of readers and students, which inevitably involves two known and unknown Aspects and their interconnection are logically linked to each other [7, 8]. We know that algebraic equations and geometric proofs are known to unknown. However, when we write, we write down the idea from the ancient times, and often ignore the characteristics of the cognitive structure of readers and learners. When writing software, we will ignore the characteristics of information processing. Therefore, UMA 18 is intended to emphasize how to understand the method, which helps us to better understand and master the geometry language [9].

References

1. Zhang, C.: Talking about the importance of geometry language in geometry teaching of middle school. J. Chengdu Teachers Coll. **20**(4) (2001)
2. Xu, F., Xu, W.: Transparent Geometry - New Practice of Internet+ Planar Geometry. Shanghai Education Publishing House, Shanghai (2017)
3. Liu, J.: Learn to express geometry logical thinking process with mathematical language. Shuxue Tongbao **45**(5) (2001)
4. Xu, F.: Basic Graphic Analysis Method. Elephant Publishing House, New York (1998)
5. He, J.: Play the role of graph language in mathematics teaching. Study Math. Teach. **30**(5) 2011
6. Wang, H.: The 'law' of junior high school plane geometry education – Basic Graphic Analysis Method, no. 1–2. School Mathematics in Shanghai (2015)
7. Zou, X., Zou, S.: Bilingual information processing method and principle. Comput. Appl. Softw. (11), 69–76, 102 (2015)
8. Zou, S., Zou, X.: Understanding: how to resolve ambiguity. In: Shi, Z., Goertzel, B., Feng, J. (eds.) ICIS 2017. IAICT, vol. 510, pp. 333–343. Springer, Cham (2017). https://doi.org/10.1007/978-3-319-68121-4_36
9. Zou, S., Zou, X., Wang, X.: How to do knowledge module finishing. In: Shi, Z., Pennartz, C., Huang, T. (eds.) ICIS 2018. IAICT, vol. 539, pp. 134–145. Springer, Cham (2018). https://doi.org/10.1007/978-3-030-01313-4_14

Image Elementary Manifold and Its Application in Image Analysis

Chao Cai[1(✉)], Lingge Li[1], and Changwen Zheng[2]

[1] State Key Laboratory for Multispectral Information Processing Technologies, School of Automation, Huazhong University of Science and Technology, Wuhan 430074, Hubei, People's Republic of China
caichao@hust.edu.cn
[2] Science and Technology on Integrated Information System Laboratory, Beijing 10080, People's Republic of China

Abstract. Image basis function plays a key role in image information analysis. Due to the complex geometric structure in image, a better image basis or frame often have a very large family with a large number of basis functions lying in a lower dimensionality manifold, such as 2D Gabor functions and Contourlets used in image texture analysis, the corresponding image transform and analysis will be very time consuming. In this article, we propose a novel image representation method called "image elementary manifold", here, an image elementary manifold can represent all the basis functions lying in the same manifold. A fast elementary manifold based image decomposition and reconstruction algorithm are given. Comparing to traditional image representation methods, elementary manifold based image analysis reduce time consumption, discovers the latent intrinsic structure of images more efficiently and provides the possibility of empirical prediction. Finally, many experiments show the feasibility of image elementary manifold in image analysis.

Keywords: Image basis · Manifold · Image elementary manifold

1 Introduction

In linear algebra, basis is a set of linearly independent vectors that can represent every vector in a given vector space via linear combination. In mathematical approximation theory, it requires only the linear combination of few vectors to reconstruct signal accurately. For example, the basis functions of Fourier transformation is Sine function and Cosine function, the input signal is limited to $L^1(R)$ [1], then it is extended to $L^2(R)$ [2]. In 1946, Gabor [3] proposed that the signal to be analyzed is first multiplied by a window function for Time-Frequency Localization. A Gabor system may be a basis for $L^2(R)$, which is generated from a single $L^2(R)$-function through phase space translations and modulations. Wavelet transform [4, 5] inherits and develops the localization performance of Gabor transform, overcomes it's shortcoming of lack of discrete

© Springer Nature Singapore Pte Ltd. 2019
F. Sun et al. (Eds.): ICCSIP 2018, CCIS 1005, pp. 132–142, 2019.
https://doi.org/10.1007/978-981-13-7983-3_12

orthogonal basis. Do and Vetterli [6, 7] constructed a double filter bank structure which results in a flexible multiresolution, local, and multidirectional image expansion using contour segments, named Contourlet Transform. The contourlet expansion is shown to achieve the optimal approximation rate for piecewise C^2 smooth images with C^2 smooth contours. For this class of functions, the decay rate of approximation error of contourlet transform is far better than wavelets and Fourier basis [5, 8].

As for images, there are still some problems in subspace decomposition and reconstruction. Traditional image decomposition method requires convolving the image with all the basis functions, but the rotation and dilation of a mother function often generate a large number of basis functions, this leads to a large amount of calculation. For example, Gabor Transform and Contourlet Transform use multidirectional basis functions to achieve better approximation, but the large time consuming limits their application. Actually, there are potential low dimensional manifolds exist in basis functions, generating through shifting, scaling, rotating and so on. Further more, one can decompose images into different sub-manifold space. In this article, we classify the basis functions based on their embedding manifold. Therefore, the computational power and the empirical predictive power of image analysis will be greatly increased.

2 Image Elementary Manifold

2.1 Manifold Embedded Property of Image Basis Functions

A manifold is an abstract mathematical space that near each point resembles Euclidean space. Many image sets vary due to a small number degrees of freedom and the set of these images lie in or near to some low-dimensional manifolds embedded in a high dimensional (e.g. equal to the number of image pixels) image spaces [9]. Manifold learning algorithms can infer global structures from locally computed geometric properties (such as distances, angles, and symmetry). Existing manifold learning algorithm includes distance-preserving methods (such as ISOmap [10], MVU [11]), angle-preserving methods (such as conformal eigenmaps [12]) and proximity-preserving methods (such as LLE [13] [14]. Wu et al. prompt a data-driven method for semi-supervised multioutput regression on image manifolds [15].

Manifold embedded property could be found in many kinds of basis functions. Shifting, rotating or scaling always exists in basis functions, and each kind of these basis images should lie in a low-dimensional manifold. Simply looking at the Gabor basis functions in Fig. 1, all basis functions in one scale are generated by rotating the zero direction image (the top image), so that these images lie in a one-dimensional manifold. These basis functions could be packaged together as a manifold, and this manifold will be treated as an elementary function in image decomposition and reconstruction. Therefore, the manifold spans the space which is spanned by Gabor basis functions.

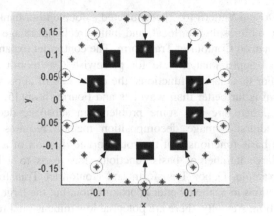

Fig. 1. Gabor basis functions and the one-dimensional manifold learned by MVU algorithm. Each asterisk stands for an elementary image which is generated by rotating a zero direction image. The picture that arrow points to is the corresponding basis function.

2.2 Image Elementary Manifold

As mentioned above, a series of basis functions that lie in a manifold could be packaged together for follow-up computation. A package model will be introduced in the following paragraphs.

Suppose that a manifold S_P of the intrinsic dimension d in the vector input space is a set of some sample points and their deformations, such as shifting, rotating. It could be formulated as follows:

$$S_P = \{x | \exists \alpha, x = s(P, \alpha)\} \tag{1}$$

Where s the deformation function, P is the sample points, $\alpha \in R^d$ is deformation parameter.

A core task of manifold learning is to find the low-dimensional structure (potential embedded manifold) of high-dimensional observed data, that is to find deformation parameter α and deformation function s. Many manifold learning algorithms can give a low dimensional global coordinates from high dimensional input data. If we take these low dimensional variables which have been learned by manifold learning algorithm as the deformation parameters, a deformation mapping between high-dimensional data and low-dimensional variables can be obtained.

In this paper, we use Maximum Variance Unfolding (MVU) algorithm, which attempts to unfold curved manifolds while preserving local geometry. After obtaining the intrinsic variables of image transformation by manifold learning algorithm, the deformation mapping between high-dimensional space and low-dimensional space is obtained by higher-order Taylor expansion, and then the nonlinear manifold is approximated by polynomial.

$$s(P,\alpha) = s(P,0) + \alpha\frac{\partial s(P,\alpha)}{\partial \alpha}\Big|_{\alpha=\vec{0}} + 0.5\alpha^2\frac{\partial^2 s(P,\alpha)}{\partial \alpha^2} + O(\alpha^3) \approx P_0 + \alpha T' + 0.5\alpha^2 T''$$

(2)

Here T' is tangent vector, T'' is the second-order partial derivative. As shown in Fig. 2: $P_0 + \alpha T'$ is the first-order Taylor expansion to approximate the point P on the manifold surface, $P_0 + \alpha T' + 0.5\alpha^2 T''$ is the second-order Taylor expansion to approximate the point P on the manifold surface.

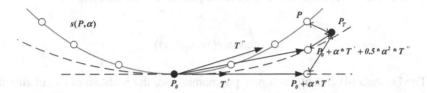

Fig. 2. Manifold distance computation based on Taylor-expansion approximation

The approximated manifold s is called an elementary manifold of basis functions. P means that a collection of similar basis functions. All these functions are generated from a central function and modeled by a multivariable polynomial. The elementary manifold s will be an elementary cell in image decomposition and reconstruction.

In many cases, the analytical expression of s is unknown, so, the partial differentiation in Eq. (2) will be represented by difference in calculation, that is:

$$\frac{\partial s(P,\alpha)}{\partial \alpha} \approx \frac{\Delta s(P,\alpha)}{\Delta \alpha}$$

(3)

Traditional transform method convolves the input image with all basis functions, which needs a huge consumption of calculation. Based on elementary manifold, we just compute correlation between input image and manifold instead of a series of basis functions. The correlation details based on manifold will be shown in next sections.

2.3 The Decomposition and Reconstruction of Images Based on Image Elementary Manifold

Figure 3 illustrates the distance between manifolds. If S_P and S_E are all represented by polynomials, the problem will be transformed into solving the distance between two polynomial surfaces.

Based on Taylor expression, manifold could be modeled by a multivariable polynomial whose dimension (D) and order (O) are settable values. Therefore, the correlation between the point and manifold is defined as:

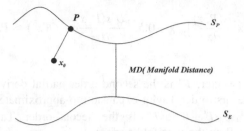

Fig. 3. Manifold distance diagram. The manifold distance (MD) between corresponding manifolds S_P and S_E. The correlation between the point x_0 and the manifold S_P.

$$r = \max_{\alpha} \text{cov}(x_0, s(P, \alpha)) \tag{4}$$

The Formula (4) constitutes a new polynomial. So, the problem of calculating the correlation between point x_0 and manifold S_P is converted to solving the maximum of polynomial with fewer variables. Solving the maximum of polynomial directly provides the possibility of empirical prediction.

From the point of linear algebra, we can decompose image $I(x, y)$ into linear combination of image basis if the image is in the space spanned by the basis, which is the synthesis equation

$$I(x, y) = \sum_i a_i \tilde{\omega}_i(x, y) \tag{5}$$

Where $\tilde{\omega}_i(x, y)$ is called the dual function of the basis function $\omega_i(x, y)$, a_i is the decomposition coefficient. According to the dual property of basis functions, we have the analysis equation

$$a_i = \langle I(x, y), \omega_i(x, y) \rangle \tag{6}$$

The process of calculating coefficient a_i according to Formula (6) can be considered as decomposition process. And the weighted summation of basis functions according to Formula (5) can be seen as reconstruction process. When the number of basis functions is large, calculating coefficients requires a huge consumption.

In this paper, we introduce the image elementary manifold. Basis functions are classified into different manifolds. Therefore, it only needs to compute the manifold distance for image decomposition and reconstruction. Formula (5) could be converted to Formula (7):

$$I(x, y) = \sum_i r_i \tilde{s}_i \tag{7}$$

Where $\tilde{s}_i$ refers to the dual elementary manifold, r_i is the corresponding decomposition coefficient which is the maximum of the polynomial in Formula (4).

In this work, the concept of inner product of elementary manifolds and the input image is introduced. It replaces the inner product of basis functions and the input image. According to the dual property of basis functions, we can also infer the equation:

$$r_i = \langle I(x, y), s_i \rangle \tag{8}$$

Similarly, the same kind of dual basis functions could be trained as a manifold in image reconstruction. According to Formula (7), using dual elementary manifolds and corresponding coefficients can reconstruct the input image.

2.4   Computation Analysis of Elementary Manifold Decomposition

Using elementary manifolds can significantly reduce the calculation of the decomposition and reconstruction. Suppose there are N basis functions, and there are t pixels in each basis image. According to Formula (6), conventional method convolves the input image (K pixels) with all basis functions. This means that $N * t * K$ times multiplication and $N * t * K$ times addition need to be calculated.

For elementary manifold method, suppose each Taylor-expansion polynomial includes P terms, there are t polynomials. The value of P is determined by the order of the polynomial O and the number of free variables D. According to Formula (4) and (8), the decomposition process needs to calculate $P * t * K$ times multiplication and $P * t * K$ times addition to construct a new polynomial that represents the correlation between point and manifold.

Generally, the number of polynomial terms is far less than the number of basis functions ($P \ll N$, $P * t * K \ll N * t * K$). Therefore, elementary manifold method will show its advantage. For example, $t = 13 * 13 = 169$, $P = 20$, $N = 90$, $K = 128 * 128$, in conventional method, $N * t * K = 249,200,640$ times multiplication and 249200640 times addition need to be calculate, while in our method, it only needs to calculate $P * t * K = 55,377,920$ times multiplication and 55377920 times addition.

3   Some Applications About Elementary Manifold

In this section, we verify the feasibility of the image elementary manifold, and show applications in image decomposition, image reconstruction and edge detection through a series of experiments. In those experiments, we first test a simple image elementary manifold composed of 13×13 pixels stepped edge images with different directions and displacements (as shown in the Fig. 4), these basis functions span a piecewise constant space.. Then, other classic basis functions like Gabor functions and Log-Gabor functions are used in elementary manifold method. We use the MVU manifold learning algorithm to get the manifold knowledge.

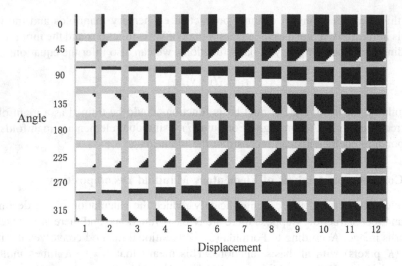

Fig. 4. Some 13 × 13 pixels stepped edge elementary images

3.1 Image Decomposition

By calculating the correlation between each small image block of the input image and the elementary manifold, namely the correlation coefficient, a correlation coefficient matrix can be generated, which is the image decomposition process. Some classic basis functions also can be used in this method, such as Gabor basis functions. As mentioned in Sect. 2.4, we now present several experiment results with elementary manifold method and compare it with the performance of Gabor transform directly. The decomposition coefficient image is shown in Fig. 5(b), stepped edge images were treated as a two-dimensional manifold for manifold learning. The transform effectively shows the fact image edges. In Fig. 5(c), Gabor basis functions are considered lying in two manifolds (real part and imaginary part). The experimental results proved the feasibility of elementary manifold method.

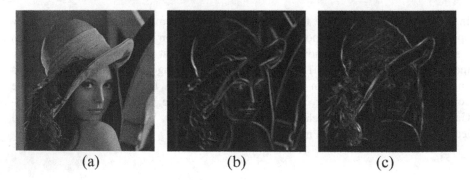

Fig. 5. Image decomposition. (a) Input image. (b) Decomposition image with stepped edge elementary manifold. (c) Decomposition image with Gabor basis function manifold.

In this experiment, we choose $t = 13 * 13 = 169$, $P = 20$, $N = 90$, the time consuming of our method is far less than the conventional two dimensional convolution method. With the unified data types ("double"), our approach takes 5 s while traditional Gabor transform takes 24 s for 512×512 pixels image in the same hardware platform.

As mentioned in Sect. 2, the computation complexity is closely related to the number of polynomial terms. Therefore, we took some experiments to discover the relationship between the terms and the processing time. A 512×512 pixels image is decomposed, with $t = 13 * 13 = 169$, $N = 90$. The result is shown in Table 1. Time consumption is proportional to the number of polynomial terms.

Table 1. The processing time according to increasing polynomial terms. The relation of the number of free variables (D) and orders (O) to polynomial terms (M) and time consumption.

(D, O)	(2,2)	(2,3)	(3,3)	(4,3)	(5,3)	(6,3)	(7,3)
P	6	10	20	35	56	84	120
Time consumption (ms)	3033	3997	4939	5889	8403	10747	14472

3.2 Image Reconstruction

According to Formula (7), calculating the linear combination of dual elementary manifolds can reconstruct the input image. In this experiment, we use two different elementary image sets reconstruct the "Lena" image (256×256 pixels). From Fig. 6 (a), we find that the result reconstructed by the stepped edge elementary image set (13×13 pixels) mentioned before describes the geometric structure information of the input image correctly, while the hair, facial features and other details are not so accurate. The straight lines in the figure are very clear, although curves are not smooth. As shown in Fig. 6(c), it is reconstructed by the stepped edge elementary image set (3×3 pixels), which can almost recover the input image. Figure 6(b) shows an example of the Log-Gabor transform on the "Lena" image. The reconstruction image is smoother, which mainly result from the different characteristics of basis functions.

3.3 Image Edge Detection

Image elementary manifold can be used for image edge detection. For example, in Fig. 4, each elementary image is expected to represent an "edge". The input image is first removed the mean image, and then decomposed into correlation coefficient image, which reflects the intensity of stepped edge. Therefore, the edges of the input image would be highlighted in the transformed image. Since the linear equations of learning samples are known, we can obtain the gradient direction and amplitude of each point of transformed image. We follow on do non-maximum suppression for gradient amplitudes. Then we use the double threshold algorithm to detect and connection edges. Finally, the clear edges would be obtained.

In this experiment, the elementary images are used to detect the edges of a cameraman image, of size 256×256 pixels. The size of each elementary image is 13×13

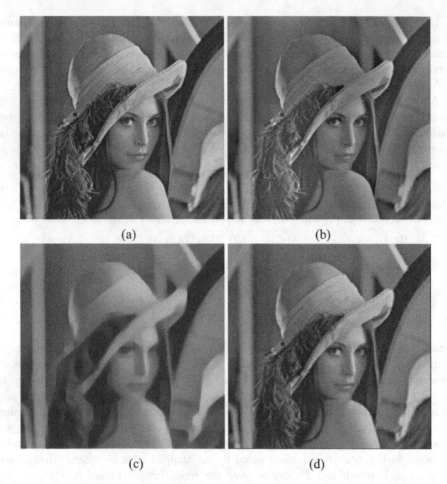

(a)   (b)

(c)   (d)

Fig. 6. Reconstruction image by elementary images with different sizes. (a) Original image. (b) The image is reconstructed by Log-Gabor transform. (c) The image is reconstructed by the stepped edge elementary images (13 × 13 pixels). (d) The image is reconstructed by the stepped edge elementary images (3 × 3 pixels).

pixels. The experimental results are shown in Fig. 7. It is shown that the edge features of the cameraman and the camera in the image are detected very well, and the lines are continuous and smooth. Due to the limited size of the elementary image, many detailed edges cannot be accurately described.

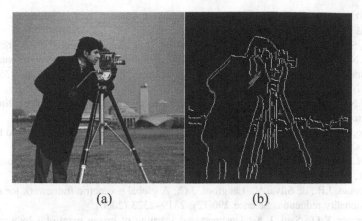

(a)   (b)

Fig. 7. Edge detection images. (a) Input image. (b) Edge image.

4 Conclusion

In this paper we proposed a new elementary manifold method in combined with image multi-scale geometric analysis. It is shown that this method can improve the computing performance of image basis function analysis. In this paper, we calculate the correlation coefficients between elementary manifold and the input image in spatial domain, whereas in traditional method, correlation coefficients image is constructed by using all basis functions convolve with the input image. In order to improve the computing speed, the traditional method of digital image processing deals with images via the transformation from the image to the frequency domain processing. The proposed algorithm could show great advantages when the number of basis functions is considerably larger than the number of Taylor expansion terms. Furthermore, the elementary manifold spans the space which is spanned by the basis functions that lying in the manifold. Experiments indicate the potential of the elementary manifold method in image processing applications. The disadvantages of this method include two aspects. For one thing, despite the manifold learning algorithm is varied, but there are still unstable situation when training basis functions; for another, the increase of the Taylor expansion order will lead to a sharply increase of computing cost, and if the order of the polynomial is too low will result in fitting error. For future work, we will try to transform the elementary manifold to the frequency domain processing to improve the algorithm efficiency.

References

1. Papoulis, A.: The Fourier Integral and its Applications, 2nd edn. McGraw-Hill, New York (1987)
2. Dym, H., McKean, H.P.: Fourier Series and Integral. Academic Press, New York (1972)
3. Gabor, D.: Theory of communication. J. Inst. Elect. Eng. (London) **93**(111), 429–457 (1946)

4. Lee, D.T.L., Yamamoto, A.: Wavelet analysis: theory and applications. Hewlett Packard J. **45**, 44 (1994)
5. Mallat, S.: A Wavelet Tour of Signal Processing, 2nd edn. Academic, New York (1999)
6. Do, M.N., Vetterli, M.: Contourlets: a directional multiresolution image representation. In: 2002 International Conference on Proceedings of Image Processing, vol. 1, pp. I-357–I-360. IEEE (2002)
7. Do, M.N., Vetterli, M.: The contourlet transform: an efficient directional multiresolution image representation. IEEE Trans. Image Process. **14**(12), 2091–2106 (2005)
8. Donoho, D.L., Vetterli, M., DeVore, R.A., Daubechies, I.: Data compression and harmonic analysis. IEEE Trans. Inf. Theory **44**(6), 2435–2476 (1998)
9. Pless, R., Souvenir, R.: A survey of manifold learning for images. IPSJ Trans. Comput. Vis. Appl. **1**, 83–94 (2009)
10. Tenenbaum, J.B., de Silva, V., Langford, J.C.: A global geometric framework for nonlinear dimensionality reduction. Science **290**(12), 2319–2323 (2000)
11. Weinberger, K.Q., Saul, L.K.: Unsupervised learning of image manifolds by semidefinite programming. Int. J. Comput. Vis. **70**(1), 77–90 (2006)
12. Sha, F., Saul, L.K.: Analysis and extension of spectral methods for nonlinear dimensionality reduction. In: Proceedings of 22nd International Conference on Machine Learning, ICML 2005, pp. 784–791. ACM Press (2005)
13. Roweis, S.T., Saul, L.K.: Nonlinear dimensionality reduction by locally linear embedding. Science **290**(5500), 2323–2326 (2000)
14. Zhang, J., Huang, H., Wang, J.: Manifold learning for visualizing and analyzing high-dimensional data. IEEE Intell. Syst. **25**, 54–61 (2010)
15. Wu, H., Spurlock, S., Souvenir, R.: Semi-supervised multi-output image manifold regression. In: IEEE International Conference on Image Processing, vol. 70, pp. 2413–2417 (2017)

SAR Image Fast Online ATR Based on Visual Attention and Scale Analysis

Hongqiao Wang[✉], Yanning Cai, Junyi Yao, Shaolei Zhang,
and Guangyuan Fu

Xi'an Research Institute of Hi-Tech, Xi'an 710025, Shaanxi, China
ep.hqwang@gmail.com

Abstract. Aiming at the online automatic target recognition for SAR images, a visual attention based scale analysis method is introduced for the feature extraction and the classifiers construction. By improving the features adaptability and robustness on speckle, a local multi-resolution analysis method is introduced for feature extraction of the SAR targets. Also a non-biased multi-scale LSSVC model is proposed to furthermore improve the classification performance. On this basis, a fast online learning algorithm based on Cholesky factorization is studied and applied to the SAR image recognition, which has smaller computation complexity than the common method with matrix inversion. Experiments testify that the presented method can give better classification precision and online performance.

Keywords: SAR ATR · Online learning · Visual attention · Scale analysis · LSSVC

1 Introduction

Synthetic Aperture Radar (SAR) is an important sensor due to its all weather, day/night, high resolution imaging, long standoff capability. Along with the development of radar technologies, as well as with increasing demands for target identification in radar applications, automatic target recognition (ATR) using SAR has become an important branch of image recognition [1].

Although there are many target recognition problems are solved by deep learning [2–4] in the current computer vision and image pattern recognition fields. But the traditional statistic machine learning models are still adopted in some conditions such as the lacking of massive data, the gradually increasing of data with time, etc. The kernel method represented by support vector machine (SVM), which is developed from statistic learning theory, shows good prediction performance. By transforming the quadratic programming problem to a linear system of equations the least squares support vector classifier (LSSVC) is a better choice as the learning efficiency of is greatly improved [5]. However, the classification precision of LSSVC method depends too much on the selection of kernel function and the kernel parameters. As different kernel functions

© Springer Nature Singapore Pte Ltd. 2019
F. Sun et al. (Eds.): ICCSIP 2018, CCIS 1005, pp. 143–154, 2019.
https://doi.org/10.1007/978-981-13-7983-3_13

have different characteristics, and the perfect theory basis of the kernel construction or the kernel selection has not been found till now, the performance of kernel functions vary greatly in different application fields. Aiming at the problem, a lot of combined-kernel methods appeared, namely the multiple kernel learning methods [6,7], the researchers expected to gain better performance by the combination of multiple kernels. Wang [8] presented a multiple kernel learning method with hybrid kernel alignment maximization for pattern classification applications. Saeid [9] proposed a similarity-based multiple kernel learning algorithms for classification of remotely sensed images. Fan [10] studied a fast multiple empirical kernel learning machine, and the machine is applied to the fast pattern recognition field. Lin [11] aimed to study the multi-kernel learning for multivariate performance measures optimization. In the regression aspects, Wang [12] studied a non-biased composite kernel machine and the online chaotic time series prediction applications. The method can give better prediction precision and speed, but the composite kernel coefficients are determined still by empirical methods. The multi-scale kernel method is a special case of multiple kernel learning, the core of the method is the fusion of multiple kernels with different scale. Bao [13] studied a multi-scale kernel learning method and its application in image classification, the conclusions shows that the multi-scale kernel methods have more flexibility and can provide more complete choice of scale than the composite kernel methods. Except for the good classifier, to gain high classification precision, another important work is the extraction of the proper features for targets. Nowadays, the vision cognition principles are widely used for feature analysis, which gives high performance of target detection, identification and classification like the biological vision.

Most of the above-mentioned examples are offline problems, which can be solved by offline learning algorithms. But in the situations with high real-time requirement, or the learning samples increase with a time series, the online learning algorithms must be used. As the least squares support vector machine (LSSVM) saved much time through solving linear equations instead of quadratic programming, some online learning algorithms based on LSSVM [14,15] appeared. The key points of these methods lie in the block of kernel matrix, and the LSSVM can be trained using inverse matrix of the blocks. But if the dimension of kernel matrix is high, the computational complexity of getting inverse matrix is still too high for online learning.

On this basis, aiming at the SAR image ATR, a visual attention and scale analysis method is introduced for feature extraction of the SAR targets. Then a non-biased multi-scale kernel LSSVC model is considered. Moreover, a fast online learning method rather than the directly inversing of the block matrix is adopted to train the multiple kernel machine. The experiments testify that the presented method can give better classification precision and online performance.

2 Visual Attention and Scale Analysis Based Feature Extraction Method

On SAR image ATR, without loss of generality, the MSTAR data set is taken as the object of investigation. The targets in MSTAR chips have some characters such as the chips have the same size with 128×128 pixels, there is only one target in one chip and the target lies in the center of the chip, the chips have the same resolution, etc. So, for the target recognition object, more attention should be paid for the area around the target in the chip. Learning from the visual attention mechanism of biological vision, the focus of visual attention of SAR target should be the gravity center of the target.

The traditional multi-resolution analyses are commonly realized by filtering and sampling. These methods have disadvantages for feature extraction, because the obtained orthogonal basis may not give the similar expression for the data having the same local characteristic. To solve this problem, borrowing the sampling filter idea of the traditional wavelet method, a new sampling method using a local extension is adopted [16], which can guarantee the generated basis pointing to the local region and can guarantee the same local characteristics having the similar projection coefficients on the basis. On the implementation, we can begin from the focus of visual attention of the SAR target (namely the gravity center of the target). Then by several times of filtering using the fast filter, a multi-scale decomposition of the image can be gained, and the difference of Gaussian (DOG) like space image of the original image is also obtained. Finally, utilizing the key pixels sampling directly from the multi-level image, we can rapidly get the local multi-scale feature of the target.

Through the above analyzing, we first can construct a multi-level DOG like scale space based on image. Then an 8-neighborhood orthogonal basis can be designed, with which the multi-level sampling filter on image can be executed, as a result, the image features in the 8 directions and a low frequency feature are derived. Then, the target image is processed by a 4-level local multi-resolution decomposition. Then, the feature vector can be obtained by choosing the pixels in each level of the image [17].

3 Non-biased LSSVC Model with Multi-scale Kernel

3.1 Non-biased LSSVC Model

To obtain better classification performance, the structural risk form of LSSVC is modified by introducing an item of $\frac{b^2}{2\lambda^2}$ ($\lambda > 0$) into the objective function, then a non-biased LSSVC (NBLSSVC) is obtained. The objective function and the corresponding restrictions are shown as (1)

$$\begin{aligned} \min \quad & \tfrac{1}{2}\mathbf{w}^{\mathrm{T}}\mathbf{w} + \tfrac{b^2}{2\lambda^2} + \tfrac{1}{2}C\sum_{i=1}^{l}\xi_i^2 \\ \text{s.t.} \quad & y_i\left[\mathbf{w}^{\mathrm{T}}\varphi(\mathbf{x}_i) + b\right] = 1 - \xi_i,\ i = 1, 2, \ldots, l. \end{aligned} \tag{1}$$

Then set $\mathbf{w}' = [\mathbf{w}, b/\lambda]$, formula (1) can be transformed as

$$\min \quad \tfrac{1}{2}\mathbf{w}'^{\mathrm{T}}\mathbf{w}' + \tfrac{1}{2}C\sum_{i=1}^{l}\xi_i^2$$

$$\text{s.t.} \quad y_i\mathbf{w}'^{\mathrm{T}}[\varphi(\mathbf{x}_i);\lambda] = 1 - \xi_i, \ i = 1,2,\ldots,l. \tag{2}$$

On this basis, the restricted optimization can be transformed to a non-restricted one, the Lagrangian function can be derived as

$$L = \frac{1}{2}\mathbf{w}'^{\mathrm{T}}\mathbf{w}' + \frac{1}{2}C\sum_{i=1}^{l}\xi^2 - \sum_{i=1}^{l}\alpha_i\left[y_i\mathbf{w}'^{\mathrm{T}}[\varphi(\mathbf{x}_i);\lambda] + \xi_i - 1\right]. \tag{3}$$

and the differential coefficients of $\mathbf{w}'$, ξ_i, α_i can be expressed as (4)

$$\begin{aligned}
\frac{\partial L}{\partial \mathbf{w}'} = 0 &\quad\rightarrow\quad \mathbf{w}' = \sum_{i=1}^{l}\alpha_i y_i [\varphi(\mathbf{x}_i);\lambda]\\
\frac{\partial L}{\partial \xi_i} = 0 &\quad\rightarrow\quad \alpha_i = C\xi_i\\
\frac{\partial L}{\partial \alpha_i} = 0 &\quad\rightarrow\quad y_i\mathbf{w}'^{\mathrm{T}}[\varphi(\mathbf{x}_i);\lambda] = 1 - \xi_i
\end{aligned} \tag{4}$$

From Eq. (4), it can be found that the equation can be transformed with a matrix form after eliminating $\mathbf{w}'$ and ξ_i as (5),

$$(\mathbf{K}' + \lambda^2\mathbf{E} + C^{-1}\mathbf{I})\alpha = \mathbf{Y}, \tag{5}$$

where $\mathbf{E}$ is a $l\times l$ matrix with all elements are 1, $\mathbf{I}$ is a $l\times l$ identity matrix, $\mathbf{K}_{i,j} = (\varphi(\mathbf{x}_i)\cdot\varphi(\mathbf{x}_j)) = k(\mathbf{x}_i,\mathbf{x}_j)$ is the kernel function, and $\mathbf{Y} = (y_1,y_2,\ldots,y_l)^{\mathrm{T}}$, $\alpha = (\alpha_1,\alpha_2,\ldots,\alpha_l)^{\mathrm{T}}$. So,

Under the KKT condition, Ultimately the decision function of the non-biased LSSVC can be derived as

$$f(\mathbf{x}) = \text{sgn}\left[\sum_{i=1}^{l}\alpha_i y_i\left(k(\mathbf{x},\mathbf{x}_i) + \lambda^2\right)\right]. \tag{6}$$

If the Eq. (5) is simplified as $\mathbf{H}\alpha = \mathbf{Y}$. Its easy to prove that $\mathbf{H}$ is a symmetric positive definite matrix, as a result, matrix $\mathbf{H}$ can be transformed by Cholesky decomposition. Suppose matrix $\mathbf{H}$ is factorized as $\mathbf{H} = \mathbf{U}^{\mathrm{T}}\mathbf{U}$ where $\mathbf{U}$ is an upper triangular matrix, then $\mathbf{U}$ can be calculated as the formulas (6)

$$\begin{aligned}
u_{ii} &= \left(h_{ii} - \sum_{k=1}^{i-1}u_{ki}^2\right)^{1/2}, \quad i = k+1, k+2,\ldots,l\\
u_{ij} &= \left(h_{ij} - \sum_{k=1}^{i-1}u_{ki}u_{kj}\right)\bigg/ u_{ii}, \quad j > i
\end{aligned} \tag{7}$$

Ultimately, the Lagrange coefficient vector α of non-biased LSSVC model may be obtained as (8)

$$
\begin{aligned}
p_i &= \left(y_i - \sum_{k=1}^{i-1} u_{ki} p_k \right) \bigg/ u_{ii}, \quad i = k+1, k+2, \ldots, l \\
\alpha_i &= \left(p_i - \sum_{k=i+1}^{n} u_{ik} x_k \right) \bigg/ u_{ii}
\end{aligned}
\tag{8}
$$

where α_i is the ith element of α.

3.2   Non-biased Multi-scale Kernel LSSVC

The foundation of multi-scale kernel method is seeking for a set of kernel functions owning the multi-scale representation capability. For kernel functions being widely used, the Gaussian radial basis function (RBF) is the most popular one,

$$
k(\mathbf{x}, \mathbf{z}) = \exp\left(-\frac{\|\mathbf{x} - \mathbf{z}\|^2}{2\sigma^2} \right).
\tag{9}
$$

it is also a typical kernel which can be easily multi-scaled as (10)

$$
k\left(\frac{\|\mathbf{x} - \mathbf{z}\|^2}{2\sigma_1^2} \right), \ldots, k\left(\frac{\|\mathbf{x} - \mathbf{z}\|^2}{2\sigma_m^2} \right).
\tag{10}
$$

where $\sigma_1 < \ldots < \sigma_m$. From (10), we can find when σ is small, the LSSVC using the RBF kernel can fit the features which have drastic variability, and when σ is large, the classifier can well classify the features with mild variability. By this way, the multi-scale kernels may bring better generalization. On practical implemented, the values of σ can be determined as

$$
\sigma_i = 2^i \sigma, \quad i = 0, 1, 2, \ldots.
\tag{11}
$$

For target recognition application, the decision function then can be deduced as

$$
f(\mathbf{x}) = \text{sgn}\left[\sum_{i=1}^{l} \alpha_i y_i \langle \Phi(\mathbf{x}), \Phi(\mathbf{x}_i) \rangle + b \right].
\tag{12}
$$

And for the typical multi-scale kernel learning method with the convex combination of kernels, the decision function is

$$
f(\mathbf{x}) = \text{sgn}\left[\sum_{j=1}^{m} \mu_j \sum_{i=1}^{l} \alpha_i y_i \langle \Phi_j(\mathbf{x}), \Phi_j(\mathbf{x}_i) \rangle + b \right].
\tag{13}
$$

By introducing the kernel functions and the multiple kernel coefficients, the function is transformed as

$$
f(\mathbf{x}) = \text{sgn}\left[\sum_{j=1}^{m} \mu_j \sum_{i=1}^{l} \alpha_i y_i k_j(\mathbf{x}, \mathbf{x}_i) + b \right].
\tag{14}
$$

By introducing the kernel functions and the multiple kernel coefficients, we can Finally get the non-biased multi-scale kernel LSSVC as

$$f(\mathbf{x}) = \text{sgn} \left[\sum_{j=1}^{m} \mu_j \sum_{i=1}^{l} \alpha_i y_i (k_j(\mathbf{x}, \mathbf{x}_i) + \lambda^2) \right]. \tag{15}$$

4   Fast Online Learning of Multi-scale Kernel Machine

To track the dynamic characteristics of the non-biased LSSVC, the online learning algorithm of the multi-scale kernel machine should be designed, following this idea, a sliding time window model of the online algorithm is introduced in this paper.

4.1   Sample Increasement

From the above-mentioned analysis, the kernel function matrix $\mathbf{K}(t)$ at time t is a $l \times l$ matrix which can be expressed as

$$\mathbf{K}(t) = \begin{bmatrix} k(\mathbf{x}_{t-l+1}, \mathbf{x}_{t-l+1}) & \cdots & k(\mathbf{x}_{t-l+1}, \mathbf{x}_t) \\ \vdots & \ddots & \vdots \\ k(\mathbf{x}_t, \mathbf{x}_{t-l+1}) & \cdots & k(\mathbf{x}_t, \mathbf{x}_t) \end{bmatrix}, \tag{16}$$

correspondingly

$$\mathbf{H}(t) = \begin{bmatrix} k(\mathbf{x}_{t-l+1}, \mathbf{x}_{t-l+1}) + \lambda^2 + C^{-1} & \cdots & k(\mathbf{x}_{t-l+1}, \mathbf{x}_t) + \lambda^2 \\ \vdots & \ddots & \vdots \\ k(\mathbf{x}_t, \mathbf{x}_{t-l+1}) + \lambda^2 & \cdots & k(\mathbf{x}_t, \mathbf{x}_t) + \lambda^2 + C^{-1} \end{bmatrix}, \tag{17}$$

Through the Cholesky decomposition, the matrix can be transformed as $\mathbf{H}(t) = \mathbf{U}(t)^{\mathrm{T}} \mathbf{U}(t)$, so $\mathbf{U}(t)$ can be obtained. Now suppose a new sample $(\mathbf{x}_{t+1}, y_{t+1})$ is added to the sliding window at time $t + 1$, the new form of $\mathbf{H}(t)$ can be represented as

$$\mathbf{H}(t + 1) = \begin{bmatrix} \mathbf{H}(t) & \mathbf{V}(t + 1) \\ \mathbf{V}(t + 1)^{\mathrm{T}} & v(t + 1) \end{bmatrix} \in \mathbb{R}^{(l+1) \times (l+1)}, \tag{18}$$

where $v(t + 1) = y_{t+1} y_{t+1} \left(k(\mathbf{x}_{t+1}, \mathbf{x}_{t+1}) + \lambda^2 \right) + C^{-1}$, $\mathbf{V}(t + 1) = \big[y_{t+1} y_{t-l+1}$ $\left(k(\mathbf{x}_{t+1}, \mathbf{x}_{t-l+1}) + \lambda^2 \right), \dots, y_{t+1} y_t \left(k(\mathbf{x}_{t+1}, \mathbf{x}_t) + \lambda^2 \right) \big]^{\mathrm{T}}$. Then the task is to seek for the $\mathbf{U}(t + 1)$ satisfying $\mathbf{H}(t + 1) = \mathbf{U}(t + 1)^{\mathrm{T}} \mathbf{U}(t + 1)$.

Obviously, $\mathbf{H}(t+1)$ is also a symmetrical positive definite matrix, by Cholesky decomposition in the same way, the result can be gained as

$$\mathbf{U}(t+1) = \begin{bmatrix} \mathbf{U}(t) & \mathbf{W}(t+1) \\ \mathbf{0}^{\mathrm{T}} & w(t+1) \end{bmatrix}, \tag{19}$$

where $\mathbf{W}(t+1)$ is a l-dimensional row vector and $w(t+1)$ is a real number, which can be calculated as

$$\mathbf{W}_i(t+1) = \left(\mathbf{H}_{i,l+1}(t+1) - \sum_{k=1}^{i-1} \mathbf{U}_{k,i}(t)\mathbf{U}_{k,l+1}(t) \right) \Big/ \mathbf{U}_{i,i}, \tag{20}$$

$$\mathbf{w}(t+1) = \left(\mathbf{H}_{l+1,l+1}(t+1) - \sum_{k=1}^{l} \mathbf{U}_{k,l+1}^2(t+1) \right)^{1/2}. \tag{21}$$

From (19), we can find that the decomposition result $\mathbf{U}(t)$ of $\mathbf{H}(t)$ at time t can be used for the decomposition of $\mathbf{H}(t+1)$ when a new sample is added at time $t+1$.

4.2   Sample Elimination

Suppose the kernel matrix is $\mathbf{H}(t+1)$ at time $t+1$, and the decomposition result is $\mathbf{U}(t+1)$. Then well eliminate the earliest sample from the training set. Suppose the new matrix is $\hat{\mathbf{H}}(t+1)$, its obvious that $\hat{\mathbf{H}}(t+1)$ is also a symmetrical positive definite matrix which can be transformed by Cholesky decomposition. Set the decomposition result is $\hat{\mathbf{H}}(t+1) = \hat{\mathbf{R}}^{\mathrm{T}}(t+1)\hat{\mathbf{R}}(t+1)$, then the matrixes with different blocks can be renewed as

$$\mathbf{H}(t+1) = \begin{bmatrix} \hat{v}(t-l+1) & \hat{\mathbf{V}}^{\mathrm{T}}(t+1) \\ \hat{\mathbf{V}}(t+1) & \hat{\mathbf{H}}(t+1) \end{bmatrix}, \tag{22}$$

$$\mathbf{U}(t+1) = \begin{bmatrix} \hat{w}(t-l+1) & \hat{\mathbf{W}}^{\mathrm{T}}(t+1) \\ \mathbf{0} & \hat{\mathbf{U}}(t+1) \end{bmatrix}. \tag{23}$$

From $\mathbf{H}(t+1) = \mathbf{U}(t+1)^{\mathrm{T}}\mathbf{U}(t+1)$, we can get

$$\hat{v}(t-l+1) = \hat{w}^2(t-l+1), \tag{24}$$

$$\hat{\mathbf{V}}(t+1) = \hat{w}(t-l+1)\hat{\mathbf{W}}^{\mathrm{T}}(t+1), \tag{25}$$

$$\hat{\mathbf{H}}(t+1) = \hat{\mathbf{U}}^{\mathrm{T}}(t+1)\hat{\mathbf{U}}(t+1) + \hat{\mathbf{W}}(t+1)\hat{\mathbf{W}}^{\mathrm{T}}(t+1). \tag{26}$$

In Eq. (26), $\hat{\mathbf{U}}(t+1) \in \mathbb{R}^{l \times l}$ and $\hat{\mathbf{W}}^{\mathrm{T}}(t+1) \in \mathbb{R}^l$ are known, $\hat{\mathbf{R}}(t+1)$ can be derived from

$$\mathbf{J}(l)\dots\mathbf{J}(1)\left[\hat{\mathbf{W}}(t+1), \hat{\mathbf{U}}^{\mathrm{T}}(t+1) \right]^{\mathrm{T}} = \left[\mathbf{0}, \hat{\mathbf{R}}^{\mathrm{T}}(t+1) \right], \tag{27}$$

where $\mathbf{J}(i) \in \mathbb{R}^{(l+1)\times(l+1)}$ is defined as

$$\mathbf{J}_{m,n}(i) = \begin{cases} 1 & m = n \neq 0, \ i \\ \sin\theta_i & m = n = 0, \ i \\ -\cos\theta_i & m = 0, \ n = i \\ \cos\theta_i & m = i, \ n = 0 \\ 0 & \text{else} \end{cases} \tag{28}$$

The matrix $\hat{\mathbf{R}}(t+1)$ obtained from (27) satisfies with $\hat{\mathbf{H}}(t+1) = \hat{\mathbf{R}}^{\mathrm{T}}(t+1)\hat{\mathbf{R}}(t+1)$, and the algorithm complexity is $\mathbf{O}(l^2)$. But if we perform the Cholesky decomposition for $\hat{\mathbf{H}}(t+1)$ again, the time complexity is $\mathbf{O}(l^3)$. So, our method can greatly improve the online training speed.

5   Experiments and Results Analysis

5.1   SAR Target Recognition Experiments

The MSTAR public data sets was provided by DARPA (Defense Advanced Research Project Agency)/AFRL (Air Force Research Laboratory). The MSTAR data is a standard dataset in the SAR ATR community, allowing researchers to fairly test and compare their ATR algorithms. The MSTAR data consisted of 128×128 pixel chips, which are 1 foot resolution, X-band, three types of ground military vehicles, BMP2, BTR70 and T72. Each chip has SAR images separated by $1°$ azimuth increments within an angular coverage between $0°$ to $360°$. All the chips are taken at depression angles of $17°$ and $15°$. Figure 1 shows several chips about the three types of targets.

Considering the MSTAR dataset, the number of the training samples is 1622 and the test sample is 1365. On feature extraction, the 4-level local multi-scale feature extraction is our main method, the feature dimension is 161. To evaluate the performance, another feature extraction method named the combined wavelet moment and entropy feature is introduced. The classifiers are the common LSSVC, the NBLSSVC, the multi-scale kernel LSSVC (MSK-LSSVC) and the multi-scale kernel NBLSSVC (MSK-NBLSSVC) with a 4 scale RBF kernels. The scale parameter of Gaussian kernels is selected from $\{0.01, 0.1, 0.5, 1\}$, the punishment parameter C is from $\{10, 100, 200, 1000, 2000\}$, we still do a cross validation for every test. The test results are the best values with different parameter selection. The parameter $\lambda = 1$ in all tests. After the features of the testing set being extracted, the feature vectors are sent to the classifier and the recognition precision is outputted. The classification result is shown in Table 1.

From the experimental results, we can see that the local multi-scale resolution feature extraction and the multi-scale kernel combined method gives a higher classification precision of 98.75% with a 161 dimension using both the LSSVC and the NBLSSVC models.

To further analyze the adaptability and robustness of the features and the classifier, the speckle with mean 0 and variance 0.04 is added to the MSTAR testing set, the final recognition results are shown in Table 2.

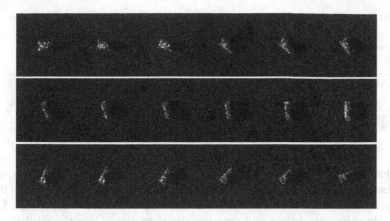

Fig. 1. Sample chips of BMP2, BTR70 and T72 targets in MSTAR dataset depression angles.

From the result in Table 2, it can be concluded that the 4-level local multi-scale feature and the 4-scale RBF kernel NBLSSVC method has higher classification precision at different speckle adding degrees than the other methods, it also shows that the 4-level local multi-resolution feature and the non-biased model have better adaptability and robustness.

Table 1. MSTAR dataset recognition result using different features and classifiers

No.	Features	Dimension	Classifier	Recognition precision
1	Wavelet moment and entropy	31	LSSVC	96.95%
2	PCA	233	LSSVC	96.47%
3	Local multi-scale feature	161	LSSVC	97.44%
4	Local multi-scale feature	161	MSK-LSSVC	98.75%
5	Local multi-scale feature	161	MSK-NBLSSVC	98.75%

5.2   Time Tests of Online Learning

The online learning test is mainly between the Cholesky decomposition method and the common matrix inversion method. The online learning process is under the following assumptions: the sliding windows length is set as 100, 200, 1600 respectively, which also represents the dimension of the kernel matrix. The training samples of BMP2, T72 and BTR70 are randomly extracted from the training set with the proportion of 40%, 40% and 20% respectively. Then the new training sample (randomly extracted from the rest training samples) is added in the sliding window one by one, meanwhile, the oldest sample in the beginning of the window is eliminated. Under every step of the window sliding, a classifier is obtained by training, then the classifier is applied to the testing set, the feature

Table 2. SAR target recognition result at different speckle adding degree

Speckle adding degree (SAD)	Recognition precision				
	No. 1	No. 2	No. 3	No. 4	No. 5
SAD = 1	91.43%	85.93%	92.31%	93.41%	94.36%
SAD = 2	80.81%	77.95%	85.79%	87.62%	87.99%
SAD = 3	72.53%	69.38%	74.14%	76.48%	77.36%

extraction methods are the 4-level local multi-resolution decomposition with a 161 dimension and the wavelet moment and entropy combined feature with 31 dimension. After feature extraction with local multi-scale decomposition for all the sample chips, we design and training the classifier. Then the multiple-class classification problem is transformed into the two-class problem by One VS One method. The online learning steps are all 10, at each step, it means the training time is the average value of 10 steps.

The test result of the average time comparison between the common online LSSVC with matrix inversion and the online NBLSSVC with Cholesky decomposition is shown in Fig. 2. The feature dimensions are 31 and 161 respectively. From the result, it can be concluded that with the increase of the sliding window length, the average time of NBLSSVC increases more slowly than the common LSSVC, and larger the window length is, more obvious the difference between two classifiers is. It confirms that the Cholesky decomposition can greatly improve the online learning efficiency than the common method.

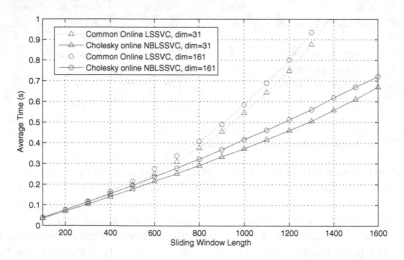

Fig. 2. Average time tests between the common online LSSVC with matrix inversion and the Cholesky decomposition NBLSSVC.

6 Conclusions

Great obstacles are brought to the usability and recognition efficiency of SAR ATR field as the strong speckle and low image resolution, especially in the high real-time application cases. By introducing a visual attention based multi-scale feature extraction method and the non-biased multi-scale kernel LSSVC, an effective classification algorithm based on the SAR image target recognition is proposed. The multi-scale feature extraction and the multi-scale classifier combined method can bring higher classifier precision, better adaptability and robustness on speckle. Meanwhile, through using the Cholesky decomposition for the kernel matrix, a fast online learning algorithm is obtained. The experiments testify that the presented method has better online learning performance than the common methods.

Acknowledgments. This work was jointly supported by the National Natural Science Foundation for Young Scientists of China (Grant No: 61202332, 61403397), China Postdoctoral Science Foundation (Grant No: 2012M521905) and Natural Science Basic Research Plan in Shaanxi Province of China (Grant No: 2015JM6313).

References

1. EI-Darymli, K., Gill, E.W., Mcguire, P., Power, D., Moloney, C.: Automatic target recognition in synthetic aperture radar imagery: a state-of-the art review. IEEE Access **4**, 6014–6058 (2016)
2. Pei, J.F., Huang, Y.L., Huo, W.B., et al.: SAR automatic target recognition based on multiview deeplearning framework. IEEE Trans. Geosci. Remote Sens. **56**(4), 2196–2210 (2018)
3. Chen, S., Wang, H., Xu, F., Jin, Y.Q.: Target classification using the deep convolutional networks for SAR images. IEEE Trans. Geosci. Remote Sens. **54**(8), 4806–4817 (2016)
4. Morgan, D.A.E.: Deep convolutional neural networks for ATR from SAR imagery. Algorithms Synth. Apert. Radar Imag. XXII **9475**, 94750F (2015)
5. Suykens, J.A.K., Gestel, T.V., Moor, B.D., Vandewalle, J.: Least Squares Support Vector Machines. World Scientific, Singapore (2002)
6. Gönen, M., Alpaydin, E.: Multiple kernel learning algorithms. J. Mach. Learn. Res. **12**(2), 2211–2268 (2011)
7. Wang, H.Q., Sun, F.C., Cai, Y.N., Chen, N., Ding, L.G.: On multiple kernel learning methods. Acta Automatica Sinica **36**(8), 1037–1050 (2010)
8. Wang, Y.Q., Liu, X.W., Dou, Y., Lv, Q., Lu, Y.: Multiple kernel learning with hybrid kernel alignment maximization. Pattern Recogn. **70**, 104–111 (2017)
9. Saeid, N., Saeid, H., Abdolreza, S.: Similarity-based multiple kernel learning algorithms for classification of remotely sensed images. IEEE J. Sel. Top. Appl. Earth Obs. Remote Sens. **10**(5), 2012–2021 (2017)
10. Fan, Q., Wang, Z., Zha, H.Y., Gao, D.Q.: MREKLM: a fast multiple empirical kernel learning machine. Pattern Recogn. **61**, 197–209 (2017)
11. Lin, F., Wang, J., Zhang, N.A., Xiahou, J.B., McDonald, N.: Multi-kernel learning for multivariate performance measures optimization. Neural Comput. Appl. **28**, 2075–2087 (2017)

12. Wang, H.Q., Sun, F.C., Cai, Y.N., Zhao, Z.T.: Online chaotic time series prediction using unbiased composite kernel machine via Cholesky factorization. Soft Comput. **14**(9), 931–944 (2010)
13. Bao, J., Chen, Y.Y., Yu, L., Chen, C.W.: A multi-scale kernel learning method and its application in image classification. Neurocomputing **257**, 16–23 (2017)
14. Chen, Q., Ren, X.M.: Chaos modeling and real-time online prediction of permanent magnet synchronous motor based on multiple kernel least squares support vector machine. Acta Phys. Sinica **59**(4), 2310 (2010)
15. Steven, C.H., Jin, R., Zhao, P.L., Yang, T.B.: Online multiple kernel classification. Mach. Learn. **90**(2), 289–316 (2013)
16. Wang, H.Q., Cai, Y.N., Fu, G.Y., Wang, S.C.: Robust automatic target recognition algorithm for large-scene SAR images and its adaptability analysis on speckle. Sci. Program. **2016**, 11 (2016). 3801053
17. Wang, H., Cai, Y., Fu, G., Wu, M.: Visual-cognition-driven SAR multiple targets robust feature extraction, recognition and tracking. In: Sun, F., Liu, H., Hu, D. (eds.) ICCSIP 2016. CCIS, vol. 710, pp. 100–112. Springer, Singapore (2017). https://doi.org/10.1007/978-981-10-5230-9_11

Image Artistic Style Transfer Based on Color Distribution Preprocessing

Yinshu Zhang[1], Jiayi Chen[2], Xiangyu Si[1], Zhiqiang Tian[1(✉)], and Xuguang Lan[2]

[1] School of Software Engineering, Xi'an Jiaotong University,
Xi'an 710049, Shaanxi, China
zhiqiangtian@xjtu.edu.cn

[2] Institute of Artificial Intelligence and Robotics, Xi'an Jiaotong University,
Xi'an 710049, Shaanxi, China

Abstract. Style transfer is an increasingly popular field that can capture the styles of a particular artwork and use them to synthesize a new image with specific content. Previous NST algorithms have the limitation to transfer styles to correct regions in the output image. Therefore, some regions in the output image have deformed structures of the source image. In this paper, we propose a color preprocessing-based neural style transfer method to overcome the limitation. To reduce impacts caused by color differences between source image and style, we propose three models based on a color iterative distribution transform algorithm (IDT). The first one is named original color-preprocessed (OCp) model, which uses IDT to transform the color probability density function (PDF) of source image into that of style image. The second one is named exposure-corrected original color-preprocessed (EC-OCp) model, which adds an automatic detail-enhanced exposure correction module before OCp model. When source image is underexposed, EC-OCp model can achieve better results than OCp model. The third one is style color-preprocessed (SCp) model. It uses IDT to transform the color PDF of style image into that of source image. The original structures are well protected in the output image. According to experiments, the proposed models are robust to the source images with more conditions. Therefore, they have more usage values than the original method.

Keywords: Neural style transfer · Color transfer · Iterative distribution transform

1 Introduction

Image style transfer is referred to the reconstruction of artistic style by computer automatically. The goal is to transfer the style of a classic art work to the daily photos. Therefore, the photos can retain the original content while presenting a unique artistic style. For a long time, the research on image style transfer mainly focuses on two issues:

1. It is hoped that the synthetic images have an artistic sense, that is, the more the output image looks like the real painting work, the better.

© Springer Nature Singapore Pte Ltd. 2019
F. Sun et al. (Eds.): ICCSIP 2018, CCIS 1005, pp. 155–164, 2019.
https://doi.org/10.1007/978-981-13-7983-3_14

2. It is hoped that the algorithm has a wide application.

Traditional style transfer or texture transfer methods are mostly strategy-based and parameterless. They protect the content and structure of the source image in various ways. Efros and Freemand [1] use various priori images extracted from the source image, including the intensity map of the source image, the intensity map of the blurred source image, and the gradient statistics of each image block of the source image, etc., to limit the selection and placement of texture image blocks, so as to protect the content and spatial structure of the source image. Ashikhmin et al. [2] regard artistic style as high-frequency information of images, and retain the low-frequency information of source images at the moment of style transfer. Later, Lee et al. [3] improve the transfer effect of this method by using the object edge direction information of the source image. Hertzmann et al. [4] propose an image analogies framework based on the actual scene of the style image, which can also be applied in the artistic style transfer.

Since the traditional style transfer method generally calculates the low-level features of pixels and image blocks and replaces the image blocks in the output image with corresponding texture image blocks, the output image has little artistic sense on the whole.

In recent years, the development of computer vision, deep learning theory and computer graphics processing (GPU) has provided new ideas for style transfer problems. Gatys et al. [5] first make use of the strong feature extraction ability of convolutional neural network to realize the extraction and use of complex art styles. From then, the Neural Style Transfer (NST) genre has been opened up. Later, Li et al. [6] give a theoretical explanation for the Gram matrix which is discovered accidentally in this method. They prove that the essence of the style loss function based on the Gram method is the maximum average difference between the data in two feature layers. Later, Risser et al. [7] consider that the high-level art style can also be measured by the mean and variance of the feature layer. In addition to the loss function of the Gayts method, a "deep histogram loss" is added. In the above three works, the way to extract the high-level art style from the deep feature layer of the style image affects the synthesis effect to some extent.

The method based on Gram global statistics can make the synthesis target present a high-level artistic style, but cannot distinguish various style textures, leading to unreasonable spatial structure of the image. Li et al. [8] propose an algorithm based on the Markov Random Field, which directly use the deep feature block of style image to replace Gram matrix as the high-level art style. However, if the style image does not have the similar structure required by the source image, or the object's category is different, the algorithm will generate an error. Liao et al. [9] propose a deep image analogy framework. The idea is that the image classification ability of VGG network makes the real photo and art image have comparability in the deep convolutional layer. However, it can only be used for style transfer between the same objects.

The purpose of this paper is to improve the existing neural style transfer frame, so that the spatial structure of the output image is more reasonable, and the frame can be applied to a variety of special environments.

The main contributions of this paper are listed as follows:

1. An OCp style transfer model has been proposed to improve the synthesis effect of original style transfer framework, when the color dynamic ranges between source image and artwork are quite different.
2. We propose an EC-OCp model to ensure the transfer quality for the case of exposure errors.
3. A SCp style transfer model is proposed to protect the color style of source image while improving the spatial rationality of the output image.

2   Method

This paper proposes a kind of style transfer method based on color probability distribution preprocessing from the perspective of the quality and matching degree of the source image itself. Firstly, we construct an Original Color-preprocessed Neural Style Transfer (OCp NST) model for the spatial irrationality caused by the difference in color dynamic range between source image and artwork. Then, an Exposure-corrected and Original Color-preprocessed Neural Style Transfer (EC-OCp NST) model is proposed to further improve the synthesis effect of OCp model, aiming at a special application of "direct artistic stylization of photos taken by mobile terminals". Finally, we propose a Style Color-preprocessed Neural Style Transfer (SCp NST) model based on color distribution transformation, which realizes a stylized requirement for retaining the color of the source image.

2.1   Style Color-Preprocessed Neural Style Transfer

When the color dynamic range of the source image is much smaller than that of the style image, the artistic style texture tends to be misplaced. Our solution is to transfer the color style of the style image to the source image before the neural style transfer, and this method is called the Original Color-preprocessed Neural Style Transfer (OCp NST). The pre-transfer of color can enhance the color dynamic range of source image. At the same time, the object boundaries in the source image will be more obvious and the content loss function will have a larger activation value at the edge of the object. Figure 1 shows our OCp style transfer model structure.

We use the Iterative Distribution Transform (IDT) [10], a nonlinear n-dimensional probabilistic distribution transform algorithm, to realize the source color pre-transfer. The IDT algorithm can change the color of all pixels in source image into the color in style image, and also can protect the color continuity in the object.

The pre-transfer module in our method can be formulated as:

$$I'_c \leftarrow t_{SC}(I_c) \tag{1}$$

where I'_c is the source image X'_c that will be input to the original style transfer framework, I_c is the source image of our OCp model and $t_{SC}(\cdot)$ is the mapping function solved by transforming the multidimensional probability distribution I_c into the multidimensional probability distribution I_s of the style image.

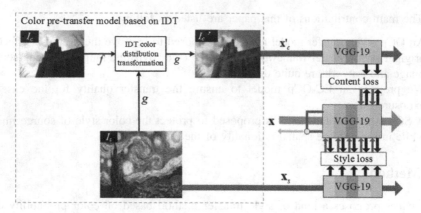

Fig. 1. OCp Neural Style Transfer model based on color preprocessing

2.2 Exposure-Corrected and Original Color-Preprocessed Neural Style Transfer

This section focuses on the photo beautification needs of mobile phone users in outdoor photography. When the photo (the image to be stylized) is taken in the open air where the light is very strong, exposure error may occur. The wrong exposure usually has the problem that the edge gradient of the object in the backlight area is smaller than normal. At the same time, the color saturation is low so that the color dynamic range is small (Fig. 2).

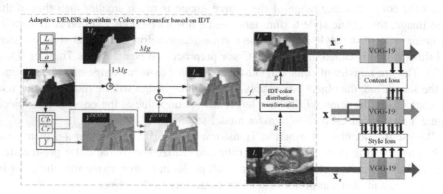

Fig. 2. EC-OCp Neural Style Transfer model for photos taken outdoors

In this case, although the OCp model proposed in the last section can get output with a more reasonable spatial structure, the local stereoscopic impression of the object is still not good. Therefore, we propose an Exposure-corrected and Original Color-preprocessed Neural Style Transfer (EC-OCp NST) which adds the adaptive DEMSR exposure correction algorithm before the OCp model.

Compared with the existing curve correction, global optimization and exposure correction algorithms, the self-adaptive DEMSR exposure correction algorithm proposed in this paper is faster and simpler, mainly including the following three steps:

First, adaptive modified region judgement is needed to judge whether to correct the exposure. The backlight area template detection method is used to realize it.

The next step is the detail-enhanced multi-scale retinex. We improve the traditional multi-scale Retinex (MSR) algorithm [11] to remove the "Halo" phenomenon and enhance edges and stereoscopic perception of the object in backlight region.

Once the backlight enhanced image is obtained, the non-backlit areas are removed. Then we fuse the backlight area of backlight enhanced image and the non-backlit area of source image to obtain a final exposure correction image I_{ec}.

The final exposure correction image is input into the OCp model to form the final EC-OCp model. At this point, the pre-transfer module formula of OCp becomes $I_c'' \leftarrow t_{SC}(I_{ec})$, that is, the source image input to VGG-19 network is X_c''.

2.3 Style Color-Preprocessed Neural Style Transfer

The model presented in this section implements a special style transfer requirement: instead of changing the color style of source image, only the texture and painting skills in the artwork are transferred. In order to protect the color style of the source image while maintaining stroke continuity, the Style Color-preprocessed Neural Style Transfer model (SCp NST) is proposed based on color pre-transfer of style image. Figure 3 shows our SCp style transfer model structure. Before starting the style transfer iteration, we first use the IDT color probability distribution transformation algorithm to transform the color distribution of artworks into the color distribution of photos. It is formulated as follows:

$$I_s' \leftarrow t_{CS}(I_s) \tag{2}$$

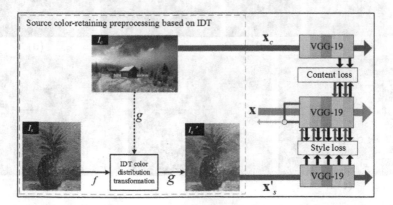

Fig. 3. SCp Neural Style Transfer model preserving the color style of source image

where I_s' is the input to the original style transfer framework, I_s is the style image and $t_{CS}(\cdot)$ is the mapping function transforming the color probability distribution I_s into the distribution I_c of the source image.

3   Experiments

3.1   Settings

The experimental environment of the proposed method is shown in Table 1. Our color preprocessing and IDT algorithm are implemented using Matlab. In all of the following experiments, we fixed the number of iterations for the algorithm of Gatys et al. 1000 times; the weight of the style loss function is 1000 times the weight of the content loss; other algorithms directly extract the results in their papers.

Table 1. The experimental environment.

Language	Deep learning tool	GPU	Operation system
Matlab	Theano	NVIDIA Tesla K40	CentOS 7

3.2   Results and Analysis

For each group of source images and style images, we controlled the number of iterations of all models to be the same, and compared the output of the proposed OCp, EC-OCp, SCp model with the output of the existing deep style transfer algorithm.

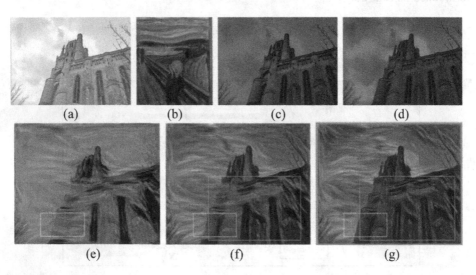

(a)   (b)   (c)   (d)

(e)   (f)   (g)

Fig. 4. The results of Gayts et al. algorithm and proposed OCp models using different color transfer algorithms. (a) the source image, (b) the style image, (c) I_c' using the Reinard's algorithm [12], (d) I_c' using IDT [10], (e) output of Gatys's algorithm [5], (f) output of OCp model using Reinard's algorithm [12], (g) output of OCp model using IDT [10], respectively. By comparing the three output, our OCp model based on IDT algorithm is more effective.

Since we are the first to propose an improved algorithm based on color preprocessing, we only compared with the algorithm of Gayts, etc. to prove the effectiveness of our algorithm.

Figure 4 shows the output of algorithm of Gayts et al. and OCp model using different color transfer algorithms when the color dynamic range of the source image is much smaller than that of the style image.

As can be seen from Fig. 4, the spatial rationality of the algorithm of Gayts et al. is very poor for the case where the color dynamic range of the source image is much smaller than that of the style image, and the color preprocessing can solve this problem well. In addition, the OCp model using the IDT color distribution transfer algorithm can protect the spatial structure of the source image more effectively and get more realistic result.

Figures 5 and 6 show the results of OCp, EC-OCp, SCp model and the existing algorithm when the source images are well exposed.

Figure 5 shows the results of each model when the source images are well exposed and have small color dynamic range. Figure 6 shows the results of each model when the source images are well exposed and have large color dynamic range. From (c), (d) and (e), our OCp and EC-OCp models have the same effect, which can better protect the content and spatial structure of the source image than the Gayts et al. algorithm. The SCp model protects the rationality of the original space from another perspective, which is far better than the algorithm of Gatys et al. as well. Therefore, the SCp model proposed in this paper enables the requirement of transferring textures but no colors from style image.

Fig. 5. The results of OCp, EC-OCp, SCp models have better spatial rationality when the source images are well exposed and have small color dynamic range. (a) the source image, (b) the style image, (c) output of Gatys's algorithm [5], (d) output of OCp model, (e) output of EC-OCp model, (f) output of SCp model, respectively.

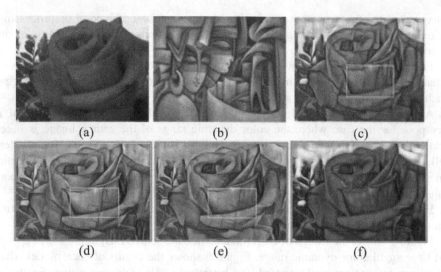

Fig. 6. (a) The source image, (b) the style image, (c) output of Gatys's algorithm [5], (d) output of OCp model, (e) output of EC-OCp model, (f) output of SCp model, respectively. When the source images are well exposed and have large color dynamic range, the results of OCp, EC-OCp, SCp models are more stereoscopic than Gayts et al. algorithm. Meanwhile, the results of SCp model retain the original color style.

Figures 7 and 8 show the results of OCp, EC-OCp, SCp models and the existing algorithm when the source images have exposure errors.

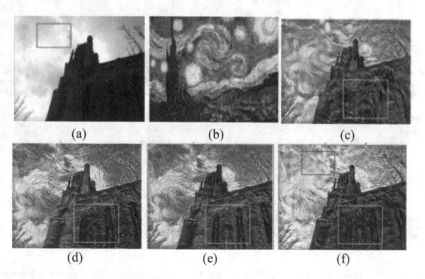

Fig. 7. (a) The source image, (b) the style image, (c) output of Gatys's algorithm [5], (d) output of OCp model, (e) output of EC-OCp model, (f) output of SCp model, respectively. The output of EC-OCp has the best spatial rationality when the source images have exposure errors.

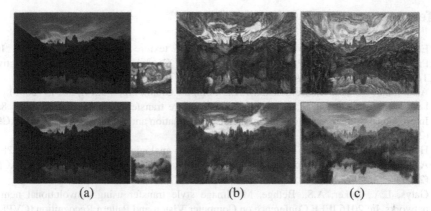

(a)   (b)   (c)

Fig. 8. (a) The source image (left), the style image (right), (b) output of Gatys's algorithm [5], (c) output of EC-OCp model, respectively. The output of EC-OCp model has the best spatial rationality when the source images have exposure errors.

The OCp model protects the content and spatial structure of the source image much better than the algorithm of Gatys. The EC-OCp model is more realistic than the OCp model in the spatial structure. The SCp model can also obtain output with correct structure, and the protection of the content and spatial structure of the source image is much better than the algorithm of Gayts et al.

4   Conclusion

Considering the influence of source image quality and matching degree on style transfer, we propose three preprocessing models to cater to a variety of application scenarios. It has been proved that the models have successfully improved the artistic sense and spatial rationality of the synthetic results.

Future work can also be deepened from the following aspects. A variety of objective evaluation methods for evaluating the output of style transfer algorithms need to be proposed. Computer art creation is a complex process that integrates computer vision, cognitive science and graphics. The research on computer autonomous artistic creation is not only a basic applied research on images and graphics, but also a basic research of cognitive science that reflect the principle of human understanding and creating vision. In the future work, we can read this basic research in many aspects to provide some ideas for the problem of style transfer.

Acknowledgement. This work was supported in part by the NSFC No. 91748208, No. 61876148, No. 61573268, and funded by China Post-doctoral Science Foundation of NO. 2018M631164 and the Fundamental Research Funds for the Central Universities of No. XJJ2018254.

References

1. Efros, A.A., Freeman, W.T.: Image quilting for texture synthesis and transfer. In: Proceedings of the 28th Annual Conference on Computer Graphics and Interactive Techniques, pp. 341–346. ACM (2001)
2. Ashikhmin, N.: Fast texture transfer. IEEE Comput. Graph. Appl. **23**(4), 38–43 (2003)
3. Lee, H., Seo, S., Ryoo, S., et al.: Directional texture transfer. In: Proceedings of the 8th International Symposium on Non-Photorealistic Animation and Rendering, pp. 43–48. ACM (2010)
4. Hertzmann, A., Jacobs, C.E., Oliver, N., et al.: Image analogies. In: Proceedings of the 28th Annual Conference on Computer Graphics and Interactive Techniques, pp. 327–340. ACM (2001)
5. Gatys, L.A., Ecker, A.S., Bethge, M.: Image style transfer using convolutional neural networks. In: 2016 IEEE Conference on Computer Vision and Pattern Recognition (CVPR), pp. 2414–2423. IEEE (2006)
6. Li, Y., Wang, N., Liu, J., et al.: Demystifying neural style transfer. In: Proceedings of the 26th International Joint Conference on Artificial Intelligence, pp. 2230–2236. AAAI Press (2017)
7. Wilmot, P., Risser, E., Barnes, C.: Stable and controllable neural texture synthesis and style transfer using histogram losses. arXiv preprint arXiv:1701.08893 (2017)
8. Li, C., Wand, M.: Combining markov random fields and convolutional neural networks for image synthesis. In: Proceedings of the IEEE Conference on Computer Vision and Pattern Recognition (CVPR), pp. 2479–2486 (2016)
9. Liao, J., Yao, Y., Yuan, L., et al.: Visual attribute transfer through deep image analogy. ACM Trans. Graph. (TOG) **36**(4), 120 (2017)
10. Pitié, F., Kokaram, A., Dahyot, R.: Towards automated colour grading. In: 2nd IEE European Conference on Visual Media Production, vol. 117 (2005)
11. Cho, S., Shrestha, B., Joo, H.J., Hong, B.: Improvement of retinex algorithm for backlight image efficiency. In: (Jong Hyuk) Park, J., Chao, H.C., Obaidat, M.S., Kim, J. (eds.) Computer Science and Convergence, vol. 114, pp. 579–587. Springer, Dordrecht (2012). https://doi.org/10.1007/978-94-007-2792-2_55
12. Reinhard, E., Adhikhmin, M., Gooch, B., et al.: Color transfer between images. IEEE Comput. Graph. Appl. **21**(5), 34–41 (2001)

Depthwise Separable Convolution Feature Learning for Ihomogeneous Rock Image Classification

Yueqin Zhu[1,2], Lin Bai[3,4,5(✉)], Weihang Peng[6], Xinyang Zhang[3,5], and Xiong Luo[7]

[1] Development and Research Center,
China Geological Survey, Beijing 100037, China
[2] Key Laboratory of Geological Information Technology,
Ministry of Natural Resources, Beijing 100037, China
[3] Geomathematics Key Laboratory of Sichuan Province,
Chengdu University of Technology, Chengdu 610059, China
bailin@mail.cdut.edu.cn
[4] College of Geophysics, Chengdu University of Technology,
Chengdu 610059, China
[5] College of Management Science,
Chengdu University of Technology, Chengdu 610059, China
[6] College of Network Security, Chengdu University of Technology,
Chengdu 610059, China
[7] School of Computer and Communication Engineering,
University of Science and Technology Beijing, Beijing 100083, China

Abstract. The issue of classifying rock images is one of most important problems in geological detection and analysis. In order to improve rock recognition performance, we use convolution neural network (CNN) based deep learning method to classify ihomogeneous rock images intelligently. We present the depthwise separable convolution method for rock image classification, which reduces the required parameters compared to normal convolution, and achieves the separation of channels and regions. In our experiments, there are 12 kinds of common rock image data collected by us. Generally, similar rocks such as limestone and dolomite are easy to be confused, which is the same as that of rock with naked eyes. Compared with the model Inception, the rock image classification accuracy can be improved 9% by using the depth separable convolution model Xception. Meanwhile, after analyzing feature maps of granite and slate generated by the proposed model, we can easily find that the color, mineral composition and structure of the rock image are extracted successfully.

Keywords: Deep learning · Rock image classification ·
Depthwise separable convolution

© Springer Nature Singapore Pte Ltd. 2019
F. Sun et al. (Eds.): ICCSIP 2018, CCIS 1005, pp. 165–176, 2019.
https://doi.org/10.1007/978-981-13-7983-3_15

1 Introduction

As a product of the earth's development and evolution, rock records the process of material cycling and evolution. It is an important research object in the field of geology, and it is also the carrier of ore deposits. One of the most important tasks in geological survey, engineering exploration and ore prospecting is rock identification [1]. However, due to the gap between professional knowledge and personal experience, some rocks can not be accurately classified. At the same time, there is a strong subjectivity in the determination of mineral content, such as plagioclase content of about 15%, resulting in classification uncertainty. Therefore, the automatic identification of rock based on computer can be convenient for field workers, fast and accurate classification. It is of great significance to study the automatic identification of rocks for quantitative analysis of rocks by computer and mathematical tools.

Rocks are named and classified according to mineral composition, content, and structure. Rock mineral assemblage, content, color, luster and other attributes information form some rock image specific visual features such as color, texture and shape. These features are the basis of computer automatic learning and image classification. There are some types of rock images in Fig. 1.

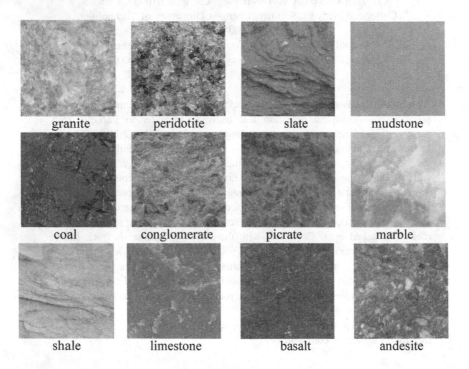

granite	peridotite	slate	mudstone
coal	conglomerate	picrate	marble
shale	limestone	basalt	andesite

Fig. 1. Rock image types

Rock texture in many cases is non-homogenous and strongly directional [2, 3]. Also mineral crystal morphology, granular size, particle spacing [4], and color of the texture may vary significantly in some rock texture types. Due to these properties, analysis and classification of rock textures is a difficult task. How to accurately extract rock information and identify rock is the challenge currently facing.

With the advent of the era of big data and the development of artificial intelligence technology, a large number of images of rock have been collected. According to this, it is possible to use computer technology such as depth learning to simulate the experience of geological workers in rock identification by naked eyes.

2 Related Work

As a typical example of image classification, rock images classification is a challenging and difficult job due to the heterogeneous properties of rocks [1]. However, with the advancement of computer vision technology, there are some achievements and distinguished results have been made in this field. The first results are about the major features to be considered and measured, such as color, morphology, texture and so on. The discussions around this issue started from single feature such as color and texture. There are some representative researches as Lepistö [3], Patel [2] and Kosi-Ulbl [4] who focus on the color feature extraction and classification. Instead, the texture of input image has been identified as an important feature for any type of rock image [5]. The second attempt about rock image attempts is the method which applied to analysis for the extracted features. The co-occurrence matrices method was first proposed in the literature, then Law' masks was performed well [6]. And then the nearest neighbor method was introduced and used by Lepistö et al. [7]. Shang and Barnes [8] proposed a reliability-based method to select features. Chatterjee [1] conducted feature selection based on the genetic algorithm, and then multiclass support vector machine (SVM) also was used to classify limestone. Bayesian analysis was adopted in grayscale by Sharif et al. [9]. The third attempts focus on the classifier or classification methods, which involve the probability vector (CPV) [3], KNN [7], probabilistic neural network [2], Bayesian [9], SVM [8–11]. Certainly, there are few new means have been verified in the last two years, for example the deep learning was introduced by Zhang [12, 13] and this papers which focus on the Convolutional neural networks. Convolutional neural networks have emerged as the master algorithm in computer vision in recent years, and developing recipes for designing them has been a subject of considerable attention. Common convolution neural networks include LeNet, VGG, Inception etc. Francois Chollet propose replacing Inception modules with depthwise separable convolutions in neural computer vision architectures, named Xception, which has a similar parameter count as Inception V3. On ImageNet, Xception shows marginally better results than Inception V3. Here we will try depthwise separable convolution feature learning for ihomogeneous rock image classification.

The convolutional neural network (CNN) was developed in the 1960s. Hubel et al. [14] found in the field of biology that visual information transmitted from the retina to the brain was stimulated by multiple levels of receptive fields. LeNet [15] is the first successful application of convolutional neural network. In CNN, the weights in the network are shared and the invariant function [16, 17] is used to sample the pool layer spatially or temporally. The larger network scale will greatly increase the amount of computation. In order to build smaller and lower models, some effective network architectures are proposed, such as deep separable convolution [18], stacked extreme learning machine [19, 20].

3   Methods

As shown in Fig. 2, a complete CNN consists of input layer, convolutional layers, pooling layers and fully connected layer. The input is rock image, and the output is the classification results. Here we have developed Inception_v3 and Xception model for rock image classification, with the framework as shown in Fig. 2.

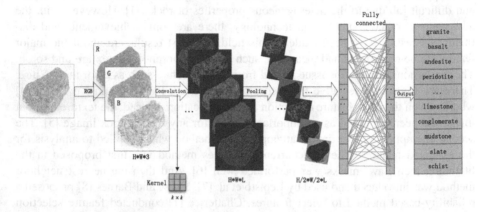

Fig. 2. Conventional convolution neural network model framework

3.1   Deep Separation Convolution Model

The steps for deep separation convolution of rock images are as follows.

(1) **Inputting the rock image.** The rock image is preprocessed (the image is processed into 399 × 399 RGB image by bilinear interpolation or randomly cropping) and input into the network.

(2) **Conducting depthwise separable convolution.** It is shown in Fig. 3. Each channel is kept separate in the depthwise separable convolutions.

Let G be the input of the convolution, size of $\mathbf{H} \times \mathbf{W} \times \mathbf{C}$, where $\mathbf{H}$ and $\mathbf{W}$ are the height and width of the feature map, respectively. And K is the kernel, size of $k \times k \times c_{out}$. In addition, s is a set of the range by sliding window, $\hat{G}_{i,j,\hat{s}}$ is the row i column j of the $\hat{s}$ th element of the set s, $K_{i,j}$ is the row i column j of K.

$$convolution(G, K) = \sum_s \sum_{i,j} \hat{G}_{i,j,\hat{s}} \cdot K_{i,j} \tag{1}$$

We assume that the input is a matrix $G_{\mathbf{H} \times \mathbf{W} \times \mathbf{C}}$. First, we expand $G_{\mathbf{H} \times \mathbf{W} \times \mathbf{C}}$ in the third dimension to get matrix $G^i_{\mathbf{H} \times \mathbf{W}}$ ($i = 1, 2, \ldots$ C). And we use C 3 × 3 kernel for

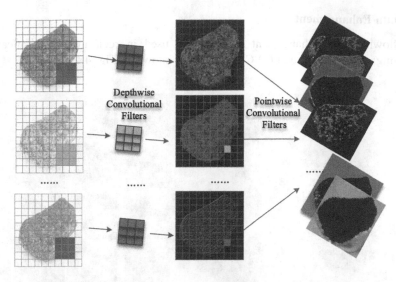

Fig. 3. Depthwise separable convolution structure

each matrix, then we get C matrixes by convolution independent. Then, we will concat all the matrixes, and we use C_out (the number of the output channel) $1 \times 1 \times C$ kernel in the convolution, finally we use ReLu to make the no nonlinear transformation and get the output of the depthwise separable convolution.

$$G_{H \times W \times C} = concat(G0, G1 \mid G(c \mid 1)) \qquad (2)$$

$$ReLu(x) = max(0, x) \qquad (3)$$

(3) **Pooling.** Reduce the complexity of the input matrix while preserving the main features as much as possible. It applies some linear or non-linear operations while the sliding window across the feature maps. These operations are usually the mean or the max of the window's area.

(4) **Designing a network.** As a network unit, several depth separation convolutions and pooling are performed. The unit is stacked continuously, and a fast channel is added between different units.

(5) **Mapping.** The fully connected layer maps the learned "distributed feature representation" to the role of the sample mark space. Converting the last fully connected layer to each class's probability by the softmax function.

(6) **Loss function.** The last layer uses softmax as the result of the classification output. The purpose is to normalize the output of the network to the probability of each category. Then use the cross entropy function as the loss function of the entire network.

3.2 Data Enhancement

The following data enhancement methods are used in rock image classification: (1) Scaling; (2) Rotating; and (3) Cropping. It is shown in Fig. 4.

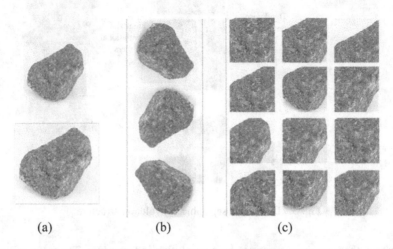

(a)   (b)   (c)

Fig. 4. Data enhancement method (a) Scaling. (b) Rotating. (c) Random cropping.

Firstly, scaling an image to a specified size is conducted through the use of bilinear interpolation. Here, bilinear interpolation is an interpolation algorithm in numerical analysis and it is widely used in the field of digital imaging proceesing.

Supposing we know the value of the functions $Q_{11} = (x_1, y_1)$, $Q_{12} = (x_1, y_2)$, $Q_{21} = (x_2, y_1)$, $Q_{22} = (x_2, y_2)$, we get the formula as follows.

$$f(R_1) \approx \frac{x_2 - x}{x_2 - x_1} f(Q_{11}) + \frac{x - x_1}{x_2 - x_1} f(Q_{21}) \quad \text{where} \quad R_1 = (x, y_1) \tag{4}$$

$$f(R_2) \approx \frac{x_2 - x}{x_2 - x_1} f(Q_{12}) + \frac{x - x_2}{x_2 - x_1} f(Q_{22}) \quad \text{where} \quad R_2 = (x, y_2) \tag{5}$$

$$f(P) \approx \frac{y_2 - y}{y_2 - y_1} f(R_1) + \frac{y - y_1}{y_2 - y_1} f(R_2) \tag{6}$$

The input rock image will be rotated by a random angle from 0 to 360°. Assuming the random angle is θ, the original image has height and width of (a, b). After rotating, the image has height and width of (c, d).

$$c = \lfloor |a \cdot cos(q)| + |b \cdot sin(q)| \rfloor \tag{7}$$

$$d = \lfloor |b \cdot cos(q)| + |a \cdot sin(q)| \rfloor \tag{8}$$

$$
\begin{bmatrix} x_1 \\ y_1 \\ 1 \end{bmatrix} = \begin{bmatrix} 1 & 0 & c \\ 0 & -1 & d \\ 0 & 0 & 1 \end{bmatrix} \begin{bmatrix} cosq & -sinq & 0 \\ sinq & cosq & 0 \\ 0 & 0 & 1 \end{bmatrix} \begin{bmatrix} 1 & 0 & -a \\ 0 & -1 & b \\ 0 & 0 & 1 \end{bmatrix} \begin{bmatrix} x_0 \\ y_0 \\ 1 \end{bmatrix}
$$
$$
= \begin{bmatrix} cosq & sinq & -a \cdot cosq - b \cdot sinq + c \\ -sinq & cosq & a \cdot sinq - b \cdot cosq + d \\ 0 & 0 & 1 \end{bmatrix} \begin{bmatrix} x_0 \\ y_0 \\ 1 \end{bmatrix}
\tag{9}
$$

Where x_0 and y_0 are the positions of the original pixel points, and x_1 and y_1 are the positions of the rotated pixel points. If the rotation angle is not an integer multiple of 90°, some blank areas was added for retaining the whole images.

Then, randomly cropping an area within the image range is conducted by a random function, and scaling the picture to a specified size is consequently performed by bilinear interpolation.

We define a function Random (min, max), which gets a Integer number from min to max. And another function Image (W1:W2, H1:H2) is defined to cut an image from (W1, H1) of the original image with a width of (W2-W1), and a height of (H2-H1).

$$
W1 = Random(w\_min, w\_max), H1 = Random(h\_min, h\_max)
\tag{10}
$$

$$
W2 = Random(0, image\_w\text{-}W1), H2 = Random(0, image\_h\text{-}H1)
\tag{11}
$$

$$
Image\_new = Image(W2:W2 + W1, H2:H2 + H1)
\tag{12}
$$

4 Experimental Result and Discussion

4.1 Rock Image Dataset

The rock images in our experiment are collected on the Internet or by photographed. After the data is cleaned and cut, the common 12 types of rocks are selected. The number of each rock image type is about 1000, and the experiment randomly divides 80% of the rocks as training set, 20% as validation set. The specific rock types include: 7 types of igneous rocks, 3 types of sedimentary rocks, and 5 types of metamorphic rocks. The specific rock types are shown in Table 1.

4.2 Experimental Setting

(1) Experimental hardware devices

The experimental hardware devices are Intel Core i7-6800K (CPU), 40 GB (memory) and Nvidia GeForce GTX 1070 (graphics cards).

Table 1. Rock type for experiment

Igneous rocks	Sedimentary rocks	Metamorphic rocks
Granite	Sandstone	Marble
Diorite	Limestone	Quartzite
Gabbro	Dolomite	Serpentinite rock
Peridotite		Slate
Rhyolite		Phyllite
Andesite		
Basalt		

(2) Experimental software environment

The experimental software environment are Windows, python3.5 and Tensorflow 1.4.0.

4.3 Comparative Experiments

(1) Inception V3 model. Training after the rock images enhancement, and setting the learning rate to 0.0001. Then, the accuracy of the model on the training set is 97%, and the accuracy on the verification set is 77% after 100000 iterations. The result can be found in Fig. 5.

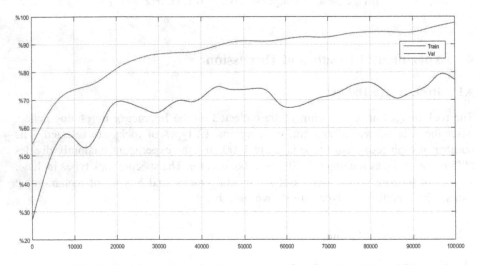

Fig. 5. Training and verification accuracy using Inception V3 model

(2) Xception model. Training after the rock images enhancement. The accuracy of the model on the training set is 98%, and the accuracy on the verification set is 86% after 80000 iterations. The result can be found in Fig. 6.

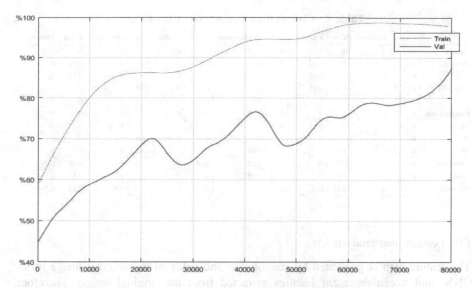

Fig. 6. Training and verification accuracy using Xception model

4.4   Discussion

(1)   Model comparison analysis

Compared to Inception, Xception's classification accuracy has increased by 9%. It means that deep separation convolution shows a better adaptation advantage than the previous CNN.

(2)   Result analysis

Table 2 provides the identification results of 12 kinds of rocks in the verification set. Each row indicates the probability that the corresponding rock is recognized as other types of rocks. The probability of recognition itself is the classification accuracy. It is recognized as other types except for itself. As can be seen from this table, there are granite, peridotite, mudstone, coal, conglomerate, picrite, shale with classification accuracy greater than 90%.

Then, we analyze the classification result to find out the reasons why some rock identification accuracy is low. Generally, rocks are made up of the same mineral composition and they are easily confused. In the classification results, limestone and marble have a 10% false positive rate. From a geological point of view, limestone and dolomite belong to carbonate rock, and marble is metamorphosed by carbonate rock. Moreover, the morphology is very similar and difficult to distinguish, and identification in the field needs to be further resolved by dilute hydrochloric acid. Basalt and andesite also have a 10% false positive rate, and their main minerals are plagioclase.

Table 2. Classification accuracy of validation set

	Granite	Peridotite	Slate	Mudstone	Coal	Conglomerate	Picrite	Marble	Shale	Limestone	Basalt	Andesite
Granite	0.85	0	0	0	0	0.05	0	0.05	0	0	0	0.05
Peridotite	0	0.95	0	0	0	0	0	0	0	0	0.05	0
Slate	0	0	0.73	0.07	0	0.07	0	0	0	0	0.13	0
Mudstone	0	0	0	0.95	0	0	0	0	0.05	0	0	0
Coal	0	0	0	0	1	0	0	0	0	0	0	0
Conglomerate	0	0	0	0	0	1	0	0	0	0	0	0
Picrite	0	0	0	0	0	0	0.94	0	0	0	0	0.06
Marble	0	0	0	0	0	0.1	0	0.75	0.05	0.1	0	0
Shale	0	0	0	0	0	0.08	0	0	0.92	0	0	0
Limestone	0	0	0.05	0	0	0.05	0	0	0.15	0.65	0.05	0.05
Basalt	0	0.15	0.1	0	0	0.05	0	0	0	0	0.6	0.1
Andesite	0	0	0.07	0	0	0	0	0	0	0.07	0.14	0.71

(3) Feature map analysis

The feature map is generated by convolution and delay of the original image in the CNN, and it can represent features extracted from the original image. Therefore, comparing the original image and the feature map of the rock, it can be seen whether the feature map extracts the features of the identified rock from the original image.

Figure 7(a) is an original image of granite. And Fig. 7(b), (c), and (d) are feature maps extracted by CNN. It is seen from this figure that Fig. 7(b) extracts the flesh red feldspar in Fig. 7(a), and (c) extracts the transparent quartz in Fig. 7(a). It is a dark mineral such as mica in Fig. 7(a).

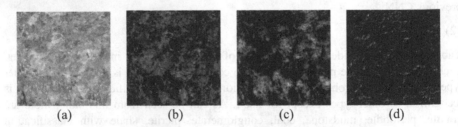

(a)   (b)   (c)   (d)

Fig. 7. Granite feature map generated by CNN

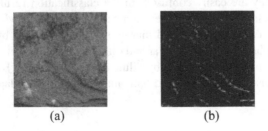

(a)   (b)

Fig. 8. Slate feature map generated by CNN

In Fig. 8, it can be seen that the feature extracted from Fig. 8(b) is the platy structure of Fig. 8(a). Similarly, it can be found that the CNN achieves obvious extraction performance on the structure of slate.

5 Conclusion

Compared with the traditional image classification objects with color, shape and other features, rock images have the features of varied color and varied shape. The geologist identifies the rocks mainly according to the structure and mineral composition of the rocks. In this paper, a CNN-based deep learning model is designed. The collected rock images are processed through different image data processing methods such as rotation, random cropping and enlarged input image. Finally, though the use of our proposed method, the classification accuracy of verification is 86%, which is average accuracy on verification data set, indicating that the deep learning method is effective in classifying rock images. The feature map generated by the CNN is also analyzed. It is found that deep learning can extract the color, structure, and mineral composition of the rock image.

In the furture, we will take some measures to improve rock images classification accuracy, such as collect more rock images for training, dividing rock images into smaller categories etc.

Acknowledgment. This work is supported by the National Key R&D Program of China under Grant 2016YFC0600510, and National undergraduate innovation and entrepreneurship training program of Chengdu University of Technology, and the Key Laboratory of Geological Information Technology of Ministry of Land and Resources under Grant.

References

1. Chatterjee, S.: Vision-based rock-type classification of limestone using multi-class support vector machine. Appl. Intell. **39**(1), 14–27 (2013)
2. Patel, A.K., Chatterjee, S.: Computer vision-based limestone rock-type classification using probabilistic neural network. Geosci. Front. **7**(1), 53–60 (2016)
3. Lepistö, L., Kunttu, I., Visa, A.: Color-based classification of natural rock images using classifier combinations. In: Kalviainen, H., Parkkinen, J., Kaarna, A. (eds.) SCIA 2005. LNCS, vol. 3540, pp. 901–909. Springer, Heidelberg (2005). https://doi.org/10.1007/11499145_91
4. Lepistö, L., Kunttu, I., Visa, A.: Rock image classification using color features in Gabor space. J. Electron. Imaging **14**(4), 040503 (2005)
5. Singh, N., Singh, T.N., Tiwary, A.: Textural identification of basaltic rock mass using image processing and neural network. Comput. Geosci. **14**(2), 301–310 (2010)
6. Fukushima, K.: Neocognitron: a self-organizing neural network model for a mechanism of pattern recognition unaffected by shift in position. Biol. Cybern. **36**(4), 193–202 (1980)
7. Lepistö, L., Kunttu, I., Visa, A.: Rock image classification based on k-nearest neighbour voting. IEE Proc. Vis. Image Signal Process **153**(4), 475–482 (2006)

8. Shang, C., Barnes, D.: Support vector machine-based classification of rock texture images aided by efficient feature selection. In: Proceedings of the International Joint Conference on Neural Network, pp. 1–8 (2012)
9. Sharif, H., Ralchenko, M., Samson, C.: Autonomous rock classification using Bayesian image analysis for rover-based planetary exploration. Comput. Geosci. **83**, 153–167 (2015)
10. Perez, C.A., Saravia, J.A., Navarro, C.F.: Rock lithological classification using multi-scale Gabor features from sub-images, and voting with rock contour information. Int. J. Miner. Process. **144**, 56–64 (2015)
11. Shu, L., McIsaac, K., Osinski, G.: Unsupervised feature learning for autonomous rock image classification. Comput. Geosci. **106**, 10–17 (2017)
12. Zhang, Y., Li, M.C.: Automatic identification and classification in lithology based on deep learning in rock images. Acta Petrol. Sin. **34**(2), 333–342 (2018)
13. Bai, L., Yao, Y.: Mineral composition analysis of rock image based on deep learning feature extraction. China Min. Mag. **27**(07), 178–182 (2018)
14. Hubel, D.H., Wiesel, T.N.: Receptive fields binocular interaction and functional architecture in the cat's visual cortex. J. Physiol. **160**(1), 106–154 (1962)
15. LeCun, Y., Bottou, L., Bengio, Y.: Gradient-based learning applied to document recognition. Proc. IEEE **86**(11), 2278–2324 (1998)
16. Litjens, G., Kooi, T., Bejnordi, B.E.: A survey on deep learning in medical image analysis. Med. Image Anal. **42**, 60–88 (2017)
17. LeCun, Y., Bengio, Y., Hinton, G.: Deep learning. Nature **521**(7553), 436 (2015)
18. Chollet, F.: Xception: deep learning with depthwise separable convolutions. In: Proceedings of the IEEE Computer Society Conference on Computer Vision and Pattern Recognition 1800–1807 (2017)
19. Luo, X., Sun, J., Wang, L.: Short-term wind speed forecasting via stacked extreme learning machine with generalized correntropy. IEEE Trans. Ind. Inf. (2018) https://doi.org/10.1109/tii.2018.2854549
20. Luo, X., Xu, Y., Wang, W.: Towards enhancing stacked extreme learning machine with sparse autoencoder by correntropy. J. Franklin Inst. **355**(4), 1945–1966 (2018)

An Efficient Network for Lane Segmentation

Haoran Li[1,2], Dongbin Zhao[1,2], Yaran Chen[1,2], and Qichao Zhang[1,2(✉)]

[1] The State Key Laboratory of Management and Control for Complex Systems,
Institute of Automation, Chinese Academy of Sciences, Beijing, China
{lihaoran2015,dongbin.zhao,chenyaran2013,zhangqichao2014}@ia.ac.cn
[2] University of Chinese Academy of Sciences, Beijing, China

Abstract. As the basis of scenes understanding for autonomous driving, lane segmentation is always a challenge due to the various illumination conditions, heavy traffics and richly-textured roads. Because of the heavily biased distribution of lane/non-lane pixels, it is hard to achieve satisfying results by using image segmentation networks such as fully convolution neural networks (FCN). In this paper, we propose a new loss function to tackle the unbalanced data distribution problem. It has shown that the loss function significantly improves the performance of available segmentation networks such as FCN on the lane segmentation task.

Keywords: Lane segmentation · Loss function · Autonomous driving

1 Introduction

Intelligent driving has received more and more attention from both academy and industry. As the basis of the intelligent driving, Sensing system locates the position of the vehicle and helps the vehicle understand the environment. Lane detection plays an important role in sensing systems. When the high definition map is available, lane detection system assists the positioning system to catch the accurate position [6]. Moreover, lane detection is the indispensable component of the Advanced Driver Assistance Systems (ADAS), since it can obtain the position and posture of the vehicle relative to the lane.

In the past decades, traditional lane detection methods can be divided into two categories [13]: feature-based methods and model-based methods. Feature-based methods [14] extract the region of interest (ROI) of the original image and detect the edges of the region. Model-based methods [10] hold the hypothesis on the lane model and estimate the best lane model parameters according to the received images. However, those methods are not robust to the complex road environments such as heavy wear, messy lane marker, and various lane models.

This work is supported by the National Key Research and Development Plan under Grants 2016YFB0101003.

© Springer Nature Singapore Pte Ltd. 2019
F. Sun et al. (Eds.): ICCSIP 2018, CCIS 1005, pp. 177–185, 2019.
https://doi.org/10.1007/978-981-13-7983-3_16

For recent years, since the deep networks can catch the robust features from the massive labeled images to image classification tasks [4], object detection tasks [3,5] and vision-based control tasks [19]. Several researchers applied the deep networks to tackle the dilemma that traditional methods are underperformance under the complex road environments [7,8,11]. Moreover, the deep networks can discover the hidden distribution rules of the lanes from the massive images, such as fixed lane interval and distribution over the different lane types. Those extra experience contribute to segmenting the lanes.

Although there are some methods based on deep networks, few of which segments the lanes in pixel-level. We propose a new loss function for deep neural network. With this loss, many deep convolution neural network can be trained by end-to-end and divide the pixels into the different lane types which include solid yellow, dashed yellow, solid white and dashed white. The performances of available segmentation networks have the noticeable improvement.

The rest of this paper is structured as follows. We review the related work about lane detection and image segmentation in next section. Then we discuss our proposed loss function. In Sect. 4 we set up experiments on our dataset and the public dataset and show that our method achieves the best performance on both datasets.

2 Related Work

In this section, we introduce the development of the lane detection methods including the traditional methods and advantaged methods based on deep networks. We also review the deep learning-based image segmentation methods briefly.

2.1 Lane Detection

The development of lane detection is accompanied by the intelligent driving system. Early work put the attention on the ROI of the images [1]. They pre-processed the region by the special color filter [16]. The edge detection operators such as Sobel operator [15] and Canny operator were used to extract the edges over the region. Finally, the edge images was post-processed to fit the lanes. However, Due to the complex conditions such as the drastically changing light, heavily wear road and various camera exposure parameters, it was virtually impossible to choose the appropriate parameters for the color filter. When the road texture is messy, for example with the vast lane markers, it was hard to fit the lanes from the detected edges.

There are several work based on deep learning. Kim et al. [9] firstly applied the convolution neural networks (CNN) to lane detection. They fed the edge images into CNN and obtained better estimations of the lanes. This network focused on the noise suppression rather than lane segmentation. Huval et al. [8] rasterized the original images and classified each grid by sliding windows. The classification model was based on CNN. The inputs of the model were the image patches in sliding windows. He et al. [7] proposed a hat-like filter to extract the image patches which had a great opportunity to be lane lines. Then they built the dual-view convolutional neural network (DVCNN) to classify the patches. This work mostly like image classification rather than segmentation. As same as Huval methods, Lee et al. [11] split images into grids. They proposed vanishing point guided network (VPGNet) which was fed the whole images and predicted each grid category. Moreover, the VPGNet detected lane marker and vanishing points simultaneously. Different from above methods, we propose a new loss function which enable the deep neural network be end-to-end trainable for the lane segmentation tasks. This networks segments the lanes on pixel-level rather than grid-level. Compared with the image rasterization, this networks achieves more delicate segmentation images.

2.2 Image Segmentation

Deep learning produces a far-reaching influence on the field of image segmentation. The milestone is fully convolution neural network (FCN) [12] which is an end-to-end trainable neural network for segmentation tasks. Then there are many variants of FCN to improve the original method performance. One of those is SegNet [2], which stored indexes during the max pooling operations and restored the segmentation labels according to the indexes during the upsampling operations. The indexes contained some spatial information of images and helped improve the segmentation performance.

For most CNN, researchers use the max pooling or large stride convolution to decrease the resolution of the images. This practice achieves the larger receptive field and cuts the memory requirements. On the other hand, it loses the spatial information for segmentation tasks. Yu et al. [18] proposed the dilated residual networks (DRN) which relieved the gridding artifact with the appropriate dilated rates and feasible network architecture. Dilated convolution [17] is another important exploration of image segmentation since it expands the receptive field with the higher resolution. The following work is aimed to seek the way to combine dilated convolutions with FCN frameworks efficiently.

3 Loss Function

Although the current segmentation methods have obtained amazing achievements on several datasets, few studies uses these methods to segment the lanes directly. The method of Huval and Lee method are classified as lane segmentation. However, those methods need to split the image into grids. This rasterization loses the accuracy and confuses the different lanes in the distance.

The difficulty of the image segmentation methods for lanes segmentation is small proportion of the lanes in the image. The proportion falls in 3%–8%. The hypothesis of the traditional softmax loss is that each pixel may belong to any class with the same probability. However, due to the heavily biased distribution of lane/non-lane pixels, there are the pixels which are the candidate to the lanes but belong to the background most of the time. This unbalanced occurrence will bias the model. The non-lane class has more contribution to update the weights.

Inspired by class-balanced cross-entropy loss function, we design the weighted softmax loss function to tackle this problem.

$$L(W) = \sum_{k \in K} L_k(W)$$

$$= \sum_{k \in K} -\alpha \sum_{i \in L} log \frac{e^{f_{il}}}{\sum_{j \in C} e^{f_{ij}}} - (1 - \alpha) \sum_{b \in B} log \frac{e^{f_{bl}}}{\sum_{j \in C} e^{f_{bj}}}. \quad (1)$$

where L is the set of lane pixels, B is the set of background pixels, k is the sample in each batch K. f is the neural network output for each pixel. l is the label for the output. α is the balance parameter. For the lane pixel, the gradient of the loss of the output is. C is the set of the classes.

$$\frac{\partial L}{\partial f_{il}} = -\sum_{k \in K} \alpha \frac{\partial}{\partial f_{il}} log \frac{e^{f_{il}}}{\sum_{j \in C} e^{f_{ij}}}$$

$$= -\alpha \sum_{k \in K} (1 - \frac{e^{f_{il}}}{\sum_{j \in C} e^{f_{ij}}}). \quad (2)$$

The gradient of the non-lane pixel is obtained in the same way.

$$\frac{\partial L}{\partial f_{bl}} = -\alpha \sum_{k \in K} (1 - \frac{e^{f_{bl}}}{\sum_{j \in C} e^{f_{bj}}}). \quad (3)$$

If the probability of the pixel belonging to the lane in the whole dataset is p, the sums of the gradients for classifying the pixel to the lane and the non-lane are

$$-\alpha p N \sum_{k \in K} (1 - \frac{e^{f_{il}}}{\sum_{j \in C} e^{f_{ij}}}) \text{ and } -(1 - \alpha)(1 - p)N \sum_{k \in K} (1 - \frac{e^{f_{bl}}}{\sum_{j \in C} e^{f_{bj}}}). \quad (4)$$

N is the number of the batches used to train the network. To make the model classify the pixels without bias, we want to have

$$\frac{-\alpha p N}{-(1 - \alpha)(1 - p)N} = 1. \quad (5)$$

It is obvious that $\alpha = 1 - p$. It is impossible to choose the precise α for each pixel. So we need make a trade-off over the whole image pixels to choose the parameter.

Another view of this loss function is the special attention mechanism. This loss improves the pixel weights and also their effect for network which makes the model focus on the lane pixels.

4   Experiments

We evaluate several networks on lane segmentation dataset and Caltech lanes dataset [1]. Those models are trained by Adam with batch size 8. All implementation are based on the Tensorflow framework.

Random flipping and random cropping are employed in augmenting the datasets. The flipping transforms the images from left-sided view to right-sided view. Random cropping imitates images changing when the camera is jittering. The $F1$ score is used to evaluate the performances. Figures 1 and 2 show the scores.

$$\text{Precision} = \frac{\text{True Positive}}{\text{True Positive} + \text{False Positive}} \tag{6}$$

$$\text{Recall} = \frac{\text{True Positive}}{\text{True Positive} + \text{False Negative}} \tag{7}$$

$$F1 = \frac{2 \times \text{Precision} \times \text{Recall}}{\text{Precision} + \text{Recall}} \tag{8}$$

4.1   Lane Segmentation Dataset Results

Lane segmentation dataset is composed of 5000 training images and 3000 test images and covers variant scenes such as the crowded urban roads, the country roads, and the highway. The labels contain solid yellow line (including single yellow line and double yellow line), dashed yellow line, solid white line and dashed white line. According to the traffic rules of China, the vehicle should not across the median strip of the road and solid yellow lines. Therefore, when the median strip or solid yellow lines appears, we only detect the lanes on the same side with the vehicle.

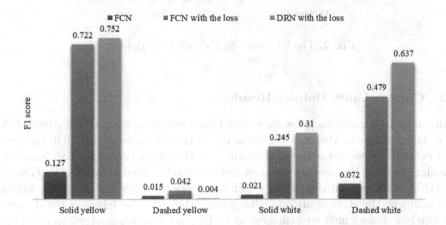

Fig. 1. The F1 scores on lane segmentation dataset. (Color figure online)

We train the FCN with normal softmax loss function and our loss function on the lane segmentation dataset. The F1 scores over different classes are shown in Fig. 1. The FCN with the loss has higher F1 score than the original FCN. The DRN whose decoder network is same as FCN is trained with our loss function and has better performance than the original FCN except on the dashed yellow type.

The original FCN almost only detects solid yellow lines and dashed white lines since these two kinds of lines nearly occur in every image. The results in the second column of Fig. 3 suggest that FCN is insensitive to lanes due to the heavy unbalance between lane pixels and non-lane pixels. Compared to the results of FCN trained with our loss function, this unbalance is eliminated. In Fig. 3, the third column segmentation results almost cover all the lanes pixels, but they also cover some non-lane pixels, which cause the lower precision. According to the fourth column results of the figure, The DRN reliefs this problem to some degree since the final feature maps have larger resolution with the same receptive field and remains more spatial information.

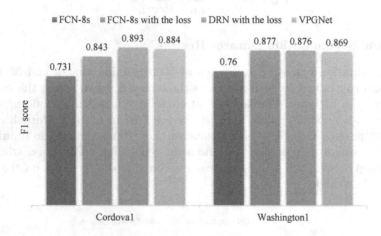

Fig. 2. The F1 scores on Caltech lanes dataset

4.2   Caltech Lanes Dataset Results

Caltech lanes dataset includes four clips taken around streets in Pasadena, CA at different times of the day. We train the networks on two clips (636 images) and evaluate those networks performance on the other two clips (585 images). We also compare the networks with vanishing point guided networks (VPGNet). VPGNet is the multi-tasks model which segments the grids instead of the pixels and achieved the state of art on Caltech lanes dataset. The labels of the dataset are the lane lines which are represented by Bezier curve parameters. In practice, the lines width is set to 8 as the ground truth maps of segmentation tasks.

The line metric [11] $F1$ score is used to evaluate the performances of different networks. It is different from $F1$ score of image segmentation. It is computed by the following way: The minimum distance from predicted lane pixel to the sampling points from Bezier curve is calculated. If the distance is less than the threshold, the pixel is true positive. Otherwise, it is a false positive. The results are shown in Fig. 2.

The DRN with the loss is slightly better than VPGNet. The loss function is helpful since the FCN with the loss has better performance than original FCN. Interestingly, The performance of DRN with the loss is as same as the FCN with the loss on the Washington1 dataset. Figure 4 is the segmentation results on Caltech lanes dataset. It is obvious that the results of the original FCN on Caltech lanes dataset are better than the results on lane segmentation dataset. The most probable reason is that the lanes positions in the images on Caltech dataset are tedious while the positions on lane segmentation dataset are

Fig. 3. The segmentation results on lane segmentation dataset. The first column is the ground truth. The second to the fourth columns respectively correspond to the results of the original FCN, FCN with the loss, DRN with the loss. Yellow, blue and purple correspond to solid yellow, solid white and dashed white. (Color figure online)

Fig. 4. The segmentation results on Caltech lanes dataset. The green means the lanes pixels. The first column is the ground truth. The second to the fourth columns respectively correspond to the results of original FCN, FCN with the loss, DRN with the loss. (Color figure online)

changeable. By comparing the second column with third column, it is conceivable that the loss function makes the FCN model focus on the lanes pixels.

5 Conclusions

In this work, we present the new loss function to train the network on the special segmentation tasks, such as heavily unbalanced pixel labels. This loss function make the deep convolution networks focus on the segmented objects. The results on lane segmentation dataset and Caltech lanes dataset show this loss function significantly improves the performance.

References

1. Aly, M.: Real time detection of lane markers in urban streets. In: 2008 IEEE Intelligent Vehicles Symposium, pp. 7–12. IEEE (2008)
2. Badrinarayanan, V., Kendall, A., Cipolla, R.: SegNet: a deep convolutional encoder-decoder architecture for image segmentation. arXiv preprint arXiv:1511.00561 (2015)
3. Chen, Y., Zhao, D.: Multi-task learning with cartesian product-based multi-objective combination for dangerous object detection. In: Cong, F., Leung, A., Wei, Q. (eds.) ISNN 2017. LNCS, vol. 10261, pp. 28–35. Springer, Cham (2017). https://doi.org/10.1007/978-3-319-59072-1_4
4. Chen, Y., Zhao, D., Lv, L., Li, C.: A visual attention based convolutional neural network for image classification. In: 12th World Congress on Intelligent Control and Automation, pp. 764–769 (2016)
5. Chen, Y., Zhao, D., Lv, L., Zhang, Q.: Multi-task learning for dangerous object detection in autonomous driving. Inf. Sci. **432**, 559–571 (2018)
6. Cui, D., Xue, J., Zheng, N.: Real-time global localization of robotic cars in lane level via lane marking detection and shape registration. IEEE Trans. Intell. Transp. Syst. **17**(4), 1039–1050 (2016)
7. He, B., Ai, R., Yan, Y., Lang, X.: Accurate and robust lane detection based on dual-view convolutional neutral network. In: 2016 IEEE Intelligent Vehicles Symposium (IV), pp. 1041–1046. IEEE (2016)
8. Huval, B., et al.: An empirical evaluation of deep learning on highway driving. arXiv preprint arXiv:1504.01716 (2015)
9. Kim, J., Lee, M.: Robust lane detection based on convolutional neural network and random sample consensus. In: Loo, C.K., Yap, K.S., Wong, K.W., Teoh, A., Huang, K. (eds.) ICONIP 2014. LNCS, vol. 8834, pp. 454–461. Springer, Cham (2014). https://doi.org/10.1007/978-3-319-12637-1_57
10. Lee, J.W.: A machine vision system for lane-departure detection. Comput. Vis. Image Underst. **86**(1), 52–78 (2002)
11. Lee, S., et al.: VPGNet: vanishing point guided network for lane and road marking detection and recognition. In: 2017 IEEE International Conference on Computer Vision (ICCV), pp. 1965–1973. IEEE (2017)
12. Long, J., Shelhamer, E., Darrell, T.: Fully convolutional networks for semantic segmentation. In: Proceedings of the IEEE Conference on Computer Vision and Pattern Recognition, pp. 3431–3440 (2015)

13. Narote, S.P., Bhujbal, P.N., Narote, A.S., Dhane, D.M.: A review of recent advances in lane detection and departure warning system. Pattern Recogn. **73**, 216–234 (2018)
14. Niu, J., Lu, J., Xu, M., Lv, P., Zhao, X.: Robust lane detection using two-stage feature extraction with curve fitting. Pattern Recogn. **59**, 225–233 (2016)
15. Sobel, I.: History and definition of the sobel operator. Retrieved from the World Wide Web (2014)
16. Wu, P.C., Chang, C.Y., Lin, C.H.: Lane-mark extraction for automobiles under complex conditions. Pattern Recogn. **47**(8), 2756–2767 (2014)
17. Yu, F., Koltun, V.: Multi-scale context aggregation by dilated convolutions. arXiv preprint arXiv:1511.07122 (2015)
18. Yu, F., Koltun, V., Funkhouser, T.: Dilated residual networks. In: Computer Vision and Pattern Recognition, vol. 1 (2017)
19. Zhao, D., Chen, Y., Lv, L.: Deep reinforcement learning with visual attention for vehicle classification. IEEE Trans. Cogn. Dev. Syst. **9**(4), 356–367 (2017)

Optimize Expert Knowledge Acquisition with Attribute Calculation: How to Understand Twin Turing Machine

Xiaohui Zou[1,2(✉)] [iD], Fang Fang[3], and Jiali Feng[4]

[1] Sino-American Searle Research Center, Beijing, China
geneculture@icloud.com
[2] Peking University, Room 415, Audio-Visual Building, Beijing 100871, China
[3] Fang Ya Physical and Mental Integration (Beijing) Health Technology Co., Ltd.,
Beijing, China
fangyalaoshi@163.com
[4] Shanghai Maritime University, Shanghai, China
jlfeng@189.cn

Abstract. This article aims to introduce how to use the attribute calculation method to achieve the purpose of optimization expert knowledge acquisition through several typical examples. The method is as follows: Firstly, the cognitive system framework in the expert's mind is transformed into the information processing mode of the computer through a typical attribute coordinate; further, through a set of typical attribute calculations, the artificial knowledge ontology can be transformed into a computer for the software model is repetitively reused; finally, the weight of the expert's mind is transformed into a software-simulated gravity judgment by a typical geometric algebraic method and geometric product, and then statistical analysis can be performed. The result: not only the property theory and its computer modeling and simulation can be realized, but also the expert knowledge acquisition from the unattainable or inscrutable altar to the classrooms and campuses of teachers and students, as that become a routine that you can operate or enjoy at any time. The significance lies in: the small-scale production of knowledge mode that lasts for thousands of years, and the attribute calculation method to optimize the human-computer collaboration and synergy paradigm of expert knowledge acquisition, which is transformed into a large-scale production of knowledge mode in daily teaching activities with teachers and students. This parallel production of cognitive systems and information processing is not only operational, but also an optimal simplification of knowledge center construction.

Keywords: Attribute calculation method · Expert knowledge acquisition · Attribute coordinate · Geometric algebraic method · Knowledge ontology

1 Introduction

This article aims to introduce how to use the attribute calculation method [1, 2] to achieve the purpose of optimization expert knowledge acquisition [3] through several typical examples [4–6].

© Springer Nature Singapore Pte Ltd. 2019
F. Sun et al. (Eds.): ICCSIP 2018, CCIS 1005, pp. 186–194, 2019.
https://doi.org/10.1007/978-981-13-7983-3_17

How to distinguish the expert's innovative knowledge and even the genius idea from the public's people and even the madness? This is a great challenge not only for artificial intelligence but also for human intelligence. The number axis and coordinate system (the invention of Descartes) is undoubtedly a good basic tool. Can they be used as the basic frame of reference for measuring expert knowledge? If the Cartesian number axis is the reference system established by the functional relationship between the geometric point and the algebraic number, then can we establish a functional relationship between the Turing machine and the calculable spaces and the integers on the number axis as reference system? These two reference systems are combined with attribute theory, not only are attribute coordinates and attribute calculations possible, but attribute learning and general learning are also possible. Figure 1 is a functional relationship between the Cartesian number axis and the Turing machine space in terms of general computability and learnability. Note that the space marked from negative to positive is a pair of linear spaces that are generated by the Turing machine. Together, they form the bridge between general computing and general learning. Such a combination can be called: a general learning function reference system.

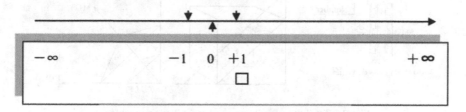

Fig. 1. General learning function reference system

The qualitative analysis and attribute calculation in this paper are based on the general learning function reference system described in Fig. 1. Various probabilistic curves and periodic curves can be established with a functional relationship to determine the specific computable and learnable basic patterns. It can be regarded as an alternative twin Turing machine and a universal learning machine. In other words, the calculation or operation, learning or memory, modeling or simulation of the human brain and the computer and even the two brains can be achieved through various equivalent twin Turing machines. It is not only understandable but also able to judge a variety of learning tasks that require expert experience and is connected with common sense.

The following describes how to understand the characteristics of the human-machine and the advantages of man-machine combination.

2   Method

The method is as follows: Firstly, the cognitive system framework in expert thinking is transformed into the information processing mode of the computer through typical attribute coordinates; further, through a set of typical attribute calculations, the artificial knowledge ontology can be transformed into a computer software model and repeated. Finally, through the typical geometric algebra method and geometric product, the weight of the expert thinking is transformed into the center of gravity of the software simulation, and then the automatic calculation of the cycle, the statistical analysis of the probability and the general learning of the model. The method steps are as follows:

2.1   Typical Attribute Coordinate

The cognitive system framework in expert thinking is transformed into a computer information processing model by typical attribute coordinates. Thus, typical three-dimensional attribute analysis and calculations can be implemented formally.

As can be seen from Fig. 2, on the right is a typical attribute coordinate and on the left is a typical twin Turing machine (understood A model). With Fig. 1, there is a functional relationship between the two under constraints.

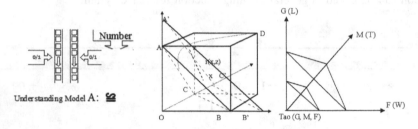

Fig. 2. Attribute coordinates and twin Turing machine

From the right side of Fig. 1, the formal method based on geometric algebra can be used to solve the problem of expert knowledge acquisition and formal expression; the model A of formal understanding can be seen on the left. They represent the universal learning model and the universal learning machine, respectively. The former can not only collect (small, medium, and big) data from zero, but also establish a specific attribute coordinate system according to the learning task and its complexity (recorded and displayed in attribute coordinates). The latter is systematically introduced in the article on formal understanding models (so omitted here).

This example presents three dimensions (multidimensional analysis is the advantage of the machine, so the superiority of the model lies in modeling and simulation in computer), that is, recording the physical dimension F (W) of real world information, and recording the mental dimension of mind information M (T) and the grammatical dimension G (L) for recording social information by using language. The starting point is the coordinate origin Tao (G, M, F). The three-dimensional coordinate frame can be divided into three small, medium and big data acquisition intervals by two cross sections (small and large two triangles). The advantage of domain experts is that they can quickly converge and make decisions based solely on clues or small data. Machine systems can use greedy algorithms to traverse (small, medium and big) data. According to the principle shown in Fig. 1, each of the numerical axes of the three-dimensional cognitive model can be converted into a learning model and a general learning machine that can be learned by the twin Turing machine shown in Figs. 1 and 2. Because, whether or not understanding can be used to judge whether to learn, knowledge summarized by human experts is familiar with five general learning evaluation levels, and is also suitable for general learning machines.

2.2 Typical Attribute Calculations

Through the typical attribute calculations, the artificial knowledge ontology can be transformed into a computer for the software model is repetitively reused.

A set of typical attribute calculations can be used to transform a human ontology into a computer reusable software model. How do experts rely on experience to make rapid, divergent and converging thinking effects and make decisions? This is a core task in expert knowledge acquisition. Fang Fang, as a senior counselor, tried to introduce her theories and methods that she developed through long-term experience to the academic peers and even the relevant aspects of society. It is to explore the symptoms of depression and the brain through actual typical cases remodeling method from damage. The steps are as follows: Firstly, the information of depression and brain damage are obtained, according to the brain in the depression state; further, the memory recombination technology in physical and mental integration therapy is used for conditioning; finally, after a certain period of time, the depression and brain state are detected. The result is the effect of physical and mental integration therapy on improving depression and reshaping the brain. The significance of this is to improve the state of depression and to reorganize memory. Only in this way a significant memory on active and healthy effect can the brain be haven. This will provide the industry with a new way to solve depression, benefiting patients, families and society. Zou Xiaohui communicated with Fang Fang, and combined with relevant research results and information from the industry, confirmed several attributes and their measurable attribute values (in combination with the experience of Princeton University brain health experts and rehabilitation information of representative patients): sleep time, excited threshold and recorded value of the graphic match test. They exactly fit the three dimensions shown in Fig. 2 (can be seen as the actual application of the attribute coordinates). In this way, according to the expert experience, the three sets of attribute data that can be collected by the information processing machine would further verify the actual effects before and after the memory reorganization (the internal information processing mechanism of the cognitive system) under the guidance of the psychological counseling expert. For example, the image information collected by the EEG can be decomposed and converted into symbolic data, as a specific application example of a certain type of learning machine, that is, the twin Turing machine, can be transformed into a joint learning of human-machine cooperation. The data collected from zero (small, medium, and big data) distinguishes between the normal value and the extreme value of the upper and lower limits.

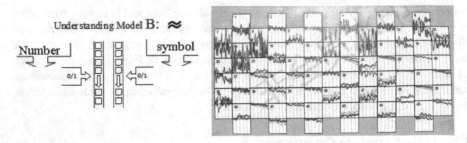

Fig. 3. Graphic-text conversion learning machine

It can be seen from Fig. 3 that a function relationship can also be established between numbers and symbols (further and generalized symbols: picture, number, table, audio and image). As long as there is enough sufficient data, the general purpose computer can complete the corresponding learning task according to the general learning machine, based on probability statistics, or periodic repetition. Since various symbols can be formally expressed, they can be acquired and collected automatically. Therefore, not only the experience of experts, but also the characteristic information (attributes and their values) of ordinary users (including patients) can be automatically learned by a dedicated learning machine or even a general learning machine. Many professional analysis can query at any time or just the clear results that users need (do not have to spend time looking at a lot of data that you don't have to look at). This can significantly simplify the acquisition of expert knowledge and its formal expression or natural language processing and its formal understanding (or its corresponding software engineering modeling and its formal pattern recognition). From this example, it can be seen that various types of waveforms can also be transformed into generalized languages that can be automatically recognized by expert systems through generalized translation.

Any pattern or schema of the world-mind-language learning tasks can be implemented in a general bilingual context.

2.3 Typical Geometric Algebraic

The weights in expert thinking are converted to the center of gravity of the software simulation by typical geometric algebra methods and geometric products, and then statistical analysis is performed. This is Professor Feng Jiali's formal attribute theory.

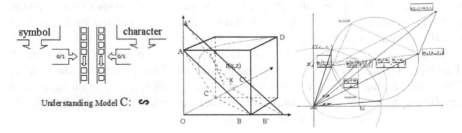

Fig. 4. Universal learning machine and dedicated learning machine

The Disposition of Clifford Product of Porizated Entangled Vector of Inner Product and Its Barycentric Combination is the result of decades of research by Professor Feng Jiali. Once it is formalized, it can make appropriate with human-computer interactions. The specific way of combining universal learning machine with the special learning machine can be quickly and clearly defined. This makes it easy for academics experts to think of a situation: where the NP problem is difficult (if it takes a few decades of experience to accumulate experts to obtain a breakthrough under certain conditions and translate into a P problem), then computer and the learning machine can be quickly and easily understood and mastered under certain constraints (at that time NP = P is also proved with in it).

So far, with Figs. 1, 2, 3 and 4 and its examples, the process of expert knowledge acquisition and formal expression is also the process of several types of twin Turing machines (as universal learning machines) to do generalized translation (starting human-computer interaction, once attribute coordinates and recordable data is sufficient, the machine's automatic learning ability will accumulate over time until it is formalized to understand the various knowledge and experience of human experts). In the past, Zou Xiaohui regarded expert knowledge acquisition with formal expression or natural language processing with formal understanding as two manifestations of a problem. Now they are regarded as the calculation and learning and creation forms of the twin Turing machine and the universal learning machine. The difference between generalized translation and narrow translation is only the difference between symbol systems.

Fig. 5. The narrow translation model is: first monolingual interpretation, then bilingual interpretation

As can be understood from Fig. 5, the English-based bilingual interpretation based on words and the Chinese interpretation based on Chinese characters are two different sets of "world-mind-language" interpretation frameworks. Due to the interpretation of many problems or the presentation of events and even the repeated reproduction of complex things, the "world-mind-language" framework cannot be separated. Therefore, it is different from the era when Turing machine (1936) can be calculated, at the same time, there are also the eras of Turing test (1950) and Searle's Chinese room (1980), the strong artificial intelligence concept, Chuyu Xiong and Xiaohui Zou exploring the era of learning (2018), whether the twin Turing machine discussed by Jiali Feng and Xiaohui Zou can be combined with attribute theory (2018), and Fang

Fang and Xiaohui Zou can discuss the memory reorganization method she said. After the expert knowledge is acquired and then formally expressed, the tasks such as repeated application (2018) are repeated and merged here. Such a large-span academic exchange and integration process is only the beginning [7–22].

Interpretation, translation, learning, understanding and creation are inevitable with the involvement of a series of cognitive systems and information processing technologies.

3   Results

The result is not only the realization of attribute theory and its computer modeling and simulation, but also the expert knowledge acquisition from difficult or incredible altars to classrooms and campuses of teachers and students (it will become an operational example for teachers and students. The program is always available.) (Table 1).

Table 1. From seizing opportunities to creating opportunities: reflecting the characteristics of several eras

Types	Information processing	Formal cognitive system
1st-Calculation	Turing machine: Can be calculated or not?	Turing test: Can be strong or weak?
2nd-Learning	Xiong and Zou: Can be learning or not?	Chinese room: Can be understanding or not?
3rd-Creation	Feng and Zou: Can be connected or not?	Fang and Zou: Can be reorganized or not?
4th-Freedom	ICIS2018: Renewable or not?	ICCSIP2018: Can it be developed or not?

It is clear that Computable and Learnable, Pervasive and Renewable are all in different levels of information processing; comprehensibility, and reorganization and even development are in the ladders of cognitive systems. The ICIS2018 Language Cognitive Forum and ICCSIP2018 Cognitive System Topic reserve a lot of room for development. For example, a wide range of talented experts in the fields of general intelligence, cognitive systems and information processing, and general information, all with their own skills and a set of theories, methods and typical examples with Strong AI or Weak AI. Therefore, the research results of this paper are only a joke (Throwing bricks for jade).

The formulas or equations are displayed:

$$\Sigma xy = I u \tag{1}$$

$$\Sigma nn = I d \tag{2}$$

$$\Sigma\, mm = I\,k \tag{3}$$

$$I\,u \approx I\,d - I\,k \tag{4}$$

$$I\,d = I\,k + I\,u \tag{5}$$

$$I\,d \equiv I\,k + I\,u \tag{6}$$

$$E_* = E_{k*} \tag{7}$$

$$Z\,t = X\,t - Y\,t \tag{8}$$

(1–6) are some mathematical expressions of Xiaohui Zou's previous discussions on information processing, data processing and knowledge processing. (7) is the mode that Chuyu Xiong's X-form wants to learn. (8) is the formula in the process of derivation of Jiali Feng's geometric product. Listed here is just a slap in the face (Throwing bricks for jade).

4 Conclusion

The significance lies in: small-scale production of knowledge modules that lasts for thousands of years can be transformed into large-scale production of knowledge modules by optimizing expert knowledge acquisition with attribute calculation methods, and even synergistic paradigms, that is, teachers and students in daily teaching by human-computer collaboration knowledge module finishing and intelligent text analysis. The parallelism between cognitive systems and information processing is not only operational, but also a simplified way to build knowledge centers.

References

1. Chang, J.S., Wong, H.J.: Selecting appropriate sellers in online auctions through a multi-attribute reputation calculation method. Electron. Commer. Res. Appl. 10(2), 144–154 (2011)
2. Thompson, J.A., Bell, J.C., Butler, C.A.: Digital elevation model resolution: effects on terrain attribute calculation and quantitative soil-landscape modeling. Geoderma 100(1), 67–89 (2015)
3. Leu, G., Abbass, H.: A multi-disciplinary review of knowledge acquisition methods: from human to autonomous eliciting agents. Knowl.-Based Syst. 105(C), 1–22 (2016)
4. Feng, J., Xu, G., Wang, X.: Pattern recognition method based on the attribute computing network. In: IEEE International Conference on Granular Computing. IEEE (2008)
5. Zou, X.: New ideas and new methods for reconstructing the "concept classification system" - from "semantic triangle" to "grammatical relationship" to "semantic triangulation". In: Chinese Lexical Semantics Seminar (2005)
6. Xu, G.: Qualitative mapping model of intelligent fusion and its implementation of attribute computing network. Shanghai Maritime University (2008)

7. Feng, J.: Entanglement of inner product, topos induced by opposition and transformation of contradiction, and tensor flow. In: Shi, Z., Goertzel, B., Feng, J. (eds.) ICIS 2017. IAICT, vol. 510, pp. 22–36. Springer, Cham (2017). https://doi.org/10.1007/978-3-319-68121-4_3

8. Xiong, C.: Universal learning machine – principle, method, and engineering model contributions to ICIS 2018. In: Shi, Z., Pennartz, C., Huang, T. (eds.) ICIS 2018. IAICT, vol. 539, pp. 88–101. Springer, Cham (2018). https://doi.org/10.1007/978-3-030-01313-4_10

9. Zuo, X., Zuo, S.: Indirect computing model with indirect formal method. Comput. Eng. Softw. **32**(5), 1–5 (2011)

10. Zou, X., Zou, S.: Two major categories of formal strategy. Comput. Appl. Softw. **24**(16), 3086–3114 (2013)

11. Zou, X., Zou, S.: Bilingual information processing method and principle. J. Comput. Appl. Softw. **32**(11), 69–76 (2015)

12. Zou, X., Zou, S.: Virtual twin Turing machine: bilingual information processing as an example. Comput. Eng. Softw. **32**(8), 1–5 (2011)

13. Zou, X., Zou, S.: Basic law of information: the fundamental theory of generalized bilingual processing. In: ISIS Summit Vienna 2015. The Information Society at the Crossroads (2015). (T9.1002)

14. Xu, X., Liu, Y., Feng, J.: Attribute coordinate comprehensive evaluation model combining principal component analysis. In: Shi, Z., Pennartz, C., Huang, T. (eds.) ICIS 2018. IAICT, vol. 539, pp. 60–69. Springer, Cham (2018). https://doi.org/10.1007/978-3-030-01313-4_7

15. Feng, J.: An intelligent decision support system based on machine learning and dynamic track of psychological evaluation criterion. In: Da Ruan, Hardeman, F., van der Meer, K. (eds.) Intelligent Decision and Policy Making Support Systems Studies in Computational Intelligence, vol. 117, pp. 141–157. Springer, Berlin (2008). https://doi.org/10.1007/978-3-540-78308-4_8

16. Zou, X.: Original Collection on Smart-System Studied. Smashwords Inc., Los Gatos (2018). ISBN 9780463607640

17. Zou, X.: Advanced Collection on Smart-System Studied. Smashwords Inc., Los Gatos (2018). ISBN 9780463020036

18. Zou, X., Zou, S., Ke, L.: Fundamental law of information: proved by both numbers and characters in conjugate matrices. Proceedings **1**, 60 (2017)

19. Zou, S., Zou, X.: Understanding: how to resolve ambiguity. In: Shi, Z., Goertzel, B., Feng, J. (eds.) ICIS 2017. IAICT, vol. 510, pp. 333–343. Springer, Cham (2017). https://doi.org/10.1007/978-3-319-68121-4_36

20. Gulcehre, C., Chandar, S., Cho, K., et al.: Dynamic neural turing machine with continuous and discrete addressing schemes. Neural Comput. **30**(4), 1–28 (2018)

21. Cerf, V.G.: Turing Test 2. Commun. ACM **61**(5), 5 (2018)

22. Heitner, R.M.: Views into the Chinese room: new essays on searle and artificial intelligence. Mind. Mach. **15**(1–111), 97–106 (2005)

Algorithms

An Unsupervised Joint Model
for Claim Detection

Xueyu Duan[1,2], Mingxue Liao[2(✉)], Xinwei Zhao[1,2], Wenda Wu[1,2], and Pin Lv[2]

[1] University of Chinese Academy of Sciences, Beijing, China
[2] Institute of Software, Chinese Academy of Sciences, Beijing, China
{xueyu2016,mingxue,xinwei2016,wenda2016,lvpin}@iscas.ac.cn

Abstract. Claim detection is one of the most important tasks in argument mining. Most existing work employs supervised methods that rely on not only good-quality and large-scale annotated corpora, but also highly engineered and sophisticated features. Unsupervised methods are a possible solution to the above problems but few work has been done from unsupervised perspective. In this paper, we propose an unsupervised joint model including position model, indicator model and TextRank model. Position information is important for argument components detection, and our position model not only considers the sentences at the beginning and the end of the whole text but also at the beginning and the end of each paragraph. Considering the discourse makers' good indication of claims, we also introduce indicator model into our joint model. Experiments on three English argumentation corpora show that our model outperforms the state-of-the-art unsupervised methods for claim detection.

Keywords: Argument mining · Claim detection · Unsupervised joint model

1 Introduction

Argument studies the act or process of forming reasons and drawing conclusions, which receives growing research interests recently [21]. Argument mining aims to automatically extract structured arguments which usually consists of a central claim (or conclusion) and several supporting or attacking premises (or evidences) from original texts [13,15]. Claim is a fundamental component in different definitions of an argument [8,26]. Thus the claim detection is one of the most significant subtasks in the argument mining pipeline. Automatic claim detection consists of claim detection in general [14,18,25] and claim detection with a topic or pre-defined concrete context as an input [11]. Our work aims to find claims in one argumentative text without a topic as an input.

The work is supported by both National scientific and Technological Innovation Zero (No. 17-H863-01-ZT-005-005-01) and State's Key Project of Research and Development Plan (No. 2016QY03D0505).

© Springer Nature Singapore Pte Ltd. 2019
F. Sun et al. (Eds.): ICCSIP 2018, CCIS 1005, pp. 197–209, 2019.
https://doi.org/10.1007/978-981-13-7983-3_18

There are plenty of studies of claim detection. Most of them solve it by employing supervised learning methods [23], based on highly engineered and sophisticated features. However, supervised methods deeply rely on a good-quality and large-scale annotated corpus, which suffers from high cost. Furthermore, the high-cost corpus annotation also limits the application of argument mining in various domains. Therefore, unsupervised methods are a possible solution to the above problems. Nevertheless, limited work has been done using unsupervised methods such as [7, 19].

Ferrara et al. presents an unsupervised ranking approach Attraction to Topics (A2T), which combines the topic information with the position information of the sentences [7]. They design a parabolic function for the position of the sentences in one text, which only focuses on the sentences at the beginning and the end of the whole text, without considering sentences at the beginning and the end of each paragraph in one text. However, we found that the first and the last sentence of a paragraph usually includes a claim in argumentative texts, so these sentences should be distinguished from those in the middle of a paragraph. We therefore propose a **position model** to model the sentences not only at the beginning and the end of the whole text, but also at the beginning and the end of each paragraph.

Discourse markers often indicate the occurrences of argument components, and indicator features have good performance for claim detection in supervised methods [10, 23, 24]. To the best of our knowledge, discourse markers have not been studied in unsupervised methods up to now. Thus we propose an **indicator model** and introduce it to our unsupervised joint model to investigate if indicators can boost the performance of unsupervised methods.

Petasis et al. applies an unsupervised graph-based algorithm, TextRank, to major claim detection, which shows that graph-based approaches and approaches targeting extractive summarization can have a positive effect on major claim detection [19]. Major claim expresses the author's stance with respect to the topic in one argumentative text. But they only employ it to major claim detection, without investigating its performance in the claim detection task. Inspired by this work, we introduce TextRank to our joint model, detecting not only major claims but also other claims. The intuition behind our joint model is that claims share significant similarities with their premises, thus are more likely to be the "hub vertices" in the graph than other non-claim sentences. Therefore, we use the **TextRank model** as a base model of our joint model.

In this work, we propose an unsupervised joint model based on position model, indicator model and TextRank model for claim detection and major claim detection. We evaluate our model on three English argumentation corpora for claim detection and major claim detection, and experiments show that our joint model achieves the best performance among all models.

The rest of the paper is organized as follows: Sect. 2 presents an overview of approaches related to argument mining focusing on the claim detection. Section 3 presents our joint model. Section 4 presents our experimental corpora. Section 5 shows evaluation results and error analysis on claim detection task, with Sect. 6

showing evaluation results and error analysis on major claim detection task. The final section concludes the work of this paper and proposes some directions for further research.

2   Related Work

There are lots of approaches trying to solve the argument components detection problem [6,11,14,22]. Almost all proposed approaches so far rely on pipeline frameworks in which the argument mining problem is split into independent subtasks. Argument components detection is one of the subtasks whose target is to classify the sentences into claims, premises or None [22]. And claim detection describes the process of identifying argument components as a binary classification task.

Argument components segmentation is often seen as the first step of an argument mining pipeline, and the granularity of argument components depends on the domain of an argumentative text [1]. For example, argument components in persuasive essays [22] are at clause-level, which means that the argument component may be a complete sentence or a clause. In Wikipedia articles studied in [20], argument components span from less than a sentence to more than a paragraph. Our work follows most of predecessors' methods for claim detection at the sentence-level granularity such as [7,27].

In order to identify argument components, proposed methods mostly employ supervised machine learning methods and use highly engineered and sophisticated features [23]. The features include six types: structural features, lexical features, syntactic features, indicator features, contextual features and word embeddings. In [2,23], structural features achieve the best result among the single feature types in persuasive essays, hotel reviews and Wikipedia articles.

Levy et al. defined the task of automatic claim detection with a topic and proposes an approach to this task [11]. The supervised method they used is designed as a cascade of three components that consist of sentence component, boundaries component and ranking component, in order to find the context dependent claims automatically. Lippi et al. proposed a method that exploits structured parsing information to detect claims without resorting to contextual information [14]. The method relies on the ability of Partial Tree Kernels to generate a rich feature set, which is able to capture structured representations without the need of a costly feature engineering process. Our joint model aims to detect claims in one argumentative text without a topic as an input.

However, not many approaches that aim to solve this problem using semi-supervised or unsupervised methods are proposed. As for semi-supervised approaches, novel unsupervised features are developed in [9] for argument components detection that exploit clustering of unlabeled data from debate portals based on word embeddings representation. Meanwhile, this work employs topic model features extracted from the vector representation of the sentences obtained by LDA model [3]. Topic information has been also used to learn argument and domain words [17] from argumentative words, based on post-processing LDA.

Besides, the topic information and position information are the main ideas of A2T [7]. The topic information indicates whether an argument component is a sentence highly focused on a specific topic, and position information indicates if an argument component appears at the beginning or the end of a text. Wachsmuth et al. used sentence position as a feature in supervised machine learning methods to indicate (1) whether a sentence is the first, second or last one within a paragraph and what its relative position is, (2) whether the sentence and the covering paragraph is the first, second or last one within the whole essay and what its relative position is [27]. Our joint model uses an improved position function to model the sentences not only at the beginning and the end of the whole text, but also at the beginning and the end of each paragraph.

Petasis et al. applied extractive summarization algorithm TextRank to identify the major claim [19]. The evaluation has been carried out in two English corpora and the results suggest that there is an overlap between extractive summarization and argument mining. Inspired by this work, we consider the similarities between sentences and build a "similarity graph" of sentences to detect claims. Besides, Levy et al. presented an unsupervised framework for corpus-wide claim detection [12].

3   Our Model

Given one argumentative text, our proposed approach, an unsupervised joint ranking model, can be applied to detect both the claims and major claims. The joint model combines position model, indicator model and TextRank model.

The intuition behind our approach includes three aspects: (1) (major) claims are usually present in the introduction or conclusion of an argumentative text and paragraphs frequently begin or conclude with a claim [22]; (2) discourse markers often indicate the components of an argument; (3) (major) claims share significant similarities with their premises, thus are more likely to be the "hub vertices" in the "similarity graph" built from sentences in a text than other non-claim sentences.

The idea of our model is that the higher the score of a sentence, the higher the probability of the sentence is a claim, and the top-ranked sentence is likely to be a major claim. Our model are described in detail as follows.

Position Model. Given a text (c) that includes a set of sentences $\{s_i | 1 \leq i \leq n\}$. Our position function (P_w) considering the position features of sentences is defined as follows:

$$score_P(s_i) = \begin{cases} 2, & \text{if } s_i \text{ is the first or last sentence in the first or last paragraph;} \\ 1, & \text{if } s_i \text{ is the first or last sentence in other paragraphs;} \\ 0, & \text{others.} \end{cases} \quad (1)$$

Different from A2T position function (P_a) where it only pays attention to the beginning and the end of the whole text, our position function considers the paragraphs information of one text, based on the first intuition abovementioned.[1] The first or the last sentence of a paragraph always includes a claim in argumentative texts, so these sentences should be distinguished from those in the middle of a paragraph. In this paper, we apply the piecewise function to separate them.

Indicator Model. Stab et al. collected a list of discourse markers that include forward indicators, backward indicators, thesis indicators and rebuttal indicators in order to classify argument components [24]. In this work, we intend to use the discourse markers to detect (major) claims, so we remove those discourse markers that indicate premises. We keep a sublist of discourse markers collected in [24] at last, containing 82 discourse markers. We use indicator function to indicate whether a sentence contains a discourse maker in the list, and it is defined as follows:

$$score_I(s_i) = \begin{cases} 1, & \text{if } s_i \text{ contains discourse maker in the list;} \\ 0, & \text{others.} \end{cases} \tag{2}$$

TextRank Model. TextRank is a graph-based ranking model that is a way of deciding the importance of a vertex within a graph, by taking into account global information recursively computed from the entire graph, rather than relying only on local vertex-specific information [16]. In this paper, TextRank is applied to solve the sentence extraction problem by building a graph that represents the text and interconnects each vertex (sentence) with similarity. The basic idea is that the higher score of a vertex, the higher its importance. Finally, top-ranked sentences are good candidates to form a summary of the text.

We use the open-source TextRank implementation which uses TF-IDF [5] similarity measure that can be found in [4], which is the same as [19]. We study both major claim detection and claim detection, while Petasis et al. studied only major claim detection [19].

Joint Model. The final score of sentence s_i in the text is defined as follows:

$$score(s_i) = \alpha \cdot score_T(s_i) + [\beta \cdot score_P(s_i) + \\ (1 - \alpha - \beta) \cdot score_I(s_i)] \cdot \overline{score_T(s_i)} \tag{3}$$

The $score_T(s_i)$ represents the score of sentence s_i in the graph built by TextRank, the $score_P(s_i)$ represents the score of sentence s_i given by the position function, and the $score_I(s_i)$ represents the score of sentence s_i given by the indicator function. We use the average score of $score_T(s_i)$ (represented as $\overline{score_T(s_i)}$) to dynamically adjust the contribution of $score_P(s_i)$ and $score_I(s_i)$ in (3). $\alpha, \beta \in [0, 1]$ are constants used to balance the similarity score, the position score and the indicator score. α and β depend on the genre. In the final step, all the sentences are ranked by $score(s_i)$. The higher the score of a sentence, the

---

[1] P_a function is defined as $\rho_{s_i}/\sum_{s_j \in c} \rho_{s_j}$. In P_a, $\rho_{s_i} = mf(pos_i)^2 + nf(pos_i) + p$. Given $L(c)$ as the number of sentences of c, $f(pos_i) = |L(c)/2 - pos_i|$. And the parameters m, n, p determine the shape of ρ_{s_i} where we set them all equal to 1.

higher the probability of the sentence being a claim. We carried out two experiments for major claim detection, one of which uses only one top-ranked sentence from each text and the other one uses two top-ranked sentences from each text. In the two experiments, we determine whether these sentences are major claims or not. Meanwhile, for claim detection, we choose the K% top-ranked sentences and check whether these sentences are claims or not.

4 Corpus

The experiments in this paper deal with argument components at sentence level, which means each document is divided into sentence-level ADU (argumentative discourse unit) types. Following [27], we also stipulate that each sentence in a text corresponds to exactly one ADU in order to prevent one sentence from having more than one ADU type. On the one hand, if a sentence contains only one ADU and the annotation is at clause-level, we have to enlarge the annotation to its complete covering sentence. On the other hand, if a sentence contains more than one ADU, we assume major claim is more important than claim than premise than None. The corpora used in experiments are as follows.

4.1 Persuasive Essays Corpus

The Argument Annotated Persuasive Essays version 1 corpus (C1) has been complied by [22]. C1 is a collection of 90 persuasive student essays in various topics. In each essay, the sentences are annotated as major claims, claims, premises or none, and each essay has only one major claim (we do not include the title in experiments). Both support and attack relations can hold between a premise and another premise, a premise and a (major) claim, or a claim and a major claim. The Argument Annotated Persuasive Essays version 2 corpus (C2) has been complied by [24] which consists of 402 persuasive student essays. There are two differences between C1 and C2. One difference is that each essay in C2 may include more than one major claims. And the other one is that C2 has removed the relation between major claim and premise. The argument components of the processed C1, C2 are showed in Table 1.

Table 1. Statistics of argument components on the corpora. MC is short for major claim, CL is short for claim and PR is short for premise.

	C1	C2	C3
MC	90	751	213
CL	418	1359	0
PR	834	3391	421
None	241	1241	1515
All	1583	6742	2149

4.2   User-Generated Web Discourse Corpus

The Argument Annotated User-Generated Web Discourse corpus (C3) has been presented by [9]. C3 contains four genres specifically: 5 articles, 46 blog posts, 73 forum posts and 216 comments to articles. The annotation model was proposed in [26]. Claims are supported or attacked by premises. Backings are additional evidence to support the claims. Rebuttals attack claims and refutations attack rebuttals. In this work, we regard backings, rebuttals and refutations as premises. The texts in C3 have implicit claims, we delete the texts which contain only implicit claims because we use the extractive summarization method in this paper. The processed C3 include 179 texts finally. Because each text in C3 has 1.19 claims in average, we regard claim as major claim on C3. The argument components of the processed C3 are showed in Table 1.

5   Claim Detection

The first task studied in this paper is Claim Detection (CD): given a non-topical argumentative text, determine how many K% top-ranked sentences contain claims. Because we regard claim as major claim in C3, we choose C1 and C2 to evaluate our model instead of C3. As for α and β in Eq. 3, we set both of them equal to 1/3. According to the statistics of C1 and C2, the proportion between the number of sentences containing a claim and the total number of sentences in the whole corpus is almost 30%, which is in line with the proportion between the number of claims and total number of sentences in each essay. Thus we set K equal to 30.

As a baseline for comparison against our approach in CD, we choose two unsupervised approaches, namely TextRank algorithm and A2T position function P_a. The TextRank algorithm is the same as [19]. Besides, P_a function can be found in [7].

5.1   Results

The results of CD can be seen from Table 2. In our experiments, we evaluate each individual model in corpus C1 and C2 to examine which model performs best for CD. We use E_k, precision, recall and macro F1 as evaluation metrics. As can be seen from Table 2, our proposed position model (P_w) performs best for CD on both corpora, based on the comparison of the four individual models. The performance of our proposed indicator model ranks second while the A2T position model performs worst. It indicates that position features and indicators features which perform well in supervised methods are also beneficial to the unsupervised claim detection. Furthermore, position model performs better with the paragraph information added, namely position information of sentences at the beginning and the end of each paragraph.

Additionally, we also evaluate our joint model on the two corpora and the results demonstrate that compared to all models (individual and joint), joint

Table 2. Results of claim detection obtained in corpus C1 and C2 when selecting the top K% sentences for each text. E_k represents the number of claims in top K% of a text. P represents precision. R represents recall. F1 represents macro F1($=\frac{2PR}{P+R}$). In approach, T represents TextRank algorithm with TF-IDF. And I represents Indicator model.

Approach	C1				C2			
	E_K	P	R	F1	E_K	P	R	F1
T	199	43.26	39.17	41.12	925	47.17	43.80	45.42
P_a	173	37.61	34.06	35.74	817	41.66	38.68	40.12
$T + P_a$	177	38.48	34.84	36.57	840	42.84	39.77	41.25
P_w	224	48.63	44.04	46.22	1027	52.37	48.62	50.43
I	217	47.08	42.63	44.75	943	48.07	44.63	46.29
$T + P_w$	227	49.35	44.69	46.90	1050	53.54	49.72	51.56
$T + I$	231	50.22	45.47	47.73	1046	53.34	49.53	51.36
$P_a + I$	212	46.09	41.73	43.80	959	48.90	45.41	47.09
$P_w + I$	239	52.06	47.14	49.48	1098	55.99	51.98	53.91
$T + P_a + I$	196	42.61	38.58	40.50	916	46.71	43.37	44.98
$T + P_w + I$	**247**	**53.70**	**48.62**	**51.03**	**1132**	**57.73**	**53.60**	**55.59**

model ($T+P_w+I$) performs best. To be more specific, in terms of precision, recall and F1, the improvements over the baseline model TextRank are 10.44%, 9.45%, 9.91% on C1 corpus and 10.56%, 9.80%, 10.17% on C2 corpus. And considering the comparison of results between joint models incorporating P_a and joint models incorporating P_w, our proposed position model performs better than the A2T position model and it shows again that including the position information of sentences in paragraphs are more beneficial to the claim detection task.

5.2 Error Analysis

The results show that model P_w is better than model P_a in both corpora C1 and C2. The difference between the two models can be seen from two sentences (showed in Table 3) which are in essay 11 of corpus C1. S1 is the third sentence of the first paragraph (there are 4 sentences in the first paragraph) and it's annotated as None. S2 is the last sentence of the third paragraph (there are 5 sentences in the third paragraph) and it's annotated as a claim. S1 is classified as a claim by model P_a due to the fact that it's in the beginning position of the text. But model P_w will take into account not only the beginning and the end position of the whole text but also the beginning and the end position of each paragraph and make the correct judgement as it's in the middle of the first paragraph. S2 is mispredicted by model P_a but predicted correctly by model P_w. S2 gets a lower ranking in model P_a because of its middle position in the text, but it gets a higher ranking in model P_w because it is the last sentence of the third paragraph. Position information along with the paragraph information added is more useful in CD.

Table 3. Examples of error analysis for CD. The true type of sentence is marked in bold in the fourth column. CL is short for claim.

No.	Sentence	P_a	P_w
S1	*Another individual might think camping as a motor home with all the amenities of their house, including the kitchen sink*	CL	**None**
S2	*Being outside in the sun is another great advantage of camping*	None	**CL**

No.	Sentence	T	$T + I$
S3	*In recently years, many countries have polished the law of the death penalty*	CL	**None**
S4	*Hence, death penalty neither controls the violent in society nor creates a violent culture*	None	**CL**

But model P_w can not solve this problem when the sentence is a claim in the middle of the paragraph.

The results of Table 3 show that joint model incorporating the model I gets a performance improvement (e.g. model T vs. model $T + I$). We keep a discourse marker list to indicate whether or not a sentence is a claim. We give examples S3 and S4 (in Table 3) to prove that indicator model is beneficial to unsupervised claim detection. S3 and S4 are in essay 373 (there are 26 sentences in essay 373) of topic "capital punishment" in corpus C2. S3 is annotated as None and S4 is annotated as a claim. S3 is classified as a claim by model T because S3 ranks 5th in model T. But model $T + I$ will take into account the textrank features and indicator features, and lower the ranking to 12th as S3 doesn't contain any indicator in the discourse marker list. In contrast, S4 ranks 17th in model T, but model $T + I$ raises its ranking to 6th and makes the correct prediction for S4 because it contains the indicator "*Hence*". These examples showed that our position model and indicator model have a better performance in CD.

Compared to the four individual models, joint models incorporating the individual model perform better than the individual models themselves, except that model $T + P_a$ and $T + P_a + I$ perform worse than model T. The results show that incorporating P_a and $P_a + I$ into the individual model T respectively to form joint models causes performance degradation on the individual model T. On the contrary, incorporating T and $T + I$ into the individual model P_a respectively to form joint models improves performance of the individual model P_a. It indicates that the quality of the position function has impacts on the performance of joint models.

6 Major Claim Detection

We evaluate our approach in the Major Claim Detection (MCD) task, another core subtask in the argument mining pipeline. The goal of MCD is to determine if each sentence in the text contains a major claim. We firstly perform the experiments on the persuasive student essays corpora (C1 corpus and C2 corpus). Following the [19], we also conduct two experiments: in the first experiment (E1), we extract the top-ranked sentence in a text, while in the second experiment (E2), we extract two top-ranked sentences, then we determine whether the major claim component is contained among these extracted sentences. Additionally, to evaluate the general performance of our approach, we conduct the two experiments aforementioned on the corpus in another domain: the Argument Annotated User-Generated Web Discourse corpus (C3).

In line with the Sect. 5, we choose the methods in [19] and [7] as our baselines.

6.1 Results

The results of MCD can be seen from Table 4. For MCD, we conduct the same experiments on corpus C1 and C2. From Table 4, we can see that the results of performance comparison among all individual models is in line with the results of CD in Sect. 5. And it shows that our intuition is verified again that sentences position information and indicators which perform well in supervised methods are beneficial to the unsupervised major claim detection. And the results show that our proposed joint model $T+P_w+I$ outperforms all other models (individual and joint) and the accuracy of E_1 and E_2 improves 17.77%, 40.00%, 36.07%, 37.06% respectively. What deserves to be mentioned is that the accuracy of E_2 on C2 corpus is up to 91.04%.

For the performance of our model on corpus C3, the results show that our model can be successfully applied to the comments.

6.2 Error Analysis

MCD focuses on the top-ranked or the two top-ranked sentences in our ranking model. The results show that model P_w is better than model P_a in corpus C1, C2 and C3. The sentence S5 (showed in Table 5) is in essay 86 of corpus C1 and it's annotated as a major claim. S5 is neither the first nor the last sentence of the text, so it won't be classified as a major claim in E_{2c} by model P_a. However, the probability of being classified as a major claim by model P_w will increase as it is the last sentence of the first paragraph. The way to use position information is important in argument components detection. We give example S6 in Table 5 to show that indicator model is useful in unsupervised MCD. S6 is in essay 402 (there are 16 sentences) of topic "study hard or play sport" in corpus C2 and it's annotated as a major claim. S6 ranks 3th in model T, but model $T + I$ raises its ranking to 2nd as it contains the indicator "In my point of view". These examples show that our position features and indicator features also have a better performance in MCD.

Table 4. Results of major claim detection in corpus C1, C2 and C3. The subscript a of E represents the accuracy of texts.

Approach	C1		C2		C3	
	E_{1a}	E_{2a}	E_{1a}	E_{2a}	E_{1a}	E_{2a}
T	15.56	21.11	37.31	53.98	25.70	41.90
P_a	3.33	21.11	8.21	28.61	32.96	44.69
$T + P_a$	3.33	18.89	9.20	53.23	32.96	49.16
P_w	23.33	45.56	45.27	75.37	26.26	49.72
I	16.67	30.00	28.86	51.24	18.44	36.87
$T + P_w$	24.44	56.67	64.68	90.80	**36.31**	**53.07**
$T + I$	27.78	36.67	51.74	69.90	22.34	38.55
$P_a + I$	32.22	48.89	59.20	75.12	22.91	42.46
$P_w + I$	**35.56**	56.67	68.66	85.82	26.26	49.72
$T + P_a + I$	16.67	36.67	48.51	73.38	30.17	46.37
$T + P_w + I$	33.33	**61.11**	**73.38**	**91.04**	33.52	52.51

Table 5. Examples of error analysis for MCD. The true type of sentence is marked in bold in the fourth column. MC is short for major claim.

No.	Sentence	P_a	P_w
S5	*This essay will argue that the main functions of universities as the highest educational institution are teaching and researching*	None	**MC**

No.	Sentence	T	$T + I$
S6	*In my point of view, both of studying hard and playing sports are part of life to children*	None	**MC**

Indicator model show a significant improvement in both corpora C1 and C2, but they achieve the worst result according to the comparison of individual models in corpus C3, and cause performance degradation on the joint model which incorporates model I. This is due to the fact that the discourse markers are extracted from corpus C1 and C2, which are domain-specific and not suitable for corpus C3. Our proposed position function P_w focuses on the sentences of the first and the last paragraph, which is the same as P_a. The position model P_a causes performance degradation on the joint model which incorporates model P_a in both corpora C1 and C2. But it works in the opposite direction in corpus C3, as can be seen from the results of comparison between P_a and $T + P_a$.

7   Conclusion and Future Work

In this paper, we propose a novel unsupervised joint model based on position model, indicator model and TextRank model for (major) claim detection.

We evaluate our joint model on Persuasive Student Essays Corpus and User-generated Web-discourse Corpus and the experiments demonstrate that our proposed model has a significant improvement than the state-of-the-art unsupervised methods. It suggests that our proposed sentence position information and discourse indicators play a significant role in the unsupervised model for (major) claim detection. Together with unsupervised extracted summarization, our joint model has a best performance.

For the future work, we would try to employ our joint model into other argument components detection tasks, such as identification of premises. And we also can apply our model to other corpora, such as larger corpus or corpus in other domains. Due to the successful application of sentence position information and discourse indicators in unsupervised method for (major) claim detection, it is interesting to try to introduce other features which work well in supervised method into the unsupervised method for argument components detection.

References

1. Ajjour, Y., Chen, W.F., Kiesel, J., Wachsmuth, H., Stein, B.: Unit segmentation of argumentative texts. In: Proceedings of the 4th Workshop on Argument Mining, pp. 118–128. Association for Computational Linguistics (2017)
2. Aker, A., et al.: What works and what does not: classifier and feature analysis for argument mining. In: Proceedings of the 4th Workshop on Argument Mining. Association for Computational Linguistics (2017)
3. Blei, D.M., Ng, A.Y., Jordan, M.I.: Latent Dirichlet allocation. J. Mach. Learn. Res. **3**, 993–1022 (2003)
4. Bohde, J.: Document summarization using TextRank (2012). http://joshbohde. com/blog/document-summarization
5. Christopher, D.M., Prabhakar, R., Hinrich, S.: Introduction To Information Retrieval, vol. 151, no. 177, p. 5 (2008)
6. Eger, S., Daxenberger, J., Gurevych, I.: Neural end-to-end learning for computational argumentation mining. In: Proceedings of the 55th Annual Meeting of the Association for Computational Linguistics (Volume 1: Long Papers), pp. 11–22. Association for Computational Linguistics (2017). https://doi.org/10.18653/v1/ P17-1002
7. Ferrara, A., Montanelli, S., Petasis, G.: Unsupervised detection of argumentative units though topic modeling techniques. In: Proceedings of the 4th Workshop on Argument Mining, pp. 97–107. Association for Computational Linguistics (2017)
8. Freeley, A.J., Steinberg, D.L.: Argumentation and Debate. Cengage Learning, Boston (2013)
9. Habernal, I., Gurevych, I.: Exploiting debate portals for semi-supervised argumentation mining in user-generated web discourse. In: Proceedings of the 2015 Conference on Empirical Methods in Natural Language Processing, pp. 2127–2137. Association for Computational Linguistics (2015). https://doi.org/10.18653/v1/ D15-1255
10. Lawrence, J., Reed, C.: Combining argument mining techniques. In: Proceedings of the 2nd Workshop on Argumentation Mining, pp. 127–136. Association for Computational Linguistics (2015). https://doi.org/10.3115/v1/W15-0516

11. Levy, R., Bilu, Y., Hershcovich, D., Aharoni, E., Slonim, N.: Context dependent claim detection. In: Proceedings of COLING 2014, the 25th International Conference on Computational Linguistics: Technical Papers, pp. 1489–1500. Dublin City University and Association for Computational Linguistics (2014)
12. Levy, R., Gretz, S., Sznajder, B., Hummel, S., Aharonov, R., Slonim, N.: Unsupervised corpus-wide claim detection. In: Proceedings of the 4th Workshop on Argument Mining, pp. 79–84. Association for Computational Linguistics (2017)
13. Lippi, M., Torroni, P.: Argument mining: a machine learning perspective. In: Black, E., Modgil, S., Oren, N. (eds.) TAFA 2015. LNCS (LNAI), vol. 9524, pp. 163–176. Springer, Cham (2015). https://doi.org/10.1007/978-3-319-28460-6_10
14. Lippi, M., Torroni, P.: Context-independent claim detection for argument mining. IJCAI **15**, 185–191 (2015)
15. Lippi, M., Torroni, P.: Argumentation mining: state of the art and emerging trends. ACM Trans. Internet Technol. (TOIT) **16**(2), 10 (2016)
16. Mihalcea, R., Tarau, P.: TextRank: bringing order into text. In: Proceedings of the 2004 Conference on Empirical Methods in Natural Language Processing (2004)
17. Nguyen, H., Litman, D.: Extracting argument and domain words for identifying argument components in texts. In: Proceedings of the 2nd Workshop on Argumentation Mining, pp. 22–28. Association for Computational Linguistics (2015)
18. Palau, R.M., Moens, M.F.: Argumentation mining: the detection, classification and structure of arguments in text. In: Proceedings of the 12th International Conference on Artificial Intelligence and Law, pp. 98–107. ACM (2009)
19. Petasis, G., Karkaletsis, V.: Identifying argument components through TextRank. In: Proceedings of the Third Workshop on Argument Mining (ArgMining2016), pp. 94–102. Association for Computational Linguistics (2016). https://doi.org/10.18653/v1/W16-2811
20. Rinott, R., Dankin, L., Alzate Perez, C., Khapra, M.M., Aharoni, E., Slonim, N.: Show me your evidence - an automatic method for context dependent evidence detection. In: Proceedings of the 2015 Conference on Empirical Methods in Natural Language Processing, pp. 440–450. Association for Computational Linguistics (2015). https://doi.org/10.18653/v1/D15-1050
21. Shnarch, E., Levy, R., Raykar, V., Slonim, N.: GRASP: rich patterns for argumentation mining. In: Proceedings of the 2017 Conference on Empirical Methods in Natural Language Processing, pp. 1345–1350. Association for Computational Linguistics (2017)
22. Stab, C., Gurevych, I.: Annotating argument components and relations in persuasive essays. In: Proceedings of COLING 2014, the 25th International Conference on Computational Linguistics: Technical Papers, pp. 1501–1510. Dublin City University and Association for Computational Linguistics (2014)
23. Stab, C., Gurevych, I.: Identifying argumentative discourse structures in persuasive essays. In: Proceedings of the 2014 Conference on Empirical Methods in Natural Language Processing (EMNLP), pp. 46–56. Association for Computational Linguistics (2014)
24. Stab, C., Gurevych, I.: Parsing argumentation structures in persuasive essays. Computational Linguistics **43**(3), 619–659 (2017)
25. Teufel, S., et al.: Argumentative zoning: information extraction from scientific text. Ph.D. thesis, Citeseer (1999)
26. Toulmin, S.: The Uses of Argument. Cambridge UP, Cambridge (2003)
27. Wachsmuth, H., Al Khatib, K., Stein, B.: Using argument mining to assess the argumentation quality of essays. In: Proceedings of COLING 2016, the 26th International Conference on Computational Linguistics: Technical Papers, pp. 1680–1691. The COLING 2016 Organizing Committee (2016)

How to Understand the Basic Structural Unit

Yongchao Gan[1] and Xiaohui Zou[2,3(✉)] [iD]

[1] Department of Physics, Hubei University, Wuhan 430062, China
ycgan@qq.com
[2] Sino-American Searle Research Center, UC Berkeley,
Berkeley 94720-3840, USA
949309225@qq.com
[3] Peking University, Room 415, Audio-Visual Building, Beijing 100871, China

Abstract. This paper aims to apply the understanding model to understand the basic structural unit of the material world. The method steps are as follows: A to understand the old terms, such as: Wave-Particle Duality, "material and space", "physical and field" and "particles and waves"; B, to understand the new terms, such as: "π-type triple-wave particle duality" and "Tai Chi particle wave"; C, to understand the statement of new and old, such as: A brief review of the process of exploring the "basic structural unit of the material world" in human history, focusing on the basic theory of material structure – "Tai Chi Particle Wave" theory on the basis of "classical electromagnetic field according to photon corresponding decomposition found classic Correspondence between the basic unit between electromagnetic field and quantum electromagnetic field. The result is to break the relationship between physical and field (particles and waves) and predict the existence of the basic structural unit of the material world - Tai Chi Particle Wave. Its significance is to make material and space, physical and field, particles and waves effectively unified. This is an interesting question that clarifies the most basic structural unit of the material world. Revealed the third wave-particle duality; and unified the three wave-particle duality revealed by Einstein 1905, De Broglie 1923 and Gan 1995 respectively, revealing the microscopic object π-type triple wave particle duality.

Keywords: Understanding model application · Material structure ·
Elementary particles · Tai Chi particle wave · Third wave-particle duality ·
Π-type triple wave particle duality

1 Introduction

The primitive structure of the world and the most basic structural unit of the material world are an unchanging and fascinating topic. Since humans have had their minds, people have been continually seeking. Not only philosophers, scientists, and even ordinary people are curious. The ancient Greek philosopher Thales proposed that water is the starting point of all things; Heraclitus believes that: fire is the origin of all things; Democritus claims that all things in the world are made up of indivisible particles (atoms) and voids composition. The dominant position in modern science is the quark theory. This paper aims to apply the understanding model to understand the basic

© Springer Nature Singapore Pte Ltd. 2019
F. Sun et al. (Eds.): ICCSIP 2018, CCIS 1005, pp. 210–219, 2019.
https://doi.org/10.1007/978-981-13-7983-3_19

structural unit of the material world that according to the π-type triple-wave particle duality and Taiji particle wave revealed by Chinese scholar Gan, is the basic material unit that constitutes our world [1–3].

2 Method

The method steps are as follows: A to understand the old terms, such as: Wave-Particle Duality, "material and space", "physical and field" and "particles and waves"; B, to understand the new terms, such as: "π-type triple-wave particle duality" and "Tai Chi particle wave"; C, to understand the statement of new and old, such as: A brief review of the process of exploring the "basic structural unit of the material world" in human history, focusing on the basic theory of material structure – "Tai Chi Particle Wave" theory on the basis of "classical electromagnetic field according to photon corresponding decomposition found classic Correspondence between the basic unit between electromagnetic field and quantum electromagnetic field.

2.1   From Wave-Particle Duality To π-type Triple Wave Particle Duality

The Revelation of the Third Wave-particle Duality and the π-type Triple Wave Particle Duality: As early as 1927, Dirac completed the classical electromagnetic field decomposition according to the model [4]:

$$A(r,t) = \sum_l \sum_\sigma \sqrt{\frac{\hbar}{2\omega_l \varepsilon_0 \tau}} \hat{e}_{l\sigma} \left[a_{l\sigma} e^{i \cdot (k_l \bullet r - \omega_l t)} + a_{l\sigma}^* e^{-i \cdot (k_l \bullet r - \omega_l t)} \right] = \sum_l \sum_\sigma A_{l\sigma}(r,t) \quad (1)$$

About seventy years later, Gan et al. further advanced Dirac's work and completed the decomposition of the classical electromagnetic field by photon [3, 5]:

$$\begin{aligned} A(r,t) &= \sum_l \sum_\sigma \sum_j \sqrt{\frac{\hbar}{2\omega_l \varepsilon_0 \tau}} \hat{e}_{l\sigma} \left[a_{l\sigma j} e^{i \cdot (k_l \bullet r - \omega_l t)} + a_{l\sigma j}^* e^{-i \cdot (k_l \bullet r - \omega_l t)} \right] \\ &= \sum_l \sum_\sigma \sum_j A_{l\sigma j}(r,t) \end{aligned} \quad (2)$$

It is proved that the energy, momentum and angular momentum of each electromagnetic fundamental wave can be equal to the energy, momentum and angular momentum of a co-frequency photon, respectively, thus establishing a relationship between the classical electromagnetic field and the quantum electromagnetic field. The correspondence between a basic unit (electromagnetic fundamental wave, photon) reveals that the classical electromagnetic field (wave) has particle structure in structure, also known as the third wave-particle duality [1–3].

As early as 1905, Einstein revealed the first wave-particle duality (wave-particle duality of light), which was verified by Millikan in 1916 and won two Nobel Prizes in Physics in 1921 and 1923 respectively. In 1923, De Broglie revealed the second wave-particle duality (wave-particle duality of physical particles), which was verified by

Davidson and Little Thomson in 1927 and won two in 1929 and 1937 respectively Nobel Prize in Physics. Now introduces the third wave-particle duality and introduces the first wave-particle duality (light wave-particle duality) revealed by Einstein in 1905, and the second type revealed by De Broglie in 1923. Wave-particle duality (wave-particle duality of physical particles) overlaps into the following form [1–3]:

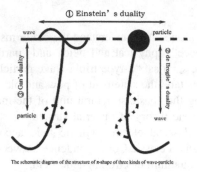

The schematic diagram of the structure of π-shape of three kinds of wave-particle

Then the contradiction between wave and particle can be solved, and the three wave-particle dualities can be unified harmoniously. It turns out that particles are particles, waves are waves, visible, tangible, and real; but the real particles have De Broglie volatility in motion - the second wave-particle duality The real wave has particle property in structure - the third wave-particle duality; under certain conditions, the real wave and the real particle can also be transformed into each other - first Wave-particle duality (essential wave-particle duality).

The other two wave-particle dualities are the wave-particle duality of phenomena. Their wave and particle have only one being real, while the other is false existence, which is the reality. The reflection of existence is like the shadow of a tree reflecting the existence of a tree. In the latter two kinds of wave-particle duality, although wave and particle exist simultaneously, they are a virtual and real, and wave and particle cannot be transformed into each other. Therefore, distinguishing between true and false waves and particles is the key to understanding the π-type triple-wave-particle duality [1–3].

This is the understanding by human brain, and further can be computer-aided understanding by means of the description of geometric figures.

2.2   The Wave-Particle Two-Image Relation and the Taiji Particle Wave

Mathematical Abstraction and Physical Interpretation of the π-type Triple Wave-particle Duality: the Wave-particle Two-image Relation and the Taiji Particle Wave.

If we regard the classical electromagnetic field and the quantum electromagnetic field as two different states (or two phases) of the same light field, then the transformation between the classical electromagnetic field and the quantum electromagnetic field is the first true wave in the wave-particle duality. The transformation between classical electromagnetic waves (represented by a wave matrix [W]) and real particles - photon gas (represented by a particle matrix [P]).

If written in a matrix transformation form, there are: [particle matrix] – [transform matrix] [wave matrix], that is,

$$\begin{bmatrix} \varepsilon \\ p \end{bmatrix} = \begin{bmatrix} \hbar & 0 \\ 0 & \hbar \end{bmatrix} \begin{bmatrix} \omega \\ k \end{bmatrix} \text{ or } P = GW \tag{3}$$

The physical mechanism contained in this mathematical expression—how the classical electromagnetic field and the quantum electromagnetic field are transformed (or how the "electromagnetic fundamental wave" and the "photon quantum" are transformed) is definitely a question worth exploring.

We believe that even an absolute vacuum is not empty, but is filled with a large number of quantum fields in the ground state (which of course includes quantum electromagnetic fields in the ground state). Since the quantum electromagnetic field of the ground state fills the entire vacuum, the basic unit of the classical electromagnetic field, the electromagnetic fundamental wave, can be absorbed by the quantum electromagnetic field in the ground state at a certain moment when it meets certain conditions (the electromagnetic fundamental wave at a certain position. The ground state quantum electromagnetic field at the same position is absorbed in situ without energy drift), thereby causing the quantum electromagnetic field to transition from the ground state to the excited state. The quantum electromagnetic field in the excited state is very unstable, and can jump from the excited state back to the ground state in a very short time and release (spit) a position and the energy of the absorbed electromagnetic fundamental wave at a certain position of the vacuum Photon. In this way, the conversion of the real electromagnetic fundamental wave to the real photon is completed, and the ground state quantum field in the vacuum only plays a mediating role - after going through a series of changes and returning to the original state. This is the physical essence of the classical electromagnetic field quantization process. Of course, the opposite process can also occur under another condition: the ground state quantum electromagnetic field absorbs a photon, transitioning from the ground state to the excited state. Since the excited state is very unstable, the quantum electromagnetic field in the excited state will be in a very short time. An electromagnetic fundamental wave with the same frequency and energy as a photon is emitted in a vacuum (this is the vacuum injection - the vacuum is everywhere, and the result of the coherent superposition of these jets just restores the electromagnetic fundamental) From the excited state back to the ground state, the conversion of photons to the electromagnetic fundamental wave is completed [1]. Behind such a picture of the mutual transformation of particles and waves, it hides the most basic structural unit of the material world - the Taiji particle wave (the π-type triple-wave particle dual-material carrier).

2.3 The Taiji Particle Wave (Material) and Space

It is the dialectical unity of the Taiji particle wave (material) and space that presents the colorful world of particles (physical) and waves (field) in real space.

Obviously, in this wonderful π-type triple-wave-particle duality picture, the real wave is completely equal to the real particle. When the Taiji particle wave appears in the face of the particle, the particle has De Broglie volatility in motion (the second wave-particle duality). When the Taiji particle wave appears in the face of the wave, the wave has the structure in the particle. Sex (the third wave-particle duality). For example, a Tai Chi photon wave, when it appears as a photon (in a vacuum embracing photon state), the photon is closely related to the whole vacuum (unlike the bullet flying freely in a vacuum, the bullet is not associated with the vacuum), and in motion It has De Broglie volatility; when it appears as electromagnetic wave (in the fundamental wave state of the particle), the electromagnetic wave is also closely related to the vacuum and exhibits particle structure; under certain conditions, the electromagnetic fundamental wave and photon Mutual transformation (the first type of wave-particle duality) can also occur between them. In this way, the Taiji photon wave is a more comprehensive description of light, and the electromagnetic wave and the photon are only the result of the scorpion image [1].

It is based on such a physical picture that we predict that the Taiji particle wave is the most basic structural unit that constitutes the material world. It completely eliminates the mechanical modes of infinite subdivision of molecules, atoms, nucleus, protons, neutrons, quarks, etc., and presents two states of vacuum embracing particle state and particle fundamental wave state, which unifies particles and waves, and unifies matter with space. Therefore, from the appearance point of view, the Taiji particle wave can change from infinitesimal to infinite waves and from infinity to infinitesimal particles—through both infinity and infinity, and unifying matter (particles) Space (field). As for the Taiji electron wave, it should be similar to the Taiji photon wave, and it has a π-type triple wave particle duality. Only so far, we only know its second wave-particle duality (electronic De Broglie volatility). However, we believe that in the near future, the first wave-particle duality and the third wave-particle duality of Taiji electronic waves will be recognized by us. We predict that electrons will be broken into electronic fundamental waves filled with the entire vacuum in the future; under certain conditions, electronic fundamental waves can be converted into electrons.

3   Results

The result is to break the relationship between physical and field (particles and waves) and predict the existence of the basic structural unit of the material world - Tai Chi Particle Wave.

Similar to the three predictions made by Einstein's general theory of relativity (the precession of Mercury's perihelion, the gravitational deflection of light, and the gravitational red shift of the spectral line), it has proved its solid foundation in the scientific community, our π-type Triple wave-particle duality can also make three predictions: 1 It can directly derive the quantization of light energy without relying on any quantum hypothesis and relying on classical theory [7]; 2 relying solely on classical theory without any quantum hypothesis It is possible to directly derive Planck's blackbody radiation formula [8]; 3 waves are completely equal to particles, the quantum theory of light and the classical electromagnetic theory of light are two independent and parallel theories, and the quantum theory of light cannot contain the classical electromagnetic of light Theory.

In order to make up for the above defects, Galileo used to overthrow Aristotle's "the faster the object falls, the faster the falling speed" (it is actually more powerful than the experiment), we can also use the power of logic to prove "the quantum theory of light" Classical electromagnetic theory that cannot contain light" - If "quantum theory of light can contain the classical electromagnetic theory of light", then we can use the quantum theory of light to dominate the world, so that classical electromagnetic theory and electromagnetic waves are both out of the historical arena. Withdrawal from the physical world, electromagnetic waves lose their place of existence. However, electromagnetic waves cannot be eliminated as a kind of real existence. Therefore, the quantum theory of light cannot contain the classical electromagnetic theory of light.

In addition, based on Dirac's "classical electromagnetic field decomposition according to mode" (or "substance quality is equal to the sum of a series of atoms and molecular masses"), it is strongly required that the sum of the energy of a series of discrete photons can be continuously changed, so Gan Yongchao A hypothesis is proposed: any positive real number R can be decomposed into a series of algebraic sums of integer multiples of positive real numbers, expressed as a formula, namely:

$$R = n_1 r_1 + n_2 r_2 + \ldots \ldots + n_i r_i + \ldots \ldots = \sum_{i=1}^{N} n_i r_i \qquad (4)$$

If you convert it into a popular expression, "a series of standard gimmicks of different sizes can be combined into any weight." Obviously, this is another mathematical problem. Surprisingly, this mathematical problem was given a clever and rigorous proof by Jihua Gan, an outstanding alumnus of Columbia University and an applied mathematician at the chief investment office of JP Morgan Chase, the largest US bank. The world's problems are subtly transformed into an easier geometric problem and give an unassailable proof [6].

4 Comparative Analysis

According to the opinions or suggestions of the reviewers, a set of verification basis is added, referred to as the 311 program.

We know that there are three ways to translate the "science hypothesis" into "scientific theory": 1 from quantitative to qualitative: when the "scientific hypothesis" is applied to scientific practice, there are more and more facts and the content of this hypothesis. In line with, and no known facts contradict it, then this "scientific hypothesis" can be transformed into "scientific theory." 2 Scientific predict is that the scientific foresight made by the "science hypothesis" can be confirmed by scientific means, then this "scientific hypothesis" can be transformed into "scientific theory." 3 Experimental judgment: Design a one-of-a-kind, very sensitive judgmental experiment to test the truth of the "scientific hypothesis."

The verification of Einstein's general theory of relativity took the second approach: making three predictions in advance (the fertility of Mercury's perihelion, the gravitational deflection of light, and the gravitational red-shift of the spectral line). When these prophecies are verified, it lays a solid foundation for the general theory of relativity in the scientific community. Specifically, Eddington and Crowlin led a small squad to the island of Principe in the Gulf of Guinea in West Africa and Sobral of

Brazil on May 29, 1919. Observed by the bias, the observations of the two places on November 6 of the same year were announced by the President of the Royal Society of Thomson (probably verifying Einstein's theory; accurate verification will wait until 1975).

Our "π-type triple-wave particle duality" and "Tai Chi particle wave" theory can also make three predictions (and also subversive, they are events that are impossible in modern physics): 1 without any help Quantum hypothesis and relying solely on classical theory can directly derive the quantization of light energy. Impossible events are difficult to prove by Chinese scholars defending dragons [3, 10]; 2 can rely on classical theory alone to derive directly from classical theory. Langke's blackbody radiation formula, impossible event, was confirmed by British scholar Marshall [8]; 3 "quantum theory of light" and "classical electromagnetic theory of light" are two independent, parallel theories, "waves (electromagnetic waves)" and "particles (photons)" are completely equal. The quantum theory of light cannot contain the classical electromagnetic theory of light, and it is also an impossible event. (As early as 1930, Fermi pointed out: "The quantum theory of light can contain the classical electromagnetic of light. The theory, which was developed by Louise et al. and regarded as the golden rule of modern physics, was confirmed by Chinese scholar Gan [11, 12], sharply pointed out For nearly 90 years, experimental evidence can not find a "classical electromagnetic theory, quantum theory of light can contain light" of.

In order to make up for the remaining half of the above defects, use Galileo to overthrow Aristotle's "the faster the object falls, the faster the falling speed" (it is actually more powerful than the experimental proof), we can also use the power of logic to prove "The quantum theory of light cannot contain the classical electromagnetic theory of light" - if "the quantum theory of light can contain the classical electromagnetic theory of light", then we can use the quantum theory of light to dominate the world, thus making "classical electromagnetic theory" And "electromagnetic waves" have both withdrawn from the historical arena and withdrawn from the physical world, so "electromagnetic waves" have lost the foundation of their existence (disappeared). However, "electromagnetic waves" cannot be eliminated as a kind of real existence. Therefore, the quantum theory of light cannot contain the classical electromagnetic theory of light.

In addition, based on Dirac's "classical electromagnetic field decomposition according to mode [4]" ("substance quality is equal to the sum of a series of atoms and molecular masses"), it is strongly required that the sum of the energy of a series of discrete photons can be continuously changed, so Gan Yongchao proposed A conjecture: any positive real number R can be decomposed into a series of algebraic sums of integer multiples of positive real numbers, expressed as a formula, namely (4).

Convert it into a popular expression, that is, "a series of standard gimmicks of different sizes can be combined into any weight." Obviously, this is another mathematical problem. Surprisingly, this mathematical problem was given a clever and rigorous proof by Jihua Gan, an outstanding alumnus of Columbia University and an applied mathematician at the chief investment office of JP Morgan Chase, the largest US bank. The world's problems are subtly transformed into an easier geometric problem and give an invulnerable proof [6].

Finally, if we can find "the phenomenon of vacuum ejection of photons or electrons" - the particles disappear in the vacuum and become the corresponding "particle fundamentals", or the "first wave-particle duality" of the "Taiji electrons" "–that is, under certain conditions, the electrons are "broken" into an "electron fundamental wave" filled with the entire vacuum (as if "photon" is converted into "electromagnetic fundamental wave"), then our "Taiji particle wave" Theory will become a matter of fact.

An exciting fact is that the photo-vacuum phenomenon of photons (photons disappear, converted into "electromagnetic fundamental waves") has long been commonplace (that is, the wave-particle duality of light revealed by Einstein), but we have not seriously the ground is compared with the analysis. If you carefully carry out the comparative analysis – "the vacuum ejection phenomenon of photons" - the photon disappears in the vacuum and transforms into the corresponding "electromagnetic fundamental wave", which is exactly the experimental evidence we dreamed of (and this is just Einstein.) The "wave-particle duality" of the light found!)

So far, the three predictions, a conjecture, and an experiment of "π-type triple-wave particle duality" and "Taiji particle wave" have been confirmed (the 311 program has been completed).

5 Conclusion

The significance is to make material and space, physical and field, particles and waves effectively unified. This is an interesting question that clarifies the most basic structural unit of the material world. Revealed the third wave-particle duality; and unified the three wave-particle duality revealed by Einstein 1905, De Broglie 1923 and Gan 1995 respectively, revealing the microscopic object π-type triple wave particle duality.

If we can find the phenomenon of vacuum ejection of photons or electrons - the particles disappear in the vacuum and turn into the corresponding particle fundamentals, or the first wave-particle duality of the Tai Chi electrons - that is, under certain conditions The electron breaks into an electron fundamental wave (like an electromagnetic wave) that fills the entire vacuum. Under another condition, the electron fundamental wave that fills the entire vacuum can be converted into electrons. Then, the Taiji particle wave theory becomes iron-fixed fact. If we can find the phenomenon of vacuum ejection of photons or electrons - the particles disappear in the vacuum and turn into the corresponding particle fundamentals, or the first wave-particle duality of the Tai Chi electrons - that is, under certain conditions The electron breaks into an electron fundamental wave (like an electromagnetic wave) that fills the entire vacuum. Under another condition, the electron fundamental wave that fills the entire vacuum can be converted into electrons. Then, our taiji particle wave theory becomes iron-fixed fact.

From the standpoint of Gan: the most fundamental structural unit of the physical world is an interesting question. More than two thousand years ago, the ancient Greeks proposed the atomic theory of the structure of matter. Today, Chinese scholars put forward the modern atomic theory—"Tai Chi particle-wave" theory. This paper briefly reviews the exploration process of the basic structural unit of the material world in human history, and mainly introduces the basic theory of material structure created by Chinese scientists, the theory of Tai Chi particle-wave. This theory presumes that based on decomposing classical electromagnetic field into a series of electromagnetic fundamental waves according to photons, a corresponding relation of fundamental units between classical electromagnetic field and quantum electromagnetic field is found, and a new wave-particle duality—the third kind of wave-particle duality, is revealed. Later, three kinds of wave-particle duality—Einstein's Wave-particle Duality of light in 1905, de Broglie's Wave-particle Duality of particle in 1923, and Gan's Wave-particle Duality of wave in 1995 are unified harmoniously. Further more, the π–type triple wave–particle duality of micro-object is revealed, and the formulation of relation between particle and wave is accomplished. The existence of Tai Chi particle-waves, the basic structural units of the material world is predicted. Thus material and space, object and field, particle and wave are unified effectively. The three subversive predictions and a conjecture based on the theory are confirmed. The theory of "Tai Chi particle-wave" of material structure has been written into textbooks of colleges and universities for six years, reprinted five times and spread widely among the people. Even in The XXIV World Congress of Philosophy, there are reports and discussions on the "Tai Chi particle-wave".

From the standpoint of Zou: this paper would aim to understand how to understand the basic structural unit of the material world from the perspective of cognitive systems and information processing: Taiji particle waves? The method is as follows: Firstly, empirical scientific methods are used to confirm or falsify the research results of Gan Yongchao, namely: formulas and models and their schematic diagrams; then, from the perspective of teaching and research, to reflect on the phenomenon; and then from the perspective of thinking and cognition, why should we follow the scientific community formed its familiar scientific paradigm to treat the Gan Yongchao phenomenon by history and society. The result is: First, through the attitude of empirical science and the attitude of rational philosophy, Gan Yongchao himself began to accept the fact that under the conditions of contemporary international internet, any scientific discovery is to accept the comprehensive international and domestic academic circles. Test or verify, otherwise, it is scientifically discovered that this is not rigorous. At the same time, relevant academic institutions and colleagues need to understand the truth: for new things and people, we should first give positive attention and support, and it is not appropriate to let them go their own way, which is not conducive to encouraging explorers is not conducive to the formation of a positive academic ecological environment. The significance of this is that many features of the scientific cognitive system have yet to be further explored, and its breadth and height are to be expanded; an important application field of information processing technology is: scientific innovation talents and their exploration spirit and if the judgment of the research results can be more automated, then the situation similar to the phenomenon can be correspondingly identified, properly handled and treated reasonably earlier. Finally, what is worth thinking about is: How to eliminate ambiguity? [13] Especially for the cognitive system of human experts, how to make the information processing system automatically eliminate ambiguity? This is a huge challenge for AI.

How to Understand the Basic Structural Unit 219

Acknowledgement. Special thanks to Feng Zhiwei and Zou Xiaohui, the host of ICIS2018 Language Cognitive Workshop, given the expansion meeting, Feng Jiali and other an experts listened to Gan Yongchao's explanation of his 311 program, and thanks for service support from Wang Xiaoqun in Peking University.

References

1. Yan, Z., Gan, Y., Zhao, J., et al.: Introduction to Natural Science, pp. 44–48. Science Press, Beijing (2012)
2. Gan, Y.: Is the basic unit of classical electromagnetic field a new substance? Philos. Rev. (Ser. 8), 276–281 (2010). Wuhan University Press
3. Gan, Y., Wang, W.: A self-consistent picture of wave-particle duality of light. In: Roychoudhuri, C., Kracklauer, A.F., Creath, K. (eds.) The Nature of Light: What Are Photons? (2007). Proceedings of SPIE, 6664: 666407
4. Dirac, P.A.M.: The quantum theory of the emission and absorption of radiation. Proc. R. Soc. (Ser. A) Lond. **144**, 243 (1927)
5. Gan, Y., Zhang, J., Shen, W., et al.: Study on the intrinsic structure of the radiation field. Acta Photonica Sinica **24**(5), 472–475 (1995)
6. Gan, Y., Gan, J.: The conflict between classics and quantum (discrete and continuous): Gan Yongchao's conjecture and its proof. Beijing J. Relativistic Res. **15**(2), 45 (2017)
7. Yan, W.: Proceedings of SPIE, 6664: 66640A (2007). Chin. Phys. **14**(12), 2514–2521 (2005)
8. Marshall, T.W.: Brownian motion of a mirror. Phys. Rev. D **24**(6), 1509–1515 (1981)
9. Gan, Y.: Proceedings of SPIE, 7421: 74210U (2009)
10. She, W.L.: Quantization of light energy directly from classical electromagnetic theory in vacuum. Chin. Phys. **14**(12), 2514–2521 (2005)
11. Gan, Y.: Can the quantum theory of light contain the classical electromagnetic theory of light? In: Roychoudhuri, C., Kracklauer, A.F., Khrennikov, A.Y. (eds.) The Nature of Light: What are Photons? III (2009). Proceedings of SPIE 2009, 7421: 74210U
12. Gan, Y., Hu, Z., Gang, Z.: Lorentz-Compton paradox and a win-win decision scattering experiment design. J. Light Scatt. **18**(1), 75–79 (2006)
13. Zou, S., Zou, X.: Understanding: how to resolve ambiguity. In: Shi, Z., Goertzel, B., Feng, J. (eds.) ICIS 2017. IAICT, vol. 510, pp. 333–343. Springer, Cham (2017). https://doi.org/10.1007/978-3-319-68121-4_36

Algorithms for Maximum Lifetime of Covering Path

Huafu Liu and Zhixiong Liu[✉]

School of Computer Engineering and Applied Mathematics,
Changsha University, Changsha, Hunan, China
hfliu9063@163.com, lzxterry@163.com

Abstract. Path coverage is an important issue in wireless sensor networks. Some algorithms are presented to solve path coverage problem in some specialized situations. However, they cannot be applied in common sensor networks applications. Moreover, energy conservation is not considered in these works. This paper presented a maximum lifetime path coverage algorithm in sensor networks. The goal is to divide the sensors into h groups, and schedule all groups such that the maximum lifetime can be achieved. We transform the problem into several sub problems and give a heuristic algorithm for it. Simulation experiments are conducted to find the impact of the size, the initial energy and the sensing radius of the sensor to the maximum lifetime.

Keywords: Wireless sensor networks · Path coverage · Maximum lifetime · Algorithm

1 Introduction

Wireless sensor network (WSN) is a self-organized network consisting of a large number of cheap wireless sensors, and its purpose is cooperative sensing, collecting and processing network within the coverage area of the object information, and transmits it to the users. Sensor nodes have a strong ability to cooperate, through the local data acquisition, preprocessing and data exchange between nodes to complete the global task. WSN can be run in an independent environment, but also through the gateway to connect to the existing network infrastructure, such as Internet.

The sensor is usually equipped with limited battery energy [2], how to maximize the lifetime of sensor network is a hot problem. Lots of attentions have been paid on this problem. Abrams *et al.* [4] gave that maximizing the lifetime of sensor network problem was NP-Complete. Cardei *et al.* [5] gave a solution by dividing the sensor into maximal number of disjoint set covers to extend the lifetime of the sensor network. When the density of target points is bounded, Lu *et al.* [6] gave a PTAS to maximize the network lifetime, and they also proved that it is NP-hard to schedule the sensors for maximum lifetime of sensor network even in special case, e.g. the sensing radius and the transmission radius of sensors are equal. Kumar *et al.* [1] gave an algorithm to a special problem when sensor nodes are deployed to form a barrier for detecting movements. There are many other literatures along his topic [3, 7–10].

Zhang *et al.* [11] gave an efficient approximation algorithm which achieves a solution for path monitoring problem. In this paper, we consider the maximum lifetime

© Springer Nature Singapore Pte Ltd. 2019
F. Sun et al. (Eds.): ICCSIP 2018, CCIS 1005, pp. 220–233, 2019.
https://doi.org/10.1007/978-981-13-7983-3_20

of sensor covering path problem. The definition of the problem is that: given a path P, and a set of sensors S, divide S into h groups and schedule them to monitor the path such that maximum lifetime can be achieved.

As can see above, existing schemes mainly focus on point coverage, area coverage and barrier coverage, only one algorithm pointing to the specialized multimedia sensor network is presented for path coverage. Moreover, energy conservation is not considered in most of these researches. This paper utilizes bipartite weighted matching technique to maximize lifetime of the network while implementing path coverage.

The main contribution of this paper is that we give a heuristic algorithm for maximum lifetime of sensor covering path problem. Through simulation experiments, we find the relationship between the number of sensors and the maximum lifetime of the sensor covering path, and how the initial energy and the sensing radius of sensor affects the maximum lifetime of the sensor covering path.

The rest of the paper is organized as follows. The symbols and definition that are used throughout the paper is given in Sect. 2. In Sects. 3, the algorithms of the problem are presented. Section 4 discusses the simulation results. Finally, we conclude the paper in Sect. 5.

2 Problem Analysis

2.1 Symbols

In this section, we introduce some symbols that will be considered in this paper.

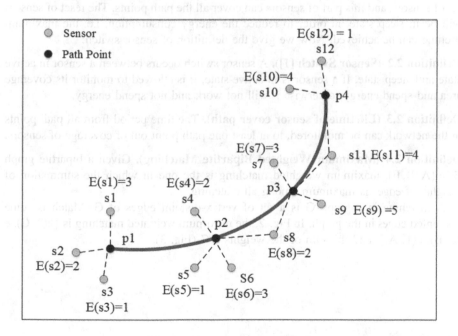

Fig. 1. A sample sensor network

- E(s): represent the energy of the sensor s, i.e. the lifetime of the sensor s. For example, $E(s) = 5$ means that s can work for 5 h.
- S(v): For each path point v, let S(v) be the set of sensors covering v. E.g., $S(v) = \{s_2, s_4, s_6\}$ means that point v is covered by sensor s_2, s_4 and s_6.
- C(s): For each sensor s, let C(s) be the path point set which is in the monitoring area of the sensor s. $C(s) = (p_1, p_5, p_7)$, means that sensor s covers three points which are p_1, p_5 and p_7.
- A − B: A, B are two sets, and $A - B = \{x | x \in A, x \notin B\}$.
- A + B: A, B are two sets, and $A + B = \{x | x \in A \text{ or } x \in B\}$.
- |A|: A is a set, and |A| is the size of A.

Let's take an example in Fig. 1, as illustrated, 12 sensors and 4 path points existed in the network. $E(s_1) = 3$, $S(p_1) = \{s_1, s_2, s_3\}$, $C(s_8) = \{p_2, p_3\}$.

2.2 Preliminaries

Definition 2.1 (Coverage weighted bipartite Graph). A coverage weighted bipartite graph of a sensor network is constructed as follows:

Let $B = (V_1, V_2, E)$ be the coverage weighted bipartite graph. The set V_1 contains the vertex which is the corresponding sensor. The set V_2 contains the vertex which is the corresponding path point. If u is in C(u), then (u, v) is an edge in B. The weight of edge (u, v) is the energy of the sensor u.

In the sensor scheduling process, in order to reduce the energy consumption of the sensor, we use the sensor switch strategy. We only need active a necessary part of the set of sensors, and this part of sensors can cover all the path points. The reset of sensors will be in sleep state, in order to reduce the energy consumption, i.e. the maximum lifetime can be achieved. Now we give the definition of sensor switch:

Definition 2.2 (Sensor Switch [1]). A sensor switch occurs between a sensor in active state and sleep state. If a sensor is in active state, it is allowed to monitor its coverage area and spend energy; otherwise it will not work and not spend energy.

Definition 2.3 (Lifetime of sensor cover path). The time period from all path points in the network can be monitored, to at least one path point out of coverage of sensors.

Definition 2.4 (Maximum Weighted Bipartite Matching). Given a bipartite graph $B = (A, B, E)$, maximum weighted matching is the one in which the summation of weights of edges is maximum among all matching.

A matching in a graph G is a set of vertex-disjoint edges of G. Match is some disjointed edges in the graph. In Fig. 2, the maximum weighted matching is {e(3, C), e (2, B), e(1, A)}, and the sum of the weights is 7 (Fig. 3).

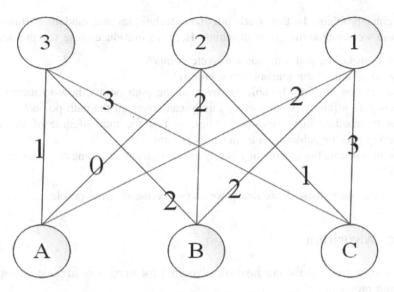

Fig. 2. Maximum weighted bipartite matching

2.3 Problem Definition

If a number of sensors are deployed at random around a path, we need to divide these sensors into h groups, and how to schedule it to achieve the maximum lifetime of the sensor covering path. Now, we formally define the problem in this paper.

Problem 1 (Maximum lifetime of sensor cover path). Given a path P, and a set of deployed sensors S, find h groups of sensors $T_1, T_2, \ldots, T_h$, and schedule them to monitor the path such that maximum lifetime can be achieved.

In Fig. 1, we give a sensor network, and there is a path and some sensors. These sensors are divided into 2 groups. $T_1 = \{s_1, s_4, s_7, s_{10}\}$, $T_2 = (s_2, s_3, s_5, s_6, s_8, s_9, s_{11}, s_{12})$. We can first use T_1 to monitor the path, then we use T_2 to monitor the path when T_1 cannot cover the path because some sensors in T_1 may exhaust their all the energy. T_1 and T_2 may not be an optimal partition, but we will use some heuristic rules to find a way that is close to the optimal partition.

2.4 Our Results and Techniques

In order to solve maximum lifetime of sensor covering path problem, we transform it into 5 sub problems. The solution of the sub problems can merge into the solution of the original problem. In this work our main techniques are random partition and maximum weight bipartite graph matching. Here we introduce these sub problems:

1. How to make the path into some discrete points?
2. How to divide all the sensors into h groups?
3. Some groups may not be able to cover all the path points, how to merge some groups into a family, so that every family can cover all the path points?
4. How to schedule these sensors families, so that the total lifetime of the sensor covering path be achieved is as much as possible?
5. How to schedule the sensors in a family to maximize the lifetime of sensor covering path?

If we can solve these 5 problems, we can solve the original problem.

3   Our Algorithm

In this section we describe our heuristic algorithm for maximum lifetime sensor covering path problem.

For maximum lifetime of sensor cover path problem, we use **discretization-path** algorithm to discretize the path into some point at first, then using **partition-sensors** algorithm divides the sensors into h groups. These groups may not cover all the path points. We use **merge-group** to merge the groups into some families that every family can cover all the path points. Finally we schedule all the families by **family-schedule.** For the scheduling any family we use **sensor-schedule** to schedule sensors of family. The sum of the maximum lifetime of each family is the maximum lifetime of the sensor covering path.

3.1   Path Discretization

For sub Problem 1, we adopt same step value to discretize the path points. Here we give a formal definition of the Problem 1.

Problem 2 (Path discretization). Given a path P, make path curve discretization, which generates a set of discrete points, denoted by Q.

In our algorithm **discretization-path** for Path discretization problem, we first set a step value d, and then we move distance d in the coordinates of x to take a point on the path, and add to the collection Q.

It is easy to see that the time complexity of **discretization-path** algorithm is $O((x_h-x_1)/d)$.

Algorithm 1 discretization-path (P, d, x_l, x_h)

Input: a path P, d, x_0, x_h

Output: discrete points of path P.

1. Set a step-value d, let the initial x-coordinate of the path be x_l, and let the last x-coordinate of the path be x_h;

2. Q is empty set; $x_i = x_l$;

3. where $x_i <= x_h$

4.   get point $p(f(x_i), x_i)$,

5   $Q = Q + \{p\}$;

6. $x_i = x_i + d$;

7. return Q;

Fig. 3. Algorithm for path discretization

3.2   Random Partition Sensor Set

Here we introduce how to solve sub Problem 2, which is to divide the sensor into h groups. Now we give a formal definition of sub Problem 2.

Problem 3 (Group Sensors). Given a path P, and a set of deployed sensors S, find h groups of sensors $T_1, T_2, \ldots, T_h$, and every group can cover some path points of the path P.

For this problem, we give a **partition-sensors** algorithm. For each path point p, S (p) is divided into k groups randomly, and the algorithm finally will generate k groups of sensors, and each of them may cover some path points. The random algorithm solving Problem 3 is given in Fig. 4.

In Algorithm 2, we loop $h * n$ times, and each time we need to randomly remove some points from each S (p_j). Then the time complexity of the random algorithm is O (hnm).

3.3   Random Merge Sensor Group

Using **partition-sensors** algorithm, we get h groups of sensors, but some of them may not able to cover all path points, thus additional works should be done to merge some groups into family, which can cover all path points independently. The formal definition of sub Problem 3 is given below.

Algorithm 2 partition-sensors(S, Q)

Input: a set of deployed sensors $S = \{v_1, v_2, ..., v_n\}$, and a set $Q=\{p_1,...,p_m\}$ of points of P

Output: a set of groups of sensors.

1.   For each point p_i, let S(p_i) be the set of sensors covering p_i;

2.   Let $T_1, T_2, ..., T_h$ be set of groups of sensors;

3. $S_1 = $;

4.   For i =1 to h do

5.   For j=1 to m do

6.   randomly choose a subset S' of S(p_j);

7. $T_i = T_i + (S' - S_1)$;

8. $S(p_j) = S(p_j) - (S' - S_1)$;

9. $S_1 = S_1 + (S' - S_1)$;

10.   return $T_1, T_2, ..., T_h$.

Fig. 4. Random algorithm for Group Sensors problem

Problem 4 (Merge Groups). Given h groups of sensors $T_1, T_2, ..., T_h$, a set of pints Q, and generate a family of sets $W_1, W_2, \cdots, W_r(r \leq h)$ such that each W_i covers all the points in Q.

We give an algorithm **merge-group** to the Problem 5 in Fig. 5. At first, we sort all groups in ascending order by the number of path points covered by them. Then we take the first group T_i from the groups, if the group T_i can cover all the path point, T_i will be put into family W_i and removed from the groups. Otherwise, we place T_i into W_i and get the next group T_{i+1}. If T_{i+1} can cover the point which is uncovered by W_i, then add T_{i+1} into W_i. Repeat above process until W_i can cover all the path points or all the groups we have been handled. If there exist some path points uncovered by W_i, then we need to decide whether there is a family W_j that can cover all the path points. If not exist, return null, otherwise the remaining groups will be placed in a family W_j, and the W_i will also be placed into W_j.

Algorithm 3 merge-group(T, Q)

Input: a set T={ T_1, T_2,$\cdots$, T_h } of groups of sensors, a set Q={p_1,…,p_m} of points of P

Output: a family of sets W_1, W_2, $\cdots$, W_r(r<=h) such that each W_i covers all the points in Q.

1.   Sort the sets in T in nondecreasing order by the number of points covered by T_i, denoted
     by T={T_1, T_2,$\cdots$, T_h}.

2. r=1; T'=T; S'= Q;

3.   While r<=h do

4. W_r=0 ; j = 1;

5.   While T' is not empty and the points in S' is not empty and j <=h do

6.   If | C(T_j)-(Q-S') | <=0   // T_j is the j-th set in T'

7. j++;

8.   continue;

9. W_j= W_r+{ T_j }; T'= T'- T_j;

10. S'=S' - C(T_j);

11. j++;

12.   If S' is empty

13. r++

14.   Else

15.   If r<=1 return NULL;

16.   else

17.   add all set in T' into W_r-1;

18.   add all set in W_r into W_r -1;

19. r--;

20. return W_1, W_2, $\cdots$, W_r.

Fig. 5. Algorithm for Get groups problem

Calculating the number of points covered by each sensor takes time $O(hnm)$. Sorting all groups takes time $O(h \log h)$, and the running time to merge groups is $O(h^2)$. Then, the total time is $O(hnm + h^2)$.

3.4   Family Schedule

Sub Problem 4 is to schedule families. The sequence of family scheduling has no impacts on maximizing the network lifetime, for lacking of relevance. We give the following definition of the problem.

Problem 5 (Family schedule). Given a families of sensors, and schedule them to achieve the maximum lifetime of the sensor covering path.

It is easy to know that the maximum lifetime can be obtained by running each family once time. Now we give an algorithm solving Problem 5 in Fig. 6.

Algorithm 4 family-schedule(W)

Input: a family of sets $W=\{W_1, W_2, \ldots, W_r\}$ ($r<=h$) such that each W_i covers all the points in $Q=\{p_1,\ldots,p_m\}$.

Output: the schedule of the sets in W

1.   compute the expected lifetime of each W_i;

2.   for $i=1$ to r do

3.   Let the sensors in W_i cover the points in P;

4.   return.

Fig. 6. Algorithm for family schedule problem

It is obvious that the time of this algorithm is $O(r)$.

3.5   Sensors Schedule

Sub Problem 5 is sensor schedule problem. Sensor schedule is mainly to find a scheduling strategy to make the sensor in activate or sleep state, so as to achieve the maximum life cycle coverage. How to schedule sensors is our crucial problem. Here we give a formal description of the problem.

Problem 6 (sensor schedule). Given a set of sensors, a path, and schedule sensor to cover the path to get the maximum lifetime.

To solve Problem 6, we construct a coverage weighted bipartite graph G, then we find a maximum weighted bipartite matching in G. Because we want to schedule some sensor with largest energy. If these sensors cannot cover all the path points, we continue to construct coverage weighted bipartite graph G' for these uncover points until all the path points are covered or the rest of the sensor cannot cover all of the path points. The **sensor-schedule** algorithm for sensor schedule problem is described in Fig. 7.

Algorithm 5 sensor-schedule(W_i, Q)

Input: a set of sensors W_i which covers all the points in Q and a set $Q = \{p_1,..,p_m\}$ of points.

Output: the schedule of the sensors in W_i

1. While the sensors in W_i which can cover all the point in Q

2. Construct a **coverage weighted bipartite graph** $G=(V_1,V_2,E)$, where V_1 denotes the set of sensors in W_i which has energy, V_2 denotes the set of points in Q; if a point p is covered by a sensor s, the corresponding two vertices of p and s have an edge, and the weight of edge (u, v) is the energy of sensor u;

3. Find a maximum weighted matching in G, denoted by M;

4. While there is an unmatched vertex in V_2 do

5. Denote the set of unmatched vertices by V_2' in V_2;

6. Induce a new subgraph G' based on V_1 and V_2';

7. Find a maximum weighted matching in G';

8. For each vertex v in V_2, let M(v) denote the vertex in V_1 which matched the vertex of v in V_2, and minimum energy in all M(v) is represent by *var_temp*;

9. For each vertex v in V_2, M(v) is scheduled to cover the point v and M(v), so each vertex in V_i which is matched by a vertex in V_2 will spend var_temp energy;

10. Delete the vertices in W_i which has no energy.

11. return

Fig. 7. Algorithm for Maximum lifetime sensor cover problem

The time complexity of the maximum weight matching algorithm is two (n^2m). The total time complexity is $O(n^2m^2w)$, where w is the maximum weight of edges.

4 Simulations

Here, we give simulation experiment to observe the impact of the number of sensors on the maximum lifetime of the sensor covering path. As only one algorithm is presented for path coverage before, and which has some specialized requirements for sensor networks, thus it is unfeasible to compare the result of our work with the former algorithm. We only investigate the impact of the size, the initial energy and the sensing radius of the sensor to the maximum lifetime in this sector.

We discretize the path into 10 points, some sensor nodes are deployed around in these path points, and each sensor has initial energy in [5, 10] at random. We need to monitor the discrete points on the path. The points covered by each sensor are also continuous. We take the same random strategy, and we assume that each sensor can cover [1, 3] discrete points on the path.

According to the experimental results, we found that when the number of sensors is very small, the lifetime of the sensor cover path is 0. The reason for this is that there are not enough sensors to cover these path points. With the increasing of number of sensors, the lifetime of the sensor covering path shows a rising trend, because there are more sensors to cover these path points. The experimental result is shown in Fig. 8.

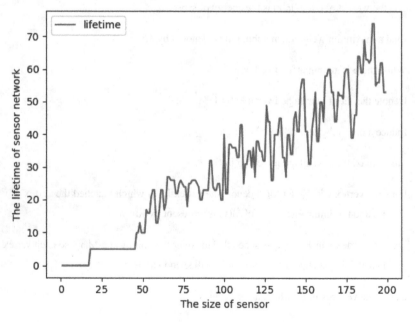

Fig. 8. The change of the lifetime with respect to the size of sensors.

The impact of the minimum initial energy of sensors on the maximum lifetime of the sensor cover path is given. We discretize the path into 10 points as the same, 200 sensor nodes are deployed around in these path points, and each sensor has the same initial energy. The points covered by each sensor are also continuous. We assume that each sensor can cover [1, 3] discrete points randomly on the path.

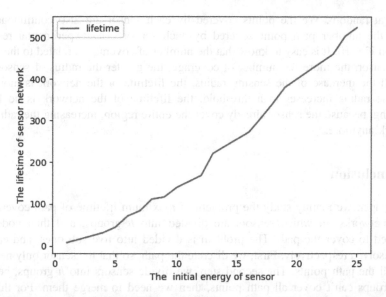

Fig. 9. The change of the lifetime with respect to the initial energy of sensors.

With the initial energy of the sensors, the lifetime of the sensor cover path also is increased, because the individual sensor has more energy spent. The experimental result is shown in Fig. 9.

We also observe how the sensing radius of sensors affect the maximum lifetime of the sensor cover path. As the same, we discretize the path into 10 points, around in these path points random deploy 200 sensor nodes, each sensor has initial energy in

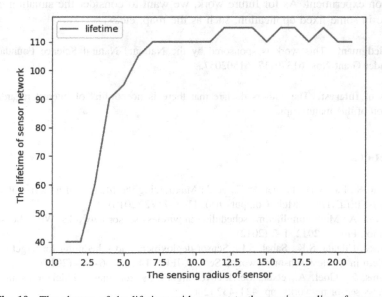

Fig. 10. The change of the lifetime with respect to the sensing radius of sensors.

[5, 10] at random. We the points covered by each sensor are also continuous. We change the number path point covered by each sensor. The experimental result is shown in Fig. 10. It is easy to know that the number of coverage is related to the radius of the sensor, the more the number of coverage, the greater the radius of sensor.

With the increase of the sensing radius, the lifetime of the network is more, but when the radius increases to a threshold, the lifetime of the network is no longer increasing, because the sensor already cover the entire region, increasing the radius, do not work anymore.

5 Conclusion

In this paper, we mainly study the problem of maximum lifetime of path coverage in sensor networks, in which sensors are divided into h groups, and then nodes are scheduled to cover the path. The problem is divided into five sub ones, and each of them is solved respectively. First, we discrete the path, so that the sensor only needs to cover all the path points. The second step, we divide sensors into h groups, because some groups can't cover all path points, then we need to merge them. For this sub problem, we adopt a strategy to merge these groups which cover points is small at first. After the merge, each family can cover all the path points, and then we just need to schedule all the families. Finally, the most important problem in the process of scheduling is the sensor scheduling, so we design a heuristic algorithm which uses maximum weight bipartite matching algorithm, and this method helps to prolong the network lifetime. In the scheduling process, we only need activate the matched sensor, and other sensors are in sleep state to reduce energy consumption for future work. It is found that the maximum lifetime of the network increases with the increase of the number of sensors, the initial energy of sensor and the sensing radius of sensor in the simulation experiment. As for future work, we want to consider the situation of path coverage in some fixed application, such as the map, etc.

Acknowledgment. This work is sponsored by the National Natural Science Foundation of China under Grant Nos. 61379117, 61502057.

Conflicts of Interest. The authors declare that there is no conflict of interest regarding the publication of this manuscript.

References

1. Kumar, S., Lai, T.H., Posner, M.E., et al.: Maximizing the lifetime of a barrier of wireless sensors. IEEE Trans. Mob. Comput. **9**(8), 1161–1172 (2010)
2. Dhawan, A.: Maximum lifetime scheduling in wireless sensor networks. Wirel. Sens. Netw. Technol. Protoc. **2012**, 1–3 (2012)
3. Mini, S., Udgata, S.K., Sabat, S.L.: Sensor deployment and scheduling for target coverage problem in wireless sensor networks. Sens. J. IEEE **14**(3), 636–644 (2014)
4. Abrams, Z., Goel, A., et al.: Set k-cover algorithms for energy efficient monitoring in wireless sensor networks, pp. 424–432 (2003)

5. Cardei, M., Du, D.Z.: Improving wireless sensor network lifetime through power aware organization. Wirel. Netw. **11**(3), 333–340 (2005)
6. Lu, Z., Li, W.W., Pan, M.: Maximum lifetime scheduling for target coverage and data collection in wireless sensor networks. IEEE Trans. Veh. Technol. **64**(2), 714–727 (2015)
7. Meguerdichian, S., Koushanfar, F., Potkonjak, M., et al.: Coverage problems in wireless ad-hoc sensor networks. In: Proceedings of IEEE INFOCOM 2001, Twentieth Joint Conference of the IEEE Computer and Communications Societies. IEEE Xplore, vol. 3, pp. 1380–1387 (2001)
8. Lu, M., Wu, J., Cardei, M., Li, M.: Energy-efficient connected coverage of discrete targets in wireless sensor networks. In: Lu, X., Zhao, W. (eds.) ICCNMC 2005. LNCS, vol. 3619, pp. 43–52. Springer, Heidelberg (2005). https://doi.org/10.1007/11534310_7
9. Gu, Y., Pan, M., Li, W.: Prolonging the lifetime of large scale wireless sensor networks via base station placement. In: Vehicular Technology Conference, pp. 1–5. IEEE (2013)
10. Gu, Y., Pan, M., Li, W.: Maximizing the lifetime of delay-sensitive sensor networks via joint routing and sleep scheduling. In: International Conference on Computing, Networking and Communications, pp. 540–544. IEEE (2014)
11. Zhang, Y., Huang, H., Sun, P., Li, Y.: Improving path-coverage for moving targets in wireless multimedia sensor networks. J. Commun. **9**(11), 843–850 (2014)

Active Learning-Based Semi-supervised Spectral Clustering Algorithm

Wei-Jin Jiang[1,2], Yi-Rong Jiang[3(✉)], Yang Wang[1(✉)], Jia-Hui Chen[1], and Li-Na Tan[1]

[1] Institute of Big Data and Internet Innovation, Mobile E-business Collaborative Innovation Center of Hunan Province, Hunan University of Commerce, Changsha 410205, China
jlwxjh@163.com, 18508488203@163.com, 810663304@qq.com, 363168449@qq.com
[2] School of Computer Science and Technology, Wuhan University of Technology, Wuhan 430073, China
[3] Tonghua Normal University, Tonghua 134002, China
307553803@qq.com

Abstract. Semi-supervised learning is one of the hottest research topics in the Machine Learning. The performance of semi-supervised clustering depends on the quality of supervision information, so it is necessary to actively learn high quality supervision information. An active learning algorithm based on pairwise constraints with error correction is proposed in this paper. The algorithm searches the pair-wise constraints information which clustering algorithm can't find, and try its best to reduce connections between this constraint information, which is used in the spectral clustering. Utilizing supervised information adjust the distance matrix in the spectral clustering, and sort the distances. The algorithm makes the learning can study actively when the learning receives the data without flags by the two-way search method, and get better clustering result with less constraints. Meanwhile, the algorithm reduces the computational complexity of the semi-supervised algorithms based on constraints and resolves the singular problem of the pair-wise constraints in the clustering process. Experimental results on UCI benchmark data sets and artificial data set states clearly the performance of the algorithm is better than other compared algorithms, and the performance of algorithm is better than the ones of the spectral clustering which randomly selects the supervision information.

Keywords: Semi-supervised clustering · Active learning · Semi-supervised learning · Pairwise constraint · Spectral clustering

1 Introduction

Semi-supervised clustering generally guides the clustering process through two kinds of prior information, namely label information and pairwise constraint information. Since the label point information can be transformed into pairwise constraint information, clustering information (must-link and cannot-link) is usually used as a priori information in semi-supervised clustering [1]. There are three main types of

© Springer Nature Singapore Pte Ltd. 2019
F. Sun et al. (Eds.): ICCSIP 2018, CCIS 1005, pp. 234–244, 2019.
https://doi.org/10.1007/978-981-13-7983-3_21

semi-supervised clustering algorithms: the first is a constraint-based semi-supervised clustering method (CBSSC) [1–5]. Such algorithms generally use the must-link and cannot-link pairwise constraints to guide the clustering process. The second category is the distance-based semi-supervised clustering method (DBSSC) [6–9]. This type of algorithm changes the distance measure function in the clustering algorithm by learning the supervised information. The third category is the constraint and distance based semi-supervised clustering method (CDBSSC) [10–15]. It is actually a combination of the above two types of methods.

Although the above three types of algorithms use pairwise constraints to guide clustering, the singular problems of pairwise constraints are often encountered in the solution process, so the clustering results are not very satisfactory. Aiming at the above problems, this paper proposes an Active learning semi-supervised spectral clustering method based on pairwise constraints, and mines the supervised information with rich clustering information and applies it to the spectral clustering algorithm. The algorithm effectively utilizes the supervised information integration data clustering, which reduces the computational complexity of the semi-supervised clustering algorithm based on constraints and solves the singular problem of pairwise constraints in the clustering process.

2 Semi-supervised Clustering Active Learning Algorithm

2.1 Learning Methods

The algorithm calculates the Euclidean distance between two points as an input parameter, $Dist(i,j) = \left(\|x_i - x_j\|^2 \right)^{\frac{1}{2}}$. And each time the algorithm needs to modify the distance matrix according to the constraint supervision information, that is, the ML constraint distance is set to 0, and the CL constraint distance is set to ∞. If $(x_i, x_j) \in ML$, then $Dist(i,j) = 0$; if $(x_i, x_j) \in CL$, then $Dist(i,j) = \infty$.

Algorithm 1.   Active Learning of pair-wise constraints based on Error Correction

Input: The data set, *Dist*, the number of constraints to be learned N, the existing paired point constraint information ML, CL, the last clustering result asgn (which contains the cluster label for each point).

Output: The new constraint new_ML, new_CL, stop evaluating the evaluation.

Step 1 The distance matrix is modified according to the constraint supervision information. Sort each distance value from small to large to get the queue; // Learning new constraints requires the results of the last clustering to find out the incorrect pairwise relationship in the last assignment.

Step 2 Initialize the newly added constraint point set $Pt\_con=\Phi$ in this learning process. The array *smalldis*=Φ, *bigdis*=Φ, saves the distance when the constraint is added. The number of constraints that have been learned during this learning process is $L=0$;

Step 3 // Start processing from two points far away.

Step 3.1 Find the first item x that is not equal to ∞ from large to small in the queue, and let the two points related to x be m and n;

Step 3.2 If $asgn(m) =asgn(n)$, then ask if m and n are the same class; // Investigate the last clustering results of the pair of points, if the same is doubtful, confirm by asking questions, and then advance to a smaller distance

If m and n are not the same class&$(m, n) \notin CL$ & $m \notin Pt\_con$ &$n \notin Pt\_con$

then   {add *(m,n)* to the new_CL constraint, record m and n to Pt_con, record x to *bigdis*, $L=L+1$;}

Step 3.3 Find the next item x in the queue from big to small. The x related points are still recorded as m and n. Go back to step 3.2, until $L>0.5*N$;

Step 4 // Start processing from two points close to each other

Step 4.1 Find the first item y that is not equal to 0 in the queue from small to large, so that the two points related to y are m and n;

Step 4.2 If $asgn(m)\neq asgn(n)$, then ask if m and n are of the same class,

If m and n are the same class&$(m, n) \notin CL$ & $m \notin Pt\_con$ &$n \notin Pt\_con$

Then {add *(m,n)* to the new_ML constraint, record m and n to Pt_con, record y to *smalldis*, $L=L+1$;}

Step 4.3 Find the next item y in the queue from small to large. The points related to y are still recorded as m and n. Go back to step 4.2 until $L=N$;

Step5   Return   new_ML,   new_CL,   calculate   and   return *evaluation=average(bigdis)-average(smalldis)*.

2.2   Semi-supervised Clustering Based on Spectral Method

At present, there are many semi-supervised spectral clustering algorithms. In this paper, the spectral clustering algorithm is matched with this pairwise constrained learning algorithm, and the spectral clustering algorithm in [3] is adopted. For the sake of simplicity, the *k-means* algorithm is used to complete the clustering of the spectral space. The specific process is shown in Algorithm 2.

Algorithm 2.   Semi-supervised spectral clustering algorithm.

Given a data set $S = \{S_1 L, S_n\}$ to be processed, divide it into k classes. The specific steps are as follows:

Step1   Calculate   the   adjacency   matrix $A \in R^{n \times n}$,   where

$$A_{ij} = \exp(-\frac{\left\| s_i - s_j \right\|^2}{2\sigma^2})i \neq j, \text{and } A_{ii} = 0,$$

Step 1.1   If a pair of points *(i, j)* belong to the must-link set, then $Aij = Aji = 1$;

Step 1.2   If a pair of points *(i, j)* belong to the cannot-link set, then $Aij = Aji = 0$;

Step2 Constructing a matrix $L = \dfrac{(A + d_{max}I - D)}{d_{max}}$, where D is a diagonal

matrix, the diagonal elements are $d_{ij} = \sum_{k=1}^{n} A_{ik}$, and *dmax* is the

maximum of the elements on the diagonal;

Step3 Calculate the feature vector corresponding $x_1, x_2, \cdots, x_k$ to the k largest

eigenvalues of L, constructing $X = [x_1, x_2, \cdots, x_k] \in R^{n \times k}$;

Step 4 Unitize each row in X to get matrix Y, that is $Y_{ij} = \dfrac{X_{ij}}{(\sum_j X_{ij}^2)^{\frac{1}{2}}}$;

Step 5 Think of each row of Y as a point in the R^k space, using the *K-means* algorithm or other methods for clustering;

Step 6 If the *i*-th line of Y is assigned to the *j*-th class, the original data point s_i is also assigned to the *j*-th class.

3   Experimental Simulation

3.1   Experimental Data

The experimental data in this paper has real-world data sets and artificial data sets. The real data set uses the UCI benchmark data *iris*, *glass*, and *heart*. The artificial dataset uses self-created data *rings*, *tripleS* and *balls*. Figure 1 shows the 2-dimensional diagram of the 3 personal data sets. Figure 1(a) consists of four spherical data clusters, one for the upper left and the lower right, and one for the lower left and upper right. Figure 1(b) is a two ring type data group, the outer ring is one type, and the inner ring is another type. Figure 1(c) consists of three S-type data clusters, with three categories from left to right.

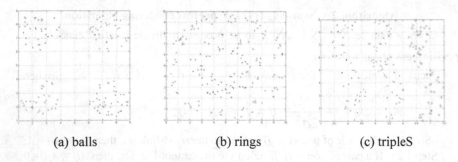

(a) balls   (b) rings   (c) tripleS

Fig. 1. Artificial data set

3.2   Experimental Results and Analysis

The experiment takes 10 runs to average, and learns 10 new constraints per iteration, up to 30 iterations. The results for the six data sets are shown in Fig. 2. It can be seen from Fig. 2 that the learning strategy in this paper can generally get a good result quickly; the

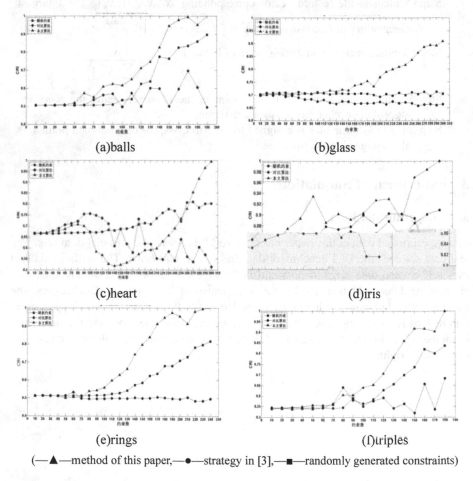

(a)balls   (b)glass

(c)heart   (d)iris

(e)rings   (f)triples

(—▲—method of this paper,—●—strategy in [3],—■—randomly generated constraints)

Fig. 2. Each set of data contrast experiment results

way of randomly generating constraints increases with the increase of constraints; but the contrast strategy yields good results with certain constraints, and the clustering effect may worsen as the constraints increase. This is because *K-means* is used as the clustering algorithm in the spectral space in the spectral clustering algorithm of this paper. Therefore, the learning method of the comparison strategy may not get a good result.

In order to verify that the learning condition *evaluation* < 0 is valid, the number of iterations and the CRI value corresponding to the *evaluation* < 0 is recorded in the above experiment, and the experiment is repeated 10 times, as shown in Table 1. As can be seen from Table 1, the algorithm in this paper has a good performance for all six data sets. The *glass* data set cannot satisfy the stop condition within 300 constraints and stops at the maximum number of learning times. Other data sets can satisfy the stop condition when less than 30 times, and CRI is also better.

Table 1. Experimental results for 6 data sets

Data set	Average number of iterations	Maximum/minimum iterations	Average CRI	Maximum/minimum CRI
Iris	5.2	10/4	0.9721	1.0000/0.9497
Glass	30	30/30	0.8987	0.9315/0.8527
Heart	27.7	29/24	0.9605	0.9852/0.9158
Balls	13.5	18/10	0.9360	1.0000/0.8891
Rings	17.7	25/15	0.9560	0.9883/0.9264
Triples	16.6	19/14	0.9681	1.0000/0.9225

Table 2 shows the cluster number and running time (average of 20 operations) obtained by clustering each algorithm with 6 data sets in each class and 2 randomly generated pairs of constraints.

Table 2. Number of clusters and running time

Data set	NEW		ASSC		RCA		CSC		SCREEN	
	Number of clusters	Time/s	Number of clusters	Time/s	Number of clusters	Time/s	Number of clusters	Time/s	Number of clusters	Time/s
Iris	3	0.16	7.23	0.39	4.12	0.33	3.75	0.26	8.65	0.43
Glass	6	4.32	13.04	10.15	8.26	7.63	7.30	12.19	14.10	9.93
Heart	2	0.29	6.91	0.79	5.09	0.53	3.22	0.43	7.19	0.65
Balls	2	0.28	6.27	0.40	7.17	0.57	3.28	0.72	7.35	0.89
Rings	2	0.31	7.10	0.42	7.57	0.87	3.94	0.63	7.12	0.76
Triples	3	0.31	7.33	0.55	7.62	0.39	3.98	0.70	6.95	0.82

The experimental results are shown in Fig. 3, which shows the *F*-index values of different clustering algorithms on different datasets under different numbers of constraint pairs. When the constraint pair is 0, the CRI index is the clustering performance of the AP algorithm. It can be seen from the figure that the clustering performance of the *NEW* method is greatly improved compared with the AP algorithm. In addition to the dataset triples, the *NEW* method gives better clustering results on several other datasets. As can be seen from the figure, RCA also got better clustering results on most datasets. This shows that in the RCA algorithm, the constraint pair information does not have any guiding effect on the data set partitioning, but it is worse than the original K-means clustering performance. However, as shown in Fig. 3(c), the clustering performance of the ASSC algorithm shows a downward trend when the number of constraint pairs is greater than 201. The *F*-index values of the other two comparison algorithms on all datasets indicate that the performance of the two algorithms is lower than the other four algorithms.

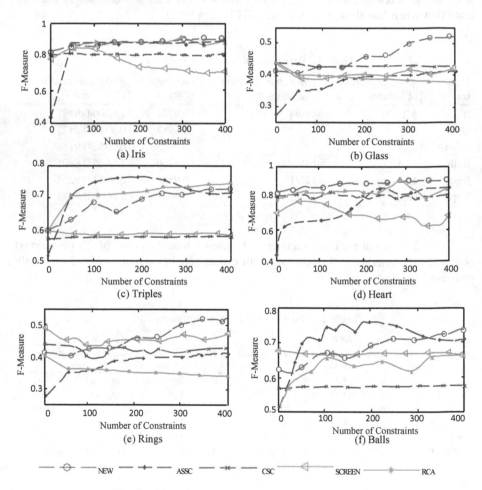

Fig. 3. Clustering performance evaluated by F index

Table 3 shows the NMI values obtained by performing five algorithms on each of the six data sets. Overall, the performance of the New algorithm is superior to the other four algorithms in the low-dimensional data set. When clustering high-dimensional data, the NMI value of the New algorithm is higher than the NMI values of the other four algorithms. Secondly, the NMI value is better than SCREEN, and the RMI is poor when the high-dimensional data is processed. Therefore, for high-dimensional data clustering, the performance of the New algorithm is better than other algorithms. The New algorithm utilizes supervised information integration data dimensionality reduction and clustering, and the singularity problem of pairwise constraints is considered in clustering. Therefore, the performance of *New* algorithm is better than the other four algorithms.

Table 3. Comparison of NMI achieved by New algorithm and four methods on 6 data sets

Dataset	Instance	Dimension	Class	ASSC	RCA	CSC	SCREEN	New
Iris	150	4	3	0.7357	0.8858	0.9231	0.9297	0.9305
Glass	214	9	6	0.4312	0.4523	0.5242	0.5325	0.5197
Heart	270	13	2	0.5738	0.5211	0.5736	0.5821	0.5915
Rings	187	2	2	0.6228	0.6102	0.6417	0.6733	0.6756
Balls	145	2	2	0.8120	0.8231	0.7983	0.8056	0.8419
Triples	176	2	3	0.5123	0.5396	0.5038	0.6234	0.7102

Next, we will experiment on the face data of the high-dimensional large sample. For the 59,217 images collected, the experimental data set information is shown in Table 4.

Table 4. Experimental data sets used by the information

Data set	Size	Dimension	Category
YALEB	2415	1024	38
CMUPIE	3328	1024	68
HeadPose	2791	1120	15
NUS-WIDE	30000	500	30
MSAR-MM	20683	225	20

In order to compare image clustering algorithms, we use the *K-means* clustering algorithm as a benchmark. The ASSC, RCA, CSC, SCREEN, and NEW algorithms first reduce the image samples to the $c - 1$ dimension (c is the number of categories of the training samples), and then use *K-means* to cluster the reduced-dimensional results.

Table 5. Comparison of NMI achieved by New algorithm and five methods on 6 data sets

Algorithm	Data set sample		
	YALEB	CMUPIE	Head Pose
K-means	0.2287 ± 0.0041	0.4160 ± 0.0035	0.4186 ± 0.0020
ASSC+ K-means	0.8893 ± 0.0096	0.8416 ± 0.0074	0.5179 ± 0.0159
RCA+ K-means	0.9058 ± 0.0045	0.8757 ± 0.0068	0.5255 ± 0.0144
CSC+ K-means	0.9111 ± 0.0038	0.8835 ± 0.0040	0.5598 ± 0.0186
SCREEN+ K-means	0.9134 ± 0.0073	0.8843 ± 0.0040	0.5620 ± 0.0181
NEW+ K-means	0.9155 ± 0.0076	0.8892 ± 0.0040	0.5699 ± 0.0182

We randomly selected 1 000 data from each data set as training samples, 300 of which have annotation information, and the remaining training samples have no annotation information. The remaining data in the data set was used as the test sample, and each set of experiments was repeated 10 times, and then the average and standard deviation of the 10 results were calculated. The experimental results are shown in Table 5.

3.3   Relevant Work Comparison

It can be seen from the above experiments that the algorithm in this paper is different from the traditional spectral clustering algorithm [15]: the Gauss kernel function often used by the spectral clustering algorithm is different as the similarity measure, and the similarity is directly calculated on the Euclidean distance measure. The computational complexity of the proposed algorithm is $O(tn_{ml}l^2)$ $(n_{ml} < n)$, where l is the number of samples, n_{ml} is the number of samples after the merged must-link pairwise constraint, n is the original sample number, and t is the number of iterations. It is not difficult to find that the computational complexity of the algorithm is less than or equal to the computational complexity of K-means $(O(tnl^2))$. Therefore, the algorithm in this paper is a simple and effective algorithm. CDBSSC adds a penalty to K-means' objective function in an attempt to solve the above problem, but choosing the appropriate penalty factor is a difficult problem for this type of algorithm. Therefore, this kind of algorithm is not only difficult to solve the singular problem, but also increases the computational complexity of the algorithm $(O(tnl^4))$.

4   Conclusion

Semi-supervised learning is an important technique that utilizes unlabeled learning. It automatically utilizes a large amount of unlabeled data to enhance the generalization of the learner over the entire data distribution without external intervention. In this paper, an algorithm for actively learning pairwise constraints is proposed. Based on the spectral feature matrix formed by the adjusted distance matrix, the objective function clustering is performed. The experimental results show that the clustering performance of the algorithm is better than the semi-supervised spectral clustering based on random selection of supervised information, and overcomes the problem of nuclear parameter sensitivity. At the same time, the conditions for learning stop are given. The experiment verifies that the stopping condition can effectively find better clustering results. The constraint set has a great influence on the clustering result, and the evaluation of the constraint set is a problem worthy of further study. The correlation between Coherence and clustering results, another evaluation index proposed in [6], is not very obvious, so other evaluation indicators need to be further studied. In addition, exploring how many marker samples are needed to achieve effective semi-supervised learning, under what circumstances semi-supervised learning works, how to avoid semi-supervised learning may result in a significant decline in learner generalization ability, and semi-supervised learning to solve more practical issues will continue to be an important part of the research.

Acknowledgments. This work was supported by the National Natural Science Foundation of China (61472136; 61772196), the Hunan Provincial Focus Social Science Fund (2016ZDB006), Key Project of Hunan Provincial Social Science Achievement Review Committee (XSP 19ZD1005), Hunan Provincial Social Science Achievement Review Committee results appraisal identification project (Xiang social assessment 2016JD05). The authors gratefully acknowledge the financial support provided by the Key Laboratory of Hunan Province for New Retail Virtual Reality Technology (2017TP1026).

References

1. Zhao, X., Liu, X.: An improved spectral clustering algorithm based on axiomatic fuzzy set. J. Electron. Inf. Technol. **40**(8), 1–7 (2018)
2. Ramon-Gonen, R., Gelbard, R.: Cluster evolution analysis: identification and detection of similar clusters and migration patterns. Expert Syst. Appl. **83**, 363–378 (2017). https://doi.org/10.1016/j.eswa.2017.04.007
3. Xia, P., Ren, Q., Wu, T., et al.: Sonar image segmentation fusion of multi-scale statistical information FCM clustering and MRF model in wavelet domain. Acta Armamentaria **38**(5), 940–948 (2017). https://doi.org/10.3969/j.issn.1000-1093.2017.05.014
4. Li, W., Zhao, J., Yan, T.: Improved Kmeans clustering algorithm optimizing initial clustering centers based on average difference degree. Control Decis. **32**(4), 759–762 (2017). https://doi.org/10.13195/j.kzyjc.2016.0274
5. Jia, H., Ding, S., Du, M.: Self-tuning p-spectral clustering based on shared nearest neighbors. Cogn. Comput. **7**(5), 622–632 (2015)
6. Huang, S.-B., Yuan, C.-F., Huang, Y.-H.: SCoS: the design and implementation of parallel spectral clustering algorithm based on spar. Chin. J. Comput. **41**(4), 868–885 (2018)
7. Hu, Q., Ding, S.: p-Spectral clustering algorithm with optimization of local similarity. J. Front. Comput. Sci. Technol. **12**(3), 462–471 (2018)
8. Xu, H.L., Long, G.Z., Bie, X.F., Wu, T.A., Guo, P.S.: Active learning algorithm of SVM combining tri-training semi-supervised learning and convex-hull vector. Pattern Recogn. Artif. Intell. **29**(1), 39–46 (2016)
9. Ye, M., Liu, W.: Large scale spectral clustering based on fast landmark sampling. J. Electron. Inf. Technol. **39**(2), 278–284 (2017)
10. Yang, J., Deng, T.: A semi-supervised multiview spectral clustering algorithm based on distance metric learning. J. Sichuan Univ. (Eng. Sci. Ed.) **48**(1), 146–151 (2016)

11. Zhang, J., Zhang, H.: Improved spectral clustering based on inflexion point estimate. J. Chin. Comput. Syst. **38**(5), 1049–1053 (2017)
12. Lu, C., Yan, S., Lin, Z.: Convex sparse spectral clustering: single-view to multi-view. IEEE Trans. Image Process. **25**(6), 2833–2834 (2016)
13. Tian, F., Gao, B., Cui, Q., et al.: Learning deep representations for graph clustering. In: Proceedings of the Association for the Advance of Artificial Intelligence, Quebec City, Canada, pp. 1293–1299 (2014)
14. Cao, S., Lu, W., Xu, Q.: Deep neural networks for the advance of artificial intelligence, Phoenix, Arizona, USA, pp. 1145–1152 (2016)
15. Yoo, S., Huang, H., Kasiviswanathan, S.P.: Streaming spectral clustering. In: Proceedings of the IEEE International Conference on Data Mining, Helsinki, Finland, pp. 637–648 (2016)

Secondary Filtering Update Algorithm for Nonlinear Systems—Based on Extended Kalman Filter

Xiaoliang Feng[1], Yuxin Feng[1], and Chenglin Wen[1,2(✉)]

[1] College of Electrical Engineering, Henan University of Technology,
Zhengzhou 450001, China
wencl@hdu.edu.cn
[2] School of Automation, Hangzhou Dianzi University, Hangzhou 310018, China

Abstract. Based on the fixed point theory, in this paper, a novel extended Kalman filtering algorithm with secondary filtering update is proposed for nonlinear systems. As we all known, the traditional extended Kalman filter which based on the Taylor series expansion of nonlinear system function, only retains the first-order approximation term, and omits the second-order and higher order terms. It is inevitable to reduce the estimation accuracy. This paper compensates and updates it by constructing a secondary filtering update algorithm. The secondary filtering algorithm constructs the filtering state estimation equation into a fixed point equation and updates the state estimate by solving the fixed point equation. The final simulation results verify the effectiveness and feasibility of the proposed method.

Keywords: Nonlinear systems · Extended Kalman filtering ·
Secondary filtering update · Fixed point equation

1 Introduction

As we all known, the filtering methods, such as, Kalman filters [1–4], H∞ filters [5, 6], and Characteristic function filters [7, 8], have been widely used in radar target tracking, information fusion, communication, navigation, and other fields.

For a system described by a linear Gaussian model, the standard Kalman filter was utilized and developed to obtain an estimate of the system state, in the sense of minimum mean square error (MMSE). However, actual systems always exhibit various of nonlinearity. In order to achieve the state estimate of nonlinear systems, we must establish the filtering algorithm for nonlinear systems [9–15]. Among them, there are two main types of nonlinear filtering methods. One kind of nonlinear filtering methods firstly linearize the system model, and then use the linear system filtering method to obtain the system state estimate, such as the extended Kalman filter (EKF) [9–11]. Another nonlinear filtering method is to approximate the statistics of the system state estimation. The representative methods include unscented Kalman filter (UKF) [12, 13], particle filter (PF) [14, 15], and so on. For the extended Kalman filter, the core idea is to linearize the system model by ignoring the secondary and more order terms of the Taylor series at certain working point. Adhere, based on the approximate linearization

© Springer Nature Singapore Pte Ltd. 2019
F. Sun et al. (Eds.): ICCSIP 2018, CCIS 1005, pp. 245–254, 2019.
https://doi.org/10.1007/978-981-13-7983-3_22

model, the standard Kalman filter algorithm could be used to estimate the system state. With simple filtering construction, EKF is easy to understand and carry out. However, EKF only retains the first-order approximation of the Taylor series expansion of the nonlinear function, and omits the second-order and above high-order terms. This results into a loss of estimation accuracy. While UKF avoided the linearization of nonlinear functions, which approximates the probability density distribution of the nonlinear function and uses a series of determined samples to approximate the posterior probability density of the state [13]. However, it requires a specific form of nonlinear function to select the sampling point. Therefore, when the system with high nonlinearity, the estimation error of UKF is still large.

Motivated by the discussion above, especial for the advantages and disadvantages of EKF, in this paper, a novel secondary filtering update algorithm is proposed on the basis of EKF. In the secondary filtering update process, the state estimate and the filtering gain is iteratively obtained by solving a fixed point equation about the filter state estimate. To some extent, the secondary filtering update method compensates for the influence of the truncation error of the Taylor series expansion on the state estimation value, and then improves the estimation accuracy of the whole method.

The rest of this article is organized as follows: A discrete nonlinear system model is formulated in Sect. 2. In Sect. 3, the standard EKF is introduced and the state estimate is updated by the secondary filtering update method. In Sect. 4, a numerical simulation is given to illustrate the effectiveness of the proposed method. Section 5 summarizes this article.

2   System Overview

Consider the following nonlinear stochastic dynamic system:

$$x(k) = f(x(k-1), k) + w(k) \tag{1}$$

which is observed by the following nonlinear measurement model:

$$y(k) = h(x(k), k) + v(k) \tag{2}$$

where, k is the system discrete time. $x(k)$ is the state of the system at time k. $f(*)$ is a nonlinear evolution function of the system state. $h(*)$ is the nonlinear observation function of the system. It is assumed that $w(k)$ and $v(k)$ are both zero-mean white Gaussian noise sequences with covariance $Q(k)$ and $R(k)$, respectively, and uncorrelated with each other. Namely, $w(k) \sim \mathcal{N}(0, Q(k))$, $v(k) \sim \mathcal{N}(0, R(k))$.

Remark 1: For the convenience of discussing the problem, both $w(k)$ and $v(k)$ are assumed to additive. However, the issues discussed below also apply to non-additive situations.

For a state filtering problem, our goal is to find the best estimate of the system state $x(k)$ given the measurement sequence $Y(k) = \{y(1), \cdots, y(k)\}$ up to the most recent time instant k. For the above general nonlinear systems, EKF is one of the most commonly used state estimation methods. In EKF, it is necessary to perform Taylor series expansion on the nonlinear equations of the system, and use the first-order terms and constant terms to approximate the original system equations to achieve linearization of the system model. On this basis, the classical Kalman filter is used to achieve system state estimation. Based on the idea of fixed point equation, this paper proposes an algorithm for quadratic filtering update of nonlinear systems based on extended Kalman filtering algorithm. To some extent, it compensates for the influence of truncation error of Taylor series expansion on state estimation.

3 Secondary Filtering Update Method

In this section, the classical EKF is first introduced. Based on the construction and solution of fixed-point equations, a quadratic filtering update method for state estimation is given. The main content includes the following two subsections.

3.1 Extended Kalman Filtering

For the nonlinear systems shown in (1) and (2), the Taylor series expansion is performed on them. First, the nonlinear function $f(*)$ is expanded by the Taylor series at the state estimate $\hat{x}(k-1|k-1)$, and the higher order terms of the second order and above are discarded to linearize the process function. The nonlinear function $h(*)$ in the observation equation is expanded by the Taylor series at the state prediction value $\hat{x}(k|k-1)$, and the higher order terms of the second order and above are discarded to linearize the observation function. The classical extended Kalman filter algorithm is given as follows.

Time update:

$$\hat{x}(k|k-1) = E\{x(k)|Y(k-1)\} \approx f(\hat{x}(k-1|k-1)) \tag{3}$$

Equation (3) is used to predict the state of the system, in which, $Y(k-1) = \{y(1), y(2), \cdots, y(k-1)\}$. However, in order to predict the covariance of the system state, the nonlinear function $f(x(k-1), k)$ needs to perform Taylor series expansion at the state estimate $\hat{x}(k-1|k-1)$ and ignore the second order and high order terms.

Denote

$$F(k, k-1) = \left. \frac{\partial f(x(k-1), k)}{\partial x(k)} \right|_{x(k)=\hat{x}(k-1|k-1)}$$

The corresponding state prediction covariance is

$$P(k|k-1) = \mathrm{cov}(x(k)|Y(k-1)) \approx F(k, k-1)P(k-1|k-1)F^T(k, k-1) + Q(k) \tag{4}$$

Measurement update:

At time k, the predicted value of the system observation is

$$\hat{y}(k|k-1) = E\{y(k)|Y(k-1)\} \approx h(\hat{x}(k|k-1)) \tag{5}$$

At time k, the systematic observation prediction error covariance is

$$P_y(k|k-1) = \text{cov}(y(k)|Y(k-1)) \approx H(k)P(k|k-1)H^T(k) + R(k) \qquad (6)$$

where,

$$H(k) = \left.\frac{\partial h(x(k), k)}{\partial x(k)}\right|_{x(k) = \hat{x}(k|k-1)}$$

On this basis, the filter gain of the extended Kalman filter can be obtained

$$K(k) \approx P(k|k-1)H^T(k)(H(k)P(k|k-1)H^T(k) + R(k))^{-1} \qquad (7)$$

Further, the state estimate of the system is obtained by

$$\hat{x}(k|k) = E\{x(k)|Y(k)\} \approx \hat{x}(k|k-1) + K(k)(y(k) - \hat{y}(k|k-1)) \qquad (8)$$

The corresponding estimated error covariance is

$$P(k|k) = \text{cov}(x(k)|Y(k)) \approx (I - K(k)H(k))P(k|k-1) \qquad (9)$$

In order to solve the state estimation of the nonlinear system at each moment by extending the Kalman filter, it is only necessary to continuously perform the iterative process described by Eqs. (3)–(9).

3.2   Secondary Update Based on Fixed Point Equation

In this section, a new filtering algorithm to update the state estimate is introduced based on the EKF. The filtered estimation result obtained by EKF is used as the initial value of the secondary filtering algorithm, and the filtering gain obtained by the extended Kalman filtering algorithm will be used as the initial value of the filtering gain of the first iteration of the fixed point filtering algorithm. Then, the initial value of the filter estimate in the fixed point filtering algorithm is substituted into the fixed point equation for iteration. If the iteration error between the previous and second is less than a given iteration threshold, the iteration is exited and the iteration value is output as a fixed point filter estimate value. Then, the filtered estimated value obtained by the iteration is substituted into the fixed point equation to update the fixed point filtering gain. The secondary system is sequentially filtered to update the nonlinear system. The specific implementation is formulated as follows.

For the nonlinear systems described in (1) and (2), construct the following form of filter:

$$\hat{\hat{x}}(k|k) = \hat{x}(k|k) + u(k) * [y(k) - \hat{y}^*(k)] \qquad (10)$$

$$\hat{y}^*(k) = h(\hat{\hat{x}}(k|k), k) + E\{v(k)\} \qquad (11)$$

In fact, the filters described by Eqs. (10) and (11) are fixed point equations with unknown parameters. Among them, $u(k) \in R^{n \times m}$ is the filter gain matrix to be estimated. $\hat{x}(k|k)$ is the state estimate obtained by extended Kalman filtering. $\hat{\hat{x}}(k|k)$ is the unknown state in the fixed point equation. $u(k)$ is the unknown filter gain of the fixed point equation. $y(k)$ is the observed value of the system. $E\{v(k)\}$ is the mean value of the observed noise of the system (which is set to zero in this paper).

We set $u_0(k) = K(k)$, and $\hat{\hat{x}}_0^0(k|k) = \hat{x}(k|k)$. Substituting Eq. (10) into Eq. (11) yields the equation:

$$\hat{\hat{x}}(k|k) = \hat{x}(k|k) + u(k) * [y(k) - h(\hat{\hat{x}}(k|k), k) - E\{v(k)\}] \tag{12}$$

The iterative process for solving the fixed point equation shown in Eq. (12) can be constructed as follows:

$$\begin{cases} \hat{\hat{x}}_0^1(k|k) = \hat{\hat{x}}_0^0(k|k) + u_0(k) * (y(k) - H(\hat{\hat{x}}_0^0(k|k), k)) \\ \hat{\hat{x}}_0^2(k|k) = \hat{\hat{x}}_0^1(k|k) + u_0(k) * (y(k) - H(\hat{\hat{x}}_0^1(k|k), k)) \\ \vdots \\ \hat{\hat{x}}_0^{m_0}(k|k) = \hat{\hat{x}}_0^{m_0-1}(k|k) + u_0(k) * (y(k) - H(\hat{\hat{x}}_0^{m_0-1}(k|k), k)) \end{cases} \tag{13}$$

Where, $m_0 = 1, 2, \cdots, n$.

When $\left| \hat{\hat{x}}_0^{m_0}(k|k) - \hat{\hat{x}}_0^{m_0-1}(k|k) \right| < \varepsilon$ (ε is the given iteration threshold), $\hat{\hat{x}}_0^{m_0}(k|k)$ is output as the fixed point filtering state estimate $\hat{\hat{x}}_1(k|k) = \hat{\hat{x}}_0^{m_0}(k|k)$ at time k.

Because $u(k)$ is an unknown parameter in the fixed point equations described in Eqs. (10) and (11), this paper intends to update the unknown parameter $u(k)$ by the following method based on the above estimation of the fixed point filtering state.

$$u_1(k) = \frac{\hat{\hat{x}}_1(k|k) - \hat{x}(k|k)}{y(k) - H(\hat{\hat{x}}_1(k|k), k)} \tag{14}$$

Using the above to obtain $u_1(k)$, further construct the following fixed point equation:

$$\hat{\hat{x}}_2(k|k) = \hat{\hat{x}}_1(k|k) + u_1(k) * [y(k) - H(\hat{\hat{x}}_2(k|k), k) - E\{v(k)\}] \tag{15}$$

Then construct an iterative solution process similar to the fixed point equation shown in (13):

$$\begin{cases} \hat{\hat{x}}_1^1(k|k) = \hat{\hat{x}}_1^0(k|k) + u_1(k) * (y(k) - H(\hat{\hat{x}}_1^0(k|k), k)) \\ \hat{\hat{x}}_1^2(k|k) = \hat{\hat{x}}_1^1(k|k) + u_1(k) * (y(k) - H(\hat{\hat{x}}_1^1(k|k), k)) \\ \vdots \\ \hat{\hat{x}}_1^{m_1}(k|k) = \hat{\hat{x}}_1^{m_1-1}(k|k) + u_1(k) * (y(k) - H(\hat{\hat{x}}_1^{m_1-1}(k|k), k)) \end{cases} \tag{16}$$

where $m_1 = 1, 2, \cdots, n$.

When $\left|\hat{\tilde{x}}_1^{m_1}(k|k) - \hat{\tilde{x}}_1^{m_1-1}(k|k)\right| < \varepsilon$ (ε is the given iteration threshold) then, $\hat{\tilde{x}}_1^{m_1}(k|k)$ is output as the fixed point filtering state estimate $\hat{\tilde{x}}_2(k|k) = \hat{\tilde{x}}_1^{m_1}(k|k)$ at time k.

Similarly, we can get the unknown parameter $u_i(k)$ of the fixed point equation in the ith iteration and its corresponding fixed point equation:

$$\hat{x}_{i+1}(k|k) = \hat{x}_i(k|k) + u_i(k) * [y(k) - H(\hat{x}_i(k|k), k) - E\{v(k)\}] \tag{17}$$

Its iterative solution process is as follows:

$$\begin{cases} \hat{\tilde{x}}_i^1(k|k) = \hat{\tilde{x}}_i^0(k|k) + u_i(k) * (y(k) - H(\hat{\tilde{x}}_i^0(k|k), k)) \\ \hat{\tilde{x}}_i^2(k|k) = \hat{\tilde{x}}_i^1(k|k) + u_i(k) * (y(k) - H(\hat{\tilde{x}}_i^1(k|k), k)) \\ \qquad\qquad\vdots \\ \hat{\tilde{x}}_i^{m_i}(k|k) = \hat{\tilde{x}}_i^{m_i-1}(k|k) + u_i(k) * (y(k) - H(\hat{\tilde{x}}_i^{m_i-1}(k|k), k)) \end{cases} \tag{18}$$

If $|u_i(k) - u_{i-1}(k)| < \varepsilon$ (ε is the given iteration threshold), then output $\hat{x}(k|k) = \hat{\tilde{x}}_i^{m_i}(k|k)$ as the final result of the auxiliary filter update.

Remark 2: When the fixed-point equation appears divergent, the above iterative process will be difficult to converge, that is, the end condition of the iterative process cannot be satisfied. At this point, it is necessary to constrain the iterative update process based on the fixed point equation. Considering that the numerical point divergence may occur in the solution process of the fixed point equation. In this article, an interrupt instruction $\alpha(k)$ is set. Each iteration, the interrupt instruction is incremented by 1. When the interrupt instruction reaches the maximum number of iterations, the iterative process tends to be scattered; At this point, the iterative process is terminated. In the simulation process of this paper, the maximum number of iterations of the fixed point equation is set to 10 times.

4 Simulation Analysis

In this section, a numerical simulation is provided to illustrate the effectiveness and feasibility of the proposed secondary filtering method. Consider the following non-linear systems:

$$\begin{cases} x(k+1) = 2.5x(k)/(1+x^2(k)) + w(k+1,k) \\ y(k+1) = x^2(k+1) + v(k+1) \end{cases} \tag{19}$$

where, $f(x(k), k)$, $H(x(k+1), k)$ are the nonlinear state function and the nonlinear measurement function, separately. $w(k+1, k)$, $v(k+1)$ are respectively the process noise and observed noise of the system, and they are uncorrelated zero-mean Gaussian white noise with the variances $Q = 0.1$, $R = 1$. The initial values are: $x(0) = 1$, $p(0) = 0.1$.

This simulation includes two parts: firstly, the proposed filtering method is compared with the basal EKF algorithm. Further, The proposed method is compared with the famous UKF method.

Part 1: Compared with the basal EKF

The simulation results are shown in the following Fig. 1:

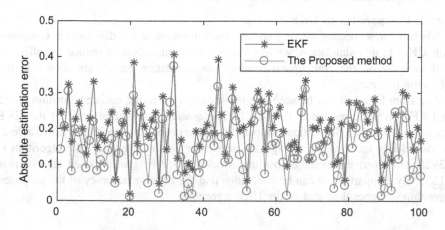

Fig. 1. The absolute estimation error curves of the proposed method and EKF

Table 1. The mean absolute estimation error (MMSE) of the proposed method and EKF

Filtering methods	EKF	The proposed method
MAEE	0.2035	0.1504

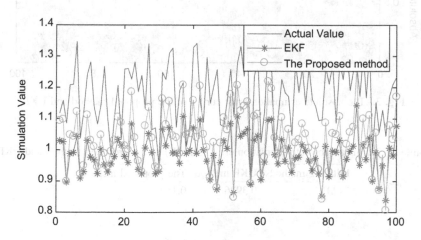

Fig. 2. The real state curve and two estimate curves

From Table 1, we can clearly see that the average absolute error obtained by the EKF method is 0.2035. However, the average absolute error obtained by the proposed method is 0.1504. As shown in Fig. 2, it can be seen that the secondary filtering update algorithm based on EKF can significantly improve the filtering performance of non-linear systems compared with EKF. The better performance of the proposed method indicates that the secondary filtering update algorithm based on EKF leads to better performed nonlinear filters if the expansion points are well selected.

Part 2: Compared with UKF
In this part, the secondary filtering update algorithm proposed in this paper is compared with UKF. In this simulation, we use Monte Carlo simulation to reduce the affect of random noise on the comparison results. The simulation results are shown in the following figures:

Just from Fig. 3, it can be seen that the secondary filtering update algorithm based on EKF also performs better than UKF. The absolute estimation error of the UKF algorithm has a large fluctuation compared with the proposed algorithm. From Table 2, we can clearly see that the average absolute error obtained by the UKF algorithm is 0.3926. However, the average absolute error obtained by the proposed algorithm is 0.1535. By comparison, it can be concluded that the filtering accuracy of the proposed algorithm is higher than that of the UKF algorithm.

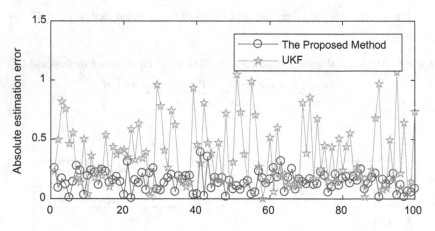

Fig. 3. The absolute estimation error curves of the proposed method and UKF

Table 2. The mean absolute estimation error (MMSE) of the proposed method and UKF

Filtering methods	UKF method	The proposed method
MAEE	0.3926	0.1535

As shown in Figs. 2 and 4, the estimation accuracy of the proposed algorithm is compared with the extended Kalman filteralgorithm and the unscented Kalman filter algorithm. The proposed algorithm has higher estimation accuracy and better filtering effect. Experiments show that using the fixed point equation to perform secondary filtering update on a class of nonlinear systems can improve the state estimation accuracy of the system and reduce the state estimation error.

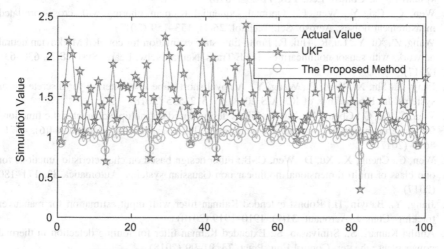

Fig. 4. The real state curve and two estimate curves

5 Summary of this Article

This paper proposes a secondary filtering update algorithm for a class of nonlinear systems. The algorithm first uses an extended Kalman filter algorithm to obtain an extended Kalman filter state estimate and filter gain. The obtained state estimation value and filter gain are used as the filter estimation initial value and the filter gain in the fixed point filter equation, and then the system is iteratively updated by the fixed point equation. Compared with the classical EKF, this method can effectively improve the estimation accuracy of nonlinear filtering. The simulation compare results verify the effectiveness of the secondary filtering update method.

Acknowledgment. This work was supported by the National Natural Science Foundation of China under grant nos. 61503174, U1804163 and 61773154, the Natural Science Foundation of Henan Province of China under grant nos. 162102210196, and the Scientific Research Foundation of Henan University of Technology under grant no. 2015RCJH14.

References

1. Qiu, A., Gu, J., Wen, C., Zhang, J.: Self-triggered fault estimation and fault tolerant control for networked control systems. Neurocomputing **272**, 629–637 (2018)
2. Wu, Z., Fu, M., Xu, Y., Lu, R.: A distributed Kalman filtering algorithm with fast finite-time convergence for sensor networks. Automatica **95**, 63–72 (2018)
3. Marelli, D., Zamani, M., Fu, M., Ninness, B.: Distributed Kalman filter in a network of linear systems. Syst. Control Lett. **116**, 71–77 (2018)
4. Wen, C., Cai, Y., Wen, C.: Optimal sequential Kalman filtering with cross-correlated measurement noises. Aerosp. Sci. Technol. **26**(1), 153–159 (2013)
5. Wang, Z., Xu, Y., Lu, R., Hui, P.: Finite-time state estimation for coupled Markovian neural networks with sensor nonlinearities. IEEE Trans. Neural Netw. Learn. Syst. **28**(3), 630–638 (2017)
6. Feng, X., Shi, X., Wen, C., Wang, Y.: A novel short dime H∞ filtering for discrete linear systems. In: Proceedings of ICCAIS 2018, pp. 512–515 (2018)
7. Wen, C., Ge, Q., Cheng, X., Xu, D.: Filters design based on multiple characteristic functions for the grinding process cylindrical workpieces. IEEE Trans. Ind. Electron. **64**(6), 4671–4679 (2017)
8. Wen, C., Cheng, X., Xu, D., Wen, C.-B.: Filter design based on characteristic functions for one class of multi-dimensional nonlinear non-Gaussian systems. Automatica **82**, 171–180 (2017)
9. Jiang, Y., Baoyin, H.: Robust extended Kalman filter with input estimation for maneuver tracking. Chin. J. Aeronaut. **31**(9), 1910–1919 (2018)
10. Anitha Kumari, S., Srinivasan, S.: Extended Kalman filter for fouling detection in thermal power plant reheater. Control Eng. Pract. **73**, 91–99 (2018)
11. Ge, Q., Shao, T., Chen, S., Wen, C.: Carrier tracking estimation analysis by using the extended strong tracking filtering. IEEE Trans. Ind. Electron. **64**(2), 1415–1424 (2017)
12. Kulikov, G.Y., Kulikova, M.V.: Accurate continuous–discrete unscented Kalman filtering for estimation of nonlinear continuous-time stochastic models in radar tracking. Sig. Process. **139**, 25–35 (2017)
13. Zheng, B., Fu, P., Li, B., Yuan, X.: A robust adaptive unscented Kalman filter for nonlinear estimation with uncertain noise covariance. Sensors **18**(3), 808–816 (2018)
14. Wang, Z., Mo, C., Dai, H.: Target detection method before tracking based on particle filter. Procedia Comput. Sci. **107**, 141–147 (2017)
15. Salmond, D.J., Smith, A.F.: A particle filter for track before detection. In: IEEE Proceedings of the American Control Conference, pp. 3755–3760 (2001)

Probabilistic Context-Aware Ambients

Lei Zhang[1], Yue Long[1], Yongzhi Cao[1,2], and Hanpin Wang[1,3(✉)]

[1] Key Laboratory of High Confidence Software Technologies (MOE),
School of EECS, Peking University, Beijing 100871, China
[2] School of Mathematics and Statistics,
Northeastern University at Qinhuangdao, Qinhuangdao 066004, China
[3] School of Computer Science, Guangzhou University,
Guangzhou 510006, China
whpxhy@pku.edu.cn

Abstract. The calculus of context-aware ambients has been introduced
for modeling mobile systems that are context-aware. However, due to the
randomness of contexts in real life, the methods to deal with it are necessary. Therefore, based on the aforementioned calculus, we present the
calculus of probabilistic context-aware ambients in this paper. We provide the syntax and semantics of our calculus. The new calculus is mainly
designed for modeling the processes and contexts both with randomness.

Keywords: Process calculus · Calculus of context-aware ambients ·
Context awareness · Calculus of probabilistic context-aware ambients

1 Introduction

In the early 1990s, Weiser proposed the pervasive computing [1] which is a
paradigm for distributed systems where portable devices appear anywhere and
anytime in humans' daily life. In pervasive computing, context-awareness is considered as the key technique about the media or transformations between physical space and information. In recent years, with the development of sensor technology, context-awareness has been widely applied in industrial products.

There are mainly two kinds of formal methods for context-aware systems.
One is based on the bigraphs, for example [2–5]. Another method origins from
process calculus. Braione and Picco [6] modeled the context-aware systems with
process calculus. In [7], Zimmer designed a new process calculus to describe and
analyze agent systems by using ambient calculus and join calculus. Similarly,
Kjærgaard and Bunde [8] proposed CONAWA calculus based on mobile ambients. In CONAWA, one can find that the actions of a system depend on its
context evidently. But the syntax of CONAWA calculus is not concise enough.

In 2011, inspired by Zimmer's calculus, Siewe et al. built a context-aware
calculus named calculus of context-aware ambients (CCA for short) [9] to model

Supported by National Natural Science Foundation of China under Grants 61572003,
61772035, 61751210 and Major State Research Development Program of China (No.
2016QY04W0804).

F. Sun et al. (Eds.): ICCSIP 2018, CCIS 1005, pp. 255–267, 2019.
https://doi.org/10.1007/978-981-13-7983-3_23

and analyze mobile systems with the capability of context-awareness. They proposed a method that describes context information by logic language formally, and changed the atomic action in Zimmer's calculus with context-guarded action. These improvements enable processes in CCA to perform different actions according to different context information. CCA has been applied in many areas since it was proposed: besides describing the exceptional handling [10], it is also used for a formal specification [11] and smart car systems.

Nowadays, there are many systems with randomness such as large distributed systems and social network. Since 1980s, there have been some probabilistic extensions of the classic process calculus (like CCS and CSP) [12,13] to deal with situations involving randomness. Some scholars replaced the non-deterministic behavior with probabilistic behavior [14,15], and others enriched the calculus with a probabilistic choice operator [16,17].

In this paper, we propose a new calculus called the calculus of probabilistic context-aware ambients (PCA for short) to model the random systems with context-awareness. We extend and refine the syntax and semantics of CCA [9] to allow probabilistic behaviors. We also enrich the context-guarded action with the ability of making decisions built on the probabilities of contexts by defining a semantics where probabilities and non-determinism co-exist.

The rest of the paper is organized as follows. Firstly, we briefly recall some basic details of CCA in Sect. 2. Then we make a preparation for PCA by combining probability into processes and contexts of CCA in Sect. 3. Section 4 is devoted to the syntax and semantics of PCA, and Sect. 5 concludes the work and identifies several interesting problems for further research.

2   Calculus of Context-Aware Ambients

In this section, we recall some basic notations and concepts of CCA from [9].

2.1   Syntax of CCA

Like the π-calculus [20], the simplest entities of the calculus are *names* which is usually denoted by n, m. For simplicity, we denote the set of *names* by $\mathbf{N}$. We let $\tilde{y}$ denote a list of names and $|\tilde{y}|$ denote the size of $\tilde{y}$. The syntax of CCA is defined as follows.

$$P, Q ::= \mathbf{0} \mid P|Q \mid (\nu n)P \mid !P \mid n[P] \mid \kappa?M.P \mid x \rhd (\tilde{y}).P$$
$$M ::= \text{in } n \mid \text{out} \mid \text{del } n \mid \alpha x\langle\tilde{y}\rangle \mid \alpha(\tilde{y}) \mid \alpha\langle\tilde{y}\rangle$$
$$\alpha ::= \uparrow \mid n\uparrow \mid \downarrow \mid n\downarrow \mid :: \mid n:: \mid \epsilon$$

There are mainly three parts: processes (denoted by P or Q), capabilities (denoted by M), and locations (denoted by α). Here we illustrate the syntax of CCA, since the syntax of PCA is based on it.

Processes are the principal part of CCA. The notation $\mathbf{0}$ represents the process that does nothing and terminates immediately. The notation $P|Q$ means that P and Q are running in parallel. The notation $(\nu n)P$ restricts the name n private and unique to P. The notation $n[P]$ means that n is the name of the ambient and P is the running process in the ambient. The notation $!P$ allows the process to make a copy of P anytime. The notation $\kappa?M.P$ is a process that waits until the environment satisfies κ, then the process performs M and continues like P. We will show the formal definition of context expression κ and explain how an environment *satisfies* it in the next subsection. The notation $x \rhd (\tilde{y}).P$ states the linking of the name x to the process P, where $\tilde{y}$ is a list of formal parameters. For simplicity, PCA will not have processes of this type.

Capabilities can be thought as terms that enable the ambients or processes to perform some actions. We group the capabilities into two categories: the first three are designed for mobility, and the last three mainly focus on message passing. The ability to go inside another sibling specific ambient n is 'in n' capability, and oppositely the ability to leave a parent ambient is the 'out' capability. Besides, 'del n' is used for dissolving a sibling and empty ambient named n.

In CCA, processes exchange messages using the output capability $\alpha\langle\tilde{y}\rangle$ to send a list of names $\tilde{y}$ to a location α, and the input capability $\alpha(\tilde{y})$ to receive a list of names from a location α. The location α can be "↑" for any parent, "n ↑" for a specific parent n; "↓" for any child, "n ↓" for a specific child n; "::" for any sibling, "n ::" for a specific sibling n; ϵ (empty string) for the executing ambient itself. For the reason that the capability $\alpha x\langle\tilde{y}\rangle$ is used for process call which PCA does not have, here we still omit its details.

2.2   Context-Awareness

In CCA, a context $\mathcal{C}$ is a process containing some (including zero) occurrence(s) of a hole '⊙'. We will formally define the contexts of CCA:

$$\mathcal{C}, \mathcal{C}' ::= \mathbf{0} \mid \odot \mid \mathcal{C}|P \mid P|\mathcal{C} \mid n[\mathcal{C}] \mid (\nu n)\mathcal{C}$$

where P is a process and $n \in \mathbf{N}$.

The context of a subprocess is obtained by replacing this subprocess by a hole '⊙'. For example, a system is modeled by the process $P \mid n[Q \mid m[R \mid S]]$. So, the context of the process R in that system is $P \mid n[Q \mid m[\odot \mid S]]$. Conversely, we can also put a process P into a context $\mathcal{C}$ by replacing all holes with the process, and then we get a process $\mathcal{C}(P)$. In the previous example, if we put the process T into the context of R, the origin process turns into $P \mid n[Q \mid m[T \mid S]]$. For spatial modality, we need the following definition:

$$\mathcal{C} \downarrow \mathcal{C}' \text{ if } \exists n, \mathcal{C}'' \text{ such that } \mathcal{C} = n[\mathcal{C}'] \mid \mathcal{C}''.$$

The definition indicates that $\mathcal{C}$ contains $\mathcal{C}'$ within exactly one level of nesting. Then, $\mathcal{C} \downarrow^* \mathcal{C}'$ is the reflexive and transitive closure of the previous relation, indicating that $\mathcal{C}$ contains $\mathcal{C}'$ at some nesting level.

Except for context, we also need *awareness*. Siewe et al. [9] defined a modal logic for specifying the properties of contexts. We usually call a formula in this logic a *context expression* (CE for short). The syntax of CE is given in Table 1.

Table 1. Syntax of CEs

Definition	Name
True	True
$n = m$	name match
$\bullet$	hole
$\neg\kappa$	negation
$\kappa_1 \wedge \kappa_2$	conjunction
$\kappa_1 \vert \kappa_2$	parallel composition
$n[\kappa]$	location
$n\circledR\kappa$	revelation
$\oplus\kappa$	spatial next modality
$\diamond\kappa$	somewhere modality
$\exists x.\kappa$	existential quantification

Table 2. Free names of CEs

Context expression	Free names
True	$\emptyset$
$n = m$	$\{n, m\}$
$\bullet$	$\emptyset$
$\neg\kappa$	$\mathbf{fn}(\kappa)$
$\kappa_1 \wedge \kappa_2$	$\mathbf{fn}(\kappa_1) \cup \mathbf{fn}(\kappa_2)$
$\kappa_1 \vert \kappa_2$	$\mathbf{fn}(\kappa_1) \cup \mathbf{fn}(\kappa_2)$
$n[\kappa]$	$\mathbf{fn}(\kappa) \cup \{n\}$
$n\circledR\kappa$	$\mathbf{fn}(\kappa) - \{n\}$
$\oplus\kappa$	$\mathbf{fn}(\kappa)$
$\diamond\kappa$	$\mathbf{fn}(\kappa)$
$\exists x.\kappa$	$\mathbf{fn}(\kappa) - \{x\}$

Since there is quantifier $\exists$ in context expressions, the variables or names may be free or bounded. We use $\mathbf{fn}(\kappa)$ to denote the set of free names over a CE κ, and the formal definition of it is shown in Table 2.

The logic of context expressions is an extension of modal logic. Its semantics is given by the *satisfaction* relations $\models$: $\mathcal{C} \models \kappa$ says that a context $\mathcal{C}$ satisfies a context expression κ. The logic is defined in Table 3.

Table 3. Satisfaction relations between contexts and CEs

Relation	Meaning	Name
$\mathcal{C} \models \mathbf{True}$		(Sat-true)
$\mathcal{C} \models n = n$		(Sat-match)
$\mathcal{C} \models \bullet$	iff $\mathcal{C} = \odot$	(Sat-hole)
$\mathcal{C} \models \neg\kappa$	iff $\mathcal{C} \not\models \kappa$	(Sat-neg)
$\mathcal{C} \models \kappa_1 \wedge \kappa_2$	iff $\mathcal{C} \models \kappa_1$ and $\mathcal{C} \models \kappa_2$	(Sat-and)
$\mathcal{C} \models \kappa_1 \vert \kappa_2$	iff there exist $\mathcal{C}_1, \mathcal{C}_2$ such that $\mathcal{C} = \mathcal{C}_1 \mid \mathcal{C}_2$, $\mathcal{C}_1 \models \kappa_1$ and $\mathcal{C}_2 \models \kappa_2$	(Sat-par)
$\mathcal{C} \models n[\kappa]$	iff there exists $\mathcal{C}'$ such that $\mathcal{C} = n[\mathcal{C}']$ and $\mathcal{C}' \models \kappa$	(Sat-amb)
$\mathcal{C} \models n\circledR\kappa$	iff there exists $\mathcal{C}'$ such that $\mathcal{C} = (\nu n)\mathcal{C}'$ and $\mathcal{C}' \models \kappa$	(Sat-rel)
$\mathcal{C} \models \oplus\kappa$	iff there exists $\mathcal{C}'$ such that $\mathcal{C} \downarrow \mathcal{C}'$ and $\mathcal{C}' \models \kappa$	(Sat-next)
$\mathcal{C} \models \diamond\kappa$	iff there exists $\mathcal{C}'$ such that $\mathcal{C} \downarrow^* \mathcal{C}'$ and $\mathcal{C}' \models \kappa$	(Sat-sw)
$\mathcal{C} \models \exists x.\kappa$	iff there exists n such that $\mathcal{C} \models \kappa\{x \leftarrow n\}$	(Sat-exist)

3   Processes and Contexts with Probabilities

In this section, we introduce processes with probability in PCA and normalization method of context distribution.

Recall that a *probability distribution* over a countable set X is a function $\mu : X \rightarrow [0,1]$ such that $\sum_{x \in X} \mu(x) = 1$. We write $Distr(X)$ for all the probability distributions over X. For any countable set X, distribution $\mu \in Distr(X)$, and subset $V \subseteq X$, we let $\mu(V) = \sum_{x \in V} \mu(x)$.

Though CCA does not have choice operator like $\sum_{i \in I} P_i$ directly, in PCA we mix the choice operator with probability such as $\sum_{i \in I} p_i.P_i$. We separate context-awareness from capabilities in the context guarded action of CCA for simplicity. With respect to the syntax of the CCA given in Sect. 2, we replace the action process $\kappa?M.P$ with $M.P$, $\sum_{i \in I} p_i.P_i$, and $\kappa_\Delta^a?P$.

Here, $M.P$ is named **action process** which comes from MA [18]. It means that the process will perform the capability M then reduce to P, and we will give the reduction rules for different capabilities later.

$\sum_{i \in I} p_i.P_i$, is named **(probabilistic) choice operator**, where I is an indexing set and p_i is a real number in the interval $(0,1]$ denoting the probability that the process becomes P_i. When the indexing set is finite, say $I = \{i_1, \ldots, i_n\}$, we can also write this process as $p_{i_1}.P_{i_1} + \cdots + p_{i_n}.P_{i_n}$. We give some notations that will be used later. Let $[\![\sum_{i \in I} p_i.P_i]\!]$ denote the distribution over PCA. For any process T in PCA:

$$[\![\sum_{i \in I} p_i.P_i]\!](T) = \sum_{i \in I \wedge T = P_i} p_i$$

and we usually let μ denote a distribution of processes in PCA. For any individual process P, there is also a distribution (like $[\![1.P]\!]$) corresponding to it, and then we denote the distribution by μ_P. This means that in PCA we will not explicitly distinguish distributions and processes if not confused.

After we combine probabilities with processes, the contexts of a process also be a probability distribution.

In the rest of the paper, we use Φ to denote a distribution of contexts. Since we can get a context from a process and conversely we can also get a process from a context, we have the following definition:

Definition 1. *For a distribution μ of processes, the contexts (distribution) of a process P, denoted by $\mu \ominus P$, is obtained by taking place of P by $\odot$ in μ. Conversely, for a distribution Φ of contexts, we can also get a distribution of processes by replacing all holes by a process P and it is denoted by $\Phi \oplus P$.*

$\kappa_\Delta^a?P$, is named **guarded action process**. It is a little different from guarded action of CCA: except the process P, there is a context expression κ but with a superscript a and a subscript Δ. Here Δ is a binary comparison operator in the set $\{=, >, <, \leq, \geq, \neq\}$ and a is a real number between 0 and 1. We name κ_Δ^a **guarded expression** to distinguish it from context expression κ.

In PCA, because we can only get a distribution of processes, for some processes there may be different contexts with some probabilities. The relation between contexts and context expressions will be very complicated: some contexts may satisfy some expression while others may not. So we need to introduce the superscript a and subscript $\triangle$ as a measurement of how the distribution satisfies the expression:

In the guarded action process $\kappa_\triangle^a ?P$, assuming the the total probabilities of the contexts which satisfy the κ is r, and the process can turn into P if the condition statement $(r \triangle a)$ is true.

We will formally define this at the end of this section. But in some cases, a process may not appear in all cases in a distribution, and this may cause some confusions, such as:

Example 1. For a processes distribution μ where

$$\mu(T) = \begin{cases} 0.1, & \text{if } T = m[\text{is\_in}(n)_>^{0.5}?P]; \\ 0.4, & \text{if } T = n[\text{is\_in}(n)_>^{0.5}?P]; \\ 0.5, & \text{if } T = n[Q]; \\ 0, & \text{otherwise.} \end{cases}$$

in the distribution is_in(n) denotes context expression $n[\oplus(\bullet \mid \textbf{True})] \mid \textbf{True}$. This context expression will be satisfied only when the process is in an ambient named n. According to our definition, the distribution of contexts of the process is_in$(n)_>^{0.5}?P$ is:

$$\mu \ominus \text{is\_in}(n)_>^{0.5}?P(\mathcal{C}) = \begin{cases} 0.1, & \text{if } \mathcal{C} = m[\odot]; \\ 0.4, & \text{if } \mathcal{C} = n[\odot]; \\ 0.5, & \text{if } \mathcal{C} = n[Q]; \\ 0, & \text{otherwise.} \end{cases}$$

We notice that $n[Q]$ is one of the contexts of process is_in$(n)_>^{0.5}?P$, but the process never appears in this context. Actually in real life, κ is always implemented by some sensor. It means that only when the process with sensor (κ in PCA) is in the system ($\mathcal{C}$ in PCA), the sensor can judge whether the environment satisfies it or not. So the context $n[Q]$ in the above example will not be observed by the context expression is_in(n). The context expression is_in(n) can only see the contexts $m[\odot]$ and $n[\odot]$. Since probabilities of the two contexts are 0.1 and 0.4 in the whole system, in the 'eye' of is_in(n) the two contexts' probabilities are $0.1/(0.1 + 0.4) = 0.2$ and $0.4/(0.1 + 0.4) = 0.8$, respectively. Meanwhile, the origin process is_in$(n)_>^{0.5}?P$ means that, if more than half of all the situations are that the process is in the ambient n, then the is_in$(n)_>^{0.5}$ will be satisfied and the process will reduce to P. But if we take context $n[Q]$ into account, the probability that is_in$(n)_>^{0.5}?P$ is in the ambient $n[\cdots]$ is 0.4, which is less than a half. This is unreasonable since the probability that the process is in $n[\cdots]$ is larger than other situations. Only when we omit the situations where is_in$(n)_>^{0.5}?P$ does not appear, the result is reasonable. That is what we will do when we measure the probabilities of the contexts in PCA: **normalization**.

The context for a process is given by replacing the process with a hole $\odot$, which means that the context may contain at least one hole. In the paper, we denote the set of all contexts containing at least one hole by Π and have the following definition:

Definition 2 (Normalization of context distribution). *For any distribution $\mu \ominus P$ of contexts of a process P, and a context C, the **normalized probability** of C of P, denoted by $Pr^n(C \mid \mu \ominus P)$, is:*

$$Pr^n(C \mid \mu \ominus P) = \begin{cases} 0, & \text{if } \sum_{C' \in \Pi} \mu \ominus P(C') = 0; \\ \frac{\mu \ominus P(C)}{\sum_{C' \in \Pi} \mu \ominus P(C')}, & \text{otherwise.} \end{cases}$$

Sometimes if not confused, we will leave out the distribution $\mu \ominus P$ in $Pr^n(C \mid \mu \ominus P)$, i.e. $Pr^n(C)$.

Now we can define the satisfying relations between distributions of contexts and guarded expressions:

Definition 3 (Satisfaction). *We say that a context distribution Φ satisfies a guarded expression κ_Δ^a, denoted by $\Phi \models \kappa_\Delta^a$, if the condition statement:*

$$\left(\sum_{C \models \kappa} Pr^n(C \mid \Phi) \right) \Delta\, a$$

is true.

Based on the new satisfaction above, it is easy to figure out that in the above example $\Phi \models \text{is\_in}(n)_>^{0.5}$, since $\sum_{C \models \text{is\_in}} (\text{n}) Pr^n(C \mid \Phi) = Pr^n(n[\odot]) = 0.8 > 0.5$. This result is reasonable as we say before.

4   Probabilistic Context-Aware Ambients

Based on the work in Sect. 3, in this section we define the probabilistic context-aware ambients for probabilistic behaviors.

4.1   Syntax of PCA

Definition 4 (Syntax of PCA). *The set of process terms, denoted by **PCA**, in PCA is given by the syntax:*

$$M, M' ::= \epsilon \mid (x) \mid \langle y \rangle \mid \text{in } n \mid \text{out} \mid \text{open } n \mid M.M'$$
$$\Delta ::= > \mid < \mid \geq \mid \leq \mid \neq \mid =$$
$$P, Q ::= \mathbf{0} \mid P|Q \mid (\nu n)P \mid n[P] \mid !P \mid M.P \mid \sum_{i \in I} p_i.P_i \mid \kappa_\Delta^a?P$$

where $n \in N$, x and y stand for the variables of the names, and $\sum_{i \in I} p_i$ is a summation over a countable indexing set I where $p_i \in (0, 1]$ for all $i \in I$ and $\sum_{i \in I} p_i = 1$.

Although PCA comes from CCA, we only use part of CCA for simplicity. In fact, there is neither process call $x \triangleright (\tilde{y}).P$, nor location α. In the definition of capabilities, (x) and $\langle y \rangle$ stand for input and output respectively. They are both communication primitives. When there are two parallel processes, one with input prefix and another with output prefix, they may communicate with each other. Besides, we replace the capability 'del n' by 'open n', since the latter comes from MA and is more applicative.

Like context expressions, names appearing in an process can either be free or bounded by an input or a restriction. For any P, we write $\mathbf{fn}(P)$ for the sets of free names in P. The definition of it related to processes is shown in Table 4. As we mentioned at the end of Sect. 2, we use $P\{a \leftarrow b\}$ to represent replacing every free a in P with b. A change of bounded names in P, such as we replace $(\nu n)n[P] \,|\, m[Q]$ with $(\nu s)s[P\{n \leftarrow s\}] \,|\, m[Q]$, is called α-conversion. Two processes are the same if we can get one from another by α-conversion.

Table 4. Free names of PCA

Process	Free names	Capability	Free names
$\mathbf{0}$	$\emptyset$	ϵ	$\emptyset$
$P\|Q$	$\mathbf{fn}(P) \cup \mathbf{fn}(Q)$	(x)	$\emptyset$
$(\nu n)P$	$\mathbf{fn}(P) - \{n\}$	$\langle y \rangle$	$\{y\}$
$n[P]$	$\mathbf{fn}(P) \cup \{n\}$	in n	$\{n\}$
$!P$	$\mathbf{fn}(P)$	out	$\emptyset$
$M.P$	$\mathbf{fn}(M) \cup \mathbf{fn}(P)$	open n	$\{n\}$
$\sum_{i \in I} p_i.P_i$	$\bigcup_{i \in I} \mathbf{fn}(P_i)$	$M.M'$	$\mathbf{fn}(M) \cup \mathbf{fn}(M')$
$\kappa_\Delta^a ? P$	$\mathbf{fn}(\kappa) \cup \mathbf{fn}(P)$		

We introduce some notations before starting the next subsection.

- For any μ, $\mu' \in \mathrm{Distr}(\mathbf{PCA})$ and process $Q \in \mathbf{PCA}$, we use $\mu|Q$, $Q|\mu$ and $\mu|\mu'$ to denote the distribution over $\mathbf{PCA}$ such that for any process $T \in \mathbf{PCA}$:

$$(\mu|Q)(T) = \begin{cases} \mu(T'), & \text{if } T = T'|Q; \\ 0, & \text{otherwise.} \end{cases}$$

$$(Q|\mu)(T) = \begin{cases} \mu(T'), & \text{if } T = Q|T'; \\ 0, & \text{otherwise.} \end{cases}$$

$$(\mu|\mu')(T) = \begin{cases} \mu(T_1) \cdot \mu'(T_2), & \text{if } T = T_1|T_2; \\ 0, & \text{otherwise.} \end{cases}$$

– For any $\mu \in \mathrm{Distr}(\mathbf{PCA})$ and $n \in N$, we use $n[\mu]$ and $(\nu n)\mu$ to denote the distributions over $\mathbf{PCA}$ such that for any process $T \in \mathbf{PCA}$:

$$n[\mu](T) = \begin{cases} \mu(T'), & \text{if } T = n[T']; \\ 0, & \text{otherwise.} \end{cases}$$

$$(\nu n)\mu(T) = \begin{cases} \mu(T'), & \text{if } T = (\nu n)T'; \\ 0, & \text{otherwise.} \end{cases}$$

Besides, we use a similar way to simplify the representation of a distribution of contexts.

4.2 Semantics of PCA

As in most process calculus, we define the operational semantics of PCA. It consists of structural congruence and reduction. The former is static while the latter is dynamic. The semantics is in the style of Milner's reaction relation [21] for the π-calculus, which was inspired by [22].

Structural Congruence $\equiv$ is the smallest congruence relation on processes that satisfies the axioms in Table 5.

Here we only explain the last three rules, since the others are trivial and you can get more information in [23]. (Struct Zero Action) states that the action ϵ does nothing when it's running. So we take these two processes as the same. (Struct Guard) means that if two processes are structural congruent, they are also congruent after we place the same guard-expression before them. This rule is like the rule (Struct Amb) where we place the processes into the same ambient. (Struct Prob), is designed for probabilistic choice operator. Firstly, we lift the relation $\equiv$ to distributions of processes in PCA, and define that for any two processes distributions μ, υ:

$$\mu \equiv \upsilon \text{ if } \forall P \in \mathbf{PCA}, \sum_{P' \equiv P} \mu(P') = \sum_{P' \equiv P} \upsilon(P')$$

Consider the following processes of PCA:

$$\frac{1}{4}.P + \frac{3}{4}.Q, \ \frac{1}{8}.P + \frac{3}{4}.Q + \frac{1}{8}.P,$$

we usually regard the two processes as the same process due to the fact that they all have the same distributions over any processes of PCA, e.g. if the processes run, the result is a distribution of processes with the probabilities 0.25 for P, 0.75 for Q, and 0 for others. Due to the definition of (Struct Prob), we do have the conclusion that the two are the same. So the rule (Struct Prob) is reasonable and necessary.

Since we want to model mobile systems with PCA, we need reduction rules in Table 6 which are the dynamic semantics of PCA.

Table 5. Structural congruence of PCA

Rule	Name
$P \equiv P$	(Struct Relf)
$P \equiv Q \Rightarrow Q \equiv P$	(Struct Symm)
$P \equiv Q, Q \equiv R \Rightarrow P \equiv R$	(Struct Trans)
$P \equiv Q \Rightarrow (\nu n)P \equiv (\nu n)Q$	(Struct Res)
$P \equiv Q \Rightarrow P\|R \equiv Q\|R$	(Struct Par)
$P \equiv Q \Rightarrow\, !P \equiv\, !Q$	(Struct Repl)
$P \equiv Q \Rightarrow n[P] \equiv n[Q]$	(Struct Amb)
$P \equiv Q \Rightarrow M.P \equiv M.Q$	(Struct Action)
$P\|\mathbf{0} \equiv P$	(Struct Par Zero)
$P\|Q \equiv Q\|P$	(Struct Par Comm)
$(P\|Q)\|R \equiv P\|(Q\|R)$	(Struct Par Assoc)
$(\nu n)\mathbf{0} \equiv \mathbf{0}$	(Struct Res Zero)
$(\nu n)(\nu m)P \equiv (\nu m)(\nu n)P$	(Struct Res Res)
$(\nu n)(P\|Q) \equiv P\|(\nu n)Q$, if $n \notin \mathbf{fn}(P)$	(Struct Res Par)
$(\nu n)(m[P]) \equiv m[(\nu n)P]$, if $n \neq m$	(Struct Res Amb)
$!\mathbf{0} \equiv \mathbf{0}$	(Struct Repl Zero)
$!P \equiv P\|!P$	(Struct Repl Copy)
$\epsilon.P \equiv P$	(Struct Zero Action)
$P \equiv Q \Rightarrow \kappa_\Delta^a?P \equiv \kappa_\Delta^a?Q$	(Struct Guard)
$\sum_{i \in I} p_i.P_i \equiv \sum_{j \in J} q_j.Q_j$ if $[\![\sum_{i \in I} p_i.P_i]\!] \equiv [\![\sum_{j \in J} q_j.Q_j]\!]$	(Struct Prob)

The first five rules are very natural since they are basic reduction rules in process calculus, and if you need more information please refer to [20]. The rule, (Red Amb), just comes from [18]. The seventh rule, (Red Cong), is for the congruence relations. The rule, (Red Comm), tells the way how two processes communicate. It comes from CCS for presenting the message passing between two processes. It is easy to see that this communication is synchronous. If needed, we can also change it into asynchronous communication with channel. The following one, (Red Prob), is introduced in Sect. 3. The last one, (Red Guard), is the only rule designed for guared expressions. The word *guard* tells us that when the context of the guarded process satisfies the expression, the process turns into the subprocess following the expression; otherwise, it does nothing and waits until the expression is satisfied. For example: there are a car (denoted by c) and a garage (denoted by g). The car will keep moving until it enters the garage. We can model this situation by the process of PCA:

$$c[\text{in } g.0 \,|\, \text{is\_in}(g)_=^1?Stop] \,|\, g[]$$

where is_in(g) is the context expression defined in Example 1 and here we only replace the ambient name n with the name g. Due to the satisfaction relations,

Table 6. Reduction rules of PCA

Rule	Name
$n[\text{in } m.P \mid Q] \mid m[R] \rightarrow m[n[P \mid Q] \mid R]$	(Red In)
$m[n[\text{out}.P \mid Q] \mid R] \rightarrow n[P \mid Q] \mid m[R]$	(Red Out)
$\text{open } n.P \mid n[Q] \rightarrow P \mid Q$	(Red Open)
$P \rightarrow \phi \Rightarrow P \mid Q \rightarrow \phi \mid Q$	(Red Par)
$P \rightarrow \phi \Rightarrow (\nu n)P \rightarrow (\nu n)\phi$	(Red Res)
$P \rightarrow \phi \Rightarrow n[P] \rightarrow n[\phi]$	(Red Amb)
$P \equiv P', P \rightarrow \phi, \phi \equiv \phi' \Rightarrow P' \rightarrow \phi'$	(Red Cong)
$(x).P \mid \langle y \rangle.Q \rightarrow P\{x \leftarrow y\} \mid Q$	(Red Comm)
$\sum_{i \in I} p_i.P_i \rightarrow [\![\sum_{i \in I} p_i.P_i]\!]$	(Red Prob)
$\Phi \oplus \kappa_\Delta^a ?P \rightarrow \Phi \oplus P$, if $\Phi \models \kappa_\Delta^a$	(Red Guard)

we find that the context of the car does not satisfy the guard is_in(g) until it is in the garage. We have the following reductions:

$$(c[\text{in } g.0 \mid \text{is\_in}(g)\overset{1}{=}?Stop] \mid g[]) \qquad \text{(Red in)}$$
$$\rightarrow g[c[0 \mid \text{is\_in}(g)\overset{1}{=}?Stop]] \qquad \text{(Struct Par Zero)}$$
$$\equiv g[c[\text{is\_in}(g)\overset{1}{=}?Stop]] \qquad \text{(Red Guard)}$$
$$\rightarrow g[c[Stop]]$$

Notice that here we do not show the reductions with distributions, since all things in the system are certain and we present this in a brief way.

5 Conclusion

We have introduced the probabilistic context-aware ambients, with the aim of modeling randomness of real-life systems. Based on the context-awareness, PCA has the ability of distinguishing different contexts. We have used normalization method of context to give PCA the ability of measuring the actual probability of context. The processes with these abilities can make different decisions with regard to different situations.

There are several problems worth further studying. Firstly, like the example in Sect. 4.2, different processes may have the same distributions over any processes of PCA. So behavioral equivalence need to be studied to enhance the equivalence relation between two processes of PCA. Secondly, in real life systems, there are not only randomness but also noise. Noise is another hot topic in process calculus, and some initial attempts have already been made for investigating this matter. For example, Abdulla et al. [24,25] and Cao [26] proposed and systemically studied the model of lossy channel systems and its probabilistic extension. Following Shannon's information theory [27], researchers usually formalize the channel noise into a probabilistic transitional semantics, and thus PCA may have the ability to deal with noise as well.

References

1. Weiser, M.: The computer for the 21st century. Sci. Am. **265**(3), 94–104 (1991)
2. Birkedal, L., Debois, S., Elsborg, E., Hildebrandt, T., Niss, H.: Bigraphical models of context-aware systems. In: Aceto, L., Ingólfsdóttir, A. (eds.) FoSSaCS 2006. LNCS, vol. 3921, pp. 187–201. Springer, Heidelberg (2006). https://doi.org/10. 1007/11690634_13
3. Birkedal, L., Debois, S., Hildebrandt, T.: On the construction of sorted reactive systems. In: van Breugel, F., Chechik, M. (eds.) CONCUR 2008. LNCS, vol. 5201, pp. 218–232. Springer, Heidelberg (2008). https://doi.org/10.1007/978-3-540-85361-9_20
4. Wang, J.S., Xu, D., Lei, Z.: Formalizing the structure and behaviour of context-aware systems in bigraphs. In: 2011 First ACIS International Symposium on Software and Network Engineering (SSNE), pp. 89–94 (2011)
5. Xu, D.Z, Xu, D., Lei, Z.: Bigraphical model of context-aware in ubiquitous computing environments. In: 2011 IEEE Asia-Pacific Services Computing Conference (APSCC), pp. 389–394 (2011)
6. Braione, P., Picco, G.P.: On calculi for context-aware coordination. In: De Nicola, R., Ferrari, G.-L., Meredith, G. (eds.) COORDINATION 2004. LNCS, vol. 2949, pp. 38–54. Springer, Heidelberg (2004). https://doi.org/10.1007/978-3-540-24634-3_6
7. Zimmer, P.: A calculus for context-awareness, Brics Research (2005)
8. Kjærgaard, M.B., Bunde-Pedersen, J.: A formal model for context-awareness. Technical report, BRICS (2006)
9. Siewe, F., Zedan, H., Cau, A.: The calculus of context-aware ambients. J. Comput. Syst. Sci. **77**(4), 597–620 (2011)
10. Rocha, L.S., Andrade, R.: Towards a formal model to reason about context-aware exception handling. In: 2012 5th International Workshop on Exception Handling (WEH), pp. 27–33 (2012)
11. Almutairi, A., Siewe, F.: Formal specification of CA-UCON model using CCA. In: 2013 Science and Information Conference (SAI), pp. 369–375 (2013)
12. Giacalone, A., Jou, C.C., Smolka, S.A.: Algebraic reasoning for probabilistic concurrent systems. In: Proceedings IFIP TC2 Working Conference on Programming Concepts and Methods (1990)
13. Deng, Y.: Semantics of Probabilistic Processes: An Operational Approach. Shanghai Jiao Tong University Press, Springer (2014)
14. Hansson, H., Jonsson, B.: A logic for reasoning about time and reliability. Formal Aspect Comput. **6**(5), 512–535 (1994)
15. Di Pierro, A., Hankin, C., Wiklicky, H.: Probabilistic KLAIM. In: De Nicola, R., Ferrari, G.-L., Meredith, G. (eds.) COORDINATION 2004. LNCS, vol. 2949, pp. 119–134. Springer, Heidelberg (2004). https://doi.org/10.1007/978-3-540-24634-3_11
16. Baier, C., Kwiatkowska, M.: Domain equations for probabilistic processes. Math. Struct. Comput. Sci. **10**(06), 665–717 (2000)
17. Herescu, O.M., Palamidessi, C.: Probabilistic asynchronous π-calculus. In: Tiuryn, J. (ed.) FoSSaCS 2000. LNCS, vol. 1784, pp. 146–160. Springer, Heidelberg (2000). https://doi.org/10.1007/3-540-46432-8_10
18. Cardelli, L., Gordon, A.D.: Mobile ambients. In: Nivat, M. (ed.) FoSSaCS 1998. LNCS, vol. 1378, pp. 140–155. Springer, Heidelberg (1998). https://doi.org/10. 1007/BFb0053547

19. Kwiatkowska, M., Norman, G., Parker, D., Vigliotti, M.G.: Probabilistic mobile ambients. Theor. Comput. Sci. **410**(12), 1272–1303 (2009)
20. Milner, R.: Communicating and Mobile Systems: the Pi Calculus. Cambridge University Press, Cambridge (1999)
21. Milner, R.: Functions as processes. Math. Struct. Comput. Sci. **2**(02), 119–141 (1992)
22. Berry, G, Boudol, G.: The chemical abstract machine. In: Proceedings of the 17th ACM SIGPLAN-SIGACT Symposium on Principles of Programming Languages, pp. 81–94 (1989)
23. Cardelli, L., Gordon, A.D.: Ambient logic. Math. Struct. Comput. Sci. **13**(3), 371–408 (2003)
24. Abdulla, P.A., Bertrand, N., Rabinovich, A., Schnoebelen, P.: Verification of probabilistic systems with faulty communication. Inf. Comput. **202**(2), 141–165 (2005)
25. Abdulla, P., Annichini, A., Bouajjani, A.: Symbolic verification of lossy channel systems: application to the bounded retransmission protocol. In: Cleaveland, W.R. (ed.) TACAS 1999. LNCS, vol. 1579, pp. 208–222. Springer, Heidelberg (1999). https://doi.org/10.1007/3-540-49059-0_15
26. Cao, Y.: Reliability of mobile processes with noisy channels. IEEE Trans. Comput. **61**(9), 1217–1230 (2012)
27. Shannon, C.E.: A mathematical theory of communication. ACM SIGMOBILE Mob. Comput. Commun. Rev. **5**(1), 3–55 (2001)

How to Understand Three Types of Cognitive Models

Xiaohui Zou[1,2(✉)] ⓘ, Yizhen Qi[3], and Dixing Wang[4]

[1] Sino-American Searle Research Center,
UC Berkeley, Berkeley 94720-3840, USA
`geneculture@icloud.com`, `949309225@qq.com`
[2] Room 415, Audio-Visual Building, Peking University, Beijing 100871, China
[3] Research Department, Tsinghua University China Knowledge Network
(CNKI), Beijing, China
[4] Beijing Wang Dixing Intelligent Computer Technology Co., Ltd.,
Beijing, China

Abstract. This paper aims to explore more efficient information processing methods through quasi-holographic space, knowledge and language cognitive systems. The method is as follows: First, the spatial computing system is understood as a formal abstract cognitive system; further, the five-loop traversal system is understood as a conceptual knowledge query system; finally, the language cognitive system is understood as a tabular text reusing system. The result is: quasi-holographic space, five-loop traversal and bit-list logic as three thinking modes or three types of cognitive systems, in the object form and knowledge content information processing on the same path. The significance is that not only the three types of cognitive systems, such as quasi-holographic space, five-loop traversal and order-sequence structure, all of them are difficult to understand, now are easily understood, and a new cognitive paradigm that is simplified is obtained.

Keywords: Attribute calculation method · Expert knowledge acquisition ·
Attribute coordinate · Geometric algebraic method · Knowledge ontology

1 Introduction

This paper aims to explore more effective information processing methods through quasi-holographic space, knowledge and language cognitive systems. Wang discovered and constructed a quasi-holographic space computing model for decades. Qi discovered and constructed a knowledge query framework in decades. Zou discovered and constructed a language chess game for decades. System, is there a connection between these three types of cognitive systems? Is there a possibility to achieve the same goal? This is an important reason for this article [1–12].

Whether from the physical mechanism, from the social significance, or even from the perspective of the mental language, such a comparative study is valuable. The key is whether a uniform evaluation scale or frame of reference can be found (preferably carried out under the support of a computer network).

© Springer Nature Singapore Pte Ltd. 2019
F. Sun et al. (Eds.): ICCSIP 2018, CCIS 1005, pp. 268–284, 2019.
https://doi.org/10.1007/978-981-13-7983-3_24

So a bold formal evaluation tool was activated by Zou Xiaohui. It is a computable and learnable automation device or system (although it is currently primarily a logical and mathematical design):

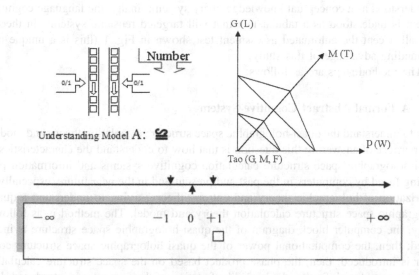

Fig. 1. Micro and macro, qualitative and quantitative cognitive evaluation system

It can be seen from Fig. 1 that the attribute coordinate system at the upper right (dividing the data acquisition area is very easy); the twin Turing machine at the upper left (the theoretical model of the fully automatic universal learning machine, which is characterized by the formal understanding that is computable and verifiable); The logical basis of the intelligent universal learning system that can establish the linkage function between the Cartesian number axis and the twin Turing machine: the structural relationship between order and position can be duplicated and easily reused in a targeted manner (in combination with the upper and lower functional systems that would be done by automatic evaluation).

The enumerability of natural numbers and the operational lattice of Turing machine (filling in 0 or 1 in spaces) can be automatically converted between decimal and binary numbers (also between other digital systems). After the consistency of the mathematical and physical of the calculation and operation on pure numbers, the logic and mathematical principles of indirect formalization and indirect calculation of any generalized symbol can be filled in by lattice spaces, and the system is set. In this way, various specific cognitive systems can be tested based on bi-list logic, linkage functions, and generalized translation.

2 Method

The method is: First, the quasi-holographic system of spatial computing is understood by us as a formal abstract cognitive system; in addition, the five-cycle traversal system is understood as a conceptual knowledge query system; finally, the language cognitive system is understood as a tabular text that will targeted reusable systems. In theory, they all accept the automated assessment test shown in Fig. 1 (this is a unique and outstanding advantage of this study).

The method steps are as follows:

2.1 A Formal Abstract Cognitive System

How to understand the quasi-holographic space structure calculation theory and model? The purpose of answering this question is that how to understand the characteristics of quasi-holographic space structure calculation cognitive systems and information processing faced by computers in the past and present and in the near future, especially in polarization of holographic theory and entropy theory, trying to understand a quasi-holographic space structure calculation theory and model. The method is as follows: firstly, the computer block diagram of the quasi-holographic space structure is introduced; then, the computational power of the quasi-holographic space structure computer is introduced; then, the phase product based on the space structure calculation theory is introduced; finally, the brain-like function of the computer is introduced. It is characterized by a quasi-holographic spatial calculation. The result: highlights the basic principles that the structural structure calculation follows. The significance can be found from the performance comparison of the two computational models. From the perspective of science and technology, quasi-holographic space structure calculation theory and model are instructive to researchers and explorers in related fields.

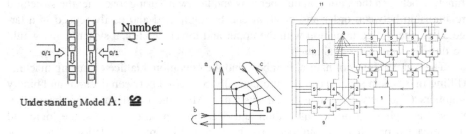

Fig. 2. Mathematical calculations and learning; physical calculations and learning

As can be seen from Fig. 2, the formal understanding model on the left, that is, the general-purpose digital learning machine, can learn from the zero-start any digits on the right of Fig. 2 and its evolution law (it can learn the data that is reused).

Machine learning is different from the rules of human brain learning. Human brain learning follows the following methods:

It can be seen from Fig. 2 that the theoretical calculation and formal learning based on the formal understanding model A (the twin Turing machine) are on the left of Fig. 2; In the middle is a simplified schematic of the bits of a hexadecimal space structure computer with three bidirectional input and output ports A, B and C. A + B = C, because the logic is reversible, so C – B = A, C – A = B. The assignment of A, B, and C can be any of the 0–15 value states (as determined by the codec), and its input and output are one of the 16-value states relative to one bit of the binary if it is 64-bit calculation. Its value range is 64 bits of 16-bit power. The right side reflects the multiplication and division of rational numbers, involving several points: 1, Core structure operator (based on Fig. 3 design), 2, choose one, 3, One or two dispensers, 4, dual port RAM, 5, the terminal, 6, the command register, 7, in and out of the read and write direction control, 8, parallel read and write control of the operator or terminal, 9, read and write control of the terminal, 10, The server of the host or server.

The Computer Block Diagram: the human brain follows multiple factors and causes each other, and the input can directly drive the output; it has logical reversible, bidirectional parallel read and write bidirectional parallel input and exit characteristics; exchange, operation, control and multi-to-many bidirectional parallel interchange bus functions are unified and can be synchronized Parallel read, write, and calculate; storage and integration, address and data unification, and quasi-multi-valued logic reasoning. The essential difference between the two is that the symbolic mechanism follows the principle of serial time calculation, and the coupling mechanism of the human brain follows the principle of parallel space structure calculation.

Based on the theory of space computing, spatial structure operations can be realized by means of binary AND, OR, and NOT gates. It can revolutionize the theory and technology of computing, switching, bus, encryption and decryption, and artificial intelligence. The specific implementation is shown in Fig. 3 - The computer block diagram of the new quasi-full-space structure.

Displayed equations with Fig. 2 in the middle the simplified schematic diagram of a bit of a hexadecimal space structure computer with three bidirectional input and output ports A, B, and C. A + B = C, because the logic is reversible, so C – B = A, C – A = B.

$$A + B = C \tag{1}$$

$$C - B = A \tag{2}$$

$$C - A = B \tag{3}$$

D in Fig. 2 is a gate array designed in the logic structure mode of Fig. 3, and represents an integer addition and subtraction relationship. Its superiority compared with traditional computers and quantum computers is that A, B, and C ports can be multi-bit parallel input and output and calculation. The input and output of the A, B, and C ports are all superimposed, and when the multi-bit operation is performed, the reading and writing calculations can be completed synchronously. It is a true one-step in-situ calculation result without intermediate or final result detection. If quantum

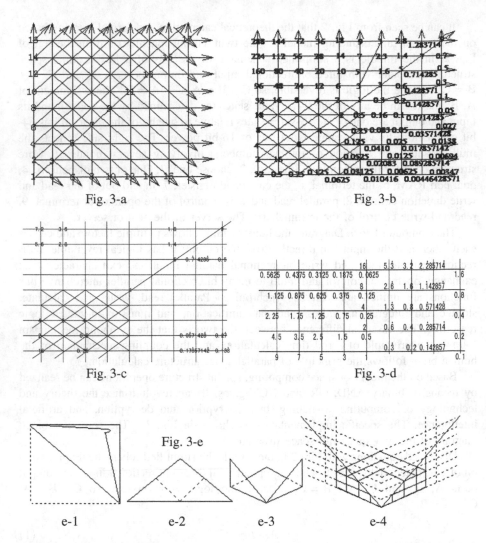

Fig. 3-a

Fig. 3-b

Fig. 3-c

Fig. 3-d

Fig. 3-e

e-1   e-2   e-3   e-4

Fig. 3. (a) reflects the addition and subtraction of integers. (b)–(d) reflects the multiplication and division of rational numbers

computing is used to complete the stable calculation of the 16-valued 64-bit that it will not be possible for another ten years, and its universal application is still unpredictable.

General system theory has only qualitative descriptions, no quantitative formal description, and cannot construct systems according to system theory, which is the fundamental shortcoming of system theory. After many years of research, the author Wang proposes a "quasi-holographic system theory" and a quasi-holographic system model (Figs. 3 and 2 on right). It embodies the emergence of complex systems and self-organizing mechanisms, which can be used to construct hexadecimal brain intelligence machines.

General system theory has only qualitative descriptions, no quantitative formal description, and cannot construct systems according to system theory, which is the fundamental shortcoming of system theory. After years of research, the author Wang proposes a "quasi-holographic system theory" and a quasi-holographic system model (Fig. 3(a)–(d)). It embodies the emergence of complex systems and self-organizing mechanisms, which can be used to construct hexadecimal brain intelligence machines.

The most essential feature of the system is that a single factor cannot be achieved, but self-organizing and emerging system functions can be achieved when the specific rules constitute the whole. Self-organizing emergence is the core of system theory. As shown in Fig. 3(a), the combination of integers and integers can bring out the addition and subtraction relationship and function of integers. And in Fig. 3(b)–(d) the combination of rational numbers can bring out the multiplication and division relationship and function. The existing electronic technology can realize the addition of integers, subtraction, rational multiplication and division, power, square, logarithm, and antilog operations.

Based on the principle of spatial structure calculation, the multi-causal purpose mechanism of brain-like intelligent machine and the quasi-multi-valued logical reasoning mechanism can be determined; the self-organizing description problems of complex systems such as human brain, thinking, artificial intelligence, society and ecology can be solved.

The new computer can solve the principle and efficiency problem of state parallel space conversion; solve the multi-causal and inter-causal interaction between states; solve the problem of inherent self-organization mechanism between states; solve the problem of separation of computer from environment and background information Problem; solve the problem of separation of storage and storage, separation of peripherals and core computing functions; solve bus bottleneck problems; solve binary logic, certainty and formal paradox. The reading and writing calculation can be completed synchronously, which not only improves the computing power, but also improves the ability of human-like brain work, such as parallel perception and parallel behavior.

The calculation of quasi-holographic space structure is based on the multi-causal and multi-causal causal logic relationship, and the self-organized emergence between states - solving the combined explosion problem of the state. It can be integrated with the environment and background information to process information, and state transitions have real-time transparency. A simple state transition relationship structure is unlikely to produce complex state transition functions, and it is expected to generate complex functions with a simple structure, which can only sacrifice time. The spatial structure calculation has the relative transparency of the calculation process, that is, the input operand and the output result, including the compiled code, are transparently connected. Thus the steps or procedures for solving a problem are the least time-consuming, the least expensive and the most simplified.

The Computational Power: the strength of the calculation function is mainly based on the principle of calculation, not on the calculation medium. If based on superconducting technology, the calculation speed will not increase exponentially. However, if we shift from time calculation theory to space calculation theory, the exponential growth of computing power can be achieved through the transformation of the calculation principle.

From the perspective of system theory, a system with computing functions must be a system factor that reflects the relationship between combination and decomposition (operation). Quantum calculations do not give a description of the computational relationship of factors [13–28].

2.2   The Five-Loop Traversal System

How to understand the virtual neuron morphological model: the subject-object unified ontology network? The purpose of answering this question is that how to understand the virtual neuron morphological model by distinguishing the two groups of known and unknown terms and exploring their connection ties: the subject-object unified ontology concept network framework. The method is: first, clear the object-based model and the concept-based model, which are known and familiar terms; furthermore, based on the twin-force-based model and the force-idea-based model, which is unknown to everyone and unfamiliar terms; finally, with the combination of algebraic symbols and geometric figures, plus a specific naming or association. It is characterized by the application of abstract and visual and intuitive thinking. The result is: this neuron morphological model is described from a virtual perspective: the subject-concept unified ontology concept network framework. The significance lies in: boldly imagine or predict a subjective and objective unity of knowledge ontology and expert terminology concept network. Regardless of its success or failure, it has the role and value of enlightening the mind and developing ideas.

As can be seen from Fig. 4, the formal understanding model B on the left, that is, the universal symbol learning machine can self-learn any symbol from the starting point and its evolution law (even learning its reused data).

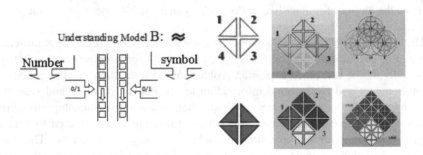

Fig. 4. Formal understanding of model B and state-structure-logic numbers

Machine learning is different from the rules of human brain learning. Human brain learning follows the following methods:

2.2.1   Basic Logic

The four hypotenuses form a solid around the core of the cross, and the four entities form a larger entity around the core of the rice. And so on, until a given five-ring worldview hologram of the same law is formed. Among them: (1) The view of the coordinate system and the reference system: the mi-shaped diamond is the coordinate system, the four-meter diamond forms the reference system; (2) the view of the quadrant: the cross-shaped diamond is the quad-tree quadrant, and the mi-shaped diamond is eight Fork tree quadrant map; (3) Matrix view: all geometric elements and texts are identified by a matrix of x, y; (4) Logic perspective: positive spin and revolution are generative deductive logic, The reverse is the interpretation of reductionism, and the overall layer-by-layer refinement is the inductive logic.

2.2.2   Basic Language

The above-mentioned relationship constitutes the language system, and further is the thinking language architecture, which is the mechanical language architecture of the thermodynamic geometry existing in the neural network of the brain. The geometric elements that characterize thermodynamics are all marked by text to give semantics. On the contrary, the text annotations are all positioned by geometric elements to give the power. The relationship between the two forms the semantics of pragmatic (environment). OCN is geared towards problem interpretation and problem solving. Pay attention to two points: First, the retrieval, query and so on of the authenticity, validity and rationality of the conceptual framework of the interpretation of things, the concept description framework must satisfy the pragmatic (environment) of the completeness of the minimum scale, and also conform to the grammar, so it is necessary to rely on the deep language power; the second is the generation of the natural language specification sentence of the problem. The generated problem statement must satisfy the semantic needs and the grammar, so it needs the grammar of the surface layer.

2.2.3   Theoretical Model

Here Transcendental Force and Force Self-consciousness have been defined as object and subject, the theorem is the relationship between the two, and so on, the law is the association of the theorem's dimensional reasoning. The final result is the philosophical model of the complete inductive reasoning of the basic ten-dimensional space, namely the five-ring worldview hologram.

2.2.3.1 Definition: Transcendental Force

The internal force of the output and the return force of the input refer to the force exerted by the inside of the human body to carry the signal reflected back after describing the external thing. There are two ways to characterize the force: geometric elements and text labels. The force refers to the hypotenuse of the isosceles right triangle to represent the magnitude and direction of the force. The text annotation is the text that sequentially marks the two endpoints of the hypotenuse. For the sake of description, we abstractly simulate the two-dimensional cold characterization of the human body. The right-angled sides of the four isosceles right triangles are sequentially joined to form a cross-diamond quaternary combination force. Since the force is Transcendental, the force is represented by TF (abbreviated by Transcendental Force):

Abstract interactions appear in pairs in a so-called pair-forces actually represented by a pair of vectors as the force-interaction.

$$TF = {}_2^1C_4^1 \ {}_2^0A_4^{1,2,3,4} \begin{matrix} {}_2^2C_4^2 \\ \\ {}_2^3C_4^3 \\ \\ {}_2^4C_4^4 \end{matrix} \qquad \text{①}$$

Here A is a function of the force in the cross diamond, and refers to the container in which the human body stores the object agent information, that is, the abstract neuron, characterized by objective terms and only two bytes. The prefix is marked with the serial number of the objective term, the subscript is the scale, 2 refer to the two hypotenuses, and so on. The subscripts of the suffix are four orthogonal orientations that can be sensed, and the superscript is the identification orientation of the stimulus source. There C is the orientation endpoint, i.e. the cold sensory source orientation marker outside the human body, i.e. the abstract dendritic, characterized by subjective terms within two bytes of four orientations. The prefix of the prefix is the serial number and the subscript is the scale. The subscripts of the suffix are the orientation positions of the four endpoints of 1 left objectivity, 2 upper image, 3 right subjectivity, and 4 abstraction, and the superscript is the current position, that is, the given assignment. It can be seen from the title that ① is an abstract combination of neuron dendrites and cell bodies.

2.2.3.2 Definition: Force Self-consciousness (FS)

FS refers to the information of excitement or inhibition obtained by humans after observing a certain FT, and abstractly stored in their respective containers Self-consciousness. The concept FS is also characterized by two ways: geometric elements and text labels. The force mind FS refers to two right-angled sides in the isosceles right-angled triangle, where the vertical edges characterize the excited flat edges to characterize the suppression. The combination FT from four FT and the combination FS form four FS. Force Self-consciousness is expressed by FS:

$$FS = {}_2^1A_4^1 \ {}_4^0C_4^{1,2,3,4} \begin{matrix} {}_2^2A_4^2 \\ \\ {}_2^3A_4^3 \\ \\ {}_2^4A_4^4 \end{matrix} = {}_4^1① \ {}_4^0C_4^{1,2,3,4} \begin{matrix} ①_4^2 \\ \\ ①_4^3 \\ \\ ①_4^4 \end{matrix} \qquad \text{②}$$

Force Self-consciousness function in the shaped diamond form is abstract synapse that the human body suppresses the orientation selection and connection of the main agent information. The power mind FS is the sociality of the human body. The pointer to the objectivity, image, subjectivity and abstract as position outside the human body, that is, the axon, is distinguished by the underline and the dendritic C. Each ① is known to consist of one objective term and four subjective terms. Thus, there are four objective terms in ② and a combination of sixteen subjective terms, and so on.

2.2.3.3 Theorem: The Relationship Between TF and FS

The power of TF and FS includes various combinations of the relationship between TF and FS in the two-dimensional conformal field, which is a two-passive traversal. Because the intentional things are not true or false, there are good and bad possibilities. That is, the physics and meaning can be inconsistent; however, the meaning itself is good or bad. Choosing good or bad has both knowledge and human problems. This model considers the choice of validity and rationality as a good choice, and the unclear and negative choices as a bad choice. In this way, a good choice is to use the counter-factual Middle Knowledge, which is used to solve the evil problem, by MK:

$$(\ ②_4^2 \ )^2$$

$$MK = (\ ②_4^1 \ )^2 \quad [\ {}_8^0 C_4^{1,2,3,4} \ ]_{\diamond, 180°} \quad (\ ②_4^3 \ )^2 \qquad\qquad ③$$

$$(\ ②_4^4 \ )^2$$

The subscripts in brackets [] are qualifiers. It is strictly forbidden to choose a combination of TF and FS that is both intermediate ◇(possible) and 180° (reverse), and the position of the synapse is unique. According to the meaning of the question, ③ consists of a combination of sixteen objective terms and sixty-four subjective terms. A logical self-consistent exhaustive traversal description of a two-dimensional conformal field of sixteen objective terms namely a basic neural loop description.

2.2.3.4 Law: The Power of the Relationship Between TF and FS

It contains the traversal of the power of the relationship between TF and FS. Since the two traversals do not have structural and logical problems in the selection, there is no limit to the choice of ③ good and bad. Further, all the choices of the first traversal, and the procedures and results in the second traversal. Good and bad appearance. In line with the Principle of the Best (Leibniz), it is also called the law of sufficient reason. Therefore, it is represented by Principle P:

$$(\ ③_4^2 \ )^2$$

$$P = (\ ③_4^1 \ )^2 \quad {}_{16}^0 C_4^{1,2,3,4} \quad (\ ③_4^3 \ )^2 \qquad\qquad ④$$

$$(\ ③_4^4 \ )^2$$

④ is a basic complete inductive reasoning whole. According to the meaning of the question, it consists of a combination of sixty-four objective terms and two hundred and fifty-six subjective terms. A two-dimensional traversal description of the two-dimensional conformal field observation of sixty-four objective terms is implemented and a closed-loop interpretation is formed, that is, the interpretation of a certain neural circuit by a basic neural loop group.

Form-structure-logic numbers in Fig. 4 shows the morphological structure logic system of the five-ring graph space grid that gives the definition of the shape, structure and logic of the things, covering the definitions of the things that are common to the things (things: all activities in human life and all social phenomena encountered by Dong Danian as the Modern Chinese Classification Dictionary in Ci Hai the edition by Shanghai Dictionary Press. 2007.11.P949).

This theoretical model can exhaust the given conceptual terminology of 8321 two bytes to explain the things in a regular way, covering all activities and all social phenomena of human consensus, because the value of a post-synaptic potential is known to be 1–8321. In the same way, the same is true for other conceptual explanations.

2.2.3.5 Proof: The Cube of the Relationship Between TF and FS

The cube of the relationship between TF and FS: that is in order to traverse the power of the relationship between TF and FS, the positioning and visual proof of all positions and elements in the two traversals are realized, which is a decisive and strict argument, that is, the basic five-ring world view hologram. Therefore, use $W\diamondsuit$:

$$W_\diamondsuit = (\;④_4^1\;)^2 \quad {}_{32}^{0}C_4^{1,2,3,4} \quad (\;④_4^3\;)^2 \qquad ⑤$$

with $(\;④_4^2\;)^2$ above and $(\;④_4^4\;)^2$ below.

⑤ is a standard complete inductive reasoning whole, also known as whole of meta-integrated inference overall. According to the title, it is composed of 256 objective terms combined with 1024 subjective terms.

A two-dimensional conformal field of 256 objective terms is observed to match the two traversal descriptions and form a closed loop proof.

2.2.3.6 Interpretation: Fourth Power of the Relationship Between TF and FS

The fourth power of the relationship between TF and FS: in order to traverse the cube of the relationship between TF and FS, you realize the intentional interpretation of all the existences and concepts of the three traversals, and the traversal of the hologram of the basic five-ring worldview. The repetition of the two possible worlds is an inevitable world, so use $W\square$ to mean:

$$W_\square = (\text{⑤}_4^1)^2 \quad {}_{64}^{0}\mathcal{C}_4^{1,2,3,4} \quad \begin{array}{c} (\text{⑤}_4^2)^2 \\[6pt] (\text{⑤}_4^3)^2 \\[6pt] (\text{⑤}_4^4)^2 \end{array} \qquad \text{⑥}$$

⑤ is a standard complete inductive reasoning whole, also known as whole of meta-integrated inference overall. According to the title, it is composed of 1024 objective terms combined with 4096 subjective terms. The logical self-consistent realization of the two-dimensional conformal field of 1024 objective terms is consistent with the observation, the definition of reductionism is formed for ④.

$$W_\square = 5 \left(\frac{C}{O} \right)_I^2 \qquad \text{⑦}$$

⑥ can be further simplified to ⑦. The coefficient 5 refers to the five-ring geometric matrix model, and the results of both the numerator and the denominator are mapped to the geometric matrix model. O is the object, that is, the entity term and is equivalent to A, because the observer acts as the agent in the identity of the object and forms a constraint on the concept term of C. Im is equivalent to the scale of the A or C prefix subscript. It is obvious that ⑦ is the parent equation of the dimensional reasoning, and all the theorems in the theoretical model, that is, all the solutions, can be inferred.

2.2.3.7 Equivalence: This Model and the Thermodynamic Equation of State

The equation of state of a simple system incorporating thermodynamics can be expressed as

$$T = T(p, V) \qquad \text{⑧}$$

The temperature is T, the pressure is P, and the volume is V. State T is determined by the parameters of p and V. In addition, state equations such as thermodynamic coefficient of expansion, pressure coefficient, and isothermal compression coefficient can be introduced.

The W in ⑦ can be abstracted as a thermodynamic temperature scale T, the C terminology can be abstracted as a pressure p, and the O entity term can be abstracted as a volume V.

From the above discussion, it is obvious that ⑦ = ⑧, the difference is only ⑦ is a given thermodynamic state equation of the rule, such as ⑦ is a rule of 5, 5 and ι are given, and the numerator and denominator can approximately divide the square. The above does not participate in the operation, which acts as a further characterization of the equation of state. From the meaning of the title, ⑦ is the model of rational mechanics [29–37].

2.3   The Language Cognitive System

The biggest feature of Chinese is that characters are not only quantitatively determined but also can be used as an indirect formalized basic structural unit to combine any level one language unit, and thus, accurate and indirect calculation can be realized.

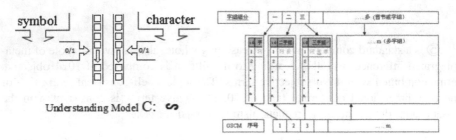

Fig. 5. Formal understanding of model C and Chinese indirect computing systems

It can be seen from Fig. 5 that the machine learning process between the formal understanding model C and the Chinese indirect computing system is essentially the value or assignment of digital symbols, Chinese character numbers and various symbols. Therefore, there is a natural fit between cognitive system of the language and information processing. Between machine formal understanding and user (human) conceptual choice or contract, there is not only the logical consistency of the bi-list structure, but also the mathematical connectivity of the linkage function, and even its negotiability with conventions and generalized translation between various symbol systems. Based on these three basic attributes, the practical application scenario (generalized translation system) of the universal learning machine (formalized understanding model of generalized translation) can be constructed.

Thus, narrow translations (and even alternative translations) are treated as special cases of generalized translation, which can complete a series of learning, understanding and interpretation. There will be a significant improvement in the (various) types of cognitive systems and (various) types of information processing. Here, natural language processing and formal understanding, expert knowledge acquisition and formal expression, pattern recognition and formal modeling will all be the same in three systems engineering of language, knowledge and software [38–55].

3   Results

The result is that information processing on the same path both in the object form and knowledge content, not only the quasi-holographic space, five-cycle traversal and bit-list logic are used as three cognitive systems and information processing, and their characteristics are highlighted. And the basic paradigm has been found (physical, biological and psychological - social) that automatically recognizes and learns by computers (Table 1).

Table 1. Physical, biological and psychological – social paradigms

Cognitive types	Information processing	Formal understanding models
1st-Rigid Law	Bit-list logic structure	Digital understanding model
2nd-Rigid Law	Synonymous conversion	Symbolic understanding model
3rd-Flexible Law	Agree to juxtaposition	Character understanding model
4th-Flexible Law	Interpretation then translation	Bilingual understanding model

It is clear that the combination of the three formalized understanding models and the generalized bilingual model of interpretive translation is the basis for formal, intelligent and social understanding. The understanding of the three types of cognitive systems and information processing can be well understood by means of a formal understanding model (i.e., a universal learning machine). For example, Dixing Wang designs a computer based on a quasi-holographic system from the hexadecimal system. In fact, it is completely possible to understand the original ideas of the designer through the formal understanding of the model A shown in Fig. 1. The enlightenment obtained is that any binary structure design or corresponding mode can be given to universal learning machine for automatic identification. As another example, Yizhen Qi constructed the state-structure-logic deductive system from the geometrical characteristics of artificial neurons. At the same time, he constructed a corresponding conceptual framework based on the characteristics of biological neurons. This gives the corresponding structural or symbolic system to the formal understanding model B to realize the automatic learning way to understand the original ideas of the designer, and also expands the scope of pattern recognition of machine learning. Then, in terms characters and Chinese, any user's repeated use can be learned by the formal understanding model C (in other words, this is equivalent to machine learning to gradually understand each user's Language usage habits). It can be seen that Xiaohui Zou understands from the perspective of Chinese characters and Chinese chess or knowledge chess and the original chess soul: Saussure's language is chess fully, and Wittgenstein's language game, and Heidegger's language is existence. The home is not a hole in the wind.

4   Conclusion

The significance is that not only are three types of cognitive systems, such as quasi-holographic spaces, five-cycle traversal, and sequential-sequence structures, all of which were once difficult to understand, but now they are easy to understand, and they all It is regarded as a new cognitive paradigm, and it has obtained a simplified expression and understanding.

Worth further exploration is: past and present many personalized cognitive systems and standardized information processing, due to the formal understanding model of general computing and general learning and further universal creation, will be free, fair and efficient. This will inevitably stimulate the comprehensive development of a new era of cognitive systems and information processing.

References

1. Chapman, S., Marrochio, H., Myers, R.C.: Holographic complexity in vaidya spacetimes II. J. High Energy Phys. **2018**(6), 114 (2018)
2. Baik, K., Dudley, C., Marston, P.L.: Acoustic quasi-holographic images of scattering by vertical cylinders from one-dimensional bistatic scans. J. Acoust. Soc. Am. **130**(6), 3838 (2011)
3. Zartman, D.J., Plotnick, D.S., Marston, T.M., et al.: Quasi-holographic processing as an alternative to synthetic aperture sonar imaging. J. Acoust. Soc. Am. **133**(5), 3295 (2013)
4. Tougbaev, V.A., Eom, T.J., Yu, B.A., et al.: Quasi-holographic solution to polarization-sensitive optical coherence tomography acceptable to nonlaboratory applications. J. Biomed. Opt. **13**(4), 044014 (2008)
5. Barbon, J.L.F., Martingarcia, J.: Terminal holographic complexity. J. High Energy Phys. **6**(6), 132 (2018)
6. Chow, H.K.H., Choy, K.L., Lee, W.B.: A dynamic logistics process knowledge-based system - an RFID multi. Knowl.-Based Syst. **20**(4), 357–372 (2007)
7. Leo Kumar, S.P.: Knowledge-based expert system in manufacturing planning: state-of-the-art review. Int. J. Product. Res. 1–25 (2018)
8. Shihabudheen, K.V., Pillai, G.N.: Recent advances in neuro-fuzzy system: a survey. Knowl.-Based Syst. **152**, 136–162 (2018)
9. Campbell, K.E., Oliver, D.E., Shortliffe, E.H.: The unified medical language system. J. Am. Med. Inform. Assoc. **5**(1), 12–16 (1998)
10. Hurwitz, J., Kaufman, M., Bowles, A.: 9 IBM's Watson as a Cognitive System. Cognitive Computing and Big Data Analytics. Wiley (2015)
11. Spiridonov, V., Ezrina, E.: The interaction of several languages in the cognitive system. Russ. J. Cogn. Sci. **2**(4), 12–29 (2015). Social Science Electronic Publishing
12. SFL Inc.: Dynamically evolving cognitive architecture system based on a natural language intent interpreter (2017)
13. Leyton, M.: Principles of information structure common to six levels of the human cognitive system. Inf. Sci. **38**(1), 1–120 (1986)
14. Leu, G., Abbass, H.: A multi-disciplinary review of knowledge acquisition methods: from human to autonomous eliciting agents. Knowl.-Based Syst. **105**(C), 1–22 (2016)
15. Chang, J.S., Wong, H.J.: Selecting appropriate sellers in online auctions through a multi-attribute reputation calculation method. Electron. Commer. Res. Appl. **10**(2), 144–154 (2011)
16. Thompson, J.A., Bell, J.C., Butler, C.A.: Digital elevation model resolution: effects on terrain attribute calculation and quantitative soil-landscape modeling. Geoderma **100**(1), 67–89 (2015)
17. Feinerer, I., Hornik, K., Meyer, D.: Text mining infrastructure in R. (2015). Text MI
18. Sapiro-Gheiler, E.: "Read my lips": using automatic text analysis to classify politicians by party and ideology (2018). Read ML
19. Angeli, G., Premkumar, M.J.J., Manning, C.D.: Leveraging linguistic structure for open domain information extraction, Leveraging LS, ACL (2015)
20. Del Corro, L., Gemulla, R.: Claus IE: clause-based open information extraction (2013). Claus IECO WWW
21. Padia, A., Ferraro, F., Finin, T.W.: KGCleaner: identifying and correcting errors produced by information extraction systems. KGC leaner I, journal CoRR, abs/1808.04816 (2018)
22. Jannin, P., Strauss, G., Meixensberger, J., Burgert, O.: Validation of knowledge acquisition for surgical process models (2018). Validation OK

23. Gordon, J., Van Durme, B.: Reporting bias and knowledge acquisition (2013). Reporting BA, AKBC @CIKM
24. Lin, Y., Liu, Z., Luan, H., Sun, M., Rao, S., Liu, S.: Modeling relation paths for representation learning of knowledge bases. In: Proceedings (2015). Modeling RP, EMNLP
25. Kuznetsov, S.O., Poelmans, J.: Knowledge representation and processing with formal concept analysis. Wiley Interdisc. Rev.: Data Min. Knowl. Discov. **3**, 200–215 (2013)
26. Manning, C., Surdeanu, M., Bauer, J., Finkel, J., Bethard, S., McClosky, D.: The stanford core NLP natural language processing toolkit. In: Proceedings Manning (2014). The SC, ACL
27. Sarikaya, R., Hinton, G.E., Deoras, A.: Application of deep belief networks for natural language understanding. IEEE/ACM Trans. Audio Speech Lang. Process. **22**, 778–784 (2014). Application OD
28. Bahdanau, D., Cho, K., Bengio, Y.: Neural machine translation by jointly learning to align and translate. Neural MT, journal CoRR, abs 1409.0473 (2014)
29. Jia, R., Liang, P.: Adversarial examples for evaluating reading comprehension systems. In: Proceedings (2017). Adversarial EF, EMNLP
30. Rajpurkar, P., Zhang, J., Lopyrev, K., Liang, P.: SQuAD: 100, 000 + questions for machine comprehension of text. In: Proceedings (2016). SQuAD10, EMNLP
31. Stanley, G.B.: Reading and writing the neural code. Nat. Neurosci. **16**, 259–263 (2013)
32. King, K.D.: Bringing Creative writing instruction into reminiscence group treatment. Clin. Gerontol. **41**, 1–7 (2018)
33. Uddin, G., Khomh, F.: Automatic summarization of API reviews. In: 2017 32nd IEEE/ACM International Conference on Automated Software Engineering (ASE), pp. 159–170 (2017). Automatic SO
34. Zou, X.: Original Collection on Smart-System Studied. Smashwords, Inc. (2018). ISBN 9780463607640
35. Zou, X.: Advanced Collection on Smart-System Studied. Smashwords, Inc. (2018). ISBN 9780463020036
36. Zou, X., Zou, S., Ke, L.: Fundamental law of information: proved by both numbers and characters in conjugate matrices. In: Proceedings, vol. 1, p. 60 (2017)
37. Zou, S., Zou, X.: Understanding: how to resolve ambiguity. In: Shi, Z., Goertzel, B., Feng, J. (eds.) ICIS 2017. IAICT, vol. 510, pp. 333–343. Springer, Cham (2017). https://doi.org/10.1007/978-3-319-68121-4_36
38. Underhill, J.W.: Humboldt Worldview and Language. Edinburgh University Press, Edinburgh (2013). pp. 12, 161
39. Joseph, J.E.: Saussurean tradition in linguistics. In: Concise History of the Language Sciences, pp. 233–239 (1995)
40. French, R.M.: Subcognition and the limits of the turing test. Mind **99**(393), 53–65 (1990)
41. Preston, J., Bishop, M.: Views into the Chinese room: new essays on searle and artificial intelligence. Minds Mach. **15**(1–111), 97–106 (2005)
42. Starks, M.R.: The Logical Structure of Philosophy, Psychology, Mind and Language as Revealed in the Writings of Wittgenstein and Searle (2016)
43. Strong, T.: Therapy as a New Language Game? A Review of Wittgenstein and Psychotherapy: From Paradox to Wonder. Psyccritiques (2015)
44. Fox, C.: Heidegger's "black notebooks". Philosophy **90**(2), 1–12 (2018)
45. Zuo, X., Zuo, S.: Indirect computing model with indirect formal method. Computer Engineering & Software (2011)
46. Zou, X., Zou, S.: Two major categories of formal strategy. Comput. Appl. Softw. **24**(16), 3086–3114 (2013)

47. Xiaohui, Z., Shunpeng, Z.: Bilingual information processing method and principle. J. Comput. Appl. Softw. **32**(11), 69–76 (2015)
48. Zou, X., Zou, S.: Virtual twin turing machine: bilingual information processing as an example. Software (2011)
49. Zou, X., Zou, S.: Basic law of information: the fundamental theory of generalized bilingual processing. In: ISIS Summit Vienna 2015. The Information Society at the Crossroads. 2015: T9.1002 (2015)
50. Loeb, I.: The role of universal language in the early work of Carnap and Tarski. Synthese **194**, 1–17 (2017)
51. Hernández-Orallo, J.: Evaluation in artificial intelligence: from task-oriented to ability-oriented measurement. Artif. Intell. Rev. **48**, 1–51 (2017)
52. Lu, W., Chen, T.: New conditions on global stability of Cohen-Grossberg neural networks. Neural Comput. **15**(5), 1173 (2003)
53. Traoré, M.K., Muzy, A.: Capturing the dual relationship between simulation models and their context. Simul. Model. Pract. Theory **14**(2), 126–142 (2018)
54. Mcgregor, A., Vu, H.T.: Better streaming algorithms for the maximum coverage problem. Theory Comput. Syst. 1–25 (2018)
55. Partala, T., Surakka, V.: The effects of affective interventions in human–computer interaction. Interact. Comput. **16**(2), 295–309 (2018)

Intelligent Measurement and Management of Aircraft Structural Deformation

Hongli He[1(✉)], Bei Chen[1], and Quanbo Ge[2]

[1] Chinese Flight Test Establishment, Testing Institute, Xi'an, China
hhhl2003@163.com
[2] School of Automation, Hangzhou Dianzi University, Hangzhou, China

Abstract. Aiming at the requirement of aircraft structural deformation measurement, a life cycle aircraft structural deformation measurement and management system based on CPS is proposed. The virtual simulation is used to select the measuring equipment and optimize the measuring scheme to form the measuring plan. Under the guidance of the measuring plan, the digital, network, data fusion and virtualization technologies are used to realize the intelligent perception, analysis and decision-making and control of the physical measuring equipment, which can fundamentally reduce the human interference and improve the quickness and efficiency of the testing.

Keywords: CPS · Intelligent measurement · System design ·
Virtual simulation

1 Introduction

With the background of "made in China 2025" and "Internet+" era, the deep integration of the new generation of information technology and manufacturing industry has become the main line to promote the development of intelligent technology [1]. Artificial intelligence is the key to unlocking the future smart world [1]. The core of its strategy is to realize real-time connectivity, mutual recognition and effective communication between people, equipment and products through CPS (Cyber Physical Systems), thus constructing a highly flexible of informationization and intelligent mode of digitization [2].

Intelligent testing starts from several aspects of test resource intensive management, specification of test process, and collection of test data. To form a "smart" test system for intelligent deployment of test resources, progressive optimization of test procedures. On the basis of tracking the development trend of intelligent testing technology at home and abroad and combining with the actual demand of flight test, this paper designs an intelligent measurement and management system of flight test aircraft structure deformation. Due to the limited space, this paper focuses on the overall design idea of intelligent measurement system, and constructs an intelligent measurement

H. He—The project is supported by the national natural science foundation (No: 91646108).

F. Sun et al. (Eds.): ICCSIP 2018, CCIS 1005, pp. 285–293, 2019.
https://doi.org/10.1007/978-981-13-7983-3_25

system using the existing measurement equipment in our hospital, which can directly output measurement reports and results.

2   System Design

Aiming at the needs of aircraft structural deformation measuremental, a full life cycle aircraft deformation intelligent measurement system is constructed to realize the intelligentization, automatic acquisition, processing, evaluation and data control of feature points, lines and surface data. The system is mainly composed of five subsystems: intelligent physical measurement subsystem, Intelligent acquisition subsystem, measurement planning subsystem, Intelligent data processing subsystem and Monitoring and result output subsystem. The architecture constitutes the cyber physical system (cps), which embodies the intelligent features of "state awareness, real-time analysis, self-determination, and precise execution".

Physical Measurement Subsystem. The physical measurement subsystem is a physical structure such as an execution unit, a transmission unit, a sensing unit, and a measuring unit of the device. Through the combined application of multimeasurement equipment, it is possible to obtain information on all points, lines and planes on the aircraft under test and point cloud information, and obtain the shape data of the aircraft through uniform processing of the coordinate system [3].

Intelligent acquisition subsystem through the construction of the information network system, real-time perception of the surrounding environment, the measured object and the state posture of the intermediate measurement link is realized. The CPS-based state-aware environment is constructed through the measurement devices, simulation devices and processing devices of different interfaces. Achieve effective collection and transmission of the required information [4, 5].

Measurement Planning Subsystem. Measurement planning is the key to optimal system configuration and the basis for automated measurements. The various designs that need to be measured during the measurement planning phase. According to the requirements of the measurement task and the knowledge of the site environment, the simulation model is built, and the measurement characteristics are simulated and calculated. The simulation selects the selection, combination, layout, and measurement tasks of the participating measurement equipment in a specific task. It is mainly used for task preparation, simulation measurement site, equipment layout, equipment interference, measurement trajectory path simulation, The measurement plan are confirmed, and the formed measurement plan is sent to the measurement and control center for control. The formed measurement plan is sent to the measurement and control center for control, and the physical system is commanded for orderly measurement [6].

Intelligent data processing, analysis, decision-making subsystem Intelligent data processing, analysis, and decision-making subsystems are the core of the system, and are mainly responsible for data processing, analysis, management, decision-making, and control. It mainly performs calibration processing, coordinate conversion, data adjustment processing, data fusion, uncertainty analysis, and is responsible for the management of various equipment states and the management of measurement data, guiding transmission, processing, evaluation, display, etc. With the functions of management decision expert system, the measured data can be managed based on the model of the aircraft m [7, 8].

Monitoring and Result Output Subsystem. Human-computer interaction, results display and output. Display the test site by visualizing the 3D virtual scene image, and according to the data processing result, form a result report according to the project requirements. The visual monitoring system provides visual management functions for 3D virtual scenes. Visual management is mainly divided into two parts: main visual switching and custom partial view representation. In the three-dimensional virtual scene, although the system provides the viewpoint switching function, it does not have the pertinence of the observation of the feature parts. According to the characteristics of the test, a plurality of reasonable observation visual points are reserved in advance in the visual monitoring, During the running of the system, you can switch to any main vision at any time, which is convenient for displaying the characteristic part data. The theoretical information can be loaded and hidden at any time [9]. The results can be output according to data and report forms.

2.1 Physical Measurement Subsystem

The physical measurement subsystem is a physical structure such as an execution unit, a transmission unit, a sensing unit, and a measuring unit of the device. The measuring device comprises a total station, a light pen, a three-dimensional scanner, a laser tracker, an image measuring system, etc., and the physical measurement subsystem is connected to the data processing subsystem through an information network, and the collected data is sent to the data processing center, The physical measurement subsystem receives commands from the control center and automatically collects data according to the control commands.

2.2 Measurement Planning Subsystem

Measurement planning is the basis for intelligent testing. According to the measurement requirements, the reasonable measurement equipment is selected through analysis, the measurement sequence and its planning are determined, the measurement process is simulated based on the selected measurement equipment, optimize the measurement path to generate a collision-free detection path. The planning result is generated by the converter to generate a measurement program file, and the measurement program file is generated by the post processor to generate a measurement device control command, and the related measurement operation is performed.

The measurement plan is divided into three levels. One is the test ability plan, which integrates the measurable design into the full life cycle guarantee of the aircraft test. In the initial stage of the test design, it considers how to solve the measurement problems at each stage, and will measure the support activities and the required Various technical means for analysis and standardization; The second is the measurement equipment station planning, using the least measurement equipment and the optimal station plan under the premise of ensuring the measurement accuracy and measurement range; the third is the optimal measurement path planning, the purpose of which is to ensure the measurement accuracy. Under the shortest path, the detection area of the object to be tested can be traversed safely and efficiently, and the optimal measurement plan can be effectively obtained through machine learning in the simulation process.

Measuring Equipment Station Intelligent Planning. During the test, the measuring device should be in a position where all the areas to be detected can be measured. If this is not possible, additional measurement equipment or transfer measurements are required. However, these measures will result in increased measurement costs, Measurement accuracy and work efficiency are reduced. Therefore, in order to obtain an optimal measurement station plan, it is necessary to arrange station planning before measurement. The minimum measurement equipment is used to ensure that the measurement accuracy and measurement range are met. The intelligent planning of the measurement equipment station usually needs to adopt the automatic solution and optimization algorithm of the station. Firstly, the station reference plane is obtained, and a series of initial station input points are obtained by discretely calculating the reference plane measurement range; Then, the hierarchical search strategy is used to search for available stations, and the measurement accessibility analysis is performed to screen all available station sets; Finally, the clustering algorithm and the chaos algorithm can be used to optimize the station, and the minimum set of available stations is obtained, and the calculation basis of the measurement accuracy is given.

Optimal Measurement Path Intelligent Planning. The planning of the measurement path is a key issue in the shape detection of aircraft components. In order to ensure the measurement accuracy, the shortest path can be used to safely and efficiently complete the traversal of the detection area of the object to be tested. In the process of detecting the shape of the aircraft, the digital model is known, and the goal of the measurement planning is to make the number of measuring points as small as possible while satisfying the requirements of measurement accuracy. At the same time, the density of the distribution of the measuring points changes with the curvature of the surface, and the adaptive distribution of the measuring points is realized.

2.3　Intelligent Acquisition Subsystem

Mainly obtain the data of each measuring device and send it to the data processing and analysis center for processing. At present, various digital measuring devices have their advantages and limitations. In order to realize the rapid positioning and attitude measurement of large aircraft, according to the design idea and the mechanism of intelligent measuring system, Multi-measurement equipment such as total station, light pen, scanner, robotic arm, etc. should be used for joint measurement. In the measurement process, the measurement reference is unified, and the quantitative measurement is collected by the on-site measurement data. Drive control system should compensate for positioning and closed-loop control achieve intelligent and accurate measurement and accurate inspection. Different measuring instruments often use different communication interface standards. Different measuring devices use different data processing and operating systems, which makes data communication and integration difficult. To this end, different types of measuring equipment such as points, lines, and surfaces are classified, and a unified standard interface and a conversion interface are designed, so that all data are controlled in the same control center; Through the secondary development of 3D CAD software (such as CATIA and UG), the unified measurement core ensures that geometric information, dimensional tolerances, inspection plans, measurement simulations, measurement results and other information are seamlessly shared between the same or different platforms. At the same time, the WEB software system is used to perform measurement result analysis report and statistical report output, thereby managing all data and realizing information integration and closed-loop feedback.

2.4 Intelligent Data Processing Subsystem

Accurate measurement data is the key and core of research and development, testing, and production. How to coordinate the scheduling of multiple measurement devices through intelligent measurement processing and management, quickly and accurately obtaining the shape data of a large space measurement object, and making whether the decision is out of tolerance based on the allowable tolerance data of the aircraft is a key issue that must be addressed. According to the work procedure and division of labor, the information processing flow chart of intelligent processing decision and display under the support of expert knowledge is given. The system diagram is shown in Fig. 1.

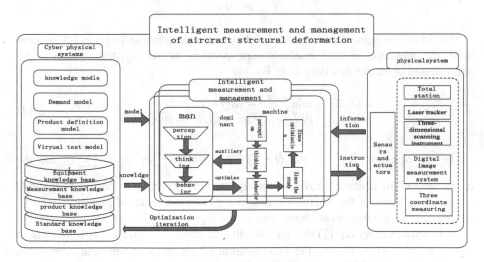

Fig. 1. Measurement processing and management subsystem processing flow chart

Data processing is the core and central nervous system of the system, responsible for the processing, analysis and control of equipment. Data processing analysis needs to carry out calibration processing, unification of large space coordinate benchmarks, data fusion processing, etc. The key algorithms of benchmark unified and fusion processing are given below.

Multi-mode large space measurement control network coordinate reference uniform In order to integrate each measurement coordinate system into the global coordinate system, the reference coordinate system of any measurement site is selected as a global coordinate system, and the measurement data of different measurement devices are spatially registered. The coordinate conversion equation for the measurement data between any two measurement stations is:

$$P = \begin{bmatrix} R & T \\ 0 & 1 \end{bmatrix} Q \tag{1}$$

Where: P is the measurement data in the global coordinate system, Q is the measurement data in the local coordinate system, R is the rotation matrix, and T is the translation vector.

In this paper, a multi-mode measurement space registration algorithm based on quaternion and global adjustment is established to spatially register the measurement data of different measurement devices. Therefore, if the unit four elements $W = [\omega_0, \omega_1, \omega_2, \omega_3]$ is selected, the rotation matrix R and the translation vector T are:

$$R = \begin{bmatrix} \omega_0^2 + \omega_1^2 - \omega_2^2 - \omega_3^2 & 2(\omega_1\omega_2 - \omega_0\omega_3) & 2(\omega_1\omega_3 + \omega_0\omega_2) \\ 2(\omega_1\omega_2 + \omega_0\omega_3) & \omega_0^2 + \omega_2^2 - \omega_1^2 - \omega_3^2 & 2(\omega_2\omega_3 - \omega_0\omega_1) \\ 2(\omega_1\omega_3 - \omega_0\omega_2) & 2(\omega_2\omega_3 + \omega_0\omega_1) & \omega_0^2 + \omega_3^2 - \omega_1^2 - \omega_2^2 \end{bmatrix} \tag{2}$$

$$T = P - RQ \tag{3}$$

Based on the same characteristics of the same measurement target point set centroid, the minimum sum of residuals corresponding to the registration data is the optimization objective function, as in Eq. (4):

$$\begin{aligned} m(R, T) &= \min \sum \| P - (RQ + T) \|^2 \\ &= \min \sum (\bar{P}\bar{P}^T - \bar{F}\bar{Q}^T R^T - R\bar{Q}\bar{F}^T + R\bar{Q}\bar{Q}^T R^T) \end{aligned} \tag{4}$$

In the equation: $\bar{P} = P - \bar{\mu}_P$, $\bar{Q} = Q - \bar{\mu}_Q$, $\bar{\mu}_P = \frac{1}{n}\sum_{i=1}^{n} P_i$, $\bar{\mu}_Q = \frac{1}{n}\sum_{i=1}^{n} Q_i$ are the coordinates of the center of gravity of the registration data group respectively; $\bar{P}$ and $\bar{Q}$ are the coordinates of the registration data group after the center of gravity; P_i and Q_i are the original measurement coordinates of the registration data group, respectively.

It is obvious from Eq. (7) that the objective function minimization is equivalent to $R\bar{Q}\bar{F}^T$ maximization, that is, the maximization of the diagonal element summation operator of matrix $R\bar{Q}\bar{F}^T$, so that $J = \sum \bar{Q}\bar{F}^T$, the objective function is transformed into:

$$M(R,T) = \max \sum RJ \tag{5}$$

$$J = \frac{1}{n}\sum_{i=1}^{4}\left[(P_i - \bar{\mu}_P)(Q_i - \bar{\mu}_Q)^T\right] \tag{6}$$

To do this, construct a 4×4 matrix H:

$$H = \begin{bmatrix} tr(J) & \Delta^T \\ \Delta & J + J^T - tr(J)I_3 \end{bmatrix} \tag{7}$$

Where Δ is $\begin{bmatrix} L_{23} & L_{31} & L_{12} \end{bmatrix}^T$, I_{ij} is $(J - J^T)_{ij}$, I_3 is a 4×4 matrix, then the unit eigenvector H corresponding to the largest eigenvalue is the quaternion vector W obtained, and the rotation matrix R can be calculated by Eq. (2) Substituting the calculation result R into the Eq. (3), the translation vector T can be solved.

The rotation matrix R and the translation vector T are used as the estimated values, and the spatial adjustment of the multi-mode measurement data is adjusted by the distance constraint, and the globally optimal spatial registration relationships R and T of the measurement stations are obtained.

2.5 Monitoring and Result Output Subsystem

The monitoring and output subsystem is the key link of human-computer interaction. This part is essential for the safety and reliability of the test. Through the subsystem, the effect display and final output of the results can be performed.

Display the results of the test site and measurement by visualizing the three-dimensional virtual scene image, and form a result report according to the requirements of the data processing result. It includes virtual scene display, image monitoring, point cloud display, out-of-tolerance labeling, etc. All data can be displayed on site, or can be accessed on a remote computer according to each person's management and access rights.

3 Application Verification

The flight test aircraft structural deformation intelligent test and management evaluation construction in accordance with the overall planning, the gradual implementation of the idea is gradually advanced.

According to the aircraft structural deformation measurement requirements of a certain transport plane (Point measurement accuracy is no more than 1 mm), Using digital measurement equipment such as total station, light pen, and image measurement to form an integrated measurement platform, Which are carried out under the support of the information network subsystem. The joint networking of multiple measurement equipment is realized, and all measurement information is introduced into the control center for centralized control and processing. The expert knowledge (the plane's outer contour, threshold information, equipment performance, etc.) are joined in the center of the measurement and control system.

The system can collect, process and convert data in real time, The guidance measurement can be performed by processing the data. The system can give fault diagnosis combined with expert knowledge (such as exceeding the tolerance threshold) and give warning if the tolerance is exceeded, which is marked in red. as shown in Fig. 2. The accuracy of measurement and the validity of coordinate transformation are verified by comparing the results of common measurement points with data of several heterogeneous measuring devices. The test system verifies the effectiveness of intelligent measurement and the effectiveness of coordinate transformation and data processing through precision testing.

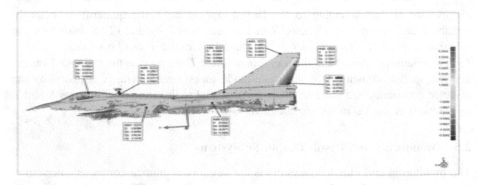

Fig. 2. Measurement results and error marking (Color figure online)

4 Summary

This paper presents an application framework of the intelligent data analysis and evaluation system for aircraft structural deformation in the whole life cycle of flight test, which has been initially implemented in a hangar. Using digital, network, virtualization and other technologies to achieve intelligent perception, analysis and decision-making, can optimize the original test process, fundamentally reduce human interference, improve the quickness, efficiency and accuracy of testing.

References

1. Outline of China's manufacturing industry development 2015–2025. Ministry of Industry and Information Technology, China Academy of Engineering (2015)
2. Hermann, M., Pentek, T., Otto, B.: Design principles for industrie 4.0 scenarios (2015)
3. Wu, L.L., Wang, Y., Liu, S.L., et al.: Research on three-dimensional optical measurement technology of aircraft skin parts. Aviat. Manuf. Technol. (2016)
4. Lei, P.: Research on Interoperation Technology and Application of Intelligent Precision Machining for Aircraft Assembly Interface. Beijing University of Aeronautics and Astronautics, Beijing

5. Li, W.P., Tian, X.T., Geng, J.H., et al.: A digital combination measurement method for aircraft assembly profile. Aviat. Manuf. Technol. **61**(1), 16–23 (2018)
6. Pan, X., Gong, J., Liu, X.: Research and application of mil automated test method based on simulink. J. Ordnance Equip. Eng. (11), 163–168 (2017)
7. Zhao, J.G., Liu, X.Y., et al.: Research on 3D digital co-measurement method for large complex components of aircraft. Aviat. Manuf. Technol. **61**(5), 55–59 (2018)
8. Wang, Y., Wang, X.N., Wang, X., Lu, Z.J., et al.: Research on construction method and key technology of intelligent production system. Aviat. Manuf. Technol. **61**(1), 16–23 (2018)
9. Wang, J.F., Liu, R., Xie, M., Guo, H.J., et al.: Field real - time data - driven 3D visual monitoring of the process of making hole in the airfoil. Aviat. Manuf. Technol. **61**(1), 36–41 (2018)

Design and FPGA Implementation of an High Efficient XGBoost Based Sleep Staging Algorithm Using Single Channel EEG

Yiqiao Liao[1], Milin Zhang[2(✉)], Zhihua Wang[1], and Xiang Xie[1]

[1] Institute of Microelectronics, Tsinghua University, Beijing, China
[2] Department of Electronic Engineering, Tsinghua University, Beijing, China
zhangmilin@tsinghua.edu.cn

Abstract. This paper proposed a high efficient 5-class sleep staging XGBoost based algorithm using a single channel electroencephalogram (EEG). The sum of spectrum absolute value, instead of Fast Fourier Transform (FFT) based spectral energy, was proposed for feature extraction, which greatly reduced the complexity. The system is synthesized using $0.18\,\mu m$, and experimental verification using Field-Programmable Gate Array (FPGA) based on Sleep-EDF database. An overall accuracy (ACC) of 79.1% is achieved, which a highest ACC of 86.3% has been measured with specified patient.

Keywords: XGBoost · Sleep staging · EEG · Classification

1 Introduction

Sleep disorder is a health issue that may happens to people in all the ages. According to the nationwide survey in the United States, more than 20% of the adult population suffer from sleep problems [1]. Sleep staging is necessary for diagnosis of sleep-related diseases, i.e., dyssomnias and parasomnias etc. In addition, sleep stages are commonly used in nursing intervention for the cure of sleep disorder.

In clinical practice, sleep staging is typically performed with Polysomnography (PSG). The results of PSG are obtained by multiple signals, i.e. multi-channel Electroencephalography (EEG), Electrocorticography (ECoG), Electromyogram (EMG) and Electrocardiography (ECG). Professional PSG device is bulky and expensive and the process is time consuming. On the other hand, commercial available wearable sleep staging devices are available in the market. The majority are designed based on single-channel parametric test and/or acceleration sensor, featuring a low accuracy. Thus, The need for a single-channel EEG based sleep staging algorithm with high accuracy, high flexible, low latency and low power consumption is urgent.

© Springer Nature Singapore Pte Ltd. 2019
F. Sun et al. (Eds.): ICCSIP 2018, CCIS 1005, pp. 294–303, 2019.
https://doi.org/10.1007/978-981-13-7983-3_26

Various studies have been reported on single-channel PSG based sleep staging using traditional machine learning and/or deep learning methods [2–6]. [2] proposed a wearable low-latency sleep stage classifier for rodent uses both EEG and EMG signals as inputs, but can't meet the demand of single channel EEG sleep staging system. [3] introduces a novel algorithm using machine-controlled decision trees, however the uses of FFT based spectral energy feature is power hungry. The growing of deep learning provided a solution of end to end learning for sleep staging. [6] proposed to compose Convolutional Neural Network (CNN) and Recurrent Neural Network (RNN) for both feature extraction and state transition of Long Short-Term Memory (LSTM) from CNN, featuring a state-of-the-art overall accuracy and F1-score for single channel EEG (Sleep-EDF:82.0%-76.9). However the network is too complex to implement in hardware. It is almost impossible to implement such a model in wearable platform in real time with satisfactory battery life. In addition, the model is too complex to overfit with small datasets.

Support vector machine (SVM) was commonly used in EEG classification for low power application scenarios, i.e. seizure detection [7], spike sorting [8]. [5] proposed a Rapid Eye Movement (REM)/Non-REM sleep classifier for Alzheimer patients based on SVM. However, single SVM is only capable for binary classification. Multiple SVM system can be applied for multiple class classification, but suffers from high power consumption due to the multiplication operations. Decision tree is good at multiple class classification problems. [3] proposed an ultra-low power SoC for sleep staging based on decision tree classifier and spectral features. However the FFT based spectral features used in this work is power hungry. In addition, the two EEG channels based algorithm features an accuracy of only 78.85%. XGBoost [9] is a gradient boosting decision tree algorithm, proposed in 2016. It features good performance in efficiency and the ability to solve practical problems [10], and a good adaptability to multiple class classification issues. It requires no multiplication operations, resulting high hardware friendly in implementation. In addition, it is friendly to both transfer learning with large dataset and fine tune with small dataset, which fits the scenario of various wearable devices development. Hardware implementation of XGBoost has been reported in literature [11], It demonstrated the implementation of large tree ensembles and speedup of XGBoost, which is not fit for the low power application of sleep staging.

This paper proposed an XGBoost based sleep staging algorithm using single-channel EEG data. The proposed algorithm features an overall accuracy (ACC) of 79.1%, and a highest ACC of 86.3% for specific patient. The proposed algorithm has been implemented in FPGA with 3.5 KB model, which is much lower than the reported results in literature [6].

2   Design of the XGBoost Based Sleep Staging Algorithm

Figure 1 illustrated the blockdiagram of the proposed XGBoost based sleep staging algorithm. It consists of two main steps: (1) feature extraction, and

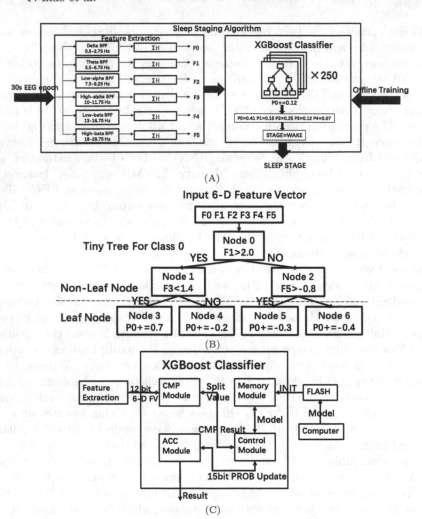

Fig. 1. (A) Blockdiagram of the proposed XGBoost based sleep staging algorithm. It consists of a feature extraction module and a XGBoost based classifier. (B) Architecture of a single tree with a depth of 3. (C) Architecture of the proposed XGBoost Classifier.

(2) XGBoost based classification. According to American Academy of Sleep Medicine (AASM), sleep stages are divided into five discrete stages: Wake, Non-rapid Eye Movement stage 1 (N1), N2, N3 and REM. Five sleep stages classification result is expected from the final output.

A 30 s epoch of single channel EEG, $X_{in}(t)$, is used as the input signal. Six bandpass filters, $h_1(t)$, $h_2(t)$ ... $h_6(t)$, are applied to the input signal as

$$X_{fi}(t) = X_{in}(t) * h_i(t) \tag{1}$$

where the passband of the filters are 0.5 Hz to 2.75 Hz (denoted as delta wave), 3.5 Hz to 6.75 Hz (denoted as theta wave), 7.5 Hz to 9.25 Hz (denoted as low-alpha wave), 10 Hz to 11.75 Hz (denoted as high-alpha wave), 13 Hz to 16.75 Hz (denoted as low-beta wave) and 18 Hz to 29.75 Hz (denoted as high-beta wave), respectively.

Spectral energy is widely used in EEG based feature extraction [12], by calculating power density function using FFT

$$p_f = \|\mathcal{F}\{X_{in}(t)\}\| \tag{2}$$

Where $\mathcal{F}$ indicated for FFT operation, $\|\cdot\|$ indicated for norm operation, p_f is the power density function with frequency f.

The sums the power density for specific frequency band is calculated as

$$\delta_{power} = \sum_{f=aHz}^{bHz} p_f \tag{3}$$

Where a and b is the frequency for specific band, for example $a = 0.5$ and $b = 2.75$ for delta band.

The calculation of spectral energy involves FFT for 3000 points which becomes a bottleneck for low power application. The power consumption and the cost of area for feature extraction based on FFT are usually 20 times of classifier [13]. In order to solve this issue, we proposed to extracts the sums of absolute value, $B_i(t)$, instead of spectral energy, as

$$B_i(t_k) = \sum_{t=t_k}^{t_k+3000} |X_{fi}(t)| \tag{4}$$

Where t_k is the time for feature extraction.

The spectral energy of each band is approximate with 6-D feature vector (FV). According to experimental result, the use of the 6-D FV features higher ACC (79.12% versus 76.24%) and lower complexity while compare to the use of spectral energy in XGBoost based sleep staging.

The outputs of the feature extraction module are pushed into the XGBoost based classifier for sleep staging. For each discrete stage, N trees are required. Thus, $5N$ trees are required for a 5-stage classification. A trade-off is performed between the performance and the complexity of the algorithm. According to quantitative analysis results as shown in Fig. 2(A). It shows the performance increases slightly when N is higher than 50.

For each tree, with a depth of M, there are in total $2^M - 1$ nodes, 2^{M-1} of which are non-leaf nodes, while $2^{M-1} - 1$ of which are leaf nodes. According to Fig. 2(B), the accuracy decreased when $M > 3$. The number of nodes and power consumption would increased exponentially with M. Thus, the depth of each tree is set to $M = 3$. For a tree with a depth of 3, two comparison operations, three read operations and one addition operation are required. The power consumption of realizing one single tree is

$$P_{single} = P_{read} \times 3 + P_{cmp} \times 2 + P_{add} \tag{5}$$

where P_{cmp} and P_{add} represent the power consumption required for single comparison operation and addition operation, respectively. P_{read} represents the power consumption for the access of model. The total power consumption of the proposed algorithm can be evaluated as $P_{single} \times 5N$. According to [14], in 45 nm process, $P_{cmp} \approx 5\,pJ$, while $P_{add} \approx 0.1\,pJ$. The power consumption for the access to Static Random Access Memory (SRAM) is $P_{SRAM} \approx 5\,pJ$, while the power consumption to read from FLASH memory is $P_{FLASH} \approx 640\,pJ$. Assume there is 3.5 KB on-chip SRAM on-chip, supporting the storage of parameters for model with $N < 50$. The total power consumption is at the level of several nJ for $N \leq 50$, at the level of several uJ for $N > 50$.

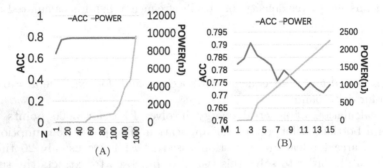

(A)   (B)

Fig. 2. (A) Accuracy/Power change with N (M = 3) (B) Accuracy/Power change with M (N = 50).

L2 regularization term was used in loss function to prevent overfitting. In order to further increase the robustness of the training process, random sample ratio of data and feature was set to 0.5 and 0.7 while tree generation, respectively. The training will be interrupt if overfitting is detected. Since sleep staging is an imbalanced problem, different weights were given to different classes to balance the dataset. In order to improve the efficiency in the use of the model parameters, learning rate is choose as 0.80. In order to further improve the accuracy for specific patient, a coarse to fine two steps training method was utilized. The dataset was split into training dataset and validation dataset. At coarse step, XGBoost training was applied to all training dataset for 40 trees. At fine step, XGBoost training as applied to training dataset of one specific patient for another 10 trees. The test of the validation dataset was also applied to the same specified patient.

3   Hardware Implementation of the Proposed Sleep Staging Algorithm

3.1   System Overview

Figure 1 illustrated the architecture of the hardware implemented algorithm. The input signal is 30 s epoch of single channel EEG with 100 Hz sampling rate.

The proposed sleep staging system consist of two part: (1) feature extraction module based on IIR filter, and (2) classifier based on XGBoost. Model of XGBoost is trained offline and stored in FLASH. The classifier loads the model from FLASH to registers at the memory INIT state. The feature extraction module extract the 6-D FV with IIR filter and absolute value addition operation. The classifier consists of four modules: CMP module, ACC module, Control module and Memory module. The classifier receive the quantization 12-bit feature vector to perform comparison in CMP module and update the classification results based on the output of the XGBoost processor every 30 s in ACC module.

3.2   Implementation of the IIR Based Feature Extraction Module

For the implementation of passband filter in feature extraction module, second order Butterworth bandpass filters with 14 bit quantization parameter is choosed. The implementation of constant coefficient multiplier use Intellectual Property (IP) provided by Vivado Design Suite provided by Xilinx. The transfer function of the Infinite Impulse Response (IIR) filter is

$$H(z) = \frac{b_0 - b_0 z^{-2}}{a_0 + a_1 z^{-1} + a_2 z^{-2}} \tag{6}$$

where a_0, a_1 and b_0 is parameter designed with scipy library. For high-beta band filter, the 3 dB cutoff frequency of that filter are 17.98 Hz and 29.7 Hz, respectively. The order and quantization bit of the filter is determined by quantitative analysis on the tradeoff between complexity and accuracy. Accumulation of absolute value of specific frequency band is used to approximate the spectral energy. FFT is widely used in the extraction of spectral energy, which is very power hungry compared to the proposed method.

a_0 is quantized as exponent of 2 to eliminate the need for divider. The output of each filter is accumulated and saved in a 26-bit feature register. If the accumulation of 30 s epoch is finished, the 12-bit Most Significant Byte (MSB) of the feature register is sent to the comparator to compare with a 12-bit split value.

3.3   Implementation of the XGBoost Classifier

The work flow of the XGBoost Classifier is as shown in Fig. 3. It starts from the initialization of the memory. The model parameters of the XGBoost are loaded from the FLASH. The quantization 12 bit 6-D feature vectors are loaded and stored in registers. The parameters of one tree are loaded and will be compared with the extracted features. A new node is found after each comparison process. The comparison process stops only when the new node is a leaf node, which means the comparison of one single tree is done. A 15 bit probability change of the specific class is output to update the probability register. When the comparison for all the trees and all the classes are done, the accumulated probability of different classes determine the final classification result according to the maximum value in probability register. The classifier load a new input every 30 s.

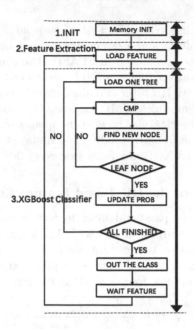

Fig. 3. Workflow of the entire process. It consists of three main steps: (1) initialization of the memory, (2) load feature from the output of the feature extraction module, (3) the XGBoost based classification.

Since the depth of the tree is chosen as 3, the model parameter of one single tree is seven 16-bit integers. Three of them is for non-leaf nodes with a structure of {1'b0, feature_index, split_data}, and four of them is for leaf nodes with a structure of {1'b1, class_prob}.

4   Experimental Result

The proposed sleep staging system is implement on FPGA Xilinx Artix-7 xc7a100tfgg484-2 with 1893 Lookup Table (LUT) elements and 1210 flip flop elements and verified with the PhysioNet Sleep database [15], which contains 79 healthy patents with overnight EEG records and corresponding sleep patterns based on AASM. The classification accuracy of the proposed system is evaluated with hold-out validation with 70% training dataset and 30% test dataset. The classification model is trained with learning rate 0.80, L2 regularization weight 0.5 and 50 rounds for 5 class classification. The overall accuracy (ACC) is define as

$$ACC = \frac{TP + TN}{TP + TN + FP + FN} \tag{7}$$

where TP, TN, FP, FN are True Negative, True Positive, False Positive and False Negative, respectively.

Table 1 compares the performance of proposed work with the work reported in literature. The accuracy of the proposed work is among the best hardware

Table 1. Performance comparison with state-of-the-art works

Methods	Stages	Input	ACC	Power	App[1]	FE[2]	Classifier
BioCAS14 [2]	3-class W, REM, NREM	2-EEG, EMG	72.54%	930 uW	Portable	FFT	Thresholding
EMBC15 [3]	5-class W, REM, N1, N2, N3	1-EEG	78.85%	N/A	Algorithm	FFT	Thresholding
ISCAS16 [4]	3-class W, REM, NREM	2-EEG, EMG	79.7%	360 uW	Portable	64 order FIR Filter	Decision trees
BioCAS17 [5]	2-class REM, NREM	1-EEG	91.7%	20.8 uW	Wearable	FFT	Thresholding
JSSC17 [13]	5-class W, REM, N1, N2, N3	1-EEG	77.84%	426 uW	Wearable	FFT	Decision trees
TNSRE17 [6]	5-class W, REM, N1, N2, N3	1-EEG	82.0%	N/A	Algorithm	CNN +Bi-LSTM	CNN +Bi-LSTM
This work	5-class W, REM, N1, N2, N3	1-EEG	79.12%	102 uW	Wearable	Multi- band 2-order IIR Filter	XGBoost

[1] App stands for Application.
[2] FE stands for Feature Extraction.

implemented 5-class sleep staging with single channel EEG. The only better accuracy was reported using deep learning, which is very hardware hungry. In addition, the feature extraction of the proposed work is more efficient than the prior works based on FFT or 64-order Finite Impulse Response (FIR) filter. Table 2 shows the test results for different sleep stages. Table 3 compares the performance of the proposed classifier with six different feature inputs. For case 1, FFT based spectral energy is used as the feature. For case 2, IIR based sums of

Table 2. Test results for different sleep stages

Class	Precision[1]	Recall [2]	F1 score[3]	Support[4]
Wake	0.78	0.90	0.84	2654
N1	0.32	0.06	0.10	607
N2	0.81	0.89	0.84	4502
N3	0.93	0.78	0.85	1722
REM	0.70	0.68	0.69	2360

[1] $\text{Precision} = \frac{TP}{TP+FP}$
[2] $\text{Recall} = \frac{TP}{TP+FN}$
[3] $\text{F1 score} = \frac{2TP}{2TP+FN+FP}$
[4] support stands for the number of test epoch to support this class.

absolute value is used as the feature. For case 3, 14-bit quantization IIR filter is used as the feature. For case 4, the accuracy for one specific patient is measured. For case 5, the ACC for algorithm implement on FPGA is measured. For case 6, the accuracy for one specific patient on FPGA is measured.

Table 3. Accuracy performance of the proposed algorithm

	Case 1	Case 2	Case 3	Case 4
ACC	76.24%	79.12%	79.07%	86.31%
Feature	FFT	IIR	IIR	IIR
Quantization	N/A	N/A	14-bit	14-bit
Test Methods	70/30% Split	70/30% Split	70/30% Split	One Specific
Order	N/A	2	2	2

5   Conclusion

This paper proposed an XGBoost based sleep staging algorithm using single-channel EEG data. The proposed algorithm utilizes the sum of spectrum absolute value instead of FFT based spectral energy as the main feature, resulting a greatly reduction in the complexity of the overall algorithm. Trade-off between performance and hardware expense has been performed. The proposed classification algorithm features an ACC of 79.1%. In order to demonstrate the transfer ability of the proposed algorithm, fine training for specific patient was performed achieving an ACC of 86.3%.

In the future, We will implement the proposed algorithm at the Application-Specific Integrated Circuit (ASIC) level, together with the EEG acquisition front-end, analog-to-digital converter, electric stimulator and power management module to realize an ultra-low power chip that integrates acquisition, processing and stimulation at the same time. We will further reduce power consumption while maintaining the same accuracy.

Acknowledgements. This work is supported in part by National Natural Science Foundation of China through grant 61674095, and Thousand Youth Talents Plan.

References

1. Hossain, J.L., Shapiro, C.M.: Sleep and breathing **6**(2), 85 (2002)
2. Chemparathy, A., et al.: 2014 IEEE Biomedical Circuits and Systems Conference (BioCAS), IEEE 2014, pp. 592–595 (2014)
3. Imtiaz, S.A., Rodriguez-Villegas, E.: 2015 37th Annual International Conference of the IEEE Engineering in Medicine and Biology Society (EMBC), IEEE 2015, pp. 378–381 (2015)
4. Li, P.Z.X., Kassiri, H., Genov, R.: ISCAS 2016, pp. 1314–1317 (2016)

5. Altaf, M.A.B., Saadeh, W.: 2017 IEEE Biomedical Circuits and Systems Conference (BioCAS), IEEE 2017, pp. 1–4 (2017)
6. Supratak, A., Dong, H., Wu, C., Guo, Y.: IEEE Trans. Neural Syst. Rehabil. Eng. **25**(11), 1998 (2017)
7. Yoo, J., Yan, L., El-Damak, D., Altaf, M.A.B., Shoeb, A.H., Chandrakasan, A.P.: IEEE J. Solid-State Circ. **48**(1), 214 (2013)
8. Ou, T., et al.: 2017 IEEE 12th International Conference on ASIC (ASICON), IEEE 2017, pp. 504–507 (2017)
9. Chen, T., Guestrin, C.: Proceedings of the 22nd ACM SIGKDD International Conference on Knowledge Discovery and Data Mining, ACM 2016, pp. 785–794 (2016)
10. Volkovs, M., Yu, G.W., Poutanen, T.: Proceedings of the Recommender Systems Challenge 2017, ACM 2017, p. 7 (2017)
11. Owaida, M., Zhang, H., Zhang, C., Alonso, G.: 2017 27th International Conference on Field Programmable Logic and Applications (FPL), IEEE 2017, pp. 1–8 (2017)
12. Hassan, A.R., Bashar, S.K., Bhuiyan, M.I.H.: ICACCI 2015, pp. 2238–2243 (2015)
13. Imtiaz, S.A., Jiang, Z., Rodriguez-Villegas, E.: IEEE J. Solid-State Circ. **52**(3), 822 (2017)
14. Han, S., Liu, X., Mao, H., Pu, J., Pedram, A., Horowitz, M.A., Dally, W.J.: 2016 ACM/IEEE 43rd Annual International Symposium on Computer Architecture (ISCA), IEEE 2016, pp. 243–254 (2016)
15. Kemp, B., Zwinderman, A.H., Tuk, B., Kamphuisen, H.A., Oberye, J.J.: IEEE Trans. Biomed. Eng. **47**(9), 1185 (2000)

How to Understand the Mathematical Basis of Two Basic Types of Computational Behavior

Chenjun Lv[1] and Xiaohui Zou[2(✉)] 🆔

[1] Nie Rongzhen Education Association, Beijing, China
1969585758@qq.com
[2] Sino-American Searle Research Center, Beijing, China
949309225@qq.com

Abstract. The purpose of this paper is to explore the possibility of computer information processing the Turing machine and the Gödel machine. The method steps are as follows: On the basis of Lvs' research on continuum hypothesis, a new theory of natural number and real number coding is proposed. Between natural numbers and real numbers, it is also possible to construct an infinite number of hierarchical topology numbers with different sizes. They are all infinite sequences of incompleteness. Then, it analyzes the calculation behavior of the Turing machine as a complete sequence, and defines a new Gödel machine, which is the computational behavior on the incomplete sequence. Next, it is illustrated that the neural network and quantum computing are Gödel machines. The result is the discovery that an interesting finding is that quantum mechanical description of the trajectory of electrons and the internal connection state of neural networks are similar or isomorphic with the topological number structure of real continuums, and are related to the choice of set theory of axiom. The significance lies in: it proves that Lv derives two basic types of computational behavior from the most basic mathematical principles: the Turing machine and the Gödel machine. This may have some inspiring new ideas for the future research of artificial intelligence.

Keywords: Real number continuum · Layered topology set ·
Incomplete sequence · Turing machine · Gödel machine · Neural networks ·
Quantum computing

1 Introduction

The purpose of this paper is to explore the possibility of computer information processing on the Turing machine and the Gödel machine: The mathematical basis of two basic types of computational behavior.

The mathematical meaning of the Gödel incompleteness theorem: the real number cannot be expressed as a coding function of a natural number.

Let us first discuss the concept of "computational behavior". In mathematics, the most basic computational behavior is to use natural numbers to construct the whole real number, which is the core problem of the whole mathematical foundation. Other complex computing behaviors are based on this foundation. As L. Kronecker said in his

© Springer Nature Singapore Pte Ltd. 2019
F. Sun et al. (Eds.): ICCSIP 2018, CCIS 1005, pp. 304–313, 2019.
https://doi.org/10.1007/978-981-13-7983-3_27

famous saying "God created natural numbers, the rest are man-made". The natural number set N is an infinite set that people must admit. The whole mathematics is gradually constructed on the basis of N. The first thing that needs to be constructed is the real set R, which is the two most infinite sets of mathematics that are also "real".

2   Method

The method steps are as follows: On the basis of Lvs' research on continuum hypothesis, a new theory of natural number and real number coding is proposed. Between natural numbers and real numbers, it is also possible to construct an infinite number of hierarchical topology numbers with different sizes. They are all infinite sequences of incompleteness. Then, it analyzes the calculation behavior of the Turing machine as a complete sequence, and defines a new Gödel machine, which is the computational behavior on the incomplete sequence. Next, it is illustrated that the neural network and quantum computing are Gödel machines.

2.1   The Basis of Lvs' Research on Continuum Hypothesis

The natural number set N is an infinite set that people must admit. The whole mathematics is gradually constructed on the basis of N. The first thing that needs to be constructed is the real set R, which is the two most infinite sets of mathematics that are also "real".

In general, any real fraction $R \in [0, 1]$ can be expressed as an infinite series.

$$r = f(N) = 0. \, f(1) \, f(2) \ldots f(n) \ldots \ldots \tag{1.1}$$

Where f (n) is a recursive function, which can be either a decimal system or a binary system. In this classical sense, any real number can be represented as a natural number encoding function f (N). It should be emphasized that if the binary system is adopted, "calculation" is completely equivalent to "judgment", for example, a real decimal

$$R = 0.101010. \ldots \ldots$$

Also be read as

$$R = 0. \; \text{True or false or true or false} \ldots \ldots$$

We call Eq. (1.1) "expansion of real numbers", and a real number can have different expansions.

In addition to expansion, real numbers also have "definitions". In general, real numbers have both geometric definitions and algebraic definitions. For example, the π is a geometric definition, that is, "$\sqrt{2}$ the ratio of the circumference length to the diameter"; it is an algebraic definition, that is, a positive real number of "$r^2 = 2$". Mathematically, a polynomial function is often used to define a real number. The definition of the real number and the expansion is not the same thing the relationship between the two is very complicated.

Next we will enter the core content. The formula (1.1) is of course a real number. In the real analysis, people also default to an axiom: any real number can be expressed in the form of Eq. (1.1). But a more detailed analysis shows that this axiom does not match the Gödel incompleteness theorem. A Gödel number is a natural number n. A Gödel arithmetic proposition is a natural number encoding function f (n), which defines a real number $r_n = f(N)$, and any expansion of the f (n) represents a true value. It is determined that either f (n) = 1 or f (n) = 0; but the Gödel incompleteness theorem states that if the definition of this real number is non-contradictory, then an expansion of an item f (n) The true value must be un-decidable, that is, f (n) = 1 and f (n) = 0 do not hold. Simply put, the essence of the Gödel incompleteness theorem is that there are real numbers that are definable (no contradiction) but un-decidable (incomplete). Like intuitional mathematicians Lej Brouwer and A. Heyting have constructed such arithmetic propositions and real numbers. For example, Heyting thinks that if Didenkind is divided, there is no guarantee that the Euler constant C is a real number because the algorithm "does not give We provide any way to determine whether any rational number A is located to the left or right of C or just equal to C" [1]. That is, C is a definable but un-decidable real number [1].

Below we will analyze where this problem lies. Dedekind segmentation is the basic method of constructing real numbers. According to classical theory, it can construct all real numbers. Intuitively, this method is based on the so-called "upper and lower bound principle": on the real axis, arbitrarily gives a point P, which divides the real set into two disjoint subsets L and R, Where L has no maximum value and R has no minimum value, so each split will generate a unique real number, as shown in the following Fig. 1.

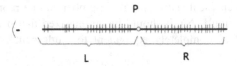

Fig. 1. Dedekind principle

The geometrical intuitive meaning of Dedekind segmentation is obvious, which is a geometric definition of real numbers. But in the sense of algebra, this method has problems: we can't say "arbitrarily give a real number P", but first we must determine whether the real number P exists. If P does not exist, then "up (down) the principle of the boundary is not established. And we say that a real number P exists, that is, for its expansion formula P = f (N) = 0. f (1) f (2) ... f (n) ..., the infinite series f (N) is Convergent, if f (N) diverges, then the P value does not exist.

Therefore, we put forward the concept of "definite but un-decidable real number", which refers to the divergent infinite series of real numbers. It does define a real number, but this real number cannot be calculated. The so-called "ghost real number" People know that these real numbers exist, but they cannot express them.

According to the geometric definition of real numbers, the counter-evidence method is universally established. We must prove that a real number R = f (N) exists, as long as it proves that non - f (N) does not hold; but according to the algebra definition of real numbers, the counter-evidence method cannot be universally established. A real number R = f (N) exists and can only be constructed step by step. Intuitionistic mathematicians do not recognize the counter-evidence law, emphasizing that existence is constructed, and the reason is here. But in fact, people do not distinguish between the geometric definition of real numbers (non-constructive proof) and algebraic definition (constructive proof), and mistakenly believe that the two are equivalent, which is the ideological root of the paradox that leads to mathematics. In mathematics, using geometric intuition to define some basic concepts, although there are logical hidden dangers, it is also inevitable. Regardless of Weierstrass, Cauchy, Dedekind, Cantor, their methods of constructing real numbers use the method of counter-evidence, and they all get the "non-constructive proof" of all real numbers; but if we construct from the natural number gradually, it is not necessarily possible to put the whole Real numbers are constructed. This is a major logical flaw in the classical real number theory we want to make clear.

One of the authors of this paper proved an important meta-theorem:

Conclusion I. For the infinite series $f(N) = 0.1 f(1) f(2) \ldots f(n) \ldots, f(N)$ converges if and only if f (N) is complete.

This is a strong conclusion, indicating that the convergence and completeness of infinite series (sequences) are equivalent. It reveals the inherent structure between mathematical analysis and mathematical logic. The value of this conclusion is that it shows that the classical computational behavior (i.e., the general Turing machine) is only the computational behavior on the complete sequence, and the calculation result is convergent, but for the incomplete sequence, the calculation result is divergent. It is a different calculation behavior than the Turing machine.

2.2 The Latest Achievement of Set Theory

The latest achievement of set theory is that the real continuum is actually an infinitely stacked topological structure.

So, what is the computational behavior of this incomplete sequence? We still hope to derive from the "source" of mathematics, that is, the relationship between natural numbers and real numbers. In set theory, the basic proposition about the structural relationship between natural numbers and real numbers is the "continuous system hypothesis" (CH). Under the axiom set theory ZFC, CH is un-decidable, but fortunately we have solved this problem. Let's talk briefly about the CH problem. According to the set theory, starting from the cardinality ω of the natural number, an infinite sequence of super-poor bases (called Aleev) can be formed:

$$\omega, \omega_1, \omega_2, \ldots, \omega_i, \ldots \ldots \tag{2.1}$$

Knowing the cardinality of real numbers 2^ω, CH is essentially to prove: 2^ω Which one is equal to which Alev ω_i (CH guess $2^\omega = \omega_1$)? Regrettably, Gödel and Cohen proved that CH is un-decidable under the existing set theory axiom system. That is to say, although the axiom set theory can derive most of the classical mathematics, it is impossible to determine whether the real number is "how big"? Therefore, we cannot make a true and deterministic description of the structural relationship between natural numbers and real numbers [2].

One of the authors of this paper has proved a surprising theorem as follows:

Conclusion II. All Alevs ω_i are smaller than 2^ω.

Due to space limitations, this article does not discuss this proof in detail. But in order to let the readers have the confidence to discuss it, we quote Cohen's paragraph, and he has already guessed the result: "The continuum provided by the construction power set is not based on the axiom of substitution to construct higher from the lower base. Any process of the cardinality can be achieved. In this way, 2^ω will be considered to be greater than $\omega_1, \omega_2, \omega_\omega$ the cardinality [2]. Intuitively, this is equivalent to saying that between the natural number and the real number, there are an infinite number of real number subsets of different sizes.

In set theory, we generally do not directly construct real numbers, but rather constructively construct the power set P (N) of the natural number set N, and its cardinality is also equal 2^ω. In the first step, we can construct a set of N finite subsets $P^\infty(N)$. First, first arrange a set g(1) of all finite subsets of only one element containing N:

$$\{1\}, \{2\}, \ldots, \{n\}, \ldots \ldots$$

Then, arrange the set g(2) of all finite subsets of only 2 elements containing N:

$$\{1,2\}, \{1,3\}, \ldots, \{1,n\}, \ldots \ldots$$
$$\{2,3\}, \{2,4\}, \ldots, \{2,n\}, \ldots \ldots$$
$$\ldots$$
$$\{n, n+1\}, \{n, n+2\}, \ldots, \{n, n+m\}, \ldots \ldots$$
$$\ldots \ldots$$

In the same way, we can arrange all the g(1), g(2),...,g(n),... in order, and can prove:

Conclusion III. $P^\infty(N)$ The cardinality is equal to ω_1.

We use the $P^\infty(N)$ called N "ω-type compact power set", in the same way, we can form an incremental infinite sequence of "ω-type compact power set":

$$P^\infty(N), P^\infty(P^\infty(N)), P^\infty(P^\infty(P^\infty(N))), \ldots \ldots$$

In the same way, it can also prove:

Conclusion IV. $P^\infty(N), P^\infty(P^\infty(N)), P^\infty(P^\infty(P^\infty(N))), \ldots \ldots$ The cardinality is equal to $\omega_1, \omega_2, \omega_3, \ldots \ldots$

By replacing the above conclusions with algebraic languages, we can get the following inferences:

Inference I. Between the natural number set N and the real number set R, there are an infinite number of super-poor cardinal sets of different sizes ω_1, ω_2, ω_3, ..., and there is a recursive function relationship as follows:

$$g^i : \omega_{i-1} \to \omega_i \tag{2.2}$$

Any set ω_i is a set of recursive functions of the set ω_{i-1}, starting from the initial set ω_0, ω_1 is the set ω_0 of first-order recursive functions, ω_2 is the set ω_0 of second-order recursive functions,......ω_i is the set ω_0 of i-order recursive functions, so that in N and R an infinitely stacked set ω_i is constructed, which can be expressed as a set of i-order recursive functions of a natural number, i.e.

$$\forall u \in \omega_i =: \forall u_1, u_2, \ldots, u_i \in \omega_0 g^i(u_1, u_2, \ldots, u_i) \tag{2.3}$$

That is to say, ω_i any element u can be expressed as ω_0 an i-order function $\forall u_1, u_2, \ldots, u_i \in \omega_0 g^i(u_1, u_2, \ldots, u_i)$. The two formulas (2.3) and (1.1) express the same meaning.

According to classical mathematics, the two definitions (2.2) and (2.3) are equivalent. But if it is strictly analyzed, according to (2.2), if you want to construct ω_i, the domain is defined ω_{i-1}, but in fact people are constructed ω_i according to (2.3), and its domain is ω_0. Therefore, the two definitions of (2.2) and (2.3) are not equivalent in form, leading to many paradoxes in mathematics, which are the same as the results of the previous analysis.

To distinguish between (2.2) and (2.3), we need to ω_i give two different definitions of "continuity":

Inference II. Let ω_i set of i-order recursive functions between N and R, if ω_i complete (convergent), then a good set of sets, we call "ω_i continuous on R", then it is a "set" (set); if it is incomplete (divergent), then ω_i is a full-order set, we call "ω_i topological continuity on R", this time ω_i is a "class" (class).

We can only intuitively understand this inference. If ω_i is complete, according to the conclusion I, any of its elements $\forall u \in \omega_i =: \forall u_1, u_2, \ldots, u_i \in \omega_0 g^i(u_1, u_2, \ldots, u_i)$ will converge to a certain value. In other words, we can prepare to "capture" or to any element, this is the so-called selection axiom (it is equivalent to the good-order theorem); if it is incomplete, one of its elements cannot converge to a certain value, that is, we cannot accurately "capture" this element, but the order between any two of its elements remains the same, which is a kind of "topology continuity".

From a structural point of view, the set ω_i of i-order recursive functions on the real continuum R is "topologically continuous" which is the constructive set of true subsets of R. Intuitively, after removing some real numbers from R, the resulting The real set is still "continuous". There are many examples like this. We only get the abstract concept of the whole real number R from a non-constructive point of view, but in the process of actual construction, we can only obtain ω_i infinite stack topological set on R. If symmetry is considered, ω_i algebraic structure may be more complicated, and even forms groups such as groups, rings, and lattices on R. We can imagine ω_i as an algebraic variety. Therefore, the real number set is more complicated than any of our imaginations. We call R "the universe of mathematics".

Therefore, even in the real continuum (one-dimensional space), the calculation behavior is very complicated, even "multi-dimensional". In the image, there are many "singular points" entering the multi-dimensional space in the one-dimensional space, the Turing machine is ineffective to calculate the values of these "singularities", but we do have other calculations.

2.3   The Expression Algorithm and Implementation

In the 1960s, when David Marr studied computer vision, he divided it into three levels of expression, algorithm, and implementation, first expressing it as a mathematical problem, then selecting an algorithm (program), and finally algorithm is implemented on hardware. In the expression (model), the Turing machine is essentially a recursive function f (N) of a natural number, and the result f (n) of each step is determined. Starting from f (1), we know that f (n) the value of that can be used to calculate the value of f (n + 1). In our concept, the Turing machine ω_{i-1} is one i-order recursive function g^i on a complete sequence (good order set). The working mode of the Turing machine is positioning and serial: each computing unit stores only one time of encoding information and after n units are successively calculated, the final output is as shown in the Fig. 2.

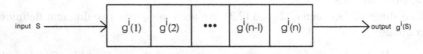

Fig. 2. Turing machine

However, if ω_{i-1} is an incomplete sequence, that is, under the binary system, a function term $g^i(n) = 1$ or $g^i(n) = 0$ is not established, and the Turing machine will fall into a "down" state. The calculations on such incomplete sequences are obviously not possible with the Turing machine. In order to make the discussion more concise and clear, we directly point out that distributed and parallel algorithms can solve the computational problems on such incomplete sequences. This algorithm, we call it the "Gödel machine" [3].

Slightly explain. Distributed means that if the Gödel machine has n calculation units, then, coded information is not stored in one of its calculation units, but is stored in a certain connection state of the n calculation units. The n calculation units are equivalent to 2^n kind of connection state, and each of the connection states can represent coding information. When the Gödel machine inputs a signal s, if the coding information of s is stored, then s will be immediately "recognized". Parallel means that s is not transmitted sequentially on the n calculation units. It is these n computing units that are both "excited" at the same time, and s will quickly "pair" out the state of the coupling of the encoded information.

Let me explain it further. The n computing units of the Gödel machine are obviously not a linear order structure, but a topological structure g^i. Intuitively, when the signal s is transmitted on g^i top, we cannot accurately "capture" s at a certain position $g^i(n)$, but we can calculate the probability that s appears on $g^i(n)$. There is no doubt that the Gödel machine is a probability calculus function. When a signal s is input, its output $g^i(s)$ is a probability distribution function (as shown) (Fig. 3).

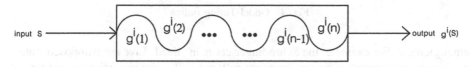

input S ⟶ $g^i(1)$ $g^i(2)$ ... ... $g^i(n-1)$ $g^i(n)$ ⟶ output $g^i(S)$

Fig. 3. Gödel machine

Obviously, the Gödel machine works completely differently from the Turing machine. From the point of view of proof theory, the Turing machine is a constructive proof. It is to prove proposition A that it is derived step by step through mathematical induction. But the Gödel machine is a non-constructive proof. It is to prove A, not directly. To derive A, we use probability calculus to exclude non-A. That is to say, it is only a probability exclusion method of "choose one of the two", which is the normal state of human thinking.

3 Results

The result is the discovery that an interesting finding is that quantum mechanical description of the trajectory of electrons and the internal connection state of neural networks are similar or isomorphic with the topological number structure of real continuums, and are related to the choice of set theory of axiom.

Logically, the Turing machine can't deal with the contradiction law and the failure of the law, but the Gödel machine can handle such problems well, thus breaking the Gödel incompleteness theorem. Therefore, if the Turing machine is "assembled" with the Gödel machine, it may solve the algorithm problem in artificial intelligence more effectively. The basic model is as follows. Input a signal s on the Turing machine. If it falls into a "stop state" on one of the computing units n, i.e. $g^i(n) = 1$ and $g^i(n) = 0$, it will pass the signal to a On the Gödel machine, a judgment of $g^i(n) = 1$ or $g^i(n) = 0$ is made by probability calculus, and then this signal is fed back to the Turing machine, and the recursive calculation is continued, and the final output is as shown (Fig. 4).

The last question is: Can this Gödel machine be implemented? What is the basis of the algorithm? It is not difficult to find that the Gödel machine is completely similar to the description of quantum mechanics. In quantum mechanics, a particle also has "uncertainty" at a certain position, and its probability is completely determined by the Schrödinger equation. Second, the particles are also in a state of quantum

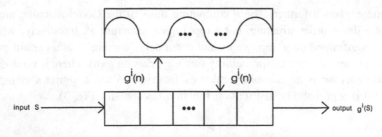

Fig. 4. Gödel-Turing online

entanglement. For example, the Schrödinger cat is in "dead- Live superimposed state," as soon as an observation occurs, quantum collapse will occur immediately, and the cat will immediately return to the dead or alive eigenstate. In this sense, the Gödel machine is a quantum computer.

4 Conclusion

The significance lies in: it proves that Lv derives two basic types of computational behavior from the most basic mathematical principles: the Turing machine and the Gödel machine. This may have some inspiring new ideas for the future research of artificial intelligence.

Distributed and parallel deep neural networks also have equivalent computational effects. We quote a classic discussion to illustrate: "Distributed representations will produce some powerful, unpredictable, spontaneously occurring features... with the ability to automatically summarize new situations"; "If there are k-level units, each of which is randomly selected for the next layer. The unit has n junction branches, then, there is n^k potential channel. It is almost certain that there will be a junction channel for any two conceptual units, so several intermediate units along this channel can be used to join the two concepts units However, these schemes end up having to assign a number of intermediate units to each valid join, and once this assignment occurs, all but one of the actual connections issued from each intermediate unit are void" [3].

This is exactly the same as the description of the Gödel machine and the "quantum collapse". Therefore, in principle, quantum computer is a more sophisticated and complex deep neural network. Recently, two Chinese scholars, Yue-Chi Ma and Man-Hong Yung, published a paper in the NPJ Quantum Information, proposing a neural network model to achieve quantum entanglement. It has been directly confirmed that neural networks are equivalent to quantum computation. If we regard the neural network as an "algorithm", the quantum state as "implementation", and the real continuum as a basic mathematical "expression" model, we clearly clarify a basic fact: no matter from expression (On the basis of mathematics, algorithms (computer software), implementation (physical hardware), the Turing machine can break through, it is not the real model of human cognition. Perhaps the Gödel machine or the Gödel-Turing online is the essence of artificial intelligence.

From a structural point of view, the continuity in the classical sense does not exist, and the one-dimensional continuum is actually only topologically continuous.

Intuitively, we can understand this: The Turing machine is the computational behavior on the discrete order, the Gödel machine is the computational behavior on the topological order, and the so-called calculation behavior means that when the machine inputs a signal s, it must pass through the internal some kind of calculation program, finally outputting a result $g^i(s)$; when the Turing machine is in the "stop state", it can "calculate" a result through the Gödel machine.

This paper explores that the quantum entanglement and the probabilistic nature of neural networks are all derived from topological order, which will be a far-reaching research direction.

It is worth thinking about: Since the Turing machine actually elaborates the computable principle, not the actual computer [4]. So when we think about or explore the Turing machine and the Gödel machine, we actually explore two types of calculations in mathematics. This is a question that must be considered in cognitive system research [5]. Another problem is that when we say twin Turing machine [6], what we are talking about is actually the Turing test [7] and the topic of the Chinese room argument proposed by Searle. The important point is that artificial intelligence (whether traditional AI or new generation AI by computer programming) can understand natural language like human beings. Therefore, the twin Turing machine is actually a formal understanding model, not an actual computer.

References

1. Heyting, A.: The intuition basis of mathematics. In: Mathematical Philosophy, p. 62. The Commercial Press (2003)
2. Cohen, P.J.: Comments on the basis of set theory. In: The Mathematical Philosophy Translations Compiled by the Logic Research Laboratory of the Institute of Philosophy of the Chinese Academy of Social Sciences, p. 134. The Commercial Press (1988)
3. Hinton, G.E., McClelland, J.L., Rumelhart, D.E.: Distributed expression. In: Boden, M.A. (ed.) Artificial Intelligence Philosophy, p. 339, 341, 350. Shanghai Translation Publishing House (2001)
4. Turing, A.M.: Appendix one (A)–on computable numbers, with an application to the Entscheidungsproblem. Ann. Rev. Autom. Program. 43(43), 230–264 (1960)
5. Leyton, M.: Principles of information structure common to six levels of the human cognitive system. Inf. Sci. 38(1), 1–120 (1986)
6. Zou, X.: Virtual twin turing machine: bilingual information processing as an example. Software 32(8), 1–5 (2011)
7. Turing, A.M.: Computing Machinery and Intelligence. Computers & Thought, pp. 44–53. MIT Press, Cambridge (1995)

Improved Direct Chaotic Nonlinear Filters

Yang Zhang$^{(\boxtimes)}$, Gang Zhang, Guo-sheng Rui, and Hai-bo Zhang

Naval Aeronautical University, Yantai 264001, Shandong Province,
People's Republic of China
zhyang_111@163.com

Abstract. With the development of electronic techniques and filter theories, nonlinear filters appear and obtain the performance beyond the traditional linear filter in a certain extent, this paper takes the chaotic nonlinear filter design as the main research object, by constructing Duffing Chaos vibrator Euler implementation and improving its structure, a new direct chaotic nonlinear filter is proposed, different from the past nonlinear signal processing method, the output results of the filter can effectively filter the noise inside and outside the band, without judging chaos phase change, the original period signal can be directly obtained, experiments show that, this method can effectively recover the input signal to noise ratio under -30 dB, which is a reliable nonlinear filtering technique, and further more, its adaptability can be improved.

Keywords: Chaotic filter · Duffing oscillator · Sinusoidal driving force · Nonlinear

PACS: 05.45.-a · 05.40.-a · 02.60.Cb

1 Introduction

In modern telecommunications equipment systems and various types of control systems, filters get wide range of applications, the research of filters has always been valued by scholars. However, the performance of traditional linear filter is limited, general band-pass filter can only filter out-band noise, while have no ideas for the noise band; with the development of nonlinear techniques, various nonlinear filtering techniques are born at the right moment, whose typical representative is the nonlinear Kalman filter, but existing nonlinear filtering techniques [1] have a common flaw: the performance of filter is very bad and efficiency is usually low under a low SNR (**Signal to Noise Ratio**); so is there a nonlinear filtering technology, which has a good filtering performance under a low noise signal to noise ratio in-band? A new nonlinear filtering system is introduced in this article-Improved Direct Chaotic Nonlinear Filter, which can effectively suppress strong internal and external noise in-band and out-band.

Because the traditional linear method is difficult to satisfy filtering demands [2] of weak signals under low SNR conditions, an effective means of detecting weak signals technology can be used to assist for filtering. With the development of modern

Project supported by three National Natural Science Foundations of China (No. 41606117, No. 41476089, No. 61671016).

F. Sun et al. (Eds.): ICCSIP 2018, CCIS 1005, pp. 314–326, 2019.
https://doi.org/10.1007/978-981-13-7983-3_28

signal-processing techniques, Duffing chaotic oscillator [3] plays an increasingly important role in the field of weak signal detection and identification, information collection and control, communications technologies; now Duffing chaotic system research is mainly focused on signal amplitude detections, and confined to the qualitative status determination, as in [4, 5], the parameters of Duffing systems are set to the threshold, and the test signal are introduced into the system as parts of its perturbation of driving force, by observing changes of Duffing oscillator phase diagram, feature signals amplitudes of weak signal are obtained. These methods can not achieve real-time determination, and are easy to appear instability detections.

In addition, scholars do a lot of research for the Duffing chaotic oscillator detection techniques, of which literature [6] used a phase plane trajectory method as the criterion of the fractal status for signal detections, but this algorithm is vulnerable to be influenced by a variety of factors as simulation time at a low efficiency; literature [7] improved the phase plane trajectory method by the form of a double oscillator, but still did not get good test results. Some quantitative detection methods, such as Lyapunov Characteristic Exponents method, Kolmogorov entropy, Fractal Dimension method and other analytical methods [8–12], the characteristics of which are their quantifiable determination on chaos but require complex calculations when determining, do not meet the requirements of engineering applications, which greatly limits the Duffing oscillator used in engineering fields.

This article fuses filter theory and Duffing chaos detection theory together, put forward a new filter theory by Duffing chaotic oscillator, the specific method adjust Duffing oscillator by re-deriving system equation to obtain a new filter form, namely improved direct chaotic nonlinear filters, the filter can achieve and go beyond the traditional linear filter filtering effect, simulation results show that the filter system in the case of a sinusoidal signal under signal to noise ratio −30 dB still has very good filtering performance, but when the signal to noise ratio reduces to −40 dB, the filtering performance will fall.

The noise add to the signal will be filtered by the improved direct chaotic nonlinear filters, which is same as traditional linear filters, but compared with traditional linear filters, the improved direct chaotic nonlinear filters in the article can not only remove the noise out-band but the noise in-band, which can obtain higher signal to noise ratio and have more excellent performance.

2 Discrete Implementations of Duffing Chaotic Oscillator

2.1 Chaotic Oscillator System Based on the Euler Equations

Chaotic oscillator can be seen as a two-dimensional Itô stochastic control system [13, 14], as the following Eq. (1),

$$dx(t) = f(x(t), u(t))dt + g(x(t), u(t))d\omega(t), t \geq 0 \tag{1}$$

Here $x(t) \in R^n$, $u(t) \in R^m$ are the state vector and input vector of the system. $\omega(t)$ is a standard p-dimensional Wiener process, $F(R^m)$ is set to the input collection, the supremum norm of u is $|u|_{\sup} = \sup\{|u(t)|, t \geq 0\} \leq \infty$; $f : R^n \times R^m \to R^n$, $g : R^n \times R^m \to R^n$, for random control systems, using the Euler method as its approximate method is mean square stable [15].

2.2 Duffing Chaotic Oscillator Euler State Model

In this paper, Duffing chaotic oscillator is the object of study, which is one of the most classic nonlinear chaotic systems, because of its sensitivity to period weak signals and high noise immunity, it is widely used in weak signal detections [16], the experiments showed that the realization of Duffing oscillator by the Euler equation, the computational complexity is much lower than traditional implementation methods, which has engineering application; the Duffing oscillator Euler implementation will be analyzed as following, and the reliable Duffing oscillator state model will be obtained.

General Duffing equation can be showed as (2),

$$\ddot{x} + k\dot{x} - ax + bx^3 = \gamma\cos(\omega t) \tag{2}$$

If intermediate variables $y = \dot{x}$ is introduced, (2) can be converted to (3),

$$\begin{cases} \dot{x} = y \\ \dot{y} = -ky + ax - bx^3 + \gamma\cos(\omega t) \end{cases} \tag{3}$$

The Jacobian matrix is calculate by (3), thus the system is linearized to (4),

$$\begin{bmatrix} \dot{x} \\ \dot{y} \end{bmatrix} = \begin{bmatrix} 0 & 1 \\ a - bx^2 & -k \end{bmatrix} \cdot \begin{bmatrix} x \\ y \end{bmatrix} + \gamma \cdot \begin{bmatrix} 0 \\ \cos(\omega t) \end{bmatrix} \tag{4}$$

From the above analysis, in fact Duffing system can be re-constructed as a state model of Euler equation, by the derivative of the difference quotient, numerical integration of the rectangle formula, as well as other ways to use the Taylor expansion method, stochastic differential equations can be converted to a single formula, namely:

$$\begin{cases} y_0 = \eta \\ y_{k+1} = y_k + hf(t_k, y_k), k = 0, 1, \cdots, n - 1 \end{cases} \tag{5}$$

The formula is called the forward Euler equation. As can be seen from the formula, the later function value y_k can be calculated directly according to the previous point. Therefore, the above formula is an explicit formula, as long as the initial value y_0 is known, it is possible to calculate the numerical solution of recursive sequence of differential equations $\{y_k (k = 0, 1, \cdots, n)\}$.

2.3 Duffing Equation Simulation of Euler Method

According to the Euler method, the following simulation is done:

Sinusoidal signals are set as the cycle driving motivation of Duffing oscillator, whose angular frequency is set $w = 1$ rad/s, amplitude is set $\gamma = 0.82$, Duffing oscillator state Euler equation phase diagram are shown as Fig. 1 based on mentocaro simulations, when Euler model is used to build Duffing system, system shows the disorderly and unsystematic chaotic motion.

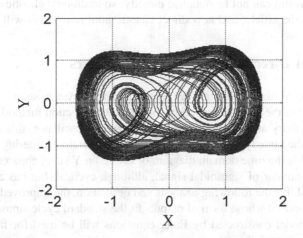

Fig. 1. Euler form of the phase diagram of the motivation amplitude $\gamma = 0.82$

Further experiments, with the increasing amplitude of the cycle driving motivation, then $\gamma > 0.83$, Duffing oscillator model built by Euler form will enter large-scale periodic state, meanwhile maintain large-scale periodic state with the further increasing of the amplitude, as Fig. 2 shows; the use of Euler constructed Duffing oscillator model, you can adjust the oscillator cycle driving motivation value, different states will arise and the qualitative change of which can be used to detect whether cycle signal is introduced.

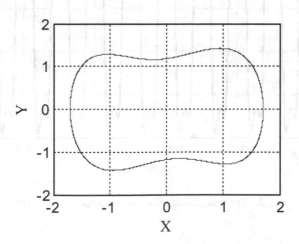

Fig. 2. Phase diagram of oscillator by Euler algorithm when $\gamma > 0.83$

The result of experiments test and verify the feasibility of the Euler algorithm using for Duffing oscillator, on the other hand for signal detections, it's necessary to accurately distinguish two kinds of states as in Figs. 1 and 2, namely the judgement of phase transformations [6], which will obviously increase the complexity and error rate, meanwhile the result can not be obtained directly, so traditional chaotic detections will be improved in the article, and new direct chaotic nonlinear filters will be proposed.

3   Improved Direct Chaotic Nonlinear Filters

From the foregoing, the traditional way sees whether the system state transforms from the chaotic state to the large-scale periodic state as the detection method, which makes use of the sensitivity and noise immunity characters of oscillator, this method is difficult to output the same type as original signal like conventional filtering techniques, as shown in Fig. 3 is the time domain diagram of Fig. 2 on Y state, apparently the output from chaotic oscillator of sinusoidal signal, although cyclical, but has a non-standard cycle sine signal. By the following analysis and derivation, the improved direct chaotic filter will be proposed whose form of outputs fit the standard cycle sinusoidal signal of inputs, and a model constructed by Euler equations will be used for fast operationa. Specific process is as follows:

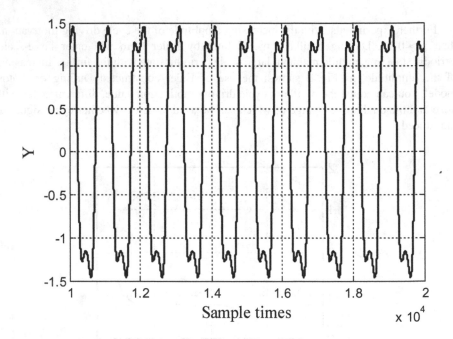

Fig. 3. The time domain diagram of outputs on Y state

According to the working principle of the filter, after noisy signals are input, and the result of outputs will be signals whose noise is filtered, as shown in Fig. 4:

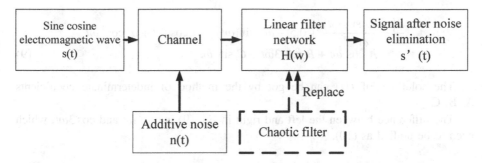

Fig. 4. Chaos filters which replace traditional linear filter network

Consider the general case, shown in Fig. 5, the electromagnetic wave signal is assumed $s(t) = a \cos \omega t$, since the additive noise $n(t)$ is introduced, so that the input signal of the filter is $s(t) = a \cos \omega t + n(t)$, the conventional linear filter network filter noisy signals by setting a reasonable pass-band filter to remove out-band noise, whereby denoised signals will be got as $s'(t)$, at the premise of high signal to noise ratio, $s'(t)$ can achieve the purpose of the subsequent signal reception or signal detection, but if the signal to noise ratio is low, noise will still retain within the passband, then it will be more difficult for subsequent signal processing.

In order to make the role of Duffing chaotic oscillators filters, it must make the whole nonlinear filter noise filter network plays the positive performance to filter noise and retain period cosine signal, while according to the mechanism of Duffing chaotic oscillator detection, Duffing oscillator has signal sensitivity, noise immunity features, and it is feasible to be a kind of filter after improved, Now the basic algorithm of direct Duffing chaotic nonlinear filter is derived as follows:

If the output values of Duffing oscillator system have the same frequency as the signal to be filtered $a \cos \omega t$, the mathematical representation of the Duffing chaotic must be changed,

$$\ddot{x} + 0.5\dot{x} - x + x^3 = f(t) \tag{6}$$

In the traditional chaotic oscillator detection algorithm, when input $f(t)$ is cosine signal driving force, namely $f(t) = \lambda \cos \omega t$, oscillator shows as the form of the same frequency and the third harmonic superimposed, namely:

$$x = M \cos \omega t + N \cos 3\omega t + K \sin \omega t \tag{7}$$

So in reverse, if the output of the system is $x = a \cos \omega t$, in order to solve the value of input $f(t)$, which has periodicity and symmetry [19], according to (7), should satisfy the combining form, namely:

$$f(t) = A \cos \omega t + B \cos 3\omega t + C \sin \omega t \tag{8}$$

Substitute $x = a \cos \omega t$ and (8) into (6) and (9) will be obtained, namely:

$$\frac{d(-a\omega \sin \omega t)}{dt} + 0.5(-a\omega \sin \omega t) - a \cos \omega t + a^3 \cos^3 \omega t$$
$$= A \cos \omega t + B \cos 3\omega t + C \sin \omega t \tag{9}$$

The solutions of $f(t)$ can be got by the method of indeterminate coefficients A, B, C.

The difference between the left and right in Eq. (9) is $\cos^3 \omega t$ and $\cos 3\omega t$, which need to be unified as (10),

$$
\begin{aligned}
\cos(3\omega t) &= \cos(\omega t + 2\omega t) \\
&= \cos \omega t \cos 2\omega t - \sin \omega t \sin 2\omega t \\
&= \cos \omega t (2 \cos^2 \omega t - 1) - 2 \sin^2 \omega t \cos \omega t \\
&= 2 \cos^3 \omega t - \cos \omega t - 2(1 - \cos^2 \omega t) \cos \omega t \\
&= 2 \cos^3 \omega t - \cos \omega t - 2 \cos \omega t + 2 \cos^3 \omega t \\
&= 4 \cos^3 \omega t - 3 \cos \omega t
\end{aligned}
\tag{10}
$$

Meanwhile (11) will be got,

$$\cos^3 \omega t = \frac{\cos(3\omega t) + 3 \cos \omega t}{4} \tag{11}$$

Calculate the right of (9) by (10), (12) will be got,

$$A \cos \omega t + B \cos 3\omega t + C \sin \omega t = (A - 3B) \cos \omega t + 4B \cos^3 \omega t + C \sin \omega t \tag{12}$$

Combine (16) and (17), (12) will be got,

$$-a\omega^2 \cos \omega t - 0.5a\omega \sin \omega t - a \cos \omega t + a^3 \cos^3 \omega t$$
$$= (A - 3B) \cos \omega t + 4B \cos^3 \omega t + C \sin \omega t \tag{13}$$

Equation (13) has the same form, let the coefficients equal both sides (14) will be got, namely:

$$
\begin{cases}
A - 3B = -a\omega^2 - a \\
4B = a^3 \\
C = -0.5a\omega
\end{cases}
\tag{14}
$$

(14) will be solved as (15),

$$B = \frac{a^3}{4} \tag{15}$$

And (16) will be further got as (16),

$$\begin{cases} A = -a\omega^2 - a + \frac{3}{4}a^3 \\ B = \frac{a^3}{4} \\ C = -0.5a\omega \end{cases} \tag{16}$$

Now the primary Duffing equations will be converted the new form for filtering as (17),

$$\ddot{x} + 0.5\dot{x} - x + x^3 = \left(-a\omega^2 - a + \frac{3}{4}a^3\right)\cos \omega t + \frac{a^3}{4}\cos 3\omega t + (-0.5a\omega)\sin \omega t \tag{17}$$

It can be known by settings, the solutions of (17) are actually the outputs of the direct Duffing chaotic filter $x = a \cos \omega t$.

The function of oscillator is converted from detections to filters, combined with the previous analysis, (17) can be solved by Euler equations, whose numerical solution can be obtained.

Duffing equation is generally expressed as (18), i.e.:

$$\ddot{x} + k\dot{x} - ax + bx^3 = \gamma \cos(\omega t) \tag{18}$$

The introduction of intermediate variables $y = \dot{x}$, (18) can be converted to (19),

$$\begin{cases} \dot{x} = y \\ \dot{y} = -ky + ax - bx^3 + \gamma \cos(\omega t) \end{cases} \tag{19}$$

As can be seen from (19), Duffing system is a two-dimensional, non-linear system.

By the previous Euler equations, conventional Duffing oscillator can be expressed by the state equations as (20), namely:

$$\begin{cases} x(n+1) = x(n) + \omega \cdot h \cdot y(n) + v(n) \\ y(n+1) = (1 - 0.5 \cdot \omega \cdot h) \cdot y(n) + \omega \cdot h \cdot [x(n) - x^3(n)] \\ \quad + \gamma \cdot \omega \cdot h \cdot \cos[\omega \cdot (h \cdot n)] \end{cases} \tag{20}$$

Combine (20) and (17), the improved direct chaotic nonlinear filters can be got as (21),

$$\begin{cases} x(n+1) = x(n) + \omega \cdot h \cdot y(n) + v(n) \\ y(n+1) = (1 - 0.5 \cdot \omega \cdot h) \cdot y(n) + \omega \cdot h \cdot [x(n) - x^3(n)] \\ \quad + \omega \cdot h \cdot \{A \cdot \cos[\omega \cdot (h \cdot n)] + B \cdot \cos[3 \cdot \omega \cdot (h \cdot n)] + C \cdot \sin[\omega \cdot (h \cdot n)]\} \end{cases} \tag{21}$$

The derivations above is in the case that the periodic signals are introduced, in order to detect the noise immunity of the filter, simulations are done as follows.

4 Simulation Tests

Simulation environments: Signals to be measured is power line signals whose main angular frequency is $w = 1$ rad/s, peak amplitude is $A = 1$ V. The effects on the outputs of different filters under different noise intensity are considered, as follows Figs. 5, 6 and 7 respectively show the comparison between the conventional linear filters and the improved chaotic filters, of which the conventional linear filters adopt Butterworth band-pass filters, whose pass band set to be same as the band of signals to be measured, the performance of filters are compared under the same conditions.

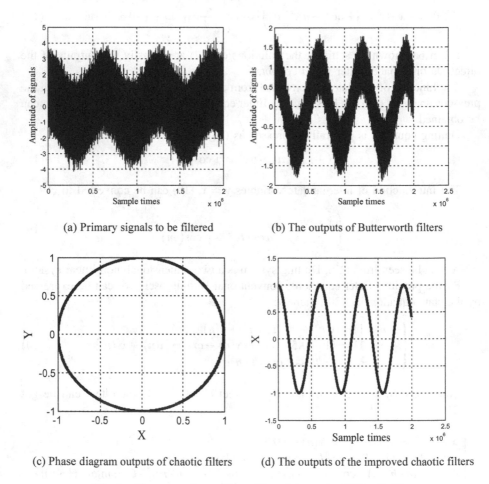

(a) Primary signals to be filtered

(b) The outputs of Butterworth filters

(c) Phase diagram outputs of chaotic filters

(d) The outputs of the improved chaotic filters

Fig. 5. The comparisons of two filter states under SNR = 0 dB

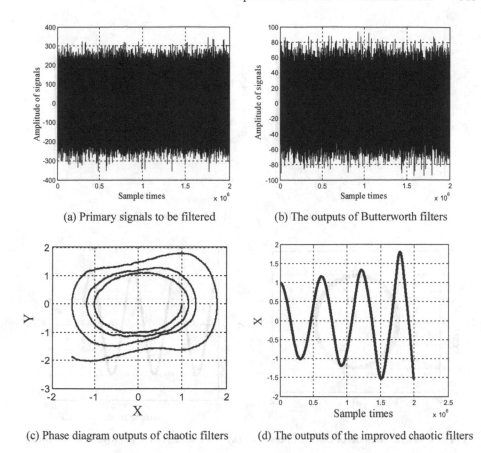

(a) Primary signals to be filtered

(b) The outputs of Butterworth filters

(c) Phase diagram outputs of chaotic filters

(d) The outputs of the improved chaotic filters

Fig. 6. The comparisons of two filter states under SNR = −40 dB

As shown in Figs. 5 and 7, when signal-to-noise (SNR) is 0 dB, −30 dB, the filtering performances of the improved direct chaotic nonlinear filters are excellent, which can filtered the noisy signal to get the pure signals. For example, when SNR = −30 dB, the outputs of conventional Butterworth filters show as Fig. 7(b), compared with the primary signals to be filtered in Fig. 7(a), SNR has hardly any improvements and the results of filters are very bad, while if the noisy signals are introduced into the improved direct chaotic filters, whose results of filters are shown in Fig. 7(d), SNR is remarkably improved, meanwhile the amplitude characteristics of the periodic signals to be measured are retained, as shown in Fig. 7(c), which shows map relations between outputs x and its differential forms $y = \dot{x}$, which just constitute unit circle features, and fit with the primary signals. Compared with traditional filters, the improved direct chaotic nonlinear filters can realize the filtering process under lower signal to noise ratios, and have better filtering performance, this is because that traditional band-pass filters can only filter the out-band noise and lack the ability to filter the in-band noise, signal to noise ratios will be very low, while the improved direct chaotic filters make full use of the long-term periodic excitations of the primary signals

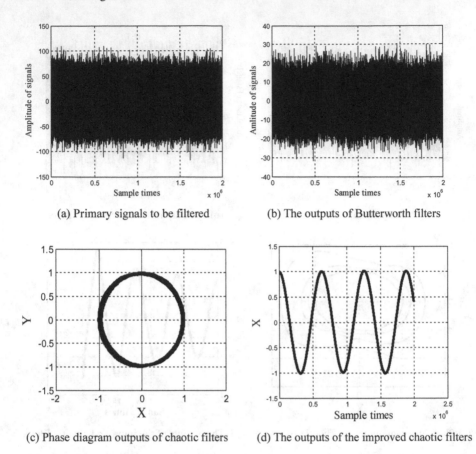

(a) Primary signals to be filtered   (b) The outputs of Butterworth filters

(c) Phase diagram outputs of chaotic filters   (d) The outputs of the improved chaotic filters

Fig. 7. The comparisons of two filter states under SNR = −30 dB

to be measured, effectively restrain in-band and out-band noise, substantially increase the signal to noise ratios of the outputs, while the result of filtering will get bad when SNR is lower than −40 dB, signal distortions will appear, as shown in Fig. 6(d), but the techniques of signal corrections can be used to satisfy the performance of filtering.

5   Summary

With the development of nonlinear scientific theories, all kinds of nonlinear techniques were born, whose typical representative is Kalman techniques, which realize the signal extractions from the noise by the recursion way. These methods have high complexities and aren't suitable for the signal processing under very low signal-to-noise ratios. In order to realize the filtering both on in-band and out-band noise, new nonlinear filters-improved direct chaotic nonlinear filters are proposed in the paper. The filters derive the new chaotic system for filtering noisy periodic signals, realize the conversion from the Duffing classics detection system to the Duffing chaotic filter system and its numerical solutions, meanwhile solve the problem of performance limitations to filter both in-band and out-band noise. Compared with traditional nonlinear methods, the filters have higher efficiencies because it can output results directly by filtering both in-band and out-band noise. Experiments show that this filter algorithm can effectively recover the signals above −30 dB, as a reliable nonlinear filter technique, compared with traditional linear filters, significant improvement in performance is got.

References

1. Lu, Z., Liao, Q., Pei, J.: A PIV approach based on nonlinear filtering. J. Electron. Inf. Technol. **32**(2), 400–404 (2012)
2. Zeng, Z., Li, R.: Design study on the high-order band-pass filters. J. Commun. **22**(10), 99–103 (2001)
3. Gan, J., Xiao, X.: Nonlinear adaptive multi-step-prediction of chaotic time series based on points in the neighborhood. Acta Physica Sinica **52**(12), 2995–3000 (2003)
4. Wang, Y., Jiang, W., Zhao, J., Fan, H.: A new method of weak signal detection using Duffing oscillator and its simulation research. Acta Physica Sinica **57**(4), 2053–2059 (2008)
5. Wang, G.Y., He, S.L.: A quantitative study on detection and estimation of weak signals by using chaotic Duffing oscillators. IEEE Trans. CAS-I **50**(7), 945–953 (2003)
6. Wang, G.Y., Chen, D.J., Lin, J.Y., et al.: The application of chaotic oscillators to weak signal detection. IEEE Trans. Ind. Electron. **46**(2), 440–444 (1999)
7. Yang, H.Y., Ye, H., Wang, G.Z.: Study on Lyapunov exponent and Floquet exponent of Duffing oscillator. J. Sci. Instrum. **29**(5), 927–932 (2008)
8. Zhang, B., Li, Y., et al.: An algorithm based on Lyapunov exponents to determine the threshold of chaotic detection for weak signal. Prog. Geophys. **18**(4), 748–751 (2003)
9. Hu, N.Q., Wen, X.S.: The application of Duffing oscillator in characteristic signal detection of early fault. J. Sound Vib. **68**(5), 917–931 (2003)
10. Nijmeijer, H., Berghuis, H.: On Lyapunov control of the Duffing equation. IEEE Trans. Circuits Syst.- 1: Fundam. Theory Appl. **42**(1), 473–477 (1995)
11. Liu, X., Liu, X.: Weak signal detection research based on Duffing oscillator used for downhole communication. J. Comput. **6**(2), 359–367 (2011)
12. Yu, B., Li, Y., Zhang, P.: Application of correlation dimension and Kolmogorov entropy in aeroengine fault diagnosis. J. Aerosp. Power **21**(1), 219–224 (2006)
13. Tian, Z., Wei, Y., Hu, L.: Mean square stability and exponential stability of Euler scheme for solving stochastic differential equations. Nat. Mag. **24**(6), 369–370 (2002)
14. Wang, W., Chen, Y.: Mean-square stability of Euler method for linear neutral stochastic delay differential equations. Mathematica Numerica Sinica **32**(2), 206–212
15. Ye, Q., Huang, H., Zhang, C.: Design of stochastic resonance systems in weak signal detection. Acta Electronica Sinica **37**(1), 216–220 (2009)
16. Fang, T.: Random Vibration of Engineering. National Defense Industry Press, Beijing (1995)
17. Gong, G.: Stochastic differential equation and its application. Tsinghua University Press, Beijing (2008)
18. Nie, C.: Chaotic system and weak signal detection. Tsinghua University Press, Beijing (2009)

19. Koukoulas, P., Kalouptsidis, N.: Nonlinear system identification using Gaussian inputs. IEEE Trans. Signal Process. **43**(8), 1831–1841 (1995)
20. Pantaleon, C., Souto, A.: Comments on "A periodic phenomenon of the extended Kalman filter in filtering noisy chaotic signals". IEEE Trans. Signal Process. **53**(1), 383–384 (2005)
21. Buckwar, E.: Introduction to the numerical analysis of stochastic delay differential equations. J. Comput. Appl. Math. **125**(1), 297–307 (2000)

A Hotel Review Corpus
for Argument Mining

Xueyu Duan[1,2], Mingxue Liao[2(✉)], Xinwei Zhao[1,2], Wenda Wu[1,2], and Pin Lv[2]

[1] University of Chinese Academy of Sciences, Beijing, China
[2] Institute of Software, Chinese Academy of Sciences, Beijing, China
{xueyu2016,mingxue,xinwei2016,wenda2016,lvpin}@iscas.ac.cn

Abstract. With the development of the network, the research of user reviews has become more important in academia and industry, because user reviews gradually influence the reputation of products and services. Argument mining has recently become a hot topic, and it is currently in the center of attention of the text mining research community. We can deeply dig out information contained in the user reviews with argument mining technology. This paper makes a corpus of hotel reviews and presents a novel scheme to model arguments, their components and relations in hotel reviews in English. In order to capture the structure of argumentative discourse, the annotation scheme includes the annotation of Major Claim, Claim, Premise, Background and Recommendation as well as Support and Attack relations. The sentiment polarity of argument components contains Positive, Negative and Neutral. We conduct a manual annotation study with 300 annotators on 1427 hotel reviews. And the final corpus collects 85 hotel reviews according to inter-rater agreement and it will encourage future study in argument recognition.

Keywords: Argument mining · Corpus · Hotel reviews

1 Introduction

With the advent of the era of big data, more and more information is generated by lots of people on the Internet. User reviews are one of the most important content. With the rapid development of e-commerce, more and more users choose online shopping. As an important decision evidence in user purchase process, user reviews increase rapidly after purchasing. A large number of user reviews lead to very unstable quality of user reviews, which is challenging for customers to obtain valuable information contained in user reviews. Therefore, it is more important to predict the quality of user reviews automatically. In the past, the focus of research on user reviews is mainly on sentiment analysis. The corpus of

The work is supported by both National scientific and Technological Innovation Zero (No. 17-H863-01-ZT-005-005-01) and State's Key Project of Research and Development Plan (No. 2016QY03D0505).

hotel reviews doesn't annotate the information related to the logic, reasoning, and persuasiveness of user reviews which has a direct impact on the quality of user reviews. For the automatic prediction of the quality of user reviews, this paper makes a corpus of hotel reviews in English in order to consider not only the lexical and syntactic information in the content but also the rich reasoning information contained in the content.

Argument mining is currently in the center of attention of the text mining research community [11]. Argumentation is an interdisciplinary research field, which focuses on the process of debate and reasoning. It runs through various disciplines, such as logic, philosophy, language, rhetoric, law, cardiology and computer science, and is inseparable from them. The availability of the current hype of big data, together with tremendous advances in computational linguistics, created fertile ground for the rise of a new area of research called argument mining [6]. Argument mining aims to automatically extract structured arguments which usually consists of a central claim (or conclusion) and several supporting or attacking premises (or evidences) from original texts [6,8]. As for argument components detection, lots of previous studies solve it by employing supervised learning methods [16]. And the frequently used machine learning methods include Support Vector Machine [7,10,14,16], Naive Bayes [12,13], Decision Trees and Random Forests [2,3,16].

The rest of the paper is organized as follows: Sect. 2 presents an overview of corpora related to argument mining. Section 3 proposes a novel annotation scheme about hotel reviews in argument recognition. Section 4 shows the statistics of our own corpus in hotel reviews. The final section concludes the work and proposes some directions for further research.

2   Related Work

As argument mining is in its infancy, the lack of corpus is an important factor limiting its development. There is a huge need for reliable annotated corpora including argument components and argument relationships, as they are required for supervised machine learning methods for extracting arguments. This paper presents a novel annotation scheme to model arguments (details in Sect. 4) and we manually annotate arguments in hotel reviews in English.

European Court of Human Rights (ECHR) corpus has been complied by [9]. ECHR is a small collection of 10 Legal documents. Mochales et al. obtains an inter-rater agreement of $\kappa = 0.75$ on a bigger corpus of 47 legal documents in their subsequent study [10]. Law has been the pioneering application domain for argument mining and it's one of the most successful applications.

Rhetorical, philosophical and persuasive essays constitute another interesting field for argument mining [8]. As for persuasive student essays, the Argument Annotated Persuasive Essays version 1 corpus (C1) has been complied by [15] and the Argument Annotated Persuasive Essays version 2 corpus (C2) has been complied by [17]. C1 is a collection of 90 persuasive student essays in various topics. In each essay, the sentences are annotated as major claims, claims, premises or none, and each essay has only one major claim. Both support and attack relations can hold between a premise and another premise, a premise and a (major) claim, or a claim and a major claim. C2 consists of 402 persuasive student essays. There are two differences between C1 and C2. One difference is that each essay in C2 may include more than one major claims. And the other one is that C2 has removed the relation between major claim and premise.

The ArguAna TripAdvisor corpus has been designed by [19], which collects 2,100 annotated hotel reviews balanced with respect to the reviews' sentiment scores $(1 - 5)$. Each hotel review is segmented into facts, positive and negative opinions. The ArguAna TripAdvisor corpus focuses mainly on sentiment analysis. Our corpus annotates the argument components and argumentative relations for hotel reviews.

3 Annotation Scheme

The ArguAna TripAdvisor corpus is created by [18] and contains 2,100 hotel user reviews from seven districts including Amsterdam, Seattle, Sydney, Berlin, Los Angeles, Barcelona and Paris. In this paper, we annotate the corpus with the argumentation relationship and collect the annotation information. We use the brat annotation tool to annotate the corpus.[1] We invite more than 300 students to study the annotations and their corresponding relationships for the hotel reviews. To ensure the reliability of the annotations, each hotel review is annotated by five different students. This paper removed the hotel reviews that are too short before annotating, and finally selected 1674 comments for annotation.

In the hotel reviews, we think that each argument must be a sentence or a clause. A sentence begins with a letter and ends with a period, question mark or exclamation point. The largest unit of annotation is one sentence and we do not allow a few sentences to form an argument component. In a sentence, each piece of text separated by a comma or semicolon is called a clause. The smallest unit of annotation is one clause.

3.1 Argument Components

We specify the argument components of the corpus as follows (the specific content of the annotation is illustrated in detail in Fig. 1):

Major Claim. Major Claim summarizes the content of the entire hotel review and is a general summary of a user's review. For example, in Fig. 1, we think that the major claim is the title of the review *"Nice Hotel"*, because throughout this review, the household has given multiple conclusions (Claim), such as *"Hotel is nice and clean"*, *"in a very convenient location"*, *"and the staff is friendly and helpful"*; these conclusions support the view of the general conclusion. We will find that the title of the review, the first sentence or the last sentence often

---

[1] http://brat.nlplab.org.

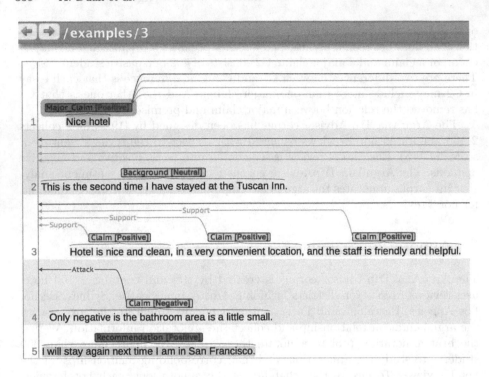

Fig. 1. Example of using the brat annotation tool. The content is in the review comment_1389 in the corpus.

summarizes the whole review, so the major claim often appears in these places. We stipulate that only one sentence in each text is marked as a major claim.

Claim. In hotel reviews, users will evaluate different aspects of the product (or service), and we consider the user's evaluation of each aspect as a claim. For example, *"The staff was amazing, and went out of their way to help us."* The first half of the sentence is a conclusion about the enthusiasm of the waiter (*the staff was amazing*), and the latter part of the sentence is the reason for this conclusion (*went out of their way to help us*). In comment_1380, we can see that users have commented on several aspects of the hotel: breakfast and coffee (the sixth sentence: *"The coffee and treats in the morning was amazing"*), wine service and dinner (the seventh sentence: *"The wine and treats at night were great also, nice touch"*) and the quietness of the room (the ninth sentence: *"Glad we did; it was very quiet"*).

Premise. When the user gives a claim, sometimes some facts are given to support or attack the claim. These facts are called premises. For example, the tenth sentence and the eleventh sentence in comment_1380: *"Some say the room are small, bur ours wasn't that tiny. A normal size hotel room compared to other hotel rooms we have stayed in,...".* In this sentence, the user's claim is *"ours wasn't that tiny"* and the user gives two relevant facts to further explain the premise for this claim: (1) The user gives some reviews from other users about the size of the room *"Some say the room are small"*. This clause attacks the user's later claim *"ours wasn't that tiny"*, so the relationship between two clauses is labelled as Attack. (2) After the claim, the user says *"A normal size hotel room compared to other hotel rooms we have stayed in"*. This sentence actually supports the claim given earlier, so mark this sentence and the previous claim as Support.

Background. We find that users often mention some background knowledge when they comment on a product or a service. Although this background knowledge is not directly related to the argument relationship, it will allow us to better position the argument relationship and help other users evaluate the credibility of the review. For example, the first sentence in the above example *"This is the second time I have stayed in Tuscan Inn"*, this sentence is a background knowledge. This sentence indicates that the user has stayed at the hotel at least twice, so other users will judge the credibility of this review based on this sentence.

Recommendation. In hotel reviews, users often give some suggestions in addition to the background knowledge. For example, the last sentence in the above example *"I will stay again next time I am in San Francisco"* can be regarded as a recommendation. Although this sentence does not directly recommend other people to stay at the hotel, it is obvious that this sentence expresses the user's love for this hotel, and indirectly recommends other users to stay at the hotel by predicting their future behavior (*"I will stay again"*).

We also need to annotate the sentiment polarity of the argument component. In comment_1389, the title *"Nice Hotel"* and the claim *"Hotel is nice and clean"* is expressing a positive sentiment, so we annotate their emotions as positive. There are some sentences, the sentiment they express are negative, such as the fourth sentence *"Only negative is the bathroom area is a little small"*, so we annotate the sentiment of this sentence as negative. In addition, there are some sentences whose sentiment is neutral, such as the second sentence *"This is the second time I have stayed at the Tuscan Inn"*. This sentence only describes a fact, so we think it is neutral.

It should be noted that in a hotel review, not every clause has a corresponding argument component type. Some sentences may not belong to any of the above mentioned types, so we don't need to mark these sentences. It should also be noted that each clause can only belong to one of the above types at most.

3.2 Argumentative Relations

In a hotel review, we not only need to annotate the argument components, but also establish the relationship between these argument components. In general, we need to annotate two relationships: Support and Attack. The rules for establishing these two relationships are as follows: A premise must support or attack a claim, but a claim cannot support or attack a premise. From here we can see that the relationship between support and attack is directional. Similarly, a claim must support or attack a major claim, but a major claim cannot support or attack a claim.

4   Our Corpus

4.1   Inter-rater Agreement

In order to evaluate the reliability of the argument annotations, we use percentage agreement and two chance-corrected measures: Fleiss's κ [1] and Krippendorff's α [4]. If all the five argument components' κ in a hotel review are greater than 0.5, they are included in the final corpus. After doing this, we finally collect 85 hotel reviews. Table 1 shows the inter-rater agreement of argument component annotations. In Table 1, we will find that the score of major claim is the highest. The inter-rater agreement of 97% and Fleiss $\kappa = 0.89$ indicates that the annotation of major claim is the most credible in hotel reviews. Among them, claim's $\kappa = 0.711$ and premise's $\kappa = 0.797$. The value of κ between 0.6 and 0.8 is considered to be substantial agreement [5].

Table 1. Inter-rater agreement of argument component annotations

	%	κ	α
Major claim	.9763	.8901	.8927
Claim	.8765	.7108	.7185
Premise	.9246	.7968	.8016
Background	.9256	.6198	.6307
Recommendation	.9465	.6827	.6930
None-argumentation	.8995	.3501	.3682

Table 2 shows inter-rater agreement of relation annotations between the argument components in the final corpus. The $\kappa = 0.560$ of the support relationship and the $\kappa = 0.625$ of the attack relationship are considered to be moderate agreement by [5].

Table 2. Inter-rater agreement of argument relation annotations.

	%	κ	α
Support	.9587	.5600	.5627
Attack	.9940	.6250	.6258

Table 3 shows inter-rater agreement of the sentiment polarity of the argument component annotations in the final corpus. Among them, positive sentiment $\kappa = 0.545$, negative sentiment $\kappa = 0.639$, neutral sentiment $\kappa = 0.413$, positive and neutral sentiment are considered to be moderate agreement, negative emotions are considered to be substantial agreement.

Table 3. Inter-rater agreement of the sentiment polarity of the argument component annotations.

	%	κ	α
Positive	.8702	.5445	.5599
Negative	.8985	.6389	.6501
Neutral	.8420	.4126	.4316

4.2   The Standard Annotation

After using the inter-rater agreement to filter out hotel reviews with low agreement, we finally collect 85 hotel reviews. For each review, there are 3–5 annotations, we follow a majority voting to get the standard annotation. For a clause, its annotation will be preserved only when over 50% of annotators take the same labeling scheme for the clause. For the five groups of comment_1389, we use the triplet (argument component, starting position in the text, ending position in the text) as the unique identifier to generate Table 4. As for annotators, the number 1 in Table 4 indicates that the annotator takes the label as shown in the row triple, and 0 indicates no. The triplet with a pass rate of more than 50% will be preserved. Finally, the clause annotations, which are located in the same clause and have the same type of argument component, are joined as an annotation. In this example, the annotations for the No 3, 4, and 5 will be joined as an annotation (Claim, 68, 161).

Table 4. The vote of annotated Comment_1389. a represents the annotator.

No.	Triplet	a_1	a_2	a_3	a_4	a_5	Total	Pass rate(%)
1	(Major claim, 0, 10)	1	0	1	1	1	4	80
2	(Background, 11, 66)	1	1	1	1	0	4	80
3	(Claim, 68, 91)	1	1	1	1	0	4	80
4	(Claim, 93, 122)	1	1	1	1	0	4	80
5	(Claim, 124, 161)	1	1	1	1	0	4	80
6	(Claim, 163, 215)	1	1	1	1	0	4	80
7	(Recommendation, 217, 266)	1	1	1	1	0	4	80
8	(Claim, 217, 266)	0	0	1	0	1	2	40
9	(Premise, 68, 91)	0	0	0	0	1	1	20
10	(Premise, 93, 122)	0	0	0	0	1	1	20
11	(Premise, 124, 161)	0	0	0	0	1	1	20
12	(Premise, 163, 215)	0	0	0	0	1	1	20

4.3   Final Corpus

Our final corpus contains 85 hotel reviews written in English, including 890 sentences and 11, 805 words. On average, each review has 10.5 sentences and 138.9 words, as shown in Table 5.

Table 5. Statistics of the final corpus.

	All	Avg. per review
Token	11805	1389
Clause	1260	15
Sentence	890	10
Major claim	85	1.0
Claim	276	3.3
Premise	143	1.7
Background	60	0.7
Recommendation	152	1.8

Error Analysis. We annotate 1674 hotel reviews in total, but there are only 85 high quality reviews in the final corpus. There are two reasons for the small amount of data in the corpus: (1) Hotel reviews are not normative texts, and do not have a certain formatal normativeness as papers or legal texts. The reviews written by the users are entirely out of user habits, and there is no special format requirement, which causes problems such as incorrect spelling, no punctuation, and irregular formatting. (2) The argument logic of hotel reviews is not as strong as that of legal texts and papers. Most users comment on a product (or service) by expressing their personal opinions, which are more emotional, followed by logical argument.

5   Conclusion and Future Work

In this paper, we propose a novel annotation scheme for arguments and manually annotate arguments in 85 hotel reviews in English in order to encourage future research in argument recognition. In addition, we show the statistics of final corpus in hotel reviews in English according to inter-rater agreement study.

For the future work, we will set the corpus as training data for reinforcement learning methods or supervised machine learning methods in order to detect argument components automatically as well as argumentative relations.

References

1. Fleiss, J.L.: Measuring nominal scale agreement among many raters. Psychol. Bull. **76**(5), 378–382 (1971)
2. Goudas, T., Louizos, C., Petasis, G., Karkaletsis, V.: Argument extraction from news, blogs, and social media. In: Likas, A., Blekas, K., Kalles, D. (eds.) SETN 2014. LNCS (LNAI), vol. 8445, pp. 287–299. Springer, Cham (2014). https://doi.org/10.1007/978-3-319-07064-3_23
3. Goudas, T., Louizos, C., Petasis, G., Karkaletsis, V.: Argument extraction from news, blogs, and the social web. Int. J. Artif. Intell. Tools **24**(05), 1540024 (2015)
4. Krippendorff, K.: Content Analysis: An Introduction to Its Methodology. SAGE Publications, Thousand Oaks (1980)
5. Landis, J.R., Koch, G.G.: The measurement of observer agreement for categorical data. Biometrics **33**(1), 159–174 (1977)
6. Lippi, M., Torroni, P.: Argument mining: a machine learning perspective. In: Black, E., Modgil, S., Oren, N. (eds.) TAFA 2015. LNCS (LNAI), vol. 9524, pp. 163–176. Springer, Cham (2015). https://doi.org/10.1007/978-3-319-28460-6_10
7. Lippi, M., Torroni, P.: Context-independent claim detection for argument mining. In: IJCAI 2015, pp. 185–191 (2015)
8. Lippi, M., Torroni, P.: Argumentation mining: state of the art and emerging trends. ACM Trans. Internet Technol. (TOIT) **16**(2), 10 (2016)
9. Mochales, R., Moens, M.F.: Study on the structure of argumentation in case law, vol. 20, no. 41, pp. 11–20 (2008)
10. Mochales, R., Moens, M.F.: Argumentation mining. Artif. Intell. Law **19**(1), 1–22 (2011)
11. Moens, M.F.: Argumentation mining: where are we now, where do we want to be and how do we get there? pp. 1–6 (2013)
12. Moens, M.F., Boiy, E., Palau, R.M., Reed, C.: Automatic detection of arguments in legal texts. In: Proceedings of the 11th International Conference on Artificial Intelligence and Law, pp. 225–230. ACM (2007)
13. Park, J., Cardie, C.: Identifying appropriate support for propositions in online user comments. In: Proceedings of the First Workshop on Argumentation Mining, pp. 29–38. Association for Computational Linguistics (2014). https://doi.org/10.3115/v1/W14-2105
14. Rooney, N., Wang, H., Browne, F.: Applying kernel methods to argumentation mining. In: FLAIRS Conference (2012)
15. Stab, C., Gurevych, I.: Annotating argument components and relations in persuasive essays. In: Proceedings of COLING 2014, the 25th International Conference on Computational Linguistics: Technical Papers, pp. 1501–1510. Dublin City University and Association for Computational Linguistics (2014)
16. Stab, C., Gurevych, I.: Identifying argumentative discourse structures in persuasive essays. In: Proceedings of the 2014 Conference on Empirical Methods in Natural Language Processing (EMNLP), pp. 46–56. Association for Computational Linguistics (2014). https://doi.org/10.3115/v1/D14-1006
17. Stab, C., Gurevych, I.: Parsing argumentation structures in persuasive essays. Comput. Linguist. **43**(3), 619–659 (2017). https://doi.org/10.1162/COLI_a_00295

18. Wachsmuth, H., Trenkmann, M., Stein, B., Engels, G.: Modeling review argumentation for robust sentiment analysis. In: Proceedings of COLING 2014, the 25th International Conference on Computational Linguistics: Technical Papers, pp. 553–564. Dublin City University and Association for Computational Linguistics, Dublin, August 2014. http://www.aclweb.org/anthology/C14-1053
19. Wachsmuth, H., Trenkmann, M., Stein, B., Engels, G., Palakarska, T.: A review corpus for argumentation analysis. In: Gelbukh, A. (ed.) CICLing 2014. LNCS, vol. 8404, pp. 115–127. Springer, Heidelberg (2014). https://doi.org/10.1007/978-3-642-54903-8_10

The Formal Understanding Models

Xiaohui Zou[1,2(✉)] (iD)

[1] Sino-American Searle Research Center, UC Berkeley,
Berkeley 94720-3840, USA
geneculture@icloud.com
[2] Room 415, Audio-Visual Building, Peking University, Beijing 100871, China

Abstract. This paper aims to introduce three types of understanding models from the perspective of human cognitive systems and machine information processing. The method steps are as follows: 1. Obtain a complete all equal formal understanding model (A) by constructing a twin Turing machine between numbers and numbers. 2. Obtain an approximately equal intelligent understanding model (B) by constructing a twin Turing machine between numbers and symbols. 3. Obtain a similar socialized understanding model (C) by constructing a twin Turing machine between numbers and characters, which is characterized by: the model A to B and then C gradually converge. As a result, it was found that the machine formal information processing and the human content information processing are opposite in convergence. It is clear that the combination of the three formalized understanding models and the bilingual model of interpretative translation is the key to formal understanding, intelligent understanding and social understanding. Based on them, ambiguity, misunderstanding and understanding are all well understood. The significance is that it proves that the three types of understanding models and the two sets of convergence modes can effectively determine the formal understanding process. Furthermore, it is clear that the ways of human and computer are combined completely which is better than pure humans or simple machines. That can be applied to cognitive systems and information processing perfectly. And its application is in the combination of human-machine-specific personalized ability training and standardized knowledge learning and management, especially based on the targeted reuse of subject knowledge centers.

Keywords: Understanding model · Cognitive system ·
Information processing · Twin Turing machine · Understanding process

1 Introduction

How to understand a piece of text? The basic question is very concerned by text analysis [1, 2], information extraction [3–5], expert knowledge acquisition [6, 7] and formal representation [8, 9], natural language processing [10] and formal understanding [11], machine translation [12], computer aided reading comprehension [13, 14] and writing expression [15, 16] and automatic digest [17]. The author's in-depth research found that it involves not only the social understanding of human language or mind in brain, but also the formal understanding of computer software or knowledge ontology

© Springer Nature Singapore Pte Ltd. 2019
F. Sun et al. (Eds.): ICCSIP 2018, CCIS 1005, pp. 337–347, 2019.
https://doi.org/10.1007/978-981-13-7983-3_30

in machine, and even the intelligent understanding of human-computer integrations with language or knowledge ontology or software both in brain and in machine as hardware those all in smart system. Therefore, this study will focus on three types of the Formal Understanding Models. This converges to the formalized aspect of socialization, formalization, and intelligent "three-in-one" understanding. Still, the subject of this research is still too big we called it as knowledge big production. However, the focus and difficulty of the problem is that it has to determine the spatial scale searching between maximum (detection rate) and minimum (precision rate).

How can we resolve this basic contradiction? Through long-term research, the author has extracted the qualitative analysis and quantitative analysis methods and tools of the three series of macroscopic, medium and micro smart model. It is effective in the interactive practice of human-machine integration smart system. Further research finds that there are very conflicts and laws between the rigid constraints of objectification, standardization and digitization and the flexible constraints of individualization, diversification and diversification. The key is the constraint mechanism. Based on cognitive system and information processing research, six questions are raised about "understanding" here:

What meaning of understanding is? How to understand? Why understand? Who understands whom? When do you understand? Where is the solution? This string of questions namely: 5W1H which is not just the most attention of journalists. In fact, people from all walks of life are concerned, but ordinary people do not have the philosopher's rational reflection training and the experimental conditions for the prophecy of scientists' experience, nor the standardization support platform of engineering technical experts and the individualized play scenes of various artists. Therefore, the 5W1H problems about understanding always exist. Contemporary Smart System Studied [18, 19] practice not only to the social understanding of interpersonal communication, but also to the formal understanding of automated processing and to the intelligent understanding of human-computer interaction, pay attention to the three-in-one understanding of rational division of co-labor between human and computer, co-intelligence and co-text-chess-board. That's the focus (Fig. 1).

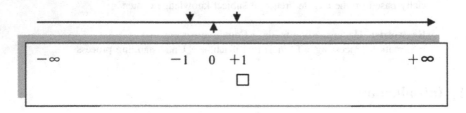

Fig. 1. The calculation of the sub-space, the number of counts

The Turing machine is best at doing the calculation of the sub-space, the number of counts. I will let it do only this thing and do it to the extreme. The way to understand it, at the same time, is the way it can be understood formally. Do the same thing with it, namely: counting. As for how to count, how to explain, how to give the operation a specific meaning (or use it to refer to what), and so on, leave it to human experts to do. The machine does what it does best.

From ignorance ($-\infty$) to omniscience ($+\infty$), there are two extremes. Not only individuals and groups of people, but humans can only be located between these two extremes. This article should not only talk about understanding from macroscopic perspective, but also understand it from microscopic operational level. Therefore, the formal bond of meson has become a bridge between human and machine, namely: the three types of twin Turing machines and Formal Understanding Models discovered by the author.

This paper aims to introduce three types of Formal Understanding Models from the perspective of human cognitive systems and machine information processing.

The formal understanding models especially refer to the three types of formal understanding models of the human, the computer, and the combination of the two. It is different from the previous socialized understanding, and is different from the formal understanding of the past. It is a formal understanding of the combination of two brains. It is characterized by: first, it understands the meaning of communication between interpersonal communication, further, it must be a formal understanding of the form that can be automatically recognized by the computer to be converted into a binary number, finally, it can also be done by human and machine interacts smoothly. The most typical is to do: a series of linkage function relationships required between the digitalized Id and the informational Iu and the knowledgeable Ik. At the same time, it must be in a rigid constrained environment of logical relationship architecture framework [20, 21].

2 Method

The method steps are as follows:

2.1 A Conformal Formal Understanding Model (A)

Obtain a conformal formal understanding model (A) by constructing a twin Turing machine between numbers and numbers that should be convertible between various hexadecimal numbers.

As can be seen from Fig. 2, two identical digital computer models (ie, the A model of the Twin Turing machine). Its characteristics are: their physical mechanism and mathematical mechanism are exactly the same. The heads and the plaids of both sides are exactly the same. Therefore, the author chooses the full ($\cong$) symbol to indicate its basic properties.

These two Turing machines are exactly the same. Both physical operation and mathematical algorithm and reasoning, that is, these thinking paths are completely consistent. Such a formal understanding model is a purely formal cognitive system and information processing system. Its practical application, first of all, can be used as a cipher machine. The number system (Number) in the upper right corner is the password book or password system. It can be any binary number system or a mixed system (how to choose it? Set by a specific user! The machine designer does not participate in the

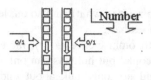

Understanding Model A: 🆚

Fig. 2. Digital understanding model

order setting). In this way, we know an important application of the Twin Turing machine: encryption and decryption.

Taking digital as an example, one of the typical embodiments is: a number box designed according to a pair of digital code locks (the password sequence that the user remembers and the password system it relies on plus the actual operation can be encrypted and decrypted).

Taking telegrams as an example, sending and receiving messages (the rules followed by the writing process or the order of remembering and the cryptosystem they rely on) are closely related to the process of encoding and decoding. Various encryption and decryption techniques can be involved here.

2.2 An Equivalent Intelligent Understanding Model (B)

Obtain an equivalent intelligent understanding model (B) by constructing a twin Turing machine between numbers and symbols. Symbols can also be distinguished between broad and narrow (Fig. 3).

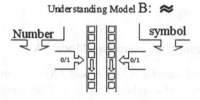

Understanding Model B: ≈

Fig. 3. Symbolic understanding model

Symbolic Understanding Model directly aids in the encryption and decryption of symbols. In fact, the general symbol understanding model must be limited to a specific symbol. Whether it is a simple or complex symbol, first of all, there must be corresponding choices and qualifications. Otherwise, it cannot directly help the encryption and decryption of specific symbols. If you first clear the basic elements, then clarify how the elements construct the combination of the hierarchical structure, and finally, clarify their specific logos, features and attributes, then you can achieve encryption and decryption of various symbol system (substance the above is to understand the various symbols in the way of encryption and decryption).

Take music as an example. Compare the piano of a keyboard instrument and string violin of the wireless spectrum to understand the symbol.

Take dance as an example. Compare the ballerina's neck and legs and feet to understand the characteristics of dance symbols.

Taking martial arts as an example, comparing the characteristics of martial arts in Southern fists northern legs, we can understand the characteristics of martial arts symbols.

With the symbolic understanding model, you can perform corresponding encryption and decryption to understand a wide variety of symbols.

2.3   A Similar Socialized Understanding Model (C)

Obtain a similar socialized understanding model (C) by constructing a twin Turing machine between numbers and characters.

Humboldt's view one word is a world [22], inspiration and reverie, that is, association is endless. This is an extremely open and flexible view in humanities. Saussure's view of that language is chess [23] gives people enlightenment and thinking is systematic and therefore scientific. By indirect formalization method and indirect computational model, not only resolves the conflict between Turing test [24] and Searle's Chinese room [25], but also further summarizes twin Turing machine, the formal understanding model. Such assertions are reasonable, legal and verifiable.

Its practical application can well understand the view of the late Wittgenstein "language game" and its early "Logical Philosophy" [26, 27] that contains the views of "world, thought, language" three-point and three-way (logical equivalence). It is even a good understanding of Heidegger's view that language is the home of existence [28].

The specific test method is to understand them in a specific language. Once the most complex language (including not only natural language, but also can further include generalized language) can also achieve formal understanding, especially the understanding of human-computer integration, which means that social interpersonal communication can be done scientific research formally (Fig. 4).

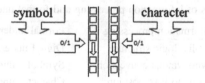

Understanding Model C: ∽

Fig. 4. Character understanding model

The Chinese character understanding model can directly help Chinese encryption and decryption. However, it cannot directly help the encryption and decryption of English. If we use the bilingual butterfly model that interprets first and then translates, then the encryption and decryption between Chinese and English can be realized (in essence, another language is understood by means of encryption and decryption).

As can be understood from Fig. 5, the internal interpretation of each of the bilinguals and the translation of each other, in fact, before the Chinese-English translation, more important, first of all, is the understanding of the mother tongue and then the foreign languages. Among them, especially for Chinese, first of all, is the understanding of characters and words. Specifically includes: matching of meaning items (ie: excluding lexical semantic ambiguity), synonym and statistical analysis of approximate phrases and sentences (callable big data and machine learning), phrase-level and sentence-level bilingual parallel corpus construction (machine Translation-supported core language resource library), computer-assisted instruction (not only for language teaching, but also for listening, speaking, reading and writing in various subjects), and so on. It can be found that the above informality and multiple formal understanding models can work together.

Fig. 5. Character-word understanding model

3 Results

As a result, it was found that the machine formal information processing and the human content information processing are opposite in convergence (Table 1).

Table 1. Basic laws of information processing and formal understanding models

Cognitive types	Information processing	Formal understanding models
1st-rigid law	Bit-list logic structure	Digital understanding model
2nd-rigid law	Synonymous conversion	Symbolic understanding model
3rd-flexible law	Agree to juxtaposition	Character understanding model
4th-flexible law	Interpretation then translation	Bilingual understanding model

It is clear that the combination of three formalized understanding models and the bilingual model of the interpretative translation which is the key to formal, intelligent and social understanding that based on, all these ambiguity, misunderstanding and understanding are well understood. The flexible law is in two kinds of manifestations.

The formulas or equations are displayed:

$$\Sigma xy = Iu \tag{1}$$

$$\Sigma nn = Id \tag{2}$$

$$\Sigma mm = Ik \tag{3}$$

$$Iu \approx Id - Ik \tag{4}$$

$$Id = Ik + Iu \tag{5}$$

$$Id \equiv Ik + Iu \tag{6}$$

Displayed equations are centered and set on a separate line that they represent the results of the practical application of three types of formal understanding models of lattice calculations (numbers) in unknown fields, all fields and known fields, and the constant relation (information identities) between the three theoretical models.

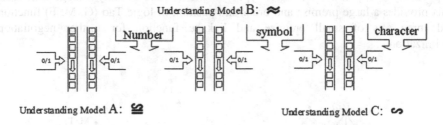

Understanding Model A: ♌   Understanding Model C: ♋

Fig. 6. Three types of formal understanding models

We can see that understanding Model A and C at two extremes from Fig. 6. Among them, from the perspective of pure formalization, the understanding model A is open, and its characteristic is that the digital system can establish a functional relationship with any symbol system. Therefore, its semantic content is uncertain. From the specific form of symbol content understanding model C is open, and its characteristic is that the writing system can establish a functional relationship with any individual's mind choice. Therefore, there is uncertainty in its pragmatic choice. Therefore, the understanding model B located in the middle is very important, and its specific symbol system can establish a specific functional relationship that with the understanding model A and a specific functional relationship with the understanding model C. In this way, a core problem is highlighted: how to determine the existence of a consistent grammatical form and its corresponding linkage function between the models and their matching formal systems? More importantly, how to establish the order and location in logic that the three types of understanding models and their matching formal systems must follow? The answers to both questions are rigid. This is clearly solved by the three types of twin Turing machines described in this study.

In the method steps are as follows: 1. Obtain a conformal formal understanding model (A) by constructing a twin Turing machine between numbers and numbers. 2. Obtain an equivalent intelligent understanding model (B) by constructing a twin Turing machine between numbers and symbols. 3. Obtain a similar socialized understanding model (C) by constructing a twin Turing machine between numbers and characters, which is characterized by: the model A to B and then C gradually converge. The first one is mathematically equivalent to; the second is mathematically equal; the third is mathematically similar which is in tow kinds of manifestations.

The three understanding models are the three types of twin Turing machines. Thus, the Turing Computability Principle (Turing Machine) and the machine-based program operation are not the human understanding of the natural language (Searle's Chinese Room) even through the Turing test, namely three types of twin Turing machines by indirect formal expression. The three understanding models (digital chess), logical order and position between machines and between human and machine or between machine and human are consistent. The only difference is the type of numbers, symbols, and characters that are chosen. They can all be included in the G (L) function as far as their relationship with the object world in the F (W) and then the choice in the concept idea in the M (T) that can use the F (W) function and the M (T) function respectively to express. These three types of functions are actually linkage functions. This provides a large premise and order and position in logic Tao (G, M, F) function and three sets of small premise and linkage function for further negotiation optimization.

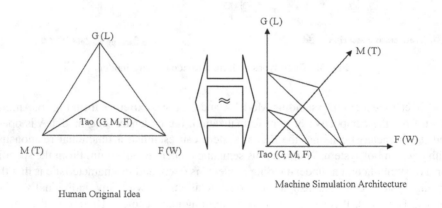

Human Original Idea

Machine Simulation Architecture

Fig. 7. How to copy it from human brain to computer

If humans can understand the expert knowledge (macronomic ontology) that expressed by the prism on the left side of Fig. 7, that is, the original idea of human beings, then the machine can understand it formally and simulate it with the three-dimensional coordinates on the right side of Fig. 7 (the accuracy is amazing, similar to the ground) is the architecture of the machine simulation.

The extraction of the remaining content information can be implemented according to the specific context. The most important thing is that the three kinds of phenomena information processing can be expressed by three types of linkage functions. In this way, the transmission of ontology information and essential and real or authentic information is contained in it.

4   Conclusion

Regarding the understanding, the author found that when talking about a certain field in particular, there are many top-level journals published and cited, but the abstract discussion is not quoted. Furthermore, the understanding of the common sense of everyday life and the expert terminology in the subject area is often different. This leads to a series of difficulties in natural language understanding and expert knowledge acquisition as well as expert knowledge representation. For example, not only the authors of philosophy, humanities and social sciences, and education and management encounter great difficulties in understanding each other's independent thinking processes and their research results, but also in psychology, physiology, and natural sciences. Even in the forefront of computer science and artificial intelligence, logic and mathematics, we often face difficulties in mutual understanding. Therefore, after IBM Deep Blue and Google Go defeated the human chess game experts, the author raised such a problem and put it into practice, namely: treating Chinese characters as chess pieces and making language chess (Saussure's understanding), The process of expressing Chinese thought is like a language game (later Wittgenstein's understanding) - its form and its path of thinking can be indirectly formalized and indirectly calculated [29], so the intelligent text analysis in NLP of human-computer integration (the natural language understanding here is easy to rule out ambiguity) and the knowledge module finishing (the expert knowledge acquisition in this way is easy to eliminate misunderstanding) lays the foundation for the large-scale knowledge big production necessary for the construction of the knowledge center [30, 31].

The significance is that it proves that the three types of understanding models and the two sets of convergence understanding modes can effectively determine the formal understanding process. Furthermore, it is clear that the ways of human and computer combined completely are better than pure humans or simple machines. That can be applied to cognitive systems and information processing perfectly.

5   Discussion: Geneculture's Questions

The order and position of the three types of twin Turing machines [32] are logically and mathematically consistent [33]. Why does it bring a series of synonymous conversions (a) and agree to juxtaposition (b)? (a) Based on the principle of hierarchical set, it is related to Tarski's language layering, formal semantics of language [34]; (b) based on the principle of attribute set, it is related to Turing machine, cryptography and test [35] and Searle's Chinese room [36] are related. Among them, encryption and decryption involve Klein's formal theory of string [37] and the P and NP problem [38] (here further involved human-computer interaction [39], cognitive system and information processing issues).

(a) Inter-machine exchange and (b) Interpersonal communication records are consistent in the logical and mathematical structure of the twin Turing machines, but their meanings and intentions not only play the standardization role of the machine equally. It can also make individualization and diversification in society and humanities from person to person. Encryption and decryption, representation and understanding, both of people and machine helping each other are reflected.

References

1. Feinerer, I., Hornik, K., Meyer, D.: Text Mining Infrastructure in R. Feinerer 2015 Text MI (2015)
2. Sapiro-Gheiler, E.: Read My lips: using automatic text analysis to classify politicians by party and ideology. Sapiro Gheiler 2018 Read ML (2018)
3. Angeli, G., Premkumar, M.J.J., Manning, C.D.: Leveraging linguistic structure for open domain information extraction. Angeli 2015 Leveraging LS, ACL (2015)
4. Corro, L.D., Gemulla, R.: Claus IE: clause-based open information extraction. Corro 2013 Claus IECO WWW (2013)
5. Padia, A., Ferraro, F., Fin, T.W.: KG Cleaner: identifying and correcting errors produced by information extraction systems. Padia 2018 KGC Leaner I, Journal CoRR, volume, abs/1808.04816 (2018)
6. Jannin, P., Meixensberger, G.S., Burgert, O.: Validation of knowledge acquisition for surgical process models. Jannin 2018 Validation OK (2018)
7. Gordon, J., Van Durme, B.: Reporting bias and knowledge acquisition. Gordon 2013 Reporting BA, AKBC @CIKM (2013)
8. Lin, Y., Liu, Z., Luan, H.-B., Sun, M., Rao, S., Liu, S.: Modeling relation paths for representation learning of knowledge bases. In: Proceedings, Lin 2015 Modeling RP, EMNLP (2015)
9. Kuznetsov, S.O., Poelmans, J.: Knowledge representation and processing with formal concept analysis. Wiley Interdisc. Rew.: Data Min. Knowl. Discov. **3**, 200–215 (2013)
10. Manning, C.D., Surdeanu, M., Bauer, J., Finkel, J.R., Bethard, S., McClosky, D.: The stanford core NLP natural language processing toolkit. In: Proceedings Manning 2014 (2014). The SC, ACL
11. Sarikaya, R., Hinton, G.E., Deoras, A.: Application of deep belief networks for natural language understanding. In: 2014 Processing of IEEE/ACM Transactions on Audio, Speech, and Language, vol. 22, pp. 778–784 (2014). Sarikaya 2014 Application OD
12. Bahdanau, D., Cho, K., Bengio, Y.: Neural machine translation by jointly learning to align and translate. Bahdanau 2014 Neural MT, Journal CoRR, volume: abs 1409.0473 (2014)
13. Jia, R., Liang, P.: Adversarial examples for evaluating reading comprehension systems. In: Proceedings, Jia 2017 Adversarial EF, EMNLP (2017)
14. Rajpurkar, P., Zhang, J., Lopyrev, K., Liang, P.: SQuAD: 100, 000+ questions for machine comprehension of text. In: Proceedings, Rajpurkar 2016 SQuAD10, EMNLP (2016)
15. Stanley, G.B.: Reading and writing the neural code. Nature Neurosci. **16**, 259–263 (2013). Stanley 2013 Reading AW
16. King, K.D.: Bringing creative writing instruction into reminiscence group treatment. Clin. Gerontologist **438**, 1–7 (2017). King 2017 Bringing CW
17. Uddin, G., Khomh, F.: Automatic summarization of API reviews. In: 2017 32nd IEEE/ACM International Conference on Automated Software Engineering (ASE), Udd in 2017 Automatic SO, pp. 159–170 (2017)

18. Zou, X.: Original Collection on Smart-System Studied. Published by Smashwords, Inc. 08 September 2018. ISBN 9780463607640
19. Zou, X.: Advanced Collection on Smart-System Studied. Published by Smashwords, Inc. 15 September 2018. ISBN 9780463020036
20. Zou, X., Zou, S., Ke, L.: Fundamental law of information: proved by both numbers and characters in conjugate matrices. In: Proceedings, vol. 1, p. 60 (2017)
21. Zou, S., Zou, X.: Understanding: how to resolve ambiguity. In: Shi, Z., Goertzel, B., Feng, J. (eds.) ICIS 2017. IAICT, vol. 510, pp. 333–343. Springer, Cham (2017). https://doi.org/10.1007/978-3-319-68121-4_36
22. Underhill, J.W.: Humboldt Worldview and Language, pp. xii, 161. Edinburgh University Press, Edinburgh (2013)
23. Joseph, J.E.: Saussurean tradition in linguistics. In: Concise History of the Language Sciences, pp. 233–239 (1995)
24. French, R.M.: Subcognition and the limits of the turing test. Mind 99(393), 53–65 (1990)
25. Preston, J., Bishop, M.: Views into the chinese room: new essays on searle and artificial intelligence. Minds Mach. 15(1–111), 97–106 (2005)
26. Starks, M.R.: The Logical Structure of Philosophy, Psychology, Mind and Language as Revealed in the Writings of Wittgenstein and Searle (2016)
27. Strong, T.: Therapy as a New Language Game? A Review of Wittgenstein and Psychotherapy: From Paradox to Wonder. PsycCRITIQUES (2015)
28. Heidegger, F.C.: Black notebooks. Philosophy 90(2), 1–12 (2018)
29. Zuo, X., Zuo, S.: Indirect computing model with indirect formal method. Comput. Eng. Softw. 32(5), 1–5 (2011)
30. Zou, X., Zou, S.: Two major categories of formal strategy. Comput. Appl. Softw. 24(16), 3086–3114 (2013)
31. Xiaohui, Z., Shunpeng, Z.: Bilingual information processing method and principle. J. Comput. Appl. Softw. 32(11), 69–76 (2015)
32. Zou, X., Zou, S.: Virtual twin turing machine: bilingual information processing as an example. Software 32(8), 1–5 (2011)
33. Zou, X., Zou, S.: Basic law of information: the fundamental theory of generalized bilingual processing. In: ISIS Summit Vienna 2015, The Information Society at the Crossroads, T9.1002 (2015)
34. Loeb, I.: The role of universal language in the early work of Carnap and Tarski. Synthese 194, 1–17 (2017)
35. Hernández-Orallo, J.: Evaluation in artificial intelligence: from task-oriented to ability-oriented measurement. Artif. Intell. Rev. 48, 1–51 (2017)
36. Lu, W., Chen, T.: New conditions on global stability of Cohen-Grossberg neural networks. Neural Comput. 15(5), 1173 (2003)
37. Traoré, M.K., Muzy, A.: Capturing the dual relationship between simulation models and their context. Simul. Modell. Pract. Theor. 14(2), 126–142 (2018)
38. Mcgregor, A., Vu, H.T.: Better streaming algorithms for the maximum coverage problem. Theor. Comput. Syst. 1–25 (2018)
39. Partala, T., Surakka, V.: The effects of affective interventions in human–computer interaction. Interact. Comput. 16(2), 295–309 (2004)

Application of PSO-LSSVM in Bias Correction of Shipborne Anemometer Measurement

Tong Hu[✉], Suiping Qi, Zhijin Qiu, Jing Zou, and Dongming Wang

Institute of Oceanographic Instrumentation, Qilu University of Technology
(Shandong Academy of Sciences), Qingdao 266001, China
tong.hu@hotmail.com

Abstract. Wind measurement from shipborne anemometer is susceptible to the airflow distortion due to ship hull and superstructure. The measurement bias needs to be minimized with regard to various meteorological and navigation applications. To address this problem, this study illustrates the feasibility to correct the measurement bias due to airflow distortion by applying Least Squares Support Vector Machine with Particle Swarm Optimization (PSO-LSSVM) method. The airflow field around hull and superstructure of an experimental ship is simulated by computational fluid dynamics (CFD) techniques. And then the nonlinear relationship between the airflow through conventional anemometer mounting sites on the main mast and the airflow through the reference point above bridge is implicitly obtained using the PSO-LSSVM regression. The dataset of relative wind observation taken during a sea trial is used to validate the effectiveness of this method. The results show that the established model efficiently eliminates most of the speed bias and reduces half of the direction bias of the mean relative wind, which indicates this method could be extended to estimate the undisturbed freestream on the open sea surface.

Keywords: Ship airflow field · Wind measurement · CFD · PSO · LSSVM

1 Introduction

Sea surface wind plays a primary role in the air-sea momentum, heat and water vapor exchange process. The field measurements of sea surface wind are mostly obtained from conventional observation platforms such as ships, buoys and offshore stations. As one data source of most marine meteorological field observations, ship platform provides long-term and continuous sea surface wind datasets. The shipborne anemometer measures the relative wind, and the true wind is calculated by the relative wind, ship speed and course. The data bias existed in the relative wind measurement is usually due to inherent characteristics of wind measurement from a moving platform of bluff-body, which leads to the necessary consideration about the airflow distortion as well as platform motion.

The airflow through the anemometer mounting site is distorted by the ship hull and superstructure, and makes the relative wind speed and direction measurements different from the undistorted freestream on the open sea surface. The measurement bias of the

© Springer Nature Singapore Pte Ltd. 2019
F. Sun et al. (Eds.): ICCSIP 2018, CCIS 1005, pp. 348–357, 2019.
https://doi.org/10.1007/978-981-13-7983-3_31

relative wind speed and direction deviates the calculation result of the true wind speed and direction, which further affects the calculation of the sea surface friction velocity u_* and the drag coefficient C_{D10N}. For example, if the freestream speed is 10 m/s, 10% wind speed bias will result in 27% bias of the momentum flux estimation [1].

The problem of wind measurement bias due to airflow distortion on ship platforms has been concerned for decades. Such measurement bias cannot be reduced by improving the accuracy of anemometers. The World Meteorological Organization suggests that the shipborne anemometer should be mounted on well-exposed position close to the front edge of the installation surface and of a certain height [2]. However, the anemometer cannot be mounted far enough away from ship hull and superstructure, and thus it is more appropriate to correct the measurement bias by post processing.

With the development of CFD techniques, the airflow distortion around ship hull and superstructure can be analyzed more conveniently, which facilitates the relevant research. Yelland et al. showed that the bias of wind speed measurements did not vary within the range of 5–25 m/s [3]. This opinion is consistent with the suggestion of Moat et al. that the airflow field around ship was insensitive to the Reynolds number in the range of $2 \times 10^5 - 1 \times 10^7$ [4, 5]. Popinet et al. showed that the mean wind speed bias depended on the upwind angle rather than the Reynolds number [6]. Griessbaum et al. presented that the wind measurement bias would lead to 30–50% deviation of the gas transport rate k_g [7]. O'Sullivan et al. suggested that more CFD simulations with different upwind angles were necessary for wind measurement bias correction [8]. Wnęk et al. verified the consistency of the CFD simulation results and the experimental data for LNG vessels on wind loads [9].

This study presents an application to correct the relative wind measurement bias using the Least Square Support Vector Machines with Particle Swarm Optimization (PSO-LSSVM). In Sect. 2, we review the basic LSSVM formulation as well as the hyper-parameter selection based on PSO. Several issues associated with the modeling process, including CFD simulation and PSO-LSSVM modeling, are discussed in detail in Sect. 3. In Sect. 4, experimental results are presented to illustrate the effectiveness of the bias correction model. Conclusions are drawn in Sect. 5.

2   PSO-LSSVM Regression

The LSSVM proposed by Suykens and Vandewalle [10] has been extensively applied to nonlinear regression and system modeling [11–13]. The algorithm complexity of LSSVM is reduced greatly by solving linear algebraic instead of the computationally hard quadratic programming problem in the standard SVM. The nonlinear regression problem can be written as:

$$\begin{cases} \min J(w, \xi) = \frac{1}{2}w^T w + \frac{1}{2}\gamma \sum_{i=1}^{n} \xi_i^2 \\ s.t. \quad y_i = w^T \varphi(x_i) + b + \xi_i \end{cases} \tag{1}$$

The Lagrange multiplier is introduced to solve the above equality-constrained optimization problem:

$$L(w,b,\xi,\alpha) = J(w,\xi) - \sum_{i=1}^{N} \alpha_i[w^T \varphi(x_i) + b + \xi_i - y_i] \tag{2}$$

The conditions for optimality are given by:

$$\begin{cases} w = \sum_{i=1}^{N} \alpha_i \varphi(x_i) \\ \sum_{i=1}^{N} \alpha_i = 0 \\ \alpha_i = \gamma \xi_i \\ w^T \varphi(x_i) + b + \xi_i - y_i = 0 \end{cases} \tag{3}$$

After eliminating w and ξ_i, one gets the following linear system:

$$\begin{bmatrix} 0 & 1_v^T \\ 1_v & \Omega + \gamma^{-1}I \end{bmatrix} \begin{bmatrix} b \\ \alpha \end{bmatrix} = \begin{bmatrix} 0 \\ y \end{bmatrix} \tag{4}$$

with:

$$\begin{cases} y = [y_1, y_2, \cdots, y_N]^T \\ 1_v = [1, 1, \cdots, 1]^T \\ \alpha = [\alpha_1, \alpha_2, \cdots, \alpha_n]^T \\ \Omega_{i,j} = K(x_i, x_j) \end{cases} \tag{5}$$

Equation (4) can be solved for the parameters α_i and b by the least squares method. Therefore, the resulting model for nonlinear regression becomes:

$$y = f(x) = \sum_{i=1}^{N} \alpha_i K(x, x_i) + b \tag{6}$$

The PSO algorithm as an optimization technique introduced by Eberhart and Kennedy well simulates the social behavior of groups such as birds randomly looking for food [14]. In PSO, each single solution is taken as a particle in the search space. All of the particles have fitness values which are evaluated by fitness function. According to the fitness values, the particles move towards better solution areas by changing the velocity and location as follow:

$$\begin{cases} v_i(t+1) = w_0 v_i(t) + c_1 r_1 (p_{best} - x_i) + c_2 r_2 (g_{best} - x_i) \\ x_i(t+1) = x_i + v_i(t+1) \end{cases} \tag{7}$$

where x_i, v_i are the location and velocity of the i th particle, w_0 is the symbol for inertial weight, c_1 and c_2 represent learning rates which are positive constants, r_1 and r_2 describe two random numbers between zero and one, p_{best} is the best previous position recorded by the ith particle, and g_{best} is the best global position among the entire particles throughout searching history.

In solving the hyper-parameter selection of LSSVM including the kernel parameter and regularization parameter, each particle is requested to represent a potential solution, namely hyper-parameters combination [15]. In this study, the LSSVM with radial basis function (RBF) kernel is trained to model the wind measurement bias, and thus each particle in PSO represents candidate values of regularization parameter γ and kernel parameter σ. To define the fitness value, five-fold cross validations with training dataset for each particle and the mean squared error (MSE) is taken as the fitness value. The bias correction modeling based on PSO-LSSVM is described in Sect. 3.2.

3 Bias Correction Modeling

The distorted airflow at the anemometer mounting site under different conditions of freestream velocity and upwind angle are obtained by CFD simulations. Then the nonlinear relationship between the distorted airflow and the undistorted freestream is modeled by means of the PSO-LSSVM.

3.1 CFD Simulation

In this study, an experimental ship is taken as an example to research on bias correction method of shipborne anemometer measurement. The dimension of the computational domain is 6L (length) × 6L (width) × 1.6L (height) where L is the length of the ship. As illustrated in Fig. 1, the ship is placed at the center of the bottom surface of the computational domain, and rotated in each CFD simulation case to achieve different upwind angles (0–360° at 10° intervals). The impact of ship swing is not considered in this study.

To simulate the relative wind measurement process onboard, the freestream entered from the inlet of the computational domain flows past the ship hull and superstructure. The velocity of freestream at the inlet is set with a logarithmic profile.

$$u = (u_*/k_v) \ln(z/z_0) \tag{8}$$

Wind speed at the height of 10 m above sea level u_{10N} is set as 5 m/s, 10 m/s and 20 m/s respectively in CFD simulation cases of the same upwind angle. The Kalman constant k_v is set as 0.4, and the roughness length z_0 is set as 2 mm.

To capture the boundary layers effects along the walls of the ship model, a tetrahedral mesh of 2×10^6 elements with 5 prismatic layers on the model's surface is generated (Fig. 2). The first layer thickness is proportional to the wall distance y+, which is close to 30. Similar to the wind tunnel test, the no-slip condition is specified on the ship hull, superstructure and the walls of the computational domain. At the outlet zero pressure condition was imposed.

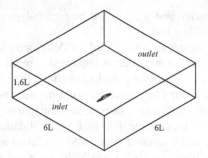

Fig. 1. Dimension of the computation domain

The turbulence closure scheme selected is *RNG k−ε* two-equation model which has been extensively used in industrial applications. The convection term is discretized using the second-order upwind scheme, and the diffusion term is discretized using the central difference scheme. Each solution was obtained by applying *SIMPLE* algorithm to solve the steady three-dimensional incompressible *RANS* equations. The convergence residual is set as 10E−4.

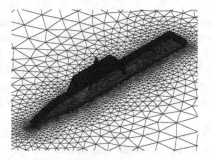

Fig. 2. Computational mesh

The speed and direction of the airflow through different wind measurement points on the experimental ship are extracted from the CFD simulation results. Besides the conventional wind measurement points on the both sides of the main mast, an additional anemometer used as reference was installed temporarily above the bridge during a sea trial.

In order to validate the CFD simulation results, the ratio of wind speed measured by the anemometers on the mast and the reference anemometer above the bridge is quantified under different upwind angles (Fig. 3). The ratio calculated from CFD simulation results is consistent with the average value calculated from the experimental dataset. Since the airflow mainly comes from the bow during ship voyage, no measurement presents in certain upwind angles.

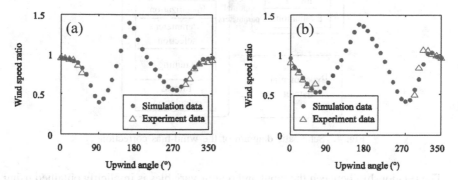

Fig. 3. Comparison of the wind speed ratios from CFD results and experimental dataset at the measurement site on the (a) port side and (b) starboard side

3.2   PSO-LSSVM Modeling

Since that it is difficult to carry out simultaneous field measurement of the undistorted sea surface wind, the relationship between the airflow through conventional anemometer mounting sites on the main mast and the airflow through the reference point above bridge is obtained based on PSO-LSSVM modeling, although the airflow through the reference measurement point will also be affected by the presence of the ship hull and superstructure. If the method could effectively reduce the wind measurement bias with respect to the reference measurement point, it could be applied to estimate the undisturbed freestream on the open sea surface by replacing the variables of airflow speed and direction taken from the reference measurement site with the one taken from the inlet of the computational domain.

The flowchart of the PSO-LSSVM modeling is shown in Fig. 4. Compared to the airflow speed, the direction of the airflow through measurement site on the main mast is relatively less affected by the ship hull and superstructure. Thus the direction of the airflow through measurement site on the main mast is selected as the input variable.

The output variables are the ratio of the airflow speed through measurement site on the main mast to the airflow speed through the reference measurement site above the bridge, as well as the direction difference between the airflow through measurement sites on the main mast and the airflow through the reference measurement site above the bridge.

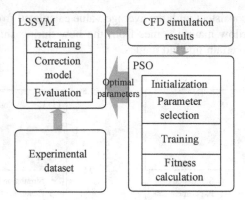

Fig. 4. Schematic diagram of the wind-bias correction

The relationship between the input and output variables is implicitly obtained using LSSVM regression with RBF kernel. The optimal hyper-parameter selection is solved by PSO, in which particles represents candidate values of regularization parameter γ and kernel parameter σ. The particle number is 30. The maximum number of iterations is 100. And the inertial weight w_0, learning rates c_1 and c_2 for the PSO algorithm are set as 0.9, 1.5, 1.5 respectively.

$$\begin{cases} f\left(wd^i_{mast}\right) = \left(r^i, \Delta\theta^i\right) \\ r^i = ws^i_{mast}/ws_{bridge} \qquad i = starboard, port \\ \Delta\theta^i = wd^i_{mast} - wd_{bridge} \end{cases} \tag{9}$$

where wd^i_{mast} is the direction of the airflow through the measurement site on the main mast, r^i is the ratio of the airflow speed through the measurement site on the main mast to the airflow speed through the reference measurement site, and $\Delta\theta^i$ is the direction difference between the airflow through measurement site on the main mast and the airflow through the reference measurement site above the bridge.

To reduce the wind measurement bias, the relative wind speed and direction are corrected according to corresponding r^i and $\Delta\theta^i$, then the corrected relative wind measurements from both sides on the main mast are merged by vector averaging.

4   Results and Discussion

In order to validate the effectiveness of the established bias correction model, the relative wind measurements from corresponding sites on the experimental ship were collected during a sea trial. The relative wind was measured at the frequency of 1 Hz and move averaged with time window of 120 s. The measurements from the anemometers installed on both sides of the main mast were input to the model respectively, then the outputs from the model were merged by vector averaging, and finally the result was compared to the measurement from the reference anemometer above the bridge.

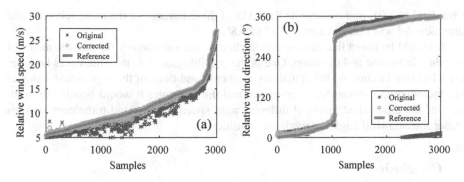

Fig. 5. Correction effects on (a) relative wind speed and (b) relative wind direction

In the sample data, the mean relative wind speed on the main mast is 92% on average of the one above the bridge. It indicates that the wind speed bias is about one tenth of the referenced mean relative wind speed. The direction difference of the mean relative wind between the measurements on the main mast and above the bridge is 13.4°. As shown in Fig. 5, after correction by the established model, the wind measurements by the anemometer installed on the main mast are closer to the measurements by the anemometer installed above the bridge, which illustrates that relationship between the airflow through different wind measurement sites is well estimated by the PSO-LSSVM regression.

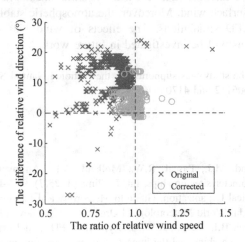

Fig. 6. Scatter plot of corrected wind speed ratio vs. direction difference

The scatter plot (Fig. 6) illustrates the ratio of the mean relative wind speed and the difference of the mean relative wind direction before and after the bias correction. The Root Mean Square (RMS) of the ratio of the mean relative wind speed r was improved from 0.92 to 1.01, and meanwhile the RMS of the difference of the mean relative wind direction $\Delta\theta$ was reduced from 13.4° to 6.8°.

It should be noted that the correction effect is not satisfactory for measurements of certain wind speed and direction. One of the possible causes is the differences between the CFD simulations and the actual environment conditions of the experimental ship at sea including the atmospheric turbulence and the sea state. It would benefit the accuracy of the established model if different wind speed profiles and turbulence settings under finer upwind angle intervals are considered.

5   Conclusion

The PSO-LSSVM method is applied to address the problem of wind measurement bias due to airflow distortion caused by the presence of the ship hull and superstructure. The empirical results demonstrated that the implicit relationship between airflow through different wind measurement sites implicitly obtained by PSO-LSSVM modeling using CFD simulation is consistent with the one in the experimental data. The established model eliminates most of the wind speed bias of the mean relative wind speed, and the direction bias of the mean relative wind measurements was reduced by half. Considering the operability to measure the undistorted sea surface wind during sea trial, the airflow through the measurement site above the bridge was selected as reference. To estimate the undisturbed freestream on the open sea surface, the referenced airflow would be replaced with the airflow at the inlet of the computational domain. It is required to validate the established model with the simultaneous field measurements of the undisturbed sea surface wind. Moreover, the atmospheric stability and sea state is not considered in CFD simulations. The effects of wind bias correction in more complicated conditions will be investigated in future work.

Acknowledgement. The study was supported by the National Natural Science Foundation of China under Grant 41606112 and 41705046.

References

1. Moat, B.I., Yelland, M.J., Pascal, R.W., Molland, A.F.: An overview of the airflow distortion at anemometer sites on ships. Int. J. Climatol. **25**(7), 997–1006 (2005)
2. World Meteorological Organization: Guide to Meteorological Instruments and Methods of Observation, 7th edn. World Meteorological Organization, Geneva (2008)
3. Yelland, M.J., Moat, B.I., Pascal, R.W., Berry, D.I.: CFD model estimates of the airflow distortion over research ships and the impact on momentum flux measurements. J. Atmos. Oceanic Technol. **19**(10), 1477–1499 (2002)
4. Moat, B.I., Yelland, M.J., Pascal, R.W., Molland, A.F.: Quantifying the airflow distortion over merchant ships. Part I: validation of a CFD model. J. Atmos. Oceanic Technol. **23**(3), 341–350 (2006)
5. Moat, B.I., Yelland, M.J., Molland, A.F.: Quantifying the airflow distortion over merchant ships. Part II: application of the model results. J. Atmos. Oceanic Technol. **23**(3), 351–360 (2006)

6. Popinet, S.: Experimental and numerical study of the turbulence characteristics of airflow around a research vessel. J. Atmos. Oceanic Technol. **21**(10), 1575–1589 (2004)
7. Griessbaum, F., Moat, B.I., Narita, Y., Yelland, M.J.: Uncertainties in wind speed dependent CO_2 transfer velocities due to airflow distortion at anemometer sites on ships. Atmos. Chem. Phys. **10**(11), 5123–5133 (2010)
8. O'Sullivan, N., Landwehr, S., Ward, B.: Air-flow distortion and wave interactions on research vessels: an experimental and numerical comparison. Methods Oceanogr. **12**, 1–17 (2015)
9. Wnęk, A.D., Guedes Soares, C.: CFD assessment of the wind loads on an lng carrier and floating platform models. Ocean Eng. **97**, 30–36 (2015)
10. Suykens, J.A.K., Vandewalle, J.: Least squares support vector machine classifiers. Neural Process. Lett. **9**(3), 293–300 (1999)
11. Mellit, A., Pavan, A.M., Benghanem, M.: Least squares support vector machine for short-term prediction of meteorological time series. Theor. Appl. Climatol. **111**(1–2), 297–307 (2011)
12. Samui, P.: Application of least square support vector machine (LSSVM) for determination of evaporation losses in reservoirs. Engineering **3**(4), 431–434 (2011)
13. Wang, Q., Qian, W., He, K.: Unsteady aerodynamic modeling at high angles of attack using support vector machines. Chin. J. Aeronaut. **28**(3), 659–668 (2015)
14. Kennedy, J., Eberhart, R.: Particle swarm optimization. In: International Conference on Neural Networks, pp. 1942–1948. IEEE Press, Perth (1995)
15. Guo, X.C., Yang, J.H., Wu, C.G., Wang, C.Y., Liang, Y.C.: A novel LS-SVMs hyper-parameter selection based on particle swarm optimization. Neurocomputing **71**(16–18), 3211–3215 (2008)

Two-Stage Weighted Regularized Extreme Learning Machine for Class Imbalanced Learning

Miaoxing Xu and Yuanlong Yu[✉]

College of Mathematics and Computer Science, Fuzhou University,
Fuzhou 350116, Fujian, China
yu.yuanlong@fzu.edu.cn

Abstract. Compared to conventional machine learning techniques, extreme learning machine (ELM) which trains single-hidden-layer feedforward neural networks (SLFNs) shows faster-learning speed and better generalization performances. However, like most representative supervised learning algorithms, ELM tends to produce biased decision models when datasets are imbalanced. In this paper, two-stage weighted regularized ELM is proposed to address the aforementioned issue. The original regularized ELM (RELM) was proposed to handle adverse effects of outliers but not target the imbalanced learning problem. So we proposed a new weighted regularized ELM (WRELM) for class imbalance learning (CIL) in the first stage. Different from the existing weighted ELM which only considers the class distribution of datasets, the proposed algorithm also puts more focus on hard, misclassified samples in the second stage. The focal loss function is adopted to update weight by decreasing the weight of well-classified samples to focus more attention on the error of difficult samples. The final decision target is determined by the winner-take-all method. We assess the proposed method on 25 binary datasets and 10 multiclass datasets by 5-folder cross validations. The results indicate the proposed algorithm is an efficient method for CIL and exceed other CIL algorithms based on ELM.

Keywords: Class imbalance learning (CIL) ·
Extreme learning machine · Cost-sensitive learning

1 Introduction

Nowadays, with the arrival of the information age, more and more data has been produced continuously in many complex, large-scale systems. Although there have been many knowledge discovery and data engineering techniques which have shown great success in many applications, imbalanced data learning is still

M. Xu—This work is supported by National Natural Science Foundation of China (NSFC) under grant 61473089.

a major challenge that has attracted academia and industry attention [1]. Most traditional machine learning algorithms, like support vector machine, expect balanced class distributions, but the most data distributions are extremely imbalanced in the real world such as medical diagnostics [2] and fraud detection [3]. Since traditional classifiers use the overall classification accuracy as the learning target, in order to obtain greater accuracy, the algorithm will inevitably lead the classifier to pay much attention to the majority class, which will reduce the performance of the minority class. However, in most cases, we draw more attention to the minority class. In other words, the cost of misclassifying minority class samples is more severe than the majority class, especially in the medical industry [4].

To address the problem of class imbalance learning (CIL), different solutions are categorized into data-level approaches and algorithm-level approaches [5]. The purpose of data-level approaches is to oversample the minority class or undersample the majority class to balance the quantity of each class [6–8]. The synthetic minority oversampling technique(SMOTE) [6] is the most representative data-level approaches by creating synthetic minority instances instead of simple resampling. On the other hand, algorithm-level approaches aim to amend traditional classifiers for matching imbalanced datasets [9–12]. Cost-sensitive learning [9,10], one-class learning [11] and ensemble methods [12] are widely employed to solve the imbalanced learning problem.

Owing to fast learning speed and great generalization performance, extreme learning machine (ELM) [13,14] has drawn more and more attention of researchers. However, like most representative supervised learning algorithms, ELM tends to produce biased decision models when datasets are imbalanced. In previous work about ELM, several CIL methods have been proposed. Weighted ELM (WELM) [9] was proposed to assign different misclassification weights empirically for each class. Boosting WELM [21] combined weighted ELM [9] with the AdaBoost framework to allocate weight of each sample adaptively. Flexible naive Bayesian (FNB) [15] classifier was applied to determined samples' weight by calculating the posterior probability of sample in naive Bayesian-based WELM (NBWELM) [16].

Although there have been some CIL algorithms based on ELM, how to assign samples' weight for better decision model is still an open and significant problem. In this paper, we propose a two-stage weighted regularized ELM (TS-WRELM) to address the aforementioned issue. The original regularized ELM (RELM) [17] was proposed to handle outliers in datasets but not target the imbalanced learning problem. So we propose a new and effective weighted regularized ELM (WRELM) for CIL. In our method, the first stage is to train the proposed WRELM. In the second stage, the focal loss function [18] is utilized to update weight based on the sample's posterior probability which can be calculated approximately by the actual outputs of the first stage WRELM [19]. The main idea of the second stage is to put more attention on hard, misclassified samples. The final decision target is determined by the winner-take-all method. We assess the proposed method on 25 binary KEEL datasets and 10 multiclass

KEEL datasets by 5-folder cross validations. The results indicate the proposed algorithm is a effective method for CIL and exceed other CIL algorithms based on ELM.

The remainder of this paper is organized as follows. Section 2 reviews related knowledge on ELM and assessment metrics used in this paper. The proposed method is described in Sect. 3. Experimental results and analyses are provided in Sect. 4. Finally, Conclusions are given in Sect. 5.

2   Preliminary Knowledge

2.1   ELM

The structure of ELM [13,14] is a single-hidden-layer feedforward neural networks (SLFNs). Different from conventional feedforward networks learning methods such as back-propagation (BP) algorithm, ELM's hidden neuron parameters are randomly initialized while the output weights need be trained by the Moore-Penrose generalized inverse. More detailly, given N training sample pairs$(\mathbf{x}_i, \mathbf{t}_i)$, where $\mathbf{x}_i$ is a feature vector and $\mathbf{t}_i$ is target vector of length m which is defined as Eq. (1), the mathematical model of the SLFNs can be described as Eq. (2).

$$t_i[j] = \begin{cases} 1 & \text{if} \quad \mathbf{x}_i \in \text{class j} \\ -1 & \text{if} \quad \mathbf{x}_i \notin \text{class j} \end{cases}, j \in \{1, \ldots, m\} \tag{1}$$

$$\underset{N \times L}{\mathbf{H}} \underset{L \times m}{\boldsymbol{\beta}} = \underset{N \times m}{\mathbf{T}} \tag{2}$$

where $\mathbf{H} = [\mathbf{h}(\mathbf{x}_1); \mathbf{h}(\mathbf{x}_2); \ldots; \mathbf{h}(\mathbf{x}_N))]_{N \times L}$ is the hidden layer output matrix , $\boldsymbol{\beta}$ with size of $L \times m$ is the output weight and $\mathbf{T} = [\mathbf{t}_1^T; \mathbf{t}_2^T; \ldots; \mathbf{t}_N^T]_{N \times m}$ is the ground truth matrix. The output of hidden layer with L nodes is denoted as a row vector $\mathbf{h}(\mathbf{x}) = [h_1(\mathbf{x}), \ldots, h_L(\mathbf{x})]$, where $h_i(\mathbf{x}) = G(\mathbf{a}_i, b_i, \mathbf{x})$ is the hidden layer node function and $\mathbf{a}_i, b_i$ are randomly initialized. Thus, the output weight $\boldsymbol{\beta}$ can be decided analytically by

$$\boldsymbol{\beta} = \mathbf{H}^\dagger \mathbf{T} = \begin{cases} (\mathbf{H}^T \mathbf{H})^{-1} \mathbf{H}^T \mathbf{T}, & \text{if} \quad N \geq L \\ \mathbf{H}^T (\mathbf{H} \mathbf{H}^T)^{-1} \mathbf{T}, & \text{if} \quad N < L \end{cases} \tag{3}$$

In order to alleviate over-fitting problem and get better generalization performance, the constrained optimization based ELM [13] is proposed as follows:

$$\text{Minimize:} \quad \mathbf{L}_{ELM} = \frac{1}{2} \|\boldsymbol{\beta}\|_F^2 + \frac{C}{2} \sum_{i=1}^{N} \|\boldsymbol{\xi}_i\|^2 \tag{4}$$

$$\text{Subject to:} \quad \mathbf{h}(\mathbf{x}_i)\boldsymbol{\beta} = \mathbf{t}_i^T - \boldsymbol{\xi}_i^T, i = 1, \ldots, N$$

where $\boldsymbol{\xi}_i$ denotes the training error vector of sample $\mathbf{x}_i$ and constant C is the regularization factor. By KKT theorem, the solution of output weight is:

$$\beta = \begin{cases} \left(\dfrac{I}{C} + \mathbf{H}^T\mathbf{H}\right)^{-1} \mathbf{H}^T\mathbf{T}, & \text{if } N \geq L \\[2mm] \mathbf{H}^T \left(\dfrac{I}{C} + \mathbf{H}\mathbf{H}^T\right)^{-1} \mathbf{T}, & \text{if } N < L \end{cases} \tag{5}$$

2.2 Assessment Metrics

In the terms of class imbalance learning, traditional assessment metrics like overall accuracy cannot provide enough information about a classifier's functionality with respect to the type of classification required [1]. For example, for a 99:1 imbalanced data set, a classifier completely misclassify a small number of samples as the majority class. In this case, the overall accuracy is still very high, that is, 99%, whereas the accuracy of minority class samples is 0%.

G-mean is the geometric means of recall values of all m classes. It is defined as

$$G\text{-}mean = \left(\prod_{v=1}^{m} R_v\right)^{\frac{1}{m}} \tag{6}$$

where $R_v = n_v/N_v$ denotes the recall value of class $v, v = 1, \ldots, m$. n_v is the number of samples which are classified correctly as class v and N_v is the number of samples belonging to class v in real. For the previous example, the G-mean is 0% since the recall of minority is 0. Due to its characteristics and widely used in the imbalanced learning field, G-mean is adopted as assessment metrics in this paper.

3 Two-Stage WRELM

3.1 Proposed WRELM for CIL

According to the preliminary knowledge about ELM from Sect. 2.1, all training samples' output vectors can form a linear representation $\mathbf{H}\beta$. In order to cope with the imbalance learning problem, the training error of each training sample is weighted by using a diagonal weight matrix $\mathbf{W}$, with size of $N \times N$. How to set initial weight matrix and update it will be discussed in Sect. 3.2. Thus the total training error of all training samples is defined as $\|\mathbf{W}(\mathbf{T} - \mathbf{H}\beta)\|_F^2$, where $\|\cdot\|_F^2$ denotes Frobenius norm of a matrix. So the training process can be represented as a constrained optimization problem:

$$\text{Minimize:} \quad \Psi(\beta, \boldsymbol{\xi}) = \frac{1}{2}\|\beta\|_F^2 + \frac{C}{2}\|\mathbf{W}\boldsymbol{\xi}\|_F^2 \tag{7}$$
$$\text{Subject to:} \quad \mathbf{H}\beta = \mathbf{T} - \boldsymbol{\xi}$$

where $\boldsymbol{\xi} = [\boldsymbol{\xi}_1, \ldots, \boldsymbol{\xi}_N]^T$ stands for training error matrix and C is used as a regularization factor to control the trade-off between the minimization of training errors and the maximization of the marginal distance. The aforementioned optimization problem can be addressed by Lagrange multiplier method:

$$L_p(\boldsymbol{\beta}, \boldsymbol{\xi}, \boldsymbol{\alpha}) = \frac{1}{2}\|\boldsymbol{\beta}\|_F^2 + \frac{C}{2}\|\mathbf{W}\boldsymbol{\xi}\|_F^2 - \boldsymbol{\alpha} \cdot (\mathbf{H}\boldsymbol{\beta} - \mathbf{T} + \boldsymbol{\xi}) \tag{8}$$

where $\boldsymbol{\alpha} \in R^{N \times m}$ is a Lagrange multiplier matrix. According to KKT optimization conditions, the partial derivatives of L_p about $\boldsymbol{\beta}, \boldsymbol{\xi}, \boldsymbol{\alpha}$ are obtained as follow:

$$\begin{cases} \dfrac{\partial L_p}{\partial \boldsymbol{\beta}} = 0 & \rightarrow & \boldsymbol{\beta} = \mathbf{H}^T\boldsymbol{\alpha} \\[2mm] \dfrac{\partial L_p}{\partial \boldsymbol{\xi}} = 0 & \rightarrow & \boldsymbol{\alpha} = C\mathbf{W}^T\mathbf{W}\boldsymbol{\xi} \\[2mm] \dfrac{\partial L_p}{\partial \boldsymbol{\alpha}} = 0 & \rightarrow & \boldsymbol{\xi} = \mathbf{T} - \mathbf{H}\boldsymbol{\beta} \end{cases} \tag{9}$$

Similar to Eq. (5), output weight can be obtained from Eq. (9):

$$\boldsymbol{\beta} = \begin{cases} \left(\dfrac{I}{C} + \mathbf{H}^T\mathbf{W}^T\mathbf{W}\mathbf{H}\right)^{-1} \mathbf{H}^T\mathbf{W}^T\mathbf{W}\mathbf{T}, & \text{if } N \geq L \\[3mm] \mathbf{H}^T \left(\dfrac{I}{C}(\mathbf{W}^T\mathbf{W})^{-1} + \mathbf{H}\mathbf{H}^T\right)^{-1} \mathbf{T}, & \text{if } N < L \end{cases} \tag{10}$$

So given a test sample $\mathbf{x}$, the output of WRELM is denoted as $\mathbf{f}(\mathbf{x}) = \mathbf{h}(\mathbf{x})\boldsymbol{\beta}$, where $\mathbf{f}(\mathbf{x}) = [f_1(\mathbf{x}), \ldots, f_m(\mathbf{x})]^T$ is the output function vector and $f_j(\mathbf{x})$ denotes the output function of the jth output node. The final predication label of $\mathbf{x}$ is determined by

$$\text{label}(\mathbf{x}) = \underset{i \in \{1, \ldots, m\}}{\arg\max} f_i(\mathbf{x}) \tag{11}$$

Inspired by [13], kernel technique can be employed into WRELM. That is, the output vector of the given test sample $\mathbf{x}$ using kernel WRELM (denoted as KWRELM) can be calculated based on Eq. (10):

$$\begin{aligned} \mathbf{f}(\mathbf{x})_{kernel} &= \mathbf{h}(\mathbf{x})\mathbf{H}^T \left(\frac{I}{C}(\mathbf{W}^T\mathbf{W})^{-1} + \mathbf{H}\mathbf{H}^T\right)^{-1} \mathbf{T} \\[3mm] &= \begin{bmatrix} \phi(\mathbf{x}, \mathbf{x}_1) \\ \vdots \\ \phi(\mathbf{x}, \mathbf{x}_N) \end{bmatrix}^T \left(\frac{I}{C}(\mathbf{W}^T\mathbf{W})^{-1} + \boldsymbol{\Phi}\right)^{-1} \mathbf{T} \end{aligned} \tag{12}$$

where

$$\boldsymbol{\Phi} = \mathbf{H}\mathbf{H}^T = \begin{bmatrix} \phi(\mathbf{x}_1, \mathbf{x}_1) & \cdots & \phi(\mathbf{x}_1, \mathbf{x}_N) \\ \vdots & \ddots & \vdots \\ \phi(\mathbf{x}_N, \mathbf{x}_1) & \cdots & \phi(\mathbf{x}_N, \mathbf{x}_N) \end{bmatrix} \tag{13}$$

and $\phi(\mathbf{x}_{n1}, \mathbf{x}_{n2})$ is a kernel function. In this paper, Gaussian function is adopted as the kernel function: $\phi(\mathbf{x}_{n1}, \mathbf{x}_{n2}) = \exp(-\sigma\|\mathbf{x}_{n1} - \mathbf{x}_{n2}\|^2)$, where σ is the kernel parameter.

3.2   Framework of TS-WRELM

How to set the diagonal weight matrix $\mathbf{W} = \text{diag}(w_{ii}), i = 1, \ldots, N$ is the key point in the proposed method. In WELM [9], with respect to a sample $\mathbf{x}_i \in$ class v, two weighting schemes based on class information are chosen as follows:

$$\text{Weighting scheme } W1 : w_{ii} = \frac{1}{N_v} \tag{14}$$

$$\text{Weighting scheme } W2 : w_{ii} = \begin{cases} \dfrac{1}{N_v} & \text{if } N_v \leq \text{AVG}(N_v) \\ \dfrac{0.618}{N_v} & \text{if } N_v > \text{AVG}(N_v) \end{cases} \tag{15}$$

where N_v is the number of samples belonging to class v and $\text{AVG}(N_v)$ denotes the average number of samples for all classes.

Different from the aforementioned two weighting schemes, we propose a two-stage WRELM framework to assign the weight of each sample. In the first stage, we initialize the weight matrix based on the class distribution of datasets as follows:

$$W_v = \sqrt{\frac{1}{N_v}} \tag{16}$$

$$\sum_{v=1}^{m} W_v^2 = 1 \tag{17}$$

where W_v denotes the weight of sample which belongs to class v, i.e., $w_{ii} = W_v$, if $\mathbf{x}_i \in$ class v. Eq. (17) is the normalization processing.

In the second stage, the focal loss function [18] is adopted to update weight based on the samples' posterior probability which can be calculated approximately by the actual outputs of samples in the proposed WRELM of the first stage [19]. According to the theory in [20], the outputs of the multilayer perceptron are proved as a posteriori probability functions of the classes being trained. Based on the method in [19], for the sack of saving time-consuming, basic sigmoid function are employed to map actual outputs of ELM to the posterior probabilities, i.e., the posterior probabilities can be calculated approximately by

$$P(y = 1|f_i(\mathbf{x})) = \frac{1}{1 + \exp(-f_i(\mathbf{x}))} \tag{18}$$

where $f_i(\mathbf{x})$ is the actual output of the i output node about the training sample $\mathbf{x}$. The normalized strategy is used to convert the posterior probabilities by

$$P'(y = 1|f_i(\mathbf{x})) = \frac{P(y = 1|f_i(\mathbf{x}))}{\sum_{j=1}^{m} P(y = 1|f_j(\mathbf{x}))} \tag{19}$$

where $P(y = 1|f_i(\mathbf{x}))$ is the original posterior probabilities, i.e., Eq. (18). In this paper, we use $P'(y = 1|f_v(\mathbf{x}))$ if $\mathbf{x} \in$ class v as the posterior probabilities of the training sample $\mathbf{x}$ about its real label.

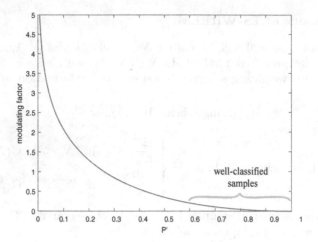

Fig. 1. Focal loss function

In the second stage, we put more attention on hard, misclassified samples. That is, the weight of samples whose posterior probabilities P' are large(i.e.well-classified samples) are decreased. the focal loss function [18] is defined as follows:

$$\text{FL}(P') = -(1 - P')^\gamma \log(P') \tag{20}$$

where $\gamma \geq 0$ is a tunable focusing parameter. In this paper, we fix γ to 1. Fig. 1 shows the focal loss function for $\gamma = 1$. From the Fig. 1, we can find that when a sample is misclassified and P' is small, the modulating factor is close to 1. It means that the sample's weight remains the same. Meanwhile, as $P' \to 1$, the factor tends to 0, i.e., the weights for well-classified samples are decreased. For a training sample $\mathbf{x}_i \in$ class v, Eqs. (21)(22) is applied to update the weight:

$$\text{Update weight: } w'_{ii} = W_v \times \text{FL}(P'(\mathbf{x}_i)) \tag{21}$$

$$\sum_{\mathbf{x}_i \in \text{class } v} w'^2_{ii} = \frac{1}{m} \tag{22}$$

where m is the total number of category and Eq. (22) is used for normalizing the weights inside each class, which keeps the weights from gathering into the majority [21]. The second stage WRELM is trained using the aforementioned updated weights. The final prediction label of a test sample $\mathbf{x}$ is determined by winner-take-all strategy:

$$\text{label}(\mathbf{x}) = \underset{i \in \{1,...,m\}}{\arg\max} \{f_i^1(\mathbf{x}), f_i^2(\mathbf{x})\} \tag{23}$$

where $f_i^1(\mathbf{x})$ and $f_i^2(\mathbf{x})$ denote the first stage and second stage WRELM, respectively. More details about two-stage WRELM are shown in Algorithm 1.

Algorithm 1. Two-Stage WRELM for CIL

1: **Input:** Training set $\aleph = \{(\mathbf{x}_i, \mathbf{t}_i), \mathbf{x}_i \in R^n, \mathbf{t}_i \in R^m, i = 1, 2, \dots, N\}$.
2: **The First Stage:**
3: **Initialization** $\mathbf{W}_1 = \mathrm{diag}(w_{ii}), i = 1, \dots, N$, where w_{ii} is determined by Eq.(16)(17).
4: Train the first stage WRELM classifier $\mathbf{f}^1$ using $\aleph$ and $\mathbf{W}_1$ by Eq.(10), where $\mathbf{f}^1(\mathbf{x}) = [f_1^1(\mathbf{x}), \dots, f_m^1(\mathbf{x})]^T$.
5: **The Second Stage:**
6: Update weight matrix: $\mathbf{W}_2 = \mathrm{diag}(w'_{ii})$, where w'_{ii} can be obtained by Eqs. (21)(22).
7: Train the second stage WRELM classifier $\mathbf{f}^2$ based on $\aleph$ and $\mathbf{W}_2$ by Eq. (10), where $\mathbf{f}^2(\mathbf{x}) = [f_1^2(\mathbf{x}), \dots, f_m^2(\mathbf{x})]^T$.
8: **Test:** Given a test sample $\mathbf{x}$, the final predication label is decided by Eq. (23).

---

4 Experiments

4.1 Datasets Description and Parameter Setting

In the experiments, 25 binary datasets and 10 multiclass datasets are used to assess the performance of the proposed algorithm. These datasets with 5-folder cross validations can be download from the KEEL dataset repository[1]. The result is averaged over 10 runs.

The imbalance ratio (IR) is a tool to quantitatively evaluate the imbalance degree of a dataset. It is defined as follows:

$$\text{Binary:} \quad IR = \frac{\#\text{majority}}{\#\text{minority}}$$
$$\text{Multiclass:} \quad IR = \frac{\max(N_v)}{\min(N_v)}, v \in 1, \dots, m \tag{24}$$

where #majority and #minority are the number of the majority class and the minority class, respectively. Tables 1 and 2 show detailed description of these datasets.

Referring to [13], 2 parameters need to be tuned for ELMs: the regularization factor C and the number of hidden nodes L. A grid search of C on $\{2^{-18}, 2^{-16}, \dots, 2^{48}, 2^{50}\}$ and L on $\{10, 20, \dots, 990, 1000\}$ is conducted in seek of the optimal result. In kernel ELMs, we need to tune the trade-off C and the kernel parameter σ. C and σ are searched in the range of $\{2^{-18}, 2^{-16}, \dots, 2^{48}, 2^{50}\}$ and $\{2^{-18}, 2^{-16}, \dots, 2^{18}, 2^{20}\}$, respectively. In focal loss function, we fix the focusing parameter γ to 1.

4.2 Experimental Results

In this paper, we compared the proposed TS-WRELM and TS-KWRELM with weighted ELM (WELM), kernel weighted ELM (KWELM) [9] and boosting

---

[1] http://sci2s.ugr.es/keel/imbalanced.php.

Table 1. Description for imbalanced binary-class datasets

DataSets	# of Attributes	# of TrainData	# of TestData	Imbalance ratio
abalone19	8	3339	835	128.21
yeast5	8	1187	297	32.89
shuttle-c2-vs-c4	9	1740	435	853
glass5	9	171	43	23.42
yeast-2_vs_8	8	385	97	23.04
yeast-1-4-5-8_vs_7	8	554	139	22.08
glass-0-1-6_vs_5	9	147	37	20
abalone9-18	8	584	147	16.67
glass4	9	171	43	16.1
ecoli4	7	268	68	15.75
yeast-1_vs_7	7	367	92	14.29
shuttle-c0-vs-c4	9	1463	366	13.77
vowel0	13	790	198	9.98
yeast-2_vs_4	8	411	103	9.28
page-blocks0	10	4377	1095	8.8
new-thyroid1	5	172	43	5.14
ecoli1	7	268	68	3.39
glass-0-1-2-3_vs_4-5-6	9	171	43	3.28
vehicle1	18	676	170	2.91
vehicle2	18	676	170	2.89
haberman	3	244	62	2.81
yeast1	8	1187	297	2.46
glass0	9	173	43	2.09
iris0	4	120	30	2
glass1	9	171	43	1.85

Table 2. Description for imbalanced multiclass datasets

DataSets	# of Attributes	# of TrainData	# of TestData	Imbalance ratio
Shuttle	9	1740	435	853
Thyroid	21	576	144	36.94
Glass	9	171	43	8.44
Balance	4	500	125	5.88
Dermatology	34	286	72	5.55
New-thyroid	5	172	43	4.84
Penbased	16	880	220	1.95
Hayes-roth	4	105	27	1.7
Wine	13	142	36	1.5
Contraceptive	9	1178	295	1.89

Table 3. G-mean (%) value on binary datasets (bold denotes the best result, underline is the second best result on each dataset.)

DataSets	WELM1	WELM2	KWELM1	KWELM2	BWELM	TS-WRELM	TS-KWRELM
abalone19	77.19	64.27	74.47	68.35	77.72	**78.25**	<u>77.94</u>
yeast5	95.39	95.16	**98.18**	<u>98.14</u>	96.74	97.34	98.07
shuttle-c2-vs-c4	100.00	100.00	100.00	<u>99.60</u>	100.00	100.00	100.00
glass5	95.99	96.60	96.51	<u>97.26</u>	94.17	93.10	**99.25**
yeast-2_vs_8	75.56	76.01	77.89	<u>78.00</u>	75.96	75.91	**79.91**
yeast-1-4-5-8_vs_7	67.10	64.26	<u>69.32</u>	65.68	65.85	66.41	**69.47**
glass-0-1-6_vs_5	98.55	98.70	**98.85**	98.85	95.60	94.08	<u>98.84</u>
abalone9-18	87.99	88.72	89.76	86.83	<u>91.10</u>	91.02	**92.25**
glass4	91.34	91.46	91.17	91.17	94.25	<u>95.71</u>	**97.71**
ecoli4	97.83	95.90	**98.24**	97.42	97.92	98.01	<u>98.08</u>
yeast-1_vs_7	77.26	76.91	77.72	74.61	77.38	**81.12**	<u>80.52</u>
shuttle-c0-vs-c4	100.00	100.00	100.00	100.00	100.00	100.00	100.00
vowel0	100.00	100.00	100.00	100.00	100.00	100.00	100.00
yeast-2_vs_4	91.56	90.02	**91.88**	90.25	90.38	90.23	<u>91.72</u>
page-blocks0	93.21	93.40	93.61	92.98	**95.26**	<u>95.22</u>	93.43
new-thyroid1	99.44	<u>99.72</u>	<u>99.72</u>	99.72	<u>99.72</u>	99.69	100.00
ecoli1	90.69	90.26	**91.04**	90.25	90.10	<u>90.92</u>	90.56
glass-0-1-2-3_vs_4-5-6	94.68	93.14	<u>95.41</u>	<u>95.41</u>	95.19	94.15	**96.48**
vehicle1	85.30	83.44	<u>86.74</u>	85.72	75.60	73.44	**86.93**
vehicle2	99.12	98.78	<u>99.45</u>	99.38	95.69	93.01	**99.60**
haberman	65.11	59.26	**66.26**	60.91	61.73	65.21	<u>65.49</u>
yeast1	72.57	70.32	<u>73.17</u>	70.33	71.93	71.70	**73.37**
glass0	81.17	82.62	**85.65**	<u>85.59</u>	76.32	74.28	81.24
iris0	100.00	100.00	100.00	100.00	100.00	100.00	100.00
glass1	78.31	79.32	<u>80.35</u>	77.48	75.49	72.55	**81.65**

Table 4. G-mean (%) value on multiclass datasets (bold denotes the best result, underline is the second best result on each dataset.)

DataSets	WELM1	WELM2	KWELM1	KWELM2	BWELM	TS-WRELM	TS-KWRELM
Wine	84.64	83.64	**97.57**	96.60	89.10	84.27	<u>97.33</u>
Balance	84.43	83.77	75.57	75.16	<u>90.72</u>	87.61	**91.78**
Shuttle	78.24	**82.81**	79.14	79.14	78.58	79.26	<u>79.39</u>
Thyroid	70.55	65.36	62.91	61.37	68.55	<u>71.84</u>	**74.93**
Glass	60.96	56.75	58.49	58.49	<u>62.22</u>	60.78	**68.37**
Dermatology	96.73	96.35	**97.60**	96.73	97.02	96.89	<u>97.59</u>
New-thyroid	<u>98.29</u>	98.28	96.19	94.77	98.12	**98.62**	96.76
Penbased	97.37	97.31	<u>98.35</u>	98.25	97.77	97.40	**98.44**
Hayes-roth	83.37	83.79	**85.08**	**85.08**	83.55	<u>83.93</u>	**85.08**
Contraceptive	56.60	54.05	55.64	50.39	56.74	<u>56.68</u>	**57.26**

weighted ELM (BWELM) [21]. Two weighting schemes are applied to WELM and KWELM, so we denote them as WELM1, WELM2, KWELM1, KWELM2, respectively.

From Tables 3 and 4, we can find that, for most datasets, our proposed method (TS-WRELM, TS-KWRELM) have the best performance. In Table 3, as for binary datasets, the proposed methods acquire best result on 17 binary datasets and second best result on 9 datasets. As shown in Table 4, the proposed methods achieve best G-mean on 7 multiclass datasets and second best result on 6 multiclass dataset. The results prove our method is helpful for settling class imbalance learning. Particularly, compared to TS-WRELM, TS-KWRELM have more efficient to address imbalanced learning problem.

5   Conclusions

This paper proposes a two-stage weighted regularized ELM (TS-WRELM) for class imbalance learning (CIL). The original regularized ELM (RELM) was proposed to handle adverse effects of outliers but not target the imbalanced learning problem. So a weighted regularized ELM (WRELM) is proposed for CIL in the first stage. Different from existing weighted ELM which assigns weight of sample by the class distribution of dataset, the proposed algorithm put more attention on hard and misclassified samples. The samples' posterior probability which can be calculated approximately by the output of WRELM, is used as the difficulty level of classifying sample correctly. The focal loss function is applied to update the weight of sample in the second stage, which decreases the weight of well-classified samples to focus more attention on the error of difficult and misclassified sample. The winner-take-all strategy is adopted to decide the final label. Experiment results on 25 binary datasets and 10 multiclass datasets indicate that the proposed algorithm is an efficient method for CIL, and outperform weighted ELM and boosting ELM in most datasets.

References

1. He, H., Garcia, E.A.: Learning from imbalanced data. IEEE Trans. Knowl. Data Eng. **9**, 1263–1284 (2008)
2. Cheng, T.-H., Hu, P.J.-H.: A data-driven approach to manage the length of stay for appendectomy patients. IEEE Trans. Syst. Man Cybern.-Part A: Syst. Hum. **39**(6), 1339–1347 (2009)
3. Zakaryazad, A., Duman, E.: A profit-driven artificial neural network (ANN) with applications to fraud detection and direct marketing. Neurocomputing **175**, 121–131 (2016)
4. Rao, R.B., Krishnan, S., Niculescu, R.S.: Data mining for improved cardiac care. ACM SIGKDD Explor. Newslett. **8**(1), 3–10 (2006)
5. Rout, N., Mishra, D., Mallick, M.K.: Handling imbalanced data: a survey. In: Reddy, M.S., Viswanath, K., K.M., S.P. (eds.) International Proceedings on Advances in Soft Computing, Intelligent Systems and Applications. AISC, vol. 628, pp. 431–443. Springer, Singapore (2018). https://doi.org/10.1007/978-981-10-5272-9_39
6. Chawla, N.V., Bowyer, K.W., Hall, L.O., Kegelmeyer, W.P.: Smote: synthetic minority over-sampling technique. J. Artif. Intell. Res. **16**, 321–357 (2002)

7. Liu, X.-Y., Wu, J., Zhou, Z.-H.: Exploratory undersampling for class-imbalance learning. IEEE Trans. Syst. Man Cybern. Part B (Cybern.) **39**(2), 539–550 (2009)
8. He, H., Bai, Y., Garcia, E.A., Li, S.: ADASYN: adaptive synthetic sampling approach for imbalanced learning. In: 2008 IEEE International Joint Conference on Neural Networks, IEEE World Congress on Computational Intelligence, IJCNN 2008, pp. 1322–1328. IEEE (2008)
9. Zong, W., Huang, G.-B., Chen, Y.: Weighted extreme learning machine for imbalance learning. Neurocomputing **101**, 229–242 (2013)
10. Zhou, Z.-H., Liu, X.-Y.: Training cost-sensitive neural networks with methods addressing the class imbalance problem. IEEE Trans. Knowl. Data Eng. **18**(1), 63–77 (2006)
11. Zhuang, L., Dai, H.: Parameter estimation of one-class SVM on imbalance text classification. In: Lamontagne, L., Marchand, M. (eds.) AI 2006. LNCS (LNAI), vol. 4013, pp. 538–549. Springer, Heidelberg (2006). https://doi.org/10.1007/11766247_46
12. Krawczyk, B., Schaefer, G.: An improved ensemble approach for imbalanced classification problems. In: 2013 IEEE 8th International Symposium on Applied Computational Intelligence and Informatics (SACI), pp. 423–426. IEEE (2013)
13. Huang, G.-B., Zhou, H., Ding, X., Zhang, R.: Extreme learning machine for regression and multiclass classification. IEEE Trans. Syst. Man Cybern. Part B (Cybern.) **42**(2), 513–529 (2012)
14. Huang, G.-B., Zhu, Q.-Y., Siew, C.-K.: Extreme learning machine: theory and applications. Neurocomputing **70**(1–3), 489–501 (2006)
15. Demšar, J.: Statistical comparisons of classifiers over multiple data sets. J. Mach. Learn. Res. **7**, 1–30 (2006)
16. Wang, J., Zhang, L., Cao, J.-J., Han, D.: NBWELM: naive Bayesian based weighted extreme learning machine. Int. J. Mach. Learn. Cybern. **9**, 1–15 (2014)
17. Deng, W., Zheng, Q., Chen, L.: Regularized extreme learning machine. In: 2009 IEEE Symposium on Computational Intelligence and Data Mining, CIDM 2009, pp. 389–395. IEEE (2009)
18. Lin, T.-Y., Goyal, P., Girshick, R., He, K., Dollar, P.: Focal loss for dense object detection. In: 2017 IEEE International Conference on Computer Vision (ICCV), pp. 2999–3007. IEEE (2017)
19. Yu, H., Sun, C., Yang, W., Yang, X., Zuo, X.: AL-ELM: one uncertainty-based active learning algorithm using extreme learning machine. Neurocomputing **166**, 140–150 (2015)
20. Ruck, D.W., Rogers, S.K., Kabrisky, M., Oxley, M.E., Suter, B.W.: The multilayer perceptron as an approximation to a Bayes optimal discriminant function. IEEE Trans. Neural Netw. **1**(4), 296–298 (1990)
21. Li, K., Kong, X., Lu, Z., Wenyin, L., Yin, J.: Boosting weighted ELM for imbalanced learning. Neurocomputing **128**, 15–21 (2014)

Covering Path with Minimum Movement: Complexity and Algorithms

Huafu Liu and Zhixiong Liu[(✉)]

Department of Mathematics and Computer Science, Changsha University,
Changsha, Hunan, China
hfliu9063@163.com, lzxterry@163.com

Abstract. In this paper, we study a special coverage problem, called *Path Coverage*, which has applications in many fields. Our objective is to move minimum steps of sensors to cover the path. Firstly, we prove that the problem is NP-hard. Then, a heuristic algorithm is given for the problem based on the analysis of the relation between sensors and points in the path. Simulation experiments are conducted to evaluate the effects of some parameters on the sensor moving distance.

Keywords: Path coverage · Move minimum steps of sensors · Algorithm

1 Introduction

Wireless sensor network (WSN) is deployed in the monitoring area by a large number of cheap sensor nodes through wireless communication to form a multi hop self-organizing network system. The purpose is to perceive collaboration, acquisition and processing of network coverage area by sensing the object information, and then send to the observer. In wireless sensor networks, there are two important research issues: path coverage and sensor movement. Path coverage aims to cover a set of specified points of path in the deployment region of a WSN. In some 0–1 models, points are required to be covered k times [1], while in some the probability model, the point is required that the covering probability to be at least d. The sensor movement problem is to minimize sensors' movement to cover target [2].

For path coverage problem, Hefeeda et al. [5] gave an efficient approximation algorithm which achieves a solution for k-coverage in dense sensor networks, and Zhang et al. [6] gave an algorithm for path coverage problem and mainly uses the probabilistic model, without considering the movability of sensors. For sensor movement problem, Liao et al. [2] gave an algorithm for problem minimizing Movement for Target Coverage. Fu et al. [7] gave an algorithm to schedule sensors for recovering a certain number of fault sensor, which has some limitations, for example, each sensor can only recover a failed sensor, and the maximum moving distance of a single sensor is limited. Moreover, there are many related works about coverage and movement [7–10].

In the paper, we consider a special case of problem. For a given path P and a set of deployed sensors, the problem is how to move sensor in minimum distance to cover the path P such that for each path point j, the covering probability of point j is at least d (the

© Springer Nature Singapore Pte Ltd. 2019
F. Sun et al. (Eds.): ICCSIP 2018, CCIS 1005, pp. 370–384, 2019.
https://doi.org/10.1007/978-981-13-7983-3_33

Path Coverage problem). We must ensure the robustness of the mobile sensor network. Therefore, the probability of each point being detected must be greater than a threshold value. Meanwhile the sensor is usually powered by an energy limited battery. Thus, energy consumption should be the primary consideration in mobile sensor networks [2]. In particular, the movement of the sensor should be minimized in order to prolong the lifetime of the network, since the movement of the sensor consumes more energy than sensing and communication do [3, 4]. Thus we want to move sensor as little as possible.

The main contribution of our paper is that we give an algorithm solving the problem, and we prove that the Path Coverage problem is NP-hard. Based on the analysis of the problem, several algorithms are given to solve the problem in heuristic way. Simulation experiments are conducted to evaluate the effects of some parameters on the sensor moving distance.

The rest of the paper is organized as follows. The problem is given in Sect. 2. In Sect. 3, the solutions to the problem are presented. Section 4 discusses the simulation results.

2 Problem Analysis

2.1 Sensor Covering Path Problem

Problem 1 (Path Coverage problem). Given a path P, a set of deployed sensors S, and a set Q of points of P, move minimum distance of the sensors to cover the path P such that for each point j in Q, the covering probability of point j is at least d.

2.2 Hardness of the Problem

To show the hardness of the Path Coverage problem, we introduce Target Coverage (TCOV) problem.

Problem 2 (Target Coverage (TCOV) problem) [2]. Given m targets with known locations and n mobile sensors deployed randomly in the task area, move sensors to new positions such that all the targets are covered and the total movement of sensors is minimized.

Theorem 1. The Path Coverage problem is NP-hard.

Proof. The proof is a reduction from the Target Coverage problem. In the Target Coverage problem: assume that there are m targets and n sensors in the network, move sensors to new positions such that all the targets are covered and the total movement of sensors is minimized. We construct The Sensor Covering path problem as follows, let path P be created by sorting these targets by x-coordinates, and set the target with minimum x-coordinate as the start point, and the target with maximum x-coordinate as the end point, respectively, then path P is formed by connecting all target points successively. If some target points possess a same x-coordinate, then they are connected according to y-coordinate, and move sensors to cover the path with minimum distance.

If there are m new positions of the sensors that can cover the m targets with movement in minimum distance, since the path P is created by m targets, we can cover the m discrete point in the path. Then m new positions of the sensors can also cover the path P with minimum distance in Path Coverage problem.

On the other hand, assume that there are m new positions of the sensors can cover the path P with movement in minimum distance. Thus, the path has m discrete points that are covered by these sensors, and the m discrete points are the m targets in the Target Coverage problem, therefore the m new positions of the Sensor can also cover m the targets with minimum in Target Coverage problem.

Ref [2] proved Target Coverage problem is NP-hard. Therefore, Path Coverage problem is NP-hard.

2.3 Preliminaries

2.3.1 Measurement of Monitoring
The probability of sensor s monitoring target t.

$$P_{ts} = 1, if\ 0 \le dist(s,t) \le R_1; \tag{1}$$

$$P_{ts} = e^{\beta(dist(s,t)-R_1)}, if\ R_1 \le dist(s,t) \le R_2 \tag{2}$$

$$P_{ts} = 0, if\ dist(s,t) \ge R_2; \tag{3}$$

If point j is covered by N sensors $(s_1, s_2, \ldots, s_N)$, then P_j is defined as the summation of all the covering probabilities of the sensors in $(s_1, s_2, \ldots, s_N)$.

$$P_j = 1 - \bigcup_{i=1}^{N}(1 - P_{ji}) \tag{4}$$

For each path point v, let $S(v)$ be the set of sensors covering v. For each sensor u, let $P(u)$ be the set of path points covered by sensor u.

Assume that Q is a set of N path points $(p_1, p_2, \ldots, p_N)$, and their x-coordinate are ordered in nondecreasing order. We define N_j$^+$ (p_i) to be p_{i+j}, and N_j$^-$ (p_i) to be p_{i-j}.

2.3.2 Redundant Sensor
For any point j in Q whose covering probabilities is at least d, if P_j is still no less than d when sensor s_i is deleted from $S(j)$, then s_i is called a redundant sensor.

To make the covering probabilities of target point k to be at least d, and for any point j in Q except point k whose covering probabilities is at least d, if P_j is still no less than d when sensor s_i is deleted from $S(j)$, then s_i is also called a redundant sensor.

2.3.3 Redundant Path
For a set of points $p_1, p_2, \ldots, p_i$, where p_{j+1} is neighbor of p_j. The covering probability of p_1 less than d, No redundant sensor can be found in $p_1, p_3, \ldots, p_{i-1}$, and p_i has

redundant sensors s_i. Find a set of sensors s_2, s_3, ..., s_i, such that s_i is moved to p_{i-1}, ..., s_2 is moved to monitor p_1, and guarantee that all points p_1, p_2, ..., p_i have coverage probability at least d. Then R−P(p_1, p_i) is called a redundant path.

2.4   Our Techniques

For sensor covering path problem, we can transform the problem into three sub-problems. If these three problems are solved, sensors covering path problem can be solved. The three sub-problems are:

1. How to make the path curve discretization?
2. There may exist some sensors that do not cover any point of the path. How to move those sensors to cover at least one point of path P?
3. How to move the sensors to cover all the path points in minimum distance?

3   The Algorithm

3.1   Discretization of Path

At first, we solve the sub-problem 1 to discretize the path curve. We formalize the problem as follows.

Problem 3 (Path curve discretization). Given a path P, make path curve discretization, which generates a set of discrete points, denoted by Q.

In our algorithm **generate-path** for this problem, we set a step-value d at first, and take a point in the path P whose x-coordinate has distance d to the current point. The specific algorithm is given in Fig. 1.

Algorithm 1 generate-path (n, min-interval, max-interval)

Input: a path P, an integer n, and the cover interval is (min-interval, max-interval)

Output: n discrete points of path P.

1. Set a step-value d to be (max-interval − min-interval) /n;

2. Q is empty set;

3. For i from 1 to n

   $x_i = d*(i - 0.5)$;

   Take the point (f(xi), xi), and add it to Q;

4. return Q;

Fig. 1. Algorithm for path curve discretization

It is easy to see that algorithm **generate-path** runs in $O(n)$ time, where n is the number points obtained.

3.2 Initialization

As for sub-problem 2, there may exist some sensors that do not cover any point of the path P. Now we study how to move those sensors to cover at least one point of path P. The problem can be defined as follows.

Problem 4 (Initializing sensor coverage). Given a set of deployed sensors S, and a set Q of points of P, move minimum distance of every sensor which covers no point of P such that each sensor covers at least one point of P.

For this problem, for every sensor, we decide whether it covers a point, if it covers no path point, then we move the sensor to the nearest path point, and let the distance between the sensor and path point be R_2. The specific algorithm solving problem 3 is given in Fig. 2.

Algorithm 2 Init (Q, n, S, m)

Input: a set Q of points of P, n is the size of Q, a set of deployed sensor S, and m is the size of S

Output: Move S in the shortest distance so that for every sensor s_i in S there exist a point p_j in Q which dist (s_i, p_j) is at most R_2;

1   For i from 1 to m

2   If the distance from sensor s_i to every point in Q is greater than R_2 then

3   Move s_i to its nearest point p_j in Q so that dist (s_i, p_j) is equal to R_2;

4   return;

Fig. 2. Algorithm for initializing sensor coverage

In algorithm **Init**, finding the nearest path point can be done in $O(n)$ time, and we need judge every sensor. Thus, algorithm **Init** runs in time $O(nm)$, where n is the number of path points and m is the number of sensors.

3.3 Moving Rules

Now we solve the sub-problem 3, i.e., how to move the sensors to cover all the path points. For this problem, we can use the following three rules to move sensors.

Rule 1. For a point p_j with coverage probability less than d, check all the redundant sensors in $S(p_j)$. If at least one sensor can be found, then move the redundant sensor which is nearest to p_j to make p_j have coverage probability no less than d.

Rule 2. If there exists a redundant path R−P(p_i, p_k) and set S(p_j) has a redundant sensor, and j is equal to i-1, then move the redundant sensor which is the nearest to p_i to make p_i have coverage probability no less than d.

Rule 3. If there exists a redundant path R−P(p_i, p_k), and set S(p_j) has a redundant sensor, and j is not equal to i−1, then move the redundant sensor which is the nearest to p_{j-1} to make p_{j-1} have a redundant sensor.

For the sub-problem 3, if the covering probability of point p_j is less than d, then we try to find a redundant sensor in S(p_j). If a redundant sensor can be found in S(p_j), we can apply Rule 1. If Rule 1 is not workable, then we need to find a redundant path. If a redundant path exists, then we apply Rules 2–3 to move redundant sensors in minimum distance.

For the above three rules, it is necessary to find the nearest redundant sensor to a point. We give the definition of how to find a redundant sensor.

Problem 5 (Finding redundant Sensor). Given a point i, a set Q of points of P, an integer n which is the size of Q, a set of deployed sensor S, an integer m which is the size of S, and an integer direct, where direct is variable indicating the left or right neighbor of current point, find the closest redundant sensor from the neighbors of point i in Q.

For this problem, we first need to determine whether there is a redundant sensor. We can use redundant sensor definition to decide whether a given sensor i is a redundant sensor or not.

Problem 6 (redundant-sensor). Given a sensor s, a set Q of points of P, an integer n which is the size of Q, a set of deployed sensor S, and an integer m which is the size of S, the objective is to determine whether s is a redundant sensor.

If the covering probability of point is at least d before removing sensor s and is less than d when removing sensor s, then sensor s cannot be a redundant sensor. The specific algorithm judging a redundant sensor is given in Fig. 3.

Algorithm 3 Judge-redundant-sensor(s, Q, n, S, m)

Input: a sensor s, a set Q of points of P, an integer m which is the size of Q, a set of deployed sensor S, and an integer m which is the size of S

Output: if s is a redundant sensor then return s, otherwise return NULL.

1   For i from 1 to n

2   If the P_i is at least d then

3   If the P_i is less than d when s is removed then

4   return NULL;

5   return s;

Fig. 3. Algorithm for judging a redundant sensor

It is easy to see that algorithm **Judge-redundant-sensor** is of running time O(nm).

If there exists a redundant sensor, we need to determine whether the redundant sensor is the nearest to the neighbors of point i. The specific algorithm to find the nearest redundant sensor to the neighbors of point i is given in Fig. 4.

Algorithm 4 Find-redundant-sensor (i, Q, n, S, m, *direct*)

Input: a set Q of points of P, an integer n which is the size of Q, a set of deployed sensor S, an integer m which is the size of S, a point i.

Output: If there exists a redundant sensor in S(i), then return the redundant sensor nearest to N_dir (i), otherwise return NULL.

1   If *direct* == left then

2   Let N_dir (i) be N_1$^+$(i)

3   Else if *direct* == right then

4   Let N_dir (i) be N_1$^-$(i)

5   Else if *direct* == self

6   Let N_dir (i) be i;

7   remove i from Q;

8   If exist a redundant sensor s which is the nearest redundant sensor to N_dir (i) then

9   add i to Q;

10   return s;

11   Else Add i to Q;

12   return NULL;

Fig. 4. Algorithm for finding a redundant sensor

Since whether a point has a redundant sensor can be found in time O(nm), which can be done by algorithm **Judge-redundant-sensor**, the algorithm **Find-redundant-sensor** runs in time O(nm^2).

By Rules1–2, we can get the following problem.

Problem 7 (Last-move-sensor). Given a point p, a sensor s, a set Q of points of P, an integer n which is the size of Q, a set of deployed sensor S, and an integer m which is the size of S, move the shortest distance of sensor s to make the covering probability of p is at least d.

Based on the algorithms **Judge-redundant-sensor** and **Find-redundant-sensor**, the specific process solving problem 6 is given in Fig. 5.

Algorithm 5 Move-sensor1 (p, s, Q, n, S, m)

Input: In S (p) has a redundant sensor s, a set Q of points of P, an integer n is the size of Q, a set of deployed sensor S, an integer m is the size of S

Output: return a point p' such that s is moved to p' in the shortest distance so that P_p is no less than d and distance between them is no more than R_2.

1   Let *pro* be the covering probability of p when remove s;

2   If $pro >= d$ then

3        $dist\_temp = dist\ (p, s)$;

4   If $dist\_temp > R_2$ then

5            $len = R_2$;

6   else $len = dist\_temp$;

7   else

8        $pro\_temp = 1 - (1 - d) / (1 - pro)$;

9        $len = -\log\ (pro) / beta + R_1$;

10   if $len > R_2$ then $len = R_2$;

11   let p' be the point that $dist\ (p, p')$ is equal to *len*, and p' is the closest point to s;

12   return p';

Fig. 5. Algorithm for moving sensors

In algorithm **Move-sensor1**, we only calculate the covering probability of p when s is removed in $O(m)$, and the minimum distance we must to move s to make P_p at least d is in $O(1)$. Therefore, the algorithm **Move-sensor1** can be done in $O(m)$ time.

How to apply Rule 3 can be defined as the following problem.

Problem 8 (Move-min-dist-sensor). Given an path point p, a sensor s, a set Q of points of P, an integer n which is the size of Q, a set of deployed sensor S, and an integer m which is the size of S, move the shortest distance of sensor s to make N_1 (p) have a redundant sensor.

For the problem 7, the first case considered is how to make sensor s_{min_index} in S $(N\_1(p))$ which is nearest to $N\_2(p)$ become a redundant sensor. It is possible that when s_{min_index} becomes a redundant sensor, there may exist a set of points P_1 (p_{i1}, p_{i2}, ..., p_{il}) (each covering probability of the points in P_1 is at least d before s_{min_index} becomes a redundant sensor) such that the covering probability of the points in P_1 is reduced to less than d in $P(s_{min\_index})$. Therefore, we need to move sensor s, and guarantee that the points in P_1 have covering probability at least d. Then the problem is transformed to seek some intersection of the circles, in which P_{pij} is at least d, and move sensor s in the shortest distance to the intersection. This position may be the only intersection between the circles, and the points of intersection of line segments from s to p_{ij} and circle. The specific process solving problem 7 is given in Fig. 6.

Algorithm 6 Move-sensor2 $(p, s, Q, n, S, m, direct)$

Input: $S(p)$ has a redundant sensor s, a set Q of points of P, an integer n which is the size of Q, a set of deployed sensor S, an integer m which is the size of S

Output: if s can be moved to a position to make N_1(p) has a redundant sensor, then move minimum finite distance to it, otherwise move-sensor1 (N_1(p), s, Q, n, S, m).

1   Let *fpoint* be the final position that s is moved to;

2   if *direct* ==LEFT then assume p_1 is the N_1$^+$ (p) and P_2 is the N_2$^+$ (p);

3   else if *direct* == RIGHT assume P_1 is the N_1$^-$ (p) and P_2 is the N_2$^-$ (p);

4   else return NULL;

5   If there is a redundant sensor s1 in $S(P_1)$ then

6   *fpoint* = s;   return;

7   If $S(P_1)$ has no sensor then

8   *fpoint*=move-sensor1 (P_1, s, Q, n, S, m);return *fpoint*;

9   In $S(P_1)$, let s_{min_index} be the nearest sensor to P_2.

10   For every point p_i in $P(s_{min\_index})$ whose covering probability is larger than d then

11   Move s to a region r_i such that covering probability p_i is still larger than d when remove s_{min_index}.

12   If there exists a position s_{opt} which is closest to the s in the intersection of all regions R(r_1, r_2, ..., r_k) then

13   *fpoint* = s_{opt};   return *fpoint*;

14   else *fpoint*=move-sensor1 (p_1, s, Q, n, S, m); return *fpoint*;

Fig. 6. Algorithm for moving sensors with guaranteed redundant sensor

In algorithm **Move-sensor2**, the positions of intersections can be found in O(m^2) time. It is easy to see that algorithm **Move-sensor2** has running time O($m^2 + nm$).

3.4   General Algorithm

Based on the algorithms for three sub-problems, now we give an algorithm to solve problem 1, as given in Fig. 7.

Algorithm 7 Move-sensor-cover-path (Q, n, S, m)

Input: a set Q of points of P, an integer n which is the size of Q, a set of deployed sensor S, an integer m which is the size of S

Output: move minimum distance of S to cover Path P, or report that no movement can achieve this.

1   Sort all the points in P by their x-coordinates;

2   Calculate the covering probability of the points in Q;

3    $mv\_dist = 0$;

4    $init(Q, n, S, m, \&mv\_dist)$;   /*initialize sensor S*/

5   For i from 0 to n do

6   For j from 1 to n do

7   If the covering probability of point p_j is larger than d then

8   Continue;

9   If there is a redundant sensor s in S $(N\_i^+ (p_j))$ or in S$(N\_i^-(p_j))$

then

10   If $i == 0$ then

11                    $s' = $move-sensor1 (p_j, s, Q, n, S, m);

12   move s to s'; $mv_dist = mv_dist + $ dist (s', s);

13   else

14   If s in S $(N\_i^+ (p_j))$ then we let $direct$ = LEFT

15   Else let $direct$ = RIGHT.

16   Assume that point x' in $N\_i^+ (p_j)$ or $N\_i^-(p_j))$ has a

redundant sensor;

17   Let the path form x' to p_j be $(p_f, p_{f-1}, ..., p_1)$;

18   For $r = f$ down to 1 do

19   If there is a redundant sensor s in $S(p_r)$ then

20   If $r >= 2$ then $s' = $move-sensor2 $(p_r, s, Q, N, S, M,$

$direct)$;

21   else $s' = $move-sensor1 (p_j, s, Q, n, S, m);

22   move s to s'; $mv_dist = mv_dist + $ dist (s', s);

23   If there is no points with covering probability less than d then End step 5 and return mv_dist;

Fig. 7. Algorithm for sensor covering path problem

Based on the algorithm **Move-sensor1**and **Move-sensor2**, algorithm **Move-sensor-cover-path** has running time $O(n^4 m + n^3 m^2)$.

4 Experiments

In Fig. 8, for the initial position of the sensor, we randomly generate 80 sensors in the region of (0, 100) *(0, 100). For the path curve function, we use $y = 0.1 *$ $(x - 10) * (x - 20)(0 < x < 100)$ to generate path point. The threshold of coverage probability $d = 0.5$, and $\beta = 0.5$, $R_1 = 2.5$, $R_2 = 5$. In Fig. 8, we change the number of points of the path. It can be seen that the curve has a turning points around 5 path points. At the beginning, the number of points is small, all the sensors should move to the nearest points. With the increasing of path points, the move distance becomes shorter. However, when the number of path points is increased to certain value n', in order to guarantee the covering probability of detection point is at least d, more movements will be involved, that is reason why after the certain value n', the move distance is increased with the increasing number of path points.

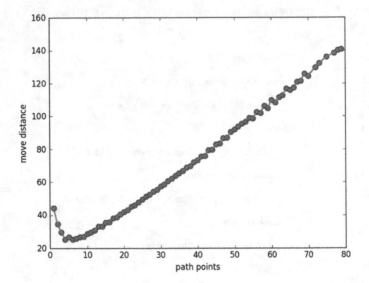

Fig. 8. The change of the number of the path points with respect to the move distance.

In Fig. 9, for the initial position of the sensor, we randomly generate 120 sensors in the region of (0,100) * (0,100). For the path curve function, we use $y = 0.1 *$ $(x - 10) * (x - 20)(0 < x < 100)$ to generate 80 path points. The threshold of coverage probability $d = 0.5$ and $\beta = 0.5$, R_1 in the range of (0, 2.5), $R_2 = 5$. We change the size of the R_1 and observe that the moving distance is decreased when R_1 is increased. For this phenomenon since sensors are in the same positions. When R_1 increases, the covering probability of the path point around it will become larger.

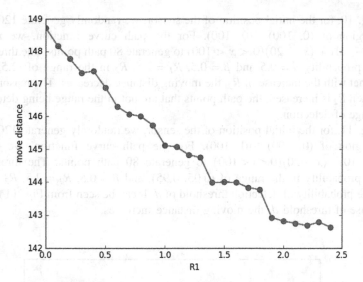

Fig. 9. The change of R_1 with respect to the move distance.

The probability of path detection is not only related to R_1, but also related to R_2. Therefore, we give the relationship between move distance and R_2 in Fig. 10.

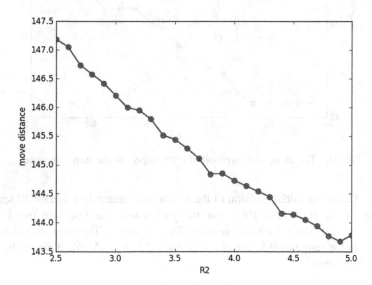

Fig. 10. The change of R_2 with respect to the move distance.

In Fig. 10, for the initial position of the sensor, we randomly generate 120 sensors in the region of (0, 100) * (0, 100). For the path curve function, we use $y = 0.1 * (x - 10) * (x - 20)(0 < x < 100)$ to generate 80 path points. The threshold of coverage probability $d = 0.5$ and $\beta = 0.5$, $R_1 = 2.5$, R_2 in the range of (2.5, 5). We observe that with the increase of R_2, the moving distance decreases. The reason for this is that when R_2 is increased, the path points that are not in the range being detected are in the range of detection.

In Fig. 11, for the initial position of the sensor, we randomly generate 120 sensors in the region of (0, 100) * (0, 100). For the path curve function, we use $y = 0.1 * (x - 10) * (x - 20)(0 < x < 100)$ to generate 80 path points. The threshold of coverage probability in the range of (0.05, 0.95), and $\beta = 0.5$, $R_1 = 2.5$, $R_2 = 5$. We change the probability of detection threshold of d. It can be seen from Fig. 11 that with the increase of threshold d, the moving distance increases.

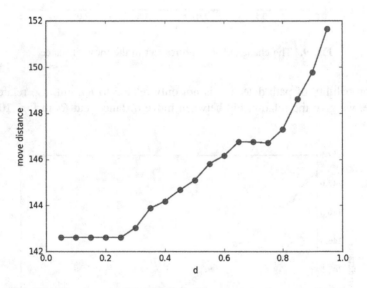

Fig. 11. The change of threshold d with respect to the move distance.

In Fig. 12, for the initial position of the sensor, we randomly generate 30 sensors in the region of (0, 100) * (0, 100). For the path curve function, we use $y = 0.1 * (x - 10) * (x - 20)(0 < x < 100)$ to generate 20 path points. The threshold of coverage probability in the range of 0.5, and $\beta = 0.5$, $R_1 = 2.5$, $R_2 = 5$. We observe the change of sensor positions.

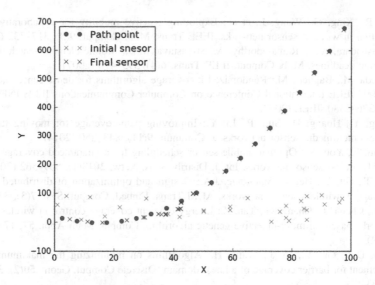

Fig. 12. The movement of the sensor.

5 Conclusions

Target tracking is one of the core applications in sensor networks. In this kind of applications, the user is often concern about the coverage of targets' moving paths, rather than in the whole area. Existing algorithms for path coverage do not consider the situation of minimum movement of sensors. Firstly, this paper proved that the problem is NP-hard, and then presented a heuristic path covering algorithm. It moved sensors through techniques of path curve discretization, redundant sensors and redundant paths, resulting in coverage of the path with minimum movement of sensors. Analysis shows, when m sensors covering n points of the path, the time complexity of the algorithm is O $(n^4m + n^3m^2)$. Simulations are conducted to evaluate the effects of some parameters, such as R_1, R_2, and the number of path points, on the moving distance of sensors.

Acknowledgment. This work is sponsored by the National Natural Science Foundation of China under Grant Nos. 61379117, 61502057.

Conflicts of Interest. The authors declare that there is no conflict of interest regarding the publication of this manuscript.

References

1. Tang, S., Mao, X., Li, X.Y.: Optimal k-support coverage paths in wireless sensor networks. In: IEEE International Conference on Pervasive Computing and Communications, pp. 1–6. IEEE Computer Society (2009)
2. Liao, Z., Wang, J., Zhang, S., et al.: Minimizing movement for target coverage and network connectivity in mobile sensor networks. IEEE Trans. Parallel Distrib. Syst. **26**(7), 1971–1983 (2015)

3. Tan, R., Xing, G., Wang, J., et al.: Exploiting reactive mobility for collaborative target detection in wireless sensor networks. IEEE Trans. Mob. Comput. 9(3), 317–332 (2010)
4. Somasundara, A.A., Ramamoorthy, A., Srivastava, M.B.: Mobile element scheduling with dynamic deadlines. Mob. Comput. IEEE Trans. 6(4), 395–410 (2007)
5. Hefeeda, M., Bagheri, M.: Randomized k-coverage algorithms for dense sensor networks. In: 2007 IEEE International Conference on Computer Communications IEEE INFOCOM, pp. 2376–2380. IEEE (2007)
6. Zhang, Y., Huang, H., Sun, P., Li, Y.: Improving path-coverage for moving targets in wireless multimedia sensor networks. J. Commun. 9(11), 843–850 (2014)
7. Zhixin, F., You, K.: Optimal mobile sensor scheduling for a guaranteed coverage ratio in hybrid wireless sensor networks. Int. J. Distrib. Sens. Netw. 2013(1), 559–562 (2013)
8. Yan, T., Gu, Y., He, T., Stankovic, J.A.: Design and optimization of distributed sensing coverage in wireless sensor networks. ACM Trans. Embed. Comput. Syst. 7(3), 33 (2008)
9. Jia, J., Chena, J., Chang, G., Tan, Z.: Energy efficient coverage control in wireless sensor networks based on multi-objective genetic algorithm. Comput. Math Appl. 57, 1756–1766 (2009)
10. Chen, D.Z., Gu, Y., Li, J., Wang, H.: Algorithms on minimizing the maximum sensor movement for barrier coverage of a linear domain. Discrete Comput. Geom. 50(2), 374–408 (2013)
11. Zhu, L., Fan, C., Wu, H., Wen, Z.: An improved algorithm for minimizing the maximum sensor movement in linear barrier coverage. Int. J. Online Eng. 12(8) 2016

Intelligence's Dilemma: AI Algorithms May Cause Anti-Intelligence

Yuhong Zhang[1,2](✉) and Umer Nauman[2]

[1] Network and Data Security Key Laboratory of Sichuan,
University of Electronic Science and Technology of China, Chengdu 610054, China
zhangyuhong001@gmail.com
[2] Information Science and Engineering College, Henan University of Technology,
Zhengzhou 450001, China
stormy.umer@gmail.com

Abstract. As the intelligent age continues and technology gets more advanced, algorithms offer some of the solutions for our better work and life. However, research suggests that the proliferation and abuse of intelligent algorithms may lead us to a decline in cognitive performance. In this paper, we first discuss the role of intelligent algorithms in terms of highlighting the value of data. Next, we analyse the non-neutrality of these data-driven algorithms. Further, we analyze the intrinsic discrimination of AI algorithm based on prejudice psychology. Next, we argue that overusing AI algorithms and strengthening the dependency on them will lead to lower our cognitive level in terms of slow thinking. Thus, the conclusion is that, in the intelligent age, the more intelligent algorithms we use, the lower our cognitive level will be. This is the dilemma of intelligence. Finally, we offer some possible principles that may apply to alleviate the above disadvantageous scenarios.

Keywords: Intelligence algorithm · Social cognitive psychology · Slow thinking · Cognitive surplus

1 Introduction

In the age of big data, whether we want to or not, most of us contribute to a growing portrait of who we are online. Whatever we do online, we are leaving our own digital footprints behind. These digital footprint paints a picture of who we are. All of behaviors like comments on social media, app use, bills pay, and so on, are electronic, and this electronic way of life and working provide massive data to some

This paper is partly supported by Henan Provincial Key Scientific and Technological Plan (no. 162300410056), Plan of Nature Science Fundamental Research in Henan University of Technology (no. 2015QNJH17), Henan Philosophy Social Science Planning Fund (no. 2017BKS007), Henan Higher Education Teaching Reform Research and Practice Project (no. 2017SJGLX002-4, 2017SJGLX056) and National Natural and Science Foundation of China (no. 61602154).

F. Sun et al. (Eds.): ICCSIP 2018, CCIS 1005, pp. 385–392, 2019.
https://doi.org/10.1007/978-981-13-7983-3_34

companies like Facebook, Tencent and Amazon. As a result, they have the opportunity to collect and take advantage of electronic data. This is the major source of big data. In essence, data is the underlying logic of intelligence [1].

We recognize that big data has great value, but the value of it is not the data. Data itself is not the solution. It is just part of the path to that solution [2]. Obviously, obtaining valuable insights from the big data is not easy. People are incapable of addressing this issue directly due to the deficiencies in terms of memory and computational power. Therefore, we often mechanize and engineer mental activities which human brain is not good at, and outsource them to machines. In a nutshell, this kind of mental activity process, in which machines replace human, can be collectively called as artificial intelligence (AI) algorithms.

2   Roles of AI Algorithms

AI is an emerging technology. For the essence of technology, the economist Brian Arthur has a deep insight into this. In his book "*The Nature of Technology*" [3], Arthur regards technology as a kind of programming of nature, a harnessing of it to human purposes. The meaning of technology is "*the entire collection of devices and engineering practices available to a culture*". This definition is very similar to what Kevin Kelly calls the "technium" in his book "*What Technology Wants*" [4].

The astronomical creation and accumulation of data generated by a plethora of sources contribute to the Big Data's huge volume and distinct characteristic. The core characteristics of big data is chaotic disorder and difficult to use (that is, the information entropy is very high). As a result, machine learning technologies (basically algorithms) are expected to stand up and reduce chaos (i.e. eliminate uncertainty).

In a real business environment, due to an enormous amount of users and a highly diverse pattern of advertisements, to find a "*best match*" among specific user and the corresponding advertisement is not easy. The biggest challenge is the large-scale optimization and search problem under complex constraints. In such scenarios, if there is no AI algorithm highly involved, it is impossible to efficiently complete the massive matching task.

During monetizing big data, researchers and the general public often show great concern over the invasion of personal privacy. This issue is indeed worthy of attention, but is that the whole truth of it? Of course not. Besides that, we have to pay more cost for that. Actually, AI algorithms have aggravated the dilemma - a trend of "anti-intellectual" in the age of AI [5]. We discuss this issue in the rest of this paper.

3   Biases of Algorithm

There is a widespread belief that, algorithm is just a collection of instructions, and they have no free will, so it is definitely objective. "*Like all technologies, AI Algorithm itself is not really good or bad; it is neutral.*"

But the above viewpoint is debatable [6]. We know that most of algorithms, especially deep learning, are driven by data, and their performances are closely related to quality, variety, and quantity of training data.

As the anthropologist and mathematician Thomas Krump emphasized in his book *"The Anthropology of Numbers"* [7], behind the data, it is actually human. Data is a form of representation of human observing the world. It is an isomorphism between a physical world and digital world. Therefore, conducting research on data, to a certain extent, is equal to the quantitative study of human beings.

It is undeniable that human behavior and perspectives are not neutral. They are often influenced by many factors such as emotions, positions, interests, and religion. In the era of big data, people's behaviors and perspectives are mapped into the data world through various applications (such as online social network, e-commerce, entertainment applications). Therefore, these data cannot be neutral. As we discussed earlier, the intelligence of algorithm comes from these biased data, how can we guarantee its neutrality? human biases and prejudices in physical world will be *synchronized* to algorithm (electronic world) through data for sure.

Beyond that, algorithms are, in part, our opinions embedded in code [8]. They are programmed and maintained by people, and algorithms can be changed based upon people's behavior. As a result, they may reflect human incorrect cognition that lead to machine learning misinterpretations. "Even if they are not designed with the intent of discriminating against some specific groups, if they reproduce social preferences even in a completely rational way, they also reproduce those forms of discrimination" [9].

Nowadays, to a great extent, our life and work run on intelligent algorithms. The data-devouring, self-improving computer algorithms have already determine Amazon online shopping recommendations, Google search results, Jinri Toutiao news feeds, and Douyin small videos.

In computer science, there is an old programmer's saying: *"Garbage In Garbage Out* (GIGO), which means that flawed input data produces nonsense output. As for intelligent algorithms, there is a similar argument *"Bias In, Bias Out* (BIBO)" to describe the potential risk brought by algorithms, which was proposed by the famous journal Nature in 2016 [10].

Through the above analysis, we can see that prejudice and bias are embedded in data and further in algorithms. In fact, prejudice and bias belong to the categories of psychology, and they are the manifestation of human cognition. Let us discuss this topic below.

4   Psychological Variables in AI Algorithm

The distinguished social psychologist Gordon Allport put forward an important academic viewpoint in his book *The Nature of Prejudice*, which emphasizes the role of social categorization in prejudice. Alport noted, "Social categorization dominates our entire thinking and life... Once the categorization is formed, it will become the basis of the normal prejudgment...the human mind must think with the aid of categories. We cannot possibly avoid this process. Orderly living depends upon it" [11].

Why do we rely on this process? Cognitive psychologists believe that human beings are "cognitive miser". From ancient times to the present, human beings often face with a complex and ever-changing world full of uncertainties. To survive in such a world, human beings have to save limited cognitive resources and simplify their cognitive processes as much as possible according to the *"Principle of Least Effort"*.

The *categorization* is a cognitive behavior that people naturally evolved in the face of an unknown world. The advantage of *categorization* is that it allows us to get used to unfamiliar world quickly, smoothly and consistently.

As a result, even though we have intricate and superior brains, we still do not want to get involved with thinking too hard or too much. If there are several ways to get something done, we tend to choose the one which is the least cognitively demanding. To this, one of the methods is to classify things (that is, categorization) in advance. But the drawbacks of *categorization* are also the root of prejudice.

Why? According to Allport, social categorization can be formed through stereotypes. The so-called *stereotypes* here is based on past experience, and forms a direct judgment and decision-making on the current. By using it, we can prejudge a new object quickly without deep understanding.

Obviously, the formation of *stereotypes* is not built in a day but accumulated through a considerable amount of perception about old objects over long time.

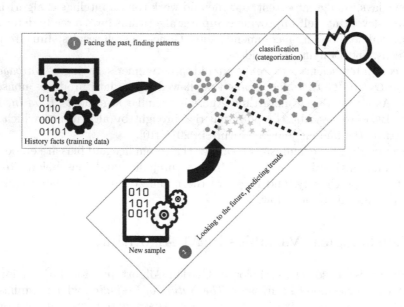

Fig. 1. Intelligent algorithm prediction process

After careful consideration, we will find that, the formation of "social categorization" and the workflow of AI algorithms are very similar. Most of AI algorithms serve for two types of task "*classification*" and "*cluster*". The former is supervised learning, which means that it infers the category of things from labeled training data, while "clustering" is unsupervised learning, that is, the training examples given to the learning algorithm are unlabeled.

The core value of intelligent algorithms is the prediction for new data samples. So how does it work? First, we use a lot of historic data (or training set) to generalize a pattern (by using classification or clustering algorithms), and then according to the pattern discovered in advance, algorithms predict which cluster or classification the new sample belongs to, as shown in Fig. 1.

Obviously, the social categorization proposed by Alport and the classification or clustering often used by algorithms, the prejudgment in stereotypes and the prediction of AI algorithms, both of them are homologous to each other. categorization, to some extent, is synonymous with prejudice. Based on this perspective, AI algorithm naturally have *genes* of prejudice.

Since the algorithm is not neutral and has prejudice and bias, why are we still inseparable from the algorithm? This is because that, faced with massive data, we are at a loss. The author of "*Homo Deus: A Brief History of Tomorrow*", Yuval Harari, noted that "the universe consists of data flows, and the value of any phenomenon or entity is determined by its contribution to data processing" [12]. But who can help to process the massive data? Only algorithms can do that. In short, we cannot get many things done without it. But an over-reliance on algorithms will raise another problem of generalizing "quick thinking", which results in reducing cognitive density of human. We will illustrate this point in the following section.

5   Generalization of Quick Thinking

As mentioned above, due to information overload, one has to rely on the help of algorithms. Algorithm, as a mirror image of human thinking, is influenced by mankind. But in turn, it will reshape human thinking. Overusing algorithm will result in a dependency on it, which further reduce our cognitive level (for example, slow thinking).

The concepts of "*slow thinking*" and "*fast thinking*" were put forward by Nobel Prize winner Daniel Kahneman in his book "*Thinking, Fast and Slow*" [13]. In this book, Kahneman explained the dichotomy between two modes of thought - "System 1" that is fast, instinctive and emotional; "System 2" that is slower, more deliberative, and more logical.

As we know, our brain is like a sophisticated machine. It is capable of processing complex patterns and regulate every aspect of our very existence. But even though we have intricate minds, we still do not want to think too hard or too much unless we have to.

In other words, most of the time, brain is dominated by quick thinking (System 1). System 1 allows us to make decisions with little-to-no mental effort.

This is what we call the *principle of least effort*. Recall the previous section of this paper, you will find that, it is the principle that also led to the generation of prejudice among people. It means that, to achieve rapid decision-making, we have to repeatedly adopt a psychological shortcut – heuristics (i.e, quick thinking), which can be offered by algorithm. However, quick thinking is flawed because it will produce more cognitive bias.

On the other hand, System 2 (i.e, slow thinking) requires more effort. More effort means more energy consumption. So our brain does not equip it easily, therefore it is usually much slower than System 1. In fact, we do not want to engage System 2 unless we really have to, because it is so cognitively demanding. In order to improve cognitive efficiency, we must pay for it. The cognitive bias of thinking fast is the one of the costs.

Perhaps you will wonder, what is the relationship between the above cognitive psychology concepts and intelligent algorithms? Let us discuss this issue in association. In the era of AI, in order to lower the cognitive threshold, most of softwares and algorithms are designed to follow such a principle, "Don't Make me Think". In essence, this is to encourage users to just start their fast thinking.

What will be the next result? Intelligent algorithms usually do not live up to its characteristic of "intelligent", and they will offer a lot of suggestions or decisions that look more appropriate. More importantly, even if we consciously switch to "slow thinking mode", because of high quality solution provided by algorithms, we find that decisions which are made by machine are usually better than ours. In the face of such frustrating scenes, we have not many options to choose. What we are likely to do is to quit the useless "slow thinking" and then outsource our cognition to AI algorithm, only leaving the low cognitive ability of fast thinking.

The follow-up consequences can be easily imagined, our cognitive density will be lower and lower, and quick thinking will generalized progressively. Here we give the definition of cognitive density (CD), described by Eq. 1.

$$CD = \frac{Thinking_{slow} \times \alpha}{Thinking_{slow} \times \alpha + Thinking_{fast} \times (1 - \alpha)} \tag{1}$$

Herein α is the proportion of slow thinking, ranging from 0 to 1. More seriously, in the era dominated by intelligent algorithms, this proportion α will be continuously reduced by them.

Fast thinking is a kind of superficial pragmatism, and the underlying logic behind it, is that cognition must conform to observation, and observation in turn binds the cognitive pattern, so that there is no *cognitive surplus*. It is constructed only by slow (critical) thinking. In addition to this, by using cognitive surplus, slow thinking can expand our cognitive boundaries and launching a saturated attack against reshaping reality.

However, the cruel reality is that, fast thinking is generalizing to erode and squeeze the space of slow thinking, resulting in a less cognitive surplus, as shown in Fig. 2.

In the book "*Homo Deus: A brief history of tomorrow*" [12], a historian Yuval Hulari pointed out that, human being can also be regarded as a kind of

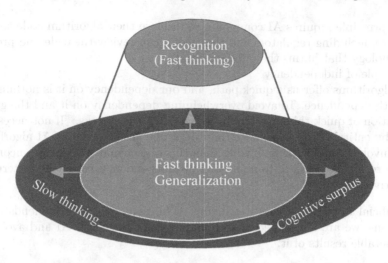

Fig. 2. Intelligent algorithm prediction process

biochemical algorithm. Over the past 70,000 years, human experience (mostly, fast thinking) has been the most effective data processing algorithm in the world, but we are likely to reach a critical point, and biochemical algorithm will be replaced by AI algorithm and then become a burden of AI. With the trend of generalization of quick thinking, many *"useless classes"* as Heral said will become possible.

6   Conclusions

From the above analysis, we can see that AI algorithms indeed make our life easier and more comfortable. However, everything has two sides. On the one hand, algorithm does not guarantee its neutrality. From the perspective of cognitive psychology, it contains the *genes* of discrimination. On the other hand, over-reliance on algorithms will reinforce our ability of "fast think (System 1)", thus weakening our cognitive level of "slow thinking" (System 2).

There seems to exist a principle of *"conservation of intelligence"*. The sum of artificial intelligence and human intelligence is a constant. If fast thinking shows more (shallow) intelligence, then slow thinking leads to less deeper intelligence. At the same time, if algorithms offer more intelligent, humans are less intelligent. there seems to exit a paradox about intelligent algorithms: the more we use them, the less intelligent we are.

To alleviate the above situation, we can try the following principles.

– Principle of transparency

"Technology creates benefits only when it is transparent" [14]. At present, many AI algorithms are not transparent in decision making, which make them almost impossible to track code violations from a technical perspective.

The principle requires AI companies to disclose their algorithm code so that people, including regulators and the media, can review the code and prevent technology that harms the public interest.
– Principle of independency
AI algorithms offer us a quick path, and our dependency on it is nothing but a path dependence. To avoid overwhelming dependency on it and the generalization of quick thinking, Occam's razor here also works. "If not necessary, not by entity". This is because that, once one entity (such as AI algorithm) get involved in our life and work, then this object may give us an uncontrollable result. So we need to maintain our independency, especially in terms of creativity.

Artificial intelligence is still evolving. While enjoying the dividends of AI algorithms, we are also expected to build trust for beneficial AI and avoid the unpredictable results of it.

References

1. Zhang, Y., Nauman, U.: Artificial unintelligence: anti-intelligence of intelligent algorithms. In: Shi, Z., Pennartz, C., Huang, T. (eds.) ICIS 2018. IAICT, vol. 539, pp. 333–339. Springer, Cham (2018). https://doi.org/10.1007/978-3-030-01313-4_35
2. Hammond, K.J.: The value of big data isn't the data. Harvard Business Review (2013) https://hbr.org/2013/05/the-value-of-big-data-isnt-the. Accessed 30 Dec 2018
3. Arthur, B.: The Nature of Technology: What it Is and How it Evolves. Free Press, New York (2011). Reprint edn
4. Kelly, K.: What Technology Wants. Penguin Books, London (2011)
5. Meredith, B.: Artificial Unintelligence: How Computers Misunderstand the World. The MIT Press, Cambridge (2018)
6. Zhang, Y., Qin, Z., Xiao, L.: The discriminatory nature of big data algorithms. Nat. Dialect. Res. **33**(5), 81–86 (2017)
7. Crump, T.: The Anthropology of Numbers (Cambridge Studies in Social and Cultural Anthropology). Cambridge University Press, Cambridge (1992)
8. Mann, G. O'Neil, C.: Hiring algorithms are not neutral. Harvard Business Review. https://hbr.org/2016/12/hiring-algorithms-are-not-neutral. Accessed 15 Nov 2018
9. Miller, C.C.: When algorithms discriminate. The NewYork Times (2015). https://www.nytimes.com/2015/07/10/upshot/when-algorithms-discriminate.html. Accessed 30 Dec 2018
10. EDITORIAL: More accountability for big-data algorithms. Nature **537**, 449 (2016) https://www.nature.com/news/more-accountability-for-big-data-algorithms-1.20653. Accessed 30 Dec 2018
11. Allport, G.W.: The Nature of Prejudice. Addison-Wesley, London (1954)
12. Harari, Y.N.: Homo Deus: A Brief History of Tomorrow. Random House, New York (2016)
13. Kahneman, D., Egan, P.: Thinking Fast and Slow. Farrar, Straus and Giroux, New York (2011)
14. Kelly, K.: Technical elements (Chinese Edition). Electronic Industry Press (2012)

Modified Method for Orbit Relative Reachable Domain with State Uncertainties

Hao Shi[(✉)], Teng Tian, Xiaoxiao Zhao, and Yujie Xiao

North Automatic Control Technology Institute, Taiyuan 030006, China
shihaounico@163.com

Abstract. State uncertainties in a spacecraft's relative motion lead to trajectory deviation. The volume that enclosing all the potential relative position due to initial state uncertainty can be geometrically described as the relative reachable domain (RRD). A general method is developed to determine the envelope of RRD in 3D space for arbitrary reference orbits. At any given time, the plane perpendicular to the instant nominal trajectory is defined as the reference plane. On each reference plane, the envelope of RRD is generated by a revolution of maximum position error vectors. Thus, the problem is transformed to a problem of solving a system of nonlinear equations. Comparison between the solved RRD and the results of Monte Carlo runs, which are propagated by nonlinear full dynamical model of relative motion and can be regarded as the true results, is presented as the numerical example to validate the effectiveness of the proposed method.

Keywords: Deviation · Relative reachable domain · Reference plane

1 Introduction

With the increasing number of nations and private companies that employ the space environment for civil, commercial, and military ventures, the importance of space situational awareness (SSA) is also increasing. SSA is defined as understanding and maintaining awareness of the orbital population of Earth, the space environment, and the possible threats posed by the European SSA Preparatory Programme [1]. With the growing demands of close-range space operations and continuously increasing number of space debris, the probability of space collisions occurring has increased significantly in recent years. Moreover, the orbital uncertainties of space objects, such as their positions being unknown in high precision, contribute to the occurrence of collisions. Therefore, high-accuracy determination of the spacecrafts' orbital accessibility becomes an important issue.

Measurement and control errors are inevitable in actual space missions. These errors cause a spacecraft's trajectory to deviate from the nominal one. Questions, such as where the spacecraft might be and whether a collision might occur, are important concerns in SSA. The relative reachable domain (RRD) [2] is a convenient tool for dealing with the issues that arise during a close-range space mission. Measurement and control errors can be regarded as initial orbital uncertainties that follow a probability distribution in the vicinity of the nominal position. In many applications [3–6], the

© Springer Nature Singapore Pte Ltd. 2019
F. Sun et al. (Eds.): ICCSIP 2018, CCIS 1005, pp. 393–405, 2019.
https://doi.org/10.1007/978-981-13-7983-3_35

random errors of the Cartesian positions of a spacecraft are assumed to be Gaussian because a spacecraft can be tracked and its error is determined within the errors associated with the corresponding position covariance ellipsoids [7]. Thus, the initial orbital uncertainties of a spacecraft can be provided by a state error ellipsoid.

The RRD concept is an extension of the reachable domain (RD) [8] from the absolute coordinate system to the relative coordinate system. Xue et al. [9–11] investigated RD for a spacecraft under a single impulse with time-free condition and obtained the upper bound of the RD envelope in 3D space. However, their result is inaccurate and conservative. Wen et al. [8, 12] employed orbit accessibility problem theory and obtained the accurate envelope of 3D RD for a spacecraft with an arbitrary maneuver position and arbitrary impulse direction. Furthermore, extensive research on the RD concept has been conducted by Refs. [13–17], and promising applications have been recognized.

Considering the gap in the description of spacecraft relative motion with the RD concept, the extension of RD research to the relative coordinate system, namely, the RRD concept, has been applied to the issue. Wen et al. [2] obtained the envelope of coplanar RRD for arbitrary reference orbits by evaluating the extreme values of the potentially accessible radius with respect to a given reference point. Shi et al. [18] extended the method of 2D RRD to a 3D case by substituting a time-varying reference plane for the reference point and obtained the envelope of 3D RRD. However, their result was overestimated because the direction constraint was not rigorous; in addition, the algorithm utilized to solve the obtained system of nonlinear equations was not prompt. The current study is a follow up to Refs. [2, 18]. The RRD problem is extended from the 2D coplanar case to general 3D space, and the method is modified so that the issue in the selection of the reference point in the previous study is eliminated.

In this study, a plane perpendicular to the instant nominal orbit is defined as the reference plane; this plane intersects RRD and forms an intersection area. The envelope of the intersection area on each reference plane indicates the maximum position error of a spacecraft at a corresponding time; it must be a closed curve and can be determined by seeking the maximum value among the potential positions obtained via propagation of the initial position and velocity errors on the given reference plane. One of the solutions to the problem of obtaining a closed curve is to solve differential equations. Thus, the problem of obtaining a closed curve is transformed to a problem of solving a system of nonlinear equations obtained by space geometry and orbital dynamics. The envelope of RRD can be identified by obtaining the closed curve on each reference plane.

This paper is constructed as follows. The determination of initial error ellipsoid is introduced in Sect. 2 firstly. Then a modified method of obtaining the 3D envelope of RRD caused by initial orbital uncertainties is presented in Sect. 3. Subsequently, an example of RRD calculation with circular reference orbit is provided in Sect. 4. Lastly, numerical simulation examples and the conclusion are presented in Sects. 5 and 6, respectively.

2   Error Ellipsoid of Initial State Uncertainty

A local-vertical, local-horizontal (LVLH) rotating frame centered in the reference orbit of a spacecraft is defined. The fundamental plane is the orbital plane, where the x axis is directed radially outward from the spacecraft, the z axis is aligned with the direction of the orbital angular momentum, and the y axis lies on the fundamental plane to complete the right-hand triad.

We consider a deputy spacecraft with state errors; this deputy spacecraft is moving in the vicinity of a chief spacecraft. The six dimensional (6D) state vector of deputy spacecraft can be defined as

$$x = \left[r^\mathrm{T}\, v^\mathrm{T} \right]^\mathrm{T} \tag{1}$$

where r and v are the position and velocity vectors in LVLH. Due to the inevitable measurement/control errors, x is a random vector with the mean value equals to the expected nominal state, which can be given as

$$\bar{x} = E(x) = \left[\bar{r}^\mathrm{T}\, \bar{v}^\mathrm{T} \right]^\mathrm{T} \tag{2}$$

where $E(\bullet)$ is the expectation operator. Therefore, the random vector can be expressed by

$$x = \bar{x} + \delta x \tag{3}$$

where $\delta x = \left[\delta r^\mathrm{T}\, \delta v^\mathrm{T} \right]^\mathrm{T}$ is the state error vector.

Suppose that the random vector x is subject to Gauss distribution, then its probability density function (PDF) is given by

$$p(x) = \frac{1}{(2\pi P)^{1/2}} \exp\left[-\frac{1}{2}(x - \bar{x})^\mathrm{T} P^{-1}(x - \bar{x}) \right] \tag{4}$$

where P is the error covariance matrix, which can be shown by

$$P = E\left[(x - \bar{x})(x - \bar{x})^\mathrm{T} \right] = \begin{bmatrix} P_{rr} & P_{rv} \\ P_{vr} & P_{vv} \end{bmatrix} \tag{5}$$

which is a symmetric positive definite (SPD) matrix.

It is found that the random vector x lies inside the hyper-ellipsoid centered at the mean state vector $\bar{x}$, which is defined by [19]

$$(x - \bar{x})^\mathrm{T} P^{-1}(x - \bar{x}) = k^2 \tag{6}$$

with the probability of

$$p(k) = \frac{1}{(2\pi)^{m/2}} \int_0^k \exp\left(-\frac{1}{2}r^2\right) f(r) dr \tag{7}$$

where k^2 is the Mahalanobis distance [20] of the state error vector δx depending on the given probability threshold; m represents the dimension of vector x; and $f(r)dr$ is the spherically symmetric volume element in an m-dimensional space.

Define a matrix A that expressed as

$$A = P^{-1}/k^2 = \begin{bmatrix} A_{rr} & A_{rv} \\ A_{vr} & A_{vv} \end{bmatrix} \tag{8}$$

Then the hyper-ellipsoid defined in Eq. (6) can be rewritten as

$$(x - \bar{x})^T A (x - \bar{x}) = 1 \tag{9}$$

Obviously, A is a SPD matrix as well.

The ellipsoid defined in Equation is the so-called error ellipsoid in the 6D full state space. Let one coordinate axis denote the 3D subspace of position error δr and the other the 3D subspace of velocity error δv. Therefore, the full state error ellipsoid centered at the origin of the frame can be expressed as a 2D sketch, as shown in Fig. 1.

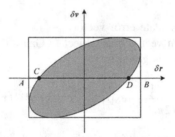

Fig. 1. The definition of error boundary.

Given the error covariance P, there are two ways of extract the position and velocity error ellipsoids from the 6D error hyper-ellipsoid. The first method is to take the inverse of P firstly, and then extract the 3×3 position submatrix A_{rr} and velocity submatrix A_{vv}, as is shown in Eq. (8). The second method is to extract the position and velocity error covariance P_{rr} and P_{vv} firstly, and then take the inverse of them, that is,

$$A_{rr} = P_{rr}^{-1}/k^2, A_{vv} = P_{vv}^{-1}/k^2 \tag{10}$$

Note that A_{rr} and A_{vv} are both SPD matrices as P is a SPD matrix.

Let's take extraction of position error submatrix as an example to show the difference between these two methods. The first method can be regarded as the intersection of the 6D error hyper-ellipsoid with the 3D position subspace in geometry, as shown in Fig. 1 by line segment CD. While the second method is taking the projection of 6D error hyper-ellipsoid onto the 3D position subspace, as shown in Fig. 1 by line segment AB. Obviously, the second method is more conservative than the first one as the line segment AB encloses CD. Given that conservativeness is legitimate for the space safety concerns, the second method will be used in the paper.

According to the finite-dimensional spectral theorem in linear algebra, for the SPD matrices A_{rr} and A_{vv} there exists real orthogonal matrices such that [21]

$$A_{rr} = R_{rr}^T D_{rr}^T D_{rr} R_{rr}, A_{vv} = R_{vv}^T D_{vv}^T D_{vv} R_{vv} \qquad (11)$$

where matrices D_{rr} and R_{rr} depend on the eigenvalues and eigenvectors of A_{rr}, D_{vv} and R_{vv} depend on the eigenvalues and eigenvectors of A_{vv}. Suppose that λ_i^r and $\lambda_i^v, i = 1, 2, 3$ are the positive eigenvalues of A_{rr} and A_{vv}, e_i^r and $e_i^v, i = 1, 2, 3$ are the corresponding normalized eigenvectors, respectively.

3 Obtaining the 3D Envelope of RRD

The RRD of the deputy spacecraft is defined as the volume formed by all possible relative positions caused by the initial orbital uncertainties; hence, RRD is a volume surrounding the nominal trajectory [2]. According to Ref. [22], the maximum envelope surface of RD is determined by the maximum control of a spacecraft. In the same manner, the envelope surface of RRD depends on the extremum of the initial orbital uncertainties. Large initial orbital uncertainties result in large RRD. When the initial orbital uncertainties decrease to zero, the envelope of RRD shrinks to the nominal trajectory.

To simplify the problem, the following assumptions are established:

(1) The time span considered is an orbital period, such that deviation from the nominal orbit caused by uncertainties is small with respect to the nominal motion;
(2) No perturbations are incorporated.

The actual initial states of the deputy spacecraft are expressed as

$$r_0(\alpha, \gamma) = \bar{r}_0 + \delta r_0(\alpha, \gamma), v_0(\beta, \theta) = \bar{v}_0 + \delta v_0(\beta, \theta) \qquad (12)$$

The trajectory deviations of the actual motion with respect to the nominal one can be expressed as

$$\delta r(t, \alpha, \beta, \gamma, \theta) = r(t, \alpha, \beta, \gamma, \theta) - \bar{r}(t), \delta v(t, \alpha, \beta, \gamma, \theta) = v(t, \alpha, \beta, \gamma, \theta) - \bar{v}(t) \qquad (13)$$

To obtain the envelope of RRD, a time-varying reference plane should be introduced to the problem to seek the envelope on the given plane. As is shown in Fig. 2, the bold line represents the envelope of RRD in LVLH; the dash line is the nominal trajectory of the deputy spacecraft; an arbitrary reference plane that perpendicular to the nominal trajectory is depicted as a quadrangle filled with fine diagonals; and the RRD intersection with the reference plane is expressed by the shadow area. Once the intersection in a given reference plane could be solved by some geometry method, then the RRD can be obtained through integrating all the intersection by moving the reference plane along the nominal trajectory in the time interval of interest. This is the basic idea employed to obtain the RRD envelope.

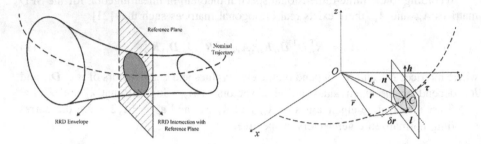

Fig. 2. Geometry of the RRD and reference plane.   **Fig. 3.** Sketch for finding the envelope of RRD.

In order to find the envelope of RRD, a geometry definition is given in Fig. 3. The notations and vectors are defined as follows: O is the origin of the reference LVLH coordinate system; the dashed arc line represents the nominal trajectory of the deputy spacecraft; the deputy spacecraft passes through point C, which is in the nominal trajectory, at $t = t_s$; $r_c = \bar{r}(t_s)$ and $v_c = \bar{v}(t_s)$ denote the relative position and velocity vectors of the nominal trajectory at point C, respectively; τ is the unit vector of v_c; n is a unit vector that lies on the orbital plane perpendicular to τ; a reference plane is built at point C, which is perpendicular to unit vector τ; the shadow represents the intersection of RRD with the reference plane; l denotes a vector from point C to the boundary of the intersection area, where l is its magnitude. Define vector p as the unit vector of l, and q the unit vector perpendicular to p in the reference plane. Obviously, vector p can be an arbitrary direction on the reference plane. If the boundaries of RRD in reference plane along the given direction p could be obtained, the entire envelope could be determined by varying the direction of vector p on the reference plane and the position of point C in the nominal trajectory.

The potential relative position vector of the deputy spacecraft, the end of which is located on the reference plane, can be expressed in the form of

$$r(t, \alpha, \beta, \gamma, \theta) = r_c + l = r_c + l \cdot p = \bar{r}(t) + \delta r(t, \alpha, \beta, \gamma, \theta) \tag{14}$$

Vector τ is perpendicular to the reference plane; therefore, τ is perpendicular to l. Hence,

$$g_1(t, \alpha, \beta, \gamma, \theta) = l \cdot \tau = \tau^{\mathrm{T}}[\bar{r}(t) + \delta r(t, \alpha, \beta, \gamma, \theta) - r_c] = 0 \tag{15}$$

The direction of l and p should be the same; therefore, l is perpendicular to q. Hence,

$$g_2(t, \alpha, \beta, \gamma, \theta) = l \cdot q = q^{\mathrm{T}}[\bar{r}(t) + \delta r(t, \alpha, \beta, \gamma, \theta) - r_c] = 0 \qquad (16)$$

Equations (15) and (16) are direction constraint functions that show that the five variables (t, α, β, γ, and θ) are not mutually independent. Only three of them are free parameters. If t, α, and β are selected as the free variables, then γ and θ are the functions of these variables expressed as $\gamma(t, \alpha, \beta)$ and $\theta(t, \alpha, \beta)$. Taking the variation of the two constraint functions results in

$$\delta g_1 = \tau^{\mathrm{T}}\left[\frac{\mathrm{d}\bar{r}}{\mathrm{d}t} + \frac{\partial(\delta r)}{\partial t}\right]\delta t + \tau^{\mathrm{T}}\frac{\partial(\delta r)}{\partial \alpha}\delta\alpha + \tau^{\mathrm{T}}\frac{\partial(\delta r)}{\partial \beta}\delta\beta + \tau^{\mathrm{T}}\frac{\partial(\delta r)}{\partial \gamma}\delta\gamma + \tau^{\mathrm{T}}\frac{\partial(\delta r)}{\partial \theta}\delta\theta = 0$$

$$(17)$$

$$\delta g_2 = q^{\mathrm{T}}\left[\frac{\mathrm{d}\bar{r}}{\mathrm{d}t} + \frac{\partial(\delta r)}{\partial t}\right]\delta t + q^{\mathrm{T}}\frac{\partial(\delta r)}{\partial \alpha}\delta\alpha + q^{\mathrm{T}}\frac{\partial(\delta r)}{\partial \beta}\delta\beta + q^{\mathrm{T}}\frac{\partial(\delta r)}{\partial \gamma}\delta\gamma + q^{\mathrm{T}}\frac{\partial(\delta r)}{\partial \theta}\delta\theta = 0$$

$$(18)$$

Thus,

$$\frac{\partial\gamma(t, \alpha, \beta)}{\partial t} = \lambda_\gamma V_r, \frac{\partial\gamma(t, \alpha, \beta)}{\partial \alpha} = \lambda_\gamma \frac{\partial(\delta r)}{\partial \alpha}, \frac{\partial\gamma(t, \alpha, \beta)}{\partial \beta} = \lambda_\gamma \frac{\partial(\delta r)}{\partial \beta}$$
$$\frac{\partial\theta(t, \alpha, \beta)}{\partial t} = \lambda_\theta V_r, \frac{\partial\theta(t, \alpha, \beta)}{\partial \alpha} = \lambda_\theta \frac{\partial(\delta r)}{\partial \alpha}, \frac{\partial\theta(t, \alpha, \beta)}{\partial \beta} = \lambda_\theta \frac{\partial(\delta r)}{\partial \beta}$$

$$(19)$$

where

$$\lambda_\gamma = \left[\left(\tau^{\mathrm{T}}\frac{\partial(\delta r)}{\partial \theta}q^{\mathrm{T}} - q^{\mathrm{T}}\frac{\partial(\delta r)}{\partial \theta}\tau^{\mathrm{T}}\right)\frac{\partial(\delta r)}{\partial \gamma}\right]^{-1}\left[q^{\mathrm{T}}\frac{\partial(\delta r)}{\partial \theta}\tau^{\mathrm{T}} - \tau^{\mathrm{T}}\frac{\partial(\delta r)}{\partial \theta}q^{\mathrm{T}}\right], V_r = \frac{\mathrm{d}\bar{r}}{\mathrm{d}t} + \frac{\partial(\delta r)}{\partial t}$$

$$\lambda_\theta = \left[\left(\tau^{\mathrm{T}}\frac{\partial(\delta r)}{\partial \gamma}q^{\mathrm{T}} - q^{\mathrm{T}}\frac{\partial(\delta r)}{\partial \gamma}\tau^{\mathrm{T}}\right)\frac{\partial(\delta r)}{\partial \theta}\right]^{-1}\left[q^{\mathrm{T}}\frac{\partial(\delta r)}{\partial \gamma}\tau^{\mathrm{T}} - \tau^{\mathrm{T}}\frac{\partial(\delta r)}{\partial \gamma}q^{\mathrm{T}}\right]$$

$$(20)$$

To obtain the envelope of RRD, the maximum value of l should be determined. From Eq. (14), we have

$$l = l \cdot p = r(t, \alpha, \beta, \gamma, \theta) - r_c = \bar{r}(t) + \delta r(t, \alpha, \beta, \gamma, \theta) - r_c \qquad (21)$$

Taking the partial derivative of l yields

$$\frac{\partial l}{\partial t} = \frac{l^{\mathrm{T}}}{l}\frac{\partial l}{\partial t} = p^{\mathrm{T}}\frac{\partial l}{\partial t}, \quad \frac{\partial l}{\partial \alpha} = \frac{l^{\mathrm{T}}}{l}\frac{\partial l}{\partial \alpha} = p^{\mathrm{T}}\frac{\partial l}{\partial \alpha}, \quad \frac{\partial l}{\partial \beta} = \frac{l^{\mathrm{T}}}{l}\frac{\partial l}{\partial \beta} = p^{\mathrm{T}}\frac{\partial l}{\partial \beta} \qquad (22)$$

Substituting Eq. (19) into Eq. (22) yields

$$\frac{\partial l}{\partial t} = p^{\mathrm{T}}\left[E + \frac{\partial(\delta r)}{\partial \gamma}\lambda_\gamma + \frac{\partial(\delta r)}{\partial \theta}\lambda_\theta\right]V_r, \frac{\partial l}{\partial \alpha} = p^{\mathrm{T}}\left[E + \frac{\partial(\delta r)}{\partial \gamma}\lambda_\gamma + \frac{\partial(\delta r)}{\partial \theta}\lambda_\theta\right]\frac{\partial(\delta r)}{\partial \alpha}$$

$$\frac{\partial l}{\partial \beta} = p^{\mathrm{T}}\left[E + \frac{\partial(\delta r)}{\partial \gamma}\lambda_\gamma + \frac{\partial(\delta r)}{\partial \theta}\lambda_\theta\right]\frac{\partial(\delta r)}{\partial \beta}$$

$$(23)$$

where E represents an 3×3 identity matrix.

The maximum value of l can be determined by letting its gradient be equal to zero,

$$\frac{\partial l}{\partial t} = \frac{\partial l}{\partial \alpha} = \frac{\partial l}{\partial \beta} = 0 \tag{24}$$

We define a parameter state vector as $X = [t, \alpha, \beta, \gamma, \theta]^{\mathrm{T}}$, and each X corresponds to a point in RRD. Then, the following equations can be obtained by combining the direction constraint functions, Eqs. (15) and (16), and the gradient function, Eq. (24).

$$\tau^{\mathrm{T}}[\bar{r}(t) + \delta r(t, \alpha, \beta, \gamma, \theta) - r_c] = 0, q^{\mathrm{T}}[\bar{r}(t) + \delta r(t, \alpha, \beta, \gamma, \theta) - r_c] = 0$$

$$p^{\mathrm{T}}\left[E + \frac{\partial(\delta r)}{\partial \gamma}\lambda_\gamma + \frac{\partial(\delta r)}{\partial \theta}\lambda_\theta\right]V_r = 0, p^{\mathrm{T}}\left[E + \frac{\partial(\delta r)}{\partial \gamma}\lambda_\gamma + \frac{\partial(\delta r)}{\partial \theta}\lambda_\theta\right]\frac{\partial(\delta r)}{\partial \alpha} = 0 \tag{25}$$

$$p^{\mathrm{T}}\left[E + \frac{\partial(\delta r)}{\partial \gamma}\lambda_\gamma + \frac{\partial(\delta r)}{\partial \theta}\lambda_\theta\right]\frac{\partial(\delta r)}{\partial \beta} = 0$$

Nonlinear equations [e.g., Eq. (25)] do not have analytical solutions and are difficult to solve numerically. We assume that the solution of Eq. (25) is denoted by $X^* = [t^*, \alpha^*, \beta^*, \gamma^*, \theta^*]^{\mathrm{T}}$; then, the boundary points can be obtained by substituting X^* back into Eq. (21).

4 3D Envelope of RRD for Circular Reference Orbits

If the chief spacecraft follows a circular orbit, then the linearization relative motion of the deputy spacecraft, which moves in the vicinity of the chief spacecraft, can be expressed as

$$\begin{bmatrix} r(t) \\ v(t) \end{bmatrix} = \Phi(t)\begin{bmatrix} r_0 \\ v_0 \end{bmatrix} = \begin{bmatrix} \Phi_{rr}(t) & \Phi_{rv}(t) \\ \Phi_{vr}(t) & \Phi_{vv}(t) \end{bmatrix}\begin{bmatrix} r_0 \\ v_0 \end{bmatrix} \tag{26}$$

The position and velocity deviation caused by initial orbital uncertainties can be obtained by the linearized relative motion expression Eq. (26).

$$\begin{cases} \delta r(t, \alpha, \beta, \gamma, \theta) = \boldsymbol{\Phi}_{rr}(t)\delta r_0(\alpha, \gamma) + \boldsymbol{\Phi}_{rv}(t)\delta v_0(\beta, \theta) \\ \delta v(t, \alpha, \beta, \gamma, \theta) = \boldsymbol{\Phi}_{vr}(t)\delta r_0(\alpha, \gamma) + \boldsymbol{\Phi}_{vv}(t)\delta v_0(\beta, \theta) \end{cases} \tag{27}$$

The nominal motion in the vicinity of r_c is approximated as

$$\begin{cases} \bar{r}(t) = \boldsymbol{\Phi}_{rr}(t - t_s)r_c + \boldsymbol{\Phi}_{rv}(t - t_s)v_c \\ \bar{v}(t) = \boldsymbol{\Phi}_{vr}(t - t_s)r_c + \boldsymbol{\Phi}_{vv}(t - t_s)v_c \end{cases} \tag{28}$$

Then Eq. (25) can be expressed as follows:

$$\begin{cases} \tau^{\mathrm{T}}[\boldsymbol{\Phi}_{rr}(t - t_s)r_c + \boldsymbol{\Phi}_{rv}(t - t_s)v_c + \boldsymbol{\Phi}_{rr}(t)\delta r_0 + \boldsymbol{\Phi}_{rv}(t)\delta v_0 - r_c] = 0 \\ q^{\mathrm{T}}[\boldsymbol{\Phi}_{rr}(t - t_s)r_c + \boldsymbol{\Phi}_{rv}(t - t_s)v_c + \boldsymbol{\Phi}_{rr}(t)\delta r_0 + \boldsymbol{\Phi}_{rv}(t)\delta v_0 - r_c] = 0 \\ p^{\mathrm{T}}\left[E + \frac{\partial(\delta r)}{\partial \gamma}\lambda_\gamma + \frac{\partial(\delta r)}{\partial \theta}\lambda_\theta\right]V_r = 0 \\ p^{\mathrm{T}}\left[E + \frac{\partial(\delta r)}{\partial \gamma}\lambda_\gamma + \frac{\partial(\delta r)}{\partial \theta}\lambda_\theta\right]\frac{\partial(\delta r)}{\partial \alpha} = 0 \\ p^{\mathrm{T}}\left[E + \frac{\partial(\delta r)}{\partial \gamma}\lambda_\gamma + \frac{\partial(\delta r)}{\partial \theta}\lambda_\theta\right]\frac{\partial(\delta r)}{\partial \beta} = 0 \end{cases} \tag{29}$$

Therefore, the equations for solving the parameters related to the envelope of RRD are obtained. The envelope for a circular reference orbit can be obtained by numerically solving Eq. (29) and substituting the solved $X^* = [t^*, \alpha^*, \beta^*, \gamma^*, \theta^*]^{\mathrm{T}}$ back into Eq. (21).

5 Numerical Examples

Given that the mahalanobis distance constant k = 3, the corresponding probability is 97.07%.

Consider an orbit injection scenario with the nominal release velocity pointing along the position R-bar direction. The launch spacecraft is moving in a circular orbit with the radius R = 7000 km. The simulation time duration of RRD is one orbital period. The magnitude of the release velocity is 2 m/s and the nominal release position is placed at the origin point of the LVLH. Thus, the initial nominal state of the nanostatellite can be expressed as

$$\bar{x}_0 = \begin{bmatrix} \bar{r}_0^{\mathrm{T}} & \bar{v}_0^{\mathrm{T}} \end{bmatrix}^{\mathrm{T}} = [0 \ \ 0 \ \ 0 \ \ 2 \ \ 0 \ \ 0]^{\mathrm{T}}.$$

The nominal trajectory with this initial state in one orbit period is presented in Fig. 4 by the bold dash line. Assume that the error covariance matrix of the initial state is

$$P = diag\left(2^2, 1^2, 0.5^2, 0.02^2, 0.01^2, 0.01^2\right),$$

which represents a standard deviation of initial position error of 2 m, 1 m, and 0.5 m along the x, y, and z directions in LVLH, respectively, and a standard deviation of initial velocity error of 0.02 m/s along the x direction and 0.01 m/s along the y and z directions. It should be noted that P can be arbitrarily set depending on the situation and it is diagonal in the paper just for simplification.

By using the method proposed, the envelope of 3D RRD corresponding to the nominal state and covariance matrix given is calculated and presented by the latticed surface in Fig. 4, and the initial nominal position is marked in the figure by a circular. Apparently, the envelope of RRD encloses the nominal trajectory entirely.

A total of 1,000 times of Monte Carlo trajectories are performed as the true results for comparison. Initial state of the Monte Carlo trajectories are generated by the "mvnrnd" function of Matlab, which can produce multivariate normal distributed random vectors upon providing the error covariance matrix P and the mean state vector $\bar{x}_0$. For a better view on the performance of the method proposed, the comparison of the solved RRD envelope with true results is shown on two section planes: one is the nominal orbit plane (the x-y plane of LVLH); and the other is the reference plane defined in Sect. 3.

The comparison on the nominal orbit plane is presented in Fig. 5. As is shown in the figure, the dash line is the nominal trajectory, solid bold lines represent the boundaries of the solved RRD's projection on the plane, and fine gray lines denote the Monte Carlo true trajectories. Note that the Monte Carlo trajectories overlap with each other and form a gray area in the plot. This gray area can be thought of as the true RRD. It can be found in Fig. 5 that the boundaries of RRD almost enclose the true RRD. However, there are a few instances lying beyond the boundaries. This is reasonable as only 97.07% of the initial error dispersion zone is considered to calculate the RRD, which means that there is a chance of 2.93% for the nanosatellite moving outside the RRD.

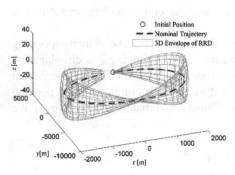

Fig. 4. Envelope of the RRD for R-bar orbit injection scenario.

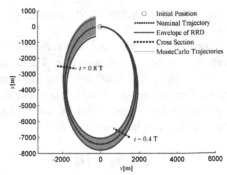

Fig. 5. Comparison on nominal orbit plane for orbit injection.

As mentioned above, the reference plane varies with the time. Two reference planes corresponding to the time of 0.4 T and 0.8 T are selected for the comparison, where T is the orbit period of circular reference orbit. As is shown in Fig. 5, the projection locations of the reference planes on nominal orbit plane are depicted as dash dot lines with the mark of corresponding time, respectively. Let XYZ axes denote the coordinate system attached on the reference plane, where X axis aligned to the vector τ, Y axis points to the vector n, and Z axis is along the direction of vector h. Then the cross section view is shown in Fig. 6, where the intersection of RRD with the reference plane is depicted as solid line, each hollow square represents an intersection point of a Monte Carlo trajectory with the reference plane, and the filled dot in the middle represents the position of nominal motion.

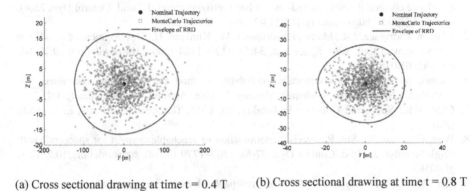

(a) Cross sectional drawing at time t = 0.4 T   (b) Cross sectional drawing at time t = 0.8 T

Fig. 6. Comparison on reference plane for orbit injection scenario.

6 Conclusion

The relative reachable domain is a geometrical description of the area that spacecraft may appear due to initial state uncertainties. A modified method was developed to obtain the envelope of 3D RRD for relative motion with initial state uncertainties. Below are the conclusions of this study.

(1) Comparison of the solved RRD envelope with true RRD area, which is generated by Monte Carlo runs, shows that the solved envelope of the RRD can define the positional volume that enclosing the possible relative trajectories due to state uncertainty successfully. This demonstrates the feasibility of the proposed method for solving for RRD.

(2) The numerical examples show that upon providing a probability threshold of the initial error ellipsoid, the probability that spacecraft may appear in the RRD is not larger than the given threshold. In other words, the case that the position of spacecraft lying beyond the RRD is a rare event.

(3) As the effects of initial state uncertainties on relative motion can be visualized intuitively by the envelope of RRD, it is convenient to use the concept of RRD to conduct trajectory deviation analysis and collision avoidance for the space mission in close range.

References

1. Rathgeber, W.: Europe's way to space situational awareness. Technical report ESPI 10, ESPI European Space Policy Institute, January 2008
2. Wen, C., Gurfil, P.: Relative reachable domain for spacecraft with initial state uncertainties. J. Guid. Control Dyn. **39**(3), 1–12 (2016)
3. Patera, R.P.: General method for calculating spacecraft collision probability. J. Guid. Control Dyn. **24**(4), 716–722 (2001). https://doi.org/10.2514/2.4771
4. Richards, A., Schouwenaars, T., How, J.P., Feron, E.: Spacecraft trajectory planning with avoidance constraints using mixed-integer linear programming. J. Guid. Control Dyn. **25**(4), 755–764 (2002). https://doi.org/10.2514/2.4656
5. Alarcón-Rodríguez, J.R., Martínez-Fadrique, F.M., Klinkrad, H.: Development of a collision risk assessment tool. Adv. Space Res. **34**(5), 1120–1124 (2004). https://doi.org/10.1016/j.asr.2003.01.015
6. Alfano, S.: Review of conjunction probability method for short-term encounters. In: AAS/AIAA Space Flight Mechanics Meeting, Sedona, Arizona, United States (2007)
7. Chan, F.K.: Spacecraft Collision Probability, pp. 1–13. The Aerospace Press, EI Segundo (2008)
8. Wen, C., Zhao, Y., Shi, P.: Precise determination of reachable domain for spacecraft with single impulse. J. Guid. Control Dyn. **37**(6), 1767–1779 (2014). https://doi.org/10.2514/1.g000583
9. Xue, D., Li, J., Baoyin, H.: Study on reachable domain for spacecraft trajectory with coplanar impulse applied. J. Astronaut. **30**(1), 88–92 (2009)
10. Xue, D., Li, J., Jiang, F.: Reachable domain of a spacecraft with a coplanar impulse applied. Chin. J. Theor. Appl. Mech. **42**(2), 337–342 (2010)
11. Xue, D., Li, J., Baoyin, H., Jiang, F.: Reachable domain for spacecraft with a single impulse. J. Guid. Control Dyn. **33**(3), 934–942 (2010). https://doi.org/10.2514/1.43963
12. Wen, C., Zhao, Y., Shi, P., Hao, Z.: Orbital accessibility problem for spacecraft with a single impulse. J. Guid. Control Dyn. **37**(4), 1260–1271 (2014). https://doi.org/10.2514/1.62629
13. Shishido, N., Tomlin, C.J.: Ellipsoidal approximations of reachable sets for linear games. In: Proceedings of the 39th IEEE Conference of Decision and Control, pp. 999–1004. IEEE (2000). https://doi.org/10.1109/cdc.2000.912904
14. Kurzhanski, A.B., Varaiya, P.: On reachability under uncertainty. SIAM J. Control Optim. **41**(1), 181–216 (2002). https://doi.org/10.1137/S0363012999361093
15. Daryin, A.N., Kurzhanski, A.B., Vostrikov, I.V.: Reachability approaches and ellipsoidal techniques for closed-loop control of oscillating systems under uncertainty. In: Proceedings of the 45th IEEE Conference on Decision and Control, pp. 6385–6390. IEEE (2006). https://doi.org/10.1109/cdc.2006.377784
16. Kurzhanskiy, A.B., Varaiya, P.: Ellipsoidal technique for reachability analysis of discrete-time linear systems. IEEE Trans. Autom. Control **52**(1), 26–38 (2007). https://doi.org/10.1109/tac.2006.887900
17. Holzinger, M.J., Scheeres, D.J.: Reachability results for nonlinear systems with ellipsoidal initial sets. IEEE Trans. Aerosp. Electron. Syst. **48**(2), 1583–1600 (2012). https://doi.org/10.1109/taes.2012.6178080
18. Shi, H., Zhao, Y., Shi, P., Wen, C., Zheng, H.: Determination of orbit reachable domain due to initial uncertainties. J. Astronaut. **37**(4), 411–419 (2016)
19. Bryson, A.E., Ho, Y.C.: Applied Optimal Control: Optimization, Estimation, and Control, pp. 309–311. Hemisphere Publishing Corporation, Washington, D. C. (1975)

20. Mahalanobis, P.C.: On the generalized distance in statistics. Proc. Natl. Inst. Sci. (Calcutta) **2**, 49–55 (1936)
21. Bapat, R.B.: Linear Algebra and Linear Models, 3rd edn. Springer, London (2012). https://doi.org/10.1007/978-1-4471-2739-0
22. Vinh, N.X., Gilbert, E.G., Howe, R.M., Sheu, D., Lu, P.: Reachable domain for interception at hyperbolic speeds. Acta Astronaut. **35**(1), 1–8 (1995). https://doi.org/10.1016/0094-5765(94)00132-6

Robotics

Gait Phase Optimization of Swing Foot for a Quadruped Robot

Guoxiong Wu, Rui Huang(✉), Jiasheng Hao, Hong Cheng, and Shanren Wang

Center for Robotics, School of Automation Engineering,
University of Electronic Science and Technology of China, Chengdu 611731, China
wuguoxiong@uestcrobot.net, ruihuang2010@gmail.com

Abstract. Quadruped robot has gained considerable interests since its wide applications in both military and entertainment scenarios. On the control and gait planning of quadruped robots, walking stability is the fundamental problem in most scenarios. In this paper, we proposed a gait phase optimization method on the swing foot of quadruped robots in walking gait. In the proposed gait optimization method, Lift-up and Touch-down phases are added in gait planning of swing foot, which aiming to improve the stability in walking phases. Finally we validate the proposed method on a quadruped robot, and experimental results indicate that the proposed gait phase optimization method has the ability to improve the stability of the quadruped robot in walking gait.

1 Introduction

Research on quadruped robots have increased significantly in recent years since they can be applied in many complex scenarios [1,2]. Compared to other autonomous robots such as wheeled robots and humanoid robots, quadruped robots not only have the ability to adapt unstructured environment (eg. field environment), but also can achieve higher speed in most scenarios. In early researches of quadruped robots, many quadruped robots with large body and high speed are developed as load carriers in field environment, such as BigDog [3], Legged-Squad 3 [4], WildCat [5], Cheetah [6] and SCalf [7] etc. These kinds of quadruped robots are hydraulic actuated which aiming to achieve higher running speed and carry heavier loads. As expanding of applications of quadruped robots, many small quadruped robots with motor actuated, such as SpotMini [8], HyQ [9,10], ANYmal [11,12], LittleDog [13,14] and Laikago [15] etc. These motor-driven quadruped robots has lower noise and most of them are focus on indoor environment.

On the research of fundamental technologies of quadruped robots, gait planning is the most important technology since suitable gait could improve the stability and motor ability of quadruped robots significantly. Gait planning methods of quadruped robots can be separated into three aspects: model-based [16], behavior-based [17] and bio-inspired methods [18]. This paper is focus on the model-based gait planning method in walking gait. Many gait models were proposed for walking gait, the most famous gait controller is proposed by Kolter

F. Sun et al. (Eds.): ICCSIP 2018, CCIS 1005, pp. 409–419, 2019.
https://doi.org/10.1007/978-981-13-7983-3_36

which named as hierarchical gait controller [19]. In the proposed hierarchical controller, three hierarchies are implemented: the perception level modeled the path of Center of Gravity (CoG) through vision sensors, the planning level calculated positions of swing foots based on planned CoG, then the control level servo actuators of the quadruped robot for achieving planned gait. In order to achieve better stability and motor ability of walking gait, many researchers focus on the planning level and build different gait models for different applications [20–22]. In gait control of quadruped robots, a critical issue is how to reduce the compact force when the robot contact the ground. For solving this problem, many control methods based on impedance control strategy are proposed in the control level [23–25]. However, the biggest drawback of these methods are the requirement of accurate and multi-dimension force detection on foots of the quadruped robot. Hence, in order to reduce the complexity of sensory system of the quadruped robot, this problem should be solved in the planning level which require less sensory information.

In this paper, a gait phase optimization method is proposed to improve the stability in walking gait of a quadruped robot. In the proposed gait optimization method, a Lift-up and a Touch-down phase are added in the gait planning of swing foots. The proposed method is validated on a quadruped robot, and experimental results indicate that the proposed gait phase optimization method has the ability to improve the stability of the quadruped robot in walking gait.

The rest of this paper is organized as follows. Section 2 introduces the system design of a quadruped robot. In Sect. 3, the proposed gait optimization method is presented. Experimental results and discussions are described in Sect. 4. Finally, we conclude the paper in Sect. 5 and suggest the future work.

2   System Design of a Quadruped Robot

In this section, a quadruped robot platform with motor-actuated is introduced. Firstly, we briefly introduce the system architecture of the quadruped robot, and then give the detail of a sensitive force sensor which installed on feet of the quadruped robot.

2.1   System Architecture of the Quadruped Robot

Figure 1 illustrates the whole structure of the quadruped robot, which total weight is 34 kg (Length × Width × Height: 64 cm × 34 cm × 56 cm). As shown in Fig. 1, the whole quadruped robot can be separated as three sub-systems: mechanical system, sensory system and control system.

On the mechanical design, the quadruped robot has totally 12 Degree-of-Freedoms (DOFs), in which 3 DOFs for each leg (knee joint, hip joint and yaw joint). As shown in Fig. 1, each joint is activated by a DC servo motor for serving active torques. Upon legs of the quadruped robot, a body structure is designed for installing the control hardware and carrying loads.

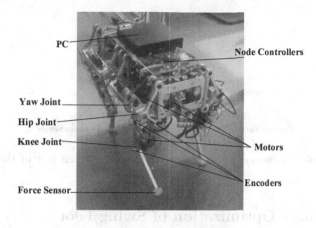

Fig. 1. The whole structure of the quadruped robot.

The sensory system of the quadruped robot consists three types of sensors: (1) Encoders for recording joints' state of the quadruped robot; (2) IMU sensor is installed on the body of the quadruped robot for obtaining the state of the body; (3) Force sensors are embedded on feet of the quadruped robot which aiming to measure the foot pressure during walking.

The control system of the quadruped robot is design as a distributed control system, with a main controller and 12 node controllers. The main controller is a PC installed on the body of the quadruped robot, which runs gait planning algorithms. Node controllers are designed for controlling each active joint, which runs control algorithms for each joint. In order to achieve real-time performance, we employ Control Area Network (CAN) for the communication between the main controller and node controllers.

2.2 Sensitive Force Sensor Design

In the design of gait control algorithms of quadruped robots (the same for the proposed gait planning method in this paper), the most important sensory information is the pressure of each foot. Hence, a sensitive force sensor is design for the quadruped robot, which aiming to obtain accurate force feedback during walking gait.

Figure 2 shows the mechanical structure of the sensitive force sensor. As shown in Fig. 2, a spring is added between the contact surface and the pressure sensor, which aiming to reduce the impact forces when the foot contacts the ground. Moreover, though the energy restored in the spring structure, the force sensor can measure the contact force immediately when the interaction force between the contact surface and the ground changes.

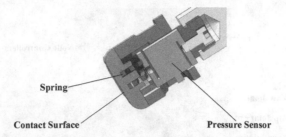

Spring

Contact Surface

Pressure Sensor

Fig. 2. Mechanical structure of the sensitive force sensor on feet of the quadruped robot.

3 Gait Phase Optimization of Swing Foot

In this section, the proposed gait phase optimization method will be presented in detail. First a gait planning method of swing foot based on a traditional gait planning method, then a gait phase optimization method is introduced which aiming to reduce compact of the swing foot.

3.1 Gait Planning of Swing Foot

In this paper, we utilize a gait planning method which plans trajectory of the swing foot with a box pattern [26]. The advantage of this method is that the quadruped robot can avoid bigger obstacles in walking gait. Figure 3 shows the schematic diagram of the gait planning method of swing foot.

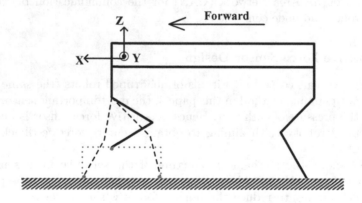

Fig. 3. Schematic diagram of the gait planning method of swing foot.

The swing movement of swing foot can be separated into three phases: lifting phase, forward phase and falling phase. In order to increase the stability of the quadruped robot, the falling phase is planned as two times longer than other two phases. Thus, assuming the whole swing phase cost time T_{swing}, duration of the lifting phase and forward phase is $T_{swing}/4$, and falling phase is $T_{swing}/2$. The detail description of foot trajectories are presented as follows.

(1) Lifting Phase: In the lifting phase, the swing foot of the quadruped robot is lifting up vertically along the Z direction, with the highest position H. The foot trajectories of the lifting phase can be described as follows:

$$\begin{cases} x(t) = 0, \\ y(t) = 0, \\ z(t) = \dfrac{4 \cdot H}{T_{swing}} \cdot t, t \in [0, \dfrac{T_{swing}}{4}]. \end{cases} \tag{1}$$

(2) Forward Phase: In the forward phase, the swing foot move in the X direction and Y direction, which aiming to move the foot to the goal position in XOY plane. Assuming that the goal position in XOY plane is $(L_x, /L_y)$, we can obtain the foot trajectories of the forward phase as follows:

$$\begin{cases} x(t) = \dfrac{4 \cdot L_x}{T_{swing}} \cdot (t - \dfrac{T_{swing}}{4}), \\ y(t) = \dfrac{4 \cdot L_y}{T_{swing}} \cdot (t - \dfrac{T_{swing}}{4}), \\ z(t) = H, t \in [\dfrac{T_{swing}}{4}, \dfrac{T_{swing}}{2}]. \end{cases} \tag{2}$$

(3) Falling Phase: In the falling phase, the swing foot of the quadruped robot is falling down vertically along the Z direction, from the highest position H to the ground. In order to ensure the foot contacts the ground during the duration of swing phase T_{swing}, we set a contact parameter β in which $\beta = 0$ indicates the foot has already touch the ground, otherwise $\beta = 1$. The foot trajectories can be described as follows in the falling phase:

$$\begin{cases} x(t) = L_x, \\ y(t) = L_y, \\ z(t) = \beta \cdot \dfrac{2 \cdot H}{T_{swing}} \cdot (t - \dfrac{T_{swing}}{2}), t \in [\dfrac{T_{swing}}{2}, T_{swing}]. \end{cases} \tag{3}$$

3.2   Gait Phase Optimization

After planning gait trajectories of the swing foot with box pattern, another issue is how to increase the stability performance in the whole swing phase. In this paper, we propose a gait phase optimization method to increase the stability performance of the quadruped robot in walking gait.

Figure 4 illustrates gait phases of the swing foot after optimization. As shown in Fig. 4, two phases are added in the swing phase of quadruped robot in walking gait: lift-up phase and touch-down phase.

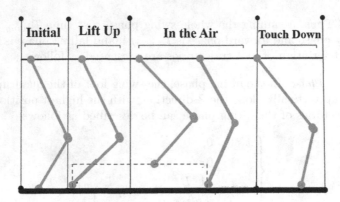

Fig. 4. Gait phase optimization of swing foot. Lift-up phase: the plantar force become smaller until the foot is off the ground; In the air: swing to the goal height and position; Touch-down phase: The plantar force become larger until the threshold.

(1) Lift-Up Phase: The goal of lift-up phase it to make the plantar force change to zero slowly. Since if the foot accelerate with a large acceleration, the quadruped robot will be not able to adjust its Center of Gravity (COG) immediately, which could make the system not stable.

(2) In the Air: This phase is the phase to run the planned gait trajectories of swing foot, which aiming to move the foot to the goal position.

(3) Touch-Down Phase: The goal of touch-down phase is decelerating the late swing phase of the swing foot. On the motor servo of gait trajectories, the controller can not servo motion trajectories accurately sometimes. Therefore, for some cases, the foot will touch the ground earlier than the planned gait. In order to increase the stability performance in these cases, the touch-down phase is added into the whole swing phase of the quadruped robot.

With the planned gait trajectory of swing foot and gait phase optimization, the quadruped robot can achieve better stability performance in walking gait in swing phase. Experiments on the quadruped robot in the next section will show the efficiency of the proposed gait phase optimization method.

4   Experiments

In this section, we evaluate the proposed gait phase optimization method on the quadruped robot. At first the experimental setup will be introduced briefly, then the experiments and results will be discussed.

4.1   Experimental Setup

The proposed gait phase optimization method is validated on the quadruped robot which introduced in Sect. 2. During all the experiments, we do not add extra loads on the quadruped robot. In order to evaluate the performance of each gait phase independently, two experiments are established: the first one is only add the touch-down phase, another one is only add the lift-up phase. At the end of experimental discussions, we discuss the stability performance of both these two situations.

4.2   Results and Discussions

The first experiment on the quadruped robot only adds the lift-up phase based on the proposed gait phase optimization method, which aiming to analysis the performance of the lift-up phase in walking gait. In the late description of figure results in this paper, we utilized LF, RF, LB, RB to represent the Left-Front leg, Right-Front leg, Left-Back leg and Right-Back leg, respectively. Figure 5 shows the comparison of RB leg and RF leg with two situations: without lift-up phase and with lift-up phase.

As shown in Fig. 5, the swing foot (RB leg in Fig. 5(a) and (c), RF leg in Fig. 5(b) and (d)) of the quadruped robot lift from the ground at around 1 second. In the original gait planning method without lift-up phase shown in Fig. 5(a) and (b), the other three legs are not stable after the swing foot lifting up (LF leg in Fig. 5(a), LB and RB leg in Fig. 5(b)).

Figure 5(c) and (d) show performances of the proposed gait phase optimization method with the lift-up phase. As shown in Fig. 5(c) and (d), the other three legs (except the swing leg) keep stable when the swing foot lifting in walking gait. From the results shown in Fig. 5, it is obviously that the quadruped robot obtained a stable gait with the proposed gait phase optimization method in lift-up phase.

The second experiment only adds the touch-down phase based on the proposed gait phase optimization method. Figure 6 compares the change on foot pressure of two situations: without touch-down phase and with touch-down phase.

As shown in Fig. 6, the LB leg (with blue line) of the quadruped robot touch the ground at around 5 second in the experiment. In the original gait planning method without touch-down phase shown in Fig. 6(a), the pressure on LB leg increases quickly and makes the quadruped robot not stable in the late swing phase (which makes the pressure on the LF leg and RB leg decrease quickly).

Figure 6(b) shows the performance of the proposed gait optimization method with touch-down phase. As shown in Fig. 6(b), the pressure on the swing foot (LB leg) increases slowly and the other three legs keeps stable in the late swing phase. From the experimental results we can see that, after adding the touch-down phase during normal gait, the quadruped robot could increase the stability in the late swing phase.

Furthermore, in order to evaluate the performance of proposed gait phase optimization method, we analyze the variation of the posture of the quadruped robot. As introduced in Sect. 2, sensory information of the IMU sensor (installed on the body of the quadruped robot) is utilized to analyze the stability of the

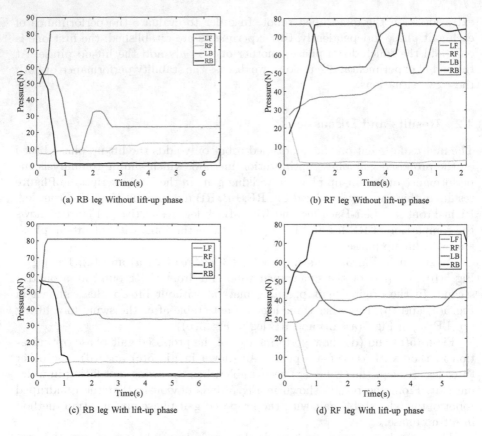

(a) RB leg Without lift-up phase

(b) RF leg Without lift-up phase

(c) RB leg With lift-up phase

(d) RF leg With lift-up phase

Fig. 5. Comparison of foot pressure with/without lift-up phase.

quadruped robot. In this experiment, we employ the proposed gait phase optimization method in a whole walking gait cycle (taking a step for each leg).

Figure 7 shows the comparison of the IMU sensory information of the quadruped robot with/without gait phase optimization method. Compared with experimental results in Fig. 7(a) and (d), it is obviously that the proposed gait phase optimization method has improved the stability of the quadruped robot significantly, in which the acceleration in both X direction and Y direction decreased. The experimental results also show that even only consider lift-up phase (in Fig. 7(b)) or touch-down phase (in Fig. 7(c)), the improved gait planning method can increase the stability of the quadruped robot in walking gait.

With experiments on the quadruped robot, the proposed gait phase optimization method improves the stability of the quadruped robot in walking gait significantly. Experimental results show that the proposed method has the ability to obtain stable gait in normal walking gait of quadruped robots.

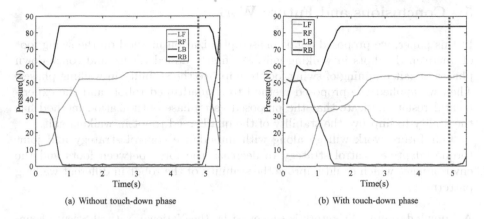

(a) Without touch-down phase

(b) With touch-down phase

Fig. 6. Comparison of foot pressure with/without touch-down phase. (Color figure online)

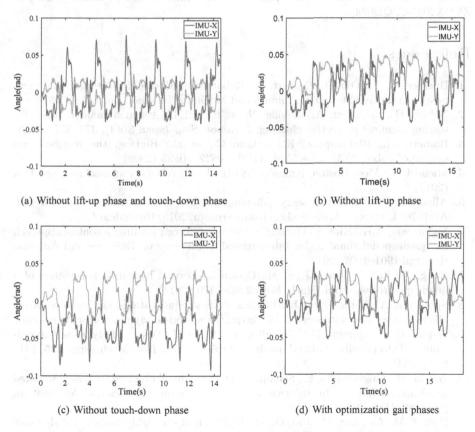

(a) Without lift-up phase and touch-down phase

(b) Without lift-up phase

(c) Without touch-down phase

(d) With optimization gait phases

Fig. 7. Comparison of the IMU sensory information of the quadruped robot with/without gait phase optimization method.

5   Conclusions and Future Work

In this paper, we proposed a gait phase optimization method on the swing foot of quadruped robots in walking gait. We firstly added lift-up and touch-down phases in gait planning of swing foot to improve the stability in walking phases. Then we applied the proposed method to a quadruped robot, and the experimental results indicate that the proposed gait phase optimization method has the ability to improve the stability of the quadruped robot in walking gait.

Our future work will go along with impedance control strategy and joint torque adaptive control strategy to decrease the force between foots and the environment, which could improve the stability of the robot in different walking patterns.

Acknowledgment. This work is supported by the National Natural Science Foundation of China (NSFC) under grant No. 61603078 and No. U1613223, and is also supported by Fundamental Research Funds for the Central Universities at University of Electronic Science and Technology of China (UESTC) under grant No. ZYGX2015KYQD044.

References

1. Buehler, M., Playter, R., Raibert, M.: Robots step outside. In: International Symposium Adaptive Motion of Animals and Machines Ilmenau, pp. 1–4 (2005)
2. Nelson, G., Saunders, A., Neville, N., et al.: PETMAN: a humanoid robot for testing chemical protective clothing. J. Robot. Soc. Japan **30**(4), 372–377 (2012)
3. Raibert, M., Blankespoor, K., Nelson, G., et al.: BigDog, the rough-terrain quaduped robot. IFAC Proc. Vol. **41**(2), 10822–10825 (2008)
4. Michael, K.: Meet Boston dynamics LS3-the latest robotic war machine. Ted Talk (2012)
5. Allen, M.: Pray that this scary galloping four-legged robot never comes for you, April 2014. http://www.wired.com/dangerroom/2013/10/wildcat/
6. Valenzuela, A.K., Kim, S.: Optimally scaled hip-force planning: a control approach for quadrupedal running. In: International Conference on Robotics and Automation, pp. 1901–1907 (2012)
7. Rong, X., Li, Y., Meng, J., et al.: Design for several hydraulic parameters of a quadruped robot. Appl. Math. **8**(5), 2465–2470 (2014)
8. Spot-mini: A nimble robot that handles objects, climbs stairs, and will operate in offices, homes and outdoors (2014). https://www.bostondynamics.com/spot-mini
9. Semini, C., Tsagarakis, N.G., Guglielmino, E., et al.: Design of HyQ - a hydraulically and electrically actuated quadruped robot. Proc. Inst. Mech. Eng. **225**, 831–849 (2011)
10. Focchi, M., Guglielmino, E., Semini, C., et al.: Control of a hydraulically-actuated quadruped robot leg. In: International Conference on Robotics and Automation, pp. 4182–4188 (2010)
11. Hutter, M., Gehring, C., Jud, D., et al.: ANYmal - a highly mobile and dynamic quadrupedal robot. In: IEEE/RSJ International Conference on Intelligent Robots and Systems, pp. 38–44 (2016)

12. Hutter, M., Gehring, C., Lauber, A., et al.: ANYmal - toward legged robots for harsh environments. Adv. Robot. 1–14 (2017)
13. Murphy, M.P., Saunders, A., Moreira, C., et al.: The littledog robot. Int. J. Robot. Res. **30**(2), 145–149 (2011)
14. Neuhaus, P.D., Pratt, J.E., Johnson, M.J.: Comprehensive summary of the institute for human and machine cognition's experience with LittleDog. Int. J. Robot. Res. **30**(2), 216–235 (2011)
15. Laikago (2016). http://www.unitree.cc/cn/showcase/
16. Kolter, J.Z., Ng, A.Y.: The stanford littledog: a learning and rapid replanning approach to quadruped locomotion. Int. J. Robot. Res. **30**(2), 150–174 (2011)
17. Brooks, R.S.: A robust layered control system for a mobile robot. IEEE J. Robot. Autom. **2**(1), 14–23 (1986)
18. Hooper, S.L.: Central pattern generators. Curr. Biol. **10**(5), 176–179 (2000)
19. Kolter, J.Z., Rodgers, M.P., Ng, A.Y.: A control architecture for quadruped locomotion over rough terrain. In: IEEE International Conference on Robotics and Automation, pp. 811–818 (2008)
20. Rebula, J.R., Neuhaus, P.D., Bonnlander, B.V., et al.: A controller for the Little-Dog quadruped walking on rough terrain. In: IEEE International Conference on Robotics and Automation, pp. 1467–1473 (2007)
21. Vukobratovic, M., Borovac, B.: Zero-moment point: thirty five years of its life. Int. J. Humanoid Robot. **1**, 157–173 (2004)
22. Hutter, M., Gehring, C., Hoepflinger, M.H., et al.: Walking and running with Star-lETH. In: International Symposium on Adaptive Motion of Animals and Machines (2013)
23. Whitney, D.E.: Historical perspective and state of the art in robot force control. Int. J. Robot. Res. **6**(1), 3–14 (1987)
24. Hogan, N.: Impedance control: an approach to manipulation. In: American Control Conference, vol. 1984, pp. 304–313 (1987)
25. Kazerooni, H., Sheridan, T.B., Houpt, P.K.: Robust compliant motion for manipulators, part I: the fundamental concepts of compliant motion. IEEE J. Robot. Autom. **2**(2), 83–92 (1986)
26. Kolter, J.Z., Rogdgers, M.P., Ng, A.Y.: A control architecture for quadruped locomotion over rough terrain. In: IEEE International Coference on Robotics and Automation, pp. 811–818 (2008)

Automatic Operating Method of Robot Dexterous Multi-fingered Hand Using Heuristic Rules

Wei Wang[1], Qiangbing Zhang[1], Zeyuan Sun[1,2,3], Xi Chen[1(✉)], and Zhihong Jiang[1,2,3(✉)]

[1] IRI, School of Mechatronical Engineering,
Beijing Institute of Technology, Beijing, China
{chenxi,jiangzhihong}@bit.edu.cn
[2] Key Laboratory of Biomimetic Robots and Systems, Ministry of Education,
Beijing Institute of Technology, Beijing, China
[3] Beijing Advanced Innovation Center for Intelligent Robotics and Systems,
Beijing, China

Abstract. Automatic grasp planning of robotic hand is always a difficult problem in robotics. Although researchers have developed underactuated hands with less degrees of freedom, automatic grasp planning is still a difficult problem because of the huge number of possible hand configurations. But humans simplify this problem by applying several usual grasp starting postures on most of grasp tasks. In this paper, a method for grasping planning is presented which can use a set of heuristic rules to limit the possibilities of hand configurations. By modeling the object as a set of primitive shapes and applying appropriate grasp starting postures on it, many grasp samples can be generated. And this is the basic content of the heuristic rules. Then, given grasp samples in finite number, a Simulink and Adams co-simulator is built to simulate these discrete grasp samples. The main purpose of the co-simulator is to simulate the dynamic behavior of robotic hand when grasping and measure the grasp quality using force closure and grasp measurement of largest-minimum resisted wrench. Last, a grasp library with force closure grasps is built where all items of grasp are sorted by the function value of grasp measurement. With the library, it's easy to plan a grasp for certain object by just selecting an appropriate grasp from the library.

Keywords: Robot grasping · Planning · Simulink and Adams co-simulator

1 Introduction

Although researchers have developed many robotic hands, such as Okada's three-fingered hands [1, 2], Stanford/JPL's three-fingered hands [3], Utah/MIT's four-fingered hands [4], BH's three-fingered hands and four-fingered hands [5, 6], DLR's four-fingered hands [7, 8] and Robonaut's five-fingered hands [9]. However, the problem of automatic grasp planning has been always challenging.

Generally, before grasp planning, it's needed to measure the grasp quality with analytical formula. The simplest function is closure, including force closure and form

© Springer Nature Singapore Pte Ltd. 2019
F. Sun et al. (Eds.): ICCSIP 2018, CCIS 1005, pp. 420–431, 2019.
https://doi.org/10.1007/978-981-13-7983-3_37

closure. At least 7 smooth point contacts can realize spatial closure of objects [10]. Salisbury and Roth [11] proposed that the force closure is equivalent to that the primitive wrench can generate the wrench space. In the contact force space, Murray et al. [12] proposed that force closure is equivalent to full rank grasping matrix and the grasp has strict internal force. Zuo and Qian [13] extended this condition to soft finger. In addition to closure, scholars also proposed grasp quality measures to evaluate grasp quality. Generally, the grasp quality measurements are classified into two groups: approaches focusing on the contact point on the object and the approaches focusing on the configuration of hand. Besides, there also are some measures developed for underactuated hand [14].

Based on the measures, experts presented many methods to plan grasping, such as optimal planning method, analytical method and experimental method. The optimal programming method is equivalent to convex optimization problem. Zhu and Wang [15] proposed an iterative algorithm. Liu [16] represented the optimal problem as the min-max-min problem and presented a solution algorithm. The analytical method is to find the hand configuration and contact point through dynamic simulation. For example, Tegin implemented a simulation of KThand based on GraspIt, where the force closure was used as grasp quality measure [17]. The experimental method planning the grasp by imitating the person's grasp experience. For example, Li et al. used BP neural network and expert system in literature [18] to realize grasp planning for fruit picking tasks. However, most of these methods can only get the position of the contact pion and the posture of the hand relative to object [19, 20]. We can also identify and grasp objects from complex environments by Deep Learning methods [21].

The method of grasp planning presented in this paper is to generate the grasp samples using a set of rules. Then these samples will be simulated in co-simulator and be sorted by grasp quality. Finally, we'll get a grasp library consisting of force closure grasp sorted by grasp quality. The overall workflow diagram is as follows (Fig. 1):

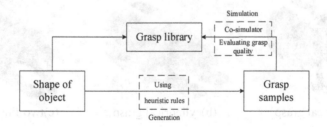

Fig. 1. Workflow of the grasp planning method

After this introduction the article is structured as follows. Section 2 summarizes the heuristic rules for generating samples of candidate grasp. Section 3 build a Simulink and Adams co-simulator and describes how the qualities of candidate grasp are evaluated. Section 4 builds a grasp library as the result of grasp planning by selecting force closure grasps and sorting them by the grasp quality and then designs an experiment to verify the results of grasp planning. Section 5 is summary and some future directions.

2 Grasp Generation

This section establishes a set of rules to generate the grasp samples, which can effectively reduce the number of possible grasps. In order to establish the rules, the following works is needed: firstly, the structure of the robotic hand is analyzed and the grasp starting posture of the robotic hand can be classified into 3 types; Then real object with complex shape is modeled by primitive geometry or there's combination. Then, we define a set of heuristic rules to determine which grasp starting postures should be applied for each primitive shape and how the parameters of the grasp should be constrained. The rest of this section will describe these works in the order as above.

2.1 Introduction to Underactuated Robotic Hand

Humans' hands have many degrees of freedom, but in most of grasp tasks, humans only use several specific postures, which are defined as grasp starting postures, to grasp various objects. In the same way, robotic hand can use several specific postures to grasp most objects. What the grasp starting postures should be depends on the mechanical structure of robotic hand. The robotic hand in this paper is a underactuated robotic hand with three fingers, as shown in the Fig. 2. The hand has three fingers, including the top single finger called thumb, and the two coupled fingers in the bottom called forefinger. Each finger has three links, which are connected by revolute joint and torsional spring. There are also four four-bar linkage to help the actuator to control the motion of the whole finger. In virtue of the gear between the base of forefingers, the two forefingers will rotate synchronously in opposite direction. This robotic hand has 10 degrees of freedom, but only four actuators. The four-bar linkage and torsional spring between the links of a finger make all the parts of the finger move as expected.

(a)spherical grasp   (b)cylindrical grasp   (c)two-finger grasp

Fig. 2. Three types of grasp starting posture

2.2 Grasp Starting Postures

The grasp starting postures of the robotic hand can be divided into three types, as shown in the Fig. 2: spherical grasping posture, cylindrical grasping posture and two-fingers grasping posture.

In the spherical grasp posture, the three fingers of the robotic hand are distributed in the palm of the hand uniformly. Because of the character of the hand that the finger's mechanical structure adapts to the shape of object, the final configuration of contact point varies with the size of the object. When grasping a bigger ball, there will be envelope grasping, that is each link of a finger have contact with the object. On the contrary, there will be fingertip pinches when grasping smaller object.

In the cylindrical grasp posture, the two forefingers and the thumb are located in the contrary side of the palm. Similarly, envelope grasping occurs when grasping bigger object and fingertip pinches occur when grasping smaller one.

In the two-finger grasping posture, the thumb of the robotic hand does not participate in the grasping, and the grasping is implemented by the rest two forefingers. This posture is applicable to the precise manipulation for objects in small size, such as picking up a pen from the ground.

2.3 Primitive Shapes

The shape of an object is usually very complex. In optimal grasp planning, the complexity of object's shape will cause much difficulty in calculation. However, complex object shapes do not cause too much difficulty in humans' grasp. It is because that humans simplify the actual shape of object into primitive shapes and their combination. Generally, there are four primitive shapes as shown in Fig. 3. In the co-simulator, the object to be tested will be modeled as combination of primitive shapes, which will largely reduce the computational complexity of the simulator.

Fig. 3. Primitive shapes and simplified shape of a cup

2.4 Heuristic Rules

This section defines a set of rules used for generating grasp samples. Generally, a grasp consists of a 6D hand's pose relative to the object, a parameter θ corresponding to the rotational angle of forefingers' base that determines the hand's grasp starting posture. therefore, there are 7 parameters to describe a grasp sample, in other word, a grasp sample has 7 degrees of freedom. All the grasps can be denoted as follows:

$$\text{Grasps} = \{(R, P, \theta) | RR^T = E_{3\times3}, P \in \mathbb{R}^3, \theta \in [0°, 90°]\} \tag{1}$$

We have discussed three grasp starting postures and four primitive shapes. According to the human grasp experience, a certain primitive shapes correspond to several grasp starting postures and different primitive shapes have different constraints on the parameters of corresponding grasp. Therefore, there is a mapping between the grasp starting postures and the primitive shapes. According to the mapping, most parameters of a grasp sample can be determinate. As for the rest degrees of freedom and corresponding parameters, it's a practical method to sample randomly over certain range. After these procedures as above, a set of grasp samples for certain object will be generated. To facilitate the following description of the rules, it is defined that the centerline vector of the robotic hand is perpendicular to the palm and pass the center point of the palm, pointing to the fingers, and the thumb vector passes the center point of the palm, is perpendicular to the centerline vector and belongs to the surface of palm, pointing to the thumb. The unconstrained parameters of grasp will be sampled uniformly over a certain range.

Cylinder: For spherical grasp starting posture, centerline of robotic hand and the centerline of cylinder coincide, forefinger's rotational Angle θ equals to $60°$; for cylindrical grasp starting posture, the center line of the robotic hand and the thumb vector are all perpendicular to the center line of the cylinder, and the forefinger's rotational Angle θ equals to $0°$. For two-fingers grasp starting posture, the center line of the robotic hand and the thumb vector are perpendicular to the center line of the cylinder, and the forefinger's rotational Angle θ equals to $90°$.

Cuboid: For two-fingers grasp starting posture, the center line of robotic hand is perpendicular to one side, and the thumb vector is parallel to the corresponding surface; for cylindrical grasp starting posture, the center line of the robotic hand is perpendicular to one side, and the thumb vector is parallel to the corresponding surface.

Sphere: For spherical grasp starting posture, robotic hand center line vector pointing toward the center of the ball; for two-fingers grasp starting posture, robotic hand center line vector points to the center of the ball.

Cone: For spherical grasp starting posture, centerline vector points to the bottom of the cone; for two-fingers grasp starting posture, centerline vector points to the bottom of the cone.

Actually, what in the above is a simple description of the rules, and the rules should be the constraints on the seven parameters in Eq. (1). And Fig. 4 summarizes the heuristic rules:

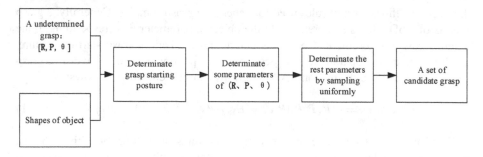

Fig. 4. The procedure to generating candidate grasp

3 Co-simulator and Grasp Quality Measure

Although the grasp samples are generated in the previous section, the actual grasp qualities are unknown. Meanwhile, it is not realistic to verify the grasp qualities of grasp samples using the real robotic hand. Therefore, it's needed to build a Simulink and Adams co-simulator, which can simulate the dynamic behavior of robotic hand when grasping. Based on the co-simulation, the grasp quality can be evaluated by force closure and grasp measurement of largest-minimum resisted wrench.

3.1 Co-simulator

Simulink is a visual simulation tool of control system developed by Mathworks. And ADAMS is an automatic analysis software of mechanical system dynamics developed by MSC in the United States. In simulation, Simulink provides the PID controller, while ADAMS is responsible for simulating the dynamic behavior of the robotic hand and outputting information such as the position and pressure of the contact point between the hand and the object.

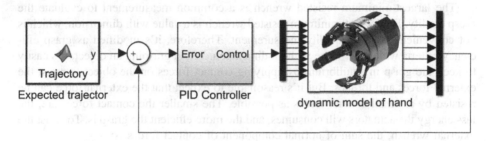

Fig. 5. Block diagram of co-simulation

The Simulink simulation system is shown in the Fig. 5 above. The Adams_sub module as shown above is the dynamic model of hand and will be used as part of the Simulink control system. The PID system of the robotic hand was built in Simulink, and the Adams_sub module was inserted into it to form the complete Simulink and Adams co-simulator of the underactuated robotic hand.

3.2 Evaluation of Grasp Quality

The most important purpose of the co-simulator is to simulate the dynamic behavior of underactuated hand and then measure the grasp quality in scalar value. In this paper, the grasp quality is measured by force closure and largest-minimum resisted wrench. A grasp is force closure when it satisfies the below condition:

$$\exists f = [f_1; \ldots f_i; \ldots], \text{st} \quad -w_{ext} = Gf \tag{2}$$

where **G** is grasp matrix and **f** is contact force vector. Generally, there are infinite possibilities for the value of contact force f when grasping. And all the possibilities of contact force can be denoted as Grasp Wrench Space $\left(W_C^U\right)$ as follow equation:

$$W_C^U = convex\,hull\{w_i = G_i f_i | \|f_i\| \geq 0, f_i \cdot n_i \leq 1\}_{i=1...n} \tag{3}$$

If there is no external wrench applied on the object, force closure is equivalent to that the origin of wrench space belong to Grasp Wrench Space. By introducing the distance function of higher dimensional space [22], force closure condition can be formulized as follow:

$$d\left(O, W_C^U\right) = \underset{u=1}{min}\,p_{W_C^U}(u) \tag{4}$$

where **O** is the origin of wrench space, and $p_{W_C^U}(u)$ represents the distance between O and W_C^U in u direction. And u is a unit direction vector in wrench space. The formula above is a problem of constrained optimal solution, and negative value means that the grasp is force closure one. The Matlab optimization function, fmincon, can solve this optimization problem easily.

The largest-minimum resisted wrench is a common measurement to evaluate the grasp quality. But largest-minimum resisted wrench is a value with dimension, which is not convenient as grasp quality measurement. Therefore, it's modified as grasp efficiency criteria which is a value without dimension. When grasping an object, it's easily to keep the grasp in equilibrium by applying contact forces on the object to resist the external forces and torques. But it's reasonable to expect that the external force can be resisted by as small contact forces as possible. The smaller the contact forces are, the less energy the actuators will consumes, and the more efficient the grasp is. To resist the external wrench, the sum of normal component of contact forces is:

$$Q_{(G, w_{ext})} = \underset{f_i = -w_{ext}}{min}\left\{\sum_{i=1}^{m}\frac{f_{in}}{f_i^U}\right\} \tag{5}$$

Generally, it's not so easy to calculate the value of $Q_{(G, w_{ext})}$. According to literature [22], the friction cone can be linearized:

$$f_i = \sum_{j=1}^{n}\lambda_{i,j}s_{i,j}, \lambda_{i,j} > 0, \sum_{j=1}^{n}\lambda_{i,j} \leq 1 \tag{6}$$

$$s_{i,j} = f_i^U\left[1, \mu_i\cos\left(\frac{2j\pi}{n}\right), \mu_i\sin\left(\frac{2j\pi}{n}\right)\right] \tag{7}$$

Therefore, grasp efficiency criteria can be formulized as follows:

$$\begin{cases} Maximize\ w_{ext}^T u \\ st.w_k^T u \leq 1, w_k \in W_C^U, u \in \mathbb{R}^6 \end{cases} \tag{8}$$

If we denote the grasp efficiency as Q, the Q equals to the maximum of $w_{ext}^T u$, which is also a constrained optimal problem.

4   Experiment Results

4.1   Library of Grasp

In this section, we'll design an experiment to verify the grasp planning method in this paper. First, it's described that how the grasp library is created for tested objects. Then, an experiment is designed to verify the top grasps in grasp library. The two objects to be tested are shown in Fig. 6. After generating samples of candidate grasp, simulating the samples and evaluating the grasp quality, we'll get a library of grasp where all the grasps are force closure and sorted by the grasp quality value.

Fig. 6. The tested objects: a cup and a phone

These two objects are a cup and a smart phone. According to the heuristic rules built in Sect. 2, the first object can be grasped by three grasp starting postures and the second object can be grasped by two grasp starting postures. As described in Sect. 2, it's need to use 7 parameters to present a grasp. These parameters are the pose of hand relative to the object and the configuration of hand. The pose consists of a 3D Euler Angle and a 3D position vector of the hand. And the configuration of hand is the rotational angle of the forefingers' base. The parameters of all possible candidate grasp generated for the cup are listed in Table 1. In the Table 1 there are totally 472 candidate grasps.

Table 1. The candidate grasps of cup

Grasp groups	Euler angle	Position vector of hand	Rotational angle	Number
First group	$(0, 0, [0, 2\pi])$	$(0, 0, [-116, 0])$	30	44
Second group	$(\pi/2, 0, [0, 2\pi])$	$(0, [38, 116], [-28, 28])$	0	192
Third group	$(-\frac{\pi}{2}, [0, 2\pi], -\pi/2)$	$(0, [38, 116], [28, 90])$	90	192
Forth group	$(\pi, 0, [0, 2\pi])$	$(0, [246, 362])$	30	44

All the candidate grasp will be simulated and the grasps which are not force closure should be discard. The rest grasps are sorted by the grasp quality value as a library of grasp. Here are all the samples of the grasp library of the cup, including totally 152 grasps (Table 2):

Table 2. The grasp library of cup

Grasp groups	Euler angle	Position vector of hand	Rotational angle	Number
First group	$(0, 0, [0, 2\pi])$	$(0, 0, [-116, 0])$	30	36
Second group	$(\pi/2, 0, [0, 2\pi])$	$(0, [38, 116], [-28, 28])$	0	48
Third group	$(-\frac{\pi}{2}, [0, 2\pi], -\pi/2)$	$(0, [38, 116], [28, 90])$	90	48
Forth group	$(\pi, 0, [0, 2\pi])$	$(0, 0, [246, 362])$	30	20

What are shown in the Fig. 7 are some of the best grasps sorted in quality value. Another object, the phone, is also tested, whose some best grasps in grasp library are also shown in Fig. 7.

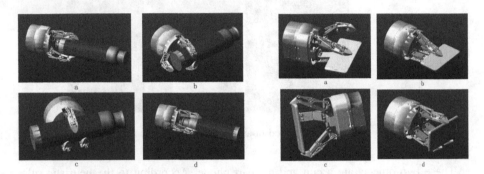

Fig. 7. The best grasps sorted in grasp quality value

4.2 Experimental Verification

The top grasps in library generated from the heuristic rules are the best grasps only in theory. It's an undetermined problem that whether the value of grasp efficiency criteria represent the grasp quality accurately. So in this section an experiment is designed to verify grasp library. Exactly, the value of grasp efficiency criteria and the current of the hand controller both reflect the amount of energy consumed when grasping an object. So it's very reasonable to verify the result of the grasp planning by measuring the current of the robotic hand controller when grasping. 9 grasps of the library are tested and their parameters are as below: Euler angle of xyz is $(\pi/2, 0, -\pi/2)$, position vector of hand is $(x, 154, 0)$, where x $= \{0, 15, 35, 55, 75, 95, 115, 135, 150\}$ and $\theta = 0$ (Fig. 8).

Fig. 8. Grasp in simulator and corresponding one in reality

All the grasp qualities of these 9 grasps are evaluated and the relationship between the grasp quality, current of controller and parameters x are described as Fig. 9. Although the two curve in Fig. 9 are not the same strictly, the value of grasp efficiency criteria and the current of the hand controller have the common trend when the parameter x varies. Therefore, it's verified that the method of grasp planning presented in this paper is reliable.

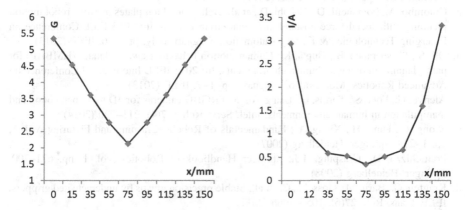

Fig. 9. Grasp quality value and current value of hand controller

5   Conclusion and Future Work

In this paper a grasp planning method based on grasp starting posture is presented and the physical platform is a underactuated three-finger robotic hand. Centering on the grasp planning and grasp quality evaluation, we have done these works as follows. Firstly, the grasp starting postures of the hand are classified into three types. Then we build a set of heuristic rules based on the grasp starting postures and primitive shapes, which can generate discrete and finite grasp samples. A Simulink and Adams co-simulator is also built to simulate the dynamic behavior of robotic hand and to evaluate the grasp quality using force closure and grasp measurement of largest-minimum resisted wrench. This method of grasp planning will generate a grasp library consist of force closure grasps. Finally, an experiment is designed to verify the grasp planning method.

There is some problem in current method of grasp planning, such as that it can't guarantee that the all the best grasps are included in the set of sample grasps generated by the rules. In the future, it's needed to apply Genetic Algorithm to extend and optimize the grasp library to include all the best grasps as much as possible. Besides, the measure of largest-minimum resisted wrench is need to improve to describe the grasp quality of the underactuated robotic hand more accurately.

Acknowledgement. The authors would like to acknowledge the National Natural Science Foundation of China (61733001, 61573063, 61503029, U1713215) for its support and funding of this paper.

References

1. Khatib, O., Yokoi, K., Brock, O., et al.: Robots in human environments. In: 1999 IEEE International Workshop on Robot Motion and Control, Kiekrz, Poland, pp. 213–221. IEEE (1999)
2. Buss, M., Carton, D., Gonsior, B., et al.: Towards proactive human-robot interaction in human environments. In: 2011 IEEE International Conference on Cognitive Info Communications, Budapest, pp. 1–6. IEEE (2011)
3. Colombo, A., Fontanelli, D., Gandhi, D., et al.: Behavioural templates improve robot motion planning with social force posturel in human environments. In: 2013 IEEE Conference on Emerging Technologies & Factory Automation, Cagliari, Italy, pp. 1–6. IEEE (2013)
4. Oli, S., L'Esperance, B., Gupta, K.: Human motion behaviour aware planner (HMBAP) for path planning in dynamic human environments. In: 2013 IEEE International Conference on Advanced Robotics, Montevideo, Uruguay, pp. 1–7. IEEE (2013)
5. Alenya, G., Foix, S., Torras, C.: Using ToF and RGBD cameras for 3D robot perception and manipulation in human environments. Intel. Serv. Robot. **7**(4), 211–220 (2014)
6. Xiong, C., Ding, H., Xiong, Y.: Fundamentals of Robotic Grasping and Fixturing, vol. 1, pp. 1–218. Springer, Heidelberg (2007)
7. Prattichizzo, D., Grasping, T.J.: Springer Handbook of Robotics, vol. 1, pp. 671–700. Springer, Heidelberg (2008)
8. Kragten, G., Baril, M., Gosselin, C., et al.: Stable precision grasps by underactuated grippers. IEEE Trans. Rob. **27**(6), 1056–1066 (2011)
9. Bridgwater, L.B., Ihrke, C.A., Diftler, M.A., et al.: The Robonaut 2 hand - designed to do work with tools. In: IEEE International Conference on Robotics and Automation, pp. 3425–3430. IEEE (2012)
10. Markenscoff, X.: The geometry of grasping. Int. J. Rob. Res. **9**(1), 61–74 (1990)
11. Salisbury, K., Roth, B.: Kinematic and force analysis of articulated hands. ASME J. Mech. Transm. Autom. Des. **105**(1), 35–41 (1983)
12. Murray, R.M., Sastry, S.S., Li, Z.: A Mathematical Introduction to Robotic Manipulation. CRC Press Inc., Boca Raton (1994)
13. Zuo, B., Qian, W.: A force-closure test for soft multi-fingered grasps. Sci. China **41**(1), 62–69 (1998)
14. Malvezzi, M., Prattichizzo, D.: Evaluation of grasp stiffness in underactuated compliant hands. In: IEEE International Conference on Robotics and Automation, pp. 2074–2079. IEEE (2013)
15. Zhu, X.-Y., Wang, J.: Synthesis of force-closure grasps on 3-D objects based on the Q distance. IEEE Trans. Robot. Autom. **19**(4), 669–679 (2003)
16. Liu, Y.H.: Qualitative test and force optimization of 3-D frictional form-closure grasps using linear programming. IEEE Trans. Robot. Autom. **15**(1), 163–173 (1999)
17. Tegin, J., Iliev, B., Skoglund, A., et al.: Real life grasping using an under-actuated robot hand simulation and experiments. In: 2009 IEEE International Conference on Advanced Robotics. Munich, Germany, pp. 1–8. IEEE (2009)
18. Li, S., Yao, S., Zhang, Y., et al.: Grasp planning analysis and strategy modeling for underactuated multi-fingered robot hand using in fruits grasping. Afr. J. Agric. Res. **6**(9), 2086–2098 (2011)
19. Saxena, A., Driemeyer, J., Ng, A.: Robotic grasping of novel objects using vision. Int. J. Rob. Res. **27**(2), 157–173 (2008)

20. Saxena, A., Chung, S., Ng, A.: 3-D depth reconstruction from a single still image. Int. J. Comput. Vis. **76**(1), 53–69 (2008)
21. Lenz, I., Lee, H., Saxena, A.: Deep learning for detecting robotic grasps. Int. J. Robot. Res. **34**(4–5), 705–724 (2014)
22. Yu, Z., Qian, W.: Linearizing the soft finger contact constraint with application to dynamic force distribution in multifingered grasping. Sci. China **48**(2), 121–130 (2005)

A Tendon-Driven Robotic Dexterous Hand Design for Grasping

Ziwei Xia[2], Jiahui Yuan[4], Bin Fang[1(✉)], Fuchun Sun[1], Chang Zhu[1], Yiyong Yang[2], and Huasong Min[3]

[1] State Key Laboratory of Intelligent Technology and Systems,
Tsinghua National Laboratory for Information Science and Technology,
Department of Computer Science and Technology, Tsinghua University,
Haidian District, Beijing 100083, China
fangbin@tsinghua.edu.cn, fangbin@mail.tsinghua.edu.cn
[2] School of Engineering and Technology,
China University of Geosciences (Beijing), Beijing 100083, China
[3] Institute of Robotics and Intelligent Systems,
Wuhan University of Science and Technology, Wuhan 430081, China
[4] Samsung Research China - Beijing (SRC-B), Beijing, China
jiahuil.yuan@samsung.com

Abstract. This paper focuses on the research of humanoid dexterous hand with tendon-driven. The structure of the dexterous hand is designed and its kinematics, dynamics and the relationship between the finger joints and the fingertip force are deduced. Then, based on the characteristics of the dexterous hand, a hierarchical control system is proposed and fuzzy adaptive PID is used as the motor control algorithm. The grasping experiments are implemented and the results indicate the hand has well performance.

Keywords: Tendon-driven · Kinematics · Dynamics · Grasping

1 Introduction

As an essential part of robotic systems, dexterous hands consist in each anthropomorphic robot. The dexterous hand can not only be used as a general-purpose operating equipment in various fields, but also can be used as disabled prosthetic [1]. The design of dexterous hands has been an active area of research for more than three decades [2].

We can divide four development stages of dexterous hands by how well they integrate with sensors. The first stage is that the type and quantity of sensors of dexterous hand are small and the function is single. Okada et al. [3] designed the multi-fingered dexterous hand to be a typical representative. This dexterous hand has no tactile sensors on its fingers but an optical sensor on the palm of the hand to determine the position of the object for grasping. In the second stage, more sensors are used and they tend to be smaller. The Stanford/JPL dexterous hand developed by Stanford

---

Z. Xia and J. Yuan—These two authors contributed equally.

© Springer Nature Singapore Pte Ltd. 2019
F. Sun et al. (Eds.): ICCSIP 2018, CCIS 1005, pp. 432–444, 2019.
https://doi.org/10.1007/978-981-13-7983-3_38

University is a typical example [4]. The hand is equipped with three fingers of the same size and each finger has 3 degrees of freedom (DOFs), corresponding to the thumb, forefinger and middle finger of the hand. A 3×3 multi-array tactile sensor with a size of 2×2 mm is installed on each fingertip. With the tactile information, the robotic hand can be used for grasping verification. In the third stage, the sensors array are used. Barrett hand has a 3×8 array of tactile sensors on both fingers and hands [5]. The tactile data of the tactile sensor can be applied for grasping attitude selection and object recognition classification [6, 7]. The fourth stage is the perceptual anthropomorphism of the dexterous hand. The BioTacsensor [8] developed by SynTouch company integrates touch, temperature, sliding sensation functions and so on. By installing the sensors, the Shadow hand enhances the operations [9]. Generally, the tactile sensor is important for the robotic dexterous hand.

In this paper, we develop a humanoid tactile to suit for an anthropomorphic robotic hand. In Sect. 2, the structure design of dexterous hand is outlined, and in Sect. 3, the control system is presented. Then, in Sect. 4 the experiment is carried out on the humanoid robotic hand to grasp. Finally, in Sect. 5 the conclusions and the future work are illuminated.

2 Dexterous Hand Design

The dexterous hand in this paper is designed with bionics referring to the fingers of normal human hands. The single finger joint of the dexterous hand can be regarded as a mechanical structure composed of multiple joints in series. In addition, the analysis of kinematics and dynamics of the dexterous hand is described.

2.1 Structural Design

The proposed dexterous hand includes five modularized fingers, a palm and a wrist. Its mechanical parts and control sections are shown as Fig. 1. The whole fingers are departed into two independent portions, phalanges and joints. It is based on modular design and has 22 articulated joints in total, wherein thumb and litter finger has 5 joints and the other four has 4 joints. They are the metacarpophalangeal joint (MP), the proximal interphalangeal joint (PIP), the interphalangeal joint (IP) and the distal interphalangeal joint (DIP). The thumb and the litter finger respectively have 5 DOFs and the other three fingers respectively have 4 DOFs. All of fingers are based on under actuated motion. DIP joint and IP joint are coupled motion, MP joint has adduction-abduction motion and PIP joint has flexion-extension motion.

The structures of two kind of fingers are shown as Fig. 2. There are two torsional springs in DIP and IP to realize the finger reset. Tactile sensors on the above of fingertip which can detect and recognize force when grasping objects. Position sensors are inside of all joints which can measure phalanges' position. The dynamics and motion are transmitted by the rope around the joint axis in DIP and IP joint. For PIP and MP joint, the dynamics and motion are transmitted by the rope around the cross shaft. On the bottom of PIP joint it is linked by two pairs of space between the vertical extension springs and the palm of the internal base.

Flexion-extension and adduction-abduction motion are driven by 17 linear stepper motors, and reset function is realized by torque springs. Motors are responsible for collect and output sensors' signals. By controlling the motor revolving speed and time to achieve each finger's precise movement. Practical transmission of linear stepper motor is shown in Fig. 3. This dexterous hand's sensors cells possess a series of transducers. This design used tactile sensors and position sensors. The adjustable capacitance pressure transducer are used as tactile sensors. Its arrangement have two forms, one is 24 fps array tactile sensor on metacarpal bone, and the other is 6 fps pressure transducer on fingertip. The position sensors employ resistive sensors. The terminal of DIP and IP joint are fixed in the center hole of sensors. They can timely measure present joints' distal position.

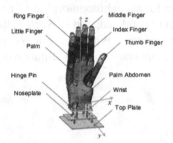

Fig. 1. The porotype of the dexterous hand

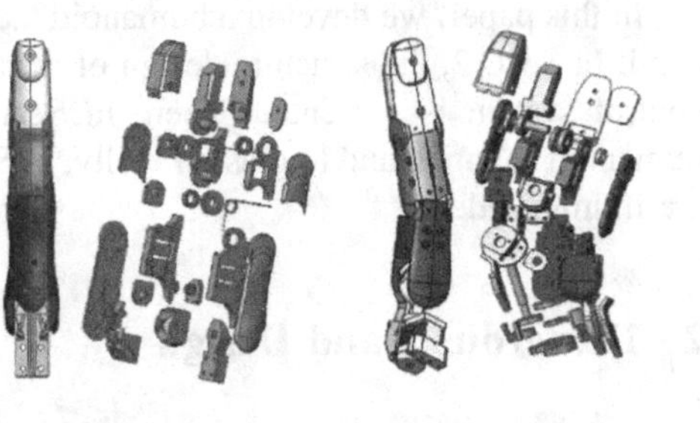

Fig. 2. Structure of 4 DOFs and 5 DOFs finger

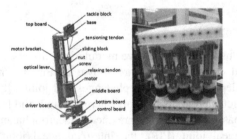

Fig. 3. Practical transmission of linear stepper motor

2.2 Kinematic Analysis

Figure 4 shows a finger joint. The middle finger of a person can generally be divided into five joints: fingertip, DIP (distal interphalangeal) joint, IP (interphalangeal) joint, PIP (proximal Interphalangeal) joint, and MP (metacarpophalangeal) joint. Each knuckle can be seen as being connected by a joint axis which can be equivalent to the coordinate system shown in Fig. 5.

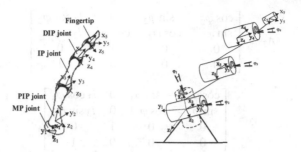

Fig. 4. Finger joint and finger structure model

By the D-H parameter method, the transformation matrix between two links can be described as follows:

$$A = Rot(z, \varphi)Trans(0, 0, d)Trans(l, 0, 0)Rot(x, \theta)$$

$$= \begin{bmatrix} \cos \varphi & -\sin \varphi \cos \theta & \sin \varphi \sin \theta & l \cos \varphi \\ \sin \varphi & \cos \varphi \cos \theta & -\cos \varphi \sin \theta & l \sin \varphi \\ 0 & \sin \theta & \cos \theta & d \\ 0 & 0 & 0 & 1 \end{bmatrix} \tag{1}$$

where Rot is rotation transformation matrix; $Trans$ is a translation transformation matrix; l is a link length; θ is a link twist angle; d is a vertical distance of two links; φ is a knuckle angle.

Assuming that the pose of the base joint of the finger is shown in Fig. 4, the pose equation at the end of the finger can be solved by Eq. (1). Take $x_1 y_1 z_1$ on the knuckle axis of the MP joint as the reference coordinate system, $x_2 y_2 z_2$, $x_3 y_3 z_3$, $x_4 y_4 z_4$ and $x_5 y_5 z_5$ are the coordinate systems on the PIP joint, IP joint, DIP joint, and Fingertip axes. l_1, l_2, l_3 and l_4 are the lengths of MP joint, PIP joint, IP joint and DIP joint. φ_1, φ_2, φ_3 and φ_4 are the rotation angles of the joints, respectively (Table 1).

Table 1. Finger model length and knuckle rotation parameters.

Joint	MP	PIP	IP	DIP
l_i (mm)	0	40	25	18
φ_1 (°)	45	90	90	90

Bring the parameters in the table into Eq. (1), and use A_1, A_2, A_3 and A_4 to indicate the change matrix for each joint.

$$A_1 = \begin{bmatrix} \cos \varphi_1 & 0 & \sin \varphi_1 & l_1 \cos \varphi_1 \\ \sin \varphi_1 & 0 & -\cos \varphi_1 & l_1 \sin \varphi_1 \\ 0 & 1 & 0 & 0 \\ 0 & 0 & 0 & 1 \end{bmatrix}$$

$$A_2 = \begin{bmatrix} \cos\varphi_2 & -\sin\varphi_2 & 0 & l_2\cos\varphi_2 \\ \sin\varphi_2 & \cos\varphi_2 & \cos\varphi_2 & l_2\sin\varphi_2 \\ 0 & 0 & 1 & 0 \\ 0 & 0 & 0 & 1 \end{bmatrix}$$

$$A_3 = \begin{bmatrix} \cos\varphi_3 & -\sin\varphi_3 & 0 & l_3\cos\varphi_3 \\ \sin\varphi_3 & \cos\varphi_3 & 0 & l_3\sin\varphi_3 \\ 0 & 0 & 1 & 0 \\ 0 & 0 & 0 & 1 \end{bmatrix}$$

$$A_4 = \begin{bmatrix} \cos\varphi_4 & -\sin\varphi_4 & 0 & l_4\cos\varphi_4 \\ \sin\varphi_4 & \cos\varphi_4 & 0 & l_4\sin\varphi_4 \\ 0 & 0 & 1 & 0 \\ 0 & 0 & 0 & 1 \end{bmatrix} \tag{2}$$

Assuming the fingertip $P_4 = [0\,0\,0\,1]^T$ in its own coordinate, then

$$
\begin{aligned}
{}^4_1P &= {}^4_1TP_4 = A_1A_2A_3A_4P_4 \\
&= \begin{bmatrix} [l_4\cos(\varphi_2+\varphi_3+\varphi_4)+l_3\cos(\varphi_2+\varphi_3)+l_2\cos(\varphi_2)]\cos\varphi \\ [l_4\cos(\varphi_2+\varphi_3+\varphi_4)+l_3\cos(\varphi_2+\varphi_3)+l_2\cos(\varphi_2)]\sin\varphi_1 \\ -l_4\sin(\varphi_2+\varphi_3+\varphi_4)-l_3c\sin(\varphi_2+\varphi_3)-l_2\sin\varphi_2 \\ 1 \end{bmatrix}
\end{aligned} \tag{3}
$$

where ${}^4_1P$ represents the coordinates of the fingertips for the MP joints.

In robot kinematics, only the position of the fingertip may be given, and the pose of each joint needs to be calculated backwards. This is called inverse kinematics solution. In this case, ${}^i_1T$ is known, and the inverse kinematics can be solved by finding the pose of the fingertip in the coordinate system.

Assuming that the coordinates of the fingertip relative to the $x_1y_1z_1$ coordinate system is (x, y, z), than it can be obtained from Eq. (3) that

$$
\begin{cases}
x = [l_4\cos(\varphi_2+\varphi_3+\varphi_4)+l_3\cos(\varphi_2+\varphi_3)+l_2\cos(\varphi_2)]\cos\varphi_1 \\
y = [l_4\cos(\varphi_2+\varphi_3+\varphi_4)+l_3\cos(\varphi_2+\varphi_3)+l_2\cos(\varphi_2)]\sin\varphi_1 \\
z = -l_4\sin(\varphi_2+\varphi_3+\varphi_4)-l_3c\sin(\varphi_2+\varphi_3)-l_2\sin\varphi_2
\end{cases} \tag{4}
$$

In formula (4), x, y, z, l_2, l_3 and l_4 are all known. Since the joint pulley ratio of the dexterous hand designed in this paper is 1:1, there is a relationship of $\varphi_4 = \varphi_3$, and the calculation is finished. You can get φ_1, φ_2, φ_3 and φ_4. It is worth noting that the solution to this equation is not unique and there may be more or no solution.

2.3 Dynamics Analysis

The dynamics of dexterous hand involves the joint speed during operation, and there is a linear change of the fingertip speed between the joint speed and the actual operation speed. In dexterous hands, the Jacobian matrix refers to a mapping relationship between each of revolute joint's speed and the position of the fingertips. Jacbi has a variety of solutions. The Jacobian matrix for finger motion in this section uses the differential method of forward kinematics.

According to the previous kinematic analysis, the relationship can be clearly defined:

$$\begin{cases} x = f_x(\varphi_1, \varphi_2, \varphi_3, \varphi_4) \\ y = f_y(\varphi_1, \varphi_2, \varphi_3, \varphi_4) \\ z = f_z(\varphi_1, \varphi_2, \varphi_3, \varphi_4) \end{cases} \tag{5}$$

where, x, y and z indicate the position of the tip of the finger; fx, fy, and fz are the corresponding function forms.

Differentiate each joint angle in Eq. (5), it can be got that

$$d\mathbf{P} = \begin{bmatrix} dx \\ dy \\ dz \end{bmatrix} = \begin{bmatrix} \frac{dx}{d\varphi_1} & \frac{dx}{d\varphi_2} & \frac{dx}{d\varphi_3} & \frac{dx}{d\varphi_4} \\ \frac{dy}{d\varphi_1} & \frac{dy}{d\varphi_2} & \frac{dy}{d\varphi_3} & \frac{dy}{d\varphi_4} \\ \frac{dz}{d\varphi_1} & \frac{dz}{d\varphi_2} & \frac{dz}{d\varphi_3} & \frac{dz}{d\varphi_4} \end{bmatrix} \cdot \begin{bmatrix} d\varphi_1 \\ d\varphi_2 \\ d\varphi_3 \\ d\varphi_4 \end{bmatrix} = \mathbf{J}d\boldsymbol{\varphi} \tag{6}$$

Where $\mathbf{P}$ is the coordinates of the end point and $\mathbf{J}$ is the Jacobian matrix.

Since the power of the dexterous hand comes from the linear movement of the slider converted by the screw motor mechanism, the two groups of tendons (relaxed and tensioned) are respectively fixed at the ends of the slider. The force is transferred through the two sets of pulleys and finally passed to the tip of the fingers of the dexterous hand to achieve the movement of the dexterous hand. In view of the driving mode, this paper uses the Lagrange equation to calculate the relationship between the fingertip force and the joint torque for dynamic analysis of single finger.

According to the displacement relationship during the motion, the following equation can be obtained as follows:

$$\begin{cases} s = r(\varphi_1 + \varphi_2) \\ v = r(\varphi_1' + \varphi_2') \\ a = r(\varphi_1'' + \varphi_2'') \end{cases} \tag{7}$$

where s, v and a are respectively the displacement, velocity and acceleration in the current state; r is the contact arc length; φ_1 is the joint rotation angle.

Using the Lagrange equation, the kinetic model equation can be obtained as follows:

$$\frac{d}{dt}\left(\frac{\partial l}{\partial \varphi_i}\right) - \frac{\partial l}{\partial \varphi_i} = F_i \tag{8}$$

where F_i is the generalized driving force of the ith joint and b is the length of the joint.

According to the finger's moment of inertia, kinematic equation and potential energy equation, the following formula is obtained:

$$\begin{cases} J_1 = 2m_1 r^2/5 \\ J_2 = m_1 d_1^2 + m_2 l_1^2 + J_2^c \\ J_3 = m_2 d_2^2 + J_3^c \\ J_4 = m_4 d_2 l_1 \end{cases} \quad (9)$$

$$E = \frac{1}{2}J_2\varphi_1'^2 + \frac{1}{2}J_3\varphi_2^2 + J_4\varphi_2'\varphi_3'\cos\varphi_3 \quad (10)$$

$$V = \frac{1}{2}k_1\varphi_2^2 + \frac{1}{2}k_2\varphi_3^2 \quad (11)$$

where m_i is the mass of the ith knuckle; J_i is the moment of inertia of the ith knuckle relative to the centroid; d_i is the distance from the centroid of the ith knuckle to the ith knuckle; and l_i is the ith knuckle Length; k_i is the ith spring constant.

According to the principle of dynamics, assuming that the joint is in contact with the object, the rotation angle φ_2 is a fixed value, then $x = r(\varphi_2 + \varphi_3)$ at this time, then the relationship between force and rotation angle is as follows:

$$\begin{bmatrix} J_1\cos\varphi_3 \\ J_2 \end{bmatrix}\varphi_3'' + \begin{bmatrix} J_3\sin\varphi_3 \\ J_2 \end{bmatrix}\varphi_3'^2 + \begin{bmatrix} k_2 \\ k_1 \end{bmatrix}\varphi_3 + \begin{bmatrix} -k_1\varphi_2 + k_2\varphi_3 \\ 0 \end{bmatrix} = \begin{bmatrix} F_1 \\ F_2 \end{bmatrix} \quad (12)$$

In Eq. (12), F_1 and F_2 are the driving forces of the first joint and the second joint, respectively.

3 Control System

The dexterous hand control system designed in this paper adopts a hierarchical control method and is mainly composed of a service layer, a real-time control layer, a sensor layer and a dynamic layer.

The service layer serves as the first layer of the control system. It distributes tasks according to the information collected by the fingers, which is the mainly task of information exchange and the operation planning process. On the PC side, the service layer is designed with a human-computer interaction interface. Through the interface, the finger's control parameters can be adjusted, and fingertip forces and joint rotation information of each finger can be collected. The layer is valuable and mainly for the planning of operational tasks, which is to adjust the gestures of the fingers of the dexterous hand in real time to ensure the stability when grabbing.

The real-time control layer of the system serves as the second layer of the control system and mainly accepts the planning instructions of the service layer. Due to the large amount of information processed at this layer, multiple real-time embedded control boards are used. The control board is roughly divided into four parts: a fingertip circuit board, a finger pulp circuit board, a palm control board, and a motor drive board. The main control chip of the fingertip circuit board is STM32L452, which is mainly used to process the tactile signal handed to the palm control board. The main control chip of the finger pulp circuit board is STM32L452 also, which mainly samples the angle values of each joint of each finger, and at the same time, the tactile information of the fingertip circuit board and the current detected angle are packaged and transmitted to the palm control board on the hand. Palm control board, whose main control chip is STM32F777, is the most important processing part of this system. It is principally not only used to analyze and process signals such as haptic and angle information, but also used to accept server action commands and to analyze and issue commands to the motor drive board. To control the various movement of each motor, the motor drive control board is utilized, and it's main control chip is STM32F051C8T6.

The sensor management layer acts as the third layer of the control system. The actual function is to collect the real-time status of the entire hand and monitor the movement of the fingers to prevent uncontrollable fingers. It uploads signals collected by various sensors for the real-time control layer of the system, and also provides an emergency stop signal for the real-time control layer of the system. The fingertip circuit board and the finger-pad circuit board serve as controllers of this layer to perform real-time control of sensors and motors. The tactile sensor samples at a sampling frequency of 200 Hz, buffers the data through DMA, and then averages each DMA value up to 10 times to obtain a tactile value at the current time. The angle sensor samples at a sampling frequency of 20 Hz and also uses DMA for data buffering. The pulp control board sends the haptic data and angle data to a palm control panel with a time-stamped data packet. The palm of the hand board accepts the action command sent by the server on the one hand, determines the current system state by analyzing the command, and issues a motor motion signal to the motor control board. After the motor control board receives the motor motion signal, it generates a response pulse motor control signal to drive each motor to do the corresponding motion.

The power layer serves as the bottom layer of the control system. It only accepts the control commands of the real-time control layer of the system. Besides providing the driving force of the dexterous hand, it also provides various information of the motor motion state, such as current information and speed information. The control system is shown in Fig. 5.

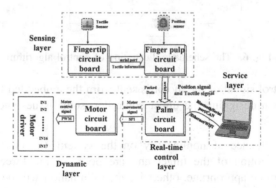

Fig. 5. Control system diagram

The dexterous hand is designed to use the motor to move the finger joint through the reins. However, this transmission method has certain defects, that is, when the rope is deformed due to the tension or the friction between the rope and the sleeve. The system has a strong nonlinearity, which makes it difficult to control the precise joint position. Therefore, the proper motor control method plays a decisive role in the reliability of the system. In order to achieve a satisfactory control result, the control of dexterous hands adopts a hierarchical control method. The control signal of the motor is determined by the controller of the system according to the position and tactile sensor. The nonlinearity of the system generated during the rotation of the joint makes the traditional PID algorithm less effective when controlling the system. Therefore, this paper adopts fuzzy self-adaptive PID control algorithm, which adds a fuzzy inference part to the traditional PID algorithm, to improve it. It is used to dynamically adjust the three parameters of P, I and D in real time and improve the real-time performance of the system. The control system of the dexterous hand determines whether to perform nonlinear compensation according to the position sensor and the tactile sensor, and then finds the displacement of the smart finger end in the space and turns into the rotation angle of each joint. According to the angle command of each motor, the fuzzy adaptive PID is used as the servo control layer, to control the rotation of the motor to the target angle. The schematic illustration of control algorithm shown in Fig. 6.

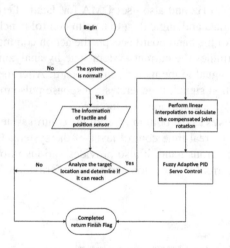

Fig. 6. The schematic illustration of control algorithm

Since the control signal of the motor is sent from the embedded board in the palm of your hand, when designing the upper controller, some issues should also be paid attention as follows:

(1) Due to the influence of nonlinearity on the system, the characteristics of the commutation motion of the finger end are poor, so the force control without overshoot is more appropriate, otherwise the elimination will be time-consuming.
(2) For the control command given by the upper computer, it must be judged whether it can be reached, otherwise the system will have uncontrollable errors.
(3) The speed of movement of the dexterous hand should be maintained properly, and the upper and lower limits should be set for the speed control of the motor, otherwise the reins will be broken due to the excessive tension.

4 Experiment Evaluation

The stability of dexterous hand movement in the fine-manipulation task is dependent on the merits if the control system, and the quality of the tactile sensor determines the precision of the dexterous hand on force control. In this part the experiment is conducted using the dexterous hand with its fingertip equipping tactile sensors for force controlling and grasping.

4.1 Force Control Test

The tactile sensor described is used to carry out force grasping experiments, and detect the distribution and size of the force. We divided 25 sensing points into the force of x, y and z in accordance with the weight of the calibration, and then set the dexterous hand grasping mode as control mode to grasp objects. The force threshold values of 1N, 5N and 10N were tested respectively, and the relationship diagram of three-dimensional force and time was obtained.

The simplest cylinder is chosen as the target object, ensuring that the fingertips of each finger are as close to the target as possible. Based on base joint rotation speed, set the dexterous hand speed slow speed that joint rotation speed is 45°/s, medium that joint rotation speed is 60°/s, high speed that joint rotation speed is 90°/s. Force control experiment in three groups, respectively set up dexterous hand running mode of low speed, medium speed and high speed, at the same time each mode set up 1N, 5N and 10N three force threshold value, the index finger in the process of fetching contact force respectively as shown in Figs. 7, 8 and 9.

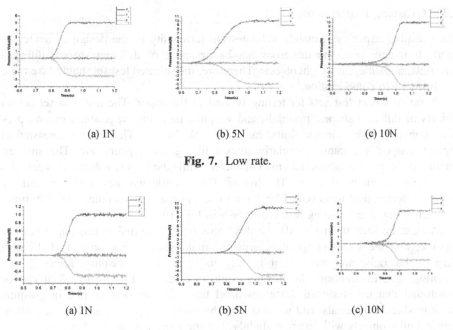

(a) 1N   (b) 5N   (c) 10N

Fig. 7. Low rate.

(a) 1N   (b) 5N   (c) 10N

Fig. 8. Median rate.

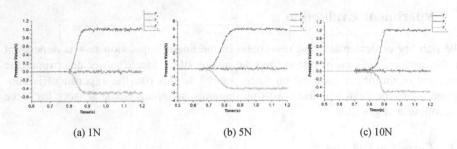

(a) 1N   (b) 5N   (c) 10N

Fig. 9. High rate.

As can be seen from Figs. 7, 8 and 9, fingertip tactile sensor performance is stable, although the fingertip pressure value has small fluctuations, but the three-dimensional force is very stable. When the force reaches the threshold at the time of grasping, the fluctuation of the force increases. This is because when the target state is reached, the motor still maintains the operating state to dynamically adjust the magnitude of the contact force. The stepper motor will generate a great amount of vibration noise at low speed. This kind of noise will affect the control system and thus affect the measurement of sensor force. In the case of the same force threshold, the rate of increase of the force corresponding to the running speed of each type of motor is different. The faster the motor runs, the faster the force rises in the curve. For the three different force threshold experiments of 1N, 5N, and 10N, the greater the force threshold is, the longer the target force is reached at the same motor running speed, and the greater the influence of the vibration noise generated by the motor at low speed startup on the system.

4.2 Grasping Experiments

The grasping experiment mainly validates the rationality of the design of dexterous hand. It mainly tests the dexterous hand's grasping of different shapes, different materials, and different weight objects. Therefore, the selected test set should take these conditions into consideration.

A set of object test sets for testing is used in the paper. The test data set covers objects of different shapes, materials, and weights, including vegetables, grapes, peppers, bananas, forks, electric drills, cans, and cola bottles. The test set consisted of regular shaped like cans, irregularly shaped like green peppers, etc. The smallest volume of grapes was about 0.5 cm in diameter, while the largest volume of vegetables was about 15 cm in diameter. The lightest Coke bottle was about 17.5 g, and the heaviest electric drill was about 3 kg. Grab the data set at a given point, grab 100 times for each thing, and grasping result as shown in Fig. 10.

As can be seen from Fig. 10, the dexterous hand designed in this paper is quite flexible, and the grasping space is large for manipulation. For objects of different shapes, materials, and weights, it is easy to make solid grasping, gripping, and pinching, etc. In addition, the finger's control is simple. From Table 2, it can be concluded that the designed dexterous hand has a higher success rate in grasping suitable shapes, materials, and weights, and the capture success rate of finer, smaller, and irregular objects will decrease slightly, but their success rate is above 84%.

(a) vegetables   (b) grapes   (c) peppers   (d) bananas

(e) forks   (f) electric drills   (g) cans   (h) cola bottles

Fig. 10. Dexterous hand object grab.

Table 2. The result of grasping

Data set	Test times	Success times	Success rate
Vegetables	100	89	89%
Grapes	100	84	84%
Peppers	100	97	97%
Bananas	100	93	93%
Forks	100	90	90%
Electric drills	100	96	96%
Cans	100	99	99%
Cola bottles	100	100	100%

5 Conclusion

This paper proposes a dexterous hand with the tendon-driven. This article first introduced the structure of the dexterous hand, deduced its kinematics, dynamics and the relationship between the finger joints and the fingertip force. Based on the characteristics of the dexterous hand, a hierarchical control system was proposed. This control method is not only overcomes the nonlinearity of the system, but also speeds up the adjustment time of the system. Finally, the dexterous hand with the tactile sensor was verified the performance by several experiments.

In future work, we will continue to study dexterous hand with tactile sensor proposed in this paper. Furthermore, we will integrate more new sensors into dexterous hands for more sophisticated operations.

Acknowledgment. This work was jointly supported by National Natural Science Foundation of China with Grant No. 61621136008, 91848206, U1613212, 61803267 and the Suzhou Special program under Grand 2016SZ0219.

References

1. Bandara, D.S.V., Arata, J., Kiguchi, K.: Towards control of a transhumeral prosthesis with EEG signals. Bioengineering **5**(2), 26 (2018)
2. Morgan, Q., Curt, S., Andrew, Y.N., Salisbury, J.K.: Mechatronic design of an integrated robotic hand. Int. J. Rob. Res. **33**(5), 706–720 (2014)
3. Okada, T.: Computer control of multijointed finger system for precise object-handling. IEEE Trans. Syst. Man Cybern. **12**(3), 289–299 (1982)
4. Loucks, C., Johnson, V., Boissiere, P., et al.: Modeling and control of the stanford/JPL hand. In: 1987 IEEE International Conference on Proceedings of Robotics and Automation, vol. 4, pp. 573–578 (1987)
5. http://www.barrett.com/products-hand.htm
6. Liu, H., Yu, Y., Sun, F., Gu, J.: Visual-tactile fusion for object recognition. IEEE Trans. Autom. Sci. Eng. **14**(2), 996–1008 (2017)
7. Liu, H., Guo, D., Sun, F.: Object recognition using tactile measurements: kernel sparse coding methods. IEEE Trans. Instrum. Measur. **65**(3), 656–665 (2016)
8. http://www.syntouchllc.com/Products/BioTac/
9. http://www.shadowrobot.com/
10. Bimbo, J., Luo, S., Althoefer, K.: In-hand object pose estimation using covariance-based tactile to geometry matching. IEEE Rob. Autom. Lett. **1**(1), 570–577 (2016)
11. Heyneman, B., Cutkosky, M.R.: Slip classification for dynamic tactile array sensors. Int. J. Rob. Res. **35**(4), 404–421 (2016)
12. Ceballos, R., Ionascu, B., Eyssel, F.A., et al.: Authoring tactile gestures: case study for emotion stimulation. Int. J. Comput. Inf. Eng. **10**(11) (2016)
13. Kappassov, Z., Corrales, J.A., Perdereau, V.: Tactile sensing in dexterous robot hands. Rob. Autonom. Syst. **74**, 195–220 (2015)

AI in Locomotion: Quadruped Bionic Mobile Robot

Lei Jiang, Jianjuan Guo, Bo Su$^{(\boxtimes)}$, Peng Xu, and Ruina Dang

China North Vehicle Research Institute, Beijing, China
bosu@noveri.com.cn

Abstract. The report begins with the requirements of quadruped robots and discusses the advantages of quadruped robots in overcoming unstructured problems. Secondly, from the main domestic and foreign research on quadruped robot, the technical status of quadruped robot is expounded; thirdly, the development process and key technologies of "Running" quadruped robot are reported; finally, the trend of 4S performance which quadruped robot urgently needs to improve is discussed.

Keywords: Quadruped robot · Bionic engineer · Legged locomotion

1 Introduction

There are a lot of mobile robots on the market. With the development of technology and the increasing demand for intelligent mobile service robots, service robots with the goal of replacing human operation have gradually become the focus of attention in the field of smart cities. Robots are expected to be used in many fields, such as transportation, security service, automatic inspection and community patrols. But their bodies are difficult to walk or overcome in complex terrain conditions. People have high expectations for robots, but the mobility of robots is so poor that the most basic mobile services are difficult to provide. Unfortunately, after the development of automotive technology for more than 200 years, the mobility of wheeled or tracked vehicles has reached the limit, and it is difficult to make a fundamental breakthrough [1]. In view of the above two problems, legged mobile is a good solution. As a result of evolution of nature for thousands of years, legged mobile is the only and the best choice for land off-road. Quadruped animals, with their super cross-country ability, can easily walk on the floor, steps, grasslands, mountain roads, snow. In 2010, Boston dynamic announced the video of "big dog" on YouTube [2]. This video has re-lighted the hotspots of global research, more and more researchers are beginning to study it. The market in this field is very huge, and a survey says that to 2020 can exceed 100 billion.

2 State of the Art of Quadruped Robot

The history of quadruped robots can be traced back to 1980. Before 2016, the modern high-performance robot was actually driven by the Boston dynamic. Some of quadruped robots are introduced as follows.

© Springer Nature Singapore Pte Ltd. 2019
F. Sun et al. (Eds.): ICCSIP 2018, CCIS 1005, pp. 445–451, 2019.
https://doi.org/10.1007/978-981-13-7983-3_39

First, LS3. Before it was called LS3, see Fig. 1, it used to be called AlphaDog [3]. This robot's self-weight 350 kg, it can be loaded 150 kg. The technical highlight of LS3 is wide angle gradient, rugged inequality, and all terrain adaptability. Even so, LS3 further integrates many advanced features, such as speech human-machine interaction, gaits (slow walk, trot, fast running gait), fall from recovery, autonomous human-machine following based on sensing system etc.

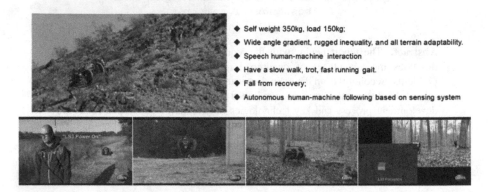

Fig. 1. Typical features in LS3 quadruped robot

Second quadruped robot called Anymal, see Fig. 2, is a robot made by ETH [4]. This robot is a quadruped robot which is holding up its body with four manipulator, named Any pulator. And of course, it is an electric drive quadruped robot, its motor named Anydrive. Anymal was used for patrol and disaster relief robots in scenes such as factories and parks. From the published video, This robot already has the ability to walk outdoors and can perform many functions, such as stand up and down, slow trot walk, climb the stairs, climbing obstacles, traversing the rain, gravel road walking.

Fig. 2. Typical features in AnyMal quadruped robot

Third robots, see Fig. 3, MIT's third generation cheetah robot [5]. This robot is supported by DARAP's Maximum Speed and Maneuverability Program. The biggest breakthrough of this robot is the use of invertable knee joint. This means that the configuration of the legs can be flexibly switched in the outer knee or inner knee structure, thereby obtaining large workspace. Cheetah3 robot have five gaits including slow trot (0.5 m/s), fast trot (1.7 m/s), bound (2.75 m/s), gallop (3 m/s) and pronk. At the same time, it also has the function of climbing steps and push recovery. Surprisingly, its vertical jump height reaches 76 cm, which is the highest jump index of all quadruped robots in the world.

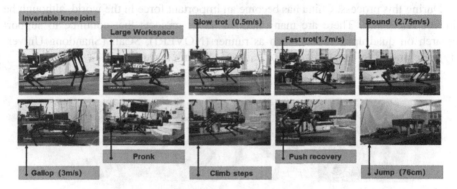

Fig. 3. Typical features in Cheetah3 quadruped robot

Boston dynamic's cheetah robot is called Wildcat [6], also supported by DARAP's Maximum Speed and Maneuverability Program, see Fig. 4. From the bench test, it can be seen that its max speed achieved 45 km/h, and the running speed of the prototype is 18 km/h. There is no doubt that it is currently the fastest quadruped robot in the world.

Fig. 4. Typical features in Wildcat quadruped robot

Finally, spot Mini is actually started with a hydraulically driven quadruped robot, see Fig. 5 named spot, which lowered its weight from 75 kg to 30 kg and its load from 35 kg to 14 kg [7]. It is reported that Boston Dynamic will produce 1000 units in 2019.

Fig. 5. Typical features in Spot-mini quadruped robot

During this process, China has become an important force in the world, although he did not start early. There are many national level projects that continue to support research on quadruped robots, such as runner (NOVERI), SCalf (Shandong University), Jueying (Zhejiang University), Laikago (Unitree), see Fig. 6.

Fig. 6. Typical quadruped robots in China

3 Research Process of the "Runner" Quadruped Robot

The "Runner" quadruped robot is one of the first prototypes of China's first-generation high-performance four-legged robots, see Fig. 7. It won the championship in the 2016 & 2018 Ground Unmanned System Competition. The robot has a weight of 140 kg, loads up to 50 kg and running speed no less than 6 km/h. Since the beginning of 2012, this project has broken through the key technologies of the four-joint bionic leg and foot mechanism, the virtual inverted pendulum balance control algorithm, and the high-performance hydraulic servo drive etc.

Fig. 7. Noveri's quadruped robot "Runner"

In order to establish proper gaits, we studied CPG (central pattern generator) algorithm [8] to setup six rhythmic gaits for this quadruped robot, such as walk, amble, pace, trot, canter and gallop, see Fig. 8. Using CPG cannot produce a good quadruped stability control strategy, but can quickly study the gait of quadruped robot.

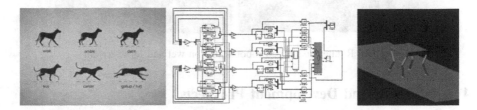

Fig. 8. From dogs gaits to quadruped robot's CPG model

Based on the virtual spring force servo model [9], a single leg compliance control model is established. The simulation analysis and research of single leg compliance is carried out, and a forward and inverse kinematics model based on force servo is established. Performance test is carried out on single leg bench and the whole machine, servo parameters are adjusted, and the bottom servo compliance control is realized (Fig. 9).

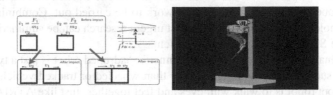

Fig. 9. Single leg compliance control model based on the virtual spring model

The basic principle of quadruped robot walking alternately is that two inverted pendulum models alternately enter the support and swing back and forth, so that at each moment one leg is responsible for supporting the body, maintaining height and posture balance; the other leg is responsible for swinging quickly to choose the best landing point. This alternating process is very fast, at least 1–2 times per second. But in the wet and loose geological conditions, because of the existence of a certain slip rate, the robot cannot maintain balance at first. Therefore, we added a slip rate prediction model to maintain stability. At present, "Runner" quadruped robot can run in grass, sand, gravel road race. We are continuing our research (Fig. 10).

Fig. 10. Runner quadruped robot walks on wet and loose terrain

4 Conclusion and Development Prospects

Four-legged robots have made tremendous progress in the past decade, including the United States, China, Switzerland, Russia and other countries have carried out substantive research, promoting the development of the world's high-performance four-legged robot. The control algorithm of the quadruped bionic robot will be adjusted according to the uncertainty of the environment, and this adjustment comes from a large number of dynamic calculations and sensor feedback results. The quadruped robot has behavioral uncertainty and very strong active adaptability when walking. Therefore, the quadruped robot is essentially a mobile robot driven by an artificial intelligence control algorithm.

Of course, compared with the traditional wheeled and tracked mobile methods, the quadruped robot still has a lot of research work to be carried out. Combining with the current technological development, the most urgent research can be summarized as four S, which are Smart, Stronger, Stability, Silent.

First is smart. It can be seen that the "runner" quadruped robot is just a type of blind walking. At such a stage, mobility is lower than wheeled or tracked vehicles. The real power of a foot robot is to walk with eyes and feet together. Just like ATRIAS's plumb pile walking research [10], wheeled or tracked vehicles can't pass anyway.

Second is stronger. Some studies show that the weight ratio of the body and the leg, if greater than 10:1, will be very useful for inverted pendulum model [11]. But in this way, the mechanism is not strong enough. This is a very relative problem. Boston Dynamic 3D printing bionic leg seems to be a very good research direction.

Third is stability. In order to adapt the robot to various terrain and stability, this requires a certain amount of creativity and training. Deepmind publish three paper are about how to generate flexible behavior in simulation environment [12]. It makes the robot more stable in resisting lateral force disturbance. This field is more important to the future of robot.

Last is silent. How to keep quadruped robot keep silent? This problem reflects the important problem is the power technology, where the engine, hydraulic pump, motor, battery and so on. They need explosive, high power density, high endurance time, low noise power unit.

Sum up above four points, we can see 4S is actually set for the goal about robustness of robots. This will lead the research direction of quadruped robots in the next few years.

Acknowledgements. This work was supported in part by National Natural Science Foundation of China (Grant No. 91748211).

References

1. Kajian, Z.: Vehicle-Terrainmechanmics, 1st edn. National Defense Industry Publishing House, Beijing (2002)
2. Bostondynamic bigdog. https://www.bostondynamics.com/bigdog. Accessed 23 Sept 2018
3. Bostondynamic ls3. https://www.bostondynamics.com/ls3. Accessed 23 Sept 2018
4. Anymal. http://www.rsl.ethz.ch/robots-media/anymal.html. Accessed 23 Sept 2018
5. Park, H.-W., Wensing, P.M., Kim, S.: High-speed bounding with the MIT Cheetah 2: control design and experiments. Int. J. Robot. Res. (2017). https://doi.org/10.1177/0278364917694244
6. Bostondynamic wildcat. https://www.bostondynamics.com/wildcat. Accessed 23 Sept 2018
7. Bostondynamic spot-mini. https://www.bostondynamics.com/spot-mini. Accessed 23 Sept 2018
8. Zhang, X.: Biological-inspired rhythmic motion & environmental adaptability for quadruped robot. Ph.D. dissertation, Tsinghua University (2004)
9. Xu, P., Su, B., Jiang, L., Yao, Q., Dang, R.: An efficient autonomous traction control method for quadruped robot. In: IEEE International Conference on Unmanned Systems (2018)
10. Hubicki, C., et al.: ATRIAS: design and validation of a tether-free 3D-capable spring-mass bipedal robot. Int. J. Robot. Res. (IJRR) **35**, 1497–1521 (2016)
11. Raibert, M., Blankespoor, K., Nelson, G., et al.: Bigdog, the rough-terrain quadruped robot. In: Proceedings of the 17th World Congress, pp. 10822–10825 (2008)
12. Josh, M., et al.: Learning human behaviors from motion capture by adversarial imitation. arXiv:1707.02201 (2017)

A Novel Rotor Position Observer for Self-sensing of Interior Permanent Magnet Synchronous Motor with Dynamic Error Compensation

Chang Deng and Jun Lu[✉]

The 32nd Research Institute of China Electronics Technology
Group Corporation, Shanghai 201808, China
athrun_chris@aliyun.com

Abstract. Among the observer models of salient permanent magnet synchronous motor for position self-sensing, equivalent electromotive force (EMF) model is simpler, independent on rotor speed, less sensitive to uncertainty of motor parameters and immune to errors caused by integrator. In this paper, a novel rotor position observer with dynamic error compensation is presented based on equivalent EMF model. A sliding mode observer is established to estimate equivalent EMF from which the rotor position can be extracted. The rotor position estimation error resulting from variation of stator current in direct axis is suppressed by a dynamic error compensator, improving position estimating performance for self-sensing direct torque control (DTC) system of salient permanent magnet synchronous motor. Compared with the observer without dynamic error compensator, the novel one has several advantages: (1) For fast torque response of DTC, position observation accuracy in speed and load transient condition are increased by 54.16% and 54.55%, respectively. (2) For high harmonic current of DTC, position observation accuracy in speed steady condition is increased by 44.89% through reducing observation error caused by current harmonics. Experiment verifies feasibility and effectiveness of the novel one.

Keywords: Permanent magnet synchronous motor · Self-sensing ·
Rotor position observer · Direct torque control · Sliding mode ·
Dynamic error compensation

1 Introduction

Permanent Magnetic Synchronous Motor (PMSM) has the advantages of simple structure, small size, low loss and high efficiency. It is widely used in industrial production, national defense, daily life and other areas. Since the installation of speed or position sensor on the shaft of the motor is essential in the governing system of PMSM, it brings the following problems: (1) Sensor is affected by working conditions such as temperature, humidity, detection distance and vibration, especially in some applications for high detection accuracy of the sensor, which limits the utilization of

© Springer Nature Singapore Pte Ltd. 2019
F. Sun et al. (Eds.): ICCSIP 2018, CCIS 1005, pp. 452–462, 2019.
https://doi.org/10.1007/978-981-13-7983-3_40

PMSM governing system in these special fields; (2) Size of the motor and inertia of the governing system are increased by sensor; (3) In order to ensure the detection accuracy, installation and maintenance of sensor should be done in a high level, which increases the complexity of drive system, reduces system reliability, and increase cost. Therefore, self-sensing control of permanent magnet synchronous motor plays an important role in the field of motor control [1], especially in modern mechanical and electrical control systems such as national defense. Many researches on self-sensing vector control [2] and self-sensing direct torque control [3] were already studied, especially the latter one. In recent years, direct torque control has caught much attention of researchers because of its fast dynamic torque response and simple structure [4]. It was already applied in "ROTOR 6004" thrust vector control actuator for launch vehicle and flight surface control actuator for aircraft developed by the United States National Aeronautics and Space Administration (NASA), as well as in "AZIPOD" electric podded propulsion system developed by ABB company [5].

Since the key technology of self-sensing DTC is accurate estimation of stator flux and torque through the current-position model, the rotor position observer must have excellent dynamic and steady observation accuracy. Some estimation methods of rotor position and speed were already presented [6–11], such as stator flux estimation method, model reference adaptive method, state observation method, high frequency injection method, artificial intelligence estimation method, etc. In general, they can be divided into two categories: methods based on motor model and methods based on external excitation. The former can be used to estimate the rotor position simply by observing the back EMF of the motor, widely used in the medium and high speed self-sensing control of non-salient pole PMSM [12]. However, the rotor position estimation of salient pole PMSM, such as interior PMSM (IPMSM), is more complicated than that of nonsalient pole PMSM due to salient pole effect. In order to achieve the IPMSM rotor position estimation based on motor model, the model is usually reconstructed and transformed into an equivalent nonsalient pole PMSM model [13]. In previous literature, the reconstruction models are divided into extended electromotive force (EEMF) model [14], active flux (AF) model [15, 16] and equivalent EMF model [17]. EEMF model is influenced by rotor speed and motor parameters, such as stator resistance and stator inductance as well as changing rate of q-axis stator current. Thus, it is difficult to design this kind of observer with robustness against both load disturbance and motor parameters uncertainty. Integrator is generally used in Active flux model to calculate stator flux, leading to some practical and difficult problems, such as steady bias of current sensor, accumulative error and initial state of integrator [18]. Compared with EEMF model and AF model, equivalent EMF model is independent on rotor speed, less sensitive to uncertainty of motor parameters and immune to errors caused by integrator. However, the differential term of d-axis stator current is neglected in its derivation. Therefore, when the motor is operating in speed and load transient or with current harmonics, the dynamic accuracy of the rotor position observer based on equivalent EMF model will be reduced. DTC has fast dynamic torque response leading to large differential of d-axis stator current, but large stator flux distortion and torque ripple leading to large harmonics of stator current [19]. Therefore, under load and speed transient or steady speed operation of DTC, position observation error caused by differential of d-axis stator current is large.

In order to achieve high performance of speed governing system through self-sensing DTC, a novel rotor position observer with dynamic error compensation is proposed based on equivalent EMF model. A sliding mode observer is established to estimate equivalent EMF from which the rotor position can be extracted. The rotor position estimation error resulting from variation of stator current in direct axis is suppressed by a dynamic error compensator, improving position estimating performance for self-sensing DTC system of IPMSM. Test bench was built based on DSP (TMS320F2812) of Texas Instruments (TI). Experiment shows excellent performance of the novel observer.

2 Rotor Position Observer Based on Equivalent EMF

2.1 IPMSM Model Based on Equivalent EMF

In $\alpha - \beta$ stationary reference frame, stator voltage and current model of IPMSM based on the equivalent EMF can be modeled as:

$$\begin{bmatrix} u_\alpha \\ u_\beta \end{bmatrix} = \begin{bmatrix} R_s + \frac{\mathrm{d}}{\mathrm{d}t}L_q & 0 \\ 0 & R_s + \frac{\mathrm{d}}{\mathrm{d}t}L_q \end{bmatrix} \begin{bmatrix} i_\alpha \\ i_\beta \end{bmatrix} + \begin{bmatrix} e_\alpha^a \\ e_\beta^a \end{bmatrix} \tag{1}$$

where e_α^a, e_β^a are equivalent EMFs, u_α, u_β are stator voltages, i_α and i_β are stator currents in $\alpha - \beta$ stationary reference frame, R_s is stator resistance, L_q is q-axis inductance.

Equivalent EMF model can be defined as:

$$\begin{bmatrix} e_\alpha^a \\ e_\beta^a \end{bmatrix} = (L_d - L_q)\mathrm{p}(i_d)\begin{bmatrix} \cos\theta_r \\ \sin\theta_r \end{bmatrix} + \omega_r\psi_d^a\begin{bmatrix} -\sin\theta_r \\ \cos\theta_r \end{bmatrix} \tag{2}$$

where p is derivative operator, i_d is d-axis stator current, θ_r is rotor electrical angel, L_d is d-axis inductance, ω_r is rotor electrical speed, ψ_f is permanent magnet flux, $\psi_d^a = (L_d - L_q)i_d + \psi_f$.

If dynamic behavior of d-axis stator current is neglected, $(L_d - L_q)\mathrm{p}(i_d)\begin{bmatrix} \cos\theta_r \\ \sin\theta_r \end{bmatrix} = 0$. The equivalent EMF model mentioned previously can be simplified as:

$$\begin{bmatrix} e_\alpha^a \\ e_\beta^a \end{bmatrix} = \omega_r\psi_d^a\begin{bmatrix} -\sin\theta_r' \\ \cos\theta_r' \end{bmatrix} \tag{3}$$

According to the simplified model, α and β component of equivalent EMF are respectively sine and cosine functions of the rotor position θ_r', from which θ_r' can be extracted by tangent function as $\tan^{-1}$.

2.2 Design and Stability Analysis of Sliding Mode Observer

For strong robustness, the state space equation of sliding mode observer based on equivalent EMF model can be expressed as follows:

$$\begin{bmatrix} \hat{i}_\alpha \\ \hat{i}_\beta \end{bmatrix} = \frac{1}{L_q}\begin{bmatrix} u_\alpha \\ u_\beta \end{bmatrix} - \frac{R_s}{L_q}\begin{bmatrix} \hat{i}_\alpha \\ \hat{i}_\beta \end{bmatrix} - \frac{l}{L_q}\begin{bmatrix} sign(\hat{i}_\alpha - i_\alpha) \\ sign(\hat{i}_\beta - i_\beta) \end{bmatrix} \tag{4}$$

where $\hat{i}_\alpha$, $\hat{i}_\beta$ are observed stator current in $\alpha - \beta$ coordinate, l is sliding mode gain, $sign$ is switch function.

Subtracting Eq. (4) from Eq. (1) yields the current error state space equation of equivalent EMF model:

$$\begin{bmatrix} \dot{\bar{i}}_\alpha \\ \dot{\bar{i}}_\beta \end{bmatrix} = -\frac{R}{L_q}\begin{bmatrix} \bar{i}_\alpha \\ \bar{i}_\beta \end{bmatrix} + \frac{1}{L_q}\begin{bmatrix} e_\alpha^a - l \cdot sign(\bar{i}_\alpha) \\ e_\beta^a - l \cdot sign(\bar{i}_\beta) \end{bmatrix} \tag{5}$$

where $\bar{i}_\alpha = \hat{i}_\alpha - i_\alpha$, $\bar{i}_\beta = \hat{i}_\beta - i_\beta$.

A Lyapunov candidate function can be defined as:

$$V = \frac{1}{2}(\bar{i}_\alpha^2 + \bar{i}_\beta^2) \tag{6}$$

For global asymptotic stability of state variables, differential of V yields:

$$\begin{aligned} \dot{V} &= \bar{i}_\alpha \cdot \dot{\bar{i}}_\alpha + \bar{i}_\beta \cdot \dot{\bar{i}}_\beta \\ &= -\frac{1}{L_q}[R_s(\bar{i}_\alpha^2 + \bar{i}_\beta^2) - (e_\alpha^a \cdot \bar{i}_\alpha + e_\beta^a \cdot \bar{i}_\beta) + l(|\bar{i}_\alpha| + |\bar{i}_\beta|)] < 0 \end{aligned} \tag{7}$$

Therefore, the range of sliding mode gain is $l > \max\{e_\alpha^a, e_\beta^a\}$.

To avoid from chattering caused by large sliding mode gain, l should be selected appropriately according to the actual effect. When the system trajectory reaches sliding surface, the observed current is converge to the actual current. After equivalent EMF, which is the equivalent control function, is extracted from the high frequency switching signal of sliding mode by low pass filter, the rotor position can be obtained as:

$$\hat{\theta}_r' = \tan^{-1}\left(\frac{-\hat{e}_\alpha^a}{\hat{e}_\beta^a}\right) = -\tan^{-1}\left(\frac{LPF(sign(\bar{i}_\alpha))}{LPF(sign(\bar{i}_\beta))}\right) \tag{8}$$

A schematic diagram of proposed sliding mode observer is shown in Fig. 1.

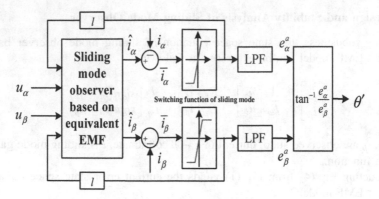

Fig. 1. Schematic diagram of proposed sliding mode observer

3 Analysis and Compensation of Dynamic Error Angle

Although equivalent EMF model overcame the disadvantages of EEMF model and AF model, a dynamic error angle caused by differential of direct axis current must be compensated in order to improve dynamic precision of rotor position observation.

3.1 Analysis of Dynamic Error Angle

As shown in Eq. (2), the related items of $\sin\theta_r$ and $\cos\theta_r$ are included in the expressions of e_α^a and e_β^a, making it quite complex to calculate the rotor position by Eq. (2). If $p(i_d)$ is zero or $(L_d - L_q)p(i_d) \ll \omega_r((L_d - L_q)i_d + \psi_f)$, the differential of i_d can be neglected, which greatly simplifies the calculation. Otherwise, a dynamic error angel will exist between the observed rotor position θ'_r from the simplified model and the actual position θ_r. To eliminate the limitation of this assumption, the definition model of equivalent EMF in Eq. (2) can be transformed into the following form:

$$\begin{cases} \begin{bmatrix} e_\alpha^a \\ e_\beta^a \end{bmatrix} = E_d^a \begin{bmatrix} -\sin(\theta_r - \varphi) \\ \cos(\theta_r - \varphi) \end{bmatrix} = E_d^a \begin{bmatrix} -\sin\theta'_r \\ \cos\theta'_r \end{bmatrix} \\ \varphi = \tan^{-1}\left(\frac{p(\psi_d^a)}{\omega_r\psi_d^a}\right) = \tan^{-1}\left(\frac{(L_d-L_q)p(i_d)}{\omega_r\psi_d^a}\right) \end{cases} \tag{9}$$

where $E_d^a = \sqrt{[(L_d - L_q)p(i_d)]^2 + (\omega_r\psi_d^a)^2}$ is the amplitude of equivalent EMF.

As shown in Eq. (9), a dynamic error angel φ exists between the observed rotor position θ'_r from and the actual θ_r. If differential of i_d can be neglected, φ is almost zero. Under some specific conditions, for example, when using the vector control of $i_d^* = 0$, the assumption can be established. However, in practical applications, this assumption is limited, especially in vector control using the maximum torque per ampere (MTPA) strategy or direct torque control. When IPMSM is operating in speed or load transient, or with large current harmonics, the change rate of i_d is large and dynamic error angle is not completely equal to zero. Lower speed and larger load lead to larger φ. Due to the inaccurate estimation of rotor position, this paper puts forward a dynamic error angle compensator. It reduces the error between the observed rotor position and the actual one, improving the performance of rotor position estimation in speed or load transient as well as with the current harmonics.

3.2 Compensation for Dynamic Error Angle

As discussed above, θ_r' is the difference between θ_r and φ, which can be obtained through the sliding mode observer. ω_r is the derivation of θ_r. In addition, φ is also a function of θ_r when i_d is transformed into a function of θ_r using Park transform in Eq. (9). Thus, the actual position θ_r and the dynamic error angle φ can be obtained as follows:

$$\begin{cases} \theta_r' = \theta_r - \varphi \\ \varphi = \tan^{-1}\left(\dfrac{\mathrm{p}((L_d - L_q)\mathrm{T}_\theta i_s)}{\omega_r(\psi_f + (L_d - L_q)\mathrm{T}_\theta i_s)} \right) \end{cases} \tag{10}$$

where $\mathrm{T}_\theta = \begin{bmatrix} \cos\theta_r & \sin\theta_r \\ -\sin\theta_r & \cos\theta_r \end{bmatrix}$, $i_s = \begin{bmatrix} i_\alpha \\ i_\beta \end{bmatrix}$.

In order to solve the above equations, the proposed dynamic error angle compensator is shown in Fig. 2. θ_r' obtained by the sliding mode observer in Fig. 1 is a known input of the compensator. When there is a deviation in both θ_r and φ, the actual value of them can be automatically tracked by the PI regulator. The parameters of regulator need to be tuned based on the characteristics of the changing φ in order to achieve best tracking effect.

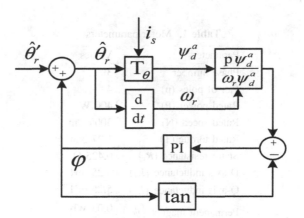

Fig. 2. Dynamic error angle compensator

4 Experimental Results

In order to verify the effectiveness of the proposed novel rotor position observer as a redundant sensor, the experiment was carried out in a PMSM-DTC speed governing system. The system composition diagram of test bench is shown in Fig. 3. In this system, permanent magnet synchronous motor has an encoder of 2500 lines, the switching frequency of inverter is 16 k and the digital signal processing chip for controller is TMS320F2812 of TI. Resolution of digital to analog converter (ADC) is 12 bit. The adjustable DC power supply and the hysteresis clutch are composed of an adjustable load.

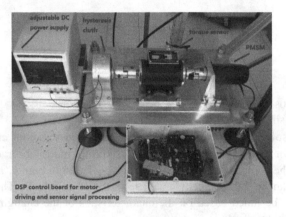

Fig. 3. Test bench

The motor parameters are shown in Table 1.

Table 1. Motor parameters

Parameters	Values
Phase number	3
Pair of poles (p)	4
Rated power (P)	400 W
Rated speed (N)	3000 r/m
Rated torque (T)	1.27 Nm
Stator resistance (R_s)	0.425 Ω
D-axis inductance (L_d)	3.25 mH
Q-axis inductance (L_q)	5.25 mH
Permanent magnet (ψ_f)	0.03 Wb

In experiments of speed variation and load variation, the difference between actual position from encoder and observed position from novel position observer was regarded as the observation precision. Compared with the observer without compensator, excellent performance of the proposed observer with dynamic error angle compensator is verified.

4.1 Speed Variation Experiment

Figure 4 shows the motor speed curve in speed variation experiment. The motor was operating under constant load of 0.1 Nm, speeding up from 200 r/min to 300 r/min and then slowing down to 200 r/min.

Figure 5 shows the comparison of the rotor position observation error before and after the compensation during above operating progress. As shown in Fig. 5, in the accelerating process from 200 r/min to 300 r/min, the observation error before and after dynamic error compensation are 0.24 rad and 0.11 rad, respectively. In the decelerating process from 300 r/min to 200 r/min, the observation error before and after dynamic error compensation are 0.04 rad and 0.02 rad, respectively. During the steady operating at speed of 200 r/min, the harmonic errors before and after dynamic error compensation are respectively 0.025 rad and 0.012 rad, while at speed of 300 r/min, the harmonic error before and after dynamic error compensation are respectively 0.021 rad and 0.01 rad. Obviously, the dynamic error angle is inversely proportional to motor speed, consistent with the theoretical model.

More results show that the novel observer with dynamic error compensator has higher observation accuracy at different operating points of the motor during steady and dynamic progress.

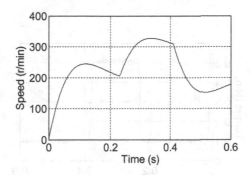

Fig. 4. The motor speed curve in speed variation experiment

4.2 Load Variation Experiment

Figure 6 shows the motor torque curve in load variation experiment. The motor was operating at constant speed of 300 r/min, loaded from 0.1 Nm to 0.5 Nm and then unloaded to 0.1 Nm.

Figure 7 shows the comparison of the rotor position observation error before and after the compensation during above operating progress. As shown in Fig. 7, in the loading process from 0.1 Nm to 0.5 Nm, the observation error before and after

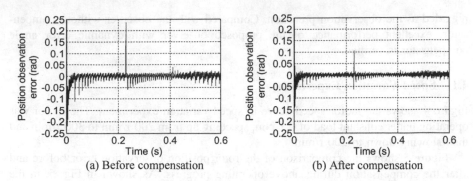

(a) Before compensation   (b) After compensation

Fig. 5. Comparison of the rotor position observation error before and after the compensation

dynamic error compensation are 0.11 rad and 0.05 rad, respectively. In the unloading process from 0.5 Nm to 0.1 Nm, the observation error before and after dynamic error compensation are 0.18 rad and 0.08 rad, respectively. During the steady operating under load of 0.1 Nm, the harmonic errors before and after dynamic error compensation are respectively 0.024 rad and 0.013 rad, while under load of 0.5 Nm, the harmonic error before and after dynamic error compensation are respectively 0.049 rad and 0.027 rad. Obviously, the dynamic error angle is proportional to motor load, consistent with the theoretical model.

More results show that the novel observer with dynamic error compensator has higher observation accuracy at different operating points of the motor during steady and dynamic progress.

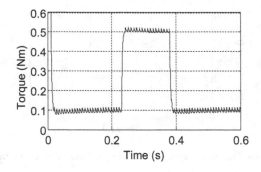

Fig. 6. The motor torque curve in load variation experiment

However, in experiments at speed below 30 r/min, due to the influence of stator resistance variation, the accurate estimation of equivalent EMF was quite difficult, which led to very large error or even failure of observer [20].

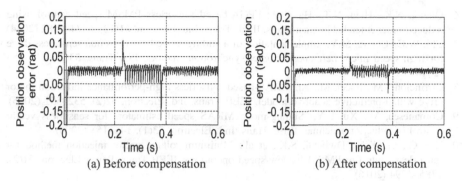

Fig. 7. Comparison of the rotor position observation error before and after the compensation

5 Conclusions

To improve position self-sensing performance for direct torque control (DTC) system of IPMSM, this paper has presented a novel rotor position observer with dynamic error compensation based on equivalent EMF model. Compared with the observer without dynamic error compensator, the novel one has several advantages:

(1) Position observation accuracy in speed and load transient condition are increased by 54.16% and 54.55%, respectively.
(2) Position observation accuracy in speed steady condition is increased by 44.89% through reducing observation error caused by current harmonics.

Due to the variation of stator resistance, the accurate estimation of equivalent EMF was quite difficult at low or zero speed, which led to very large error or even failure of observer. High frequency signal injection method and other external excitation methods should be utilized to achieve self-sensing control at low or zero speed.

Acknowledgments. This work was supported by the National Science and Technology Major Project of China under Grants 2013ZX04001-141.

References

1. Kim, S.J., Lee, Y.K., Lee, J.S., et al.: Sensorless control method in IPMSM position sensor fault for HEV. J. Electr. Eng. Technol. **8**(5), 1056–1061 (2013)
2. Oksuztepe, E., Omac, Z., Kurum, H.: Sensorless vector control of PMSM with non-sinusoidal flux using observer based on FEM. Electr. Eng. **96**(3), 227–238 (2014)
3. Foo, G., Rahman, M.F.: Sensorless direct torque and flux-controlled IPM synchronous motor drive at very low speed without signal injection. IEEE Trans. Ind. Electron. **57**(1), 395–403 (2010)
4. Kim, J.H., Kim, R.Y.: Sensorless direct torque control using the inductance inflection point for a switched reluctance motor. IEEE Trans. Ind. Electron. **65**(12), 9336–9345 (2018)
5. Sinha, B.S., Deshmukh, A., Jassal, J.S.: Contra rotating azipod propellers. J. Inst. Eng. (India) Part MR: Mar. Eng. Div. **92**(7), 11–17 (2011)

6. Quang, N.K., Hieu, N.T., Ha, Q.P.: FPGA-based sensorless PMSM speed control using reduced-order extended kalman filters. IEEE Trans. Ind. Electron. **61**(12), 6574–6582 (2014)
7. Chi, W.C., Cheng, M.Y.: Implementation of a sliding-mode-based position sensorless drive for high-speed micro permanent-magnet synchronous motors. ISA Trans. **53**(2), 444–453 (2014)
8. Cirrincione, M., Pucci, M.: An MRAS-based sensorless high-performance induction motor drive with a predictive adaptive model. IEEE Trans. Ind. Electron. **52**(2), 532–551 (2005)
9. Comanescu, M., Xu, L.Y.: Sliding-mode MRAS speed estimators for sensorless vector control of induction machine. IEEE Trans. Ind. Electron. **53**(1), 146–153 (2006)
10. Xie, G., Lu, K.Y., Dwivedi, S.K., et al.: Minimum-voltage vector injection method for sensorless control of PMSM for low-speed operations. IEEE Trans. Power Electron. **31**(2), 1785–1794 (2016)
11. Medjmadj, S., Diallo, D., Mostefai, M., et al.: PMSM drive position estimation: contribution to the high-frequency injection voltage selection issue. IEEE Trans. Energy Convers. **30**(1), 349–358 (2015)
12. Qiao, Z.W., Shi, T.N., Wang, Y.D., et al.: New sliding-mode observer for position sensorless control of permanent-magnet synchronous motor. IEEE Trans. Ind. Electron. **60**(2), 710–719 (2013)
13. Wang, G.L., Li, Z.M., Zhang, G.Q., et al.: Quadrature PLL-based high-order sliding-mode observer for IPMSM sensorless control with online MTPA control strategy. IEEE Trans. Energy Convers. **28**(1), 214–224 (2013)
14. Chen, Z., Tomita, M., Doki, S., et al.: An extended electromotive force model for sensorless control of interior permanent-magnet synchronous motors. IEEE Trans. Ind. Electron. **50**(2), 288–295 (2003)
15. Boldea, I., Paicu, M.C., Andreescu, G.D.: Active flux concept for motion-sensorless unified AC drives. IEEE Trans. Power Electron. **23**(5), 2612–2618 (2008)
16. Barnard, F.J.W., Villet, W.T., Kamper, M.J.: Hybrid active-flux and arbitrary injection position sensorless control of reluctance synchronous machines. IEEE Trans. Ind. Appl. **51**(5), 3899–3906 (2015)
17. Liu, J., Nondahl, T.A., Schmidt, P.B., et al.: Rotor position estimation for synchronous machines based on equivalent EMF. IEEE Trans. Ind. Appl. **47**(3), 1310–1318 (2011)
18. Ma, S.K., Wu, P.J., Ji, J.H., et al.: Sensorless control of salient PMSM with adaptive integrator and resistance online identification using strong tracking filter. Int. J. Electron. **103**(2), 217–231 (2015)
19. Shinnaka, S., Kishida, H.: New simple torque-sensorless torque control for quasi-perfect compensation of sixth-harmonic torque ripple due to nonsinusoidal distribution of back EMF of PMSM. Electr. Eng. Jpn. **185**(2), 51–63 (2013)
20. Paicu, M.C., Boldea, I., Andreescu, G.D., et al.: Very low speed performance of active flux based sensorless control: interior permanent magnet synchronous motor vector control versus direct torque and flux control. IET Electr. Power Appl. **3**(6), 551–561 (2009)

Robotic Knee Prosthesis Real-Time Control Using Reinforcement Learning with Human in the Loop

Yue Wen[1,2], Xiang Gao[3], Jennie Si[3(✉)], Andrea Brandt[1,2], Minhan Li[1,2], and He (Helen) Huang[1,2(✉)]

[1] Joint Department of Biomedical Engineering,
University of North Carolina at Chapel Hill, Chapel Hill, NC 27599, USA
hhuang11@ncsu.edu
[2] North Carolina State University, Raleigh, NC 27695, USA
[3] Department of Electrical, Computer, and Energy Engineering, Arizona State
University, Tempe, AZ 85281, USA
si@asu.edu

Abstract. Advanced robotic prostheses are expensive considering the cost of human resources and the time spent on manually tuning the high-dimensional control parameters for individual users. To alleviate clinicians' effort and promote the advanced robotic prosthesis, we implemented an optimal adaptive control algorithm, which fundamentally is a type of reinforcement learning method, to automatically tune the high-dimensional control parameters of a robotic knee prosthesis through interaction with a human-prosthesis system. The 'human-in-the-loop' term means that the learning controller tunes the control parameters based on the performance of the robotic knee prosthesis while an amputee subject walking with it. We validated the human-in-the-loop auto-tuner with one transfemoral amputee subject for 4 hour-long lab testing sessions. Our results demonstrated that this novel reinforcement learning controller was able to learn through interaction with the human-prosthesis system and discover a set of suitable control parameter for the amputee user to generate near-normative knee kinematics.

Keywords: Robotic knee prosthesis · Reinforcement learning · Amputees · Machine learning · Prosthetic knee kinematics · Gait symmetry

1 Introduction

Advanced robotic knee prostheses have greatly helped restoring more natural locomotion functions and improved walking efficiency for individuals with lower

This work was partly supported by National Science Foundation #1563454, #1563921, #1808752 and #1808898.

limb amputation compared with conventional passive prostheses [1–4]. Those advanced robotic prostheses are typically controlled by finite state machine impedance controller [3–5], which has about 12 to 16 configurable control parameters [3,5,6]. And the number of parameters grows when the number of included locomotion modes increases. These control parameters need to be customized for individual user due to differences in weight, physical ability, etc. [7].

Currently in clinics, prosthesis control has been personalized manually. Usually a prosthetist tunes a couple of these parameters based on the observation of an amputee's gait and his/her verbal feedback. This manual tuning procedure can be time and labor intensive [8]. In addition, the prosthesis users often need to re-visit the clinic and have the parameter re-tuned when they further adapt to the device or their physical condition changes [7]. Such a manual, heuristic tuning procedure significantly increases the associate cost of amputees for using these advanced robotic prostheses.

Researchers have been working on easing the configuration burden through 3 major approaches. One approach is to estimate of the control parameters with either muscular model [9] or inverse dynamic model [10], which haven't been validated on prosthesis control; Another approach is to reduce the number of control parameters through associating the impedance parameters with the joint angle and/or prosthesis load [8], or introducing advanced control method as virtual constraint control [11]. But the remaining control parameters still to be manually tuned; Another recently emerged approach is to automatically optimize the control parameter with measurement from human and device interaction (human-in-the-loop), such as using a cyber expert system, which encoded human expert's knowledge into computer rules, to tune the robotic knee prosthesis for individual users [12]. This method relied on the knowledge of human experts (i.e. prosthetists), which is inefficient and might be biased.

Currently, some optimization approaches have been applied to personalize wearable robotics (i.e. prosthetics and exoskeletons). Koller et al. used gradient descent methods to optimize the on-set time of an ankle exoskeleton [13]. Zhang et al. used evolution strategy to optimize the four control parameters for an ankle exoskeleton [14]. Ding et al. applied Bayesian optimization to identify the 2 control parameters of hip extension assistance [15]. However, those approaches have only been validated on able-bodied people with low dimension control parameters. To our knowledge, no one has successfully demonstrated the optimization of high-dimensional prosthesis control parameters with amputee in the loop.

Reinforcement learning is an alternative solution for optimal adaptive control of lower limb prostheses. Reinforcement learning, also called adaptive dynamic programming (ADP), has been applied to many optimal control problems of nonlinear systems with large-scale state and control spaces [16,17], in which not only an optimal control solution was found, but also the control method, which potentially can adapt to changing conditions, was learned. Direct heuristic dynamic programming (dHDP) [18] is an ADP method and works in an on-line manner without system dynamic model, and the dHDP has many applications

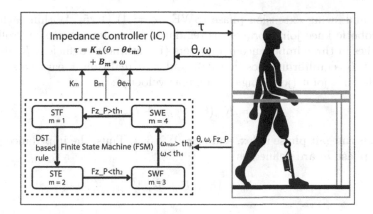

Fig. 1. Block diagram of human-prosthesis system.

to control complex, nonlinear, and high uncertainty systems [19–23]. And in our previous study, a novel ADP-based auto-tuner had been designed and validated on a OpenSim model to automatically tune the control parameters of a simulated knee prosthesis [24].

In this study, we applied the novel ADP-based auto-tuner to automatically tune the control parameters of an experimental robotic knee prosthesis while amputee walking with it, which is more challenging due to human's reactions and walking variance. The tuning goal is to allow amputee generating normative knee kinematics, which has been widely used as the control goal/evaluation criteria of robotic knee prosthesis control [1–4].

2   Problem Description

Human-prosthesis system (Fig. 1) refers to people with transfemoral amputation wearing a robotic knee prosthesis, in which the robotic knee prosthesis is controlled to mimic biological knee behavior and restore amputee's locomotion functions. Thus, clinicians/experts tuned the control parameters of the robotic knee prosthesis so that the user can generate the normative prosthetic knee kinematics when walking with the robotic knee prosthesis. The control method of the robotic knee prosthesis and the evaluation of the robotic knee kinematics were described as following.

2.1   Controller of Robotic Knee Controller

Finite state machine (FSM) impedance control has been commonly applied to control the robotic knee prostheses [1–4]. With the ground reaction force and the knee joint angle information, the FSM cyclically transits through 4 finite states based on preset thresholds (th_1, th_2, th_3, th_4 in Fig. 1): stance flexion phase (STF, $m = 1$), stance extension phase (STE, $m = 2$), swing flexion phase (SWF,

$m = 3$), and swing extension phase (SWE, $m = 4$) [4,25]. Within each phase m, the robotic knee joint torque τ is regulated by an impedance controller (1), which takes in three impedance parameters (i.e. stiffness coefficient K, damping coefficient B, equilibrium position θe), and two real-time measurements from prosthetic knee joint (joint angle θ, angular velocity ω).

$$\tau_m = K_m(\theta - \theta e_m) + B_m\omega \tag{1}$$

where m is the gait phase index, and $m = 1, 2, 3, 4$. Thus, the impedance parameters for phase m are defined as

$$I_m = [K_m, B_m, \theta e_m]^T. \tag{2}$$

2.2   Evaluation of Robotic Knee Kinematics

The normative knee kinematics in one stride can be characterized by four distinct phases: (1) stance flexion phase, where knee flexes due to loading response, (2) stance extension phase, where knee extends after maximum flexion, (3) swing flexion phase, where knee flexes for foot clearance, and (4) swing extension phase, where knee extends to get ready for next heel strike. To reduce the dimensionality while retaining most of the prosthetic knee joint kinematics information, we extracted 2 features from each phase (i.e. 8 total features from each stride): the extreme angle P_m and the duration D_m of each phase (e.g. maximum flexion angle during stance flexion phase or minimum extension angle during stance extension), where $m = 1, 2, 3, 4$ is the phase index. Similarly, the given normative knee kinematics can be characterized by $\bar{P}_m$ and $\bar{D}_m$.

The goodness of the prosthetic knee kinematics can be quantified by the peak angle errors and duration errors between the features of robotic knee kinematics and the normative knee kinematics.

$$\begin{aligned} \Delta P_m &= P_m - \bar{P}_m \\ \Delta D_m &= D_m - \bar{D}_m \end{aligned} \tag{3}$$

Thus, the kinematics performance of robotic knee prosthesis is defined as

$$x_m = [\Delta P_m, \Delta D_m]^T. \tag{4}$$

3   Reinforcement Learning Based Auto-tuner

Due to the phase-based design of the human-prosthesis dynamic system, we implemented the ADP-based auto-tuner with 4 parallel dHDP blocks corresponding to four finite states or gait phases: STF, STE, SWF, and SWE gait phases (Fig. 1). All 4 dHDP blocks were identical, including one action neural network (ANN), and one critic neural network (CNN) (Fig. 2). We present the detailed dHDP implementation in this section without specifying the phase index.

3.1 Interface Implementation

We implemented an interface module between the human-prosthesis system and the ADP auto-tuner to (1) normalize the output of the human-prosthesis system $x(n)$ to the state input $X(n)$ of the ADP auto-tuner; (2) denormalize the action of the ADP auto-tuner $U(n)$ to the same scale of impedance parameters $I(n)$ of the human-prosthesis system; (3) generate reinforcement signals $r(n)$ to ADP auto-tuner based on the status of the human-prosthesis system. n denotes the time index of each tuning iteration.

$$X(n) = \gamma \circ [x(n); x^{'}(n)] \tag{5}$$

$$I(n+1) = I(n) + \beta \circ U(n) \tag{6}$$

where $\beta \in \mathbb{R}^{3 \times 1}$ and $\gamma \in \mathbb{R}^{4 \times 1}$ are scaling factors, and $\circ$ is the Hadamard product of two vectors. We used the state $x(n)$ of the human-prosthesis system and its' derivation $x^{'}(n) = x(n) - x(n-1)$ as the state input of the ADP auto-tuner.

3.2 Utility Function/Reinforcement Signal

The reinforcement signal $r(n) \in \mathbb{R}$ was a instantaneous cost from the human-prosthesis system at tuning iteration n, which was determined by the performance of the human-prosthesis system. We set $r(n)$ to -1 if failure happens (i.e. the state of the human-prosthesis system is out of safety exploration range). And we set $r(n)$ to -0.8 if the dHDP block continued to tune the impedance parameter in an unfavorable direction that continually increased the angle error and/or duration error. Otherwise, $r(n)$ is set to 0. More detailed reinforcement rules can be find in [24].

Due to dynamic influences between phases [26], only one of the dHDP blocks could receive -1 reinforcement signal in one iteration if multiple phases failed.

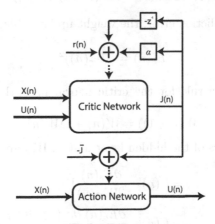

Fig. 2. Block diagram of dHDP.

Based on empirical experience, the priority of each phase was defined as (from high to low): STF, SWF, SWE, STE.

The total cost-to-go $J(n) \in \mathbb{R}$ at time instance n was given by

$$J(n) = r(n+1)) + \alpha r(n+2) + ... \\ + \alpha^N r(n+N+1) + ... \tag{7}$$

where α is a discount rate $(0 < \alpha < 1)$, and N is infinite.

3.3   Critic Neural Network

The CNN was implemented using three layers of neurons (7-7-1), which took the state $X(n) \in \mathbb{R}^{4 \times 1}$ of the system and the action $U(n) \in \mathbb{R}^{3 \times 1}$ from ANN as inputs, and the CNN predicted the total cost-to-go as $\hat{J}(n)$ at time instance n.

$$\hat{J}(n) = W_{c2}(n)\varphi(W_{c1}(n)[X^T(n), U^T(n)]^T)) \tag{8}$$

where $W_{c1} \in \mathbb{R}^{7 \times 7}$ is the weight matrix between the input layer and the hidden layer, $W_{c2} \in \mathbb{R}^{1 \times 7}$ is the weight matrix between the hidden layer and the output layer. And,

$$\varphi(v) = \frac{1 - exp^{-v}}{1 + exp^{-v}} \tag{9}$$

$$v_{c1}(n) = W_{c1}(n)[X^T(n), U^T(n)]^T \tag{10}$$

$$h_{c1}(n) = \varphi(v_{c1}(n)) \tag{11}$$

where $\varphi(v)$ is the activation function, $v_{c1}(n)$ is the input to the hidden neuron, and $h_{c1}(n)$ is the output of the hidden neuron.

The prediction error $e_c \in \mathbb{R}$ of the critic neural network can be written as

$$e_c(n) = \hat{J}(n) - [\alpha \hat{J}(n-1) - r(n)] \tag{12}$$

To correct the prediction error, the weight update objective is to minimize

$$E_c(n) = \frac{1}{2}(e_c(n))^2 \tag{13}$$

The weight update rule for the critic neural network is a gradient-based adaptation given by

$$W(n+1)) = W(n) + \Delta W(n) \tag{14}$$

The weight updates of the hidden layer matrix W_{c2} are:

$$\Delta W_{c2}(n) = l_c(n)[-\frac{\partial E_c(n)}{\partial W_{c2}(n)}] \\ = l_c(n)[-\frac{\partial E_c(n)}{\partial e_c(n)} \frac{\partial e_c(n)}{\partial \hat{J}(n)} \frac{\partial \hat{J}(n)}{\partial W_{c2}(n)}] \tag{15}$$

The weight updates of the input layer matrix W_{c1} are:

$$\Delta W_{c1}(n) = l_c(n)[-\frac{\partial E_c(n)}{\partial W_{c1}(n)}]$$

$$= l_c(n)[-\frac{\partial E_c(n)}{\partial e_c(n)}\frac{\partial e_c(n)}{\partial \hat{J}(n)}\frac{\partial \hat{J}(n)}{\partial h_{c1}(n)}\frac{\partial h_{c1}(n)}{\partial v_{c1}(n)}\frac{\partial v_{c1}(n)}{\partial W_{c1}(n)}] \tag{16}$$

where $l_c \in \mathbb{R}_{>0}$ is the learning rate of the critic neural network at time n.

3.4   Action Neural Network

The action neural network consisted of three layers of neurons (4-7-3), which took in the state $X(n) \in \mathbb{R}^{4\times1}$ from the human-prosthesis system and output the control $U(n) \in \mathbb{R}^{3\times1}$ to influence the human-prosthesis system. Furthermore, the relation between input $X(n)$ and output $U(n)$ was represented by

$$U = \varphi(W_{a2}(n) * \varphi(W_{a1}(n)X(n))) \tag{17}$$

where $W_{a1} \in \mathbb{R}^{7\times4}$ and $W_{a2} \in \mathbb{R}^{3\times7}$ are the weight matrix of the action neural network. And,

$$\varphi(v) = \frac{1 - exp^{-v}}{1 + exp^{-v}} \tag{18}$$

$$v_{a1}(n) = W_{a1}(n)x(n) \tag{19}$$

$$h_{a1}(n) = \varphi(v_{a1}(n)) \tag{20}$$

$$v_{a2}(n) = W_{a2}(n)h_{a1}(n) \tag{21}$$

Under certain state and cost-to-go function, the objective of adapting the action neural network is to back propagate the error between the desired ultimate objective, denoted by $\bar{J}$, and the approximated total cost-to-go $\hat{J}$. And $\bar{J}$ is set to 0 indicating for 'success'. The weights update rule for action neural network is to minimize the following performance error:

$$E_a(n) = \frac{1}{2}(\hat{J}(n) - \bar{J})^2 \tag{22}$$

Similarly, the weight matrix is updated based on gradient-based adaptation rule:

$$W(n+1)) = W(n) + \Delta W(n) \tag{23}$$

The weight updates of the hidden layer matrix W_{a2} are:

$$\Delta W_{a2}(n) = l_a(n)[-\frac{\partial E_a(n)}{\partial W_{a2}(n)}]$$

$$= l_a(n)[-\frac{\partial E_a(n)}{\partial \hat{J}(n)}\frac{\partial \hat{J}(n)}{\partial U(n)}\frac{\partial U(n)}{\partial W_{a2}(n)}] \tag{24}$$

The weight updates of the input layer matrix W_{a1} are:

$$\Delta W_{a1}(n) = l_a(n)[-\frac{\partial E_a(n)}{\partial W_{a1}(n)}]$$

$$= l_a(n)[-\frac{\partial E_a(n)}{\partial \hat{J}(n)}\frac{\partial \hat{J}(n)}{\partial U(n)}\frac{\partial U(n)}{\partial h_{a1}(n)}\frac{\partial h_{a1}(n)}{\partial W_{a1}(n)}]$$

(25)

where $l_a \in \mathbb{R}_{>0}$ is the learning rate of the action neural network.

4   Experiment

4.1   Experiment Protocol

One unilateral, transfemoral amputee (male, 58 years) provided written, informed consent to participate in this feasibility study, which was approved by the Institutional Review Board at the University of North Carolina at Chapel Hill. Prior to testing, a certified prosthetist fitted a experimental robotic knee prosthesis [4] to the subject. Then, the subject practiced to walk with the robotic knee prosthesis at a speed of 0.6 m/s on treadmill until he felt comfortable and confident with the testing setup without holding the handrail.

We ran 4 testing sessions each with different initial parameter configuration. For each testing session, we used the ADP-based auto-tuner to tune the impedance parameters over multiple 3-min trials with 3-min breaks between each trial to prevent fatigue from confounding our results. At the start of each trial, the subject walked for 30 s to acclimate to the testing environment. We then activated the ADP-based auto-tuner, which evaluated the prosthetic knee kinematics performance and updated any combination of impedance parameters

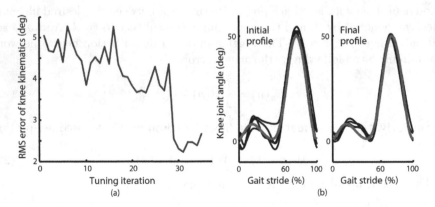

Fig. 3. The robotic knee prosthesis performance. (a) The RMS error of the robotic knee kinematics relative to the normative knee kinematics decreased along tuning procedure. (b) The final robotic knee kinematics (right, black lines) after ADP tuning procedure were more consistent and closer to normative knee kinematics (red line) compared with the initial ones (left, black lines). (Color figure online)

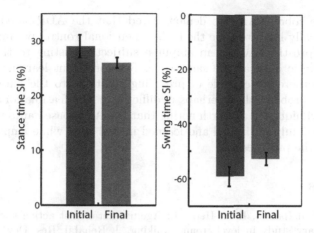

Fig. 4. Human-prosthesis performance comparison between the initial condition and final condition. Both the stance time symmetry and the swing time symmetry index improved when amputee walked with ADP-tuned impedance parameters.

every 7 strides for 2.5 min. The tuning procedure was terminated if either of 2 criteria were met: (1) the tuning iterations accumulated to 70 iterations in order to prevent subject fatigue; (2) the feature errors of prosthetic knee kinematics remained in the tolerance range for 3 of the last 5 tuning iterations.

During testing, we recorded the prosthetic knee joint angle from a potentiometer (100 Hz) and vertical GRF from the split-belt treadmill (Bertec Corp, OH, USA, 1000 Hz). The stance time and swing time were detected with ground reaction force. And symmetry index of stance time and swing time was calculated between prosthetic and intact sides.

4.2 Experiment Results

The root-mean-squared (RMS) error between the robotic knee kinematics and the normative knee kinematics decreased along the tuning iteration from $5.1°$ to $2.7°$ (Fig. 3a). With the final impedance parameters, amputee generated normative robotic knee kinematics when walking with the robotic knee prosthesis (Fig. 3b). The promising results indicated that the ADP-based auto-tuner was able to learn the control policy through interacting with human-prosthesis system and tune the impedance parameters to allow the amputee subject generating desired normative knee kinematics. In addition, the stance time symmetry index and swing time symmetry index improved after tuning procedure (Fig. 4).

5   Conclusion

In this study, we explored solutions to the human-machine co-adaptation problem, which posed greater challenge for the control of the robot than typical machine-alone robots. And we demonstrated that the ADP-based auto-tuner can automatically learn to tune the high-dimensional control parameters of the robotic knee prosthesis while an amputee subject adjusting to the computer controlled robotic knee at the same time. Reinforcement learning based control design is therefore capable of providing solutions to the human-machine co-adaptation problem that perhaps is difficult or not feasible for classic control design techniques. It is worth noting that the ADP-based auto-tuner in this study was randomly initialized and learned in real time while amputee subject walking with the prosthesis.

References

1. Martinez-Villalpando, E.C., Herr, H.: Agonist-antagonist active knee prosthesis: a preliminary study in level-ground walking. J. Rehabil. Res. Dev. **46**, 361–373 (2009)
2. Ambrozic, L., et al.: CYBERLEGs: a user-oriented robotic transfemoral prosthesis with whole-body awareness control. IEEE Robot. Autom. Mag. **21**, 82–93 (2014)
3. Sup, F., Varol, H.A., Mitchell, J., Withrow, T.J., Goldfarb, M.: Preliminary evaluations of a self-contained anthropomorphic transfemoral prosthesis. IEEE/ASME Trans. Mechatron. **14**, 667–676 (2009)
4. Liu, M., Zhang, F., Datseris, P., Huang, H.: Improving finite state impedance control of active-transfemoral prosthesis using Dempster-Shafer based state transition rules. J. Intell. Rob. Syst. **76**, 461–474 (2014)
5. Lawson, B.E., Varol, H.A., Huff, A., Erdemir, E., Goldfarb, M.: Control of stair ascent and descent with a powered transfemoral prosthesis. IEEE Trans. Neural Syst. Rehabil. Eng. **21**, 466–473 (2013)
6. Brandt, A., Liu, M., Huang, H.: Does the impedance of above-knee powered prostheses need to adjusted for load-carrying conditions? In: 38th Annual International Conference of the IEEE Engineering in Medicine and Biology Society, Orlando (2016)
7. Brandt, A., Wen, Y., Liu, M., Stallings, J., Huang, H.H.: Interactions between transfemoral amputees and a powered knee prosthesis during load carriage. Sci. Rep. **7**, 14480 (2017)
8. Simon, A.M., et al.: Configuring a powered knee and ankle prosthesis for transfemoral amputees within five specific ambulation modes. PLoS ONE **9**, e99387 (2014)
9. Pfeifer, S., Vallery, H., Hardegger, M., Riener, R., Perreault, E.J.: Model-based estimation of knee stiffness. IEEE Trans. Biomed. Eng. **59**, 2604–2612 (2012)
10. Shamaei, K., Sawicki, G.S., Dollar, A.M.: Estimation of quasi-stiffness of the human knee in the stance phase of walking. PLoS ONE **8**, e59993 (2013)
11. Gregg, R.D., Lenzi, T., Hargrove, L.J., Sensinger, J.W.: Virtual constraint control of a powered prosthetic leg: from simulation to experiments with transfemoral amputees. IEEE Trans. Rob. **30**, 1455–1471 (2014)
12. Huang, H., Crouch, D.L., Liu, M., Sawicki, G.S., Wang, D.: A cyber expert system for auto-tuning powered prosthesis impedance control parameters. Ann. Biomed. Eng. **44**, 1613–1624 (2016)
13. Koller, J.R., Gates, D.H., Ferris, D.P., Remy, C.D.: 'Body-in-the-Loop' optimization of assistive robotic devices: a validation study. In: Robotics: Science and Systems XII, Ann Arbor (2016)

14. Zhang, J., et al.: Human-in-the-loop optimization of exoskeleton assistance during walking. Science **356**, 1280–1284 (2017)
15. Ding, Y., Kim, M., Kuindersma, S., Walsh, C.J.: Human-in-the-loop optimization of hip assistance with a soft exosuit during walking. Sci. Robot. **3**, eaar5438 (2018)
16. Prokhorov, D.V., Wunsch, D.C.: Adaptive critic designs. IEEE Trans. Neural Networks **8**, 997–1007 (1997)
17. Si, J., Barto, A.G., Powell, W.B., Wunsch, D.: Handbook of Learning and Approximate Dynamic Programming. Wiley, New Jersey (2004)
18. Si, J., Wang, Y.-T.: On-line learning control by association and reinforcement. IEEE Trans. Neural Networks **12**, 264–276 (2001)
19. Enns, R., Si, J.: Helicopter trimming and tracking control using direct neural dynamic programming. IEEE Trans. Neural Networks **14**, 929–939 (2003)
20. Lu, C., Si, J., Xie, X.: Direct heuristic dynamic programming for damping oscillations in a large power system. IEEE Trans. Syst. Man Cybern. Part B Cybern. **38**, 1008–1013 (2008)
21. Yang, L., Si, J., Tsakalis, K.S., Rodriguez, A.A.: Direct heuristic dynamic programming for nonlinear tracking control with filtered tracking error. IEEE Trans. Syst. Man Cybern. Part B Cybern. **39**, 1617–1622 (2009)
22. Enns, R., Si, J.: Helicopter flight-control reconfiguration for main rotor actuator failures. J. Guidance Control Dyn. **26**, 572–584 (2003)
23. Enns, R., Si, J.: Apache helicopter stabilization using neural dynamic programming. J. Guidance Control Dyn. **25**(1), 19–25 (2002)
24. Wen, Y., Si, J., Gao, X., Huang, S., Huang, H.H.H.: A new powered lower limb prosthesis control framework based on adaptive dynamic programming. IEEE Trans. Neural Netw. Learn. Syst. **28**, 2215–2220 (2017)
25. Wen, Y., Liu, M., Si, J., Huang, H.H.: Adaptive control of powered transfemoral prostheses based on adaptive dynamic programming. In: 38th Annual International Conference of the IEEE Engineering in Medicine and Biology Society, Orlando, October 2016
26. Wen, Y., Brandt, A., Liu, M., Huang, H., Si, J.: Comparing parallel and sequential control parameter tuning for a powered knee prosthesis. In: IEEE International Conference on Systems, Man, and Cybernetics, SMC 2017, January 2017

Robust and High-Precision End-to-End Control Policy for Multi-stage Manipulation Task with Behavioral Cloning

Wei Ge, Weiwei Shang[✉], Fangjing Song, Hongjian Sui, and Shuang Cong

Department of Automation, University of Science and Technology of China, Hefei, China
wwshang@ustc.edu.cn

Abstract. In this paper, we propose a multi-stage task learning method that trains an end-to-end policy to control a 6-DoF robot arm to accomplish pick-and-place operation with high precision. The policy is mainly composed of CNNs and LSTMs, directly mapping raw images and joint angles to velocities command. In order to acquire a robust and high-precision policy, several techniques are introduced to boost performance. Augmentation trajectories are designed to alleviate compounding error problem, and dataset resampling is used to solve imbalanced data issue. Moreover, Huber loss for auxiliary outputs is illustrated to be very effective in multi-objective optimization problems, especially in robot learning field where sample complexity needs to be reduced desirably. To verify the effectiveness of our method, experiments are carried out in Gazebo simulator with UR5 arm and Kinect v1 camera. Our visuomotor policy can achieve a success rate of 87% on the pick-and-place task. The results of our experiments demonstrate that, with the skills we mention, behavioral cloning can effectively help us to learn good visuomotor policies for long-horizon tasks.

Keywords: Robot manipulation · Multi-stage task learning · Behavioral cloning

1 Introduction

With the development of robot technology, programming robots to accomplish routine tasks in our daily life like human becomes a research hotspot in robotics. Various tasks as well as complex and changeable environments in our life make it challenging to program the missions directly. Many learning methods such as reinforcement learning, imitation learning, are exploited to resolve this issue. While reinforcement learning emphasizes learning from scratch in general, imitation learning makes it possible for the robots to utilize experts' experience efficiently, so as to reduce sample complexity.

© Springer Nature Singapore Pte Ltd. 2019
F. Sun et al. (Eds.): ICCSIP 2018, CCIS 1005, pp. 474–484, 2019.
https://doi.org/10.1007/978-981-13-7983-3_42

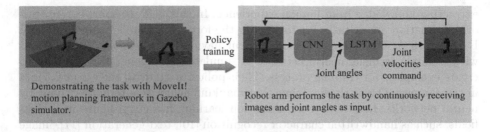

Fig. 1. An overview of our approach to end-to-end learning.

One of the best-known approaches in imitation learning is behavioral cloning, in which supervised learning methods are employed to solve sequential problems. Neural networks are designed elaborately to represent the control policies to make full use of its strong generalization ability. There have been studies about controlling the robots with neural network policies learned by behavioral cloning [1–4]. Great progress has been made in this field. Nevertheless, these methods do not tackle the problems that require long-horizon operation and high precision. What we strive to do is training policies that can not only generalize well but also be robust and high-precision. In order to achieve this goal, we design a LSTM-based network to capture the temporal information in sequential data. This network takes consecutive frames of images along with corresponding joint angles as input, and velocities command to be executed as output. The training set consists of expert's trajectories constructed via inverse kinematics using MoveIt! motion planning framework. To increase robustness, some augmentation trajectories are designed in advance to assist the policy in recovering from errors. When learning gripper action, we resample our dataset to handle imbalanced data problem. In addition, auxiliary outputs including cube position and gripper position are introduced to improve learning efficiency, which is inspired by [5–7]. We also find that we can accomplish pick-and-place task with higher precision by using Huber loss [8] rather than MSE loss as the loss function of these auxiliary outputs. For multi-objective optimization problems, Huber loss can not only stabilize the training process with same effect as gradient clipping, but also make it more intuitively for us to tune the coefficients of multiple objectives. Our approach is sketched in Fig. 1. The experimental results of this paper show that our method can help to learn robust and high-precision end-to-end policies for multi-stage tasks in robotic manipulation. And the policy exhibits good characters such as generalizing well to new object positions, automatically replanning the path while the target moves, robust to distractors and occlusions.

2   Related Work

Imitation learning, also known as apprenticeship learning or learning from demonstration, aims at acquiring policies mapping from states to actions via extracting knowledge from human experience. In this field, to some extent, priori information about tasks is provided in the form of human's behavioral data. Early in 1988, Pomerleau [9] succeeded in navigating a vehicle on real roads with a simple artificial neural network. A simulated road generator was built to create exemplars for training process. Their policy could drive the car at 0.5 m/s in the campus. This is the first time that mankind achieves automatic driving by neural networks. In recent years, imitation learning has cut a figure in various fields, such as handwritten character recognition [10], text generation [11], image captioning [12]. It is also used in the research field of robotics and achieves good results [13–19].

Last year, Rahmatizadeh *et al.* made two important achievements [20,21]. In the first study, Mixture Density Network (MDN) was utilized to represent the mapping from low-dimension inputs to gripper positions, then inverse kinematics solver was used to control Baxter robot. Two simple tasks were learned in this work, including pick-and-place as well as pushing. The second study focused on replacing direct position states with raw images, deriving an end-to-end policy. Additionally, a task selector was introduced into the network to deal with multiple tasks. Although this method can get good performances in several tasks, it is unable to handle scenes with real-time requirements owing to outputting joint angles rather than velocities or torques. James *et al.* [5] designed a network which outputs joint velocities directly, and the network was transferred to control a real robot. Despite acquiring high success rate, the target object was large thus making it easier for the policy to perceive in this work. In light of these problems, we introduce several techniques to train a robust, high-precision, real-time policy.

3 Approach

In this section, we first introduce what tasks are expected to be solved and how we collect expert demonstrations. Given these training data, we design a LSTM-based policy to accept raw images along with joint angles, and output joint velocities as well as gripper actions. Finally, policy learning details are discussed in our work.

3.1 Task Design and Data Collection

To verify that our methods can dig up implicit information useful for learning a long-horizon task, we test the learned policy in a pick-and-place task [5]. We human beings often need to pick up something from one location and then place it in another, so pick-and-place is one of the most desired behavior that we want the robots to learn. This task is divided into 5 stages, including pre-grasp stage, gripper-closing stage, lift-up stage, above-basket stage and gripper-opening stage. In the beginning, the arm is reset to a fixed configuration as initial state. Stage one places a waypoint near the cube preparing for grasping it. The second stage executes gripper closing command to grab the cube. In the

Fig. 2. Specified ranges to place cube and basket, during both training and testing. The yellow area displays the area where the cube is randomly placed, and the green areas represent the possible locations of the basket center. (Color figure online)

third stage, a waypoint is put a few inches above the cube. And the fourth stage places a waypoint above the basket. Finally, the last stage commands the gripper to open allowing the cube to drop into the basket. It is worth mentioning that all the paths are assumed to be linear in Cartesian space, hence the policy is unable to do obstacle avoidance now. In order to gather valid trajectories which accomplish the task, we check whether the cube is in the basket after these control stages. If not, the trajectory is thrown away.

When collecting data, we record raw RGB images, joint angles, joint velocities, gripper actions, cube positions and basket positions, at 10 Hz. Cube and basket are randomly placed within specified ranges so as to improve generalization (see Fig. 2). In order to handle compounding error problem and to increase robustness, some augmented trajectories are designed and added to the dataset. Firstly, we plan a linear path by MoveIt! framework. Then a uniformly distributed disturbance in Cartesian space is added to a waypoint chosen from this path randomly. Finally, we replan the path from the disturbed waypoint to the end of the stage, and latter half of this replanned trajectory is saved for error recovery. These augmented trajectories are helpful in reducing compounding errors and making the policy more robust. Besides compounding error problem, imbalanced data issue should also be taken into account. The data of a certain timestep is referred to as transition. And we could find that there are few transitions that own gripper-opening or gripper-closing tags. The gripper action tag is no-operation of almost all the transitions saved in one trajectory. To alleviate this problem, we resample the dataset, abstracting those transitions with gripper-opening or gripper-closing tags to form an additional dataset. During training process, samples are drawn from additional dataset according to a given probability. The dataset creation process is described in Algorithm 1. There are altogether 2500 trajectories in our training set, 2000 of which are ordinary trajectories, and the rest are augmented trajectories.

Algorithm 1. Dataset Creation

1: Initialize $\mathcal{D}_{total} \leftarrow \emptyset, \mathcal{D}_o \leftarrow \emptyset, \mathcal{D}_a \leftarrow \emptyset,$
2: **for** $i = 1...N$ **do**
3:     Execute trajectory T_i planned by expert π_e (using MoveIt!)
4:     **if** Task not completed **then**
5:         Delete T_i
6:     **else**
7:         Add $\{s_{\pi_e}, \pi_e(s_{\pi_e})\}$ pairs of T_i into $\mathcal{D}_o$
8:     **end if**
9: **end for**
10: **for** $i = 1...M$ **do**
11:     Randomly sample a stage r_i and execute partial trajectory T_{p_i} before r_i
12:     Plan trajectory T_{r_i} for r_i
13:     Randomly pick a waypoint p_{r_i} in T_{r_i} and disturb it
14:     Execute partial trajectory before p_{r_i}
15:     Plan residual trajectory T_i to the end of the task
16:     Execute T_i
17:     **if** Task not completed **then**
18:         Delete T_{p_i}, T_{r_i}, T_i
19:     **else**
20:         Add $\{s_{\pi_e}, \pi_e(s_{\pi_e})\}$ pairs in the latter half of T_i into $\mathcal{D}_o$
21:     **end if**
22: **end for**
23: Extract the transitions with gripper-opening or gripper-closing tags
24: Add these transitions into $\mathcal{D}_a$
25: $\mathcal{D}_{total} = \mathcal{D}_o \bigcup \mathcal{D}_a$
26: **return** $\mathcal{D}_{total}$

3.2   Network Design and Loss Function Selection

To predict velocities command, the policy should be able to excavate temporal information from consecutive images and joint angles. Thus a LSTM-based network is designed as shown in Fig. 3. This network takes as input n consecutive images and corresponding joint angles from time $t - n + 1$ to time t, then outputs joint velocities command, gripper action, as well as two auxiliary terms including cube position and gripper position, at time $t + 1$. Two auxiliary terms are employed to impel the network to master inferring position information from raw images. During testing, these position terms are used only for visualization and debugging.

Detailed architecture of our network is presented as follows. There are 8 convolutional layers, 1 LSTM layer and a few dense layers. All convolutional layers maintain $3 * 3$ convolutional kernels except the last layer, which has a $2 * 2$ kernel. Additionally, max pooling operation with a stride of 2 is performed to reduce dimensionality of the feature maps. After these interleaved layers, the feature maps are flattened and then merged with joint angles, as the input of LSTM module. The tensor output from LSTM layer is then taken as input by a fully connected layer with 128 neurons. In the end, dense layers are utilized to integrate information and to provide the final outputs.

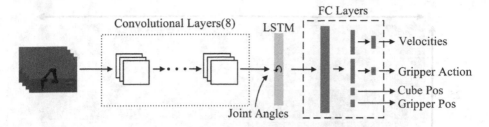

Fig. 3. Network architecture. Our policy directly maps four consecutive images and corresponding joint angles to control commands along with two auxiliary terms.

Three types of loss function are applied to the outputs of the network. For joint velocities, MSE loss is computed. Gripper action prediction problem is treated as a multi-class classification problem, and the gripper action is represented by one-hot encoding. Cross-entropy loss is utilized to be the loss function of this target. It should be noted that we use Huber loss to deal with the position regression problem. Huber loss is piecewise defined as:

$$L_\delta(a) = \begin{cases} \frac{\gamma}{2}a^2, & \text{for } |a| \leq \delta, \\ \gamma(\delta|a| - \frac{1}{2}\delta^2), & \text{otherwise.} \end{cases} \tag{1}$$

where a is the error between ground truth and the prediction. This loss is often used in robust regression, being not susceptible to outliers. We can tune γ and δ to intuitively set the gradient of loss when $|a| > \delta$. Thus, the gradient of position loss can update the weights of neural network more effectively, avoiding to be overwhelmed with other errors like velocity error and gripper action error. Additionally, Huber loss also helps our network to learn the multi-objective optimization problem smoothly, achieving similar effect as gradient clipping. We set $\gamma = 6.67$ and $\delta = 0.03$, thus when the absolute value of error is greater than 0.03, the gradient of loss with respect to prediction maintains constant 0.2 or -0.2. Combining these loss discussed above, total loss function $\mathcal{L}_{total}$ can be obtained:

$$\mathcal{L}_{total} = \alpha_{vel} * \mathcal{L}_{vel} + \alpha_{ga} * \mathcal{L}_{ga} + \alpha_{cp} * \mathcal{L}_{cp} + \alpha_{gp} * \mathcal{L}_{gp} \tag{2}$$

in which $\mathcal{L}_{vel}$, $\mathcal{L}_{ga}$, $\mathcal{L}_{cp}$, $\mathcal{L}_{gp}$ are the losses of velocities, gripper actions, cube positions and gripper positions respectively, and α_{vel}, α_{ga}, α_{cp}, α_{gp} are the coefficients of the loss terms. We weight these loss terms equally except for the gripper action term, whose weight is set as one-fifth of other terms.

3.3 End-to-End Policy Learning

After designing the network architecture, an end-to-end policy is trained. There are several key points needing to be considered during this process, including gripper action resampling, unroll timesteps and transition interval. Gripper action resampling has been discussed in Sect. 3.1, so it is not analyzed in this section.

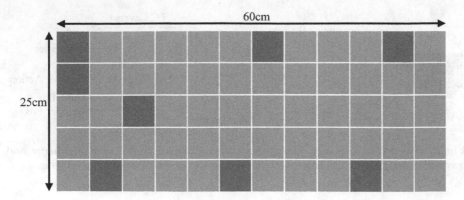

Fig. 4. Policies are evaluated by this grid. Cube generation area is split into 60 cells. Successes are marked as green, while failures are marked as orange. In this case, success rate is 87%. (Color figure online)

As is well known, LSTM belongs to recurrent neural networks, in which parameters are shared by different timesteps, thus allowing our model to synthesize information span over a period of time. We set timesteps $\hat{t}$ as 4 to enable our network to learn sequential data effectively. That is to say, four consecutive transitions compose a new data sample used for training the network. As is mentioned earlier, transitions are collected at 10 Hz. We need to determine the time interval between four transitions that compose one training data. Time interval $\hat{u}$ is set as 2 to avoid the case when four transitions have similar state input so that it is much harder for LSTM to learn temporal information. Same parameters are used to generate control commands to drive the robot when running the learned policy.

4   Experiments

In the following, a series of experiments are set up to validate the effectiveness of our method. Experiments are done in Gazebo simulator with UR5 arm, Robotiq-G85 gripper and Kinect v1 camera. Some of the issues that we are concerned about are listed below:

1. How does control effect vary when time interval changes?
2. Is the policy robust to disturbances?
3. What about the success rate of pick-and-place task?

Experimental Setup. To evaluate our method, we divide the predefined area of cube generation into 60 small cells (shown in Fig. 4), size of which are all 5 cm × 5 cm. Then cube is randomly placed in each cell, so 60 experiments are conducted. The success rate is expressed as a percentage of these trials.

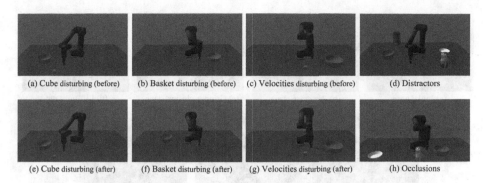

(a) Cube disturbing (before)　(b) Basket disturbing (before)　(c) Velocities disturbing (before)　(d) Distractors

(e) Cube disturbing (after)　(f) Basket disturbing (after)　(g) Velocities disturbing (after)　(h) Occlusions

Fig. 5. Disturbing test. For cube disturbing test, the cube is moved by about 3 cm, and for basket disturbing test, the basket is moved from one side to the other side. Velocities disturbances are introduced by adding a Gaussian noise (rad/s) according to $\mathcal{N}(0.0, 0.03)$.

Time Interval Experiment. Our first experiment is focused mainly on the influence of different interval setups to the performance of the control policy. We can imagine that it hinders the agent from performing well if the interval $\hat{u}$ is set inappropriately. Take an extreme example, if $\hat{u}$ is 0, then the inputs at different timesteps accepted by LSTM are same, thus no sequential information is contained. As for a large number, we can assume that two consecutive timesteps will be not very much related to each other. A set of values are tested for comparison, including 1, 2, 4. Our experimental results show that set $\hat{u} = 2$ can derive a better policy. The training process sometimes oscillates when $\hat{u}$ is set as 1 or 4, and the control policy is less accurate for pick-and-place. Therefore, we choose 2 to be the time interval.

Disturbance Test. In order to verify the robustness of the neural network control policy, we design five subtests: (1) cube position disturbing test, (2) basket position disturbing test, (3) velocities disturbing test, (4) distractors situation test, (5) occlusions situation test. For the first test, disturbances are added during pre-grasp stage. As to the second test, we move the basket while the policy tries to drive the robot to above-basket stage. Both two disturbing tests are used to confirm the replanning ability of our policy. The velocity disturbing test is aimed to check whether the policy is robust to the velocities disturbance from the robots. And the last two tests are used to see the resistance against distractors and occlusions appearing in the environments. These situations are depicted in Fig. 5. During testing, the cube is placed in the cell randomly picked from the grid. Experimental results are listed in Table 1. The control policy has a relatively good performance on disturbing tests except the occlusions test. One explanation for this behavior is that occlusions appearing in the environments make it difficult for the policy to conclude position information, such as cube position, gripper position and basket position. The results suggest that our policy shows

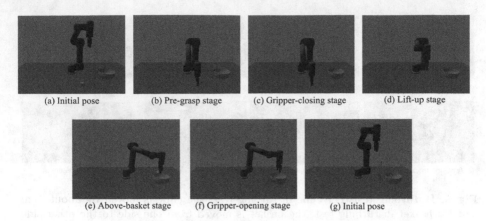

(a) Initial pose   (b) Pre-grasp stage   (c) Gripper-closing stage   (d) Lift-up stage

(e) Above-basket stage   (f) Gripper-opening stage   (g) Initial pose

Fig. 6. An example of test run.

Table 1. Disturbing tests.

Disturbance test	Cube position	Basket position	Velocities	Distractors	Occlusions
Success ratio	8/10	7/10	7/10	9/10	5/10

a certain robustness to these random disturbances though no disturbances are considered in the training set.

Task Completion Rate. For the purpose of providing better assessment of our method, successes are divided into three categories, containing cube vicinity, cube grasped and task completion. Cube vicinity is said to be achieved if the midpoint between two fingers reaches within 3 cm near the center of cube, where the cube can be grabbed by the gripper (cube size is 4 cm × 4 cm × 4 cm). We consider cube to be grasped successfully when the cube is lifted up. And task completion means that the policy accomplishes the whole pick-and-place task stage by stage. The experiments are conducted according to the experimental setup with no disturbances introduced. An example of test run is illustrated in Fig. 6. Statistical results are listed in Table 2. As is shown in this table, the neural network policy can reach cube vicinity in almost all the experiments. And 87% of 60 trials can achieve cube grasped and task completion phase. Although there are circumstances where the policy does not accomplish the whole task, it is able to achieve promising results. Moreover, it is worth mentioning that, our controller can control the gripper to achieve poses that are less than 2 cm near the cube center in about half trials.

Table 2. Policy evaluation.

Successes	Cube vicinity	Cube grasped	Task completion
Rate	92%	87%	87%

5 Conclusions

In this work, we have shown that a robust, high-precision, end-to-end controller for long time span task can be acquired with our method. As a classic problem, pick-and-place could be learned effectively by using a neural network policy. And the neural network control policy has some good features such as generalizing well to new object positions, automatically replanning the path while the target moves, robust to distractors and occlusions.

Despite these advantages mentioned above, there are some limitations. Firstly, the control policy cannot handle the situations where obstacles exist for the reason that we only collect linear paths to simplify the problem. Secondly, even our policy knows to approach the cube again if the cube falls to the table, it does not realize that the gripper should open again. That is to say, the control policy has no knowledge about regrasping. In addition, a single camera is used to capture RGB images as input, different from human beings. Most importantly, we have not transferred our control policy from simulation to real world, we will focus on this issue in the following days.

To sum up, we are able to derive good policies for robots to imitate simple behaviors of our human beings. In future work, we intend to explore how to solve these problems listed above, and we are excited to see the progress in this field.

Acknowledgment. This work was supported by the National Natural Science Foundation of China with Grant No. 51675501 and 51275500, the State Key Laboratory of Robotics and System with Grant No. SKLRS-2018-KF-07, and the Youth Innovation Promotion Association CAS with Grant No. 2012321. The authors would like to thank Information Science Laboratory Center of USTC for the hardware & software services.

References

1. Torabi, F., Warnell, G., Stone, P.: Behavioral Cloning from Observation, arXiv: 1805.01954, May 2018
2. Sun, W., Venkatraman, A., Gordon, G.J., et al.: Deeply Aggrevated: Differentiable Imitation Learning for Sequential Prediction, arXiv: 1703.01030, March 2017
3. Stadie, B.C., Abbeel, P., Sutskever, I.: Third-Person Imitation Learning, arXiv: 1703.01703, March 2017
4. Sheh, R., Hengst, B., Sammut, C.: Behavioural cloning for driving robots over rough terrain. In: IEEE/RSJ International Conference on Intelligent Robots and Systems, San Francisco, 25–30 September 2011, pp. 732–737 (2011)
5. James, S., Davison, A.J., Johns, E.: Transferring End-to-End Visuomotor Control from Simulation to Real World for a Multi-Stage Task, arXiv: 1707.02267, October 2017

6. Jaderberg, M., Mnih, V., Czarnecki, W.M., et al.: Reinforcement Learning with Unsupervised Auxiliary Tasks, arXiv: 1611.05397, November 2016
7. Dilokthanakul, N., Kaplanis, C., Pawlowski, N., et al.: Feature Control as Intrinsic Motivation for Hierarchical Reinforcement Learning, arXiv: 1705.06769, November 2017
8. Huber, P.J.: Robust estimation of a location parameter. Ann. Math. Stat. **35**(1), 73–101 (1964)
9. Pomerleau, D.A.: ALVINN: an autonomous land vehicle in a neural network. In: Advances in Neural Information Processing Systems, Denver, pp. 305–313 (1988)
10. Chung, J., Kastner, K., Dinh, L., et al.: A recurrent latent variable model for sequential data. In: Advances in Neural Information Processing Systems, Montreal, 07–12 December 2015, pp. 2980–2988 (2015)
11. Wen, T., Gasic, M., Mrksic, N., et al.: Semantically conditioned LSTM-based natural language generation for spoken dialogue systems. In: Empirical Methods in Natural Language Processing, Lisbon, 17–21 September 2015, pp. 1711–1721 (2015)
12. Karpathy, A., Li, F.: Deep visual-semantic alignments for generating image descriptions. In: Computer Vision and Pattern Recognition, Boston, 08–10 June 2015, pp. 3128–3137 (2015)
13. Schaal, S.: Learning from demonstration. Robot. Auton. Syst. **47**(2–3), 65–67 (2004)
14. Abbeel, P., Coates, A., Ng, A.Y.: Autonomous helicopter aerobatics through apprenticeship learning. Int. J. Robot. Res. **29**(13), 1608–1639 (2010)
15. Zucker, M., Ratliff, N., Dragan, A.D., et al.: CHOMP: covariant hamiltonian optimization for motion planning. Int. J. Robot. Res. **32**(9–10), 1164–1193 (2013)
16. Zhang, T., McCarthy, Z., Jow, O., et al.: Deep Imitation Learning for Complex Manipulation Tasks from Virtual Reality Teleoperation, arXiv: 1710.04615, March 2017
17. Yu, T., Finn, C., Xie, A., et al.: One-Shot Imitation from Observing Humans via Domain-Adaptive Meta-Learning, arXiv:1802.01557, February 2018
18. Duan, Y., Andrychowicz, M., Stadie, B.C., et al.: One-Shot Imitation Learning, arXiv: 1703.07326, March 2017
19. Finn, C., Yu, T., Zhang, T., et al.: One-Shot Visual Imitation Learning via Meta-Learning, arXiv: 1709.04905, September 2017
20. Rahmatizadeh, R., Abolghasemi, P., Behal, A., et al.: From Virtual Demonstration to Real-World Manipulation Using LSTM and MDN, arXiv: 1603.03833, March 2016
21. Rahmatizadeh, R., Abolghasemi, P., Boloni, L., et al.: Vision-Based Multi-Task Manipulation for Inexpensive Robots Using End-to-End Learning from Demonstration, arXiv: 1707.02920, July 2017

An Adaptive Behavior Under Uneven Terrains for Quadruped Robot

Peng Xu, Bo Su$^{(\boxtimes)}$, Lei Jiang, Qichang Yao, Ruina Dang, Wei Xu, Chenxing Jiang, Yuchuan Lu, Yunfeng Jiang, and Lindong Mu

China North Vehicle Research Institute, Beijing, China
bosu@noveri.com.cn

Abstract. In order to improve the adaptive behavior performance of the quadruped robot under uneven terrains, based on the locomotion characteristic of the trot gait, the robot is simplified as the model of the body and virtual leg. The virtual leg dynamics is established and analyzed. Also, on the basis of the dynamic model, the foothold and the trajectory during the stance duration are planned. Combined with the extern force exerted on the robot, the contact compliance control model is established to map to multi-DOF joints. The body posture balance could be achieved by compensating the foot position. The experiment is built in the uneven terrain with the trot gait, and the experimental result validates the feasibility of the method.

Keywords: Quadruped robot · Adaptive behavior · Virtual leg dynamics · Uneven terrains · Contact compliance · Posture balance

1 Background

Currently, quadruped robots are developing towards high performance. More and more domestic and foreign research institutions are carrying out in-depth research. Most quadruped mammals in nature locomote with their legs and feet, and have the huge advantages in environmental adaptability and kinematic flexibility. The study of quadruped bionic robot is playing a key role in promoting the application of quadruped robot in the future military, space exploration, safety and explosion protection, injuries rescue etc.

In order to realize the locomotion control of quadruped robot, the research on locomotion control of quadruped robot has been carried out at home and abroad. Boston Dynamics researched the mechanism of one-legged and multi-legged dynamic stability, and an inverted pendulum model was established, and also, the stable locomotion of quadruped robot under the complex terrain was realized [1]. Based on the principle of energy, Massachusetts Institute of Technology (MIT) established a model of the impulse force for quadruped robot, and the stability of the robot during bounding was realized [2], moreover, the impedance control model of foot was studied [3, 4]. ETH Zürich studied the virtual model of quadruped robot, and virtual forces are distributed to each stance leg by the distribution optimization algorithm, the joint compliance control was realized by mapping the joints [5]. Italian Institute of Technology presented a planning method of foot trajectory for quadruped robot based on

© Springer Nature Singapore Pte Ltd. 2019
F. Sun et al. (Eds.): ICCSIP 2018, CCIS 1005, pp. 485–495, 2019.
https://doi.org/10.1007/978-981-13-7983-3_43

linear inverted pendulum [6], at the same time, the impedance control model of foot was studied and the active compliance control of joint is realized [7]. Shandong University in China researched the locomotion planning model of quadruped robot, and established the impedance compliance control model between the foot and terrain [8–10].

Because the traditional wheel and tracked ground vehicle adapt to the complex terrain passively, therefore, it is difficult to maximize the mobility performance, compared with traditional ground vehicles, stride movements could be made by selecting discrete points of contact to pass across the rough terrain and complex obstacles, and adjust the attitude of the body in real time according to changes of the environment with the higher adaptability and flexibility. Complex environments such as plat eau, mountain, jungle, desert etc. are usually accompanied with disturbance of terrain fluctuation and other types of disturbance, the quadruped robot will be disturbed by external forces in the process of crossing through obstacles. To adapt different disturbed environments, the quadruped robot needs to adapt the posture of the body according to changes of environment, and establishes the adaptive control method to achieve the stable adjustment in complex environment.

Based on the situation above, to achieve the stable adaptation of quadruped robot in complex disturbance environment, we will design another different, simple and effective method with the lower cost to achieve the adaptive control under uneven terrain by simplifying the system as the virtual leg model, designing the foot behavior and establishing the foot and joint compliance controller based on the foot position and extern force. This research plans the foot trajectory of the robot based on the analysis of virtual leg dynamics model, and establishes the balance control model and compliance model between foot and environment to map to multi-DOF joints. The experimental verification of this method is carried out by establishing typical working conditions. Finally, the work of this paper is summarized and prospected.

2 Virtual Leg Model

As shown in Fig. 1, the quadruped robot includes four stance legs, each stance leg consists of three degrees of freedom, and the lateral and swing motion of legs could be realized. The robot could be simplified as the virtual leg model.

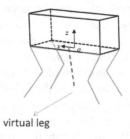

virtual leg

Fig. 1. The quadruped robot

During the motion of the quadruped robot, the leg state is divided into swing state and stance state. According the motion characteristic of trot gait, diagonal legs could be simplified the virtual leg. The virtual leg could generate the locomotion behavior equivalent to diagonal legs, and the stance state and the swing state could be seen as the two state of the virtual leg. The phase sequence of the trot gait is as follows.

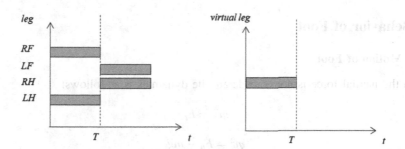

Fig. 2. Phase sequence of trot gait

As shown in Fig. 2, *LF*, *RF*, *LH*, *RH* are the left front, right front, left hind, right hind leg respectively. The rectangle filling area represents the stance duration of the leg, and the rest of the region corresponds to the swing cycle. The trot gait sets the same swing and stance duration, and the swing duration is set as T.

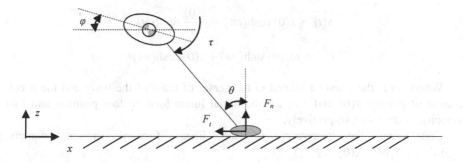

Fig. 3. Virtual leg model

According the virtual leg model, as shown in Fig. 3, the dynamics is established as follows:

$$m\ddot{x} = F_t - \frac{\tau}{l}\cos\theta \tag{1}$$

$$m\ddot{z} = F_n + \frac{\tau}{l}\sin\theta - mg \tag{2}$$

$$I\ddot{\varphi} = \tau \tag{3}$$

Where, x and z are the linear forward and vertical position of the body respectively. m is the mass of the body. F_t and F_n are the linear forward and vertical force of the foot respectively. l and θ are the length and the direction of the virtual leg respectively. φ is the pitch angle of the body. I is the moment of inertia. τ is the actuated torque. g is the acceleration of gravity.

3   Behavior of Foot

3.1   Motion of Foot

When the inertial force is not considered, the dynamics is as follows:

$$m\ddot{x} = F_t \tag{4}$$

$$m\ddot{z} = F_n - mg \tag{5}$$

According the Eq. 4, the linear forward motion is planned as follows:

$$\ddot{x} = \frac{g}{z}x \tag{6}$$

When z is the constant, Eq. 6 is calculated as follows:

$$x(t) = x(0)\cosh(\omega t) + \frac{\dot{x}(0)}{\omega}\sinh(\omega t) \tag{7}$$

$$\dot{x}(t) = \omega x(0)\sinh(\omega t) + \dot{x}(0)\cosh(\omega t) \tag{8}$$

Where, ω is the constant related to the center of mass of the body and the acceleration of gravity. $x(0)$ and $\dot{x}(0)$ are the initial linear forward foot position and foot velocity of the robot respectively.

Considering the symmetry of the linear forward motion, namely, $x(0) = -x(T_s) = \frac{\lambda}{2}$, $\dot{x}(0) = \dot{x}(T_s)$.

Where, λ is the linear forward span in the stance duration. T_s is the stance duration.

$$\dot{x}(0) = -\frac{\omega[1 + \cosh(\omega T_s)]}{\sinh(\omega T_s)}x(0) \tag{9}$$

The method that the lateral stance position of the foot is designed is the same as in the linear forward direction.

The trajectory of the vertical foot position is designed as follows (Fig. 4):

$$z(t) = -A\cos(\frac{\pi}{\lambda}x) - z_0 \tag{10}$$

Where, z_0 is the constant height of the robot. A is the vertical amplitude in the stance duration.

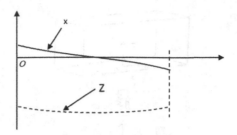

Fig. 4. Foot stance trajectory

The swing trajectory is planned according to the foothold position and swing height of the leg smoothly. The swing phase could be designed as the simple trigonometric trajectory. The trajectory is designed as follows (Fig. 5):

$$x = \lambda\left[1 - \cos(\tfrac{\pi}{T}t)\right] \quad 0 \leq t \leq T \tag{11}$$

$$z = \begin{cases} \frac{H_m}{2}\left[1 - \cos(\tfrac{\pi}{T_h}t)\right] & 0 \leq t \leq T_h \\ \frac{H_m}{2}\left[1 + \cos(\pi\tfrac{t-T_h}{T-T_h})\right] & T_h < t \leq T \end{cases} \tag{12}$$

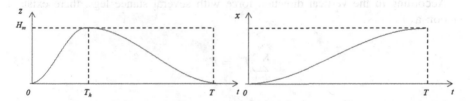

Fig. 5. Swing trajectory of foot

3.2 Balance Control

Combining the control target of the controller with its own characteristics, spring-damp virtual components are established in the vertical direction of the robot (see Fig. 6). The changes in the posture of the body could be compensated by the planned foot trajectory with the corresponding stance legs.

$$\Delta\mathbf{p} = \mathbf{k}_{pb}(\mathbf{\psi}_d - \mathbf{\psi}) \tag{13}$$

Where, $\mathbf{k}_{pb}$ is the dynamics matrix between the body posture and the foot position. $\mathbf{\psi}_d$ and $\mathbf{\psi}$ are the desired and actual body posture vector respectively. $\Delta\mathbf{p}$ is the foot position offset vector.

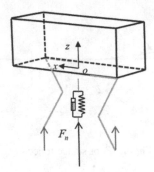

Fig. 6. Spring-damp virtual components

According to Eq. 5, considering the height and the weight of the body in the stance duration, the external force of the body could be established as follows:

$$F_n = mg + k_p(z_d - z) - k_d \dot{z} \tag{14}$$

Where, k_p and k_d are the stiffness and the damping coefficients of body height controller respectively. z_d and z are the desired and actual body height of the robot respectively. $\dot{z}$ is the actual body vertical velocity of the robot.

According to the vertical direction force with several stance legs, there exists a relation as follows:

$$\sum_{i=1}^{N} F_n^i = F_n \tag{15}$$

Where, F_n^i is the foot-terrain force of the i th stance leg. N is the number of stance legs. F_n could be distributed according to the symmetry of the trot gait.

According to the planned foot stance trajectory and the designed external force of the body, a compliance controller between the foot and the terrain is established as follows:

$$\mathbf{F}_c^i = k_{fp}(\mathbf{p}_d^i - \mathbf{p}^i) - k_{fd}\dot{\mathbf{p}}^i + \begin{bmatrix} 0 & 0 & F_n^i \end{bmatrix}^T \tag{16}$$

Where, k_{fp} and k_{fd} are the stiffness and the damping coefficients of compliance controller respectively. $\mathbf{p}_d^i$ and $\mathbf{p}^i$ are the desired and actual foot position vector of the robot respectively. $\dot{\mathbf{p}}^i$ is the actual foot velocity vector of the robot. $\mathbf{F}_c^i$ is the foot-terrain compliance force vector.

The force vector $\mathbf{F}_c^i$ is mapped to joints by the Jacobian matrix $\mathbf{J}$ of multi-DOF joints in the leg to achieve joint compliance control, namely, $\mathbf{T}_a^i = \mathbf{J}^T \mathbf{F}_c^i$, where, $\mathbf{T}_a^i$ is the torque vector of joints for the i th stance leg. The Jacobian matrix $\mathbf{J}$ represents the relationship between the foot linear velocity vector and joints velocity vector, namely, $\dot{\mathbf{p}}^i = \mathbf{J}\dot{\mathbf{q}}^i$, where, $\dot{\mathbf{q}}^i$ is the angular velocity vector of joints for the i th stance leg. Based on the leg kinematics, the Jacobian matrix $\mathbf{J}$ could be calculated as follows:

$$\mathbf{J} = \begin{bmatrix} 0 & -(a_2 c_2 + a_3 c_{23}) & -a_3 c_{23} \\ c_1(a_1 + a_2 c_2 + a_3 c_{23}) & -s_1(a_2 s_2 + a_3 s_{23}) & -a_3 s_1 s_{23} \\ s_1(a_1 + a_2 c_2 + a_3 c_{23}) & c_1(a_2 s_2 + a_3 s_{23}) & a_3 c_1 c_{23} \end{bmatrix} \quad (17)$$

Where, $s_j = \sin(q_j)$, $c_j = \cos(q_j)$, $s_{jk} = \sin(q_j + q_k)$, $c_{jk} = \cos(q_j + q_k)$, q_j is the angle for the j th joint, a_j is the link length for the j th joint of the leg.

$$\mathbf{u}_j(t) = \mathbf{k}_{qt}(\mathbf{q}_d - \mathbf{q}) - \mathbf{k}_{vt}\dot{\mathbf{q}} + \mathbf{T}_a^i \quad (18)$$

Where, $\mathbf{k}_{qt}$ and $\mathbf{k}_{vt}$ are the stiffness and the damping coefficients of joint controller respectively. $\mathbf{q}_d$ and $\mathbf{q}$ are the desired and actual joint position vector of the robot respectively. $\dot{\mathbf{q}}$ is the actual joint angular velocity. $\mathbf{u}_j(t)$ is the joint controller input.

3.3 Measurement of Robot

The actual posture angular of the robot could be measured by the IMU (Inertia Measurement Unit) mounted on the robot respectively. The actual foot position could be measured by the leg kinematics (see Fig. 7).

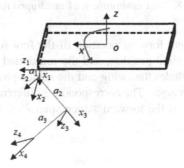

Fig. 7. Leg kinematics

The actual forward linear velocity of the robot could be estimated by the forward step length during the support period approximately.

$$\dot{x} = \frac{\lambda}{T_s} \quad (19)$$

4 Simulation Experiment

A quadruped robot and interactive environment is established using real-time inter-active multi-body dynamic engine Vortex developed by CM-Labs in Canada. The correctness and effectiveness of this method are validated by setting up obstacles and slope in the simulation environment with the trot gait. The heights of obstacles are set to 5 cm, 8 cm and 12 cm respectively, and the slope is set to 20°, and the interval between obstacles is set to 1 m.

The quadruped robot is about 135 kg in weight, and it is 1 m in length and 0.4 m in width, the height is 0.72 m when stopping and 0.8 m when walking. The robot parameters are set based on the real-world application of the quadruped robot. In the initial stage, the robot is in a flat condition far away from the obstacle. The maximum velocity is set to 0.4 m/s. The robot passes through obstacles and the slope with the trot gait, as shown in Fig. 8.

Fig. 8. Test environment of quadruped robot

Figure 9 shows the linear forward position of the foot for the robot, and the blue solid line represents the desired position, and the red dotted line represents the actual position. The trajectory includes the swing and the stance phase. The swing and stance phase realize the smooth changes. The corresponding difference between the maximum and minimum of the curve is the forward stance span λ of the foot.

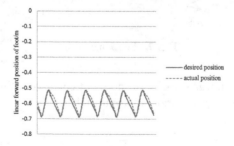

Fig. 9. The vertical foot motion (Color figure online)

Figure 10 shows the vertical position of the foot for the robot, the blue solid line represents the desired position, and the red dotted line represents the actual position.

The trajectory includes the swing and the stance phase. The robot uses trajectory planning method of foot in the process of motion. By changing the value of T_h to adjust the time of the foot step height, the ability crossing obstacles could be improved to a certain extent (see Fig. 10b). The swing height of the leg is set to 0.16 m. The difference between the maximum and the value at the end of the swing phase is close to the swing height. In the whole process, the robot always tracks the desired position generated by the controller during the movement, and meets the requirements of the control accuracy.

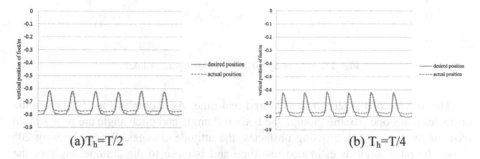

(a)T_h=T/2   (b) T_h=T/4

Fig. 10. The vertical foot motion (Color figure online)

Figure 11 represents the vertical force between the foot and the terrain, the blue solid line represents the desired force, and the red dotted line represents the actual force.

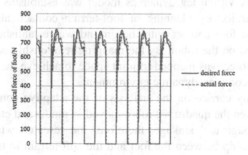

Fig. 11. The vertical force of foot (Color figure online)

The compliant contact between the foot and the terrain is realized by using the compliance controller in this research. The change of the force meets the requirement of the height compliance of the robot. The actual force between the foot and the terrain is estimated by the dynamic model, which is used to test the effectiveness of the impedance force compliance controller.

The posture of the robot is as shown in Fig. 12, the red solid line represents the pitch angle, the green dotted line represents the yaw angle, and the blue dash-dotted line represents the roll angle.

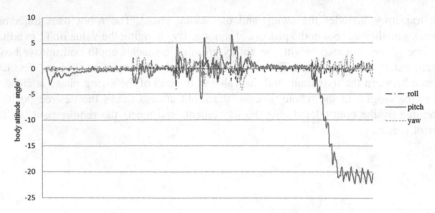

Fig. 12. The body posture (Color figure online)

The attitude of the terrain is measured real-time. As shown in Fig. 12, before the obstacles and slope passing though, the body roll angle and pitch angle are near zero in most of the time, when crossing obstacles, the attitude changes. When climbing 20° slope, the pitch angle is estimated real-time and is close to the attitude angle of the terrain, and the body posture is stable in the process of motion.

5 Conclusion and Prospect

The multi-DOF mechanism of quadruped robot was simplified as the body-virtual leg system, and the body virtual leg dynamics model was established, on this basis, this paper finished the trajectory planning of foot-terrain contact, also, the compliance control model of the foot contact with the ground was established according to the external force exerted on the robot. By the mapping relationship between the foot and the joint space, the force was mapped to joint space to achieve the adaptive control of the robot under the complex dynamic environment.

This paper mainly carried on the analysis of the adaptive control under the rigid terrain, however, when the quadruped robot moved in mud, sand etc. terrains, the robot will occur the slippage and sinkage, therefore, the research will consider the terramechanics relationship between the foot and the soft terrain in the future work, and design the foot structure with the high performance to improve the mobility under the soft terrain.

Acknowledgements. This work was supported in part by National Natural Science Foundation of China (Grant No. 91748211) and the Grant 2016QNRC001.

References

1. Raibert, M., Blankespoor, K., Nelson, G., et al.: Bigdog, the rough-terrain quadruped robot. In: Proceedings of the 17th World Congress, pp. 10822–10825 (2008)
2. Park, H., Chuah, M.Y., Kim, S., et al.: Quadruped bounding control with variable duty cycle via vertical impulse scaling. In: Intelligent Robots and Systems, pp. 3245–3252 (2014)
3. Hyun, D.J., Seok, S., Lee, J., et al.: High speed trot-running: Implementation of a hierarchical controller using proprioceptive impedance control on the MIT Cheetah. Int. J. Robot. Res. 33(11), 1417–1445 (2014)
4. Sprowitz, A., Tuleu, A., Vespignani, M., et al.: Towards dynamic trot gait locomotion: design, control, and experiments with Cheetah-cub, a compliant quadruped robot. Int. J. Robot. Res. 32(8), 932–950 (2013)
5. Gehring, C., Coros, S., Hutter, M., et al.: Control of dynamic gaits for a quadrupedal robot. In: International Conference on Robotics and Automation, pp. 3287–3292 (2013)
6. Semini, C., Tsagarakis, N.G., Guglielmino, E., Focchi, M., Cannella, F., Caldwell, D.G.: Design of HyQ – a hydraulically and electrically actuated quadruped robot. Proc. Inst. Mech. Eng. Part I: J. Syst. Control Eng. 225(6), 831–849 (2011)
7. Ugurlu, B., Havoutis, I., Semini, C., et al.: Dynamic trot-walking with the hydraulic quadruped robot — HyQ: analytical trajectory generation and active compliance control. In: Intelligent Robots and Systems, pp. 6044–6051 (2013)
8. Chai, H., Meng, J., Rong, X., et al.: Design and implementation of SCalf, an advanced hydraulic quadruped robot. Robot 36(4), 486–491 (2014)
9. Wang, L., Wang, J., Wang, S., et al.: Strategy of foot trajectory generation for hydraulic quadruped robots gait planning. J. Mech. Eng. 49(1), 39–44 (2013)
10. Li, Y., Li, B., Rong, X., et al.: Mechanical design and gait planning of a hydraulically actuated quadruped bionic robot. J. Shandong Univ. (Eng. Sci.) 41(05), 32–45 (2011)

Survey of Pedestrian Action Recognition in Unmanned-Driving

Li Chen[2], Nan Ma[1(✉)], Pengfei Wang[3], Guilin Pang[1],
and Xiaojun Shi[1]

[1] College of Robotics, Beijing Union University, Beijing, China
xxtmanan@buu.edu.cn
[2] Beijing Key Laboratory of Information Service Engineering,
Beijing Union University, Beijing, China
[3] Communication and Information Centre,
State Administration of Work Safety, Beijing, China

Abstract. With the development of unmanned-driving car technology, there are higher requirements for the intelligence, safety and stability of intelligent vehicle driving. Especially in a complex and uncertain environment, the driverless car can accurately detect the pedestrian action, which can effectively realize the autonomous driving of the vehicle. This requires that vehicles detect pedestrians firstly, then identify pedestrian body language and try to understand their intentions, predict pedestrian's actions, which form a good interaction cognition between human and vehicle. In this paper, we give a detailed survey about the recent and state-of-the-art research methods in the filed of human action recognition and discuss their advantages and limitations. We analysis the main framework of motion recognition, and summarize the common datasets of this filed. Finally, suggestions for future research directions are offered, which is expected to benefit the follow research.

Keywords: Unmanned-driving · Human active recognition ·
Convolutional neural networks · Recurrent neural networks · Activity datasets

1 Introduction

Pedestrian detection and recognition is widely applied in intelligent surveillance, human-machine interaction, content-based video retrieval and image compression. It has great economic and social value, and more and more researchers have interests in this field. Pedestrian movement detection and recognition applied to intelligent monitoring can increase the detection of abnormal behavior, and take measures timely. Meanwhile, its application in human-computer interaction is more extensive. Machines can identify human movements and understand human intentions, and can better fulfill the requirements of human beings. Its application in video retrieval and image compression can also reduce the cost of video retrieval greatly and facilitate people's lives.

In recent years, with the development of artificial intelligence (AI) technology, more and more studies have applied AI technology to unmanned driving, so that the driverless car has become a typical application scenario of artificial intelligence.

© Springer Nature Singapore Pte Ltd. 2019
F. Sun et al. (Eds.): ICCSIP 2018, CCIS 1005, pp. 496–510, 2019.
https://doi.org/10.1007/978-981-13-7983-3_44

Autonomous driving is mainly combined with intelligent sensing equipment through intelligent debugging and predictive software to achieve autonomous driving technology. In order to enable the unmanned vehicle to operate safely and steadily in complex and uncertain environment, it is necessary to realize friendly interaction between the vehicle and pedestrians [1]. This requires the car not only to detect pedestrians, but also to identify the movements of pedestrian, accurately judge the intentions of pedestrians, then make decisions.

The main process of pedestrian movement recognition is human detection and action recognition. First, find out the region of interest (ROI) which may contain pedestrians, and then detect and extract the human body from ROI. On the result of extraction, concrete action recognition is performed, the obtained motion is identified according to the agreed motion content, so that the computer can understand the pedestrian intention and make a decision.

2 The Basic Frame of Pedestrian Movement Detection and Recognition

Most researchers divide pedestrian motion recognition into two steps: pedestrian detection, motion recognition. According to the process, in this chapter, we summarize the related research work of this field, and analyze and compare different research work. Pedestrian detection is the basis of this research. Whether we can accurately and efficiently detect people and extract feature will affect the accuracy and robustness of the whole experiment. Action recognition, understanding the meaning of pedestrian actions, analyzing their behavior intentions, outputting the results of information, through decision-making judgment, to achieve the ultimate human-computer interaction. Motion recognition requires that intelligent vehicle can understand the meaning of pedestrian actions, then analyze their behavior intentions, output result information, and achieve final human-car interaction through decision-making.

2.1 Pedestrian Detection

In fact, pedestrian detection belongs to target detection, and the detection label is pedestrian or person. Target detection method can be divided into two directions, traditional algorithm and depth learning algorithm. Typical representative of traditional algorithms include HOG feature and SVM algorithm, DPM algorithm, pedestrian detection based on motion features, etc. While pedestrian detection based on deep learning includes R-CNN based region proposal and CNN classification detection framework, such as Faster R-CNN. Meanwhile, the target detection method is converted to target detection framework for the End-to-End of regression problem. YOLO is the representative.

2.1.1 HOG Characteristic and SVM Algorithm

Histogram of Oriented Gradient (HOG) is proposed by French scholar Dalal et al. [2], which is an image descriptor for human object detection.

The edge feature and gradient feature extracted by HOG can describe the local shape very well, and reduce the influence of light small offset on human detection effectively. Therefore, it is widely used in human detection, gesture recognition and face recognition.

The extraction of HOG features contain the following steps.

(1) input image
(2) normalized image
(3) calculating the gradient
(4) weighted gradient histogram projection
(5) normalization of cell contrast in overlapping block
(6) combine to obtain the feature vectors

Support Vector Machine (SVM) was first proposed by scholars in 1995 [3], and is widely used in machine learning.SVM has the advantages of simple structure and strong generalization ability [4, 5].

SVM is used to solve the two-classification problem. By introducing the kernel method, the researchers used SVM to solve the nonlinear problems. By replacing the core, we can obtain different separating surfaces, thereby achieving the purpose of classification.

Since HOG features can reduce the impact of lighting and offset on detection, Dalal et al. first attempted to apply HOG to human detection. After that, many scholars have expanded HOG and SVM, which achieves more results in pedestrian detection.

Liu et al. [6] combined the advantages of Adaboost and SVM classifier, proposed a human detection framework based on RHOG feature cascaded Adaboost and SVM classifier, which achieved good detection results.

As the most successful pedestrian detection algorithm, HOG + SVM takes a long time. Pang et al. [7] put forward two improved ways. One is to reuse the features of blocks to construct HOG features of cross detection windows. Another is to apply the sub-cell based interpolation to efficiently calculate the HOG characteristics of each block, and to improve detection speed on the accuracy of the detective.

Han et al. [8] proposed a robust detection method for human and vehicle in static images based on extended direction gradient histogram and support vector machine. Strong robustness detection is realized through focus of attention generation and hypothesis verification.

2.1.2 DPM Algorithm

Pedestrian detection based on HOG + SVM has achieved good results in related experiments. However, when human body is occluded, the accuracy of pedestrian detection of HOG + SVM has decreased. Some scholars have proposed the application of deformable component model (DPM) for pedestrian detection, and achieved some results [9].

In pedestrian detective, Yuan et al. [10] proposed a detector applying coordinate descent process for iterative learning resolution-aware transformation and based on DPM for, which obtained good detection results.

Zeng et al. [11] proposed a pedestrian detection method based on single pedestrian and dual pedestrian DPM model, which can detect the obscured pedestrians effectively.

Yan et al. [12] solved the speed bottleneck problem of DPM, while maintaining the detection accuracy of complex datasets.

Tian et al. [13] studied the extension of DPM from 2D images to 3D space-time volumes. Each action model select the most discriminating 3D sub-component automatically as a component and learn the temporal and spatial relationship between its positions. The model in this paper can adapt to intra-class variation and exhibit strong robustness.

2.1.3 Pedestrian Detection Based on Motion Characteristics

Most of the pedestrians are in motion. In recent years, some researchers have combined motion features with pedestrian detection technology, which can identify pedestrians in the scene by recognition of motion characteristics. The representative algorithm is proposed by Viola et al. [14] in 2005. They put forward a Haar-like feature on different images for static scene, and then combined the gray information of the image and the motion information to construct a pedestrian detection system. This method can detect low-resolution images in rain and snow weather, but the applicability to detect the occluded pedestrians is poor.

In addition, in view of dynamic scenes, Dalal et al. [2] proposed a method of combining visual description and optical flow features to construct pedestrian detector, which achieve pedestrian detection in moving video. However, this method can only detect pedestrians in a single window, and the detection effect of the whole image is relatively poor.

2.1.4 Pedestrian Detection Framework for Faster R-CNN

In recent years, convolution neural network (CNN) has made great breakthroughs in the application of target detection. Girshick et al. [15] proposed a regional convolution neural network (R-CNN) object detection framework t, which transform the image's target detection problem into a classification problem. Firstly, a number of candidate regions (region proposal) were generated in the image. Then the target feature is extracted from each region proposal by convolution network, and a classifier is trained by SVM to assort the region proposal. Finally, according to the classification scores of each region, the final target boundary is obtained by using the non-maximum suppression algorithm.

However, the R-CNN feature extraction convolutional network and the classifier used for classification need to be separately trained, resulting in a large amount of time and storage space in the training process. Moreover, the training of the classifier is not related to the feature extraction network, which affect the accuracy of target detection. Therefore, Girshick [16] also proposed a fast regional convolution neural network (Fast R-CNN) model, which integrates feature extraction and classification into a classification framework, improving the speed of training model and the accuracy of target detection. However, it is time-consuming for Fast R-CNN to generate region proposal separately by using selective search algorithm, which makes the algorithm not real-time. Therefore, Ren et al. [18] increase the area recommendation network (RPN) on Fast R-CNN to generate candidate regions, and form an end-to-end accelerated regional convolution neural network called Faster R-CNN model, which improves the computation speed greatly.

In reference [19], Faster R-CNN is used to detect pedestrian detection in nighttime infrared images. RPN is used to generate region proposal, and Fast R-CNN is used to extract features, classification and location refinement. Because the RPN and Fast R-CNN convolution layer uses parameter sharing mechanism, the whole framework is end-to-end, which improve the speed of pedestrian detection and realize the real-time pedestrian detection in night. In reference [20], the author improves Fast R-CNN and proposes a scale aware pedestrian detection model, which is divided into two sub networks to detect pedestrians at different scales respectively. Reference [21] combines the Region Proposal Network (RPN) in the Faster R-CNN framework with the cascaded random forest classifier to achieve the best detection results at that time. In [22], on the basis of Faster R-CNN framework, PRN has been improved to suit pedestrian detection, and a multi-level feature extraction and fusion method is proposed to improve the detection effect of small pedestrian.

2.1.5 YOLO Pedestrian Detection Framework

You Only Look Once(YOLO) is the first target detection system based on a single neural network proposed by Redmon and Farhadi in 2015 [23]. Reference [24] proposed a real-time pedestrian target detection method, which is based on the YOLO network structure and combined with the characteristics of pedestrians showing small aspect ratio in the image, and clustering selects the appropriate number and specifications of candidate frames, improves the YOLO network structure, and adjusts the distribution density of candidate frames in the X and Y axis directions, which form a network structure suitable for pedestrian detection.

In literature [25], a pedestrian detection and recognition method based on depth residual network and YOLO model is proposed. By analyzing the expression and distribution characteristics of pedestrians in images, a CNN model with 9:19 rectangle input is proposed to enhance pedestrian expression. In addition, a YOLO pedestrian detection method based on 50 level pre-activated depth residual network is proposed to make the model represent pedestrians better. In the work of reference [26], based on the YOLO network framework, according to the characteristics of vehicle video resolution and target pedestrian size in video, they optimize the size of network input, and use additional pedestrian data and data augmentation strategy to propose a highly robust model of pedestrian detection and location in traffic environment.

2.2   Action Recognition

The research of motion recognition analysis can be traced back to an experiment in Johansson [27] in 1975. The mobile spot experiment, which identifies human movements by observing the light signals connected to the human body, proposed 12-elements human body model. The 12-elements model method describing human behavior, plays an important guiding role for the later human body structure based behavior description algorithm. Since then, the progress of research on motion recognition can be roughly divided into the following 3 stages, the first is the preliminary research stage of action analysis in 1970s, the second is the gradual development stage of action analysis in 1990s, and the third is the rapid development stage of human movement analysis in recent years.

After the pedestrian is detected, we need to identify the movement, and extract the movement characteristics, so as to prepare for the later training. In simple and static background, recognition and extraction of human motion can use frame difference method to segment pedestrian motion, and then match and assign according to feature descriptors. However, in the complex, uncertain and dynamic environment, human motion recognition is more difficult. In order to better recognize pedestrian movements, it is necessary to extract the characteristics of pedestrian movements. Feature extraction is the core technology of human action recognition.

Feature extraction can be divided into surface feature extraction and deep learning method feature extraction. Apparent feature extraction is to extract the shallow features of the action on the surface of the graph by traditional algorithm, and get the expected feature information. Traditional representation extraction algorithms include two features: optical flow and gradient. In method of deep learning, feature extraction uses deep learning framework to automatically extract action features at multiple levels, which can obtain unexpected feature information. Typical represent of deep learning feature extraction is Convolutional Neutral Network (CNN).

2.2.1 Characteristics of Optical Flow

The formation of the optical flow is the movement of the image object in successive two frames of images due to the movement of the detected target or the camera. Therefore, optical flow can be used to represent the movement between two consecutive frames. Optical flow features contain a lot of motion information, which is an important method in motion recognition research.

The first optical flow computation is the HS optical flow algorithm [28] proposed by Horn and Schunk. On the assumption of optical flow invariance, they proposed the motion smoothness assumption. After, the objective function is constructed and the estimation of the light flow is solved. Since then, Optical flow computing has entered a stage of rapid development. Researchers have proposed many classical algorithms. For example, the LK optical flow algorithm proposed by Lucas and Kanade [29] is a two-frame differential optical flow estimation algorithm. In order to solve the problems of luminance non-conservation and motion discontinuity in practical problems, Black and Anandan proposed BA optical flow algorithm [30] and Brox and Malik proposed optical flow method [31] with resolution for large displacement. In recent years, new optical flow estimation algorithms have been put forward continuously, such as the DeepFlow method proposed by Weinzaepfel et al. [32]. By combining the matching algorithm with the optical flow difference method, a six-layer matching framework is constructed by convolution and maximum pooling operation, which is similar to deep converlutional network.

Most optical flow estimation algorithms are based the assumption of optical flow invariance, which makes the optical flow algorithm particularly sensitive to light. In order to solve this problem, researchers have proposed some new methods based on the assumption of optical flow invariance. It is popular to use Gaussian smoothing technique to filter images, such as optic flow in harmony (OFH) proposed in reference [33]. Some researchers have proposed to transform the brightness characteristic of pixels into the gradient feature, and calculate the optical flow by the gradient feature. For example, the SIFT Flow method proposed by Liu et al. [34] and the Constrained Optical Flow (COF) proposed by Mozerov [35].

Optical flow characteristics can characterize human motion information well. Many researches also extract feature from optical flow, and then perform action recognition. However, relying on optical flow characteristics only can not guarantee the high accuracy of motion recognition. In order to perform high-precision actions, optical flow features are often combined with other motion features, such as the work of [36–38].

2.2.2   Gradient Characteristics

Gradient feature is the most widely used action feature. Although gradient computation only needs to make the difference between the pixel of the image and the brightness of its adjacent area, the form is single. But after combination, transformation and statistics, the movement can be highly characterized. Based on the gradient feature, many motion recognition methods are proposed by domestic and foreign researchers.

Histogram of Oriented Gradients (HOG) is the most widely used feature extraction method. It was proposed by Dalal and Triggs [2] who came from the French Institute of computer science and automatic control at the CVPR conference. This method is to characterize the local information of the input image, statistics the local information of the image, which can express the features very well. Scale-invariant feature transform (SIFT) [39] is also used frequently in early study. This method searches for extreme points in space, and extracts its location and angle rotation invariant number. In addition, the PCA-SIFTT method [40] improves SIFT, and uses the Principal Components Analysis (PCA) to reduce the dimension, reduce the use of memory, and speed up the matching speed.

Combining gradient feature with optical flow feature through histogram is the most effective method to realize motion representation. The idea was first proposed by Laptev et al. [41]. He fused the gradient histogram with the optical flow histogram (HOF), first extracted the extreme points of the gradient features in the three-dimensional neighborhood, calculated the optical flow between two adjacent pixels, and finally used histogram to calculate the gradient and optical flow distribution, and normalized operation to achieve the characterization of the action.

2.2.3   CNNs for Feature Extraction

Human action recognition in a sequence of videos has always been a research field with important academic value. In recent years, CNN has matured in the field of image. Since the release of the 2012 ImageNet Challenge model, the CNN-based method has shown prominently in the image and video field. In video human action recognition, Simonyan and Zisserman [42] integrates CNN based on image and optical flow, which further gains the performance of manual features.

Sharma et al. [43] explored the application of attention models in the field of video action recognition. Zha et al. [44] used CNN features to classify video on TRECVID MED dataset. However, the study did not specify how to select the appropriate CNN model and hidden layer, nor did it use the more commonly used RNN for classification. Zeiler et al. [45] invented a convolutional network visualization technology, called deconvolution network Deconvolutional Network, which helps to check different activation characteristics and their relationship with input space. Lin et al. [46] proposed a bilinear CNN model, which consists of two feature extractors whose outputs are multiplied and pooled by an external product (WiKi). The model achieves 84.1% accuracy in training on CUB200-2011 dataset.

Jaderberg et al. [47] put forward a spatial deformation module Spatial Transformer module, which transforms and distorts input images in a dynamic way, which makes the subsequent layer processing more time-saving and labor-saving. Cao et al. [48] put forward a method based on training graph CNN feature. The algorithm extracted features from the image RGB data by using the existing CNN model, and used RNN of LSTM units to classify, and focuses on the selection and optimization of CNN model and hidden layer, as well as feature vectorization and dimensionality reduction. This experiment used ImageNet training model. Experiments on HMDB-51 and UCF-101 datasets show that the proposed method has the advantages of 42.87% and 80.14% accuracy respectively.

3 Several Commonly Used Public Action Datasets

Action dataset is an essential tool for action recognition research. An open and comprehensive dataset can not only improve the efficiency of action recognition process, reduce the time and cost of data collection, but also provide a standard and unified test platform for the advantages and disadvantages of various action recognition algorithms, so as to promote the development of action recognition field. Typical commonly used datasets are as follows: KTH action dataset, Weizmann action dataset, UCF series action dataset, HOLLYWOOD action dataset.

3.1 KTH Action Dataset

The KTH action datasets, which was published by the Royal Swedish Institute of Technology in 2004, was the first truly popular and universal dataset, and was widely used in the next decade and was a milestone in the field of computer vision. The action dataset is composed of 25 subjects performing 6 actions in 4 different scenarios. Among them, four different scenes were: outdoor scene s1, outdoor scene s2 with variable visual scale, experimenter dressed different outdoor scene s3, and indoor scene s4. The six movements are walking, jogging, running, boxing, hand waving and clapping. At present, there are 2391 data sequences in the dataset. The sample example is shown in Fig. 1.

Fig. 1. Example of KTH dataset sample official website

KTH datasets contains movements with large differences such as running and waving. But there are also some movements with small differences, such as jogging and running. So that it can be a good test of the accuracy and robustness of motion recognition methods. Although many motion recognition techniques have achieved more than 95% accuracy in the KTH test results, the openness and completeness of their data have attracted much attention from researchers in recent years, such as literature [41, 49, 50].

3.2 Weizmann Action Dataset

In 2005, the Weizmann action dataset was released by the Wizmann Academy of Sciences in Israel. It was originally published to study the human characteristics of spatiotemporal silhouettes, and was gradually applied to the entire field of motion recognition. The Weizmann action dataset is a nine-person action dataset. Although the view is fixed and the scene is relatively simple, it contains 10 complex and highly similar actions: Walk, Run, Jump, Gallop sideways, Bend, One-Hand Wave. Two-hands wave, Jump in place or Pjump, Jumping Jack, Skip. The sample example is shown in Fig. 2.

The dataset plays an important role in detecting the accuracy of motion recognition methods because of its complex and highly similar actions (such as pjump and skip). However, the experimental results of many motion recognition methods on Weizmann dataset have achieved more than 95% accuracy, such as the research in literature [51–53]. The dataset is gradually replaced by more complex dataset.

Fig. 2. Example of Weizmann action datasets

3.3 UCF Series Action Dataset

Since 2007, the University of Central Florida (UCF) has published a series of dataset, such as UCF101, UCF50, UCF Sports (2008), UCF YouTube (2008), which have attracted wide attention in the field of motion recognition.

Among them, the UCF Sports action dataset contains a set of actions collected from various sports. These movements are usually obtained from radio and television channels such as BBC and ESPN. The dataset contains 150 motion videos with a resolution of 740 × 480 and includes the following 10 actions: Diving, Golf Swing, Kicking, Lifting, Riding Horse, Running, Skate Boarding, Swing-Bench, Swing-Side, Walking. Compared with KTH action dataset and Weizmann action dataset, UCF Sports action dataset has more complex motion scenes and more action differences. The sample example is shown in Fig. 3.

Fig. 3. UCF sports dataset example

UCF Sports action dataset plays an important role in detecting the accuracy of action recognition algorithm and the adaptability to dynamic scenes because of the differences between actions and the diversity of scenes. UCF Sports action dataset is a popular dataset for small-scale motion detection and recognition, and many methods have achieved more than 85% experimental results on the modified platform.

3.4   Hollywood Action Dataset

Hollywood Action dataset was released in 2008 by the Institute of IRISA in France. The data set was basically captured in controlled scenes, which is not enough to meet the needs of researchers. So in 2009, the institute released Hollywood-2 Action dataset, an updated version of the Hollywood Action dataset. The Hollywood-2 action dataset contains 12 action categories in 10 scenarios, with 3669 videos. All the videos were intercepted from Hollywood movies. The dataset provides a real and challenging detection platform for pedestrian action recognition. The sample example is shown in Fig. 4.

Fig. 4. Example of Hollywood-2 action datasets

In addition, there are some popular datasets, the HMDB dataset published by Brown University in 2011 and the MuHAVi dataset published by Hossein Ragheb in 2010.

4   Conclusion

Pedestrian movement detection and recognition, as an important research content in the field of image detection and classification, is a hot research topic at this stage. Detection (judging whether there are pedestrians), positioning (separating pedestrians from the complex environment) and recognition (accurately understanding the meaning of specific actions) constitute the research content of pedestrian action recognition. This paper summarizes the related research contents and research progress, and gets the difficulty of pedestrian action recognition research.

1. Complex background. The complexity of the background and the degree of noise aggregation in the background will interfere with the accuracy and efficiency of pedestrian movement detection and recognition. By studying the fixed relationship

between objects and pedestrians in the image, researchers can effectively segment and separate pedestrians from complex background. By combining the intrinsic characteristics of pedestrians, the significance of pedestrians will be improved, so as to obtain a more complete and accurate separation of pedestrian content.

2. Pedestrian occlusion. In addition to the influence of complex background on pedestrian detection, the problems of occlusion from either pedestrian or other objects also have a certain impact on accurate detection and recognition. Through different firmware models, pedestrians and pedestrians are effectively separated to ensure the accuracy of the final identification.

3. Action definition. In the existing study of action recognition, the action semantic definitions are rich, but still can not meet all the action detection and recognition results. Through more detailed classification and definition of actions, more intelligent and humanized recognition results will be produced.

Pedestrian action recognition will play an important role in the areas of unmanned driving, safety monitoring, urban human settlement environment management and so on. Accuracy, speed of recognition and recognition of intelligence will become a new research focus of pedestrian action recognition.

Acknowledgment. We really thank anonymous reviewer's constructive suggestions. This part of study is partially founded by the national natural science foundation of China with the numbers 61871038 and 61672178, Beijing Natural Science Foundation with the numbers 4182022.

References

1. Aggarwal, J.K., Ryoo, M.S.: Human activity analysis: a review. ACM Comput. Surv. (CSUR) **43**(3), 16 (2011)
2. Dalal, N., Triggs, B.: Histograms of oriented gradients for human detection. In: Proceedings of IEEE Conference on Computer Vision and Pattern Recognition, San Diego, USA, pp. 886–893 (2005)
3. Cortes, C., Vapnik, V.: Support vector networks. Mach. Learn. **20**, 273–295 (1995)
4. Singh, D., Khan, M.A., Bansal, A., et al.: An application of SVM in character recognition with chain code. In: Communication, Control and Intelligent Systems (CCIS), pp. 167–171. IEEE (2015)
5. Ahmad, A.S., Hassan, M.Y., Abdullah, M.P., et al.: A review on applications of ANN and SVM for building electrical energy consumption forecasting. Renew. Sustain. Energy Rev. **33**(1), 102–109 (2014)
6. Liu, H., Xu, T., Wang, X., Qian, Y.: Related HOG features for human detection using cascaded adaboost and SVM classifiers. In: Li, S., et al. (eds.) MMM 2013. LNCS, vol. 7733, pp. 345–355. Springer, Heidelberg (2013). https://doi.org/10.1007/978-3-642-35728-2_33
7. Pang, Y., Yuan, Y., Li, X., et al.: Efficient HOG human detection. Sig. Process. **91**(4), 773–781 (2011)
8. Han, F., Shan, Y., Cekander, R., et al.: A two-stage approach to people and vehicle detection with hog-based SVM. In: Performance Metrics for Intelligent Systems 2006 Workshop, pp. 133–140 (2006)

9. Felzenszwalb, P.F., Girshick, R.B., McAllester, D., et al.: Object detection with discriminatively trained part-based models. IEEE Trans. Pattern Anal. Mach. Intell. **32**(9), 1627–1645 (2010)
10. Yan, J., Zhang, X., Lei, Z., et al.: Robust multi-resolution pedestrian detection in traffic scenes. In: Proceedings of the IEEE Conference on Computer Vision and Pattern Recognition, pp. 3033–3040 (2013)
11. Zeng, J.X., Chen, X.: Pedestrian detection combined with single and couple pedestrian DPM models in traffic scene. Acta Electronica Sinica (2016)
12. Yan, J., Lei, Z., Wen, L., et al.: The fastest deformable part model for object detection. In: Proceedings of the IEEE Conference on Computer Vision and Pattern Recognition, pp. 2497–2504 (2014)
13. Tian, Y., Sukthankar, R., Shah, M.: Spatiotemporal deformable part models for action detection. In: Proceedings of the IEEE Conference on Computer Vision and Pattern Recognition, pp. 2642–2649 (2013)
14. Viola, P., Jones, M.J., Snow, D.: Detecting pedestrians using patterns of motion and appearance. Int. J. Comput. Vision **63**(2), 153–161 (2005)
15. Girshick, R., Donahue, J., Darrell, T., et al.: Rich feature hierarchies for accurate object detection and semantic segmentation. In: Proceedings of the IEEE Conference on Computer Vision and Pattern Recognition, pp. 580–587 (2014)
16. Girshick, R.: Fast-RCNN. In: Proceedings of the IEEE International Conference on Computer Vision, pp. 1440–1448 (2015)
17. Uijlings, J.R.R., Sande, K.E.A., Gever, T., et al.: Selective search for object recognition. Int. J. Comput. Vision **104**(2), 154–171 (2013)
18. Ren, S., He, K., Girshick, R., et al.: Faster R-CNN: towards real-time object detection with region proposal networks. In: Advances in Neural Information Processing Systems, pp. 91–99 (2015)
19. Ye et al.: Night pedestrian detection based on accelerated region convolutional neural network. Progress Laser Optoelectron. **54**(08), 123–129 (2017)
20. Li, J., Liang, X., Shen, S.M., et al.: Scale-aware fast R-CNN for pedestrian detection. IEEE Trans. Multimedia **20**(4), 985–996 (2018)
21. Zhang, L., Lin, L., Liang, X., He, K.: Is faster R-CNN doing well for pedestrian detection? In: Leibe, B., Matas, J., Sebe, N., Welling, M. (eds.) ECCV 2016. LNCS, vol. 9906, pp. 443–457. Springer, Cham (2016). https://doi.org/10.1007/978-3-319-46475-6_28
22. Guo, A.I., Yin, B.Q., et al.: Small-scale pedestrian detection based on deep convolutional neural network. Inf. Technol. Netw. Secur. **37**(07), 50–53+57 (2018)
23. Redmon, J., Divvala, S., Girshick, R., et al.: You only look once: unified, real-time object detection. In: Proceedings of the IEEE Conference on Computer Vision and Pattern Recognition, pp. 779–788 (2016)
24. Gao, Z., Li, S., Chen, J., Li, Z.: Pedestrian detection method based on YOLO network. Comput. Eng. **44**(5), 215–219, 226 (2018)
25. Hao, X.Z., Chai, Z.Y.: An improved deep residual network pedestrian detection method. Comput. Appl. Res. (06), 1–3 (2019)
26. Zhu, P., Huang, L.: Pedestrian detection based on deep neural network in traffic environment. Inf. Commun. (05), 69–72 (2018)
27. Johansson, G.: Visual perception of biological motion and a model for its analysis. Percept. Psychophys. **14**(2), 201–211 (1973)
28. Horn, B.K.P., Schunck, B.G.: Determining optical flow. Artif. Intell. **17**(1–3), 185–203 (1981)
29. Lucas, B.D., Kanade, T.: An iterative image registration technique with an application to stereo vision (1981)

30. Black, M.J., Anandan, P.: The robust estimation of multiple motions: parametric and piecewise-smooth flow fields. Comput. Vis. Image Underst. **63**(1), 75–104 (1996)
31. Brox, T., Malik, J.: Large displacement optical flow: descriptor matching in variational motion estimation. IEEE Trans. Pattern Anal. Mach. Intell. **33**(3), 500–513 (2011)
32. Weinzaepfel, P., Revaud, J., Harchaoui, Z., et al.: DeepFlow: large displacement optical flow with deep matching. In: Proceedings of the IEEE International Conference on Computer Vision, pp. 1385–1392 (2013)
33. Zimmer, H., Bruhn, A., Weickert, J.: Optic flow in harmony. Int. J. Comput. Vision **93**(3), 368–388 (2011)
34. Liu, C., Yuen, J., Torralba, A.: Sift flow: dense correspondence across scenes and its applications. IEEE Trans. Pattern Anal. Mach. Intell. **33**(5), 978–994 (2011)
35. Mozerov, M.G.: Constrained optical flow estimation as a matching problem. IEEE Trans. Image Process. **22**(5), 2044–2055 (2013)
36. Wang, H., Schmid, C.: Action recognition with improved trajectories. In: Proceedings of the IEEE International Conference on Computer Vision, pp. 3551–3558 (2013)
37. Peng, X., Zou, C., Qiao, Yu., Peng, Q.: Action recognition with stacked fisher vectors. In: Fleet, D., Pajdla, T., Schiele, B., Tuytelaars, T. (eds.) ECCV 2014. LNCS, vol. 8693, pp. 581–595. Springer, Cham (2014). https://doi.org/10.1007/978-3-319-10602-1_38
38. Chaudhry, R., Ravichandran, A., Hager, G., et al.: Histograms of oriented optical flow and binet-cauchy kernels on nonlinear dynamical systems for the recognition of human actions. In: IEEE Conference on Computer Vision and Pattern Recognition, CVPR 2009, pp. 1932–1939. IEEE (2009)
39. Lowe, D.G.: Object recognition from local scale-invariant features. In: The Proceedings of the Seventh IEEE International Conference on Computer Vision, vol. 2, pp. 1150–1157. IEEE (1999)
40. Ke, Y., Sukthankar, R.: PCA-SIFT: a more distinctive representation for local image descriptors. In: Proceedings of the 2004 IEEE Computer Society Conference on Computer Vision and Pattern Recognition, CVPR 2004, vol. 2, p. II. IEEE 2004
41. Laptev, I., Marszalek, M., Schmid, C., et al.: Learning realistic human actions from movies. In: IEEE Conference on Computer Vision and Pattern Recognition, CVPR 2008, pp. 1–8. IEEE (2008)
42. Simonyan, K., Zisserman, A.: Two-stream convolutional networks for action recognition in videos. In: Advances in Neural Information Processing Systems, pp. 568–576 (2014)
43. Sharma, S., Kiros, R., Salakhutdinov, R.: Action recognition using visual attention. Comput. Sci. (2015)
44. Zha, S., Luisier, F., Andrews, W., et al.: Exploiting image-trained CNN architectures for unconstrained video classification. Comput. Sci. (2015)
45. Zeiler, M.D., Fergus, R.: Visualizing and understanding convolutional networks. In: Fleet, D., Pajdla, T., Schiele, B., Tuytelaars, T. (eds.) ECCV 2014. LNCS, vol. 8689, pp. 818–833. Springer, Cham (2014). https://doi.org/10.1007/978-3-319-10590-1_53
46. Lin, T.Y., Roychowdhury, A., Maji, S.: Bilinear CNNs for fine-grained visual recognition, pp. 1449–1457 (2015)
47. Jaderberg, M., Simonyan, K., Zisserman, A., et al.: Spatial transformer networks, pp. 2017–2025 (2015)
48. Cao, J., Jiang, X., Sun, W.: Video human motion recognition algorithm based on CNN features of training diagram. Comput. Eng. **43**(11), 234–238 (2017)
49. Derpanis, K.G., Sizintsev, M., Cannons, K.J., et al.: Action spotting and recognition based on a spatiotemporal orientation analysis. IEEE Trans. Pattern Anal. Mach. Intell. **35**(3), 527–540 (2013)

50. Goudelis, G., Karpouzis, K., Kollias, S.: Exploring trace transform for robust human action recognition. Pattern Recogn. **46**(12), 3238–3248 (2013)
51. Blank, M., Gorelick, L., Shechtman, E., et al.: Actions as space-time shapes, pp. 1395–1402. IEEE (2005)
52. Vishwakarma, D.K., Singh, K.: Human activity recognition based on spatial distribution of gradients at sublevels of average energy silhouette images. IEEE Trans. Cogn. Dev. Syst. **9** (4), 316–327 (2017)
53. Melfi, R., Kondra, S., Petrosino, A.: Human activity modeling by spatio temporal textural appearance. Pattern Recogn. Lett. **34**(15), 1990–1994 (2013)

A Real-Time Gait Switching Method for Lower-Limb Exoskeleton Robot Based on sEMG Signals

Xunju Ma[1,2,3], Can Wang[1,2(✉)], Ruizhu Zhang[3], and Xinyu Wu[1,2]

[1] Guangdong Provincial Key Lab of Roboticsand Intelligent System, Shenzhen Institutes of Advanced Technology, Chinese Academy of Sciences, 1068 Xueyuan Avenue, Shenzhen, China
{xj.ma,can.wang,xy.wu}@siat.ac.cn

[2] CAS Key Laboratory of Human Machine Intelligence-Synergy Systems, Shenzhen Institutes of Advanced Technology, 1068 Xueyuan Avenue, Shenzhen, China

[3] School of Mechanical Engineering, North China University of Water Resources and Electric Power, No. 36, Beihuan Road, Zhengzhou, China
zangruizhu@ncwu.edu.cn

Abstract. When patients wear an exoskeleton for rehabilitation to walk and encounter obstacles or stairs, they often need manual operation by themselves or other people to switch the gait of the exoskeleton robot, which leads to a poor human-machine synergy of common exoskeleton robots. In this paper, the surface electromyography (sEMG) signals of rectus femoris (RF), semimembranosus (SM) and sartorius (SR) muscles of the subjects were collected and the time domain features - root mean square (RMS) of the sEMG were extracted. A back propagation (BP) neural network was used to predict knee joint angles in real time, when the exoskeleton wearer's knee angle was greater than 70°, the exoskeleton performed gait switching across the obstacle in real time. Experiments show that when encountering obstacles, the method can realize the real-time gait switching of the exoskeleton across obstacles by the wearer using sEMG signals, and the method has good real-time characteristic and accuracy.

Keywords: Exoskeleton · sEMG · BP network · Gait switching

1 Introduction

At present, the number of disabled people in China has exceeded 85 million [1]. Among them, the number of patients with lower limb dysfunction caused by stroke and spinal cord injury has increased year by year, and the number of stroke patients has increased by about 2 million per year. By 2030, there will be more than 30 million stroke patients in China [2]. The exoskeleton robot has the advantages of high degree of automation, strong human-machine synergy, ease of wearing and usableness, and has greatly promoted the rehabilitation of patients.

When a patient wearing an exoskeleton encounters an obstacle or a stair, the patient often needs manual operation or other person's assisted operation to switch the gait of

© Springer Nature Singapore Pte Ltd. 2019
F. Sun et al. (Eds.): ICCSIP 2018, CCIS 1005, pp. 511–523, 2019.
https://doi.org/10.1007/978-981-13-7983-3_45

the exoskeleton robot, so the human-machine synergy of common exoskeleton robots is poor. Studies have shown that in the middle and late stages of rehabilitation [3], the patient's motor nervous system is gradually awakened, and the affected limb has been able to detect a certain degree of sEMG signals. Especially in the later stage of rehabilitation, the electromyography (EMG) signals are strong and can be completely used as a signal source for motion control signals. The generation of human EMG signals are about 100 ms earlier than the contraction of skeletal muscles [4]. Therefore, researchers can predict the contraction intention and contraction state of human muscles in advance through sEMG signals, and then predict the body's movement intentions. So, it is possible to use sEMG signal to control the exoskeleton online in real time.

With the increasing application and research of sEMG signal in the field of human-computer collaboration and human-computer interaction, more and more researchers have begun to use sEMG signal to predict joint angles. Li et al. proposed an algorithm for least squares support vector regression (LS-SVR). They utilized the multi-channel sEMG to predict the knee joint and the hip joint angle of human body by LS-SVR algorithm in different motion conditions [5]. Shengxin Wang et al. used the radial basis function (RBF) neural network method to estimate the angle of elbow joint [6]. Zhang et al. used Back Propagation (BP) neural network to successfully predict the joint angles of hip, knee and ankle of six normal subjects and four spinal cord injury (SCI) patients [7]. Wang et al. proposed a general regression neural network turned by genetic algorithm (GA-GRNN) to predict the knee joint angle utilizing sEMG signals [8]. Chen et al. used a deep belief network (DBN) to extract features from multi-channel sEMG signals, and finally utilized BP neural network to estimate lower limb joint angles by the extracted feature values [9]. Tang et al. selected four time-domain features and 19 fuzzy entropies of wavelet subspace as the features of sEMG signals. And a BP neural network was used to establish models for the recognition of standing up, flexion, extension and the estimation of knee joint angles [10].

The human body's maximal flexion angle of knee joint generally does not exceed $70°$ [11], and the maximum angle of knee joint is greater than $70°$ when the human body crosses an obstacle. Thence, $70°$ can be set as the threshold of the knee joint angle, and when the knee joint angle of the patient predicted by sEMG signal is greater than $70°$, the exoskeleton robot is switched to the gait across the obstacle. The sEMG signal is generated before the muscle contraction for 100 ms, making the above gait switching more free and timely. In this paper, the multi-channel sEMG signals are collected, and the RMS of sEMG signal is extracted as the feature value. The BP neural network is used to establish the prediction model of knee joint angle to realize the real-time prediction of the knee joint angle. When the predicted angle is greater than $70°$, the exoskeleton robot automatically switches the gait across obstacles.

2   Establishment of Angle Prediction Model

2.1   Data Acquisition

In order to obtain the required experimental data, five healthy subjects (male, 22 27 years old) will participate in the experiment. All subjects should ensure to have adequate rest before the experiment to avoid muscle fatigue. The experimental action requirements for collecting experimental data are as follows: the subject puts his or her feet together and stands upright facing the step, then raises the right leg and places the right foot on the step to simulate the movement across the obstacle, then the right foot is retracted and return to the initial state. Finally, an action cycle is completed and it can be called a movement of lifting leg (LL). For 10 consecutive cycles as a group of actions, the subjects should rest for 5 min between each group of actions to avoid muscle fatigue. Two sets of data need to be collected, the first set of data is used to train the BP model, and the second set of data is used to validate the model. Then, the subject simulates the moment when the leg is raised across the obstacle, and tries to ensure that the strength of the leg muscle at this time is the same as the force when actually lifting the leg. Subjects should perform the above action once and their sEMG signals data are acquired simultaneously. This movement can be called a want to lift the leg (WLL).

During the experiment, Biometrics's DataLOG (MWX8 PS850) Wireless EMG System (shown in Fig. 1(a), (b), (c)) was used to collect sEMG signals, and the sampling frequency can be selected as 2000 Hz. The number of sEMG channels collected was 10, and the muscles were rectus femoris (RF), vastus lateralis (VL), vastus medialis (VM), biceps femoris (BF), semitendinosus (ST), gracilis (GC), semimembranosus (SM), sartorius (SR), medial gastrocnemius (MG) and lateral gastrocnemius (LG). The placement of sEMG signal sensors and the human muscles are shown in Fig. 2(a) and (b). Meanwhile, the knee joint angle was measured using Biometrics's angle sensor (shown in Fig. 1(d)), which also has a sampling frequency of 2000 Hz. Before signal acquisition, the surface of the skins where sEMG signals are collected should be processed, comprising shaving and wiping with alcohol cotton to remove grease and dead skin in order to reduce the input impedance and the external interference. During the experiment, the myoelectric acquisition system should be kept away from the electronic equipment as much as possible to reduce external power frequency interference.

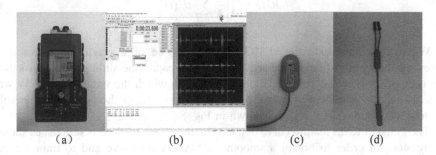

(a)　　　　　(b)　　　　　(c)　　　(d)

Fig. 1. sEMG collection device and angle sensor (a) DataLOG Wireless EMG System; (b) DataLOG software; (c) sEMG sensor; (d) Angle sensor

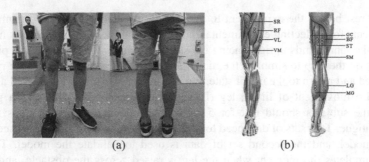

Fig. 2. (a) Location map of sEMG sensors; (b) Schematic diagram of human lower limb muscles

2.2 Signal Processing and Feature Extraction

The industrial frequency is 50 Hz in China, so a notch filter with 50 Hz should be used to pre-filter the original sEMG signals obtained to eliminate industrial frequency interference. The voltage amplitude of sEMG ranges from 0 to 1.5 mV, and the frequency is mainly concentrated at 10 to 500 Hz [12]. Therefore, after eliminating the power frequency interference of the raw sEMG, it needs to use the second-order Infinite Impulse Response (IRR) to perform band-pass filtering with a bandwidth of 10–500 Hz.

Nowadays, the commonly used feature extraction methods are: time domain analysis, frequency domain analysis and time-frequency domain analysis. In this paper, we choose the method of RMS feature extraction in time domain analysis. The RMS value can reflect the variation of EMG signal amplitude in time dimension, which is directly related to the electrical power of EMG signal, and RMS has better real-time characteristic. The RMS calculation formula is shown in (1).

$$RMS = \sqrt{\frac{1}{N}\sum_{i=1}^{N} d^2(i)} \tag{1}$$

Where $d(i)$ represents the sEMG signal sequence of a single channel and N represents the length of the signal sequence. In this paper, the sliding window method was used to segment the sEMG sample sequence, in which the window width W was set to 20 and the increment M was also set to 20, that is, the method of continuous split window was adopted [13, 14]. As shown in Fig. 3.

The glitch of RMS feature curve obtained by the above method is serious, as shown in Fig. 4(a). In order to obtain a smoother RMS feature curve and to train a more accurate BP neural network model, the obtained RMS feature sequence needs to be low-pass filtered by a Butterworth low-pass filter with a cutoff frequency of 1 Hz. And the RMS feature curve after low-pass filtering are shown in Fig. 4(b).

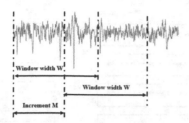

Fig. 3. sEMG signals data segmentation

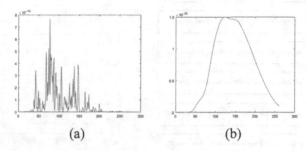

(a)   (b)

Fig. 4. (a) RMS feature curve before low-pass filtering; (b) RMS feature curve after low-pass filtering.

2.3 Muscle Selection

According to Table 1, the muscles associated with knee joint movement are: ST, SM, BF, MG, LG, SR, GC, and PL. We selected the first ten muscles to perform sEMG data collection according to the above experimental requirements for crossing the steps. The raw data curves of ten muscles are shown in Fig. 5(a). The processed RMS feature curves are shown in Fig. 5(b). It can be seen that the RMS characteristic curve of the corresponding data of the rectus femoris (RF), semimembranosus (SM) and Sartorius (SR) is more consistent with the movement law of the knee joint angle.

Table 1. Knee joint exercise pattern and the effects of major related muscles [15]

Joint name	Direction of movement	Normal range of motion	Main muscles	
			Active muscles	Antagonistic muscles
Knee joint	Flexion	0–130°	ST, SM, BF, MG, LG, SR, GC, PL (popliteus)	Quadriceps

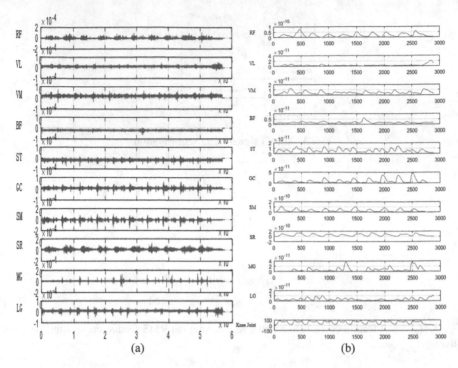

Fig. 5. (a) Ten muscle raw data graphics; (b) RMS feature curve of ten muscle data and knee joint angle curve

Since the normalized parameters of the training set are utilized to normalize the WLL data set, the WLL data set should be between the normalized parameters xmin and xmax. It can be seen from Table 2 that the muscles whose maximum voltage value of sEMG of the LL training set data is larger than the maximum voltage value of sEMG of the WLL data are: RF, BF, ST, GC, SM and SR. To sum up, the data of three muscles of RF, SM and SR were selected as the input channels of the neural network model.

Table 2. Maximum voltage value of sEMG of the corresponding muscle in each type of experimental motion data

Acquisition location	WLL action data	Training set data of LL action	Verification set data of LL action
RF	3.40545857779526e−11	8.44784929191757e−11	7.59143956189150e−11
VL	1.16598061562284e−10	1.99628699510055e−11	2.04840954914564e−11
VM	8.91757091921480e−11	1.64698243065868e−11	1.26187522083162e−11

(continued)

Table 2. (continued)

Acquisition location	WLL action data	Training set data of LL action	Verification set data of LL action
BF	3.74154466097622e−12	3.79759907587579e−12	6.06372198419947e−12
ST	5.75970267628068e−12	1.21242883799291e−11	1.37422732579256e−11
GC	7.76854132772601e−12	4.06828296713027e−11	4.74607253487347e−11
SM	5.64746293287254e−11	9.68689396052406e−11	1.10668728821098e−10
SR	1.72696781324460e−11	2.02715274811866e−10	1.41698396948146e−10
MG	1.63452423177095e−09	1.06741240855082e − 10	3.56241678567319e − 11
LG	7.01811662888870e−12	9.49004688784028e−12	1.03647843774220e − 11

2.4   Joint Angle Estimation Using BP Neural Network

A three-layer BP network can complete any n-dimensional to m-dimensional mapping [16]. Therefore, this paper selected a three-layer BP neural network to construct an angle estimation model, as shown in Fig. 6. The number of nodes in input layer is 3, which is the number of channels in the sEMG. The input vector is a sequence of the sEMG feature values corresponding to each channel. And the output vector is the knee joint angle.

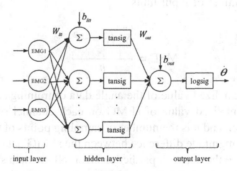

Fig. 6. Structure of the BP neural network.

The transfer functions from the input layer to the hidden layer and the hidden layer to the output layer are tansig function and logsig function, respectively. And traingdm function can be chosen as the training function of the BP neural network. The learning rate is set to 0.01. The output angle of the BP network is shown in Eq. (2).

$$\dot{\theta} = \frac{1}{1 + e^{-W_{out}\left[\frac{2}{1 + e^{-2(W_{in}x + b_{in})}} - 1\right] + b_{out}}} \cdot \tag{2}$$

Where θ is the predicted angle value, W_{in} is the weight matrix of hidden layer, W_{out} is the weight matrix of output layer, and b_{in} and b_{out} are the threshold vectors corresponding to the hidden layer and the output layer, respectively.

According to the empirical formula (3), (4), (5), the value of the number of hidden layer units can be limited to the range of [12, 35]. Then, the number of hidden layer units is gradually increased from 12 to 35 and the corresponding MSE (Mean Square Error) value is obtained according to Eq. (6) while the corresponding neural network model is saved. When the MSE has a minimum value, the corresponding hidden layer number and neural network model are the optimal hidden layer number and neural network model. The best hidden layer number is 28 in this paper.

$$\sum_{i=0}^{n} C_{n1}^{i} > k. \tag{3}$$

Where k is the number of samples, $n1$ is the number of hidden units, and n is the number of input units. If $i > n_1$, then $C_{n1}^{i} = 0$.

$$n_1 = \sqrt{n + m} + a. \tag{4}$$

Where m is the number of output neurons, n is the number of input units, and a is a constant between [1, 10].

$$n_1 = \log_2 n. \tag{5}$$

Where n is the number of input units.

$$\text{MSE} = \frac{\sum_{i=1}^{n} (y - x)^2}{n}. \tag{6}$$

Where x is the normalized value of the angle data of training set, and y is the result of simulating the normalized value of sEMG on each channel of the training set by using the trained model, and n is the number of sampling points of the training samples.

Since the order of mgnitude difference between the sEMG data and the angle data is large, in order to reduce the network prediction error, all the data should be normalized and converted into a number between [0, 1]. The mapminmax function can be used in MATLAB to normalize the data and the normalized parameters should be saved simultaneously. Then, the new training set and the verification set data are obtained, and the model is trained and verified. The normalized parameters which were saved before are utilized to normalize the data set of the WLL movements, and the obtained data is imported into the trained BP model for simulation, and then the normalized parameters are used to denormalize the simulation results to obtain the predicted angles. The training results of the training set, the verification results of the verification set, and the test results of the WLL data set are shown in Figs. 7(a), (b), and 8, respectively.

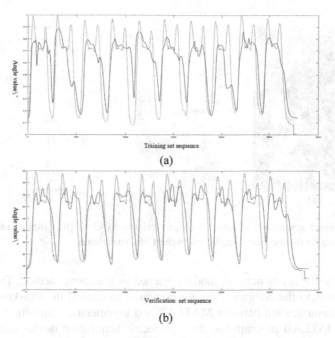

Training set sequence

(a)

Verification set sequence

(b)

Fig. 7. Fitting map of knee joint angles of the LL movements which are predicted by BP neural network; The red line represents the actual value; the blue line represents the predicted value (a) network training results; (b) network prediction results (Color figure online)

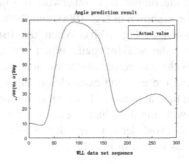

Fig. 8. Prediction results of the knee joint angle of the WLL movement

3   Real-Time Control of Exoskeleton Gait Switching

The exoskeleton robot used in this experiment is the fourth generation of lower limb exoskeleton SIAT-4 for rehabilitation developed by our project team, as shown in Fig. 9(a). The robot has the advantages of light weight (only 15 kg), easy to wear, multiple gaits, and it can be well controlled online in real time.

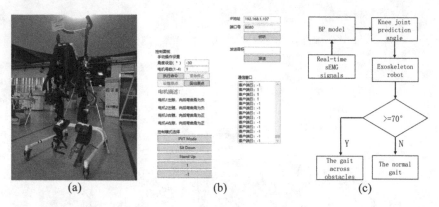

(a)   (b)   (c)

Fig. 9. (a) Fourth generation of lower limb exoskeleton SIAT-4; (b) Control interface of the exoskeleton; (c) Real-time gait switching flowchart of exoskeleton

Firstly, the BP neural network model is trained by the above method. Then, connect the exoskeleton to the computer, use the computer to control the exoskeleton; set up real-time communication between MATLAB and myoelectric acquisition device, and enable the MATLAB program and the myoelectric acquisition device to run simultaneously; open the exoskeleton control code and run it through VisualStutio2015, call up the exoskeleton control interface (shown in Fig. 9(b)) to listen for control signals. The data collected in real time by the surface myoelectric sensors is continuously imported into the BP model trained by MTALAB. When the predicted maximum angle value is greater than 70°, the output is 1, otherwise the output is −1. The sEMG measured online in real time is shown in Fig. 10(a), and the angle graph obtained from real-time prediction is shown in Fig. 10(b). When the listening result is −1, the exoskeleton robot performs the walking gait. When the listening result is 1, the exoskeleton robot performs the gait across obstacles, and the listening result is shown in Fig. 9(b). After switching the gait, the exoskeleton robot will perform a complete gait across the obstacle and then automatically return to normal gait unless 1 is listened again. The Real-time gait switching flowchart of exoskeleton is shown in Fig. 9(c). The subject wore the lower limb exoskeleton to switch the gait across obstacles based on sEMG online in real time, as shown in Fig. 11.

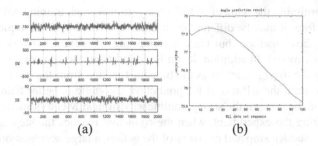

(a)   (b)

Fig. 10. (a) SEMG graphic measured online in real time; (b) Angle graphic predicted online in real time

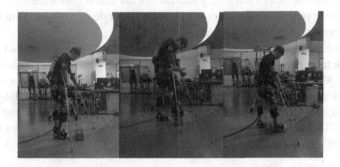

Fig. 11. Real-time online gait switching experiment

4 Discussion

In this study, the extracted RMS data set was low-pass filtered using a Butterworth filter with a cutoff frequency of 1 Hz. Combined with Fig. 4(a) and (b), it can be concluded that the method not only reduces the burrs of the characteristic curve, but also makes the RMS characteristic curve more obvious, highlighting the relationship between the characteristic curve of the EMG and the actual angle curve. There are many muscles associated with knee joint movement, but not every one of them can be used for knee joint angle prediction. It can be seen from Fig. 6 that the variation of the RMS characteristic curve of RF, SM and SR is closer to the actual angle, and the corresponding sEMG voltage value is gradually increased as the angle is gradually increased. It indicates that the voltage change of the sEMG is positively correlated with the change of the knee joint angle. The data needs to be normalized to [0, 1] before training and using the BP model. When using the BP neural network model for knee joint angle estimation, the input data value must be guaranteed in the range of [xmin, xmax]. Otherwise, the normalization of the test set data using the normalization parameters of the training set will result in erroneous results and affect the angle estimation. From Table 2, it can be concluded that the data of the RF, BF, ST, GC, ST and SR meet the above requirements.

When determining the number of hidden layer units, each training will get different models. Therefore, it may be different each time to find the optimal number of hidden layers by the above method, but the corresponding BP neural network model is the optimal network model. In addition, it can be found from the comparison with [7] and [10] that using the logsig function as the transfer function from the hidden layer to the output layer to train the BP model for predicting the angle is better than utilizing the purelin function, because of the strong nonlinearity from sEMG to joint angle. Figure 8 shows that during the experiment, when the right foot reaches the step and leaves the step, due to the sudden stop and recovery of the action, a large acceleration is generated and the muscle vibration is drastic, so that the angle and the sEMG change at this time are more severe. Therefore, the RMS value of the prediction angle and the actual angle is relatively large, but it can be seen that the curve of the prediction angle and the actual angle curve are close before the knee joint reaches the actual maximum angle. What we need is only the predicted angle before the maximum angle of the knee joint appears, so this model can be used for gait switching.

This study is to collect normal human sEMG in real-time to predict knee joint angle, and determine whether to switch gait by judging whether the predicted angle is greater than 70°. Although the sEMG from patients with central nervous system injury can be used as a source of exoskeleton control in the middle and late stages of rehabilitation, at this time the patient's muscles are not strong enough and the amplitude of sEMG is small. So, the threshold can be adjusted for such patients to improve the sensitivity and accuracy of gait switching.

5 Conclusion

This paper proposes an intelligent gait switching method based on knee joint angle estimation. The sEMG signals of five subjects' RF, VL, VM, BF, ST, GC, SM, SR, MG and LG were collected. It was found that the RF, SM and SR had a great correlation with the knee joint angle and the choice of muscle had a great influence on the prediction accuracy of the knee joint angle when lifting the leg. In this paper, the BP neural network algorithm is used to train the prediction model of knee joint angle. When the predicted angle is greater than 70°, the exoskeleton switches the gait across obstacles. The experiment shows that the method can well predict the human intention and switch the gait in real time. In the next step, we will add a variety of sensors, such as angle sensors and interaction sensors, combined with sEMG for multi-sensor fusion to form closed-loop control to better control the exoskeleton for gait switching in real time and invite appropriate patients to wear the exoskeleton for an experiment to verify the versatility of the method.

Acknowledgments. This research was supported by the National Key Research and Development Program of China (2017YFB1302303), and the National Natural Science Foundation-Shenzhen Joint Research Program (U1613219).

References

1. Guo, J.H.: China's aging global positioning and China's aging research problems and solutions. J. Acad. Res. 61–67 (2016). (in Chinese)
2. Hou, Z.G., Zhao, X.G., Cheng, L., Wang, Q.N., Wang, W.Q.: Recent advances in rehabilitation robots and intelligent assistance systems. J. Acta Automatica Sin. **42**, 1765–1779 (2016). (in Chinese)
3. Fan, Y.J.: Lower extremity exoskeleton rehabilitation robot based on sEMG and multi-source signal fusion and its clinical experiment. Doctoral Thesis. Shanghai Jiaotong University (2014). (in Chinese)
4. Ding, Q.C., Xiong, A.B., Zhao, X.G., Han, J.D.: A review on researches and applications of sEMG-based motion intent recognition methods (in Chinese). J. Acta Automatica Sin. **42**, 13–25 (2016)
5. Li, Q.L., Song, Y., Hou, Z.G.: Estimation of lower limb periodic motions from sEMG using least squares support vector regression. J. Kluwer Acad. Publishers **42**, 371–388 (2015)
6. Wang, S., Gao, Y., Zhao, J., Yang, T., Zhu, Y.H.: Prediction of sEMG-based tremor joint angle using the RBF neural network. In: The International Conference on Mechatronics and Automation, pp. 2103–2108. IEEE, Chengdu (2012)
7. Zhang, F., Li, P., Hou, Z.G., et al.: sEMG-based continuous estimation of joint angles of human legs by using BP neural network. J. Neurocomput. **78**, 139–148 (2012)
8. Wang, F., Yin, T., Lei, C., Zhang, Y.K., Wang, Y.F.: Prediction of lower limb joint angle using sEMG based on GA-GRNN. In: The IEEE International Conference on Cyber Technology in Automation, Control, and Intelligent Systems, pp. 1894–1899. IEEE, Shenyang (2015)
9. Chen, J., Zhang, X., Cheng, Y., Xi, N.: Surface EMG based continuous estimation of human lower limb joint angles by using deep belief networks. J. Biomed. Sig. Process. Control **40**, 335–342 (2018)
10. Tang, G., Wang, H., Tian, Y.: sEMG-based estimation of knee joint angles and motion intention recognition. In: the International Conference on Intelligent Human-Machine Systems and Cybernetics, pp. 390–393. IEEE, Hangzhou (2017)
11. Hu, X.Y., Yan, X.P., Guo, Z.W., Ding, H.: Study on gait characteristics of normal adults. Chin. J. Rehabil. Theory Pract. J. **12**, 855–857 (2006). (in Chinese)
12. Chu, J.U., Moon, I., Lee, Y.J., Kim, S.K., Mun, M.S.: A supervised feature-projection-based real-time EMG pattern recognition for multifunction myoelectric hand control. IEEE/ASME Trans. Mechatron. J. **12**, 282–290 (2007)
13. Zou, L.: Research on lower-limb muscle force prediction based on surface electromyography. Master Thesis. Wuhan University of Technology (2015). (in Chinese)
14. Scheme, E.J., Englehart, K.B., Hudgins, B.S.: Selective classification for improved robustness of myoelectric control under nonideal conditions. IEEE Trans. Biomed. Eng. J. **58**, 1698–1705 (2011)
15. Wang, Y.F.: sEMG control the lower limbs exoskeletons rehabilitation robots of research. Master Thesis. Hebei University of Technology (2011). (in Chinese)
16. The Product Development Center of Freescale Technology: Neural Network Theory and MATLAB 7 Implementation. Publishing House of Electronics Industry, Beijing (2005). (in Chinese)

A Multi-robot System for High-Throughput Plant Phenotyping

Chenming Wu, Rui Zeng, and Yong-Jin Liu[⊠]

Department of Computer Science and Technology,
Tsinghua University, Beijing 100084, China
liuyongjin@tsinghua.edu.cn

Abstract. In this paper, we present a multi-robot system for high-throughput plant phenotyping. The proposed system consists of a view planning algorithm and three robotic arms each equipped with a depth camera. The algorithm extends conventional next-best view plan to fit multi-robot systems and is capable of processing hundreds of RGB-D frames per second to generate collision-free motions. The robotic arms in our multi-robot system can move simultaneously in accordance with the planned motions. Compared to single-robot systems, our multi-robot system exhibits significantly better flexibility and planning time in our experiments, making high-throughput phenotyping practical.

Keywords: Multi-robot · High-throughput · Phenotyping

1 Introduction

As an active research area of biology, phenomics uses sensors, devices, software, and other techniques to acquire physical and biochemical traits of an organism and study the potential connections between visible phenotypes and the underlying genomic variants [11]. Traditional phenotyping of individual plants needs many manual operations, which is laborious and expensive. The rapidly growing need for high-throughput phenotyping motivates robotic research towards a more effective and efficient solution [7].

Researchers have mainly relied on automation to increase the throughput of phenotyping. They design systems to streamline the process of imaging a plant and reconstructing its 3-D structure with cameras or range sensors, but the principles and designs of those systems are specialized for their tasks. For example, the leave is an essential food-producing organ in most vascular plants and relevant grain yield formation [1] and photosynthetic active area optimization [9]. Phenotyping on plant leaves has been conducted with the assistance of robots [2,4,8]. Those works focus on developing a single-robot system that can probe a plant at different viewpoints. The efficiency of single-robot systems needs to be improved, and the effectiveness of these methods is sometimes limited by the accessibility of a robot.

© Springer Nature Singapore Pte Ltd. 2019
F. Sun et al. (Eds.): ICCSIP 2018, CCIS 1005, pp. 524–533, 2019.
https://doi.org/10.1007/978-981-13-7983-3_46

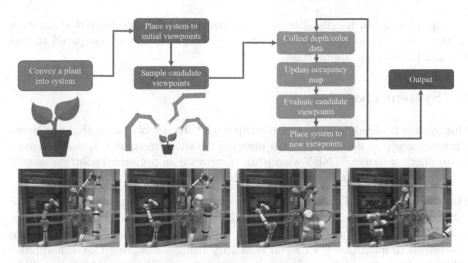

Fig. 1. (Top) the pipeline of our multi-robot system. First, the robots are driven to initial viewpoints. After sampling the candidate poses, our system runs in a cycle to plan the viewpoints for a few rounds. (Bottom) the robots move to different viewpoints to collect data in a phenotyping task.

In most robot-assisted phenotyping tasks, viewpoints are positioned by a robot sequentially, which is similar to *coverage planning* [12] and can be solved by the *Next-Best View* (NBV) approach. The NBV approach computes a sequence of locations for a sensor until the target object is entirely covered, which have motivated a wide range of applications from environment explorations [3] to model reconstructions [16]. A promising direction towards high-throughput phenotyping is adopting multi-robot systems because of better flexibility. In this case, an efficient algorithm to drive multi-robot systems is needed. However, existing NBV algorithms exhibit long processing time on evaluating viewpoints, and exponentially longer for multi-robot systems. To address the problem of multi-robot coverage, Dornhege et al. [6] present a algorithm based on sampling and ranking a number of viewpoints. To further improve the efficiency of multi-robot coverage, they offer variants of the algorithm that adopt a greedy strategy, optimal strategy or decompose planning scenarios. In this paper, we tackle the problem of robotic arms and improves the greedy approach by a beam search strategy.

We design and implement a multi-robot system for high-throughput phenotyping and propose a new algorithm to compute covered viewpoints, then the viewpoints are planned to motions that can be simultaneously executed by the robots. The major challenge is how to efficiently plan viewpoints to maximize the coverage in a fixed number of rounds. Our system has great improvements regarding effectiveness and efficiency as the running time is linear to the number of samples. By contrast, the straightforward extension of traditional NBV algorithms leads to exponentially growing samples to evaluate, which is intractable for any planner to handle. Besides, we provide a GPU-accelerated evaluation method to rank candidate poses at orders of magnitude faster compared to traditional CPU-based approaches.

2   System Overview

Our system is based on a hardware setup with three robotic arms that can move simultaneously in accordance with planned collision-free motions, and software is running a volumetric NBV algorithm to provide an optimized solution as well as convert it to the motions for our hardware system.

Hardware Setup. The hardware setup of our system composes of three UR-5 robotic arms (Odense, Denmark) with six degrees-of-freedom (DOF), and every arm is mounted with an Intel RealSense SR-300 depth camera. The robots are positioned to maximize the overall flexibility using a sampling-based manipulability analysis. Controllers of the robots are connected to an adaptive switchboard with 100 Mbps Ethernet interface to ensure low latency and high-quality communications. The SR-300 depth cameras are connected to a USB 3.0 hub with power adapter in case of an insufficient power supply. The switchboard and USB hub are connected to a controlling computer. The depth cameras will be positioned to different viewpoints for a few rounds, and each round has three viewpoints belonging to three depth cameras respectively. The robots are moving simultaneously in each round for efficiency.

Software Method. An overview of plant leaves can be obtained after postprocessing steps including noise filtering and registration. We implement a GPU-accelerated NBV algorithm to select the most promising set of viewpoints for each round. We also consider the angle to probe the leaves as a heuristic in our algorithm. The low-level software components for controlling the operation of our system are based on the Robot Operating System (ROS). Data from RealSense cameras including depth, color, and their transformations, is processed by Intel librealsense[1] and published in the format of ROS sensor messages.

3   Covered Views Planning

The core of our software method lies in constructing an overview of a plant's leaves, and we name it as *covered views planning* in this paper. To meet the requirement of high-throughput phenotyping, a short processing time for each plant is desirable.

We assume that a bounding box $\mathcal{W}_b$ of a given plant is predefined. All point clouds are combined and represented as a probabilistic octree during the phase of view planning. The octree is structured by octomap [10] where the probability of each voxel is modeled as a recursive binary Bayes filter and can be updated by log-odds strategy. Possible attributes belonging to each voxel are (1) occupied,

---

[1] https://github.com/IntelRealSense/librealsense.

(2) unknown and (3) free, which directly relate to whether a voxel has been touched by rays originated from depth cameras.

Our system acts similarly to "space carving" to phenotype a target plant, and we show the pipeline of our system in Fig. 1: (1) initialize cameras by positioning robots to initial viewpoints, (2) collect and process RGB-D information, (3) planning a set of new viewpoints for the multi-robot system and (4) move the system to a set of newly planned viewpoints. Once the initialization step 1 is done, step 2–4 will be iterated for fixed rounds to accomplish the task of phenotyping.

3.1   Candidate Viewpoints Sampling

In our paper, a viewpoint is used to describe the pose of cameras, which is a tuple of position and orientation in essence. The cameras used in our system are mounted on the end-effectors of robotic arms. Thus viewpoints and corresponding configurations of robots are interconvertible by Forward Kinematics (FK) and Inverse Kinematics (IK). Before planning a set of viewpoints that can maximize the efficiency of the phenotyping task, we sample a large set of candidate viewpoints inside the space to be explored. Typically, we can describe the sampling space as either Cartesian space or joint-space. The Cartesian-space-based strategy samples points around $\mathcal{W}_b$ and then apply IK to obtain maps between sampled viewpoints and joints. As a comparison, joint-space-based method directly samples joints in the robot's configuration, and reversely applying FK to get viewpoints.

For a multi-robot system like ours, the Cartesian space-based method is not an efficient and stable solution for the following two reasons: first, even though two close viewpoints are given, the distance between two sets of joints generated by IK solvers may be large, which makes multi-robot motion planning intractable. Second, intensive IK computations and collision checking are also time-consuming. Therefore, we choose the joint-space-based methods. For a robot $R \in \mathbb{R}^3$, we denote its configuration as $q = (\theta_1, ..., \theta_6)$, which is a six-dimensional vector. The working environment in our system $\mathcal{W}$ consists of three robotic arms $\mathcal{R} = R_1 \cup R_2 \cup R_3$, the predefined bounding box $\mathcal{W}_b$ and a Aluminum frame $\mathcal{W}_f$, i.e., $\mathcal{W} = \mathcal{R} \cup \mathcal{W}_b \cup \mathcal{W}_f$. A collision-free configuration $\mathcal{C}_{free}$ should not result in any intersection among objects in $\mathcal{W}$, and a feasible set of candidate samples $\{q_1, q_2, q_3\}$ should satisfy $R_1(q_1) \cap R_2(q_2) \cap R_3(q_3) \cap \mathcal{W}_b \cap \mathcal{W}_f = \varnothing$. Besides, to ease the motion planning problem of our multi-robot system, we have a heuristic that the covered volume by our multi-robot system is sufficient within a limited length of movements as follows.

$$\|q_i - q_i^o\|_1 < \alpha \tag{1}$$

where q_i^o is the initial configuration state of the i_{th} robot and α is an empirical value, and we use 4π in all our experiments (Fig. 3).

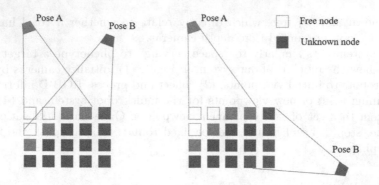

Fig. 2. Since the robots in our multi-robot system move simultaneously, the order of search should be taken into consideration <- Change this. The left figure shows that pose A and pose B share many overlapped voxels to be touched by rays, while the right figure shows a more efficient pair of poses that have more regions to be covered.

3.2   Efficient Beam Search

High-throughput phenotyping needs a short turnaround time, so an efficient algorithm to evaluate the candidate viewpoints is decisive. A straightforward extension of traditional NBV algorithm makes exponential running time, and intuitively high-throughput phenotyping becomes impossible. We observe that a large number of sampled viewpoints are overlapped with each other. A more efficient solution can be found by skipping these overlapped combinations of viewpoints during evaluation.

Greedy approaches tend to select non-overlapped viewpoints, but they are easily stuck in local solutions [6]. Instead, beam search is an efficient search technique which has been widely used in improving the results of best-first greedy algorithms, and it uses breadth-first strategy to build a search tree while exploring the search space by expanding a set of most promising nodes instead of only the best node in each level [13]. We use the beam search algorithm in our system to overcome the disadvantages of greedy approaches while maintaining the advantage in speed.

In the phase of evaluation, the order of cameras being evaluated needs to be considered because intermediate results affect the occupancy map and the probabilistic values of voxels will change simultaneously, see Fig. 2. We tackle this problem as a search problem in order of priority. Three robotic arms are adopted in our system, so we have overall six different orders of traversal $\mathcal{T}$. It is not necessary to evaluate every combination of traversal in $\mathcal{T}$ with the help of beam search because of its ability to jump from local solutions. In our system, we simply pick a traversal $(R_1, R_2, R_3) \in \mathcal{T}$. Our algorithm starts from robot R_1 and evaluate all N candidate viewpoints of R_1's camera, and the most promising b poses with a sufficient inter-distance $d = 1$ are kept. Thereafter, the algorithm evaluates all candidate viewpoints of R_2 by expanding the kept b poses of R_1 and only kept b best promising results as before. The procedure is finished when

---

Algorithm 1. Efficient Beam Search

Input: Candidate poses $\mathcal{P}_1, \mathcal{P}_2, \mathcal{P}_3$ belong to R_1, R_2, R_3 respectively,
       occupancy map $\mathcal{O}$.
Output: A set of poses $S = (p_1, p_2, p_3)$ corresponding to next best views.
1   $F \leftarrow \varnothing, \mathcal{B} \leftarrow S(\varnothing)$
2   **foreach** $m \in (1, 2, 3)$ **do**
3      $F \leftarrow \varnothing$
4   **while** $\mathcal{B}$ *is not* $\varnothing$ **do**
5          $S_t \leftarrow Top(\mathcal{B})$
6   **foreach** $p \in \mathcal{P}_m$ **do**
7              $S_p \leftarrow S_t$
8              $S_p + = p$
9              $F + = f(\mathcal{O}, S_p)$
10   **end**
11         $Pop(\mathcal{B})$
12   **end**
13   **while** $|\mathcal{B}| < b$ **do**
14          $S_o \leftarrow \arg\max F$
15          $\mathcal{B} + = S_o$
16   **end**
17 **end**
18 **return** $\arg\max \mathcal{B}$

---

all N poses of R_3 are completely evaluated. Finally, our algorithm outputs the best promising result among all b kept results. It is obvious that our algorithm produces $O(n)$ time complexity while the brute-force evaluation strategy gives $O(n^3)$ time complexity. The pseudo-code of the proposed algorithm can be found in Algorithm 1.

3.3 Evaluation and Motion Generation

Evaluation Function. The proposed search algorithm produces a set of viewpoints with the guidance of an evaluation function. Different choices on evaluation functions certainly result in different preferences on plant phenotyping. Inspired by the utility function proposed in [16], we define an evaluation function $f_s(\mathcal{O}, p)$ to rank candidate viewpoints with the consideration of normal property of leaves: we observe that the shape of leaves is near planar, the unexplored region near the explored region would have the similar normals according to the growing characteristic of plants. We prefer to cover the plant leaves in perpendicular viewpoint and formulate an evaluation function as follows.

$$f_s(\mathcal{O}, p) = free(p) \cdot dis(p) \left[\lambda \cdot leaf(\mathcal{O}, p) + (1 - \lambda) \cdot vox(\mathcal{O}, p) \right] \qquad (2)$$

The evaluation function $f_s(\mathcal{O}, p)$ has four terms, $free(p)$ is 1 if the robot is collision-free at the state of p and otherwise it is 0. $leaf(\mathcal{O}, p)$ models the relative position between the camera and the occupied voxels, $vox(\mathcal{O}, p)$ measures the

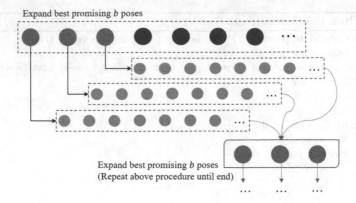

Fig. 3. An example of the beam search algorithm for finding next best views for our multi-robot system. Here we use $b = 3$ for an illustration.

number of explored unknown voxels and $dis(p)$ is related to the L_1 norm of the joint values from the previous state to the current state of p. We use $\lambda = 0.2$ in all our experiments.

$$\begin{cases} leaf(\mathcal{O}, p) &= -\sum_{o_i \in \mathcal{O}_o} p_{look} \cdot \mathbf{n}(o_i)/n_{total} \\ vox(\mathcal{O}, p) &= n_u(p)/n_{total} \\ dis(p) &= \frac{1}{1+\|q_p - q_o\|_1} \end{cases} \tag{3}$$

where $\mathbf{n}(o_i)$ is the estimated normal of the occupied voxel $\mathcal{O}_o \subset \mathcal{O}$, $n_u(p)$ is the number of unknown voxels $\mathcal{O}_u \subset \mathcal{O}$ and p_{look} is the look-at direction of the view point p. As the order of views matters in the evaluation, we define a function to evaluate an ordered vector of viewpoints $S = (p_1, ..., p_n)$ as follows.

$$f(\mathcal{O}, S) = \sum_{p_i \in S} f_s(\mathcal{O}_{1 \sim i}, p_i) \tag{4}$$

where $\mathcal{O}_{1 \sim i}$ is the occupancy map updated by simulating ray castings at pose p_1 to p_i sequentially.

GPU-Accelerated Evaluation. A straight-forward approach to evaluate a given viewpoint is to cast uniform rays towards $\mathcal{O}$ from the viewpoint. However, it is very time-consuming even with a *Hierarchical Ray Tracing* (HRT) acceleration [16] - average processing time for a frame is 0.185 s when the size of a voxel is 0.02 m. In the case of 1,000 candidate viewpoints to be evaluated, the overall processing time by this method will exceed 185 s. To fit our application of high-throughput phenotyping, we tailor raycasting from CPU to GPU, and apply to use state-of-the-art GPU ray tracing engine Optix [14]. Optix is a low-level ray tracing engine designed for high-performance ray-tracing. It is based on highly parallel GPU architectures to provide object model acceleration. The programs of Optix follow CUDA programming rules. In our implementation, the calibrated parameters of RealSense cameras are used to build a pinhole camera model for evaluation. Each candidate viewpoint performs a round of ray tracing and the intersected primitive has a corresponding result in the format of a pixel value. After the ray tracing, the composition of intersected results is computed by CUDA atomic operations.

Motion Planning. In order to move cameras to target viewpoints safely, a collision-free motion for the multi-robot system is essential. Two types of planning methods can be used in multi-robot planning - centralized (coupled) and decentralized (decoupled) approaches. Centralized motion planners treat all robots as a single combined robot and solve the motion planning problem in a high-dimensional space, while decentralized motion planners either compute the motion for each robot in its own space and use a coordination program to solve collision problems, or plan robots orderly considering previously planned robots as obstacles. Because of the need for short possible processing time in high-throughput phenotyping tasks, for example, at most 6 s in each round, we simply adopt RRT-based centralized and decentralized planners in parallel and use any of the successfully planned motions to avoid re-plannings. A better solution to this problem is using the multi-robot dRRT* method proposed in [5], and we leave it as our future work.

4   Experiments

We implemented the proposed algorithms in C++ on top of ROS and tested them on a PC with Intel Xeon Skylake Gold 6146 CPU and NVIDIA Titan V graphics card. Our system can process up to 300 frames per second, i.e., 0.003 s for each round of rays casting, which is around 200 times faster than the HRT method [16]. We set up an experimental environment that consists of a plant with disorderly leaves on which we conduct different algorithms. A comparison of greedy algorithm and our efficient beam search algorithms in terms of different choices of b is provided in Table 1, which demonstrates our efficient beam search algorithms lead to better results.

Table 1. Different values of $f(\mathcal{O}, S)$ (Eq. 4) w.r.t. different methods.

Method	Map A	Map B	Map C
Greedy	0.0268	0.0213	0.0244
Beam $b = 2$	0.0281	0.0421	0.0258
Beam $b = 3$	0.0362	0.0421	0.0311
Beam $b = 4$	0.0362	0.0488	0.0324

We also simulate an environment of diseased infection phenotyping, which is one of the most important phenotyping tasks in the level of morphology and

Image 1

Image 2

Fig. 4. 3-D positions of the marks can be obtained by mapping the detected pixels onto the composite point clouds. Points without color information are showing in blue due to different fields of view between color and depth sensors. (Color figure online)

anatomy [15]. In our experiment, we place some red marks on the front sides of the leaves. Our system first constructs an overview of leaves in accordance with the proposed viewpoints planning algorithm. Then a post-processing step is performed by noise reduction and points registration. We use a simple clustering-based method to detect red rectangles in color space and map the detected regions onto point cloud to localize the marks. The number of candidate viewpoints is 300 for each robot and beam width $b = 3$ in real-robot experiments. Note that our system is designed for viewpoints planning, the marks are only used to simulate the case of diseased infection phenotyping. Experimental results are encouraging, which show that our system works well in this application (see Fig. 4). We also provide a supplementary video to demonstrate our system[2].

5   Conclusion

In this paper, we present a multi-robot system that can be used in high-throughput plant phenotyping. The system consists of three robotic arms each equipped with a depth camera. An efficient beam search algorithm to improve traditional next-best viewpoints planning is proposed. The planned viewpoints can be further planned to the motions that can be simultaneously executed by robotic arms. Experiments demonstrate the ability of our system in a high-throughput task of phenotyping diseased infections.

Acknowledgement. The authors would like to thank Xiangyu Bu at Facebook for valuable comments and suggestions to improve the quality of this paper. This work is supported by the Royal Society-Newton Advanced Fellowship (NA150431).

---

[2] https://youtu.be/C69HHQuNY2Y.

References

1. Acquaah, G.: Principles of Plant Genetics and Breeding. Wiley, New York (2009)
2. Alenya, G., Dellen, B., Foix, S., Torras, C.: Robotized plant probing: leaf segmentation utilizing time-of-flight data. IEEE Robot. Autom. Mag. **20**(3), 50–59 (2013)
3. Bircher, A., Kamel, M., Alexis, K., Oleynikova, H., Siegwart, R.: Receding horizon "next-best-view" planner for 3D exploration. In: 2016 IEEE International Conference on Robotics and Automation (ICRA), pp. 1462–1468, May 2016
4. Chaudhury, A., Barron, J.L.: Machine vision system for 3D plant phenotyping. IEEE/ACM Trans. Comput. Biol. Bioinf. (2018)
5. Dobson, A., Solovey, K., Shome, R., Halperin, D., Bekris, K.E.: Scalable asymptotically-optimal multi-robot motion planning. In: 2017 International Symposium on Multi-Robot and Multi-Agent Systems (MRS), pp. 120–127, December 2017
6. Dornhege, C., Kleiner, A., Hertle, A., Kolling, A.: Multirobot coverage search in three dimensions. J. Field Robot. **33**(4), 537–558 (2015)
7. Fiorani, F., Schurr, U.: Future scenarios for plant phenotyping. Annu. Rev. Plant Biol. **64**(1), 267–291 (2013)
8. Foix, S., Alenyá, G., Torras, C.: 3D sensor planning framework for leaf probing. In: 2015 IEEE/RSJ International Conference on Intelligent Robots and Systems (IROS), pp. 6501–6506, September 2015
9. Haboudane, D., Miller, J.R., Pattey, E., Zarco-Tejada, P.J., Strachan, I.B.: Hyperspectral vegetation indices and novel algorithms for predicting green LAI of crop canopies: modeling and validation in the context of precision agriculture. Remote Sens. Environ. **90**(3), 337–352 (2004)
10. Hornung, A., Wurm, K.M., Bennewitz, M., Stachniss, C., Burgard, W.: OctoMap: an efficient probabilistic 3D mapping framework based on octrees. Auton. Robots **34**(3), 189–206 (2013)
11. Houle, D., Govindaraju, D.R., Omholt, S.: Phenomics: the next challenge. Nat. Rev. Genet. **11**, 855 (2010)
12. LaValle, S.M.: Planning Algorithms. Cambridge University Press, Cambridge (2006)
13. Lowerre, B.T.: The Harpy speech recognition system. Ph.D. thesis, Carnegie Mellon University, Pittsburgh, PA, USA (1976). aAI7619331
14. Parker, S.G., et al.: Optix: a general purpose ray tracing engine. ACM Trans. Graph. **29**(4), 66:1–66:13 (2010)
15. Rousseau, C., et al.: High throughput quantitative phenotyping of plant resistance using chlorophyll fluorescence image analysis. Plant Methods **9**(1), 17 (2013)
16. Vasquez-Gomez, J.I., Sucar, L.E., Murrieta-Cid, R.: View/state planning for three-dimensional object reconstruction under uncertainty. Auton. Robots **41**(1), 89–109 (2017)

Wall-Following Control of Multi-robot Based on Moving Target Tracking and Obstacle Avoidance

Kongtao Zhu$^{(\boxtimes)}$, Chensheng Cheng, Can Wang, and Feihu Zhang

Northwestern Polytechnical University, Xi'an 710072, China
banxian2008@163.com, chengchensheng@163.com, wangcan2017@mail.nwpu.edu.cn,
feihu.zhang@nwpu.edu.cn

Abstract. Studies on wall-following problem mostly focus on an single robot only. This study proposes a wall-following method of multi-robot, which is based on moving target tracking. The leader robot moves along walls by using position information include angle and distance between robots and walls. The follower robot moves along the walls, tracks its leader and avoids collision at convex corner of walls. Two E-puck robots are used in experiment in this study. The results of experiment verify the feasibility of this method.

Keywords: Wall-following · Obstacle avoidance ·
Tracking moving target

1 Introduction

The wall-following control problem is characterized by moving the robot along a wall in a desired direction at the same time maintaining a constant distance to that wall [1]. It is worth mentioning that a map of the environment is not needed. There are several reasons why autonomous mobile robots must be able to follow walls, or in a more general sense, to follow the contours of an object. Mobile robots need to have the ability to follow walls in these scenes:

- obstacle avoidance [1–3]: When a mobile robot can't get the shape of the obstacle, it can't plan an effective path to avoid the coming collision. Therefore, moving along the contours of the obstacle become a reasonable strategy.
- navigation in unknown environment [1,4]: When a robot is moving in an unknown environment, following the walls should be a reasonable and effective strategy of path planing for it.
- mapping and localization [1,5,6]: When the location of the robot is known, the modeling of the environment can be realized by using wall-following strategy. On the contrary, if the robot moving along walls in a certain environment, it is possible to localize the robot.

Supported by organization School of Marine Engineering Northwestern Polytechnical University.

F. Sun et al. (Eds.): ICCSIP 2018, CCIS 1005, pp. 534–541, 2019.
https://doi.org/10.1007/978-981-13-7983-3_47

At present, many researches have been done on wall-following problem of a single mobile robot. Juang e.g. proposed a reinforcement ant optimized fuzzy controller (FC) design method and applied it to wheeled-mobile-robot wall-following control under reinforcement learning environments [7]. Braunstingl e.g. designed a fuzzy logic controller and local navigation strategy [8]. Dain e.g. demonstrated the use of genetic programming (GP) for the development of mobile robot wall-following behaviors [9].

But all these studies focus on wall-following control of a single robot only. In our study, a simple controller is designed using the angle and distance measured by infrared sensors. On this foundation, a wall-following navigation of multi-robot based on moving target tracing is designed and implemented.

A simple method used to make one robot move following a wall is given in Sect. 2. Section 3 proposes tracing and obstacle avoidance algorithm. In Sect. 4, the wall-following of multi-robot is realized in experiments and a discussion is given. Finally, a brief summary is provided in Sect. 5.

2 Wall-Following Control of a Single Robot

A diagrammatic description of wall-following problem is shown in Fig. 1. The position of the robot in the Cartesian space is given by x, y and θ. The kinematics model of two wheeled robot is given as below.

$$
\begin{cases}
\dot{x} = v \cdot \cos\theta \\
\dot{y} = v \cdot \sin\theta \\
\dot{\theta} = \omega
\end{cases}
\tag{1}
$$

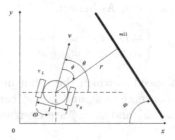

Fig. 1. Wall following of a single robot.

The mobile robot can be considered as a system with two inputs and three outputs. The three outputs are the position coordinates x, y and θ. The two inputs are the speeds of the two wheels. However, instead of the wheel speeds, the translation and rotation speeds of the robot as a whole are more interesting. The relation of them can easily be found as

$$
\begin{cases}
v = \frac{1}{2}(v_R + v_L) \\[2mm]
\omega = \frac{1}{l}(v_R - v_L)
\end{cases}
\tag{2}
$$

$$\begin{cases} v_R = R_w \cdot \omega_R \\ v_L = R_w \cdot \omega_L \end{cases} \tag{3}$$

with R_w the wheel radii, ω_R the palstance of the right wheel, ω_L the palstance of the left one, and l the distance between the two wheels.

In order to move along the wall, the robot needs to keep the wall on its right side (or left side) and maintain a safe distance from the wall. Therefore, the angle between the direction of the robot and the tangent direction of the wall needs to be stabilized at a particular angle which is marked as Φ, while the distance should be maintained at a constant which is described as R. The forward direction of robot is defined as $0\,\text{rad}$, and counterclockwise is positive while clockwise is negative. In general sense, when the robot is wanted to keep and move on the right side of the robot, the value of Φ is usually $\frac{\pi}{2}$. On the contrary, Φ is equal to $-\frac{\pi}{2}$ while the robot is supposed to move on the other side. The palstance of the wheel toward the wall is recorded as ω_I, and the palstance of another is ω_O. The relationship between ω_I, ω_O and ω_L, ω_R is represented as follows:

$$\begin{cases} \omega_L = \frac{1}{2}(1 - \sin\Phi) \cdot \omega_O + \frac{1}{2}(1 + \sin\Phi) \cdot \omega_I \\ \omega_R = \frac{1}{2}(1 + \sin\Phi) \cdot \omega_O + \frac{1}{2}(1 - \sin\Phi) \cdot \omega_I \end{cases} \tag{4}$$

The equations above represent that, while Φ is fixed on $\frac{\pi}{2}$, the wall is kept on the left side of the robot, ω_L is equal to ω_I and ω_R is equal to ω_O as a result. The opposite is true, while Φ is equal to $\frac{\pi}{2}$ and the wall is on the other side of the robot, $\omega_L = \omega_I$ and $\omega_R = \omega_O$.

To move the robot along the wall, the palstances of its two wheels ω_O and ω_I can be divided into three parts. As below:

$$\begin{cases} \omega_O = \omega_k + \omega_\phi + \omega_r \\ \omega_I = \omega_k + \omega'_\phi + \omega'_r \end{cases} \tag{5}$$

in which, ω_k is a constant speed at which the robot moves forward, ω_ϕ, ω'_ϕ are speeds used to make ϕ to converge to Φ, and ω_r, ω'_r can regulate the distance r and make it stable at R. ω_ϕ, ω'_ϕ and ω_r, ω'_r are designed as:

$$\begin{cases} \omega_\phi = k_{p\phi} \cdot e_\phi + k_{i\phi} \cdot \dot{e}_\phi \\ \omega'_\phi = -\omega_\phi \end{cases} \tag{6}$$

$$\begin{cases} \omega_r = k_{pr} \cdot e_r + k_{ir} \cdot \dot{e}_r \\ \omega'_r = -\omega_r \end{cases} \tag{7}$$

where $e_\phi = \phi - \Phi$, $e_r = r - R$, which are the angle error and distance error of the system, $\dot{e}_\phi$, $\dot{e}_r$ are their rate of change, and $k_{p\phi}$, $k_{i\phi}$, k_{pr}, k_{ir} are parameters which can be adjusted artificially as required. This is a simple PD controller. Proper parameters can make the system stable.

3   Wall-Following Control of Multi-robot Based on Moving Target Tracking

Because of the subtle differences between the robots, it is difficult to use the same algorithm to keep multiple robots moving in a row along the wall. And the different efficiencies of the motors, make it easy to drift away or collide with each other when robots move in formation. In order to avoid this situation, the method based on moving target tracking is adopted to realize the multi-robot motion along the wall in this study.

3.1   Tracking Moving Target

Sketch of the problem tracking a moving target has been displayed in Fig. 2 which is similar to the previous one. In the wall following problem, when robot is wanted to move along walls stably, the azimuth of the robot relative to walls ϕ is supposed to equal $\frac{\pi}{2}$ or $-\frac{\pi}{2}$, and r the distance between them should keep at R. Similarly in this moving target tracking problem:

- $\phi_f \to 0$: the follower must always face to its target, so its path angle is wanted to be 0;
- $d \to D$: the distance between the two robots should be kept at a safe value which is described as D.

where ϕ_f is the angle from the direction of the follower to the connection between the follower and the leader, and d is the distance between them, while D is a constant. Detailed information has been shown is Fig. 2.

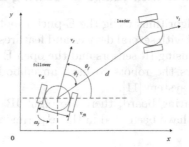

Fig. 2. Moving target tracking problem.

The follower robot should face to and keep a safe distance with its leader. As a result, speeds of the follower's two wheels can be designed as:

$$\begin{cases} \omega_{fL} = \omega_{f\phi} + \omega_{fd} \\ \omega_{fR} = \omega'_{f\phi} + \omega_{fd} \end{cases} \tag{8}$$

$$\omega'_{f\phi} = -\omega_{f\phi} \tag{9}$$

where $\omega_{f\phi}$, $\omega'_{f\phi}$ are speeds which are related to path angle and used to rotate the robot and keep ϕ_f at 0, while ω_{fd} is related to distance and supposed to maintain a safe distance.

3.2   Obstacle Avoidance

Figure 3 shows the process of the obstacle avoidance algorithm. When there is any obstacle, robot will avoid the coming collision first instead of continuing to follow the leader. If the obstacle is on the right side, the robot will turn left; if the obstacle on the left side the robot will turn right; if there is no obstacle close enough to it, the robot will move toward the target.

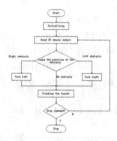

Fig. 3. Flowchart of obstacle avoidance algorithm.

4   Experiment

4.1   The E-Puck Robot with Range & Bearing Board

This article verify the algorithms using the E-puck robote [10].

E-puck was equipped with several devices and features. The idea of this study is to navigate the robot using IR sensors and the open E-puck Range & Bearing board. The board allows the robots to have an embodied, decentralized and scalable communication system [11].

Beside Range & Bearing board, there are eight IR sensors on the E-puck robot. These IR sensors have been used in the experiment of obstacle avoidance algorithm.

4.2   Wall-Following of a Single Robot

Using the R&B board, the robot can measure the position and signal intensity which is inversely proportional to the distance between the robot and signal source, if the robot constantly sends out signals, it can calculate the position and distance of the obstacle according to the signal reflected by the obstacle.

Figure 4 shows the experiment of the wall-following controller of one robot given in Sect. 2. In this experiment, the distance between robot and walls is set to 5 cm, and Φ is fixed at $-\frac{\pi}{2}$ (robot keeps wall on its right side). The trajectory of the robot is marked by a red line. In this experiment, the distance from the wall to the robot remains stable, while the wall is a straight line. The robot can well track walls, whether in a convex corner or a concave one. In general, robot using this method can move well along the wall.

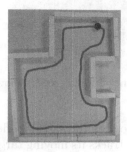

Fig. 4. Experiment a single robot moving along walls.

4.3   Moving Target Tracking and Obstacle Avoidance

Due to the leader moving along walls according to signals reflected by the walls, signals reflected by the follower robot will also have an impact on the leader when they are close enough to each other. In order to reduce the impact of the follower on its leader, the distance between them is set at 10 cm. The threshold of sensors output is set at 150. When a certain sensor output is greater than the threshold, the robot will make such a judgment that there is an obstacle in the direction of this sensor, and obstacle avoidance algorithm will work then.

Figure 5 shows the results of the experiment of double robots moving along walls based on moving target tracing and obstacle avoidance. The red points describe the trajectory of the leader robot, while the green ones show how the other robot follows it. Obviously, the follower can track its target stably whether in the straight wall, the convex corner or the concave corner. While robots in the convex corner, the obstacle avoidance strategy given in Sect. 3 is adopted. The follower robot will not track the leader until its IR sensors output is below the threshold. However, while in the concave corner, the robot in the rear slows down because the robot in front makes a turn, and the distance between them will become smaller if the follower keeps its speed. Therefore, the trajectory of the follower is not agreement with the trajectory of the leader in concave corners. In addition, the trajectory of the follower appears wavy and zigzag at a straight wall. The cause of this phenomenon will be given in the discussion below.

4.4   Discussion

The robot taking wall-following strategy get orientation of obstacles from receiving and calculating signals which are transmitted by the robot and reflected on the surface of obstacles. The signals are also received and calculated by the follower robot and used for tracking the moving one. Robot not only receives signals

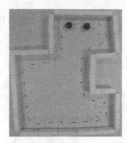

Fig. 5. Experiment of double robots moving along walls.

sending by its target, but also gets the signals reflected by walls. The result is that when the following robot tracks its moving target, it can not distinguish the real target and the mirror target produced by reflection. Therefore, the robot sometimes tracks the real target, and sometimes moves towards walls. While it is close enough to the wall, the robot will move away from the wall with the operation of obstacle avoidance algorithm. And go on like this. This is why the trajectory of the follower appears wavy and zigzag at a straight wall.

A filter can be used to reduce the effect of this mirror target. The distance between follower and the virtual robot which is caused by reflections must be longer than what between follower and the real target. So, mistakes can be reduced if the distant target, which is possible to be a virtual one, is filtered away. What needs to be noted is that the filter can only reduce the impact, instead of completely eliminated it. In fact, the filter described above has been adopted in this experiment.

5 Conclusion

This study provides a wall-following control method of multi-robot based on moving target tracing. The leader robot calculates position information of walls in real-time measurement and moves along the walls. The follower tracks the leader and takes obstacle avoidance algorithm into use while it gets close to walls. The results of experiment show that the leader can move along walls stably, and the follower tracks its target well.

Acknowledgement. This work was supported by the National Natural Science Foundation of China (NSFC) under Grants 61703335, and the Fundamental Research Funds for the Central Universities under Grants G2017KY0302.

References

1. van Turennout, P., Honderd, G., van Schelven, L.J.: Wall-following control of a mobile robot. In: Proceedings 1992 IEEE International Conference on Robotics and Automation, vol. 1, pp. 280–285, May 1992
2. Jung, I.-K., Hong, K.-B., Hong, S.-K., Hong, S.C.: Path planning of mobile robot using neural network. In: Proceedings of the IEEE International Symposium on Industrial Electronics, ISIE 1999, vol. 3, pp. 979–983 (1999)
3. Chancharoen, R., Sangveraphunsiri, V., Navakulsirinart, T., Thanawittayakorn, W., Boonsanongsupa, W., Meesaplak, A.: Target tracking and obstacle avoidance for mobile robots. In: 2002 IEEE International Conference on Industrial Technology IEEE ICIT 2002, vol. 1, pp. 13–17 (2002)
4. Bemporad, A., Marco, M.D., Tesi, A.: Wall-following controllers for sonar-based mobile robots. In: Proceedings of the 36th IEEE Conference on Decision and Control, vol. 3, pp. 3063–3068, December 1997
5. Katsev, M., Yershova, A., Tovar, B., Ghrist, R., LaValle, S.M.: Mapping and pursuit-evasion strategies for a simple wall-following robot. IEEE Trans. Rob. **27**(1), 113–128 (2011)
6. Crowley, J.L.: Mathematical foundations of navigation and perception for an autonomous mobile robot. In: Dorst, L., van Lambalgen, M., Voorbraak, F. (eds.) RUR 1995. LNCS, vol. 1093, pp. 7–51. Springer, Heidelberg (1996). https://doi.org/10.1007/BFb0013953
7. Juang, C.F., Hsu, C.H.: Reinforcement ant optimized fuzzy controller for mobile-robot wall-following control. IEEE Trans. Ind. Electron. **56**(10), 3931–3940 (2009)
8. Braunstingl, R., Mujika, J., Uribe, J.P.: A wall following robot with a fuzzy logic controller optimized by a genetic algorithm. In: Proceedings of 1995 IEEE International Conference on Fuzzy Systems, vol. 5, pp. 77–82, March 1995
9. Dain, R.A.: Developing mobile robot wall-following algorithms using genetic programming. Appl. Intell. **8**(1), 33–41 (1998). https://doi.org/10.1023/A:1008216530547
10. E-puck: E-puck education robot. http://www.e-puck.org
11. Gutierrez, A., Campo, A., Dorigo, M., Donate, J., Monasterio-Huelin, F., Magdalena, L.: Open e-puck range & bearing miniaturized board for local communication in swarm robotics. In: 2009 IEEE International Conference on Robotics and Automation, pp. 3111–3116, May 2009

Robot Simulation and Reinforcement Learning Training Platform Based on Distributed Architecture

Yun-Liang Jiang[1,2], Zeng-Qiang Huang[1(✉)], Jun-Jie Cao[3],
Yong Liu[3], Xinqiang Ma[4], and Yi Huang[4]

[1] School of Computer Science, Hangzhou Dianzi University,
Hangzhou 310018, China
huangzengqiang@foxmail.com
[2] School of Information Engineering, Huzhou University,
Huzhou 313000, China
[3] Institute of Cyber Systems and Control, Zhejiang University,
Hangzhou 310027, China
[4] Institute of Intelligent Computing and Visualization Based on Big Data,
Chongqing University of Arts and Sciences, Chongqing 402160, China

Abstract. In recent years, reinforcement learning, which enables robots to learn previously missing abilities, plays an increasingly important role in robotics, such as learning hard-to-code behaviors or optimizing problems without an accepted closed solution. The main problem of RL in robotics is that it is expensive and takes a long time to learn and operate. Another problem: advanced robot simulators like Gazebo are inefficient and time-consuming. In order to cope with these problems, a hybrid computing platform based on traditional robot simulation architecture and distributed architecture (hereinafter referred to as RDTP) is proposed in this paper, which helps to save cost, shorten time and speed up simulation and training. Additionally, the platform is optimized to a certain extent in terms of ease of use and compatibility.

Keywords: Robot · Simulation · Reinforcement learning · Distributed

1 Introduction

Currently, most of the well-performed robots are trained based on the traditional control methods, which requires an established model in advance with certain cost. Compared with the traditional control methods, model is unnecessarily set for reinforcement learning, but to obtain an excellent model by training a large amount of sample data. However, the problems existing in the training process of reinforcement learning are mainly reflected as follows: a large amount of sample data needs to be obtained through the interaction between lots of robots, while large sample collection from robots is slow with large loss, and even may be dangerous, especially for flying robots like quadrotor. To overcome the difficulty of data sampling, the University of Southern California has developed advanced robot simulators like Gazebo, which is conducive to saving cost, shorten time and speeding up data collection. For simple

© Springer Nature Singapore Pte Ltd. 2019
F. Sun et al. (Eds.): ICCSIP 2018, CCIS 1005, pp. 542–553, 2019.
https://doi.org/10.1007/978-981-13-7983-3_48

environment simulation and robot training, there are already many excellent projects, such as Gym [1] and RoboSchool which provided by OpenAI. Only after a large amount of robotic environment interaction and training can a satisfactory training effect be obtained. However, limited to the computing power of a single computer, training time has become a bottleneck in the field of robotics. There are a lot of people who are trying to train on distributed robots, but there is no excellent distributed processing framework to support them, so they can't get satisfactory results [2].

In order to deal with these problems, this paper proposes a robot simulation and reinforcement learning training platform based on distributed architecture, and optimizes the evolutionary strategy in terms of parallelism and distributed reliability, making it more suitable for this platform, and this distributed platform architecture also validates the role of this platform in reinforcement learning training. Finally, the comparison experiment between the platform and the single-node GPU training platform was carried out in many aspects. It is proved that this platform effectively improves the training speed and reduces time cost of the robot's reinforcement learning model; specifically, the platform provides distributed support for the reinforcement learning and robot simulation sampling, besides, remote desktop and other operation support are available with its high compatibility.

2 Related Works

In 2012, AMP lab at the University of California, Berkeley, open-source Spark, a generic parallel framework for Hadoop MapReduce. Spark's system architecture is a classic master-slave structure, and memory calculation enables it to well support the operation of common machine learning algorithms, especially when it with the help of massive data training. However, Spark's distributed iteration assignments are task-based [3], so it is not well supported for reinforcement learning tasks that require frequent parameter exchanges.

In order to solve the problem of Spark fails to support the algorithms such as for reinforcement learning efficiently, Berkeley RISELab in 2017 open source framework of general parallel Ray for reinforcement learning design [4], a distributed iterative operation decreases from the task level to function level, which effectively improves the support to reinforcement learning algorithm, but it is limited for there is no expansion of multi-simulation environment for the robot simulation.

In 2015, Google released AlphaGo based on neural network and long-term prediction [5]. The match between AlphaGo and top players effectively proved the potential of AI. At the same time, abundant training also further revealed the shortcomings of computing ability from traditional training platform. To accelerate AlphaGo's training, Google built a distributed training platform. In 2017, Google released the Tensor Processing Unit that supports reinforcement learning and other training tasks from the aspect of hardware [6], and updated the architecture constantly to provide better support and reduce the energy consumption of the Computing Unit. However, the capacity and price still cannot be widely used.

3 Instruction to System Architecture Design

In this section, detailed architecture of the platform and the major framework of the combination of all parts are presented. Considering that the distributed architecture of the platform is based on the open source framework Ray provided by AMP laboratory which adopts the master and multi-slavers, our mixed architecture adopts the typical distributed architecture extending from the traditional master and multi-slavers. The overall architecture of the system is shown in Fig. 1. Each part is described specifically as below.

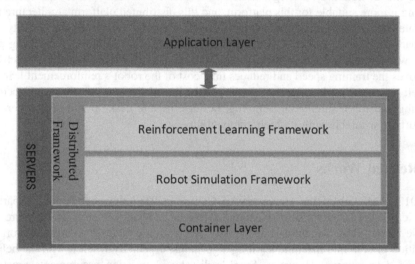

Fig. 1. The platform mainly consists of four parts: the application layer interacting with users, principal distributed framework, the simulation framework integrating multiple ones and the container layer improving platform compatibility.

3.1 Application Layer

The application layer is composed of LXDE [7] lightweight desktop environment and VNC [8] remote control software. With the purpose of providing users with a convenient and intuitive operation interface and checking the simulation and training effects of the robot in real-time. The client implementation architecture is shown in Fig. 2.

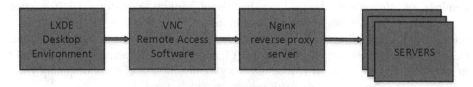

Fig. 2. Client architecture is composed of lightweight desktop environment, remote control software and reverse proxy service

Starts the service, the LXDE desktop can be accessed through the browser, and the effect is shown in Fig. 3. The training task is submitted through the operating interface similar to the Ubuntu system, which is more convenient to submit the simulation environment for obtaining sampling number and checking training effect. The Nginx [9] reverse proxy service effectively protects clusters in the LAN.

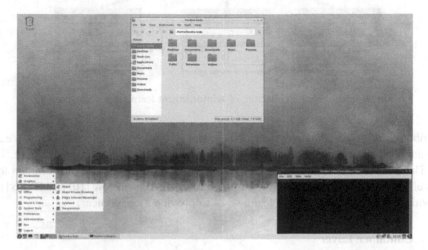

Fig. 3. LXDE Desktop is a desktop environment which is lightweight and fast. It is designed to be user friendly and slim, while keeping the resource usage low.

3.2   Distributed Framework

As the subject of the platform, the distributed framework critically impacts the computing performance of the platform. Considering that reinforcement learning and training requires frequent parameter collection and redistribution, the distributed framework uses Ray, a high-performance distributed execution framework designed for reinforcement learning. Ray adopts a computational abstraction method different from the traditional distributed computing framework, which endowed a deeper task abstraction capability than Spark, thus achieving excellent performance that is more suitable for distributed reinforcement learning and computing. To adapt Ray to more robot simulation frameworks, the API interacting with the robot simulation framework is modified. The architecture diagram is shown in Fig. 4.

3.3   Robot Simulation Framework and Reinforcement Learning
Framework

The simulation framework of this platform integrates Torcs, a racing simulation game that can be used to test autonomous driving, VizDoom, A FPS (First Person Shoot) game framework that can be used to test image recognition and situational interaction, and gazebo, a popular robot simulation software. Since the design of each simulation framework itself is mostly based on the single-machine, in order to adapt to the

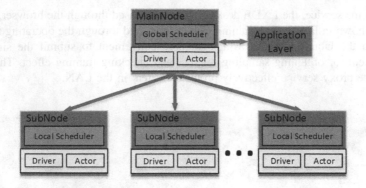

Fig. 4. Distributed architecture of reinforcement learning and computing

distributed and container deployment, the content of the deployment and startup in each simulation framework needs to be modified to adapt to the platform architecture.

The reinforcement learning framework of this platform integrates the common tool sets of reinforcement learning algorithm, such as Gym, TensorFlow [10] and RLlib [11] provided by Ray's development team, so as to provide more choices.

3.4 Container Layer

Most of the existing excellent robot simulation, reinforcement learning and training frameworks are developed based on the Ubuntu platform. However, the systems used are different and the versions are diversified. In order to make the platform flexible and compatible with multiple system platforms, Docker [12] container technology is introduced to realize container deployment.

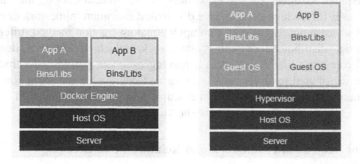

Fig. 5. Docker architecture and VM architecture. In Docker, All container are run by a single operating system kernel and thus more lightweight than virtual machines.

The emergence of Docker technology solves the urgent problems such as effective coordination between teams, quick deliver and deploy, as well as business requirements achieving. Container's deployment, volume, resource utilization and other aspects are better than virtual machine technology, and the implementation frameworks are shown in Fig. 5.

After the platform is containerized, its management can use hardware more fully and flexibly.

4 Parallel Optimization of Evolutionary Strategy Algorithm

For the past years, evolutionary algorithm is more frequently used to solve the problem of reinforcement learning. As an evolutionary algorithm, the evolutionary strategy algorithm is mainly used to generate strategies, which can be directly used as an alternative to traditional reinforcement learning algorithms such as strategy gradient algorithm and Q learning. In the optimization of strategies represented by neural network, there is no backpropagation of gradient in the optimization process of evolutionary strategy algorithm. Therefore, compared with many reinforcement learning algorithms, it is equipped with little computational complexity and the approximation of value function is omitted, which weakens the influence of delay reward on reinforcement learning. Like other evolutionary algorithms, evolutionary strategies have good parallelism and scalability. Based on the parallel training framework proposed in this paper, the improved evolutionary computing algorithm integrates low computational complexity and high parallelism, which can greatly accelerate the speed of reinforcement learning and training.

The improved evolutionary strategy algorithm in this paper is based on the natural evolution strategy algorithm [13]. The definition θ is the parameter of the neural network representing the strategy, and $F(\theta)$ is the fitness function, expressed by the average return value of the strategy that performs the parameter σ as a parameter. A strategy parameter population $(\theta_i = \theta + \sigma \epsilon_i)$ is formed by sampling multiple times in a Gaussian distribution with θ as the mean and σ as the standard deviation. The θ_i is distributed to each node, and the strategy is executed to calculate the average return $F_i = F(\theta_i)$. The update of the policy parameters is calculated by summarizing the $F(\theta_i)$ of all nodes:

$$t\theta_{t+1} \leftarrow \theta_t + \alpha \frac{1}{n\alpha} \sum\nolimits_{i=1}^{n} F_i \in i$$

Based on the above basic algorithm, by using the characteristics of generating a pseudo random number by means of a computer, it is possible to avoid transmitting the parameter vector θ_i to each node, and it is only necessary to reconstruct the θ_i of other nodes at each node by using the commonly agreed random seed. Each node only needs to send the average return F_i (scalar value) calculated by the node to other nodes, and then each node uses the above update formula to follow the new original parameter θ. Repeat the above process until convergence. The improved algorithm transforms the master-slave distributed architecture into a zone-centric parallel architecture, and will avoid vector parameter transfers, requiring only one scalar value to be transmitted, thus significantly reducing the communication load. Combined with the parallel computing framework proposed in this paper, the optimization training of depth strategy can be made more efficient.

```
Algorithm1 Parallelized Evolution Strategies
  Input: Learning rate α, noise standard deviation σ, initial policy parameters
θ₀
    Initialize: n workers with known random seeds, and initial parameters θ₀
      for t = 0,1,2,... do
      for each worker i = 1,...,n do
        Sample εᵢ~N(0,I)
        Compute returns Fᵢ = F(θₜ + σεᵢ)
      end for
      Send all scalar returns Fᵢ from each worker to every other worker
      for each worker i = 1,...,n do
        Reconstruct all perturbations εⱼ for j = 1,...,n using known random seeds
        Set θₜ₊₁ ← θₜ + α(1/nσ)Σⱼ₌₁ⁿ Fⱼ εⱼ
      end for
    end for
```

5 Experiment and Evaluation

In this chapter, performances of the platform are tested from the aspects of the streaming data processing performance of the platform and other traditional ones, test on computing cost and the platform's node expansion performance. Tables 1 and 2 respectively show the hardware and system configuration instructions of CPU and GPU experimental platform. The experiments in this paper are carried out based on these two platforms. The purchase time of equipment is different, so the price is subject to the one when the experiment is conducted.

Table 1. Hardware and system configuration instructions of CPU experimental platform

Hardware	Description	Software	Description
CPU	Intel Xeon E5-2630,2*6*2 cores per node	JDK	8u60
Memory	128G per node	Python	3.6.5
Drive	2T per node	Docker	1.13.1
Physical nodes	Huawei servers*18	Spark	1.60
Network	15.6Tbps	OS	CentOS7.2

Table 2. Hardware and system configuration instructions of GPU experimental platform

Hardware	Description	Software	Description
CPU	Intel Xeon E5-2650,4*6*2 cores per node	JDK	8u60
GPU	GTX 1080Ti*4	Python	3.6.5
Memory	64G per node	Spark	1.60
Drive	1T per node	Docker	1.13.1
Physical nodes	Dell server*1	OS	Ubuntu 16.04
Network	15.6Tbps	OS	CentOS7.2

In addition to Mujoco [14] used by common ground Gym provided by Ray, the platform integrates several environments such as RoboSchool similar to Mujoco, racing game environment Torcs [15] and game environment VizDoom [16] of FPS (First Person Shoot).

In the following simulation environments, RoboSchool simulation environment 1 is used, and a new SimpleDog simulation environment is established. As shown in Fig. 6, simple robot needs to step over the horizontal bar on the ground and move forward, and the robot moving distance is used as the evaluation score of the algorithm.

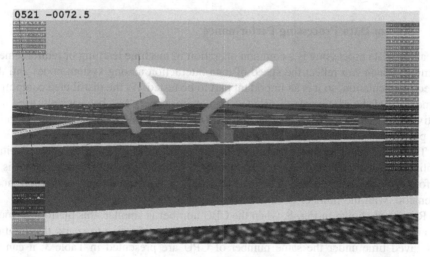

Fig. 6. Simulated robot SimpleDog with the horizontal bar, and In the background is the playground.

5.1 Parallel Improvement of Evolutionary Strategy Algorithm

The comparison algorithm in the experiment is PPO (Proximal Policy Optimization) [17]. PPO is a new strategy gradient method proposed by John Schulman et al. The traditional strategy gradient method will conduct simulated sampling again in each iteration, while PPO chooses to update in batches periodically, and PPO better adapts to the needs of multi-thread training, which is more representative.

Based on the simulation environment, the training results of ES and PPO are presented in Fig. 7. The statistical results are the comprehensive consideration of multiple experiments; the shaded part is the variance of multiple results. It can be found that the ES algorithm is capable to achieve target faster than the PPO algorithm; moreover, its alternation is stable.

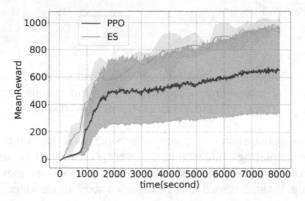

Fig. 7. Performance comparison between ES and PPO algorithms under RDTP platform

5.2   Stream Data Processing Performance

Streaming data processing is a common operation in machine learning or reinforcement learning, which can reflect the speed of data interaction among system nodes and the speed of calculation, so it is an important part to be tested. As the distributed computing framework of the platform's distributed framework, Spark has been widely used and cultivated a mature ecosystem. The comparison experiment with Spark fully verifies the performance of traditional streaming data processing in this platform.

The basic data for the experiment are referred from 10 articles about capitals published in wikipedia.com, which are about 26 Mb in English. The experiment is to perform WordCount on the articles and make a horizontal comparison on node extension, with the number of nodes from 1 to 10.

Results as shown in Fig. 8, when the CPU number is smaller, this platform is more advantageous; to increase the number of nodes is more effective to spark; the duration and saved time under the same number of CPU are presented in Table 3; it can be found that for streaming data processing, 2% to 9% of the running time is saved.

5.3   Scalability

In the actual environment of usage, factors such as the different cluster configuration and the number of nodes, as well as the calculation performance required by different experiment setting strict demands to the platform, so the distributed node extensibility is a very important performance indicators, that is to say, A available distributed platform must be equipped with proper extensibility

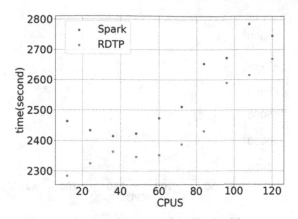

Fig. 8. Performance comparison of stream data processing

Table 3. Stream data processing performance comparison

CPUs	Spark	RDTP	Saved (%)
12	2463.7830	2284.7536	7.2660
24	2433.0000	2324.7226	4.4500
36	2414.2370	2362.9105	2.1260
48	2423.2370	2346.4801	3.1680
60	2473.0000	2351.7481	4.9030
72	2510.7840	2386.7815	4.9390
84	2653.2960	2430.1698	8.4089
96	2672.2010	2589.4157	3.0980
108	2785.8730	2615.4939	6.1160
120	2745.8200	2669.9919	2.7620

Under the simulated environment SimpleDog, the number of CPU used to increase training taking 24 as the step size and repeat training experiment, the experimental results are shown in Fig. 9. For the same training task, the increase of training nodes can effectively reduce the training time when the number of nodes is relatively small. With the increase of nodes, and the reduction of training time, the effect is gradually decreased; the communication loss between nodes is not excessively increased with the increase of nodes.

5.4 Comparison of Calculation Cost

In terms of computing hardware, GPU training is limited by the number of nodes, expensive equipment and restricted purchase quantity. Due to the limited experimental environment, and clusters performance with same number is higher than that of CPU clusters, so the computing cost of CPU clusters and GPU single nodes is taken as a

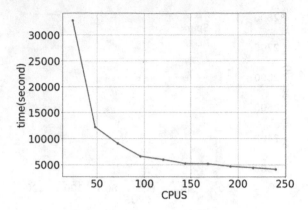

Fig. 9. The platform node extension

comparison indicator. As for the calculation cost, the price of hardware is defined as P, the time of training tasks is set as t, and the calculation formula of cost C is defined as:

$$C = 10^6/(P * t)$$

In the simulation environment SimpleDog, the training tasks are respectively carried out in CPU cluster and GPU single node, and the computing cost is compared under the two environments. The hardware environment of the comparison experiment is that CPU environment selects 96 cores according to the previous experiment, while GPU selects a core.

The experimental results are shown in Table 4. 10% of calculating cost is saved by using 96 CPU cores comparing that of 1 GPU core.

Table 4. Comparison of CPU and GPU computing cost

	Cores	Price	Time	C
CPU	96	1399/24	6608.3956	0.0270
GPU	1	7899/1	5184.5149	0.0240

6 Conclusion

In order to meet the demand of robot simulation and reinforcement learning in distributed computing, this platform combines several open source frameworks and makes modification and integration to complete a training platform with certain availability, stability and expansibility. Finally, it is proved through several experiments that compared with the traditional framework, the platform is conducive to flow data processing, utilization ability and scalability of the traditional cluster platform. Still, it is possible to conduct a further performance optimization.

Acknowledgement. This work was supported by the National Natural Science Foundation of China under Grants (U1509210 and 61771793), the Chongqing Research Program of Basic Research and Frontier Technology (No. cstc2015jcyjA40026, No. cstc2016jcyjA0568), the Science and Technology Research Program of Chongqing Municipal Education Commission (No. KJ1711278, KJ1601129, KJ1501134), the Natural Science Foundation of Yongchuan Science and Technology Commission (No. Ycstc, 2016nc2002), and the Open Research Project of the State Key Laboratory of Industrial Control Technology, Zhejiang University, China (No. ICT170330, ICT1800413).

References

1. Brockman, G., et al.: OpenAI gym. arXiv preprint arXiv:1606.01540 (2016)
2. Fan, B., Pan, Q., Zhang, H.: A method for multi-agent coordination based on distributed reinforcement learning. Comput. Simul. **22**(6), 115–117 (2005)
3. Zaharia, M., et al.: Resilient distributed datasets: a fault-tolerant abstraction for in-memory cluster computing. In: Proceedings of the 9th USENIX Conference on Networked Systems Design and Implementation, p. 2. USENIX Association, April 2012
4. Moritz, P., et al.: Ray: a distributed framework for emerging AI applications. In: 13th USENIX Symposium on Operating Systems Design and Implementation (OSDI 2018), pp. 561–577 (2018)
5. Tian, Y., Zhu, Y.: Better computer go player with neural network and long-term prediction. arXiv preprint arXiv:1511.06410 (2015)
6. Jouppi, N.P., et al.: In-datacenter performance analysis of a tensor processing unit. In: 2017 ACM/IEEE 44th Annual International Symposium on Computer Architecture (ISCA), pp. 1–12. IEEE, June 2017
7. LXDE Homepage. https://lxde.org/. Accessed 20 Sept 2018
8. VNC Homepage. https://www.realvnc.com/en/. Accessed 20 Sept 2018
9. Nginx Homepage. https://www.nginx.com/. Accessed 20 Sept 2018
10. Abadi, M., et al.: TensorFlow: a system for large-scale machine learning. In: OSDI, vol. 16, pp. 265–283, November 2016
11. Liang, E., et al.: Ray RLLib: a composable and scalable reinforcement learning library. arXiv preprint arXiv:1712.09381 (2017)
12. Docker Homepage. https://www.docker.com/. Accessed 20 Sept 2018
13. Wierstra, D., Schaul, T., Peters, J., Schmidhuber, J.: Natural evolution strategies. In: IEEE Congress on Evolutionary Computation, CEC 2008 (IEEE World Congress on Computational Intelligence), pp. 3381–3387. IEEE, June 2008
14. Mujoco Homepage. http://www.mujoco.org/. Accessed 20 Sept 2018
15. Torcs Homepage. http://torcs.sourceforge.net/index.php. Accessed 20 Sept 2018
16. Kempka, M., Wydmuch, M., Runc, G., Toczek, J., Jaśkowski, W.: VizDoom: a doom-based AI research platform for visual reinforcement learning. In: 2016 IEEE Conference on Computational Intelligence and Games (CIG), pp. 1–8. IEEE, September 2016
17. Schulman, J., Wolski, F., Dhariwal, P., Radford, A., Klimov, O.: Proximal policy optimization algorithms. arXiv preprint arXiv:1707.06347 (2017)

Robotic Knee Parameter Tuning Using Approximate Policy Iteration

Xiang Gao[1], Yue Wen[2,3], Minhan Li[2,3], Jennie Si[1(✉)],
and He (Helen) Huang[2,3]

[1] Department of Electrical, Computer, and Energy Engineering,
Arizona State University, Tempe, AZ 85281, USA
si@asu.edu
[2] Joint Department of Biomedical Engineering,
North Carolina State University, Raleigh, NC 27695, USA
hhuang11@ncsu.edu
[3] University of North Carolina at Chapel Hill, Chapel Hill, NC 27599, USA

Abstract. This paper presents an online model-free reinforcement learning based controller realized by approximate dynamic programming for a robotic knee as part of a human-machine system. Traditionally, prosthesis wearers' gait performance is improved by manually tuning the impedance parameters. In this paper, we show that the parameter tuning problem can be formulated as an optimal control problem and thus solved by dynamic programming. Toward this goal, we constructed an quadratic instantaneous cost, which resulted in a value function that could be approximated by a neural network. The control policy is then solved by the least-squared method iteratively, a framework of which we refer to as approximate policy iteration. We performed extensive simulations based on prosthetic kinetics and human performance data extracted from real human subjects. Our results show that the proposed parameter tuning algorithm can be readily used for adaptive optimal tuning of prosthetic knee control parameters and the tuning process is time and sample efficient.

Keywords: Approximate dynamic programming (ADP) ·
Policy iteration · Lower limb prosthesis · Sample efficient learning

1 Introduction

Compared to traditional passive prostheses, robotic lower limb prosthesis can provide greater functionalities and more natural gait patterns. A robotic prosthesis and its wearer can be seen as a human-machine integrated system where the controller of the prosthesis may adapt to or fight against the human body. Such interaction or co-adaptation between the two adaptive systems, namely the human and the learning machine, has been rarely studied. Therefore, it is important yet challenging to design an adaptive optimal controller to improve

© Springer Nature Singapore Pte Ltd. 2019
F. Sun et al. (Eds.): ICCSIP 2018, CCIS 1005, pp. 554–563, 2019.
https://doi.org/10.1007/978-981-13-7983-3_49

the gait performance of the human-prosthesis system, and make it tolerant to external disturbances and environmental uncertainties.

The finite state impedance controller (FS-IC) [5] is the most commonly used controller for lower limb prostheses. It prescribes different sets of impedance parameters to the robotic prosthesis corresponding to different gait phases. These impedance parameters need to be adjusted carefully to meet each amputee's physical needs. However, fine-tuning the prosthesis parameters manually and heuristically involves a lot of time and effort. Therefore researchers have proposed methods that can automatically tune the impedance parameters. For example, Huang *et al.* [7] proposed a cyber expert system to configure wearable robot control. However, the cyber expert essentially is an open-loop controller and it still requires human experts' knowledge, which greatly limits its usage. Therefore, the prosthesis control problem calls for a design that can automatically and adaptively learn the optimal impedance parameters from scratch.

In our previous work [12–14], we first demonstrated that the prosthesis control problem can be solved by approximate dynamic programming (ADP) [10,11]. In optimal control, the analytic solution to Hamilton-Jacobi-Bellman (HJB) equation for nonlinear systems is usually intractable or difficult to obtain, and ADP circumvent this issue by finding an approximate solution for the HJB equation. Policy iteration [6] is a classic algorithm for solving optimal decision and control problems. It has been discussed and expanded extensively within an ADP context [3,4]. Policy iteration has several important properties that makes itself a good candidate for optimizing the human-prosthesis system, such as nonincreasing and convergent value functions, and stable iterative control policies [4,8].

To improve the performance of the human-prosthesis system in a sample efficient manner, this paper develops an impedance tuning algorithm based on approximate policy iteration. First, a FS-IC framework [9] is established where gait phases are determined by knee kinematic and kinetic measurements including prosthesis knee joint angle, joint angular velocities and ground reaction forces. Then, gait performance is quantified by an quadratic cost function in terms of errors between measured knee motions and target knee motions. These errors are considered as the states that needs to be regulated in the optimal control problem. During an online tuning process, an model-free approximate policy iteration controller iterate between policy evaluation and policy improvement to find an optimal policy.

The remainder of this paper is organized as follows. Section 2 introduces the finite state impedance control framework in prosthesis control. In Sect. 3, the approximate policy iteration algorithm is proposed for the prosthesis control problem. Simulation results and conclusion are presented in Sects. 4 and 5.

2   Problem Description

Figure 1 shows a block diagram of the human-prosthesis simulation platform. In finite state impedance control (FS-IC) [9], a gait cycle was divided into four gait phases based on knee joint kinematics and ground reaction force.

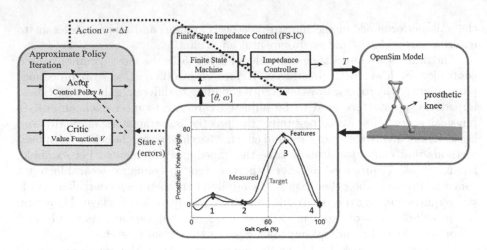

Fig. 1. Block diagram of the prosthesis control problem

These four gait phases are stance flexion (STF), stance extension (STE), swing flexion (SWF) and swing extension (SWE). Then the finite state machine in Fig. 1 determines the current phase and a set of impedance parameters I is applied to the impedance controller

$$I = [K, B, \theta_e] \in \mathbb{R}^3, \tag{1}$$

where K is stiffness, B is damping coefficient and θ_e is equilibrium position. In other words, for all four phases there are 12 impedance parameters in total. For each phase, the knee joint torque $T \in \mathbb{R}$ is generated from the impedance control law

$$T = K(\theta - \theta_e) + B\omega, \tag{2}$$

where θ and ω are knee joint angle and angular velocity, respectively.

We used OpenSim [2], a widely used simulator of human movements, to simulate walking patterns of the human-prosthesis system. In the OpenSim model, five rigid-body segments linked by one degree-of-freedom pin joints were used to represent the human body. The right knee was treated as a prosthetic knee and controlled by FS-IC as in (2), while the other joints followed prescribed motions. After each gait cycle, the differences (errors) between the measured knee angle profile and the target knee profile at the feature points (peaks marked with 1–4 in the bottom block of Fig. 1) are computed and treated as state x of the ADP controller,

$$x = [\Delta P, \Delta D]^T,$$

where $\Delta P \in \mathbb{R}$ is the peak error and $\Delta D \in \mathbb{R}$ is the duration error. Correspondingly, the action u is the impedance adjustment ΔI. More details about the FS-IC framework, the OpenSim model and the peak/duration errors can be found in our previous work [14].

3   Approximate Policy Iteration

3.1   Policy Iteration

In Fig. 1, the OpenSim model as well as the FS-IC framework can be treated as a deterministic discrete-time affine nonlinear system with unknown dynamics,

$$x_{k+1} = F(x_k, u_k), k = 0, 1, 2, \ldots \tag{3}$$

where $x_k \in \mathbb{R}^n$ is the state vector, $u_k \in \mathbb{R}^m$ is the action or control vector, and k is the time index (i.e. gait cycle in this study). Action u_k is determined by policy h as

$$u_k = h(x_k). \tag{4}$$

The instantaneous cost function or utility function $U(x, u)$ is defined in terms of both state x and action u as

$$U(x, u) = x^T R_x x + u^T R_u u, \tag{5}$$

where $R_x \in \mathbb{R}^{n \times n}$ and $R_u \in \mathbb{R}^{m \times m}$ are positive definite matrices.

The value function or cost-to-go function $V(x_k)$ is defined in an infinite horizon form with a discount factor $0 < \gamma < 1$,

$$V(x_k) = \sum_{j=k}^{\infty} \gamma^{j-k} U(x_j, h(x_j)). \tag{6}$$

The optimal value function $V^*(x_k)$ can be represented by

$$V^*(x_k) = \min_h V(x_k), \tag{7}$$

and according to the Bellman optimality principle, we can obtain the following HJB equation

$$V^*(x_k) = \min_{u_k} \{ U(x_k, u_k) + \gamma V^*(x_{k+1}) \}. \tag{8}$$

Then the optimal control policy $h^*(x_k)$ can be determined from

$$h^*(x_k) = \arg \min_{u_k} \{ U(x_k, u_k) + \gamma V^*(x_{k+1}) \}. \tag{9}$$

Before introducing the policy iteration algorithm, we first make the following assumptions such that policy iteration can be applied.

Assumption 1. System (3) is controllable; state $x_k = 0$ is an equilibrium state of system (3) under the control $u_k = 0$, i.e., $F(0,0) = 0$; the state feedback controller $u_k = h(x_k)$ satisfies $u_k = h(0) = 0$; the utility function $U(x, u)$ is a positive definite function for $\forall x, u$.

The policy iteration algorithm can solve the HJB equation 8 iteratively using the policy evaluation step and policy improvement step as follows.

Policy Evaluation

$$V^{(i)}(x_k) = U(x_k, h^{(i)}(x_k)) + \gamma V^{(i)}(x_{k+1}), i = 0, 1, 2, \dots \tag{10}$$

In the above equation, i is the iteration number; $h^{(i)}(x_k)$ is the control policy being evaluated in the ith iteration. In the first iteration $i = 0$, the initial control policy $u_k = h^{(0)}(x_k)$ needs to be an admissible control policy of system (3).

Policy Improvement

$$h^{(i+1)}(x_k) = \arg\min_{u_k}\{U(x_k, u_k) + \gamma V^{(i)}(x_{k+1})\}, i = 0, 1, 2, \dots \tag{11}$$

In general, solving (10) and (11) requires exact representations of both the value function and the control policy, which is often not tractable in practice. In Subsect. 3.2, an value function approximation (VFA) approach aims to address this issue by approximating (10).

The properties of policy iteration for discrete time nonlinear has been discussed in [3,4,8]. The following Theorems 1 and 2 presents two important properties of policy iteration.

Theorem 1. *For $i = 0, 1, \dots$, let $V^{(i)}(x_k)$ and $h^{(i)}(x_k)$ be obtained by (10) and (11). If Assumption 1 holds, then for $\forall x_k \in \mathbb{R}^n$, the iterative value function $V^{(i)}(x_k)$ is a monotonically nonincreasing sequence for $\forall i \geq 0$*

$$V^{(i+1)}(x_k) \leq V^{(i)}(x_k). \tag{12}$$

Theorem 2. *For $i = 0, 1, \dots$, let $V^{(i)}(x_k)$ and $h^{(i)}(x_k)$ be obtained by (10) and (11). If Assumption 1 holds, then the iterative value function $V^{(i)}(x_k)$ converges to the optimal value function $V^*(x_k)$, as $i \to \infty$,*

$$\lim_{i \to \infty} V^{(i)}(x_k) = V^*(x_k). \tag{13}$$

3.2 Implementation of Approximate Policy Iteration

To implement (10), a linear-in-parameter function approximator is used to approximate the value function $V^{(i)}(x_k)$,

$$\hat{V}^{(i)}(x_k) = W^{(i)T}\phi(x_k, h^{(i)}(x_k)) = \sum_{j=1}^{L} w_j \varphi_j(x_k) \tag{14}$$

where $W^{(i)} \in \mathbb{R}^L$ is a weight vector and $\phi(x_k, h^{(i)}(x_k)) : \mathbb{R}^n \times \mathbb{R}^m \to \mathbb{R}^L$ is a vector of the basis functions. The basis function $\phi(x_k, h^{(i)}(x_k))$ can be neural networks, polynomial functions, radial basis functions, etc.

The policy evaluation step (10) can be written as

$$\hat{V}^{(i)}(x_k) = U(x_k, u_k) + \gamma \hat{V}^{(i)}(x_{k+1}). \tag{15}$$

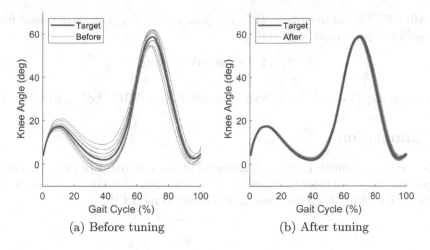

(a) Before tuning

(b) After tuning

Fig. 2. Before-after comparison of knee angle profile

Substituting (14) into (15), we have

$$W^{(i)T}(\phi(x_k, h^{(i)}(x_k)) - \gamma\phi(x_{k+1}, h^{(i)}(x_{k+1}))) = U(x_k, u_k). \quad (16)$$

Equation (17) can be solved by batch least-squares. Alternatively, it can be solved by recursive least-squares. In iteration i, N samples of state-action pairs (x_k, u) at time $k, k+1, \ldots, k+N-1$ are aligned in rows to form two vectors $\varphi^{(i)} \in \mathbb{R}^{L \times (N-1)}$ and $\mu^{(i)} \in \mathbb{R}^{1 \times (N-1)}$ in order to evaluate the ith policy $h^{(i)}(x_k)$. Hence, the least square solution of $W^{(i)}$ can be obtained from (16)

$$W^{(i)} = (\varphi^{\dagger(i)})^T(\mu^{(i)})^T, \quad (17)$$

where $\varphi^{\dagger(i)}$ is the Moore-Penrose pseudo-inverse of $\varphi^{(i)}$.

Table 1. Parameter table

Name	Symbol	Value
Discount factor	γ	0.8
Batch size	N	20
Dimension of state	N_x	2
Dimension of action	N_u	3
Weight matrix for state	R_x	$[1,1] \cdot I_2{}^*$
Weight matrix for action	R_u	$[0.1, 0.1, 0.1] \cdot I_3{}^*$
Number of unknown weights in critic $\hat{V}^{(i)}(x_k)$	L	15

${}^*I_2$ and I_3 are the identity matrices with dimensions of 2 and 3, respectively.

After $W^{(i)}$ is obtained from (17), the policy $h^{(i+1)}(x_k)$ can be obtained from the policy improvement step (11),

$$h^{(i+1)}(x_k) = \arg\min_u W^{(i)T}\phi(x_k, u). \qquad (18)$$

The above Eq. (18) can be explicitly computed from $\partial(W^{(i)T}\phi(x_k, u))/\partial u = 0$.

4   Simulation

This section demonstrates the effectiveness of the approximate policy iteration algorithm through OpenSim simulation experiments. The OpenSim model settings were adopted from the lower limb OpenSim model [1].

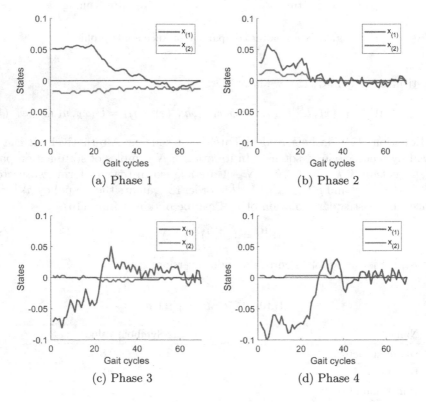

Fig. 3. Tuning results for all four phases. The units of $x_{(1)} = \Delta P$ and $x_{(2)} = \Delta D$ are radian and ratio of the full gait cycle, respectively.

Table 1 shows the parameters of approximate policy iteration during simulation. A zero-output policy is chosen as the initial control policy. At the beginning of each trial, the FS-IC was assigned with an initial IC parameter I_0. After collecting every N samples, approximate policy iteration was used to update the control policy $h^{(i)}(x_k)$ and $\hat{V}^{(i)}(x_k)$ iteratively to find an optimal policy that can drive state x_k to zero. A trial was considered successful if the absolute values of peak error ΔP_k and duration error ΔD_k were smaller than the lower bounds for 10 consecutive gait cycles before reaching 500 gait cycles; if not, then this trial was failed. The definitions and values of the lower bounds can be found in [14, Table I]. Note that a small Gaussian noise was added to the control to obtain persistence of excitation in the simulation.

Figure 2 shows 15 pairs of the prosthetic knee angle profiles before-tuning $(k = 0)$ and after-tuning $(k = 100)$. The fine-tuned knee angle profiles are much improved compared to the initial profiles. Both the peak error ΔP_k and duration error ΔD_k were reduced after tuning. In other words, the proposed ADP controller can make the knee motion closely match the target knee motion.

Figure 3 shows how the state x_k, namely the peak angle error ΔP_k and duration error ΔD_k varied during one of the trials. After the first policy update at $k = 20$, both errors were decreased significantly and oscillated around zero thereafter, which means the method converges fast and it can stabilize the system. The oscillations comes from the noise being added to the system. Notice that the errors in phases 3 and 4 are usually larger than those in phases 1 and 2, because the phases 3 and 4 are the swing phases which have larger variation in knee motion.

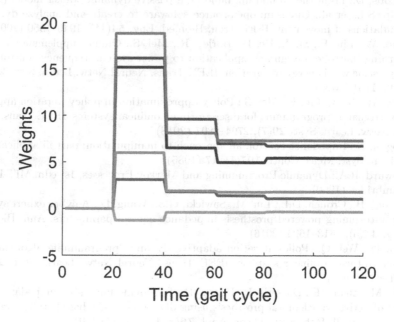

Fig. 4. Convergence of the critic weights $W^{(i)}$

Six out of 15 elements of the critic's weights $W^{(i)}$ as defined in (17) are illustrated in Fig. 4. It can be observed that $W^{(i)}$ is updated every 20 samples.

The weights are piecewise continuous with respect to time. In 120 gait cycles, the elements of $W^{(i)}$ converged, and so does the feedback gains since they are fully determined by $W^{(i)}$.

5 Conclusion

In this paper, we propose an approximate policy iteration algorithm to solve the robotic knee parameter tuning problem. The problem is formulated as an optimal control problem with unknown dynamics which can be solved online by approximate policy iteration. For implementation purpose, a linear-in-parameter structure with polynomial basis is constructed to approximate the value function. Finally, the effective of the approximate policy iteration scheme are demonstrated in the simulation results.

Acknowledgement. This work was partly supported by the National Science Foundation under grants #1406750, #1563454, #1563921, #1808752 and #1808898.

References

1. Jacobs, D.: From the ground up: building a passive dynamic walker model (2014)
2. Delp, S.L., et al.: Opensim: open-source software to create and analyze dynamic simulations of movement. IEEE Tran. Biomed. Eng. **54**(11), 1940–1950 (2007)
3. Guo, W., Liu, F., Si, J., He, D., Harley, R., Mei, S.: Online supplementary ADP learning controller design and application to power system frequency control with large-scale wind energy integration. IEEE Trans. Neural Netw. Learn. Syst. **27**(8), 1748–1761 (2016)
4. Guo, W., Si, J., Liu, F., Mei, S.: Policy approximation in policy iteration approximate dynamic programming for discrete-time nonlinear systems. IEEE Trans. Neural Netw. Learn. Syst. **29**(7), 2794–2807 (2018)
5. Hogan, N.: Impedance control: an approach to manipulation: part iii applications. J. Dyn. Syst. Meas. Contr. **107**(1), 17 (1985)
6. Howard, R.A.: Dynamic Programming and Markov Processes, 1st edn. MIT Press, Cambridge (1960)
7. Huang, H., Crouch, D.L., Liu, M., Sawicki, G.S., Wang, D.: A cyber expert system for auto-tuning powered prosthesis impedance control parameters. Ann. Biomed. Eng. **44**(5), 1613–1624 (2016)
8. Liu, D., Wei, Q.: Policy iteration adaptive dynamic programming algorithm for discrete-time nonlinear systems. IEEE Trans. Neural Netw. Learn. Syst. **25**(3), 621–634 (2014)
9. Liu, M., Zhang, F., Datseris, P., Huang, H.: Improving finite state impedance control of active-transfemoral prosthesis using dempster-shafer based state transition rules. J. Intell. Rob. Syst. Theor. Appl. **76**(3–4), 461–474 (2014)
10. Si, J., Wang, Y.T.: Online learning control by association and reinforcement. IEEE Trans. Neural Netw. **12**(2), 264–276 (2001)
11. Si, J., Barto, A.G., Powell, W.B., Wunsch, D. (eds.): Handbook of learning and approximate dynamic programming. Wiley, Piscataway (2004)

12. Wen, Y., Brandt, A., Liu, M., Huang, H., Si, J.: Comparing parallel and sequential control parameter tuning for a powered knee prosthesis joint department of biomedical engineering. In: IEEE International Conference on Systems, Man and Cybernetics, pp. 1716–1721 (2017)
13. Wen, Y., Liu, M., Si, J., Huang, H.: Adaptive control of powered transfemoral prostheses based on adaptive dynamic programming. In: Proceedings of the Annual International Conference of the IEEE Engineering in Medicine and Biology Society, pp. 5071–5074 (2016)
14. Wen, Y., Si, J., Gao, X., Huang, S., Huang, H.: A new powered lower limb prosthesis control framework based on adaptive dynamic programming. IEEE Trans. Neural Netw. Learn. Syst. **28**(9), 2215–2220 (2017)

Visual-Tactile Fusion for a Low-Cost Desktop Robotic Manipulator Grasping

Liming Fan[1](✉), Ziwei Xia[2](✉), and Yiyong Yang[2]

[1] China Aerospace Science and Technology Corporation, No. 16,
South 3rd Street, Zhongguancun, Haidian District, Beijing 100083, China
fanliming@sunwiserobot.com
[2] School of Engineering and Technology,
China University of Geosciences (Beijing), Beijing 100083, China
2002170014@cugb.edu.cn

Abstract. Desktop manipulators have found extensive applications in the factory, home, and classroom. However, existing customized desktop manipulators have hardly equipped sensors to percept the environment. In this paper, we develop a low-cost solution to this issue, by equipping an ordinary camera and tactile sensors to an off-the-shelf desktop manipulator. This integrated system uses the image to coarsely localize the objects on the desk and drives the end-effector to approach the object. During the grasping procedure, a flex sensor is used for precisely localizing the objects and a set of force sensors fixed on the gripper can be used to classify the objects according to their materials or deformability. All of the hardware units can be easily purchased and the total cost is under $500. We also made extensive experimental validation on the fruits classification task to show the advantages of the developed manipulator.

1 Introduction

With the increasing maturity of robot technology, miniaturization of robotic manipulators becomes a new development direction. The desktop robotic manipulator is such an example with compact volume and lightweight, making it possible to appear in our households. Additionally, the high cost of traditional robotic manipulators prevents them from wider adoption. Research on robotics may also advance more rapidly if robotic manipulators could maintain reasonable performance while the cost was reduced greatly [1].

However, current commercial desktop robotic manipulators lack visual or tactile perception capability, which limits the application of these robotic manipulators. On the other hand, tactile sensing has proven to be significant for advanced robotic manipulators besides visual perception. As humans get to know object properties like hardness, elasticity, thermal conductivity, roughness, etc. by touching the object, robots can also benefit from tactile feedback for object exploration and recognition, material classification, better grasp stability and force control [2–6]. In some cases, visual feedback only is not enough. For example, the appearance of the objects may seem the same, or the light condition is limited. Using tactile sensors could potentially be useful

© Springer Nature Singapore Pte Ltd. 2019
F. Sun et al. (Eds.): ICCSIP 2018, CCIS 1005, pp. 564–577, 2019.
https://doi.org/10.1007/978-981-13-7983-3_50

but there is still a lot of work to do for a deep understanding of the mechanism and common implementation in robotic manipulators [7].

Various types of tactile sensors have been developed such as piezoresistive, capacitive, piezoelectric, optical, vibrational-based, and multi-modal tactile sensors, to name a few. There are some commercial tactile sensor products from companies including Interlink, Tekscan, Weiss Robotics, Pressure Profile Systems (PPS) and SynTouch LLC [8–12]. In the meantime, researchers have come up with self-built experimental tactile sensors in the laboratory like conductive rubber based piezoresistive sensors, PVDF polymer based piezoelectric sensors, "GelSight" sensor and structure-borne sound tactile sensors [13–16].

Different sets of tasks and experiments have been carried out using tactile sensors. References [17, 18] both used the piezoresistive material to fabricate tactile-array sensors and their classification methods both relied on tactile images. Reference [17] classified ten household objects with the Schunk Parallel Gripper. In their experiment, however, bad oranges and fresh oranges are hard to distinguish. Reference [18] exploited FCRM algorithm as discrimination functions and examined different positions of flex wires in the experiments.

References [16, 19] both depended on the capacitive tactile sensors on PR2 robot grippers. Reference [16] detected slip information in order to control the pick-up and set-down of objects. Reference [19] used tactile information to distinguish the internal state of different bottles with average recognition rate around 80%. Another research reported in [20] also demonstrated the usage of tactile sensors on slippage detection with the platform of Robotic robot gripper. A recent study given by [21] utilized a V-groove cavity structure on the parallel-jaw gripper to passively reorient prismatic objects from a horizontal resting pose to an upright secure grasp.

In this paper, we develop a desktop robotic manipulator with mature tactile sensors. In order to achieve higher resolution and sensitivity, we form a multi-point sensor array with low-cost force sensors and implement Gaussian interpolation. Based on a k nearest neighbor classifier, the system is able to classify different kinds of genuine and artificial fruits, which is difficult for visual approaches. We also compare the k nearest neighbor classifier with Support Vector Machine and Naive Bayesian classification. Experimental results validate the feasibility of our system to classify objects. More importantly, the total cost of our hardware system is dramatically lower than the systems mentioned in [17–21].

The main contributions are listed as follows:

(1) We set up the architecture of the desktop robotic manipulator, which can be easily resized in other labs or even households with a small amount of cost ($414 in this paper). Our method may cast light on low-cost solutions to robotic sensing systems and promote the population of household robotic manipulators.

(2) Besides monocular vision, we employ both a flex sensor and force sensors to collect tactile information. We design a position adjustment strategy based on the force sensor array so that the contact point is exactly or close to the center of the object. This strategy leads to higher repeatability and correctness.

(3) We validate the feasibility of our system for fruit classification with three different methods. We also build a dataset that can be expanded in the future.

This paper is organized as follows: Sect. 2 will first introduce the overall architecture of our desktop robotic manipulator and its operation procedure, Sect. 3 will demonstrate the function of monocular vision used before grasping. In Sect. 4, we will have a detailed look at the features and limitations of the tactile sensors, along with the design of our tactile sensor system. Section 5 will focus on the classification based tactile information. Two separate features are extracted and compared. Then Sect. 6 will demonstrate the experiments and compare the results from three classification methods. Analysis of the experimental results will be discussed and possible explanation will be given. At the end, we will conclude our work.

2   Architecture

The desktop robotic manipulator shown in Fig. 1 consists of a robotic arm from UFactory [22], a Torobot gripper [23], the tactile sensor system and an additional ordinary camera.

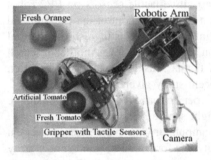
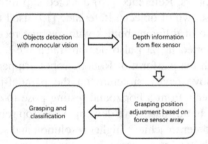

Fig. 1. Desktop robotic manipulator with objects.

Fig. 2. Operation flowchart.

The 4-DOF robotic arm uses three high torque servos to achieve a semicircular working area with a radius of 35 cm and 0 to 30 cm height. Meanwhile, another micro servo contributes to 180-degree rotation of the end-effector of the robotic arm, in our case, the gripper. The gripper weighs 45 g and is fixed to the robotic arm via an angled aluminum connecting piece. The gripper's opening width is from 0 to 54 mm which can be extended to 154 mm by adding a broadening device. On the gripper is the tactile sensor system mounted, which will be discussed in detail in the next section. In general, the tactile sensor system includes a flex sensor on one lateral side of the gripper and a $M \times N$ force sensor array on each interior side. Control of both the robotic arm and the gripper, altogether 5 degree-of-freedom, depends on an Arduino based main board while the upper monitor provides a C# based interface. Along with the robotic manipulator is an ordinary 12 megapixel CMOS camera with 1024×768 maximum resolution.

Figure 2 demonstrates the operation process of our system. The camera first takes a picture of the target area in front of the desktop robotic manipulator. The picture is then processed based on the BING Code [24] in order to identify the objects of interest. Next, the robotic manipulator will go for the objects from left to right. In order to grasp the objects, a flex sensor [25] is used to get depth information. After catching the object, the gripper will squeeze it slightly while the force sensors [8] receive tactile information. By training the robotic manipulator with different objects, classification can be achieved in the test. The image sequential frames are displayed in Fig. 3.

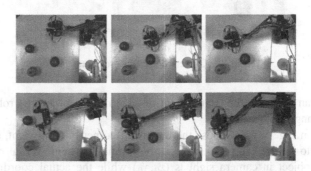

Fig. 3. Image sequential frames of a grasping process.

Plus, a brief summary of the hardware components used in our system is presented in Table 1. Again we emphasize on the transportability, reusability and low-cost of the system.

Table 1. Hardware components

Hardware	Robotic arm	Gripper	Tactile sensor		Camera
			Flex sensor	Force sensor	
Cost[a]	$339	$16	$8	$45[b]	$6
Company	UFactory	Torobot	MicroController Pros LLC	Interlink electronics	X-LSWAB
Reference	[22]	[23]	[25]	[8]	/

a. Shipping cost is not included.
b. The cost includes 4 small force sensors plus 1 large force sensor.

3 Visual Information

Before the desktop robotic manipulator grasps objects, visual information from the monocular camera is processed in order to detect the position of the objects. The procedure is illustrated in Fig. 4. BING Code [24] is used to detect areas that contain objects and draw rectangles around the objects. We then choose those rectangles with area smaller than 1300 and delete the bigger ones. After that, we fulfill the remaining rectangles and segment the picture according to the connected rectangles.

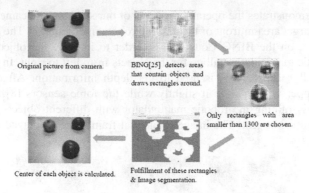

Fig. 4. Objects detection procedure.

Then we can calculate the center point of each object so that the robotic manipulator gets the angle information.

As shown in Fig. 5, we suppose the upper left corner in fresh sight, as well as the camera sight, to be the origin of Cartesian coordinate system. We also suppose the coordinate of object in camera sight is (x_0, y_0) while the actual coordinate on table (labeled as fresh sight in Fig. 5) is (x_0', y_0'). The coordinate of object's center in camera sight can be transformed into the actual coordinate on table according to Eqs. (1) and (2). The camera sight is a rectangle and the actual sight is a trapezoid. The bigger the depression angle of camera is, the smaller $(w_u - w_b)$ is. In other words, if the depression angle of camera is small enough, the fresh sight can be treated as a rectangle.

$$x_0' = \frac{x_0}{w_f}[w_d + (w_u - w_d)\frac{h_f - y_0}{h_f}] \tag{1}$$

$$y_0' = \frac{y_0}{h_f}h \tag{2}$$

where (x_0, y_0) and (x_0', y_0') refer to the coordinate of object mass center in camera sight and in fresh sight separately, w_f and h_f means the width and height of the camera sight, w_u, h, and w_b are the upper width, height, and lower width in fresh sight, d is the distance between the footer of camera and the lower edge of fresh sight.

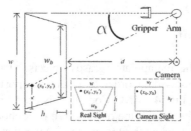

Fig. 5. Diagram for transforming the object's coordinate in camera sight to its actual coordinate on the table.

After finishing transforming the coordinate, the rotation angle α of the robotic manipulator can be calculated by the formula below.

$$\alpha = \arctan(\frac{w - x_0'}{h - y_0' + d}) \tag{3}$$

With the α information, the robotic manipulator will go for the objects from right to left.

4 The Tactile Sensor System

In this section, the details of the tactile sensor system on the gripper will be unclosed. Figure 6 is an illustration of the tactile sensor system. Due to the monocular vision in our system, a flex sensor is used to get depth information. Then follows a description of the force sensors attached to the interior sides of the gripper, including the pros and cons. In view of the sensors' shortcomings and previous research, a package of pragmatic improvements is presented. Instead of averaging the feedback data of the sensor array, we use them to adjust the point of grasping, which is critical to guarantee the repeatability of every grasping result. Finally, we will show the calibration results of the force sensors.

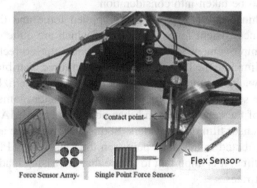

Fig. 6. Gripper with tactile sensor system. The flex sensor is used to detect the depth information of objects. The force sensor array on the left provides information for grasping position adjustment, and the single point force sensor on the right provides information for classification.

4.1 Flex Sensor

The idea of applying the flex sensor is simply from the cane for the blind to detect the circumstance around. After the Bing Code calculates the alpha-coordinate of each object's mass center, the flex sensor at the forefront of the desktop robotic manipulator aims to touch the object with corresponding alpha-coordinate. Heuristics can be regarded as a simple and effective method in this case. By controlling the robotic manipulator, the flex sensor goes forward in a zigzag way until reaching the object. The zigzag path is found to be effective and efficient when the extreme angle is three degrees more or less than alpha. The flex sensor selected is a 4.5″ long bi-directional flex sensor from SparkFun Electronics. The sensor is made of non-memory elastic material with a nominal resistance of approximately 10,000Ω, but the resistance increases as it is bent. The largest resistance can reach 40,000Ω in the condition of maximum flex.

4.2 The Force Sensor

The force sensor used in this article is 'Force Sensing Resistors' from Interlink Electronics. While the force applied to the sensor film increases, the resistance of the film will decrease. The specific relation between force and resistance is approximately linear in dual logarithmic coordinate system. Typically, the part-to-part repeatability tolerance ranges from ±15% to ±25% of established nominal resistance and the force resolution is better than ±0.5% of full use force. The force sensitivity ranges from less than 100 g to 10 kg.

Though the sensor is sensitive to tiny changes in force, it suffers from a critical defect that the distribution of resistance change over the whole film is not uniform. In other words, if the contact point doesn't remain the same in the measurement, the output cannot accurately reflect the force applied, let alone the little change of the force. In addition, mechanical setting time of the sensor, which is usually on the order of seconds, should also be taken into consideration.

The use of a thin elastomer between the applied force and the sensor can help absorb error from inconsistent force distributions which are quite common in reality. However, further improvement is needed to guarantee the correctness of the sensor output in order to eliminate the limitation of consistent force distributions. We come up with a special sandwich structure that helps get rid of the problem. Instead of applying force directly to the sensor film, we fix some five-millimeter-diameter PMMA wafers on selected points of the sensor film, and then add another PMMA sheet which is the same shape as the sensor film on the wafers. In this way, the force applied to the above sheet is always distributed to the same points on the sensor film. Plus, considering the mechanical setting time, it is important to assure that increasing loads are applied to the sensor at consistent rates.

Apart from the mechanical structure, appropriate interface electronics can improve the correctness as well. A current-to-voltage converter is recommended. This circuit produces an output voltage that is inversely proportional to the sensor's resistance. Since the resistance is roughly inversely proportional to applied force, the end result is a direct proportionality between force and voltage. To be short, the circuit provides linear increases in output voltage for increases in applied force. This linearization of the response optimizes the resolution and simplifies data interpretation.

4.3   Force Sensor Array

In order to get the pressure distribution of the object surface, we propose to build a M × N force sensor array by composing the above force sensors. Instead of averaging the feedback data of these sensor cells, we use them to determine the center point of grasping, which is critical to guarantee the repeatability of every grasping procedure. Furthermore, by employing Gaussian interpolation, we can have a more detailed knowledge of the surface pressure of the object. Before the desktop robotic manipulator grasps objects, the force sensors on the gripper need to be calibrated so that the feedback data from different force sensors are comparable. In our experiment, a two by two force sensor array is implemented to make sure that the object is in the middle of the gripper. After two or three minor adjustments, another relatively larger force sensor is used to detect the pressure applied to the object. Specific analysis of the tactile information will be discussed in the next section.

5   Classification Based Tactile Information

5.1   Raw Data

With our tactile sensor system, we can learn about the surface properties of the object. The data format is (RotateAngle, FlexSensorValue, Force11, Force12, Force13, Force14, SingleForce), where RotateAngle is the rotating angle of the gripper servo, FlexSensorValue is the feedback from the flex sensor, Force11, Force12, Force13, Force14 are values from the force sensor array and SingleForce is the value of another single point force sensor. In the training process, the desktop robotic manipulator grasps the same object repeatedly. After 30 times grasping, all the data are recorded to a txt file.

5.2   Feature Extraction

Figure 7 shows a group of raw data for fresh and artificial tomato. It can be seen from the graph that each grasping process (each peak) has a largest SingleForce value when the gripper closes to the narrowest. This largest SingleForce value is selected to be the first feature. Besides, we can get the angle of the gripper servo corresponding to the largest SingleForce. At last, 49 vector formatting like (largest SingleForce, angle) can be achieved from each data file. In our experiment, each object has 2 recorded data file, so each object can get 98 feature vectors. All of these feature vectors contribute to the training data set.

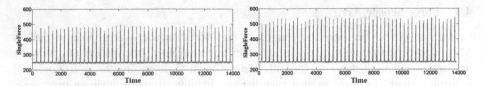

Fig. 7. Feedback from the large force sensor. Left: Fresh Tomato. Right: Artificial Tomato.

5.3 Classification

Several different classification methods are used to classify different objects [26].

SVM: The SVM type is C-SVC, kernel type is Linear. All data do not need to scale.
KNN: Calculating the average Euclidean distance between the largest SingleForce value of test sample and each value in train data set. The test object is classified to the smallest one.
NaiveBayes: Gaussian is used to estimate the probability distribution of different object. And we cheat two features as independent variables.

6 Experimental Evaluation

In this section, we present one application of our desktop robotic manipulator which cannot be completed by visual approach only but needs the help of tactile feedback. Considering the following situation: a person wants to eat some fruit, an orange for example, and then the desktop robotic manipulator is able to select the ripe orange among the fruit basket. In our experiment, we first classify genuine and artificial fruit which is easy due to the material difference. Next, we choose nine kinds of fruit including genuine and artificial oranges, fresh tomato, bad tomato, artificial tomato, fresh apple, fresh pear, artificial lemon, and fresh kiwifruit. The dataset is available upon request.

6.1 Grasping Strategy

The robotic manipulator firstly detects the position of objects with the camera. After receiving the feedback angle α from visual analysis program, the manipulator will rotate α degrees pointing to the target object. Secondly, the manipulator moves toward target object until the value from bending sensor changes 20 (this value is different for different bending sensor) which shows that the gripper touches the target object. The manipulator keeps moving a bit further and then, the gripper opens and catches the object. In order to collect better data, the gripper needs to catch the object at the center of the large single force sensor. This can be realized by our position adjustment strategy shown in Algorithm 1, where f_1, f_2, f_3, f_4 refer to the feedback from four small force sensors separately.

Algorithm 1. Position adjustment strategy.

for i = 1 to 5 **do**

  if $| f_1 + f_2 - f_3 - f_4 | > 50$ **then**

    if $(f_1 + f_2 - f_3 - f_4) > 50$ **then**

      gripper moves backward for 3 degrees

    else

      gripper moves forward for 3 degrees

    end if

  end if

end for

for i = 1 to 5 **do**

  if $| f_2 + f_3 - f_1 - f_4 | > 50$ **then**

    if $(f_2 + f_3 - f_1 - f_4) > 50$ **then**

      gripper moves downward for 3 degrees

    else

      gripper moves upward for 3 degrees

    end if

  end if

end for

After adjusting to the center, the gripper begins to collect data for classification. A complete process of data collection contains two steps, touching and pressing. The gripper grasps an object gradually until the value of the large single point force sensor reaches 300, which indicates that the gripper has touched the object. Then, the servo of the gripper rotates another 5° to let the gripper press the object. In order to get enough train and test data, the gripper would repeat this process 50 times as a group. In our experiment, each object has two groups of data. When finishing collecting a group of data, the gripper releases and begins to grasp the next object.

6.2 Result

In our experiment, data from 9 objects have been collected, each having two groups of data. The feature vector for every object is defined as: (RotationAngle, SingleForce).

Figure 7 shows the difference of SingleForce between a fresh tomato and an artificial tomato. The SingleForce starts from 250, which is in accordance with our measuring circuit. Obviously, the largest SingleForce is very different between these two objects. Therefore, the largest SingleForce can be a good feature.

According to the grasping strategy, after touching the object, the gripper begins to press it by rotating the gripper servo for 5°. However, these 5° can actually apply different force to the object in different position. In other words, the position where the gripper presses the object is very important. Thus we use the smallest servo angle in grasping each object to represent this value, which is the second feature we choose. It needs to be noted that the second feature doesn't necessarily mean the size of the object. For example, if the robotic manipulator grasps two objects of the same size, the first servo angle when it touches the objects is almost the same due to the size. However, after pressing the two objects by rotating the gripper servo another 5°, the final servo angle for the harder object will be larger than the other softer one due to the different surface properties and resistance. In the end, we have chosen two features: the largest SingleForce and the smallest angle of the gripper servo in the grasping process.

After dealing all groups of raw data, we get 883 feature vectors. We label all these feature vectors as seen in Fig. 8. For each object, 10 test samples are chosen randomly and at last we get 90 test samples and 793 train samples. Three different classification methods are used to classify these 9 objects: KNN, SVM and Naive Bayes. The classification results are shown in Table 2.

Table 2. Result with two feature combined for test data

Method	Accuracy
SVM	85.67% (77/90)
KNN (k = 1)	86.67% (78/90)
KNN (k = 3)	85.56% (77/90)
KNN (k = 5)	88.89% (80/90)
KNN (k = 7)	86.67% (78/90)
NaiveBayes	93.33% (84/90)

It shows that Naive Bayes is the most suitable classifier for this situation. Besides, for KNN, a large k does not always lead to a better result.

In order to analyze the influence of two features, we plot all feature vectors on a 3-axis graph. From two perspectives, we can get two sectional drawings. Every label represents one object. From the perspective of first feature (largest SingleForce) and second feature (Angle), the train data of 9 objects are shown in Fig. 8.

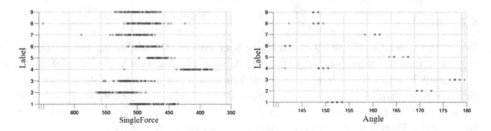

Fig. 8. Relation between features and classifier. Each row represents an object class, and each point represents one feature characteristic of samples. Upper represents SingleForce characteristic of samples while down shows the angle characteristic. For different labels, the smaller the overlapping on horizontal axis is, the clearer the distinction is.

Figure 8 shows that some objects such as 4 and 8, cannot be classified correctly by the feature of angle, but can be classified exactly by largest SingleForce. And some objects like 6, 7 and 8 cannot be classified correctly by largest SingleForce, but can be classified by angle. Some objects like 1 and 4 can be classified by two features at the same time.

The different effect of classification with single feature used is tested in our experiment. The result is shown in Table 3.

Table 3. Result with single feature for test data

Method	With feature 1	With feature 2
SVM	41.11% (37/90)	90% (81/90)
KNN (k = 1)	27.78% (25/90)	85.56% (77/90)
KNN (k = 3)	34.44% (31/90)	85.56% (77/90)
KNN (k = 5)	38.89% (35/90)	85.56% (77/90)
KNN (k = 7)	34.44% (31/90	85.56% (77/90)
NaiveBayes	33.33% (30/90)	88.89% (80/90)

Table 4. Result with two features combined for bad tomato prediction

Method	Accuracy
SVM	100% (48/48)
KNN (k = 1)	100% (48/48)
KNN (k = 3)	100% (48/48)
KNN (k = 5)	100% (48/48)
NaiveBayes	95.83% (46/48)

In order to test the predict function of the classifier, we choose a bad tomato randomly from a supermarket and use our classifier to predict its type. Since the tomato is a bad one, its label is given 4. This procedure uses 793 train samples and 48 test data from the bad tomato. The classification result is shown in Tables 4 and 5.

Table 5. Result with single feature for bad tomato

Method	With feature 1	With feature 2
SVM	97.92% (47/48)	0% (0/48)
KNN (k = 1)	100% (48/48)	0% (0/48)
KNN (k = 3)	100% (48/48)	0% (0/48)
KNN (k = 5)	100% (48/48)	0% (0/48)
KNN (k = 7)	100% (48/48)	0% (0/48)
NaiveBayes	100% (48/48)	0% (0/48)

The results show that a bad tomato is very different from a fresh one regardless of the size. Our tactile classifier can identify a bad tomato from a fresh one easily while it is difficult to do so via visual approaches.

The accuracy of the classifier with single feature varies a lot. Table 3 shows that the feature of angle is more useful than the feature of SingleForce, but Table 5 shows an opposite conclusion. For the bad tomato used to test the performance of the classifier, the first feature performs better than the second feature. In Table 4, combined with both two features, the classifier correctly classifies the tomato as a bad one, ignoring the influence of the second feature. Therefore, we cannot simply come to the conclusion that one feature is more important than the other, but it can be concluded that the classifier with two features combined is more accurate.

We also analyze the confusion matrixes of three classifiers to compare the divisibility of different objects in Fig. 9.

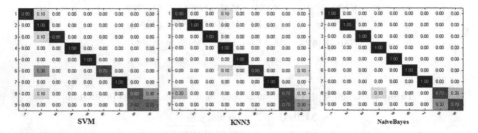

Fig. 9. Confusion matrixes of three classifiers.

7   Conclusion

In this paper, we developed a low-cost desktop robotic manipulator with visual and tactile perception capability. The camera is used to coarsely localize the objects and the tactile sensor is used to precisely localize and classify the objects. Such a low-cost system is flexible customized to many tasks. In the experimental validation, we use the developed system to collect the tactile sensor data for various fruits and obtain promising classification results. In the future, we will try to use the developed system to study the visual-tactile fusion object classification problem.

References

1. Quigley, M., Asbeck, A., Ng, A.: A low-cost compliant 7-DOF robotic manipulator. In: IEEE International Conference on Robotics & Automation (ICRA), pp. 6051–6058 (2011)
2. Decherchi, S., Gastaldo, P., Dahiya, R.S., Valle, M., Zunino, R.: Tactile data classification of contact materials using computational intelligence. IEEE Trans. Robot. **27**(3), 635–639 (2011)
3. Wettels, N., Loeb, G.: Haptic feature extraction from a biomimetic tactile sensor: force, contact location and curvature. In: IEEE International Conference on Robotics and Biomimetics, (ROBIO), pp. 2471–2478 (2011)

4. Liu, H., Song, X., Bimbo, J., Seneviratne, L., Althoefer, K.: Surface material recognition through haptic exploration using an intelligent contact sensing finger. In: IEEE/RSJ International Conference on Intelligent Robots and Systems, (IROS), pp. 52–57 (2012)
5. Bekiroglu, Y., Laaksonen, J., Jorgensen, J.A., Kyrki, V., Kragic, D.: Assessing grasp stability based on learning and haptic data. IEEE Trans. Robot. **27**, 616–629 (2011)
6. Teshigawara, S., et al.: Highly sensitive sensor for detection of initial slip and its application in a multi-fingered robot hand. In: IEEE International Conference on Robotics and Automation, (ICRA), pp. 1097–1102 (2011)
7. Dahiya, R., Valle, M.: Tactile sensing technologies. In: Robotic Tactile Sensing, pp. 79–136. Springer, Dordrecht (2013). https://doi.org/10.1007/978-94-007-0579-1_5
8. Interlink electronics products. http://www.interlinkelectronics.com/standard-products.php
9. Tekscan, Flexiforce. http://www.tekscan.com/flexiforce.html
10. W. Robotics Tactile sensors. http://weiss-robotics.de/en/tactile-sensors.html
11. PPS, Tactile sensors. http://www.pressureprofile.com/products.php
12. Balasubramania, R., Santos, V.J.: The Human Hand as an Inspiration for Robot Hand Development. Springer Tracts in Advanced Robotics, vol. 95. Springer, Cham (2014). https://doi.org/10.1007/978-3-319-03017-3
13. Teshigawara, S., Shimizu, S., Tadakuma, K., Aiguo, M., Shimojo, M., Ishikawa, M.: High sensitivity slip sensor using pressure conductive rubber. In: Sensors, pp. 988–991. IEEE (2009)
14. Seminara, L., Capurro, M., Cirillo, P., Cannata, G., Valle, M.: Electromechanical characterization of piezoelectric PVDF polymer films for tactile sensors in robotics applications. Sens. Actuators, A **169**(1), 49–58 (2011)
15. Li, R., Adelson, E.: Sensing and recognizing surface textures using a gelsight sensor. In: IEEE Conference on Computer Vision and Pattern Recognition, (CVPR), pp. 1241–1247 (2013)
16. Romano, J., Hsiao, K., Niemeyer, G., Chitta, S., Kuchenbecker, K.: Human-inspired robotic grasp control with tactile sensing. IEEE Trans. Robot. **27**(6), 1067–1079 (2011)
17. Drimus, A., Kootstra, G., Bilberg, A., et al.: Design of a flexible tactile sensor for classification of rigid and deformable objects. Robot. Auton. Syst. **62**(1), 3–15 (2014)
18. Su, J., Ko, W., Liu, Y., et al.: Design of tactile sensor array on electric gripper jaws for wire gripping recognition. In: IEEE International Conference on Automation Science and Engineering (CASE), pp. 1014–1019 (2014)
19. Chitta, S., Sturm, J., Piccoli, M., et al.: Tactile sensing for mobile manipulation. IEEE Trans. Robot. **27**(3), 558–568 (2011)
20. Heyneman, B., Cutkosky, M.: Biologically inspired tactile classification of object-hand and object-world interactions. In: IEEE International Conference on Robotics and Biomimetics, (ROBIO), pp. 167–173 (2012)
21. Chavan-Dafle, N., et al.: A two-phase gripper to reorient and grasp. In: IEEE International Conference on Automation Science and Engineering (CASE), pp. 1249–1255 (2015)
22. Robotic arm from UFactory. http://store.ufactory.cc/uarm-metal/
23. Torobot gripper. https://item.taobao.com/item.htm?spm=a1z10.5-c.w4002-3333837250.41. AG3VEM&id=15612603053
24. Cheng, M., Zhang, Z., Lin, W., et al.: BING: binarized normed gradients for objectness estimation at 300fps. In: IEEE Conference on Computer Vision and Pattern Recognition (CVPR) (2014)
25. MicroController Pros LLC, Flex sensor. http://microcontrollershop.com/product_info.php? products_id=4496
26. Bishop, C.: Pattern Recognition and Machine Learning. Information Science and Statistics. Springer, New York (2006). https://doi.org/10.1007/978-1-4615-7566-5

Author Index